THE NEW TESTAMENT

A TRANSLATION FOR LATTER-DAY SAINTS

A Study Bible

THE NEW TESTAMENT

A TRANSLATION FOR LATTER-DAY SAINTS

A Study Bible

THOMAS A. WAYMENT

Published by the Religious Studies Center, Brigham Young University, Provo, Utah, in cooperation with Deseret Book Company, Salt Lake City.
Visit us at rsc.byu.edu.

Printed in the United States of America by Sheridan Books, Inc.

DESERET BOOK is a registered trademark of Deseret Book Company.
Visit us at DeseretBook.com.

Cover and interior design by Emily V. Strong.

ISBN: 978-1-9443-9467-7

The new testament: a translation for latter-day saints
Library of Congress Cataloging in Publication Control Number: 2018025576

CONTENTS

NOTE TO THE READER

The language of the King James Bible will always be part of the Latter-day Saint cultural fabric in English: it is woven into our hymns, our ordinances, and our scriptural canon. It has been one of the primary vehicles through which we encounter the word of God, and it represents scripture. This translation is not an attempt to replace the King James Bible for Latter-day Saint readers, but it is an invitation to engage again the meaning of the text for a new and more diverse English readership.

Translation is both an art and a science, and every translation exists along a pendulum of precise or even mechanical translation of words to rendering the intent and meaning of a text. No translation is perfect, nor is any translation sufficient to never be revisited or reconsidered. All translations must consider technical vocabulary, jargon, humor, irony, and other forms of speech. This translation intentionally engages the possibility that the New Testament can be rendered into modern language in a way that will help a reader more fully understand the teachings of Jesus, his disciples, and his followers. When the language of translation becomes too foreign, too distant from the present age, it is time to consider the possibility of another translation.

I hope this attempt to translate the Greek of the New Testament will not be seen as combative or even controversial. Instead, I hope it can become a study tool, an aid to inviting readers into the text so that new meaning can be discovered, and new inspiration can be found. Its flaws are my own, a result of not always being able to know the intent of the Greek text or of the New Testament authors' abbreviated style of writing. But I also hope that the remaining flaws will not become the focus. I felt encouraged that an effort to retranslate the New Testament was in order based on the following statement:

> If [the Bible] be translated incorrectly, and there is a scholar on the earth who professes to be a christian, and he can translate it any better than King James's translators did it, he is under obligation to do so, or the curse is upon him. If I understood Greek and Hebrew as some may profess to do, and I knew the Bible was not correctly translated, I should feel myself bound by the law of justice to

the inhabitants of the earth to translate that which is incorrect and give it just as it was spoken anciently. Is that proper? Yes, I would be under obligation.[1]

PRINCIPLES OF TRANSLATION

The textual basis for this translation is the Nestle-Aland *Novum Testamentum Graece* in its 28th edition, with variations to that text following standard text critical methods. The Nestle-Aland Greek text preserves without bias the most widely acknowledged and accepted edition of Greek manuscripts. No text is perfect, and no surviving text is an original. Today we have access to thousands of Greek manuscript copies, each of which contains important differences and textual nuances. All of the differences between those copies have been carefully collated and published so that translators may know precisely the differences between the manuscripts and then weigh which texts are likely to be in error and which are more likely to be closer to the original. Most modern translations use an edition of the Nestle-Aland text as their basis for translation, although a few still rely upon an eclectic textual tradition.

As a general rule, I have not attempted to translate Greek words exactly the same in each instance, nor in the same order in which the words appear in their Greek sentences. I have given preference to readability in place of reflecting a foreign language word order. This practice can be helpful in many instances, but it has its own limitations. Also, I have chosen to err on the side of context in determining the meaning of words and have subsequently attempted to draw attention to issues associated with this in the notes. Older translations tended to favor following the order of Greek words and to note words in italics as a means of alerting the reader to words that were not contained in the Greek manuscripts being used. This practice is subjective, for example, because Greek can express ideas such as "then he will go" using a single word. This practice also assumes that additional words used to render the Greek into clear English are suspicious and perhaps unnecessary. I have avoided this practice and have attempted to render the Greek into English in a straightforward manner with as little interpretation as possible. The notes will alert the reader to instances where the Greek is unclear.

The New Testament is written in a variety of different Greek styles, with some of it being quite refined (Luke, Hebrews, and 1 Peter) while other books are quite simple (Mark and John). The language of the New Testament was not elevated or refined Greek, and the speeches and discourses that are recorded in the New Testament were given in everyday simple Greek. A translation that can represent the simple power of the language of Jesus and his followers is truly a gift, and as we are further and further removed from the seventeenth century, we have begun to lose sight of the realization that Jesus spoke like everyday people. Jesus did not speak using archaic English terms and phrases. His speech was quite ordinary, his meaning was quite profound, and his intent was often clear. As language evolves, so too translations need to evolve.

This translation intentionally uses quotation marks to designate what was said and by whom. This is generally easy to do because of the way Greek is written. Also, Greek tends to report speech by saying, "he responded saying," or "he told them saying." I have rendered these terms into a more readable text by removing what is now redundant in English. Also, the Greek New Testament was not written in sentence-length verses, but in short paragraphs. This translation adopts a paragraph structure, and so the intrusion

---

1. Brigham Young, "Remarks," New Tabernacle, Salt Lake City, 27 August 1871, in *Deseret Evening News*, 2 September 1871, 2.

of verse divisions has been minimized by placing verse designations in a smaller super-script font. This has been done to improve readability and to help facilitate comparison between the gospels when a story is told by another author. The New Testament authors frequently refer to someone as a "brother." I have translated that term inclusively, where possible, to reflect "brothers and sisters" because the original context of the word was not intentionally exclusionary but rather an artifact of first-century common usage and parlance. The New Testament does not use the term exclusively to represent only males, but instead it often uses the term generically to refer to those who believe alike, regardless of gender. However, there are numerous examples where the authors appear to have in-tended "men" exclusively. I have rendered those passages using gender-exclusive language (for example, Matthew 2:16; 8:28; 14:21, and so forth).

In the headings of each section of the Gospels, I have included parallel references to stories that are told by another author. The dates of historical figures are also included in the notes when those individuals appear in the story. The notes are included at the bottom of each page for ease of access. To keep the notes to a manageable length, I have rendered quotations of the text in the footnotes into italics. In the text of the New Tes-tament, I have used italics to designate quotations of the Old Testament, and the notes will direct the reader to the source of those quotations.

The notes favor intertextuality, especially with the Book of Mormon and the Doc-trine and Covenants. I have included those references to help the reader see how New Testament texts are engaged, developed, and interpreted in the Book of Mormon and the Doctrine and Covenants. The notes refer to these intertextual parallels as quotes, allusions, or echoes. Those three divisions are intended to designate strong shared lan-guage (using the word *compare* or *quote*), clear allusions to a story or idea (allusion), and parallels that are more distant, but clearly share similar ideas or language (echo). Select references to the Joseph Smith Translation of the Bible have been included in the notes.[2] However, I have been selective in doing so because many of the changes that he made are inextricably linked to the King James Version. I have also included alternate readings in the notes, where manuscripts differ in the Greek text. I offer an informed academic opinion regarding which version is likely to be original, but where appropriate, I have included the alternate text for the reader to consider. Sometimes even when a variant reading is unlikely to be original, it has been included in the notes so that readers will understand why those words appear in other familiar translations such as the King James Version. I have used double brackets "[[" and "]]" to indicate when a verse or short passage is not likely to be original. Those passages marked by a double bracket have a questionable origin, but they have been included for the reader because in some cases they are quite ancient readings and have a chance of being historically accurate, and they help show how the text of the New Testament developed over time. The notes offer an opinion regarding the authenticity of each passage marked by double brackets. When a spurious verse is clearly not original, it has been removed from the text and placed in the notes, and the verse number has been omitted in the translation to signal the omission.

---

2. Passages have been quoted from Thomas A. Wayment, ed., *The Complete Joseph Smith Translation of the New Testament: A Side-by-Side Comparison with the King James Version* (Salt Lake City: Deseret Book, 2005).

ACKNOWLEDGMENTS

This project would not have been possible without the generous assistance of friends and assistants who graciously offered feedback and criticism. This project is truly indebted to them. Specifically, I would like to thank Zakarias D Gram, Haley Wilson-Lemmon, Colby Townsend, Julia Min-tsu Chiou, and David A. LeFevre. I appreciate the work of the Religious Studies Center, including Daniel K Judd, Joany O. Pinegar, Brent R. Nordgren, R. Devan Jensen, Don L. Brugger, Shirley S. Ricks, and Emily V. Strong. The remaining mistakes are, of course, my own.

I would also like to thank my family, who sacrificed their time to make this production possible. Family vacations were adapted so that I could devote sufficient time to this project, and I am thankful that it has reached a point where it can be shared more broadly.

Finally, I would like to acknowledge that the impetus to begin this project started with a hope that biblical literacy could improve through reading the Bible in a modern translation. I hope this translation can find its way into homes, classrooms, and personal study, but I also hope that it can be viewed as respectful of its great biblical heritage, namely the King James translation. For Latter-day Saints, the King James Version has come to represent the word of God and scripture, and so I acknowledge an indebtedness not only for the ways in which the KJV has preserved the word of God, but also to the eloquence with which it has presented that word for the past four hundred years.

THE GOSPEL OF MATTHEW

WHO WAS MATTHEW?

Matthew's name has been associated with the First Gospel since at least the second century and possibly even as early as the late first century. Because the surviving historical record is spotty, and no manuscripts of the First Gospel survive from the first century, scholars have not been able to establish firmly how far back the tradition goes that Matthew wrote the Gospel bearing his name. Matthew is mentioned by name five times in the New Testament (Matthew 9:9; 10:3; Mark 3:18; Luke 6:15; Acts 1:13), mostly in the context of the lists of names of Jesus's earliest disciples. He was one of the twelve disciples, the first discernible group of followers of Jesus who received special recognition for their devotion and discipleship. The First Gospel does not claim to be written by Matthew, and nowhere does the author openly claim to be one of the early disciples of the Lord. Instead, readers have come to know this Gospel as the Gospel of Matthew through later traditions and remembrances. While Latter-day Saints tend to accept Matthew's authorship of the First Gospel, the evidence for making that claim is rarely discussed in detail.

The author of the First Gospel relied heavily on the Gospel of Mark, and nearly 90 percent of the Gospel of Mark is repeated in the Gospel of Matthew, thus making Matthew in some respects a second edition of Mark. The author also incorporated other information not contained in Mark, and Matthew shares a little over sixty short sayings and stories with the Gospel of Luke that are not from Mark. In addition to those materials, the Gospel of Matthew contains a number of passages that are unique. Most of this unique information comes in the form of parables (the parables of the weeds among the wheat, the field, the pearl, the net, the unforgiving servant, the laborers in the vineyard, the two sons, and the ten maidens). Therefore, the author of the Gospel of Matthew was someone who was appreciative of Mark's Gospel, who shared material with the Gospel of Luke, and who recorded the overlooked parables from Jesus's life. The author also edited and corrected the order, grammar, syntax, matters relating to geography, and other details relating to the content of Jesus's teachings from Mark's Gospel.

The earliest surviving references that mention the First Gospel call it the Gospel according to Matthew (Eusebius, *Hist. Eccl.* 3.39.15), a tradition that goes back to Papias (died about 163 CE), who cited an otherwise unknown "elder" concerning the tradition. This information conforms well with the earliest surviving manuscripts of

the Gospel that also call it either the *Gospel according to Matthew* or simply *According to Matthew*. Some manuscripts spell the name differently, preferring *Matthaion* instead of *Maththaion*, as Papias reported. This variation in spelling is also present in manuscripts for Matthew 9:9.

Three of the Gospels list Matthew as one of the twelve disciples (Matthew 10:3; Mark 3:18; Luke 6:15), but only the Gospel of Matthew refers to him as a tax collector. This was probably an attempt to connect Matthew with the person who was collecting tax receipts, named Matthew in the Gospel of Matthew but named Levi in Mark and Luke (Matthew 9:9; Mark 2:14; Luke 5:27). Thus, at least in one sense, the First Gospel had a different tradition concerning the conversion of a disciple named Matthew and how he became a follower of Jesus. Despite older claims, it is very unlikely that there was an individual named Levi Matthew or vice versa, given that such a name is otherwise unattested and first-century Jews did not have two Hebrew first names.

Beginning in the late nineteenth century, many scholars started questioning the traditional claim that the disciple Matthew wrote the Gospel bearing his name. The question seems to arise out of a consistent concern that an eyewitness (Matthew) relied heavily upon the account of someone who was not an eyewitness (Mark). The second challenge has been that the material shared by Matthew and Luke has increasingly been thought to belong to a lost Gospel source, today known simply as Q. That hypothetical source is recovered through comparing the shared material between Matthew and Luke, which is strikingly similar, suggesting that they did have access to an earlier source. This piece of information raises the further possibility that the author did not rely on his or her own eyewitness account. Finally, the material unique to the First Gospel comes down to corrections of Mark's Gospel regarding grammar, locational references, and setting, as well as the addition of parables. The difficult question becomes, could this represent the work of an eyewitness to Jesus's ministry?

Against those who think that Matthew could not have written the Gospel bearing his name are a number of other important considerations. All of the earliest Christian historians attributed the First Gospel to Matthew, and there is not an alternative tradition attributing the Gospel to another author. The earliest historians wrote that Matthew arranged the Gospel in a "Hebrew manner" (Epiphanius, *Haer.* 30.13.2–3). The meaning of that claim is difficult to determine, although it could mean that it was arranged in a Hebrew manner of storytelling. But the reality is that early Christians believed that Matthew wrote the Gospel attributed to him.

THE MANUSCRIPTS

Today there are over one hundred manuscripts of the Gospel of Matthew written in Greek, each of them offering a slightly different text for the Gospel. When the modern reader picks up a Bible, that person encounters a text that has been produced through the consultation of numerous ancient manuscripts. In working through these manuscripts, scholars are forced to make decisions to accept or reject differences between the available manuscripts. Sometimes the differences are quite small, but other times manuscripts omit entire verses or, conversely, add entire verses.

Most of the earliest Greek manuscripts of the New Testament contain only a single book, but several nearly complete or complete Bibles have survived from the fourth century and later. Greek manuscripts of the New Testament are referred to using a somewhat confusing system: papyri, uncials, and minuscules. The papyri are quite obviously

written on papyrus, and they are generally the earliest copies of any of the books of the New Testament. The uncials are described by their type of writing, namely capital letters called uncials. Those manuscripts are typically written on parchment, and they represent the earliest complete Bibles. The minuscules describe copies of the New Testament written on parchment or other materials but that are written in a cursive script called minuscule. These manuscripts date to the later Middle Ages. Typically, when scholars reconstruct the exact wording of a New Testament book, earlier manuscripts are given precedence over later ones. This is important when verses and phrases are omitted because scribes tended to add material to explain Jesus's sayings rather than removing sayings or entire verses.

The most important manuscripts of the Gospel of Matthew are twenty-three papyri, all of which are quite fragmentary and range between preserving a verse or two to an entire chapter. The Gospel of Matthew is largely reconstructed based on Codex Sinaiticus (fourth century CE) and Codex Vaticanus (fourth century CE). Modern translations almost always favor these two manuscripts, especially in instances where they are the same, with supplements from other early witnesses. Older modern translations from the nineteenth century and earlier tended to favor later manuscripts as well as those that have since been determined to be eclectic (Codex Bezae).

STRUCTURE AND ORGANIZATION

Any effort to provide a precise and agreed-on outline and structure of the Gospel of Matthew will be met with frustration. The reason for this is that there is no obvious organizing structure. Instead, there are several main features that are widely agreed upon that influence the structure in competing ways. Matthew incorporated five major discourses of Jesus, and each of them could function as an independent unit (Matthew 5–7; 10; 13:1–53; 18; 23–25). Earlier scholars had suggested that Matthew inherited these units and composed his Gospel around them, but this idea has fallen out of favor because of other indications that the Gospel is not simply a collection of interconnected discourses. Other obvious organizing features are that Matthew follows the sequence of the Gospel of Mark after Matthew 12 with some notable divergences. Additionally, Matthew likes to group things like parables (Matthew 13 and 25) or organize passages by themes. Matthew also likes keyword associations like *angel* and *Lord* (4 times in 1:18–2:23), *righteousness* (5 times in Matthew 5–7), and *follow* (9 times in chapter 8, and 6 times in chapter 19). Matthew likes doublets or repetitions (Matthew 4:23/9:35; 19:30/20:16; 10:17–22/24:9–13). Finally, Matthew likes to frame ideas, sometimes referred to as *inclusio*. For example, Matthew 1:24 and 28:20, the beginning and ending of the Gospel, refer to the idea of "Immanuel," or the promise that "God is with us."

Therefore, a few organizing features can be drawn out from this discussion. The book of Matthew is not simply a collection of texts that were reproduced without shaping and adjusting by the author. Matthew had a strong hand in presenting the story. The Gospel of Matthew is intentionally formulated from units of tradition while accepting much of what Mark wrote as authoritative. Also, Matthew did not write a biography of the Hellenistic type, nor did he write a novel. In some features, the Gospel approaches a biography, particularly in the birth and death sequences: the genealogy makes it thoroughly Jewish. And the great speeches are not philosophical but salvation oriented; thus Jesus is more akin to Moses than to Socrates. Ultimately, the Gospel of Matthew continues to defy categorization in simple terms, but its message is forward-looking, hopeful, and ever centered on the Son of Man. ✷

THE GENEALOGY OF JESUS
(MK 1:1; LK 1:1–4)

1 ¹A book of the genealogy of Jesus Christ, son of David, son of Abraham.

²Abraham was the father of Isaac, Isaac was the father of Jacob, Jacob was the father of Judah and his brothers, ³Judah was the father of Perez and Zerah (with Tamar), Perez was the father of Hezron, Hezron was the father of Aram, ⁴Aram was the father of Aminadab, Aminadab was the father of Nahshon, Nahshon was the father of Salmon, ⁵Salmon was the father of Boaz (by Rahab), Boaz was the father of Obed (by Ruth), Obed was the father of Jesse, ⁶Jesse was the father of King David.

David was the father of Solomon (by the wife of Uriah), ⁷Solomon was the father of Rehoboam, Rehoboam was the father of Abijah, Abijah was the father of Asaph, ⁸Asaph was the father of Jehoshaphat, Jehoshaphat was the father of Joram, Joram was the father of Uzziah, ⁹Uzziah was the

father of Jotham, Jotham was the father of Ahaz, Ahaz was the father of Hezekiah, ¹⁰Hezekiah was the father of Manasseh, Manasseh was the father of Amos, Amos was the father of Josiah, ¹¹Josiah was the father of Jechoniah and his brothers at the time of the captivity in Babylon.

¹²After the Babylonian captivity, Jechoniah was the father of Salathiel, Salathiel was the father of Zerubbabel, ¹³Zerubbabel was the father of Abiud, Abiud was the father of Eliakim, Eliakim was the father of Azor, ¹⁴Azor was the father of Zadok, Zadok was the father of Achim, Achim was the father of Eliud, ¹⁵Eliud was the father of Eleazar, Eleazar was the father of Matthan, Matthan was the father of Jacob, ¹⁶Jacob was the father of Joseph, the husband of Mary, of whom Jesus, who is called the Christ, was born.

¹⁷All the generations from Abraham until David are fourteen generations, and from David until the carrying away

---

This Gospel is formally titled *The Gospel according to Matthew*. A shortened form of it was also used: *According to Matthew*. This title conveys the idea of a single Gospel that is told in different forms or by different witnesses. In Roman contexts, the term *gospel* can refer to a public declaration of good news or a civic function that is for the public good. The term *gospel* is used once in the Greek translation of the Old Testament, in 2 Samuel 4:10. The Joseph Smith Translation refers to the Gospel of Matthew as *The Testimony of Matthew*.

1:1 An allusion to Genesis 2:4; 5:1 (compare Nehemiah 7:5). By referring to Jesus as the *Christ*, the Greek translation of the Hebrew title *Messiah*, Matthew here fully asserts the divine and human origins of the Messiah, who in the following verses descends from the patriarchs, kings, and commoners as well as from the Holy Spirit. There is also an intentional reference to Abraham to draw upon the idea that Jesus furthers the promises made to Abraham. **1:2** Abraham is also the father of all nations, including Gentiles, and the allusion helps Matthew look forward to the ending of his Gospel (Genesis 17:4–5; Matthew 28:18–19), when the disciples would take the gospel of Jesus Christ to all nations. **1:2–17** For Luke's different genealogy, see Luke 3:23–38. **1:3** Four women are mentioned in the genealogy (apart from Mary): Tamar (Genesis 38), Rahab (Joshua 2:1–21), Ruth (Ruth 2), and Bathsheba (2 Samuel 11–12). All four were either Gentiles or married to a Gentile (Bathsheba), which may foreshadow the gospel being taken to all nations. They are placed in parentheses because they appear as explanatory additions. **1:7** Some manuscripts spell the name Asaph as Asa. **1:11** The Babylonian captivity refers to the period of Babylonian exile when the city of Jerusalem fell and many Jews were carried away as captives into Babylon. The exile took place beginning in 597 BCE and lasted for approximately sixty years. The Book of Mormon also begins shortly before the exile (1 Nephi 1:4). Jeremiah was a prophet at the time of the exile. **1:16** Jesus's mother was named Mariam, but modern convention has changed the name to Mary. Some Greek manuscripts spell the name as Marias or Mary. **1:17** The Babylonian captivity occurred 597–539 BCE.

to Babylon are fourteen generations, and from the captivity in Babylon until the birth of Christ are fourteen generations.

THE BIRTH OF JESUS (LK 2:1–7)

¹⁸Now, the birth of Jesus Christ happened in this manner. When his mother was engaged to Joseph, before they came together, she was found to be with child of the Holy Spirit. ¹⁹And her husband Joseph, being a righteous man and not wanting to make a public example of her, wanted to send her away privately. ²⁰While Joseph was pondering these things, an angel of the Lord appeared to him in a dream, saying, "Joseph, son of David, do not be afraid to take Mary as your wife, because that which is conceived in her is of the Holy Spirit. ²¹She will bear a son, and you will name him Jesus because he will save his people from their sins." ²²All of this took place to fulfill the word of the Lord through the prophet, saying, ²³"*Behold, the virgin shall conceive and bring forth a son and they shall call his name Emmanuel,*" which is interpreted "God with us." ²⁴Joseph arose from his sleep and did as the angel of the Lord commanded him, and took her as his wife, ²⁵and they were not intimate until she bore a son, and he named him Jesus.

THE MAGI BRING GIFTS

2 ¹In the days of Herod the king, after Jesus was born in Bethlehem in Judea, magi came from the east to Jerusalem, ²saying, "Where is the newborn king of

---

1:18 Matthew wishes to clarify the time when Mary became pregnant as having taken place between the month of the engagement and the wedding ceremony. See Deuteronomy 20:7; 22:13–21 for law of Moses directives on engagements and separation while engaged. The Book of Mormon describes this in greater detail (1 Nephi 11:13–20). **1:19** The idea that Joseph was *just* or *righteous* is most likely not looking forward to obedience to the teachings of Jesus Christ but rather looking back to the law of Moses. His actions would be equivalent to divorce, and Matthew focuses on the issue of public embarrassment (a practice alluded to in Alma 14:3). **1:20** Joseph the dreamer recalls Joseph of Egypt (Genesis 37:5–11). The Book of Mormon twice speaks of Mary by name (Mosiah 3:8; Alma 7:10). Language from this verse is used in Mosiah 27:11. **1:21** Compare Genesis 17:19. The name Jesus is the English spelling of the Greek rendering of the Hebrew/Aramaic name *Yeshua* (*Joshua* in English). **1:22–23** Matthew frequently draws the reader's attention to the idea that Jesus fulfills scripture. These references are known as the formula quotations, and they explicitly set out an Old Testament foundation for the ministry of Jesus (Matthew 1:22–23; 2:5–6; 2:15; 2:17–18; 2:23; 4:14–16; 8:17; 12:17–21; 13:35; 21:4–5; 27:9–10). Most of them directly represent the author's insertion into the story. **1:23** Quotation from Isaiah 7:14 and allusion to Isaiah 8:8, 10. The word *virgin* in the context of Isaiah 7:14 refers to a young woman or a young girl before marriage. First Nephi 11:13 also uses the word *virgin* as a description of Mary, probably drawing upon Isaiah 7:14. Matthew here quotes the Greek translation, the Septuagint or LXX, of Isaiah 7:14 and not the Hebrew text. **1:25** Some late manuscripts read *she bore the firstborn son*. Matthew appears to draw the reader's attention to the fact that Mary did not remain a perpetual virgin when he says *until she bore a son*. Matthew uses the traditional way of speaking about Joseph and Mary prior to the birth of Jesus and says literally that *Joseph did not know Mary until she bore a son*.

2:1 Herod the King or Great ruled from 37 to 5/4 BCE. The Greek word *magos* can mean a wise man, an interpreter of dreams, or an astrologer. There may be some emphasis on these individuals being *magi* because it draws attention to their status as Gentiles. *Magi* are mentioned in the Old Testament as the priests of Babylon (Jeremiah 39:3, 13), and historically they were likely Zoroastrian priests or adherents. Matthew does not ascribe to them any particular spiritual meaning or prophetic fulfillment, and the other Gospels do not tell the story. **2:2, 9** Many translators render the phrase *rising star* as *a star in the east*. The reason for this is that Matthew explicitly speaks of the star *in the east*. The phrase, when used to describe the rising of the sun or stars, simply refers to the direction from which they arise: the east.

the Jews? We have seen his rising star, and we have come to worship him." ³When King Herod heard this he was troubled together with all Jerusalem, ⁴and after gathering all the chief priests and scribes of the people, he inquired of them where the Messiah would be born. ⁵And they said to him, "In Bethlehem of Judea," for so it has been written by the prophet, ⁶"*And you, Bethlehem, in the land of Judea, are not least among the rulers of Judah; from you shall come a ruler who will shepherd my people Israel.*"

⁷Then Herod privately called the magi and asked diligently concerning the time when the star appeared, ⁸and he sent them to Bethlehem and said, "Depart from here and search diligently for the child, and when you find him, send a message to me so that I may go and worship him." ⁹After hearing the king, they departed, and the rising star which they saw led them until it stood above where the child was. ¹⁰When they saw the star, they rejoiced with great joy, ¹¹and entering the house, they saw the child with Mary his mother, and kneeling down, they worshipped him, and opening their gifts, they offered him gold, frankincense, and myrrh. ¹²After being forewarned in a dream not to return to Herod, they traveled another way to their homeland.

THE ESCAPE TO EGYPT

¹³And after they departed from him, an angel of the Lord appeared in a dream to Joseph, saying, "Arise, and take the child and his mother and flee to Egypt, and stay there until I tell you. For Herod intends to seek out the child to destroy him." ¹⁴He arose and took the child and his mother and fled to Egypt in the night, ¹⁵and he was there until Herod passed away so that the word of the Lord through the prophet would be fulfilled, saying, "*I called my son out of Egypt.*"

¹⁶When Herod saw that he was mocked by the magi, he was very angry, and he sent men to kill all the children in Bethlehem and in all the region surrounding it

---

The phrase therefore may not be intentionally directional, and likely refers to the rising of the star. Given that the magi travel from the east (Matthew 2:1), it makes little sense for the star to also arise in the east, since they would be looking backward while traveling west to visit the newborn Messiah. Book of Mormon prophets spoke extensively of the star and its splendor (Helaman 14:5; 3 Nephi 1:21). **2:3** Some manuscripts read *all Judea* instead of *all Jerusalem*. **2:4** Greek *Christos* or *Christ* is the usual translation for the Hebrew title *Messiah*. Matthew begins early developing the concept that Jesus is the Messiah who fulfills scripture. *Scribes* are not copyists, but trained experts in the law of Moses. **2:6** Quotation from Micah 5:2. **2:11** *Frankincense* was used in the temple as part of the incense offerings. *Myrrh* was frequently used in the care of the body of a deceased person. The mention of these gifts in Matthew's birth story may have intentionally been included because they prefigure different elements of Jesus's death. Matthew speaks of a *house* and not a manger, perhaps reflecting differences in his sources or a later stage after the birth when Jesus was older. **2:13** The location of their flight into Egypt is unknown. Some later manuscripts report that the magi, after *they departed from him*, traveled *to their own land*. **2:13–23** Herod Archelaus (4 BCE–6 CE) ruled Samaria, Judea, and Idumea. Because of his cruelty and capriciousness as a ruler, he was banished to Gaul and was replaced by a Roman appointee. Bethlehem is a small village located about six miles south of Jerusalem. David reportedly lived in or near the city, and during New Testament times it was referred to as the *City of David* (compare 1 Samuel 20:6). **2:15** The scriptural allusion comes from Hosea 11:1. **2:16** The fact that Herod ordered his soldiers to kill all children under two years of age further draws attention to Herod's lack of precise information about the timing of the birth of Jesus. The magi may have come up to two years after Jesus's birth, but it is also possible that Herod's lack of information led to the order to kill older or younger children so that the baby Jesus would be caught and executed.

from two years old and under, according to the time which had been given him by the magi. ¹⁷Then was fulfilled the word through Jeremiah the prophet, saying, ¹⁸"*A cry in Rama was heard, mourning and much weeping, Rachel crying for her children, and she would not be comforted because they are not.*"

THE MOVE TO NAZARETH
(LK 2:39–40)

¹⁹After Herod died, the angel of the Lord appeared in a dream to Joseph in Egypt, ²⁰saying, "Arise, and take the child and his mother, and return to the land of Israel, because those who seek the life of the child are deceased." ²¹So he arose and took the child and his mother and came to the land of Israel, ²²but when he heard that Archelaus ruled Judea in the place of his father, he was afraid to go there, and having been warned in a dream, he departed into the regions of Galilee, ²³and he came and lived in a village called Nazareth so that the word through the prophets might be fulfilled that he would be called a Nazarene.

JOHN THE BAPTIST (MK 1:1–8;
LK 3:1–18; JN 1:19–23)

3 ¹In those days, John the Baptist came near the wilderness of Judea, declaring, ²"Repent for the kingdom of heaven

---

2:18 Quotation from Jeremiah 31:15. Jeremiah wrote this oracle during the time of Babylonian exile. Rama is located north of Jerusalem in the hill country in the region allotted to the tribe of Benjamin. Matthew has quoted a truncated version of the verse from Jeremiah, leaving out the verb *lamenting*. The language of Alma 28:4 is similar to this verse and Lamentations 2:5. **2:19** The death of Herod occurred in conjunction with a lunar eclipse, which has often been used to calculate the precise date of his death. His death is often dated to early spring of 5 or 4 BCE. He was buried at the fortress named after him, Herodium. The Greek word *angel* refers to a messenger. Sometimes those messengers, as in this instance, are clearly heavenly messengers, whereas at other times they are earthly messengers. **2:22** Herod Archelaus ruled 4 BCE–6 CE. **2:23** The source of the quotation is unknown. Matthew may have had in mind the idea that Jesus would take on a Nazarite vow (Numbers 6:1–21), and hence he would be a Nazarene. Or Matthew may have had in mind Isaiah 11:1, which refers to a branch, or *netzer*, that would grow out of the root of Jesse. Although more difficult on grammatical grounds, it may be that *Nazarene* refers to a person hailing from Nazareth and thus of lowly origins. Matthew explains why the family moved without mention of familial connections in the town. See 1 Nephi 11:13. Luke 1:26 indicates that Mary already lived in Nazareth when she became pregnant. The Joseph Smith Translation adds these sentences to the end of the verse: *And it came to pass, that Jesus grew up with his brethren, and waxed strong, and waited upon the Lord for the time of his ministry to come. And he served under his father, and he spake not as other men, neither could he be taught; for he needed not that any man should teach him. And after many years, the hour of his ministry drew nigh.*

3:1 Josephus, *Antiquities* 18.116–17 mentions John the Baptist. Josephus, a first-century Jewish historian, wrote that some Jews held the idea that Herod's army had been destroyed because of what Herod had done to John, whom he calls a *good man* who also taught *virtue and righteousness*. **3:1–5** Compare John 1:26–33; 1 Nephi 10:7–8. **3:2** The meaning *draws near* can also be rendered in English by *approaches*, which places less emphasis on the temporal coming of the kingdom. The New Testament defines *repentance* using the Greek word *metanoeo*, a word that means to *change one's mind*. The concept is similar to changing one's heart, but the Greek idea is more intentional with a decided and purposeful course of action. Paul notes that godly sorrow leads to repentance (2 Corinthians 7:10), and Mark notes that both Jesus and John began their teaching ministry with a message of repentance (Mark 1:14–15). Matthew almost always speaks of the *kingdom of the heavens* with a singular verb. The concept of multiple heavens may be implied, but for Matthew the *kingdom* is singular. The Gospel of Mark prefers *kingdom of God*. The Book of Mormon also begins with a call to repent (1 Nephi 1:4).

draws near." ³This is the one spoken of by Isaiah the prophet when he said, "*A voice shouting in the wilderness, prepare the way of the Lord, make his pathways straight.*" ⁴This same John had his clothing made of camel's hair with a leather belt around his waist, and his diet was locusts and wild honey. ⁵Then Jerusalem and all Judea and all the region around Jordan went to him, ⁶and they were baptized by him in the Jordan River, professing their sins.

⁷When he saw many Pharisees and Sadducees coming to his baptism, he said to them, "You offspring of snakes, who warned you to flee from the coming wrath? ⁸Bear fruit worthy of repentance, ⁹and do not think to say to yourselves, 'We have father Abraham,' because I say that God is able to raise up children to Abraham from these stones. ¹⁰Already the ax lies at the root of the trees, and every tree that does not bear good fruit will be cut down and thrown in the fire.

¹¹"I baptize you in water for repentance, but the one who comes after me is greater than I. I am not able to carry his sandals, but he will baptize you in the Holy Spirit and fire, ¹²whose winnowing fork is in his

---

Compare Matthew 4:17; 10:17; Alma 7:9; 9:25; 10:20; Helaman 5:32; Doctrine and Covenants 33:10; 39:19, etc. **3:3, 11** Quotation from Isaiah 40:3. The evangelists are united in drawing attention to Isaiah 40:3 as a foundational prophecy concerning John the Baptist (Mark 1:3; Luke 1:76; John 1:23). The prophecy is also repeated in the Book of Mormon (1 Nephi 10:7–8; compare John 1:23). Compare Doctrine and Covenants 65:1. **3:4** John the Baptist's dress and diet recall Elijah's manner of living (2 Kings 1:8; Zechariah 13:4). Jews were permitted to eat locusts according to the law of Moses (Leviticus 11:22). **3:6** John's audience does not express any surprise at seeing John the Baptist baptizing fellow Jews. First-century Jews would have been familiar with the practice of an individual washing in a *mikveh* (plural *mikva'ot*), which also required immersion. John's baptism would have differed from that practice because it was performed for another person and was probably not repeated multiple times throughout a person's lifetime. Also, John's baptism was not associated with ritual purity in preparation for holy days and temple worship. Instead, John's baptism clearly had in mind personal repentance that looked forward to a future baptism of the Holy Spirit (Matthew 3:11). The practice of washing is described in Numbers 19:7, 18. **3:7** Matthew notes the presence of Pharisees and Sadducees. These much-maligned groups were religious, political, and social in nature. The Pharisees broadly traced their origins to the Maccabean period, when John Hyrcanus established a priestly dynasty (152 BCE) to govern Judea. These separatists, the meaning of the Hebrew term *Pharisee*, encouraged obedience to the law of Moses as well as emphasizing purity, and they fought against Hellenizing trends in Jewish religious life. Likewise, the Sadducees were active in the second century BCE, although the precise influences leading to their organization are unknown. The Sadducees composed the wealthy, aristocratic Judean hierarchy, and they were influential in controlling the Jerusalem temple. Less is known about the Sadducees, and not all Jewish elites were associated with the Sadducees: some were Pharisees, and some maintained no affiliation. See Doctrine and Covenants 121:23. **3:8** Compare Acts 26:20; Alma 5:35–36; 9:30. The Joseph Smith Translation renders this verse as *Why is it that ye receive not the preaching of him whom God hath sent? If ye receive not this in your hearts, ye receive not me; and if ye receive not me, ye receive not him of whom I am sent to bear record; and for your sins ye have no cloak. Repent therefore, and bring forth fruits meet for repentance.* **3:10** *Thrown in the fire* is the first allusion to eternal judgment. See Luke 3:9; Jacob 5:42; Alma 5:52. Quoted in Doctrine and Covenants 97:7. **3:11** Compare 3 Nephi 12:1. Matthew speaks elsewhere of the coming one (compare Matthew 11:3; 21:9; 23:39). The fulfillment of this prophecy and the one in Matthew 11:3 is found in Matthew 21:9. **3:12** The imagery is that of a facility for threshing wheat. The winnowing fork refers to an instrument used to separate the kernels of wheat from the chaff by lifting the wheat and tossing it into the air.

hand, and he will purge his threshing floor and will gather his wheat into the granary, but the chaff he will burn with unquenchable fire."

THE BAPTISM OF JESUS (MK 1:9–11; LK 3:21–22; JN 1:29–34)

¹³Then Jesus came from Galilee to the Jordan River to John to be baptized by him. ¹⁴But John opposed it, saying, "I need to be baptized by you, and yet you come to me?" ¹⁵Jesus answered him and said, "Let it be so now, for thus it is fitting to fulfill all righteousness." Then he baptized Jesus. ¹⁶After being baptized, Jesus came up out of the water, and, behold, the heavens were opened to him, and he saw the Spirit of God descending like a dove and landing on him, ¹⁷and, behold, a voice from heaven, saying, "This is my beloved Son, in whom I am pleased."

THE TEMPTATION OF JESUS (MK 1:12–13; LK 4:1–13)

4 ¹Then Jesus was led into the wilderness by the Spirit, to be tempted by the devil. ²And since he had fasted for forty days and forty nights he was afterward hungry. ³And the tempter came and said to him, "If you are the Son of God, command these stones to be made into bread." ⁴But he responded to him, "It is written, *'Man will not live by bread alone, but by every word spoken by the mouth of God.'*"

⁵Then the devil took him to the holy city, and placed him upon the pinnacle of the temple, ⁶and said to him, "If you are the Son of God, throw yourself down, for it is written that *'He will command his*

Some translations prefer to translate this as a *fan*. King David purchased the threshing floor of Ornan the Jebusite as the site on which the temple would later be built (2 Chronicles 3:1). Compare Doctrine and Covenants 101:65–66. **3:13** The fact that Jesus walked some 100 kilometers, or 60 miles, from Galilee to the Jordan River near Judea, assuming he was in Nazareth (Matthew 2:23), to be baptized by John shows the importance he placed in being baptized specifically by John, who had the authority to do so. **3:14–15** Alluded to in 2 Nephi 31:5. **3:15** The Greek says simply *then he consented* in place of *then he baptized Jesus*, but the reference is clearly in reference to the act of baptism. Second Nephi 31:5–7 also offers an explanation for why Christ's baptism was needed. **3:16** Matthew does not specifically note the presence of a dove but that the Spirit descended gently like a dove. Luke 3:22 notes that the Spirit descended *bodily* like a dove. Compare 2 Nephi 31:8. **3:17** The saying of the Father echoes Abraham's declaration regarding Isaac (Genesis 22:2, 12, 16; Hebrews 1:2). Compare Psalm 2:7; Isaiah 42:1. At the end of this verse, the Joseph Smith Translation adds *hear ye him*.

4:1 In New Testament times, the terms *devil* and *Satan* had become interchangeable. The Greek *diabolos* means *slanderer* or *backbiter*. Matthew's language here implies that the devil led Jesus into the wilderness *in order to be tempted*, and the scribes who copied the Bible did not attempt to alter the passage to avoid this theological conundrum of whether the devil could lead the Christ into temptation. First Corinthians 10:13 teaches that God will limit temptation so that we are not tempted beyond our own strength and that God will provide a way for our escape. The Joseph Smith Translation alters this verse so that the Spirit does not lead Jesus into temptation. The Book of Mormon develops the idea of Christ's temptations more fully in Mosiah 15:5 (compare Mosiah 3:7; Alma 7:11). *Forty days* has many parallels in the Old Testament (Genesis 7:12; Exodus 24:18; Deuteronomy 8:2–5; 9:18, 25). Here Matthew takes forty days as literal. **4:4** Quotation from Deuteronomy 8:3. Compare Moroni 7:25; Doctrine and Covenants 98:11; Moses 5:15. **4:5** The place that the *pinnacle of the temple* refers to is not clear. Some have thought that it would have referred to the area near the place of trumpeting, located on the southwest corner. Whatever the location, the pinnacle would have been broadly visible to people in the city of Jerusalem. The story may report a spiritual encounter like that of Moses 1:11–12, in which Satan confronts Moses. **4:6** Quotation from Psalm 91:11–12.

angels concerning you' and '*they will lift you up in their hands so that you do not strike your foot against a stone.*'" ⁷Jesus said to him, "Again it is written, '*You shall not tempt the Lord your God.*'"

⁸Again the devil carried him to a very high mountain and showed him all the kingdoms of the world and their glory, ⁹and he said to him, "I will give you all these things if you fall down and you worship me." ¹⁰Then Jesus said to him, "Depart, Satan! For it is written that '*You shall worship the Lord your God, and you shall serve him alone.*'" ¹¹Then the devil departed from him, and angels came and were ministering to him.

THE EARLY GALILEAN MINISTRY (MK 1:14–15; LK 4:14–15; JN 4:1–3; 43–46A)

¹²Hearing that John had been arrested, Jesus went up to Galilee. ¹³And he left Nazareth and came to reside in Capernaum near the lake in the region of Zebulon and Naphtali ¹⁴so that the word of Isaiah the prophet might be fulfilled, saying, ¹⁵"*The land of Zebulon and the land of Naphtali, the way of the sea, near the Jordan, Galilee of the Gentiles,* ¹⁶*the people residing in darkness have seen a great light, and for those who sat in the region and shadow of death a light has dawned.*" ¹⁷After those things, Jesus began to declare, "Repent, for the kingdom of heaven is near."

4:7 Quotation from Deuteronomy 6:16. Jesus does not tempt or try (the Greek verb means both *to try* and *to tempt*) God in the way that Israel tempted God while in the wilderness. The devil, it is implied, is tempting God with his questions. **4:9** Compare Alma 11:22. **4:10** Quotation from Deuteronomy 6:13. **4:13** Having overcome the temptations of the devil, Jesus moves to Capernaum, a small fishing and farming village on the north shore of the Sea of Galilee. Such a move for convenience stands out to Matthew because it was not typical for individuals to randomly move away from family and ancestral roots. **4:13–16** The tribes of Zebulon and Naphtali had been deported by the Assyrians in 723 BC, and the area was repopulated by Gentiles. **4:15–16** Quotation from Isaiah 9:1–2. The message of the gospel includes *Galilee of the Gentiles*, which interprets Galilee as a home to Gentiles. Matthew appreciates the forward-looking reference to the Gentiles receiving the gospel message (Matthew 12:18). **4:16** This verse is echoed in Doctrine and Covenants 57:10. **4:17** Matthew notes *after those things*, signaling a shift to the beginning of Jesus's public ministry. The tempted Messiah now reaches out to save. Compare Alma 9:25; 10:20; Helaman 5:32; Doctrine and Covenants 42:7.

Decapolis, Judea, Galilee, and Samaria
Map by Brandon Whitney, ThinkSpatial, BYU Geography

JESUS CALLS HIS FIRST DISCIPLES (MK 1:16–20; LK 5:1–11; JN 1:35–51)

¹⁸Walking by the Sea of Galilee, he saw two brothers, Simon called Peter and Andrew his brother, throwing a net into the sea, for they were fishermen. ¹⁹And he said to them, "Come and follow me, and I will make you fishers of men and women." ²⁰And they immediately left their nets and followed him. ²¹And he went away from that place and saw two other brothers, Jacob the son of Zebedee and John his brother, in a ship with their father Zebedee mending their nets, and he called to them. ²²They immediately left the boat and their father and followed him.

EARLY MIRACLES (MK 3:7–12; LK 6:17–20A)

²³And he traveled around all of Galilee, teaching in their synagogues and declaring the gospel of the kingdom and healing all the sick and ill among them. ²⁴And his fame spread through all of Syria, and they brought to him all the sick, those having various illnesses and tormented by pain, possessed by demons, epileptics, and disabled, and he healed them. ²⁵And a crowd followed him, many from Galilee, Decapolis, Jerusalem, Judea, and beyond the Jordan.

THE BEATITUDES (LK 6:20B–23)

5 ¹When he saw the crowds, he went up the mountain, and after he sat down his disciples came to him, ²and he opened

---

4:18 *Simon called Peter* (literally *Simon the rock*) looks forward to Matthew 16:17–19, where Jesus names Simon the *rock*. The earliest disciples included two sets of brothers: Andrew and Peter, and Jacob and John. **4:21** The name James does not appear in the New Testament, and all individuals who bear that name in modern translations were formally named Jacob in their lifetimes. The origin of the shift from Jacob to James appears to be the Latin translation of the New Testament, which changed the name *Jacob* in Greek to *Jacobus* in Latin. Owing to verbal shifts in the language, *Jacobus* was later rendered as *Jacomus* and then through French was shortened to *James*. For the importance of John in the later New Testament, see Galatians 2:9, where he became a pillar of the Church. John is mentioned three times in the Book of Mormon (1 Nephi 14:27; 3 Nephi 28:6; Ether 4:16). Nephi appears to have this disciple in mind when speaking about the "apostle of the Lamb" who would write the end of his revelation. Matthew uses the word *apostle* only one time in reference to Jesus's earliest followers (Matthew 10:2). Instead, he prefers to call them *disciples* (= *students*). **4:23** In the Book of Mormon, Jesus heals according to the faith of the individual (3 Nephi 17:8). The Book of Mormon also testifies to the importance of Jesus's miracles (2 Nephi 10:4; Mormon 9:18). **4:24** The New Testament frequently describes illness and sickness as a result of demonic possession (Matthew 12:22; Mark 5:15; Acts 16:16). Many of the symptoms associated with demonic possession are today described in medical terms. The Old Testament does not describe illness in the same way (see Alma 46:40). **4:25** The crowds in Matthew are most often interested in Jesus, and they follow him in faith (Matthew 7:28; 12:23; 21:45–46).

5:1 The Sermon on the Mount (Matthew 5–7) portrays Christ as the new Moses (compare Exodus 24:12), teaching the Israelites God's commandments as Moses taught from Mount Sinai. The commandments that Jesus gives are spiritual and internal. While Matthew devotes three chapters to this sermon, the Sermon on the Mount's parallel in Luke has only thirty-two verses (Luke 6:17–49). A similar version of the Matthean sermon is recorded in 3 Nephi 12–14. Jesus often sat in preparation to teach (see Matthew 13:1). **5:1–11** These verses likely allude to Isaiah 61:1–2 in how they describe the ministry of the Messiah to the poor. **5:2** The Joseph Smith Translation adds *Blessed are they who shall believe on me; and again, more blessed are they who shall believe on your words when ye shall testify that ye have seen me and that I am. Yea, blessed are they who shall believe on your words and come down into the*

his mouth and taught them, saying, [3]"Blessed are the poor in spirit, for theirs is the kingdom of heaven. [4]Blessed are those who mourn, for they will be comforted. [5]Blessed are the meek, for they will inherit the earth. [6]Blessed are those who hunger and thirst for righteousness, for they will be filled. [7]Blessed are the merciful, for they will receive mercy. [8]Blessed are the pure in heart, for they will see God. [9]Blessed are the peacemakers, for they will be called the children of God. [10]Blessed are those who are persecuted for righteousness' sake, for theirs is the kingdom of heaven.[11]Blessed are you when they insult you and persecute you, and falsely say all manner of evil against you for my sake.[12]Rejoice and be glad because your reward is great in heaven, for they likewise persecuted the prophets before you.

SALT AND LIGHT OF THE WORLD
(MK 9:49–50; LK 14:34–35)

[13]"You are the salt of the earth, but if the salt loses its flavor, how can it function as salt? It is no longer good for anything, but to be thrown out and walked on.

[14]You are the light of the world. A city built on a hill cannot be hid: [15]no one who lights a lamp places it under a basket but on a lampstand, and it gives light to all those in the house. [16]Therefore, let your light shine before people so they may see your good works and give glory to your Father who is in heaven.

THE LAW AND THE PROPHETS
(LK 16:16–17)

[17]"Do not think that I have come to destroy the Law or the Prophets; I have not come to destroy but to fulfill. [18]Truly I say to you, until heaven and earth pass away, not one iota or stroke of a letter will fail from the Law until all is accomplished. [19]Whoever breaks one of the least of these commandments and teaches others in like manner will be called least in the kingdom of heaven. Whoever does them and teaches them will be called great in the kingdom of heaven. [20]I say to you that if your righteousness is not greater than that of the scribes and Pharisees, you will never enter into the kingdom of heaven.

---

depth of humility and be baptized in my name; for they shall be visited with fire and the Holy Ghost, and shall receive a remission of their sins. **5:3, 10** The blessing, *theirs is the kingdom of God*, is the same for the poor in spirit and for those who are persecuted for righteousness' sake. The form of saying *blessed are . . .* is common throughout all books of scripture (see Psalm 119:2; Helaman 12:23; Doctrine and Covenants 34:4–5). **5:4** Some early manuscripts read *Blessed are those who mourn now*, although the addition of *now* is probably not original. The Joseph Smith Translation reads *Yea, blessed are the poor in spirit, which cometh unto me; for theirs is the kingdom of heaven.* **5:6** The Joseph Smith Translation adds *filled with the Holy Ghost.* Compare Psalm 107:9; Mosiah 5:7. **5:8** Interpretation of this verse is found in Doctrine and Covenants 56:18 (compare Doctrine and Covenants 97:16). **5:11** Some early manuscripts read *may persecute you*, while other late manuscripts lack *falsely*. **5:13** The Greek reads *trampled by mankind* instead of *walked on*. First Nephi 19:7 develops the theme of trampling on the teachings of God (compare 3 Nephi 16:15). Doctrine and Covenants 103:10 interprets this verse (compare Alma 34:29; Doctrine and Covenants 101:40). **5:15** The word *basket* designates a vessel that could be used to extinguish an oil lamp. **5:16** The meaning of *good works* is expanded in Alma 5:41. **5:17** The Old Testament contains three main divisions: the Law, the Prophets, and the Writings. Here Jesus seems to draw attention to the authority of the Law and the Prophets. See 2 Nephi 25:28; 3 Nephi 15:10; Doctrine and Covenants 59:22. **5:18** Alma 34:13 expands the meaning of this verse. Compare 3 Nephi 1:25.

PERSPECTIVES ON THE LAW
(LK 6:27–36; 12:57–59)

²¹"You have heard that it was said to the ancients, '*Do not kill*,' and 'whoever kills will be in danger of the judgment.' ²²But I say to you that anyone who is angry with a sibling will be in danger of the judgment, and whoever says to his brother or sister, 'Raqa,' will be brought to the council, and whoever says 'fool' will be sent to a fiery hell. ²³When you bring your gift to the altar and there remember that your brother or sister has something against you, ²⁴leave your gift there before the altar and first be reconciled to your brother or sister, and then go and offer your gift. ²⁵Agree quickly with your accuser while you are in the way with him, or your accuser may hand you over to the judge, and the judge to the guard, and you will be thrown into prison. ²⁶Truly I say to you, you will not leave there until you have paid your last bronze coin.

²⁷"You have heard that it was said, '*You shall not commit adultery*.' ²⁸But I say to you that everyone who looks at a woman to lust for her has already committed adultery with her in his heart. ²⁹If your right eye causes you to sin, tear it out and throw it away from you! It is more profitable to you that one of your body parts be destroyed than for your whole body to be thrown into hell. ³⁰And if your right hand causes you to sin, cut it off and throw it away from you! It is more profitable to you that one of your body parts be destroyed than for your whole body to be cast into hell.

³¹"It was said, '*Whoever divorces his wife, let him give her a certificate of divorce*.' ³²But I say to you that all who divorce, with the exception for immoral behavior,

---

5:21 Quotation from Exodus 20:13 (compare Leviticus 24:17; Numbers 35:16–18; Deuteronomy 5:18) with a possible echo of Numbers 35:30. The second half of the quotation is from an unknown source, which has caused some commentators to question whether it is a quotation of scripture. **5:22** Some later and inferior manuscripts add *without a cause* following *his brother*. The Joseph Smith Translation omits *without a cause*, as does 3 Nephi 12:22. Compare Mormon 8:17. The council here is the Sanhedrin, a governing body that judged religious matters in Jewish communities (the Greek word *sanhedrin* refers to a gathering). There were multiple community or regional sanhedrins, and here Jesus speaks in the singular as though he had a specific one in mind. When speaking of judgment, Jesus speaks specifically of the *hell of fire* or the *Gehenna of fire*. The emphasis is not on a place or location (hell), but rather the torment of its fiery existence. *Gehenna* was the Greek transliteration of the Hebrew *ge-hinnom*, or the Hinnom Valley on the southern side of the city of Jerusalem. Jeremiah 7:31 notes that it was a place where human sacrifices were offered. *Raqa* is an Aramaic word meaning *fool*. **5:25** The Greek of this verse lacks a verb in the phrase *and the judge to the guard*, which is supplied in some manuscripts so that it reads *and the judge might hand you over to the guard*. The verse appears to describe imprisonment for debt, even though the Torah treats the inability to repay a debt with great leniency (Exodus 22:25; Deuteronomy 24:10–12). Matthew 18:23–35 also describes punishment associated with the inability to repay a debt, a topic that Matthew felt was important. **5:26** Often translated as *penny*, this coin is the Latin *quadrans*, a bronze coin that was one-fourth of an *as* (a larger Roman bronze coin that was in greater circulation). Its purchasing power was quite low, and Mark 12:42 notes that two *lepta*, or widow's mites, had the same value as a *quadrans*. This coin was therefore worth twice that of a *lepton*. **5:27** Quotation from Exodus 20:14; Deuteronomy 5:18. **5:28** The meaning of this verse is commented on in Doctrine and Covenants 63:16 (an allusion is found in Doctrine and Covenants 42:23). **5:30** The Joseph Smith Translation adds at the end of this verse *And now this I speak, a parable concerning your sins; wherefore, cast them from you, that ye may not be hewn down and cast into the fire*. **5:31** Quotation from Deuteronomy 24:1. **5:32** The Greek word *porneias* signifies sexual impropriety and impurity, and the written form of it has been passed on as

cause her to commit adultery, and whoever remarries the divorced woman commits adultery.

³³"Again, you have heard it said by the ancients, '*You shall not make false promises, but carry out the promises you have made to the Lord.*' ³⁴But I say to you, do not swear oaths at all, neither by heaven, because it is the throne of God, ³⁵nor by the earth, because that is his footstool, nor by Jerusalem, because that is the city of the great King, ³⁶nor by your head, because you are not able to make one hair black or white. ³⁷Let your speech be 'Yes, yes,' or 'no, no.' Whatever is more than this is evil.

³⁸"You have heard it said, '*An eye for an eye, and a tooth for a tooth.*' ³⁹But I say to you, do not resist the evildoer, but whoever strikes you on the right cheek, turn the other to him also. ⁴⁰And if someone hopes to sue you and take your tunic, give your outer coat also, ⁴¹and if someone compels you to go a mile, go two miles. ⁴²Give to those who ask you, and do not turn away those who hope to borrow money from you.

⁴³"You have heard it said, '*Love your neighbor,*' but 'hate your enemy.' ⁴⁴But I say to you that you shall love those who hate you and pray for those who persecute you. ⁴⁵In this way you will be the children of your Father in heaven: he makes the sun rise on the wicked and good, and he causes it to rain on the righteous and unrighteous. ⁴⁶If you love those who love you, what reward do you have? Do not tax collectors do the same thing? ⁴⁷And if you greet your brothers and sisters only, what are you doing better than others? Do not the people of other nations do the same? ⁴⁸Therefore, you will be perfect, even as your heavenly Father is perfect.

OFFERINGS AND PRAYER
(LK 11:1–3)

6 ¹"Be careful to not do your good acts in front of others for them to see. If so, you have no reward from your Father in heaven. ²When you make an offering, do not blow a trumpet before you as the hypocrites do in the synagogues and in the

---

the English word *pornography*. Many translations prefer the word *fornication*, but the meaning of the word is much broader and includes all immoral behavior. Compare Doctrine and Covenants 42:74. **5:33** Quotation from Leviticus 19:12; Deuteronomy 5:11, 20; 23:22. **5:34–35** The wording of these verses is reflected in 1 Nephi 17:39. **5:37** Many translators prefer to translate *ponerou* as *evil*, but the sense is of an obstacle to Christian faith. In ethical contexts, it can mean evil. **5:38** Quotation from Leviticus 24:20; Deuteronomy 19:21. **5:40** The shirt in this verse refers to the Roman tunic, a type of shirt that extended below the waist. Laborers, soldiers, and most noncitizens would wear the tunic slightly above the knee. Stripes, varying length, and colors indicated wealth and status. Roman citizens could wear the tunic underneath the toga in formal settings and likely also in winter. Standard daily dress would have been the short single-colored tunic. **5:43** Quotation of Leviticus 19:18 (Deuteronomy 7:2; 20:16; 23:4, 7), but the second half of the quotation is probably from popular oral tradition. This is not a commandment in the law of Moses but may stem from a teaching of the Essenes (see also Mosiah 23:15). The Essenes, like the Pharisees and Sadducees, were a political, social, and religious movement. An Essene community existed on the western shore of the Dead Sea, and the community may have produced the Dead Sea Scrolls. The Essenes are not directly mentioned in the New Testament, and they were extremely conservative in their religious views. **5:44** Most later manuscripts read *But I say to you, love your enemies, bless those who curse you, do good to those who hate you, and pray for those who despitefully use you and persecute you.* **5:48** A possible allusion to Psalm 18:30.

6:1 The word translated as *good acts* is the Greek word *righteousness*. The idea is fundamentally that of generosity to the poor. Some later manuscripts change *good acts* to *alms*, which may have influenced early English Bible translations. Compare Mosiah 5:11. **6:2** A *hypocrite* is a stage actor in a Greek drama. The Greek reads literally *they may have the glory of men*, but the phrase is not intended to exclude

streets so that they may have the glory of others. Truly I say to you, they have their reward. ³When you are giving, do not allow your left hand to know what your right hand is doing ⁴so that your giving may be in secret, and your Father, who sees in secret, will reward you.

⁵"And when you pray, do not be like the hypocrites: they love to pray in the synagogues and on the corners of broad streets so that people can see them. Truly I say to you that they have their reward. ⁶When you pray, go to your room and close the door, and pray to your Father in secret. Your Father, who sees in secret, will reward you. ⁷When you pray, do not pray empty words as the Gentiles do, for they think that in saying much they will be heard. ⁸Do not be like them, for your Father knows what things you need before you ask him.

⁹"Therefore, pray in this manner:

Our Father in heaven,
let your name be holy,
¹⁰may your kingdom come,
may your will be done on earth even as
    it is heaven.
¹¹Give us enough bread for today,
¹²and take away our debts, to the extent
    we have forgiven our debtors,
¹³and do not lead us toward tempta-
    tion, but save us from evil.

¹⁴"If you forgive others of their their misdeeds, your Father in heaven will

---

men or women. Third Nephi 27:11 alludes to Matthew 6:2, 5, and 16. **6:5** *Synagogue*, in this verse, may not be the physical location of worship but simply a gathering for religious discussion. The Greek term ranges in meaning from *a synagogue* to *a gathering* or *meeting*. **6:6** Some late manuscripts add *openly* to the end of the verse. The Book of Mormon preserves the adverb *openly* (3 Nephi 13:6). **6:7** One early important Greek manuscript reads *hypocrites* in place of *Gentiles*. **6:8** One important Greek manuscript reads *God your Father* in place of *your Father*. **6:9–13** These verses preserve the Lord's Prayer, which represents, for Matthew, Jesus's most important teaching on the subject of prayer. A slightly different version is found in Luke 11:2–4 (but not in the Sermon on the Plain; see note to Matthew 5:1). Other examples of Jesus's prayers include Matthew 26:39–42, 44; Luke 22:42; John 17. For scriptural teachings on prayer, see Acts 1:24; Alma 10:23; Mormon 5:21; Doctrine and Covenants 42:14; 112:10. Some translations render the wording of the prayer into elegant and flowing English prose, but the wording of the prayer uses everyday language that intentionally rhymes some of the line endings. **6:11** The idea of *bread for today*, also rendered as *daily bread*, contains a subtle critique of amassing wealth for future needs. The teaching echoes Deuteronomy 8:3. Jesus may have been commenting on the Roman acceptance of amassing wealth. Luke's translation of the saying (Luke 11:3) is more forceful in its teaching: *give us our daily bread day by day*. The word translated as *daily* appears nowhere else in the New Testament. Matthew avoids the typical Greek word for *daily*. *Daily* is translated as *supersubstantialem* in the Vulgate of Matthew 6:11 and means *life-sustaining*. Matthew's wording equates financial debt with spiritual sin. **6:12** Matthew here prefers *debts* (also *trespasses*) to Luke's *sins* (Luke 11:4). Matthew may have intended the idea of *debts* to represent the weight or impact of sin. Origen (died ca. 254 CE), an early patristic father who quoted the Lord's Prayer, translated it as *trespasses*, using a different word than Matthew or Luke did. **6:13** Later manuscripts add the final sentence of the Lord's Prayer, known as the doxology, that is familiar from other translations: *For yours is the kingdom, and the power, and the glory, forever. Amen.* The manuscripts are not very reliable that support this reading, but a version of it is recorded in the *Didache* and 3 Nephi 13:13. A similar petition by David is found in Psalm 141:4. James 1:13 treats the theme of temptation, but in this verse it can also mean *trial* or *temptation*. *Amen* is a Hebrew word signifying agreement to something that is true and firmly agreed upon, although this prayer does not end with *Amen* unless the doxology is original. **6:14** The word translated *misdeeds* is not the same word that is used elsewhere for *sins*. Jesus may have intended to refer to common infractions

forgive you. ¹⁵But if you do not forgive others, then your Father will not forgive your misdeeds.

ON FASTING

¹⁶"When you fast, do not be like the downcast hypocrites, for they make their faces appear to others to be fasting. Truly I say to you, they have their reward. ¹⁷But you, when fasting, anoint your head and wash your face. ¹⁸Thus, you will not appear to others to be fasting but to your Father, who is in secret, and your Father, who sees in secret, will reward you.

ON DISCIPLESHIP (LK 12:22–34)

¹⁹"Do not store your treasures on the earth, where moth and rust destroy, and where thieves break in and steal. ²⁰Store your treasures in heaven, where neither moth nor rust destroy, and where thieves do not break in and steal. ²¹Where your treasure is, there your heart will be.

²²"The light of the body is the eye. If your eye is healthy, then your whole body will be full of light: ²³if your eye is unhealthy, then your whole body will be full of darkness. If the light in you is darkness, then your whole body will be full of darkness. If the light in you is darkness, how great a darkness it will be!

²⁴"No one is able to serve two masters, for he will either hate one and love the other, or esteem one and despise the other. You cannot serve God and money.

²⁵"Because of this I say to you, do not worry about your life, about what to eat and drink, nor for your body and what you wear. Is not life more than food and the body more than clothing? ²⁶Look at the birds of heaven. They do not sow seeds or reap crops or gather the harvest into storehouses, but your Father in heaven cares for them. Are you not greater than they are?

---

against others and not specifically to the idea of sin against God. Alluded to in Doctrine and Covenants 82:1. **6:16** For examples of fasting, see Zechariah 7:5; 8:19; Luke 18:12 (the Pharisees fast twice a week). For fasting in the Book of Mormon, see Omni 1:26; Mosiah 27:23; Alma 8:26; 17:3; 3 Nephi 13:18; 4 Nephi 1:12; Moroni 6:5. **6:16–18** The Book of Mormon treats the subject of the interconnectedness of outward appearance and spiritual well-being using clothing as a metaphor (1 Nephi 13:7 [which uses language similar to Revelation 18:12]; 2 Nephi 28:13; Helaman 6:13; Ether 10:24). **6:19–34** These sayings are recorded in different places in the Gospel of Luke. Compare Matthew 6:19–21 = Luke 12:33–34; Matthew 6:22–23 = Luke 11:34–36; Matthew 6:24 = Luke 16:13; Matthew 6:25–34 = Luke 12:22–32. **6:20** Many translations favor the language of *storing up treasures* or *accumulating treasures*. The Greek verb can indicate those ideas, but the saying does not appear to be an encouragement to accumulate wealth, but rather a directive to store it in a new location. Compare Helaman 8:25. Alluded to in 3 Nephi 27:32; Doctrine and Covenants 6:27. **6:21** This verse shifts to singular pronouns, perhaps as a means of emphasis. **6:22** The idea of the eye being healthy also implies that it is sound and simple in its outlook. **6:24** The origin of the word *money* in this verse (*mammon*) is not precisely known, but it appears to refer to *treasure* or *acquired wealth*. The Doctrine and Covenants (82:22) cites Luke's phraseology and not Matthew's (Luke 16:9) regarding *mammon*. **6:25** Compare Luke 8:14; 21:34; Philippians 4:6. The earliest manuscripts are divided on whether the text should be *what it eats and drinks* or *what it eats*. The Joseph Smith Translation adds to the beginning of this verse *And again, I say unto you, go ye into the world and care not for the world; for the world will hate you, and will persecute you, and will turn you out of their synagogues; nevertheless, ye shall go forth from house to house, teaching the people; and I will go before you, and your Heavenly Father will provide for you, whatsoever things ye need for food, and what you shall eat; and for raiment, what ye shall wear or put on.* **6:25, 28–29** These verses are interpreted in Doctrine and Covenants 84:81–82. **6:25, 31** A similar injunction is observed in Alma 31:37.

²⁷Who is able to add one measure to his height by worrying? ²⁸And why do you worry about clothing? Think about the lilies of the field, how they grow, but they do not work or spin. ²⁹But I say to you that Solomon in all his glory was not dressed like one of them. ³⁰If God so clothes the grass of the field that today is alive and tomorrow is thrown into the oven, how much more will he clothe you of little faith? ³¹Do not worry, saying, 'What will we eat, what will we drink, or what will we wear?' ³²The Gentiles seek after all these things, but your Father in heaven knows that you need all these things. ³³Seek first the kingdom of God and his righteousness, and all these things will be given to you. ³⁴Do not worry about tomorrow, because tomorrow can worry for itself. Today's evil is sufficient for today.

ON JUDGING (MK 4:24–25; LK 6:37–42)

7 ¹"Do not judge so that you may not be judged. ²With the judgment you administer you will be judged, and with the measure you use, it will be measured to you. ³Why do you look at the splinter in the eye of your brother or sister and do not consider the log in your own eye? ⁴Or how do you say to your brother or sister, 'Let me take the splinter out of your eye,' when there is a log in your own eye? ⁵Hypocrite, first take the log out of your own eye, and then you will see clearly the splinter in the eye of your brother or sister.

⁶"Do not give that which is holy to dogs or throw your pearls before pigs, or they will trample them under their feet and turn on you and tear you apart.

⁷"Ask and it will be given to you, seek and you will find, knock and it will be opened to you. ⁸Everyone who asks receives, and those who seek find, and those who knock will have a door opened to them. ⁹Is there a person among you who, if his child asks for bread, will give him a stone? ¹⁰Or if a child asks for a fish will give him a snake? ¹¹If you being evil know how to give good gifts to your children, how much more will your Father in heaven give good things to those who ask of him. ¹²In all things, do the same to others

---

6:27 A cubit, or *one measure*, is the length from the end of the middle finger to the elbow, and in this context the directive to not worry about adding to one's overall height can also be interpreted to mean worrying about *adding an hour to one's lifespan*. **6:28** For examples of the clothing of kings, see Esther 8:15; Daniel 7:9. **6:28–29** These verses are quoted in a slightly different form in Doctrine and Covenants 84:82. **6:32** This verse is quoted in Doctrine and Covenants 84:83. **6:33** The phrase could also be rendered *its righteousness* in place of *his righteousness*. Alluded to in Doctrine and Covenants 11:23. **6:34** This verse is interpreted in a missionary context in Doctrine and Covenants 84:80–81, 84.

7:1 Given the context of Matthew 6:14–15 (paralleled in Luke 6:37), the phrase should mean *judged by God*. Other teachings of Jesus regarding judging include Matthew 12:27 and John 7:24; 8:15; 12:47. **7:2** Alluded to in Moroni 7:18; Doctrine and Covenants 1:10. **7:3** An alternative form of the saying is found in Luke 6:41–42, where the question is applied to one's neighbor. **7:4** Matthew uses the familiar *brother*, which implies both brothers and sisters, as it has been translated here. **7:5** The hypocrite in this verse is the recipient-reader of the text and hence a believer. **7:6** Dogs were sometimes thought of as contemptuous creatures that would lick blood and devour carcasses (1 Kings 14:11; 16:4), thus making them unclean. The concept of consecrated food is set forth in Exodus 29:33; Leviticus 22:10. The meaning of trampling underfoot is interpreted in 1 Nephi 19:7. Compare Doctrine and Covenants 41:6. **7:7** A parallel saying is found in Proverbs 8:17 (compare 3 Nephi 27:29). **7:7–8** These verses are paraphrased in 3 Nephi 27:29; compare John 16:24; Luke 11:9–10; Doctrine and Covenants 4:7; 6:5. **7:12** The Golden Rule was known in antiquity in many different forms and versions, and it is often called the law of reciprocity. The *Didache* (1:2) begins with a version of the Golden Rule that is similar

as you desire them to do to you. This is the Law and the Prophets.

WARNINGS (LK 6:43–49)

[13]"Enter through the narrow gate, because the gate is wide and the way is easy that leads to ruin, and there are many who find it. [14]The gate is narrow and the way is hard that leads to life, and there are few who find it.

[15]"Beware of false prophets, who come to you in sheep's clothing but inwardly are hungry wolves. [16]You will know them by their fruits. Do they gather grapes from thorns or figs from briars? [17]Thus every good tree bears good fruit, and every bad tree bears evil fruit. [18]A good tree cannot bear evil fruit, nor can an evil tree bear good fruit. [19]Every tree that does not bear good fruit is cut down and thrown in the fire. [20]Therefore, by their fruits you will know them.

[21]"Not everyone who says to me, 'Lord, Lord,' will enter into the kingdom of heaven, but only the one who does the will of my Father in heaven. [22]Many will say to me in that day, 'Lord, Lord, have we not prophesied in your name, and in your name cast out spirits, and in your name done many miracles?' [23]I will declare to them, 'I never knew you; *depart from me, you lawbreakers.*'

[24]"Everyone who hears my words and does them is like a wise person who built his house on bedrock. [25]And the rain came, and the rivers ran, and the winds blew, and they beat on that house, and it did not fall because it was built upon bedrock. [26]Everyone who hears my words and does not do them is like a foolish man who built his house on sand. [27]And the rain came, and the rivers ran, and the winds blew, and they beat on that house, and it fell, and it was a great fall!"

[28]And it came to pass that when Jesus finished speaking these words, the crowds were surprised at his teaching [29]because he taught them as one who had power and not as their scribes.

---

to the one Jesus gave: *love your neighbor as yourself, and do not do to another what you would not want done to you.* This saying appears in 3 Nephi 15:10 (compare Luke 16:16; Doctrine and Covenants 59:22). **7:13–14** The idea that there are two paths or ways was a common theme in antiquity and became known as the Two Ways. The most detailed discussion of the idea is found in *Didache* 1–6; compare Jacob 6:11; 3 Nephi 14:13; 27:33. **7:15–20** The warning about listening to wandering prophets looks forward to a time when the Christian community was under threat by hostile Christian communities seeking out converts among other Christians. **7:16–18** The word translated as *fruit* represents a plural noun, but it seems to be better represented in English by the abstract concept of fruit rather than by multiple types of fruit. **7:19** Compare Alma 5:52. **7:21** The plural is used here, *kingdom of heavens.* Some late manuscripts add *will enter into the kingdom of heaven* to the end of the verse, although this thought is already implied by the parallel structure of the verse. That they would call him *Lord, Lord* either insinuates a master-servant relationship in which the servant would use the respectful term *Lord,* or it could refer to the Old Testament idea of *The Lord.* See Matthew 25:11 for a similar idea when the five maidens cry out *Lord, Lord.* James 1:22 asserts a similar idea that the doers of the word of God will be saved. Language shared between Matthew 7:21; 12:50 appears in 3 Nephi 14:21; 27:13. **7:22** One early manuscript reads *cast out many spirits.* **7:23** Some translations choose to render this *you workers of iniquity* or *you evildoers.* The last phrase beginning with *depart* is a quotation of Psalm 6:9. Mosiah 26:27 refers to this verse, combining it with language from Matthew 25:41. **7:24, 26** Compare 3 Nephi 15:1. Echoed in Doctrine and Covenants 11:24. **7:25, 27** Alluded to in Doctrine and Covenants 90:5. **7:26** Second Nephi 28:28 alludes to this parable and also Mark 4:16 (see Matthew 16:18; 3 Nephi 18:13). **7:26–27** Compare 3 Nephi 18:13. **7:28** This is the end of the first of Matthew's five longer discourses. For the endings of the other four, see 11:1; 13:53; 19:1; 26:1. Compare 3 Nephi 15:1; 27:33. **7:29** Some later

HEALING OF A MAN WITH LEPROSY (MK 1:40–45; LK 5:12–16)

8 ¹When Jesus came down from the mountain, a large crowd followed him. ²And a man with leprosy knelt down and said to him, "Lord, if you wish, you can purify me." ³And he reached out his hand and touched him, saying, "I do want this. Be cleansed." And right away his leprosy was cleansed. ⁴Then Jesus said to him, "Share this with no one, but go show yourself to the priest, and offer the gift as instructed by Moses as a witness to them."

THE CENTURION'S SON IS HEALED (LK 7:1–10; JN 4:46B–54)

⁵And when he came to Capernaum, a centurion came to him and called him, ⁶saying, "Lord, my son is lying at home motionless, in terrible pain." ⁷And he said to him, "I will come and heal him." ⁸And the centurion responded, saying, "Lord, I am not worthy that you should come under my roof, but say the word only, and my son will be healed. ⁹For I am a man with authority, having soldiers under my command, and I say to one, 'Go,' and he goes, and to another, 'Come,' and he comes, and to my servant, 'Do this,' and he does it." ¹⁰Jesus, when he heard this, marveled and said to those following him, "Truly I say to you, I have not found such faith in Israel. ¹¹I say to you that many will come from the east and west and will eat with Abraham, Isaac, and Jacob in the kingdom of heaven. ¹²But the children of the kingdom will be thrown into the outer darkness, where there will be weeping and grinding of teeth." ¹³And Jesus said to the centurion, "Go, and as you have believed, let it be done." And his son was healed in that same hour.

HEALING OF PETER'S MOTHER-IN-LAW (MK 1:29–34; LK 4:38–41)

¹⁴And Jesus came to Peter's house and saw his mother-in-law cast down with fever.

manuscripts add the Pharisees so that the end of the verse reads *and not as their scribes and Pharisees.*

8:1–9:38 Matthew collects many of the miracle stories from Jesus's ministry in these two chapters. Together they help demonstrate to the reader that Jesus is the Promised One, or the One who would come (Matthew 3:11). **8:1** *Leprosy* in the New Testament period described a variety of skin diseases, including Hansen's disease (see Leviticus 13:45–46). **8:2** The verb indicates cleansing or purifying in a Levitical or priestly sense and is not the typical verb of healing. Compare Matthew 8:7. **8:3** The act of touching the man would have rendered Jesus unclean (Leviticus 14:1–32). **8:4** The command to not tell anyone about a miracle or healing is reminiscent of the Gospel of Mark. See Mark 1:34; 7:36; 9:30. Compare also Matthew 16:20; 17:9; Mark 7:24; 8:30; 9:9; Luke 5:14; 9:21, 36. The gift that Moses commanded to be given is set forth in Leviticus 14:2–32. **8:5** Some Syriac manuscripts refer to the centurion as a *chiliarch*, a commander of one thousand soldiers (see also 8:13). A centurion commands one hundred soldiers in the Roman army, thus indicating that this individual was a Roman citizen and a retired soldier of some rank. **8:6** The centurion could also be asking about his servant. The care that he shows for the boy may indicate that he is his son, but the Greek word can refer to either a son or servant. **8:11** See Isaiah 2:2–4 for converts from the east and west. Compare Luke 1:70; Alma 7:25; Helaman 3:30. **8:11–12** An allusion to Psalm 107:3 (compare Alma 5:24). **8:12** The image of grinding of teeth appears to contrast with those who will dine with Abraham, Isaac, and Jacob and will presumably have their mouths full of food. Grinding of teeth may refer to chewing without any food. Compare Matthew 22:13; 25:30; Alma 40:13; Doctrine and Covenants 19:5; 101:91. **8:13** The manuscript support for the final sentence, *and his son was healed in that same hour*, is not unanimous, and several different early versions exist. Some early manuscripts add a second somewhat redundant sentence to the end, *the centurion returned to his house and found his son in that same hour healed.* **8:14** First Corinthians 9:5 also refers to Peter's being married.

¹⁵And he took her hand, and the fever left her, and she began to minister to him. ¹⁶When evening came, they brought to him many under the power of demons, and he cast out the spirits with a word, and he healed all those who were ill, ¹⁷that the word of the prophet Isaiah might be fulfilled, saying, "*He took away our weaknesses and bore our sicknesses.*"

FOXES HAVE HOLES (LK 9:57–62)

¹⁸When Jesus saw the crowd around him, he commanded them to depart for the other side, ¹⁹and a scribe came to him and said, "Teacher, I will follow you wherever you may go." ²⁰And Jesus said to him, "The foxes have holes and the birds of heaven have nests, but the Son of Man does not have a place to lay his head." ²¹Another of his disciples said to him, "Lord, let me go and bury my father." ²²Jesus said to him, "Follow me, and let the dead bury their own dead."

THE STILLING OF THE STORM (MK 4:35–41; LK 8:22–25)

²³And he entered into a boat, and his disciples followed him, ²⁴and a great storm arose in the lake so that the ship was swamped by the waves, but he was asleep. ²⁵And they came and woke him, saying, "Lord, save us, we are about to die." ²⁶But he said to them, "Oh, you of little faith, why are you afraid?" Then he arose and rebuked the winds and the sea, and there was a great calm. ²⁷And the men were amazed, saying, "What kind of man is this that the waves and the lake obey him?"

HEALING OF A MAN AT GADARA/ GERASA (MK 5:1–20; LK 8:26–39)

²⁸When he came to the other side, to the land of the Gadarenes, two men who were possessed came out from the tombs to meet him. They were so fierce that it was difficult for anyone to pass down

---

8:15 When Peter's mother-in-law was healed, she ministered to Jesus. Her actions are described using the verbal form of the noun *deacon*, and the primary meaning of the noun and verb is that of service. This is one of the earliest recorded references to the actions of someone offering service as a deacon; see also Mark 1:31; Luke 4:39, and especially John 12:2. **8:16** Jesus, like God, commands by the word of his mouth. **8:17** Quotation from Isaiah 53:4. **8:18, 23** It appears that Matthew recorded additional teachings that were given after Jesus had requested to depart for the other side of the Sea of Galilee. From the physical locations noted in the chapter (Capernaum verse 5; Gadara verse 28), it appears that Jesus was traveling from the northwest to the southeast part of the lake. **8:20** The verse may allude to the Son of Man in Daniel 7:13–14. Compare Moses 1:12, where Satan calls Moses by this term as opposed to *son of God*. Others see a stronger allusion to Ezekiel 2:3, 6, 8; 3:3. In Ezekiel, the son of man is a mortal who has been given a mission to carry out. **8:22** The practice of burying the dead included directions on how to avoid defilement from coming in contact with the body of the deceased (Numbers 19:16; Deuteronomy 21:22–23). **8:26** Mark is more critical of the disciples in telling this same story (Mark 4:40). **8:28** There are multiple spellings of the name

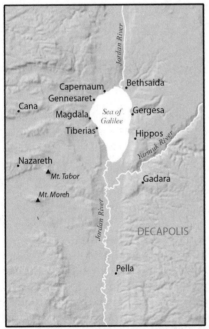

Towns and Villages of the Early Galilean Ministry
Map by Cassie Howe and Ryan Shields, ThinkSpatial, BYU Geography

that road. ²⁹And they cried out, saying, "Why do you concern yourself with us, Son of God? Did you come here to afflict us before the time?" ³⁰There was a great herd of swine feeding at a distance from them. ³¹Then the demons called to him, saying, "If you cast us out, send us into the herd of swine." ³²So Jesus said, "Get out!" And they departed into the swine, and all the herd ran down the steep hillside to the sea, and they were drowned in the water. ³³Those who tended the herd fled, and they came to the town to report everything that had taken place and what happened to the possessed men. ³⁴And the entire town went out to meet Jesus, and upon seeing him they begged him to leave from their land.

HEALING OF A PARALYZED MAN
(MK 2:1–12; LK 5:17–26; JN 5:8–9A)

9 ¹And he entered a ship and crossed over and came to his own town. ²And they brought a paralyzed man to him, resting on a mattress, and when Jesus saw their faith, he said to the man, "Cheer up, son, your sins are forgiven." ³But some of the

scribes said among themselves, "This man speaks blasphemy." ⁴Jesus perceived their thoughts and said, "Why do you ponder wickedness in your hearts? ⁵Is it easier to say, 'Your sins are forgiven' or to say, 'Get up and walk'? ⁶But so that you may know that the Son of Man has power on earth to forgive sins," then he said to the paralyzed man, "Rise, and take your mattress and go to your home." ⁷And he got up and went to his house. ⁸When the crowd saw this, they were afraid and gave glory to God, who had given this power to humans.

THE CALL OF MATTHEW
(MK 2:13–17; LK 5:27–32)

⁹And Jesus passed by that place and saw a man named Matthew sitting at the tax collector's booth, and he said to him, "Follow me." And he arose and followed him. ¹⁰While Jesus was reclining to eat in Matthew's house, many tax collectors and sinners came and dined with Jesus and his disciples. ¹¹When the Pharisees saw this, they said to his disciples, "Why does your teacher eat with tax collectors and sinners?" ¹²When he heard this, Jesus said, "Those

---

of the town where Jesus performed this healing. The likely spelling is the one translated in the text, but other possibilities are *Gergasenes* or *Gazarenes*. Gadara was about six miles to the south and east of the Sea of Galilee, and it appears to be too far for the pigs to have plunged into the Sea of Galilee. The other evangelists place the story in Gerasa (Mark 5:1; Luke 8:26). **8:29** *The time* refers to the day of judgment.

9:1 *His own town* implies Nazareth, but by this time in the ministry it is clear that Matthew means Capernaum (see Matthew 4:13). **9:3** The accusation of blasphemy was serious (see Exodus 20:7; Leviticus 24:16). **9:4** Many translations imply that Jesus read their thoughts, but the wording seems to suggest that Jesus became aware of their thoughts only after they began complaining among themselves. **9:6** The Son of Man has *power* to forgive sins. The word *power* could also be rendered as *authority*, but the idea is fundamentally that of *license, power,* and *authority*. **9:8** The crowd felt religious *fear* or *awe* at seeing the miracles, and they were thankful that God had granted such incredible *power* to heal. This story highlights the *power* that God had given to Jesus in comparison to the inability of Jesus's accusers to heal the man. **9:9** Only the Gospel of Matthew mentions the tax collector Matthew being called as a disciple. Mark and Luke tell of a tax collector named Levi that was called as a disciple. **9:10** Roman tax collection was significantly different from a modern tax system, as it depended on individuals who had bought an allotment to collect the taxes for a specific region or city. Most people were not sympathetic to these tax collectors (*publicani*), especially since they were known for taxing more than necessary for their personal benefit; see Luke 3:12–13. Matthew's name is not specifically mentioned in the Greek manuscripts, but the Greek is clear that he is the owner of the house. **9:12–13** Compare Mark 2:17; Moroni 8:8.

who are healthy do not need a physician, but those who are ill. [13] Go and learn what this means, '*I desire mercy and not sacrifice.*' I did not come to call the righteous, but sinners."

A QUESTION ABOUT FASTING
(MK 2:18–22; LK 5:33–39)

[14] Then the disciples of John came to him and said, "Why do we and the Pharisees fast often, but your disciples do not fast?" [15] Jesus said to them, "The wedding guests cannot mourn while the bridegroom is with them, but the days will come when the bridegroom will be taken from them, and then they will fast. [16] No one puts a new piece of cloth on an old garment, because the new piece of cloth lifts up at the edges and the tear is made worse. [17] Nor does anyone put new wine in old wineskins; otherwise the wineskins burst, and the wine spills and the wineskins are ruined. Instead, they put new wine in new wineskins, and both are preserved."

JAIRUS'S DAUGHTER AND A WOMAN HEALED (MK 5:21–43; LK 8:40–56)

[18] While he was saying these things, a ruler came to him and knelt before him and said, "My daughter just now passed away, but come and put your hand on her and she will live." [19] Jesus arose and followed him, and his disciples also followed. [20] But a woman, hemorrhaging at times for twelve years, came up behind him and touched the tassels of his cloak. [21] For she had said to herself, "If I can only touch his cloak, I will be saved." [22] Jesus turned and saw her and said, "Cheer up, daughter, your faith has saved you." And the woman was healed that very hour. [23] When Jesus arrived at the ruler's house, he saw the flute players and the crowd mourning the girl, [24] and he said, "Make room, for the young girl is not dead but asleep." And they mocked him. [25] When the crowd had been cast out, and after he entered and took her hand, the young girl arose. [26] And the report of this spread through that entire region.

HEALING OF TWO BLIND MEN
(MT 20:29–34; MK 10:46–52; LK 18:35–43)

[27] And as he passed through there, two blind men followed Jesus and cried out to him, saying, "Have mercy on us, Son of David!" [28] And after he entered the house, the blind men came to him, and Jesus said to them, "Do you believe that I am able to do this?" They said to him, "Yes, Lord." [29] Then he touched their eyes, saying, "According to your faith, let it be done to you." [30] And their eyes were opened, and Jesus charged them, saying, "See that you let no one know of it." [31] But when they departed, they spread word of him throughout that entire region.

9:13 Quotation from Hosea 6:6. **9:14** The disciples of John the Baptist are also mentioned in Matthew 11:2. For Old Testament counsel on fasting, see Psalms 35:13; 69:10. **9:15** The *wedding guests* are literally *children of the bridegroom*, and here Jesus envisions them being related to the bridegroom. This saying looks forward to fasting only after Jesus has died. **9:18** A *ruler* probably refers to a leader of the local synagogue. Matthew does not note what capacity this individual served in, and it is possible that he was a Roman government officer. **9:20** The *tassels of his cloak* = *tallit* or *tzitzit*. Clothing in general, and especially the hem of a garment, was symbolically meaningful in the ancient Near East. The hem of the garment was an extension of the wearer's power, authority, and persona in a variety of contexts, including royal power, divine power, and business transactions. The tassels were there as part of a commandment; see Numbers 15:37–41. The woman was unclean according to Leviticus 15:19–30. **9:22** When Enos's sins are forgiven, the language used is similar to that of this verse (Enos 1:8). See also Mark 5:34; 10:52. **9:28** Compare 2 Nephi 27:21. **9:30** *Let no one know of it* (see Matthew 8:4).

HEALING OF A MUTE INDIVIDUAL (LK 11:14–15)

³²After they had departed, a possessed man who could not speak was brought to Jesus, ³³and after the demon was cast out, the man spoke. And the crowd was amazed and said, "Never before has anyone seen things like this in Israel." ³⁴But the Pharisees said, "By the ruler of the demons he casts out demons."

THE HARVEST IS GREAT (LK 10:2)

³⁵And Jesus traveled around to all the towns and villages, teaching in their synagogues and declaring the gospel of the kingdom and healing all who were sick and ill. ³⁶When he saw the crowds, he was moved with compassion for them because they were afflicted and cast aside, like sheep without a shepherd. ³⁷Then he said to his disciples, "The harvest is plentiful, but the workers are few in number. ³⁸Ask the Lord of the harvest to send out workers to his harvest."

JESUS CALLS THE TWELVE (MK 3:13–19; LK 6:12–16)

10 ¹Then Jesus called his twelve disciples, and he gave them power over unclean spirits, to cast them out and to heal all sickness and illness. ²The names of the twelve apostles are as follows: first, Simon called Peter, and Andrew his brother, and Jacob son of Zebedee, and John his brother, ³Philip and Bartholomew, Thomas and Matthew the tax collector, Jacob son of Alphaeus and Thaddeus, ⁴Simon the Canaanite, and Judas Iscariot, who betrayed him.

SENDING OUT THE TWELVE (MK 6:7–13; LK 9:1–6)

⁵Jesus sent out these twelve, charging them, saying, "Do not go by way of the Gentiles nor enter any town of the Samaritans, ⁶but rather go to the lost sheep of the house of Israel. ⁷As you go, declare the word, teaching, 'The kingdom of heaven is near!' ⁸Heal the sick, raise the dead, cleanse the leprous, cast out spirits. Freely

---

9:34 Some later manuscripts lack this verse, but the earliest manuscripts preserve it. Satan is the ruler of the demons and is also at this time referred to as Beelzebul (Matthew 10:25; 12:24). The name is found in 2 Kings 1:2–3, 6, 16 and is often understood to mean *lord of the flies*. The name is built on the title of the Philistine deity *Ba'al* (Baal) and the title *zebub* (prince). Thus, Beelzebul was the prince of the gods, but owing to manipulation of the spelling of the name, it had taken on a derogatory meaning of *lord of the flies*. **9:35** The two adjectives describe differing types of affliction, namely illness and a general state of weakness. **9:36** Compare 5:37.

10:1 First Nephi 12:7 seems to be describing the events associated with the call and commissioning of the disciples, with the added detail that the Holy Spirit fell on the twelve and they were ordained and chosen. **10:1–11:1** This section contains the Mission Discourse. **10:2** The Gospels rarely refer to the twelve disciples as *apostles*. This is the only instance where Matthew does so. The term occurs once in Mark (Mark 3:14) and six times in Luke. The Gospel of John does not use the term. **10:4** Canaanite probably means *zealot* based on the Aramaic *qan'an*. He was possibly a zealot at one time (Josephus, *Jewish War* 2.651; 4.158–61) or was connected to a family of zealots. Matthew is unclear on how strongly this term should be interpreted with respect to Simon. Judas is more properly referred to as Judah, but tradition has favored the Greek spelling of his name. *Iscariot* is probably a regional designation, or *one from Kerioth*. The primary meaning of the clause following Judas's name is the one *who handed him over*. Given the later application of this term to his actions on the night of Jesus's arrest, it has often been translated as the *one who betrayed him*. **10:6** Jesus sends his disciples, who are believing Israelites, to find Israelites (the *lost sheep of Israel*) who have lost their way in their ancestral faith. **10:7** Alluded to in Doctrine and Covenants 39:19.

you received; therefore give freely. [9]Do not carry gold, silver, or copper coins in your belts, [10]or a bag for the way, or two tunics, or sandals, or a walking staff, because the laborer is worthy of his food. [11]Whatever town or village you enter, search out whoever in it is worthy and remain there until you depart. [12]When you enter a house, greet those inside, [13]and if the household is worthy, leave your peace on it, but if it is not worthy, let your peace return to you. [14]If anyone will not accept you and hear your words, after you depart from the house or village, shake the dust from your feet. [15]Truly I say to you, it will be more tolerable for the land of Sodom and Gomorrah in the day of judgment than for that village.

PERSECUTION FORETOLD (MK 13:9–13; LK 21:12–19)

[16]"Behold, I send you as sheep in the midst of wolves, therefore be as wise as serpents and as innocent as doves. [17]Beware of men: they will deliver you to councils, and they will flog you in their synagogues, [18]and you will be brought before rulers and kings because of me and to testify to them and the Gentiles. [19]When they hand you over, do not think about what you will say: it will be given to you in that hour what to say. [20]It will not be you speaking, but the Spirit of your Father speaking in you. [21]A brother will hand over a brother to death, and a father a son, and children will rise up against parents and have them put to death. [22]And you will be hated by all because of my name, but the one who endures to the end shall be saved. [23]And when they pursue you in that village, flee to another village. Truly I say to you, you will not pass through all the villages in Israel until the Son of Man comes.

[24]"A disciple is not greater than his teacher, nor the servant greater than his lord. [25]It is enough for the disciple to be like his teacher and the servant like his lord. If they called the master of the house Beelzebul, how much more will they defame the members of the household.

DO NOT FEAR (LK 12:2–9)

[26]"Do not fear them, for there is nothing that is hidden that will remain secret and nothing hidden that will not be made known. [27]What I say to you in the dark, say it in the light, and what you hear in a whisper, proclaim on the housetops. [28]Do not fear those who can kill the body: they are not able to kill the soul. Rather, fear the one who can destroy the soul and body in hell. [29]Are not two sparrows sold for a copper coin? And yet one of them will not fall to the earth without your Father's notice. [30]All of the hairs of your

---

10:9–10 Alluded to in Doctrine and Covenants 24:18. **10:9–15** Jesus encourages the disciples to travel without personal financial support. **10:10** Jesus refers to the fact that if the disciples do well in declaring the gospel message, they will be rewarded with food, clothing, and shelter. Mark 6:8 permits the disciples to take a *walking staff.* **10:11, 14** Alluded to in Doctrine and Covenants 24:15 (compare 60:15; 75:20). **10:12** Since the earliest Christians met in houses, this verse could imply rejection by a house church and therefore an early gathering of believers in Jesus. **10:12–15** The story of Sodom and Gomorrah is found in Genesis 18:16–19:22. **10:13** Compare 3 Nephi 27:10. **10:14** The practice of dusting the feet is interpreted in Doctrine and Covenants 24:15. **10:15** Alluded to in Doctrine and Covenants 75:21–22. **10:17** On Jewish scourging/flogging, see Deuteronomy 25:1–3. **10:18** This verse is alluded to in Doctrine and Covenants 124:3. **10:19** Echoed in Doctrine and Covenants 24:6; 84:85. **10:21** Allusion to Micah 7:6. **10:22** See 2 Nephi 31:15 (compare Matthew 24:13); Alma 32:13; 38:2 (compare Doctrine and Covenants 53:7). **10:25** See note on Matthew 9:34 for the title *Beelzebul.* **10:28** The Greek word translated as *hell* is *Gehenna* (see note on Matthew 5:22). **10:29** This is probably the Roman bronze coin known as the *as* (see note on Matthew 5:26).

head are numbered. ³¹Do not fear; you are more valuable than many sparrows.

³²"Everyone who acknowledges me before others I will acknowledge before my Father in heaven. ³³Whoever denies me before others, I will deny that person before my Father in heaven.

THE COST OF DISCIPLESHIP
(LK 12:51–53; 14:25–27)

³⁴"Do not suppose that I have come to send peace on the earth: I have not come to send peace but a sword. ³⁵'I have come to set *a man against his father, a daughter against her mother, a daughter-in-law against her mother-in-law,* ³⁶*and the enemies of a man will be those of his own house.'* ³⁷Whoever loves father or mother more than me is not worthy of me, and whoever loves son or daughter more than me is not worthy of me. ³⁸Whoever does not take up his cross and follow me is not worthy of me. ³⁹The person who finds his life will lose it, and whoever loses his life for my sake will find it.

WELCOMING A PROPHET
(MK 9:41)

⁴⁰"Whoever welcomes you welcomes me, and whoever welcomes me welcomes him who sent me. ⁴¹Whoever welcomes a proph-

et in the name of a prophet will receive a prophet's reward, and whoever welcomes the righteous in the name of righteousness will receive the reward of the righteous. ⁴²And whoever gives a drink to one of these little ones in the name of a disciple, truly I say to you that none of these will lose their reward."

JOHN'S DISCIPLES VISIT JESUS
(LK 7:18–23)

11 ¹And it came to pass that after Jesus had finished directing his twelve disciples, he departed from that place to teach and declare his message in their cities. ²When John heard in prison the works of the Christ, he sent his disciples ³and said to him, "Are you the coming one, or should we look for another?" ⁴And Jesus answered them, "Return and tell John what you hear and see: ⁵the blind can see, the lame walk, the leprous are cleansed, the deaf can hear, the dead are raised, and the poor hear the gospel. ⁶And blessed are those who are not offended by me."

JESUS DECLARES JOHN TO BE ELIJAH (LK 7:24–35)

⁷As they departed, Jesus began to say to the crowd concerning John, "What did you go to the wilderness to see, a reed shaken by

---

10:33 This may be an allusion to Peter's denial in Matthew 26:70. **10:35–36** An allusion to Micah 7:6. **10:38** Adapted and reinterpreted in Doctrine and Covenants 56:2. **10:39** This verse is quoted in Doctrine and Covenants 98:13; 103:27 (compare Matthew 16:25). **10:40** An altered version of this saying is found in Doctrine and Covenants 39:5. **10:41** The wording of the verse states that *a righteous person who accepts a righteous person will receive the reward of the righteous*. The emphasis is on *righteous* and not a fellowship of individuals, and therefore the meaning of the verse appears to be accepting someone on the basis of good works. **10:42** *Little ones* would usually be children, but in this context it may refer to new Christian missionaries (compare Matthew 18:6, 10). Quoted in Doctrine and Covenants 58:28; 84:90.

11:1 Compare 3 Nephi 17:18; 18:36; 19:35. **11:2** Some later manuscripts read *Jesus* in place of *Christ*. A number of manuscripts indicate specifically that there were two disciples sent, probably as a result of harmonizing Matthew's account to Luke's (Luke 7:18). **11:3** *The coming one* refers to the Messiah (see Matthew 3:11; 11:3). See Psalm 118:26 and Matthew 3:11; 21:9. **11:5** This verse describes in general terms the fulfillment of prophecy (Isaiah 26:19; 29:18–19; 35:5–6; 61:1). Alluded to in Mosiah 3:5. **11:6** This verse is similar in form to the Beatitudes given in Matthew 5:3–11.

wind? [8]But what did you go to see, a man in soft clothing? Behold, those who wear soft clothing are in the houses of kings. [9]But what did you go to see? A prophet? Yes, I say to you, and more than a prophet. [10]This is the one of whom it is written, *'Behold, I will send my messenger before your face, who will prepare the way before you.'*

[11]"Truly I say to you, among those born of women there has not arisen one greater than John the Baptist, even though the least in the kingdom of heaven is greater than he. [12]From the days of John the Baptist until now, the kingdom of heaven suffers violence, and the violent seize it. [13]All of the prophets and the Law have prophesied until John, [14]and if you are willing to receive it, this is Elijah who is to come. [15]Whoever has ears to hear, let him hear.

[16]"To what shall I compare this generation? It is like little children sitting in the marketplace who call out to friends. [17]They say, 'We piped to you and you did not dance; we lamented and you did not smite your breast.' [18]John came to you neither eating or drinking, and they say, 'He has a demon.' [19]The Son of Man came eating and drinking, and they say, 'Behold, a man, a glutton and wine drinker, a friend of tax collectors and sinners.' Wisdom is justified by her works."

WOES ON GALILEAN CITIES
(LK 10:13–16)

[20]Then he began to rebuke the cities in which the majority of his miracles had been done, because they did not repent. [21]"Woe

---

11:8–10 The allusion to a king wearing soft clothing, as opposed to rough, scratchy clothing, may be to Herod Antipas, who had imprisoned John the Baptist. **11:10** Quotation from Exodus 23:20 and Malachi 3:1. **11:11** The term rendered as *least (mikroteros)* can also mean *smallest, shortest, least significant,* and *youngest.* The comparison may be to Jesus himself since he alludes to the fact that he has a smaller

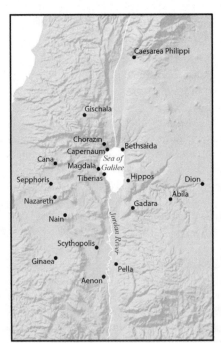

reputation than John had among some early followers. **11:13** The wording suggests that Jesus is drawing out the point that a new age has arrived. **11:14** Quoted in Doctrine and Covenants 77:9. **11:17** The quotation of what the children in the marketplace say is an echo of Ecclesiastes 3:4. **11:18** Most manuscripts lack *to you,* but the context of the passage implies that Jesus is speaking directly to a crowd. **11:19** Some manuscripts revise the saying so that it reads *Wisdom is justified by her children.* The older and better manuscripts contain the word *works* in place of *children* (Luke 7:35 also has *children*). For a note on tax collectors, see Matthew 9:10. **11:20** The word *miracles* is perhaps better translated as *deeds of power* from the Greek word *dunameis,* but in this context it appears that Matthew is referring to the miracles of Jesus, which he refers to as acts of power. **11:20–23** For the story of Sodom and Gomorrah, see Genesis 18:16–19:22. **11:21** Chorazin is located a short distance from Capernaum to the northwest and was a center of olive production. Bethsaida was a small fishing town on the north shore of the Sea of Galilee. Bethsaida may refer to Bethsaida-Julius,

Towns and Villages of the Apostolic Mission
Map by Brandon Whitney, ThinkSpatial, BYU Geography

to you, Chorazin, woe to you, Bethsaida! If the miracles were done in Tyre and Sidon that were done among you, they would have repented long ago in sackcloth and ashes. ²²But I say to you that on the day of judgment it will be more tolerable for Tyre and Sidon than for you. ²³And you, Capernaum, will you be exalted to heaven? No, you will be brought down to Hades, because if the miracles were done in Sodom that were done among you, it would have remained to this day. ²⁴But I say to you that it will be more tolerable for the land of Sodom in the day of judgment than for you."

COME UNTO ME (LK 10:21–22)

²⁵At that time Jesus said, "I praise you, Father, Lord of the heaven and the earth, because you have hidden these things from the wise and learned and did reveal them to infants. ²⁶Yes, Father, because it was your gracious will. ²⁷All things were given to me by my Father, and no one knows the Son except the Father, nor does anyone know the Father but the Son and he to whom the Son may wish to reveal him. ²⁸Come

unto me, all who are tired and burdened, and I will give you rest. ²⁹Take upon you my yoke and learn from me, because I am meek and humble of heart, and you will find rest for your souls, ³⁰for my yoke is easy and my burden is light."

THE SON OF MAN IS LORD OF THE SABBATH (MK 2:23–28; LK 6:1–5)

12 ¹At that time, Jesus went through the wheat fields on the Sabbath, and his disciples were hungry and began to pluck the grains of wheat and eat them. ²But when the Pharisees saw it, they said to him, "Your disciples do that which is not lawful on the Sabbath." ³Jesus said to them, "Have you not read what David did when he and his companions were hungry? ⁴How he went into the house of God and they ate the bread of the presence, which was not lawful for him or those with him to eat, but for the priests alone? ⁵Or have you not read in the Law that on the Sabbath the priests in the temple defile the Sabbath and are innocent? ⁶I say to you that one here is greater than the

---

which was built up by Philip. It was also home to several of the early disciples (Peter, Andrew, and Philip). Mosiah 11:21 provides context for the teaching on repentance in this verse. **11:22** Jesus spoke of both Hades and Gehenna as metaphors for hell (compare Isaiah 14:13, 15 and note on Matthew 10:28). The wording of this verse appears in Alma 9:15 as a condemnation of the wicked generally (compare Doctrine and Covenants 75:22). **11:24** Echoed in Doctrine and Covenants 75:21–22 (compare Matthew 10:15). **11:25** Jesus here speaks of heaven in the singular. In phrases such as the *kingdom of heaven*, the reference to heaven is almost always plural. **11:29** The phrase *you will find rest for your souls* is an echo of Jeremiah 6:16 and Deuteronomy 12:9. For the *meek and humble* (KJV *lowly*) *of heart*, compare Alma 37:33–34. Alluded to in Doctrine and Covenants 32:1; 54:10.

12:1 Matthew states that Jesus went through *on the Sabbaths*, suggesting perhaps that this was a regular occurrence and that he did not have a single event in mind (Deuteronomy 23:25). Compare Mosiah 13:18–19 (Mosiah 13:12–24 is a quotation of Exodus 20:2–17). **12:1–14** These two stories demonstrate that human needs are more important than rigid Sabbath observance. **12:2** For the commandment against harvesting wheat on the Sabbath, see Exodus 34:21. **12:4** What David did is described in 1 Samuel 21:1–6. The bread that David and his men consumed would have been placed in the temple to represent the presence of the Israelites before the Lord (Leviticus 24:5–9). The *bread of the presence* is also referred to as the shewbread. The reference is to the twelve loaves placed in the tabernacle and later the table that stood across from the lampstand (Exodus 26:35). Priests were permitted to eat the loaves once the new loaves were placed in the temple each week. **12:5** Jesus draws attention to the requirements for priests to prepare sacrifices and replace the bread of the presence on the Sabbath day (Numbers 28:9–10).

temple. [7]If you had known what it means, '*I desire mercy and not sacrifice*,' you would not have judged the innocent. [8]The Son of Man is Lord of the Sabbath."

HEALING OF A MAN WITH A WITHERED HAND (MK 3:1–6; LK 6:6–11)

[9]And he left that place and came to their synagogue, [10]and a man having a withered hand was there. And they asked him, saying, "Is it lawful to heal on the Sabbath?" They asked this to accuse him. [11]And he said to them, "Who from among you, who has one sheep, and if it falls into a pit on the Sabbath, will not take hold of it and lift it out? [12]How much more valuable is a person than a sheep? Therefore, it is lawful to do good on the Sabbath." [13]Then he said to the man, "Stretch out your hand," and he extended it, and it was restored to health like the other. [14]Then the Pharisees came together in council so that they could take him in order to kill him.

MY SERVANT

[15]Jesus knew this and departed from that place. And a large crowd followed him, and he healed all of them. [16]And he admonished them that they would not make him manifest [17]so that the words of Isaiah the prophet might be fulfilled, saying, [18]"*Behold, my servant whom I have chosen, my beloved who delights my soul, I will place my Spirit on him, and judgment to the nations will he declare.* [19]*He will not strive or shout out, nor will anyone hear his voice in the streets.* [20]*He will not break a shaken reed, or extinguish a smoldering flax plant, until*

he establishes judgment to victory. [21]*And in his name shall the nations hope.*"

BEELZEBUL (MK 3:22–27; LK 11:14–15, 17–23)

[22]Then a blind and deaf individual who was also possessed by a demon was brought to him, and he healed him so that he could see and speak. [23]Then all the crowd was amazed and said, "Perhaps this is the Son of David." [24]And the Pharisees heard this and said, "He did not cast out the spirit except by means of Beelzebul, the prince of the demons." [25]But he knew their thoughts, and he said to them, "Every kingdom divided against itself is left desolate, and every city or house divided against itself cannot stand. [26]And if Satan casts out Satan, he is divided against himself, and then how does his kingdom stand? [27]If I by Beelzebul cast out spirits, how do your sons cast them out? Because of this they will be your judges. [28]But if I, by the Spirit of God, do cast out spirits, then the kingdom of God has already arrived for you. [29]Or how does one enter the house of a strong person and take his belongings without first tying up the strong person? Then one is free to rob the house. [30]Whoever is not with me is against me, and whoever does not gather with me scatters. [31]Therefore, I say this to you, every sin and blasphemy by men and women will be forgiven, but blasphemy against the Spirit will not be forgiven. [32]And whoever speaks a word against the Son of Man will be forgiven, but whoever speaks a word against the Holy Spirit, it will not be forgiven either in this age or in the coming one.

12:7 Quotation from Hosea 6:6 (see also Matthew 9:13). **12:8** The verse may represent an intentional pun and could be intended to say that Jesus, as the Son of Man, is Lord of the Sabbath *or* that the Sabbath is created for the son of man (= a human) and therefore for all humanity. **12:11** See Deuteronomy 22:4. The Damascus Document, a text from the Qumran community, forbids assisting animals on the Sabbath. Jesus's question may have had the Qumran community in mind. **12:18–21** Quotation from Isaiah 42:1–4. **12:20** Echoed in Doctrine and Covenants 52:11. **12:24** Beelzebul (see note on Matthew 9:34). **12:30** Compare 2 Nephi 10:16.

A TREE AND ITS FRUIT
(LK 6:43–45)

³³"Either make the tree good and its fruit good or make the tree rotten and its fruit rotten. A tree will be known by its fruit. ³⁴You, offspring of snakes! Being evil, how are you able to speak of the good? The mouth speaks out of the abundance of the heart. ³⁵The good person takes out of his good treasure good things, and the wicked person takes out of his wicked treasure wicked things. ³⁶I say to you that in the day of judgment they will give an account of every careless word they speak. ³⁷By your words you will be justified, and by your words you will be condemned."

THE PHARISEES SEEK A SIGN
(MK 8:11–12; LK 11:29–32)

³⁸Then some of the scribes and Pharisees answered him, "Teacher, we want to see a miracle from you." ³⁹Then he answered them, "A wicked and adulterous generation seeks after a miracle, but no sign will be given to it except for the miracle of Jonah the prophet. ⁴⁰Just as Jonah was three days and three nights in the belly of a whale, even so the Son of Man will be three days and three nights in the heart of the earth. ⁴¹The people of Nineveh will rise up in judgment against this generation and will judge it because they repented be-cause of the teachings of Jonah, and one greater than Jonah is here. ⁴²A queen of the South will rise up in judgment against this generation and will judge it, because she came from the ends of the earth to hear the wisdom of Solomon, and one greater than Solomon is here.

⁴³"When the unclean spirit departs from a person, it travels through arid plac-es seeking rest, but it finds none. ⁴⁴Then it says, 'Let me return to my house where I came from,' and it goes and finds it un-occupied, swept, and decorated. ⁴⁵Then it departs and takes with it seven other spirits wickeder than itself, and they go and re-side there. And the last state of that person will be worse than the first. Thus, it will be for this wicked generation."

THE FAMILY OF JESUS (MK 3:31–
35; LK 8:19–21)

⁴⁶While he was speaking to the crowd, his mother and brothers stood outside seek-ing to speak to him. [[⁴⁷A certain man said to him, "Behold, your mother and brothers stand outside seeking to speak to you."]] ⁴⁸He responded to him, "Who is my mother and who are my brothers and sisters?" ⁴⁹And stretching forth his hand on his disciples, he said, "Behold, my mother and my brothers and sisters. ⁵⁰Those who do the will of my Father

---

12:33 Compare Alma 5:36. **12:36** The Greek word *argon*, translated as *careless*, also has the sense of *lazy* or *not well considered*. **12:38** The word translated as *miracle* can also mean a *sign*. The Gospel of John consistently uses this word to refer to the miracles of Jesus, and in this context in Matthew, it appears that they are asking for the repetition of one of the miracles. **12:39** Adultery was strongly condemned by the prophets (Isaiah 57:3–13; Mosiah 13:22 [a quotation of Exodus 20:14]; Helaman 4:12). Compare Doctrine and Covenants 42:25. **12:40** Compare Alma 38:8. **12:42** The *queen from the South* is the queen of Sheba (1 Kings 10:1–13). **12:43–45** Compare Luke 11:24–26. The Joseph Smith Translation interprets these verses to refer to those who sin against the Holy Spirit. **12:46** Je-sus's mother and brothers were standing outside the synagogue (Matthew 12:9). See also Matthew 13:55–56 and Mark 6:3 for the names of Jesus's siblings. **12:47** This verse is likely not original to the Gospel of Matthew, and several early and important manuscripts omit it. The verse was likely added to make sense of the introduction of an unnamed person in 12:48, where it states *Jesus answered him*. **12:49–50** Jesus here defines all disciples as his *mother and brothers and sisters*. **12:50** Compare Matthew 7:21.

in heaven are my brother and sister and mother."

THE PARABLE OF THE SOWER
(MK 4:1–9; LK 8:4–8)

13 ¹On that same day, Jesus went out of the house and sat by the lake, ²and a large crowd gathered near him, so he got into a boat and sat while the crowd stood on the shore. ³He spoke many things to them in parables, saying, "Behold, a sower went out to sow, ⁴and while sowing some fell on the pathway, and the birds came and ate them. ⁵But others fell on rocky ground where there was not much earth, and immediately they sprouted because the soil was not deep. ⁶And they were scorched by the rising sun, and because they did not have enough root, they withered. ⁷Others fell on thorns, and the thorns grew up and choked them. ⁸Others fell on good ground and gave fruit, some a hundredfold, some sixty, and some thirty. ⁹Whoever has ears to hear, let that person hear."

THE REASON FOR TEACHING IN PARABLES (MK 4:10–12; LK 8:9–10)

¹⁰And the disciples came to him and said, "Why do you speak to them in parables?" ¹¹He answered them, "To you it has been given to know the mysteries of the kingdom of heaven, but to them it has not been given. ¹²Because whoever has, it shall be given to that person and it will be in abundance, and whoever has not, it will be taken from that person. ¹³For this reason I speak to them in parables, so that seeing they see not, and hearing they hear not, nor do they understand. ¹⁴The prophecy of Isaiah is fulfilled in them when he said, *'Hearing you will hear but you will not understand, and seeing you will see but not perceive. ¹⁵The heart of this people grew fat, and their ears heavy, and they closed their eyes so that they would not see with their eyes and hear with their ears and understand in their heart and turn that I might heal them.'* ¹⁶Blessed are your eyes that see and your ears that hear. ¹⁷Truly I say to you that many prophets and righteous people desired to see what you see, but they did not see it, and to hear what you hear, and they did not hear it.

THE PARABLE OF THE SOWER EXPLAINED (MK 4:13–20; LK 8:11–15)

¹⁸"Therefore, hear the parable of the sower. ¹⁹Everyone who hears the word of the kingdom and does not understand it, the wicked one comes and seizes what is sown in the heart; this is the seed sown by the road. ²⁰The one sown on rocky ground is the one who hears the word and immediately receives it with joy, ²¹but that person does not have root but is short-lived, and when trial or persecution comes because of the word, he immediately stumbles. ²²The one sown on thorns is the one who hears the word, but the cares of the age and concern for riches choke the word,

---

13:1 Matthew is unclear about what house he is thinking of. This could refer to Jesus's own home in Capernaum or Peter's. This chapter gathers several of Jesus's parables into a single discourse intended to teach the reader about the kingdom of heaven. **13:3** The *parables* of Jesus are oriented toward farming and agriculture and the disparity between wealth and poverty. See Doctrine and Covenants 86:2; Mosiah 8:1. **13:6** Alluded to in Alma 32:38. **13:8** *A hundredfold* may be an allusion to Genesis 26:12. **13:11** On mysteries, see Alma 12:10; Moroni 7:15. The meaning of this verse is expanded in Doctrine and Covenants 107:19 (compare Doctrine and Covenants 6:7; 42:65; 63:23). **13:12** This saying is connected to repentance in Doctrine and Covenants 1:33. **13:14–15** Quotation from Isaiah 6:9–10. **13:17** The word translated as *righteous* is often used in the New Testament sense of being justified according to the law of Moses. **13:21** The word translated as *stumble* can also mean to *be offended* (compare Matthew 18:6).

and they become unfruitful. ²³The one sown on good earth is the one who hears the word and understands and brings forth fruit and yields a hundredfold, and another yields sixty, and another yields thirty."

THE PARABLE OF THE WEEDS AMONG THE WHEAT

²⁴Another parable he gave to them, saying, "The kingdom of heaven is like a person sowing good seed in a field, ²⁵and while the people were asleep, the enemy of the sower came and sowed weeds among the wheat and then left. ²⁶Then the grain sprouted, and the weeds appeared. ²⁷The servants of the master came and said to him, 'Lord, did you not sow good seed in the field? Where did these weeds come from?' ²⁸And he said to them, 'An enemy did this thing.' And the servants said to him, 'Do you want us to go and pull them up?' ²⁹And he said, 'No, because in gathering the weeds you pull up the wheat also. ³⁰Let them grow together until the harvest, and then in the time of the harvest I will say to the harvesters, Gather up first the weeds and bind them in bundles in order to burn them; and the wheat, gather it for my storehouse.'"

THE PARABLE OF THE MUSTARD SEED (MK 4:30–31; LK 13:18–9)

³¹Another parable he gave to them, saying, "The kingdom of heaven is like a mustard seed, which a man sowed in his field. ³²It is the smallest of all seeds, but when it grows it is greater than all herbs and becomes a tree, so that the birds of heaven come and build nests in its branches."

THE PARABLE OF THE LEAVEN/ TEACHING IN PARABLES (MK 4:33–34; LK 13:20–21)

³³He spoke another parable to them. "The kingdom of heaven is like yeast, which a woman took and hid in three measures of dough until the entire batch rose." ³⁴These things Jesus spoke in parables to the crowds, and he did not speak to them without a parable, ³⁵that the word of the prophet might be fulfilled, saying, "*I will open my mouth in parables. I will utter things hidden from the foundation of the earth.*"

EXPLANATION OF THE WEEDS AMONG THE WHEAT

³⁶Then he left the crowd and came into the house, and his disciples came to him, saying, "Explain for us the parable of the weeds of the field." ³⁷He answered, "The sower of good seed is the Son of Man, ³⁸the field is the world, the good seed are the children of the kingdom, and the weeds are the children of the wicked one. ³⁹The enemy who sowed them is the devil, the harvest is the end of the age, and the harvesters are the angels. ⁴⁰As they gather the weeds and they are burned in the fire, even so will it be in the end of the age. ⁴¹The Son of Man will send his messengers, and they will gather from his kingdom all the stumbling blocks and those acting without law. ⁴²They will cast them into a furnace of fire, and there will be

---

13:24 Matthew shifts to reporting the discourse in third person. The preceding verses (1–23) had been delivered in first person. The shift may indicate that some of the parables were delivered on a different occasion. **13:32** An allusion to Psalm 104:12. **13:33** Perhaps an allusion to Leviticus 7:13. The *measure* refers to roughly 16 pounds (7 kg) of flour, indicating that three measures constituted a substantial amount of flour. **13:35** Quotation from Psalm 78:2. Some copyists mistakenly ascribed the quotation to Isaiah. The word *world*, which appears in some translations at the end of this verse, is missing in some manuscripts. **13:38–40** Alluded to in Doctrine and Covenants 86:2–3, 7. **13:41** The Son of Man sends messengers or *angels*. The Greek word can mean both heavenly *angels* and earthly *messengers*. **13:42** The phrase *They will cast them into a furnace of fire* contains an allusion to Daniel 3:6.

weeping and grinding of teeth. [43]Then *the righteous will shine forth as the sun in the kingdom of their Father*. Whoever has ears, let that person hear.

PARABLES OF THE FIELD, THE PEARL, AND THE NET

[44]"The kingdom of heaven is like a treasure hidden in a field, which a man discovered and then hid, and out of joy he goes and sells all that he has and buys that field.

[45]"Again, the kingdom of heaven is like a merchant seeking fine pearls, [46]who finding one very valuable pearl, went and sold all that he had and bought it.

[47]"Again, the kingdom of heaven is like a net cast into the sea, and it gathered all different sorts of fish. [48]When it was filled, it was brought to the seashore, and sitting down they collected the good into baskets, and the bad they threw out. [49]Thus it will be in the end of the age: the messengers will go out and divide the wicked from among the righteous, [50]and they will be cast into a furnace of fire, where there will be weeping and grinding of teeth.

NEW AND OLD TREASURES

[51]"Do you understand all these things?" They said to him, "Yes." [52]He said to them, "Therefore, every scribe that has been taught about the kingdom of heaven is like a master of a house who brings out of the treasury new and old things."

REJECTION OF JESUS AT NAZA-RETH (MK 6:1–6; LK 4:16–30)

[53]And it came to pass that Jesus finished speaking in parables, and he departed from that place. [54]And when he came to his own region, he taught them in their synagogue so that they were astonished and said, "Where did this man learn such wisdom and gain such power? [55]Is not this the son of the carpenter? Is not his mother named Mary, and are his brothers Jacob, Joseph, Simon, and Judas? [56]And his sisters, are they not all with us? From where does he know all these things?" [57]And they were offended at him. And Jesus said to them, "A prophet is not without honor except in his own country or in his own house." [58]And he did not do many miracles in that place because of their unbelief.

THE DEATH OF JOHN THE BAP-TIST (MK 6:14–29; LK 3:19–20; 9:7–9)

14 [1]At that time, Herod the tetrarch heard the rumors about Jesus, [2]and

---

The reference to being cast into the fire may be important because in the story of Daniel a person could avoid being cast into the fire if they worshipped God. The allusion draws attention to the need to worship God the Father. The image of grinding teeth is a favorite of Matthew's (Matthew 8:12; 13:50; 22:13; 25:30; Psalm 112:10; Mosiah 16:2). **13:43** Quotation of Daniel 12:3, see also Alma 40:25. **13:54** *His own region* would typically refer to Nazareth. In Matthew 13:1, Jesus is near the Sea of Galilee, and hence Capernaum. Luke records the rejection of Jesus at the Nazareth synagogue (Luke 4:16–30). **13:55** Jesus's father is here referred to as a *tekton*, a word that describes people who work in stone and in building larger structures like homes. Jesus is not referred to as a *tekton* in the Gospel of Matthew even though it is often assumed that he was trained as a carpenter. See Matthew 1:16 for the name of Jesus's mother. See note on Mark 6:3. **13:56** The plural *sisters* would indicate at least two. The verb *know* must be supplied since the Greek lacks a finite verb. It could be that Matthew intended to raise the question of where Jesus learned such things, or where he obtained such things. **13:57** There are numerous women prophets in the Bible that may also be in mind here, including Miriam (Micah 6:4), Huldah (2 Kings 22:14), Noahdiah (Nehemiah 6:14), Deborah (Judges 4:4), and Anna (Luke 2:36).

14:1 Herod Antipas (born circa 20 BCE, died 40 CE), or simply Antipas, ruled in Galilee in the region

he said to his servants, "This is John the Baptist. He has risen from the dead, and because of this the miracles are at work in him." [3]For Herod had arrested John and bound him and put him away in prison because of Herodias, the wife of Philip his brother, [4]because John said to him, "It is not legal for you to have her." [5]Herod wanted to kill him, but he feared the crowd because they accepted him as a prophet. [6]When the birthday of Herod was celebrated, the daughter of Herodias danced in their midst, and she pleased Herod [7]so much that he swore with an oath that he would give her whatever she asked. [8]Being persuaded by her mother, she said, "Here, on a serving tray, give me the head of John the Baptist." [9]The king was grieved, but because of the oath and his dinner guests, he commanded it to be given. [10]So he sent and had John beheaded in the prison. [11]And his head was brought on a serving tray and given to the young girl, and she gave it to her mother. [12]Then his disciples came and asked for the corpse, and they buried it, and they went and reported it to Jesus.

FEEDING THE FIVE THOUSAND
(MK 6:30–44; LK 9:10–17; JN 6:1–15)

[13]When he heard this, Jesus departed from there in a boat to a deserted place to be alone, but the crowds from the cities heard this and followed him on foot. [14]When he went ashore, he saw the large crowd and was moved with compassion for them, and he healed their sick. [15]When it was evening, his disciples came to him, saying, "This place is deserted and the hour is already late; dismiss the crowd so that they can go to the villages and purchase food for themselves." [16]Jesus said to them, "It is not necessary for them to leave; give them something to eat." [17]But they said to him, "We have only five loaves and two fish here." [18]He said, "Bring them here to me." [19]And he commanded the crowd to

---

to the north and west of the Sea of Galilee. His brother, Herod Philip, ruled north of the Decapolis and to the east of Antipas's territory. Jesus on one occasion referred to Antipas as *that fox* (Luke 13:32). Antipas imprisoned John the Baptist because John had criticized the marriage of Herodias and Antipas, which was expressly forbidden (Leviticus 18:6–16). Herodias had been previously married to Herod Philip II (but not Philip the Tetrarch, Josephus, *Antiquities* 17.8, 11). **14:2** The peculiar wording of the last phrase of the verse suggests that Herod Antipas thought that the spirit of John had come back from the dead and now resided in Jesus. It does not appear that he believed Jesus was the resurrected John the Baptist but that John or the spirit of John lived on in Jesus and could be seen through the miracles. **14:4** John had likely cited Leviticus 18:6–16. **14:5** The death of John the Baptist has been famously recorded by the Jewish historian Josephus (*Antiquities* 18:118–19). **14:6** The daughter of Herodias was *Salome* (died between 62 and 71 CE). She was originally married to Herod Philip the tetrarch, and she later married Aristobulus of Chalcis and became queen of Chalcis. **14:12** *His disciples* refers to John's disciples (Matthew 11:2). **14:19** Matthew intentionally draws out sacramental imagery.

Tetrarchies of Antipas, Archelaus, Philip, and the Decapolis
Map by Ryan Shields, ThinkSpatial, BYU Geography

sit down on the grass, and taking the five loaves and two fish, he looked up to heaven and blessed and broke them and gave the bread to his disciples, and the disciples gave it to the crowd. ²⁰And everyone ate and was satisfied, and they took and gathered up the broken bread, twelve baskets full. ²¹Without numbering the women and children, the number of men eating was five thousand.

JESUS WALKS ON WATER
(MK 6:45–52; JN 6:16–21)

²²And immediately he made the disciples enter a boat and go before him to the other side while he dismissed the crowds. ²³And after he dismissed the crowds, he went up a hill alone to pray, and when evening came he was by himself. ²⁴And the ship was already many stadia from the land, being battered by waves, because the wind opposed them. ²⁵In the fourth watch of the night, he came to them walking on the sea. ²⁶When the disciples saw him walking on the lake, they were troubled and said, "It is a ghost," and they cried out in fear. ²⁷And Jesus immediately called out to them, saying, "Cheer up. It is I; do not fear." ²⁸Peter answered him, "Lord, if it is you, call to me to come to you on the waters." ²⁹He said, "Come." Peter got out of the boat and walked on the water and came toward Jesus. ³⁰But seeing the strength of the wind, he was afraid, and

he began sinking and called out, saying, "Lord, save me!" ³¹Jesus immediately extended his hand and lifted him up and said to him, "Oh you of little faith, why did you doubt?" ³²When they got into the boat, the wind stopped. ³³Then those in the boat worshipped him, saying, "Truly you are the Son of God."

HEALING IN GENNESARET
(MK 6:53–56; JN 6:22–25)

³⁴And after they crossed over, they came to the land of Gennesaret. ³⁵And the people of that place, when they recognized him, sent for all those in that region, and they brought to him all those who were ill, ³⁶and they begged him that they might touch the fringe of his clothing, and as many as touched it were cured.

EATING WITH UNWASHED
HANDS (MK 7:1–23; LK 6:39;
11:37–41)

15 ¹Then scribes and Pharisees from Jerusalem came to Jesus and said, ²"Why do your disciples transgress the precepts of the elders, because they do not wash their hands when they eat?" ³He responded to them, "Why do you transgress the commandments of God because of your precepts? ⁴For God said, '*Honor your father and mother*,' and '*Whoever speaks evil of a father or mother must certainly die.*'

14:24 Matthew gives this measurement in *stadia*, or the length of a Greek athletic stadium, which was about 180 meters/600 feet. **14:25** This would technically be the last watch of the night, and hence near early morning. **14:27** *It is I* could be rendered also as *I am*. **14:28** Matthew is the only Gospel to name Peter as the disciple who attempted to walk on water. **14:34** Matthew here reports the welcome reception that Jesus received in Gennasaret (Mark 6:53; Luke 5:1). Gennesaret, or the *land of Gennesaret*, was located on the northwest shore of the Sea of Galilee and is often spelled *Kinneret* (Numbers 34:11; Deuteronomy 3:17). Luke 5:1 refers to the Sea of Galilee as the Lake of Kinneret. **14:36** The word translated as *cured* has a sense of being rescued or preserved as well as a spiritual sense of being saved. The crowds again try to touch the *tallit* of Jesus's tunic (Matthew 9:20–21). See note on Matthew 23:5.

15:2 *The precepts of the elders* refers to the oral interpretation of the law of Moses advocated by the Pharisees. **15:3** Jesus was not opposed to interpreting the law of Moses since many of his teachings clearly do so (see Matthew 12:1–8), but in this story he is highly critical of the oral law. **15:4** Quotation from Exodus 20:12; 21:17; Deuteronomy 5:16.

⁵But you say, 'Whoever says to a father or mother, what you would have received from me is given to God, ⁶that person does not need to honor his father and mother.' Therefore, you violate the word of God because of your precepts. ⁷Hypocrites, Isaiah rightly prophesied of you, saying, ⁸'*This people honor me with their lips, but their heart is far from me;* ⁹ *in vain they honor me, teaching things that are the precepts of men.*'"

¹⁰Then he called the crowd and said to them, "Hear and understand. ¹¹It is not what enters the mouth that defiles a person, but what comes out of the mouth that defiles a person." ¹²Then the disciples came to him and said, "Do you know that the Pharisees were offended at hearing this teaching?" ¹³He responded, "Every plant that was not planted by my heavenly Father will be torn up by the roots. ¹⁴Disregard them; they are the blind guides leading the blind, and if the blind lead the blind, both will fall into a pit."

¹⁵But Peter said to him, "Explain to us this parable." ¹⁶Jesus said, "Are you also without understanding? ¹⁷Do you not understand that everything entering the mouth goes into the stomach and exits to the sewer? ¹⁸But what comes out of the mouth originates in the heart, and that defiles a person. ¹⁹From the heart comes wicked thinking, murder, adultery, immoral behavior, thefts, false witnesses, and evil speaking. ²⁰These things are what defile a person, but to eat with hands that are not washed does not defile a person."

THE SYROPHOENECIAN WOMAN'S DAUGHTER (MK 7:24–30)

²¹Jesus left that place and came to the region of Tyre and Sidon, ²²and a Canaanite woman from those regions came to him and cried out, "Have mercy on me, Lord, Son of David, my daughter is ill with a demon." ²³And Jesus did not answer her a word. But his disciples came to him and urged him, "Dismiss her because she keeps crying after us!" ²⁴He answered, "I have not been sent except to the lost sheep of the house of Israel." ²⁵But she came and knelt before him and said, "Lord, help me!" ²⁶He answered, saying, "It is not right to take the children's bread and give it to the dogs." ²⁷But she said, "Yes, Lord, but the dogs eat from the crumbs that fall from the table of their master." ²⁸Then Jesus said to her, "Woman, great is your faith; let it be done for you as you wish." And her daughter was healed in that very hour.

15:5 Mark refers to this concept as *Corban*, or a gift. According to this idea, once an offering was made to the temple it could no longer be used for the care of parents. Once made, the gift may have had a sense of being sacred and consecrated, and one could then argue that a greater gift was made by giving an offering to the temple than for the care of parents. **15:6** Some early and important Greek manuscripts omit *and mother*. **15:8** Compare 2 Nephi 27:25 and Joseph Smith—History 1:19. **15:8–9** Quotation from Isaiah 29:13 from the Septuagint (LXX). **15:10** Compare 3 Nephi 15:1; 17:23; 18:17. **15:12** Here Matthew uses the word *logon* to describe the teachings or words of Jesus. The singular stands out because the reader expects to hear that they were offended at his *teachings* or *his words*, but here the reader finds that a singular word or saying caused offense to the Pharisees. It may be that Matthew has envisioned Jesus teaching the word of God, also a singular concept. The word translated as *were offended* can also mean *stumbled*. **15:19** In listing the things coming from the heart, Jesus here lists *immoral behavior*, or *porneia* (see Matthew 5:32). **15:22** The reference to the woman's Canaanite origins expressly designates her as a Gentile. Mark is less clear on her ethnicity (Mark 7:26). **15:26** Alluded to in Doctrine and Covenants 41:6. **15:27** On using the derogatory term *dogs*, see Mark 7:27; Philippians 3:2. **15:28** The statement regarding the woman's faith is unique to Matthew's account, as is the reference to working exclusively among the Israelites (verse 24).

HEALING OF A DEAF PERSON (MK 7:31–37)

[29]Jesus departed from that place and came near the Sea of Galilee and climbed a hill and sat there. [30]And a great crowd came to him with their maimed, injured, blind, mute, and many others, and they laid them at his feet, and he healed them. [31]The crowd was amazed at seeing the mute speaking, the injured healthy, the maimed walking, and the blind seeing. And they gave glory to the God of Israel.

FEEDING OF THE FOUR THOUSAND (MK 8:1–10)

[32]Jesus called his disciples and said, "I am moved with compassion for the crowd because they have been three days with me now and they have had nothing to eat. I do not want to send them away hungry lest they collapse on the way." [33]The disciples said to him, "Where in this desolate place will we find bread in order to feed this crowd?" [34]And Jesus said to them, "How much bread do you have?" They answered, "Seven loaves and a few small fish." [35]And he commanded the crowd to sit upon the ground, [36]and he took the seven loaves and the fish, and he blessed and broke them and gave them to the disciples, and the disciples gave them to the crowd.

[37]And everyone ate and was satisfied, and afterward the disciples gathered seven baskets full of broken pieces. [38]Without numbering the women and children, the number of those eating was four thousand men. [39]And he dismissed the crowd and entered a ship, and they went to the region of Magadan.

THE SIGNS OF THE TIMES (MK 8:11–13; LK 12:54–56)

16 [1]The Pharisees and Sadducees came to tempt him, and they asked him to show them a sign from heaven. [2]And he said, "When evening comes you say, 'It will be fair weather because the sky is red,' [3]and in the morning, 'It will be bad weather today because the sky is red and darkening.' You know how to judge the face of heaven, but you are not able to judge the signs of the times. [4]A wicked and adulterous generation seeks a sign, but a sign will not be given to it except for the sign of Jonah." And he left them and went away.

THE YEAST OF THE PHARISEES (MK 8:14–21; LK 12:1)

[5]Then the disciples came to him on the other side, but they failed to bring bread. [6]Jesus said to them, "Beware and attentive to the yeast of the Pharisees and Saddu-

---

15:30 Jesus's willingness to heal those of the crowd demonstrates a shift from the preceding story (15:21–28). Jesus is now back in the land of Israel. **15:31** Compare 4 Nephi 1:5. **15:39** Some later manuscripts change *Magadan* to *Magdala*, likely because the latter is a known village on the west shore of the Sea of Galilee near Tiberias. *Magadan* is not known unless it is the same as *Magdala*. Mark states that this event took place in Dalmanutha (8:10), although even in Mark some later manuscripts change the name to *Magadan*. Given the current state of the evidence, it appears that this was either a relatively unknown region or that ancient *Magadan* awaits discovery.

16:2b–3 Half of verse 2 and all of verse 3 are missing from some of the earliest New Testament manuscripts. The reason for their removal may have been inadvertent because the text is nonsensical when these verses are removed. **16:3** Jesus draws attention to the fact that the Pharisees and Sadducees do not understand *the signs*. Jesus likely intended to refer to the signs of their day or time, and hence the *signs of the times* most closely approximates what he said. **16:3–4** Compare Alma 10:17. **16:4** The *sign of Jonah* (see Matthew 12:39–41). **16:5** The disciples have just crossed over the Sea of Galilee to the *other side*. **16:6, 12** The verbs of watchfulness, here translated as *beware* and *attentive*, are not necessarily negative terms, and therefore *beware* or *be on the lookout* are possibly too strong. Jesus appears to be drawing

cees." ⁷They discussed this among themselves, saying, "It is because we took no bread." ⁸Knowing this, Jesus said, "Why do you discuss among yourselves, you of little faith, that you have no bread? ⁹Do you not understand, and do you not remember the five loaves for the five thousand and how many baskets you gathered? ¹⁰Or the seven loaves for the four thousand and how many baskets you gathered? ¹¹How do you not understand that I was not speaking to you about bread? Beware of the yeast of the Pharisees and Sadducees." ¹²Then they understood that he had not told them to be attentive to the yeast in bread but to the teachings of the Pharisees and Sadducees.

PETER'S DECLARATION AT CAESAREA PHILIPPI (MK 8:27–30; LK 9:18–20; JN 6:67–71)

¹³Jesus then came to the region of Caesarea Philippi and questioned the disciples, saying, "Who do people say the Son of Man is?" ¹⁴They said, "Some say John the Baptist, others Elijah, others Jeremiah or one of the prophets." ¹⁵He said to them, "Who do you say that I am?" ¹⁶Simon Peter answered, "You are the Christ, the Son of the living God." ¹⁷Jesus answered him, "Blessed are you, Simon son of Jonah, because flesh and blood has not revealed this to you, but my Father in heaven has revealed it. ¹⁸I say to you that you are Peter, and on this rock I will build my church, and the gates of Hades will not overpower it. ¹⁹I will give to you the keys of the kingdom of heaven, and whatever you bind on earth, it will be bound in the heavens, and whatever you undo on earth, it will be undone in the heavens." ²⁰Then he commanded the disciples that they should tell no one that he was the Christ.

JESUS FORETELLS HIS DEATH AND RESURRECTION (MK 8:31–33; LK 9:22)

²¹From that time, Jesus began to show his disciples that he should go to Jerusalem and suffer many things at the hands of the elders, chief priests, and scribes and

---

attention to their teachings. **16:9–10** The feeding of the four thousand (Matthew 15:32–38) and the feeding of the five thousand (Matthew 14:15–21). **16:13** Caesarea Philippi became the capital of Philip the Tetrarch's (died 34 CE) government, and the area was sacred to the Greek god Pan. Herod the Great built a temple there, and the area flourished in New Testament times. **16:14** On the return of Elijah, see Malachi 4:5; on the return of Jeremiah, see 2 Esdras 2:18. **16:16** *The living God*, Joshua 3:10; Jeremiah 10:9–10; 2 Nephi 31:16. Compare Mormon 5:14; Doctrine and Covenants 42:1. Peter's declaration *You are the Christ* is meant to convey his realization that Jesus is the *Messiah* or *Anointed One*. **16:18** The Greek is built on a pun between two words for *rock*, one a masculine noun and the other a feminine noun. The masculine name Peter refers to a smaller rock, perhaps even a pebble, and the feminine word *rock* refers to bedrock. Jesus promises to build the church on the bedrock of Peter's witness, which appears to be the most obvious reading of Matthew's Greek for this verse. This is the first use of the word *church* in the Gospel of Matthew (see Matthew 18:17). The word does not appear in the other Gospels. The word *church* appears three times in two verses in the Gospels, but it is used extensively in the book of Acts. Compare 1 Nephi 13:4–5; 3 Nephi 11:39. A similar promise is made in Mosiah 27:13, and the original meaning of the verse is expanded in Doctrine and Covenants 10:69. This verse is quoted in Doctrine and Covenants 33:13. **16:19** Jesus promises Peter the *keys of the kingdom of heaven*. The idea of binding on the earth is built on the Greek word *deo*, a word that can mean to *tie, fasten*, or *be married to*. When used in an abstract sense, the word implies a contractual obligation to a partner. In a concrete sense, the verb describes tying shoes or a rope. Compare Helaman 10:7 (also Matthew 18:18); Doctrine and Covenants 1:8; 90:2; 124:93; 128:9–11. The words of Jesus in this verse allude to Isaiah 9:6; 22:22. **16:20** Jesus again commands his disciples to not spread the word (Matthew 8:4). **16:21** See 1 Nephi 19:10.

be killed and then resurrected on the third day. ²²But Peter took him and began to rebuke him, saying, "God forbid, Lord! May this not happen to you." ²³Jesus turned and said to Peter, "Get behind me, Satan. You are a stumbling block to me because you do not think about the things of God but rather the things of man."

TAKING UP A CROSS (MK 8:34–9:1; LK 9:23–27)

²⁴Then Jesus said to his disciples, "If anyone wishes to follow me, let that person deny himself and take up his cross and follow me. ²⁵Whoever desires to save his life will lose it, and whoever loses his life on account of me will find it. ²⁶What profit is there if a person gains the whole world and then loses his life? Or what will a person give in exchange for his life? ²⁷The Son of Man is about to come in the glory of his Father with his angels, and then he will give each person according to his deeds. ²⁸Truly I say to you that there are those standing among you that will not taste

death until they have seen the Son of Man coming in his kingdom."

THE MOUNT OF TRANSFIGURATION (MK 9:2–8; LK 9:28–36)

17 ¹After six days, Jesus took Peter, Jacob, and John, his brother, and brought them alone up a high mountain. ²And he was transformed before them, and his face shone like the sun, and his clothes were bright like a light. ³And Moses and Elijah appeared to them, speaking with him. ⁴Then Peter said to Jesus, "Lord, it is good that we are here. If you wish, I will make three booths here, one for you, one for Moses, and one for Elijah." ⁵While he was speaking, a bright cloud enveloped them, and a voice from the cloud declared, "This is my beloved Son. I am pleased with him; hear him." ⁶The disciples, when they heard this, fell on their faces, and they were very afraid. ⁷But Jesus came and embraced them and said, "Arise and do not be afraid." ⁸After they lifted up their eyes, they saw no one except for Jesus alone.

16:22 The force of Peter's rebuke is similar to the modern phrase *look out for yourself.* **16:24** This is the second statement about the cross in Matthew (see 10:38). Compare 3 Nephi 27:14; Moses 7:55; Doctrine and Covenants 23:6; 56:2. **16:25** The Joseph Smith Translation reads *And now for a man to take up his cross, is to deny himself from all ungodliness, and from every worldly lust, and keep my commandments. Break not my commandments, for to save your lives; for whosoever will save his life in this world, shall lose it in the world to come; and whosoever will lose his life in this world for my sake shall find it in the world to come.* **16:27** An allusion to Psalms 28:4; 62:12. The word translated as *angels* could also be translated as *messengers.* Given the context, it would appear that Jesus intended to speak of heavenly messengers, and hence angels, although he could have also meant the messengers of his gospel, and hence the disciples. Doctrine and Covenants 1:10; 65:5; 101:65 echo this verse.

17:1 *After six days* refers to the period immediately after Peter testified of Jesus the Christ at Caesarea Philippi. The only mountain that would qualify as *high* in the region of Caesarea Philippi is Mount Hermon. See Doctrine and Covenants 63:21. **17:2** Many translations use the word *transfigured* to denote the change that Jesus underwent. The Greek word is built from the same root from which English *metamorphosis* is derived, and it denotes a physical change to his body. One manuscript notes that Jesus's cloak was white as snow. Compare 3 Nephi 28:15. **17:3** On the death of *Moses,* see Deuteronomy 34:6; on the death of *Elijah,* see 2 Kings 2:11. The Joseph Smith Translation adds John the Baptist to Mark's account of the Mount of Transfiguration (Mark 9:4; Doctrine and Covenants 138:45). **17:4** Most manuscripts have the plural verb *let us make.* On the grounds of the quality of the manuscripts, the singular *I will make* is to be preferred. **17:5** Peter refers to this event in 2 Peter 1:18. There may be an echo of Deuteronomy 18:15 in the injunction *hear him.* Compare 3 Nephi 11:7.

THE COMING OF ELIJAH (MK 9:9–13)

⁹While coming down from the mountain, Jesus commanded them, saying, "Do not relate this vision until the Son of Man is risen from the dead." ¹⁰And the disciples asked him, "Why do the scribes say that Elijah must come first?" ¹¹Jesus answered and said, "Elijah is coming to restore all things. ¹²But I say to you that Elijah has already come, and they did not know him, but they did to him as they wanted, and so also the Son of Man is about to suffer at their hands." ¹³Then the disciples understood that he was speaking about John the Baptist.

A BOY IS HEALED (MK 9:14–29; LK 9:37–43A)

¹⁴And they came to a crowd, and a man approached him and fell to his knees ¹⁵and said, "Lord, have mercy on my son; he is possessed and suffers terribly. Often it throws him in the fire and in the water. ¹⁶I brought him to your disciples, and your disciples were not able to heal him." ¹⁷Jesus answered and said, "This is a faithless and corrupt generation. How long will I be with you? How long will I endure you? Bring him to me." ¹⁸And Jesus rebuked the demon, and it left him, and the boy was healed in that same hour. ¹⁹Then the disciples came to Jesus alone and said, "Why were we not able to cast it out?" ²⁰He said to them, "Because of your lack of faith. Truly I say to you that if you have faith as small as a mustard seed, you will command this mountain to move from this place, and it will move, and nothing will be impossible for you. [[²¹Because this kind is not cast out except through prayer and fasting."]]

JESUS FORETELLS HIS PASSION AGAIN (MK 9:30–32; LK 9:43B–45)

²²And when they gathered in Galilee, Jesus said to them, "The Son of Man is about to be handed over to the hands of men, ²³and they will kill him, and on the third day he will rise." And they were very sad.

THE TEMPLE TAX

²⁴And they came to Capernaum, and those who collected the temple tax came to Peter and said, "Does your teacher pay the temple tax?" ²⁵And he said, "Yes." And when he came to the house, Jesus spoke to him first, "What do you think, Simon? The kings of the earth, from whom do they collect taxes or tribute? From their children or from foreigners?" ²⁶Peter answered, "From foreigners." And Jesus said to him, "Then the children are free. ²⁷But so that they are not offended,

---

17:9 The disciples are finally told that they can reveal the Son of Man when he is risen, thus giving them a time when they can declare Jesus to everyone openly. **17:12** Jesus refers to John the Baptist as Elijah who has already come. Alluded to in Doctrine and Covenants 49:6. **17:16** The story of the disciples and their inability to heal the man's son is told in all three synoptic Gospels (Mark 9:18; Luke 9:40). The story must have been the cause of some embarrassment to early Christians and to the disciples themselves. **17:20** Compare Mosiah 4:6; Alma 60:12. **17:21** Given the poor quality of the Greek manuscript evidence for this verse, it is unlikely that it was part of the original Gospel of Matthew. It appears that it was added to explain the disciples' inability to heal in this instance. **17:24** On the temple tax, see Genesis 23:15; Exodus 30:13; 2 Chronicles 24:9. The tax was intended to cover the incidental costs of the temple that were not otherwise covered with regular tithes and offerings. The tax was often paid in shekels, and every Israelite male was required to pay a half shekel (equal to two drachma or denarii) every year. After Vespasian conquered Jerusalem and destroyed the temple (66–69 CE), he ordered that the tax still be collected in order to pay for the building of a temple to Zeus. **17:27** A Roman stater, or a shekel, is the equivalent of four drachma, and hence enough to pay the tax for Peter and Jesus.

go to the lake and throw in a fishing hook and take up the first fish you catch, and when you open its mouth you will find a stater: take it and give it to them for you and me."

On Greatness (Mk 9:33–37; Lk 9:46–48)

18 ¹At that time, the disciples came to Jesus, saying, "Who is greater in the kingdom of heaven?" ²He called a child and placed him in their midst ³and said, "Truly I say to you that if you do not change and become as a child, you will not enter into the kingdom of heaven. ⁴Whoever becomes humble like this child, that person will be greatest in the kingdom of heaven. ⁵And whoever welcomes such a child in my name, that person welcomes me.

Causing Others to Stumble (Mk 9:42–50)

⁶"Whoever puts a stumbling block in front of one of these little ones who believe in me, it is better that that person has a millstone hung around his neck so that he may be drowned in the depths of the sea. ⁷Woe to the world because of stumbling blocks, for it is necessary that stumbling blocks

come, but woe to that person by whom the stumbling blocks come. ⁸If your hand or your foot is a stumbling block to you, cut it off and throw it from you. It is better to enter life maimed or lame than having two hands or two feet and to be thrown into everlasting fire. ⁹And if your eye is a stumbling block to you, cut it out and discard it. It is better to enter life having one eye than having two eyes and to be cast into the fire of hell.

The Parable of the Lost Sheep (Lk 15:1–7)

¹⁰"Be watchful that you do not despise one of these little ones. I say to you that their angels in heaven always look on the face of my Father in heaven. [[¹¹For the Son of Man came to save the lost.]] ¹²What do you think, if a certain person has a hundred sheep and one of them wanders off, does he not leave the ninety-nine in the mountains and search out the wandering sheep? ¹³And if that person finds it, truly I say to you that he will rejoice more over it than over the ninety-nine that did not wander. ¹⁴Therefore, it is the will of your Father in heaven that not one of these little ones be lost.

18:1 The question in Mark is different (10:35–36). **18:3** Mosiah 3:18 seems to have this teaching in mind (compare Alma 12:36; 3 Nephi 11:38). **18:4** The superlative adjective *greatest* seems to have in mind the twelve disciples and who might be greatest among them. Given that Matthew has retold this story immediately after they crossed the Sea of Galilee (Matthew 17:27) and before they encountered a crowd or anyone else, it is likely that the story is meant to convey a concern among the disciples. The metaphor of becoming like a little child is developed more fully in the Book of Mormon (Mosiah 3:18–19; Moroni 8:10). **18:6** The act of putting a stumbling block in front of little children comes from the Greek word *skandalizo*. Matthew 5:29–30 speaks of this same concept that if a body part offends (*skandalizo*), then it should be removed. Alluded to in Doctrine and Covenants 54:5; 121:22. **18:7** Jesus speaks of a causative agent of offense. **18:9** The Greek reads literally *the Gehenna of fire*. **18:10** The idea that one would *despise* a child is built on a Greek word that means to *think down on* or to *think critically about*. Compare Hebrews 1:14. **18:11** The textual sources for Matthew 18:11 are quite weak, and it is likely that this verse was not originally included in the Gospel of Matthew, although it is attested in Luke 19:10. **18:14** The preceding analogy of the shepherd who seeks after the one who is lost may imply that the one is more important than the ninety-nine, but the addition of verse 14 envisions the same level of concern for all sheep, not just the lost sheep.

JUDGING A BROTHER OR SISTER

[15]"If a brother or sister sins against you, point out the problem to that person alone. If that brother or sister listens to you, then you have gained a brother or sister. [16]If that individual will not listen to you, take one or two others so that in the mouths of two or three witnesses every word will be established. [17]And if that person will not obey, tell it to the church. If that person will not obey the church, let that person be to you just like the Gentile and tax collector. [18]Truly I say to you, whatever you bind on earth, it will be bound in the heavens, and whatever you undo on earth, it will be undone in the heavens. [19]Again I say to you that if two of you agree on earth regarding any matter, whatever you ask, it will be given to you by my Father in heaven. [20]Wherever two or three are gathered in my name, I am there in their midst."

FORGIVENESS

[21]Then Peter came to him and said, "Lord, how many times can a brother or sister sin against me and I forgive that person? Seven times?" [22]Jesus said to him, "I do not say seven times, but seventy times seven.

THE PARABLE OF THE UNFORGIVING SERVANT

[23]"Because of this, the kingdom of heaven is like a ruler who wanted to settle accounts with his servants. [24]When he began to settle accounts, a debtor was brought to him owing a myriad of talents. [25]Because that person did not have the money to pay the debt, the master ordered that the servant, his wife, his children, and all his belongings be sold in order for payment to be made. [26]Then the servant fell on his knees and said, 'Be patient with me, and I will repay everything to you.' [27]The master had compassion on that servant and released him and forgave the loan. [28]That servant went out and found a fellow servant who owed him one hundred silver coins, or denarii, and he seized him by the throat, saying, 'Give me what you owe!' [29]The fellow servant fell down and begged him, saying, 'Be patient with me,

---

18:15 Some manuscripts lack the words *against you*. **18:15–20** These verses have in mind the structure of the church that would be organized after Jesus's death. **18:16** This verse quotes the rule of witnesses from Deuteronomy 19:15 (compare 1 Nephi 18:32). **18:17** In other places, Jesus speaks positively about Gentiles (Matthew 12:18, 21), but here his words appear to have negative implications about Gentiles and their status in the kingdom of heaven. Given the context of this saying, Jesus's statement regarding Gentiles refers to their not participating in the kingdom of heaven and to how the offending person should be expelled from the kingdom even like the Gentile who exists outside the kingdom. The saying plays on the common negative stereotype of tax collectors who are despised and hated (compare Matthew 9:10). This verse is one of two in the Gospels that use the word *church* (see Matthew 16:18). **18:18** See note for Matthew 16:19. In the earlier reference, the saying is delivered to Peter directly, whereas here it is to the group of disciples in the second-person plural. The promise found in this verse is again promised in Doctrine and Covenants 124:93 (compare Helaman 10:7; Doctrine and Covenants 1:8; 127:7; 128:8, 10). **18:19–20** Compare Doctrine and Covenants 6:32 for an extension of this concept in the Restoration (compare Doctrine and Covenants 32:3; 61:36). **18:22** See Genesis 4:24. **18:23–35** This parable is unique to Matthew. **18:24** The Greek word *myriad* can also refer specifically to ten thousand (compare Mormon 6:10–15). Given that a talent was the equivalent of a dozen or more years of labor for a day laborer, it should probably be taken as a general reference to thousands and thousands of talents. The number was too large for an average day laborer, for whom two to three talents would represent far more than what the average day laborer would earn in a lifetime. **18:28** A *hundred denarii* is still a significant amount of money, assuming that the average laborer would earn between five and eight denarii on a typical day. The parable is built on a disagreement between wealthy individuals.

and I will repay everything to you.' ³⁰But he would not do it, and he threw him into prison until he could repay what he owed. ³¹When his fellow servants saw what had happened, they were deeply saddened, and they went and told their master everything that had taken place. ³²Then the master called him and said, 'You wicked servant. I forgave your entire debt to me because you asked me. ³³Could you not have mercy on your fellow servant even as I had mercy on you?' ³⁴And the master was angry with him, and he handed him over to the torturers until he would repay his entire debt. ³⁵Thus my Father in heaven will do the same to you if you do not forgive your brother or sister from your heart."

INSTRUCTIONS ABOUT DIVORCE
(MK 10:2–12)

19 ¹And it came to pass that after Jesus finished these words, he departed from Galilee and came to the regions of Judea across the Jordan River. ²And a great crowd followed him, and he healed them there. ³And some Pharisees came to him, trying him and saying, "Is it permissible for a man to divorce his spouse for any reason?" ⁴He answered, "Have you not read that he who created them from the beginning *made them male and female*?" ⁵And he said, "*For this reason a man will leave his father and mother and will be joined to his wife, and being two they will be one flesh.* ⁶So they are no longer two, but one flesh. What God joined together, let no one separate." ⁷They said to him, "Why did Moses command us to give a document of divorce and to divorce her?" ⁸He replied to them, "Because of the hardness of your hearts, Moses permitted you to divorce your wives, but from the beginning it was not so. ⁹I say to you that whoever divorces his wife, except for immoral behavior, and marries another commits adultery."

¹⁰The disciples said to him, "If this is the case for a man and a woman, it is good to not marry." ¹¹He said to them, "Not everyone can accept this teaching, but only those to whom it is given. ¹²There are some eunuchs that were born eunuchs from their mother's womb, and there are some eunuchs that were made such by men, and there are some eunuchs that made themselves eunuchs for the sake of the kingdom of heaven. Whoever is able to receive it, let that person receive it."

JESUS BLESSES LITTLE CHILDREN
(MK 10:13–16; LK 18:15–17)

¹³Then some little children were brought to him so that he would lay hands upon them and pray, but the disciples rebuked them. ¹⁴But Jesus said, "Allow the little children to come to me, and do not hinder them, because the kingdom of heaven belongs to ones like these." ¹⁵And he laid his hands upon them and then departed from that place.

19:1 Jesus began his journey to Jerusalem, where he would be scourged and crucified. **19:1–9** Jesus's enemies among the Pharisees had supposed that he would contradict their interpretation of Moses's directives on divorce. The dispute surrounding permissible divorce arose over how the Pharisees and others interpreted Deuteronomy 24:1. A question about divorce and remarriage caused Herod Antipas to take John the Baptist's life (Leviticus 18:6–18). **19:4** Quotation from Genesis 1:27; 5:2. **19:5** Quotation from Genesis 2:24. **19:7–8** An allusion to Deuteronomy 24:1, 3. **19:10** The conclusion of the disciples contradicts Genesis 2:18. **19:10–12** This is considered one of Jesus's hard sayings. Jesus may have been referring to the Essenes when he said that some have *made themselves eunuchs for the sake of the kingdom of heaven*. Some Essenes had dedicated themselves to a life of celibacy in order to serve God. The saying may also be a general criticism of celibacy. A eunuch is a castrated male. **19:13** Luke 18:15 uses the word *infants* where Matthew uses *little children*.

THE RICH YOUNG MAN
(MK 10:17–31; LK 18:18–30)

¹⁶And behold, someone came to him and said, "Teacher, what good must I do that I may inherit an eternal life?" ¹⁷He said to him, "Why do you speak to me about what is good? There is one who is good. If you wish to enter into life, keep the commandments." ¹⁸He said to him, "Which ones?" Jesus said, *"Do not murder, do not commit adultery, do not steal, do not bear false witness,* ¹⁹*honor your father and mother,* and *love your neighbor as yourself."* ²⁰The young man said to him, "All of these things I have observed. What is there left for me?" ²¹Jesus said to him, "If you want to be perfect, go and sell your belongings and give to the poor, and you will have a treasure in heaven, and come and follow me." ²²When the young man heard this teaching, he went away sorrowful, for he had many possessions.

²³Then Jesus said to his disciples, "Truly I say to you that it will be difficult for a rich person to enter the kingdom of heaven. ²⁴Again, I say to you that it is easier for a camel to pass through a needle's eye than for a rich person to enter into the kingdom

of God." ²⁵When the disciples heard this they were greatly amazed and said, "Who can be saved?" ²⁶Jesus looked at them and said, "For humans this is impossible, but for God everything is possible." ²⁷Then Peter responded, "We have given up all things and have followed you. What will happen to us?" ²⁸Jesus said to them, "Truly I say to you, in the renewal of all things, you who have followed me, when the Son of Man sits on his throne of glory, you will sit on twelve thrones judging the twelve tribes of Israel. ²⁹And everyone who gives up homes, brothers, sisters, father, mother, children, or lands on account of my name will receive a hundredfold and will inherit an eternal life. ³⁰Many who are first will be last, and many who are last will be first.

THE PARABLE OF THE LABORERS
IN THE VINEYARD

20 ¹"The kingdom of heaven is like a householder who went out in the morning to hire workers for his vineyard. ²And he agreed with the workers for a silver coin per day, and he sent them into his vineyard. ³And the third hour came,

---

19:16 Compare Alma 22:15. **19:16–22** Compare Luke 18:18–23, which has different points of emphasis such as the connection between perfection and obedience and the departure of the man. Luke records only that the man *became sad,* but he does not depart from Jesus. **19:17** The one who is good is God. **19:18** Quotation from Exodus 20:12–16 (Deuteronomy 5:17–20). **19:19** Quotation from Leviticus 19:18. **19:21** Matthew 5:48 also speaks of being *perfect.* **19:22** Compare Helaman 13:20. **19:24** Jesus emphasizes the impossibility of an individual having the ability to save oneself. The saying was popular among Jesus's contemporaries, and sometimes an elephant replaced the camel in the comparison. No ancient sources mention a city gate in Jerusalem known as the eye of the needle. **19:28** Compare 1 Nephi 12:9. **19:30** The saying is given in an abbreviated form and literally reads *and many first will be last, and last first* (compare Matthew 20:16; Luke 13:30; 1 Nephi 13:42). The word *many* has a distributive meaning so that many who are first will find themselves last and many who are last will find themselves first. The word translated as *first* also has the connotation of *leading, first in a position of honor,* or *of high rank.*

20:1 The wage for the worker who worked the entire day (= one denarius) would have been considered quite low in some regions and for certain types of work. Work contracts from North Africa indicate wages between three and eight denarii per day. Jesus's audience would have anticipated a looming problem because of the low wage promised to the first worker. Doctrine and Covenants 88:70, 74 refers to missionaries as the *first laborers in this last kingdom,* a clear allusion to this verse. **20:1–16** This parable is unique to Matthew.

and he saw others standing in the market-place idle, ⁴and he said to them, 'Go to the vineyard, and whatever is just I will pay you.' ⁵And they went. Again he went in the sixth and ninth hours, and he did the same. ⁶About the eleventh hour, he came and found others standing, and he said to them, 'Why did you stand here idle all day long?' ⁷They said to him, 'Because no one hired us.' He said to them, 'Go to the vineyard.' ⁸When it was evening, the master of the vineyard said to his care-taker, 'Call the workers and give them their wages beginning from the last until the first.' ⁹And those hired in the eleventh hour came, and each received a silver coin. ¹⁰And those who came first thought they would be paid more, but each received a silver coin. ¹¹And when they accepted their pay, they murmured against the mas-ter, ¹²saying, 'These last worked one hour, and you made them equal to us, who bore the burden and the heat of the day.' ¹³He replied to one of them, 'Friend, I have done no injustice to you. Did you not agree to work for me for one silver coin? ¹⁴Take what is yours and go. I want to give to the last worker the same as you. ¹⁵Is it not lawful for me to do what I want with my belongings? Is your eye evil because I am good?' ¹⁶Thus the last will be first and the first last.'"

JESUS FORETELLS HIS DEATH A THIRD TIME (MK 10:32–34; LK 18:31–34)

¹⁷And Jesus went up to Jerusalem, and took his twelve disciples on the way alone and said to them, ¹⁸"We are going up to Jeru-salem, and the Son of Man will be handed over to the chief priests and scribes, and they will condemn him to death, ¹⁹and they will deliver him to Gentiles to mock, scourge, and crucify him, and on the third day he will rise again."

THE REQUEST OF JACOB AND JOHN (MK 10:35–45; LK 22:24–27)

²⁰Then the mother of the sons of Zebe-dee came to him with her sons, and she knelt before him and asked something of him. ²¹And he said to her, "What do you want?" She answered him, "Declare that my two sons may sit one on your right and the other on your left in your kingdom." ²²Jesus answered her, "You do not under-stand what you ask for. Are you able to drink the cup that I am about to drink?" They said to him, "We are able." ²³He said to them, "You will drink my cup, but to sit on my right and on my left is not mine to give. Rather, it is for those for whom it is prepared by my Father."

²⁴When the ten heard this, they were displeased with the two brothers. ²⁵But Jesus called them and said, "You know that the rulers of the Gentiles govern them, and their great ones have power over them. ²⁶It will not be so among you, but whoever

---

20:6–9 Echoed in Doctrine and Covenants 33:3. **20:13** That the owner would refer to the worker as a *friend* is surprising. The expected term would be *servant*. **20:14** The word *worker* is missing in the Greek text. **20:16** This verse is alluded to in Doctrine and Covenants 29:30 and 1 Nephi 13:42 (compare Doctrine and Covenants 121:34). Some late and inferior manuscripts add *many are called but few are chosen* to the end of this verse. **20:19** Compare 2 Nephi 6:9. **20:21** Even though the mother of Jacob and John asked regarding the fate of her two sons, the response implies that Jacob and John answered. In Mark 10:35, Jacob and John ask instead of their mother. Some manuscripts add a phrase to this verse: *or to be baptized with the baptism that I am baptized with.* This saying is found in Mark 10:38, but it was probably not originally included by Matthew. **20:26** This is the first time that Jesus has de-fined the meaning of the word *deacon*, here translated as *servant*. The word typically describes someone

wants to be great among you will be your servant. ²⁷Whoever wants to be first among you will be your slave, ²⁸just as the Son of Man did not come to be served but to serve and to give his life as a ransom for many."

THE HEALING OF TWO BLIND INDIVIDUALS (MK 10:46–52; LK 18:35–43)

²⁹And they departed from Jericho, and a large crowd followed him. ³⁰And two blind men sitting by the road heard that Jesus drew near, and they cried out, "Have mercy on us, Lord, Son of David!" ³¹And the crowd called on them to be silent, but they cried out more, saying, "Have mercy on us, Son of David." ³²And Jesus stopped and called to them and said, "What do you want me to do for you?" ³³They said to him, "Lord, that our eyes may be opened." ³⁴And Jesus had compassion on them and touched their eyes, and immediately they recovered their eyesight, and they followed him.

THE TRIUMPHAL ENTRY (MK 11:1–11; LK 19:28–40; JN 12:12–19)

21 ¹Then they drew near to Jerusalem and came to Bethphage, to the Mount of Olives, and Jesus sent two disciples, ²saying to them, "Go into the village in front of you, and immediately you will find a donkey tied, and a colt with her. Untie them and bring them to me. ³And if anyone says something to you, tell them that the Lord has need of them, and he will return them immediately." ⁴This fulfilled the word of the prophet, saying, ⁵"*Tell the daughter of Zion, behold your king comes, meek and riding a donkey, a colt that is the foal of a donkey.*" ⁶The disciples went and did as Jesus instructed them. ⁷And they led the donkey and the colt, and put their cloaks on them, and he sat on them. ⁸Most of the crowd spread their cloaks in the road, and others cut branches from the trees and spread them on the road. ⁹And the crowds that went before him and his followers cried out, saying, "*Hosanna to the Son of David, blessed is the one who comes in the name of the Lord,* Hosanna in the highest." ¹⁰And

who waits upon another person to help them, who waits tables, and who cares for the physical needs of another. **20:27** Jesus offers a parallel saying regarding being a deacon, or servant, of others by equating the work of a deacon with that of a slave. **20:28** The development of the concept of being a deacon continues when Jesus, in saying that the Son of Man did not come to be served, uses the verbal form of the noun *deacon*. The Son of Man came literally to be a servant/deacon to others, and thus the deacons of the kingdom have their model in the Son of Man. *A ransom for many* could imply a single, final event in contrast to the annual ritual ransoms of the law of Moses. **20:29–34** Mark and Luke preserve different versions of this story (Mark 10:46–52; Luke 18:35–43). The individual who is healed in Mark is named *Bartimaeus*. **20:32** See 3 Nephi 27:2; 28:4. Compare Ether 2:23, 25.

21:1 The location of Bethphage is unknown, but Jesus was traveling from the direction of Jericho and approaching Jerusalem from the east. **21:2** The village is probably Bethany. **21:3** The Greek of the last part of the verse reads literally *he will send them at once*, but the meaning is that Jesus or his disciples will *send them back at once*. **21:5** Quotation from Zechariah 9:9 (compare Isaiah 62:10). The last phrase of this verse has been rendered in the King James translation as *riding upon an ass, and upon a colt the foal of an ass*, insinuating that there were two animals present on this occasion (see Matthew 21:2, 7). The Hebrew of this passage reads *an ass, the foal of an ass*, implying that it was a young animal and that there was only one. The JST corrects this confusion and notes that there was only one animal. The error was ancient and may go all the way back to the author of the Gospel. **21:8** The crowd treats the event like a royal procession, reminiscent of 2 Kings 9:13. **21:9** Quotation from Psalm 118:25–26. *Hosanna* means *save* or *rescue now!* Jesus is also declared to be the Messiah with the phrase *the one who comes* (see note on Matthew 3:11; 11:3). **21:10–17** Matthew preserves the most extensive account of

when he entered Jerusalem, the entire city was agitated, saying, "Who is this?" [11]The crowds said, "This is the prophet, Jesus from Nazareth of Galilee."

CLEANSING THE TEMPLE (MK 11: 15–19; LK 19:45–48; JN 2:14–22)

[12]Then Jesus entered the temple, and he threw out all the sellers and buyers in the temple, and he overturned the tables of the money changers and the seats of the dove sellers. [13]And he said to them, "It is written, *'My house will be called a house of prayer,'* but you have made it *'a den of robbers.'*" [14]The blind and the lame came to him in the temple, and he healed them. [15]When the chief priests and scribes saw the marvelous things that he did, and heard the children crying out in the temple, saying, "Hosanna to the Son of David," they were displeased. [16]And they said to him, "Do you hear what these people say?" Jesus said to them, "Yes, and have you not read, *'Out of the mouth of infants and nursing babies you have prepared praise for yourself'*?"

[17]And he left them and went out of the city toward Bethany, and he spent the night there.

CURSING A FIG TREE (MK 11:12–14)

[18]When it was morning, as he was returning to the city, he was hungry. [19]And he saw a solitary fig tree by the road and went to it, but he found nothing on it but leaves, and he said to it, "May no fruit come to you forever." And the fig tree withered at once. [20]When the disciples saw it they were alarmed and said, "How did the fig tree wither at once?" [21]Jesus answered them, "Truly I say to you, if you have faith and do not doubt, you will not only do likewise to the fig tree, but even if you say to this mountain, 'Remove and be thrown into the sea,' it will be done, [22]and everything you may ask in prayer, believing, you will receive it."

THE QUESTION ABOUT AUTHORITY (MK 11:27–33; LK 20:1–8)

[23]And when he entered the temple, and while he was teaching, the chief priests and the elders of the people came to him, saying, "By what authority do you do these things? And who gave you this authority?" [24]Jesus answered and said to them, "I will also ask you one question, which if you answer I will also tell you by what authority I do these things. [25]The baptism of John, where did it come from, from heaven or from humans?" But they discussed it among themselves, saying, "If we say, 'From heaven,' then he will say to us, 'Why did you not believe him?' [26]But if we say, 'From humans,' we fear the crowd, for they all consider John to be a prophet." [27]They answered Jesus and said, "We do not know." He responded to them, "Neither will I tell you by what authority I do these things.

---

the temple cleansing (compare Mark 11:15–17; Luke 19:45–46; John 2:13–22). **21:11** *This is the prophet* is an allusion to Deuteronomy 18:18. Compare Acts 3:22; 7:37; 1 Nephi 22:20; 3 Nephi 20:23. **21:12** The *money changers and buyers* and *those who sold doves* were there to exchange Roman and other coinages into Tyrian shekels and to provide animals for sacrifice in the temple. See Leviticus 1:14–17 for requirements on the purity of animals used in sacrifice (also Leviticus 5:7). **21:13** The quotations come from Isaiah 56:7 and Jeremiah 7:11 (Matthew omits Isaiah's *for all people* at the end of the verse). **21:16** Quotation from Psalm 8:2. **21:17** Bethany is located a short distance from Jerusalem, approximately a mile and a half away, on the southeastern slope of the Mount of Olives. See John 11:18. **21:21** Compare Helaman 10:9. **21:22** The language of this verse is reflected in 1 Nephi 15:11; Enos 1:15; Mosiah 4:21.

MATTHEW 22 | 47

THE PARABLE OF THE TWO SONS

28"What do you think? A man had two children, and he came to the first and said, 'Child, go out and work today in my vineyard.' 29But he answered him, 'I will not,' but later he changed his mind and went. 30Then he came to the other child and said the same thing, and he answered, 'I, lord, will go,' but he did not go. 31Which of these two did the will of his father?" They said, "The first." Jesus said to them, "Truly I say to you that tax collectors and prostitutes will go before you into the kingdom of God. 32John came to you in the way of righteousness, and you did not believe him, but the tax collectors and prostitutes believed him. And when you saw it, you did not repent and believe in him.

THE PARABLE OF THE WICKED TENANTS (MK 12:1–12; LK 20:9–19)

33"Listen to another parable. There was a landowner who planted a vineyard and put a hedge around it, and built in it a winepress and a tower, and rented it to farmers and then went abroad. 34Then the time of harvest drew near, and he sent his servants to the farmers to collect the fruits of the vineyard. 35But the farmers seized his servants and one they beat, one they murdered, and one they stoned. 36Again he sent other servants, greater in number than the first, and they did the same to them. 37Later he sent his son to them, saying, 'They will show reverence to my son.' 38When the farmers saw the son, they said among themselves, 'This is the heir. Let us kill him so that we will collect his inheritance.' 39And they seized him and threw

him out of the vineyard and killed him. 40When the owner comes to the vineyard, what will he do to those farmers?" 41They said to him, "He will completely destroy those wicked people, and he will rent the vineyard to other farmers who will give him the fruit at the time of harvest."

42Jesus said to them, "Have you not read in the scriptures, *'The stone which the builders rejected, this has become the keystone, this was done by the Lord, and it is marvelous in our eyes'*? 43Because of this I say to you that the kingdom of God will be taken from you and given to another people who bear its fruit. 44The one who falls on this stone will be broken, and it will crush anyone on whom it falls." 45When the chief priests and Pharisees heard his parables, they knew that he spoke about them. 46And they sought to arrest him, but they feared the crowds, who accepted him as a prophet.

THE PARABLE OF THE WEDDING FEAST (LK 14:15–24)

22 1And Jesus spoke to them again in parables, saying, 2"The kingdom of heaven is like a king who held a marriage feast for his son. 3And he sent his servants to call those invited to the wedding, but they would not come. 4Again he sent other servants, saying, 'Tell those who have been called, I have prepared my feast. My oxen and fattened calves have been slaughtered, and everything is ready. Come to the wedding.' 5But they were uninterested and departed, one to his own field and one to his business. 6The others seized his servants, insulted them, and murdered them. 7And the king was angry, and he sent his guards

---

21:28–32 The parable of the two sons is unique to Matthew. **21:31** Compare Matthew 7:21. **21:32** *Repent* in this instance could also be *change your minds*. **21:33** The parable is built on Isaiah 5:1–7. **21:42** Quotation from Psalm 118:22–23. An allusion to the church being built on Christ as the cornerstone/keystone is found in Ephesians 2:20–22, where the image of a *cornerstone* is employed. **21:44** Some early manuscripts omit this verse, but the earlier and better manuscripts include it. It may have been omitted by scribes because it seems to interrupt the flow of the story. It may contain an allusion to Daniel 2:45.

to destroy those murderers and to burn their city. ⁸Then he said to his servants, 'The wedding is ready, and those who were called were not worthy. ⁹Go out on the main roads, and as many as you find, call them to the marriage feast. ¹⁰And those servants went out on the roads and gathered everyone they found, both wicked and good, and the marriage feast was filled with guests. ¹¹But when the king entered to see the guests, he noticed a person there who was not dressed in wedding clothing, ¹²and he said to him, 'Friend, how did you enter without wearing wedding clothing?' But he was speechless. ¹³Then the king said to his servants, 'Bind him hand and foot and throw him into the outer darkness, where there will be weeping and grinding of teeth.' ¹⁴Many are called but few are chosen."

A QUESTION ABOUT TAXES (MK 12:13–17; LK 20:20–26)

¹⁵Then the Pharisees departed and planned how they might be able to entangle him in his words. ¹⁶And they sent their disciples to him together with the Herodians, saying, "Teacher, we know that you are truthful and that you teach the way of God in truth and that you do not pander to anyone, nor do you show partiality. ¹⁷Tell us therefore what you think. Is it lawful to pay the poll tax to Caesar or not?" ¹⁸Knowing their wicked intentions, he said to them, "Why do you test me, hypocrites? ¹⁹Show me the coin of the poll tax." And they brought to him a silver coin. ²⁰And he said to them, "Whose image and inscription is on it?" ²¹They answered, "Caesar's." Then he said to them, "Give to Caesar what belongs to Caesar and to God what belongs to God." ²²When they heard this, they were amazed, and they departed and left him.

A QUESTION ABOUT THE RESURRECTION (MK 12:18–27; LK 20:27–40)

²³On the same day the Sadducees, who say there is no resurrection, came to him and questioned him, ²⁴"Teacher, Moses said, '*If someone dies without having children, his brother must marry his widow and raise children for his brother.*' ²⁵Now there were seven brothers among us, and the first married and then died not having children, and he left his wife to his brother. ²⁶The

---

22:10 The word translated as *guests* describes the act of eating while reclined, so in a generic way it refers to the guests at the wedding. **22:11** Wedding clothing is probably an allusion to Zephaniah 1:7–8. In Zephaniah, those who are dressed as foreigners are thrown out. **22:13** The word translated as *servants* is *diakonois*, or *deacons*, who are depicted in this story in their primary capacity of waiters at a table. Compare Matthew 8:12; Alma 40:13. **22:14** In some manuscripts of the Gospel of John, Jesus is called the "chosen Son" using the same adjective that is used here to describe the chosen. The Doctrine and Covenants expands the meaning of the chosen (121:34–35). The Joseph Smith Translation reads *For many are called, but few chosen; wherefore all do not have on the wedding garment.* **22:16** The claim by the disciples of the Pharisees and Herodians is difficult to translate because it is unclear whether their words were meant to hurt Jesus (in which case they are intentionally offensive), or whether they are representative of an attitude that was praiseworthy because Jesus did not allow the opinions and emotions of others to affect his teachings. The *Herodians* probably refers to supporters of Herod Antipas, or generally to those who supported the Herodian dynasty. (See also Mark 3:6; 12:13 for the only other references to the *Herodians*). **22:17** The poll tax was not an optional or voluntary tax, but it was a census-based tax that all adult males were required to pay. Tiberius, referred to as *Caesar* in this verse, died 16 March 37 CE. **22:20** Tiberius (14–37 CE) was the Roman emperor during Jesus's adult life. **22:21** Jesus elsewhere supported the payment of taxes (Matthew 17:24–27). This verse is quoted in Doctrine and Covenants 63:26. **22:24** Quotation from Deuteronomy 25:5 and Genesis 38:8 (Ruth 1:1–12 deals with the difficulties of the practice of levirate marriage).

same happened to the second and third brothers until the seventh. ²⁷Last of all, the wife died. ²⁸In the resurrection, whose wife of the seven will she be, because they all married her?" ²⁹Jesus answered them, "You go astray, not knowing the scriptures nor the power of God. ³⁰In the resurrection, they neither marry nor are given in marriage, but they are as angels in heaven. ³¹Concerning the resurrection of the dead, have you not read the word of God to you, saying, ³²*I am the God of Abraham, the God of Isaac, and the God of Jacob.*' He is not a God of the dead but of the living." ³³When the crowd heard this, they were amazed at his teaching.

THE GREATEST COMMANDMENT (MK 12:28–34; LK 10:25–28)

³⁴ When the Pharisees heard that he silenced the Sadducees, they gathered together. ³⁵And one among them, a lawyer, questioned him in order to test him, ³⁶"Teacher, what is the greatest commandment in the Law?" ³⁷He said to him, "'*Love the Lord your God with all your heart and all your soul and in all your understanding.*' ³⁸This is the greatest and first commandment. ³⁹The second is like it, '*Love your neighbor as yourself.*' ⁴⁰The entire Law and Prophets depend on these two commandments."

THE QUESTION ABOUT DAVID'S SON (MK 12:35–37; LK 20:41–44)

⁴¹Jesus asked a question of the Pharisees who were gathered together. ⁴²"What do you think about the Christ? Whose son is he?" They said to him, "The son of David." ⁴³He said to them, "How did David, while in the Spirit, call him 'Lord,' saying, ⁴⁴'*The Lord said to my Lord, Sit on my right until I make all your enemies your footstool*'? ⁴⁵If David called him 'Lord,' how is he also his son?" ⁴⁶And no one was able to answer him a word, nor did they ask him any questions from that day forward.

DENUNCIATION OF THE SCRIBES AND PHARISEES (MK 12:38–40; LK 11:37–54)

23 ¹Then Jesus spoke to the crowds and his disciples, ²saying, "The scribes and the Pharisees sit upon Moses's seat. ³Therefore, do everything they tell you and observe it, but do not act according to their works. They do not do what they teach. ⁴They bind together heavy burdens that are difficult to bear and then lay them on the shoulders of others, but they are not willing to lift a finger to move them. ⁵Every work that they perform they do to be seen by others. They broaden their phylacteries and enlarge the fringes of their robes.

22:29 The reference to *scriptures* can refer simply to what is written, and hence the scriptures, but also to any of the writings of the Old Testament such as the Law or the Prophets. **22:30** This verse is echoed in 3 Nephi 28:30. Jesus's response to the Sadducees seems directed to contradict their erroneous conclusions regarding resurrection. Its implications for deriving a broader view about marriage are limited to the question at hand, namely, whether the resurrection could solve difficulties surrounding levirate marriages. **22:32** Quotation from Exodus 3:6, 16. **22:37** Quotation from Deuteronomy 6:5 (compare 1 Corinthians 13:13; Doctrine and Covenants 59:5). **22:39** Quotation from Leviticus 19:18. **22:44** Quotation from Psalm 110:1.

23:1–36 These verses are almost entirely unique to Matthew (compare Mark 12:38–40; Luke 20:45–47). This condemnation of the Pharisees and scribes is placed shortly before the Last Supper and subsequent arrest of Jesus and provides some context for the hostility directed toward Jesus. **23:2** *Moses's seat* was a seat of prominence in the synagogue. In this passage, it may refer to an actual physical seat or to the practice of representing Moses in the act of teaching the Law. **23:4** The *burdens* appear to be their burdensome interpretations of the Law (compare Mosiah 2:14). **23:5** For the *fringe* of Jesus's clothing, see Matthew 14:36 (compare Deuteronomy 22:12). A *phylactery*, from the Greek word *to guard*, was a

⁶They love to have the prominent places at dinners and the first seat in the synagogues ⁷and to be greeted at the markets and to be called 'Rabbi.' ⁸You are not to be called 'Rabbi,' because you have a teacher, and you are all brothers and sisters. ⁹And call no one 'father' on the earth, because you have a Father in heaven. ¹⁰You are not to be called 'master teacher,' because you have one master teacher who is the Christ. ¹¹The greatest among you will be your servant. ¹²All who lift themselves up will be brought low, and those who abase themselves will be lifted up.

¹³"Woe to you, scribes, Pharisees, and hypocrites, because you close the kingdom of heaven to others, and you do not enter, and for those who are entering, you do not permit them to enter. ¹⁴[[Woe to you scribes, Pharisees, and hypocrites! You eat up the houses of widows, and for the sake of appearance you offer long prayers; therefore you will receive the greater condemnation.]] ¹⁵Woe to you scribes, Pharisees, and hypocrites! You travel sea and land to make a single proselyte, and when you make one you make that proselyte twice the child of hell that you are.

¹⁶"Woe to you, guides of the blind, who say, 'Whoever swears by the temple, is bound by nothing, but whoever swears by the gold of the temple is bound by an oath.' ¹⁷Blind fools, what is greater, the gold or the temple that sanctified the gold? ¹⁸And, 'Whoever swears by the altar is bound by nothing, but whoever swears by the gift on it is bound by an oath.' ¹⁹You are blind. What is greater, the gift or the altar that sanctified the gift? ²⁰Whoever swears by the altar swears by it and everything on it. ²¹Whoever swears an oath by the temple swears by it and him who dwells in it. ²²And whoever swears by heaven swears by the throne of God and by him who is sitting on it.

²³"Woe to you, scribes, Pharisees, and hypocrites! You tithe mint, dill, and cumin and neglect the weightier matters of the law: judgment, mercy, and faith. You should have done these things without neglecting the others. ²⁴Blind guides! You filter out gnats but swallow a camel.

²⁵"Woe to you scribes, Pharisees, and hypocrites! You purify the outside of the cup and the dish, but inside you are full of greed and lack self-control. ²⁶Blind Pharisee, first cleanse the inside of the cup so that the outside is clean also.

²⁷"Woe to you, scribes, Pharisees, and hypocrites! You are like whitewashed tombs in which the outside appears beautiful but inside they are full of the dead and all uncleanness. ²⁸Even so, you look righteous to others on the outside, but inside you are full of hypocrisy and lawlessness.

---

small leather box tied to the arm and a second one tied to the forehead. They contained a small scroll with the passages from scripture that mention wearing a phylactery (Exodus 13:1–16; Deuteronomy 6:4–9; 11:13–21). Israelites were commanded to attach fringes (*tallit*) to the corners of their clothing (Numbers 15:38–39; Deuteronomy 22:12). Jesus criticized the practice of enlarging the size of the phylactery and fringes. **23:7** *Rabbi* means *my master* or *my teacher*, and in Jesus's day it did not refer to people who were officially designated as *rabbis* because they had been trained as such, but rather it was a term of respect. Later generations codified the practice of how one could become a rabbi. **23:11** The idealization of the role of the *servant* or *deacon* in this verse is the highest praise given to being a deacon. **23:12** Alluded to in Doctrine and Covenants 112:3. **23:14** This verse is missing in the best Greek manuscripts, and only a few later manuscripts preserve it. The verse was almost certainly not original. **23:15** For a *proselyte*, see Exodus 12:43. **23:23** The *tithe* mentioned here is the requirement to pay a tenth of one's crops for the maintenance of the temple and the priests (Deuteronomy 14:22–29). Only specific crops were required to be tithed. **23:24** Some Jews strained their drinks to remove tiny insects. **23:26** Alluded to in Alma 60:23.

²⁹"Woe to you, scribes, Pharisees, and hypocrites! You build the tombs of the prophets and decorate the graves of the righteous. ³⁰And you say, 'If we were in the days of our fathers, we would not have participated in shedding the blood of the prophets.' ³¹Therefore, you testify against yourselves that you are the children of those who murdered the prophets. ³²Fulfill, then, the measure of your ancestors. ³³Snakes, born of vipers, how can you flee from the judgment of hell?

³⁴"Behold, because of this I send you the prophets and wise men and scribes, and some of them you kill and crucify, and some you flog in your synagogues and pursue them from city to city, ³⁵that the righteous blood that is poured out on the earth may come upon you, from the blood of the righteous Abel to the blood of Zacharias son of Barachias, whom you murdered between the temple and the altar. ³⁶Truly I say to you that all these things will come upon this generation.

JESUS'S LAMENT OVER JERUSALEM (LK 13:34–35)

³⁷"Jerusalem, Jerusalem, whose inhabitants kill the prophets and stone those who are sent to her. How often did I desire to gather your children together as a hen gathers her own chickens under her wings, but you would not accept it? ³⁸Behold, your house is deserted. ³⁹I say to you, you will not see me again until you say, '*Blessed is the one who comes in the name of the Lord.*'"

THE DESTRUCTION OF THE TEMPLE FORETOLD (MK 13:1–8; LK 21:5–11)

24 ¹Jesus came from the temple and was leaving when his disciples came to him to show him the buildings of the temple, ²but he answered them, "Do you not see all these things? Truly I say to you, there will not be left here a stone upon another stone that will not be overthrown."

³Then he sat on the Mount of Olives, and the disciples came to him privately, saying, "Tell us when these things will be, and what will be the sign of your coming and the end of the world?" ⁴Jesus answered them, "Beware that no one leads you astray. ⁵Many will come in my name, saying, 'I am the Christ,' and they will lead many astray. ⁶You will begin to hear of wars and rumors of war. Look and do not be troubled: these things must be, but it is not the end. ⁷Nation will rise against nation, kingdom against kingdom, and

---

23:30 Compare Helaman 13:25. **23:33** *Hell* is the Greek *Gehenna*. See Matthew 10:28; Doctrine and Covenants 112:23. **23:34** The *flogging* would be of the type enforced by a local synagogue and not the official Roman practice of scourging. Echoed in Doctrine and Covenants 63:31. **23:35** *Zacharias son of Barachias* is the murdered prophet mentioned in 2 Chronicles 24:20–22 (compare Zechariah 1:1). **23:36** Compare 3 Nephi 20:46. **23:37** *As a hen gathers her chickens.* Helaman 13:33, 3 Nephi 10:4–6, and Doctrine and Covenants 10:65; 29:2; 43:24 draw on this metaphor. **23:38** Compare Isaiah 5:9; Helaman 15:1. **23:39** Quotation from Psalm 118:26.

24:1 A significantly different version of this sermon, known as the Olivet Discourse, is found in Joseph Smith—Matthew. This is the last of Matthew's five great sermons (see note on Matthew 7:28). Compare 1 Nephi 12:22; 13:37; Doctrine and Covenants 45:37–43; 88:87–116; 133. **24:2** Jesus asks his disciples whether they *see all these things*, meaning the signs and portents of his approaching death and the calamities following it. The city of Jerusalem was besieged by the Roman army under Vespasian and Titus. The temple fell in the summer of 70 CE to Titus's army. Quoted in Doctrine and Covenants 45:20. **24:3** The *end of the world* can also mean the *end of the age*. Zechariah 14:1–10 speaks of the return of the Lord at the temple mount. **24:4** Acts 21:38 mentions a false prophet who led a group of followers into the desert. **24:6** Compare 1 Nephi 12:2; Doctrine and Covenants 45:26, 35. **24:6–7** Alluded to in Mormon 8:30. **24:7** Acts mentions a later and severe famine (Acts 11:28).

there will be famines and earthquakes in different places. [8]All of these things are the beginning of the birth pains.

PERSECUTION FORETOLD
(MK 13:9–13; LK 21:12–19)

[9]"Then they will hand you over to afflict you and kill you, and you will be hated by all people because of my name. [10]And then many will stumble, and they will betray one another and hate one another. [11]And many false prophets will arise and lead away many. [12]And because of the increase of lawlessness, the love of many will grow cold, [13]but those who endure to the end will be saved. [14]And then the gospel of the kingdom will be taught throughout the entire world as a testimony to all nations, and then the end comes.

THE DESOLATING SACRILEGE
(MK 13:14–20; LK 21:20–24)

[15]"When you see the desolating sacrilege, according to the word of the prophet Daniel, standing in the temple (let the reader understand), [16]then let those who are in Judea flee to the mountains, [17]and the one who is on the housetop, let him not go down and take anything from the house, [18]and the one in the field, let him not return to take his cloak. [19]Woe to those who are pregnant and nursing in those days. [20]Pray that your flight may not be in winter or on a Sabbath. [21]There will be great tribulation such as has not happened from the beginning of the world until now or that will even come. [22]If those days were not shortened, no flesh would be saved, but because of the elect those days will be shortened. [23]Then if someone will say to you, 'Behold, the Christ,' or 'There he is,' do not believe it. [24]It will come to pass that there will be false Christs and false prophets, and they will give great signs and wonders so that, if possible, they will cause the elect to wander. [25]Behold, I told you this beforehand. [26]If they say to you, 'Behold, he is in the desert,' do not go, or 'Behold, he is in secret rooms,' do not believe it. [27]Just as lightning arises from the east and appears in the west, even so the coming of the Son of Man will be. [28]Wherever there is a carcass, there will the vultures be gathered.

Several later manuscripts add *and plagues* to the list of *famines and earthquakes*. Compare Doctrine and Covenants 45:33. The earlier and better manuscripts omit it (compare Luke 21:11). **24:7–8** The Gentile nations will rise against other Gentile nations. **24:9** Compare Acts 4:3–5, where Peter and John were delivered to a council. **24:12** Compare 2 Nephi 1:7. Quoted in Doctrine and Covenants 45:27. **24:15** Daniel's desolating sacrilege, sometimes translated as the *abomination of desolation*, is spoken of in Daniel 9:27; 11:31; 12:11. The idea is of a pollution that leaves the holy place of the temple desolate. First Maccabees 1:54 refers to the event as the desecration of the temple under Antiochus IV Epiphanes (ruled Judea 175–164 BCE). Compare Joseph Smith—Matthew 1:12, 32. Matthew interrupts the discourse to say *let the reader understand*. **24:16** An early patristic father recalled that the Christian community fled to Pella in Jordan when the Roman army came (Eusebius, *Ecclesiastical History* 3.5.3). **24:19** Compare Mark 13:17; Luke 21:23; Helaman 15:2. **24:20** Observance of the Sabbath is still important in the end-times. **24:22** This verse presents a purpose for which these signs and portents were revealed, namely, to show God's everlasting love for his people. See also Doctrine and Covenants 68:11. **24:24** The elect will literally *wander away* from the paths of the Lord. For *false Christs*, see Words of Mormon 1:15. **24:27** Alluded to in Doctrine and Covenants 43:22. **24:28** The word translated as *vultures* typically refers to eagles. Here Jesus appears to be referring to the common sight of vultures gathered around an animal carcass to feed. The word *eagle* may be an allusion to the standards carried by the Roman army.

The Coming of the Son of Man (Mk 13:24–27; Lk 21:25–28)

²⁹"Immediately after the tribulation of those days, '*The sun will be darkened, and the moon will not give its light, and the stars will fall from heaven, and the powers of heaven will be shaken.*' ³⁰Then the sign of the Son of Man will appear in heaven, and all the tribes of the earth will mourn, and they will see the *Son of Man coming on the clouds of heaven* with much power and glory. ³¹And he will send his messengers with a loud trumpet, and they will gather his elect from the four winds and from one end of heaven to the other.

The Meaning of the Fig Tree (Mk 13:28–32; Lk 12:29–33)

³²"Learn this parable from the fig tree: When its branch is soft and it puts forth its leaves, you know that summer is near. ³³So it will be for you: when you see all these things, you will know that it is near, even at the doors. ³⁴Truly I say to you that this generation will not have passed until all these things have occurred. ³⁵Heaven and earth will pass away, but my words will not pass away.

The Need to Be Watchful (Mk 13:33–37; Lk 12:40; 21:36)

³⁶"Concerning that day and hour, no one knows it, neither the angels of heaven nor the Son, but only the Father. ³⁷Just as it was in the days of Noah, so will the coming of the Son of Man be. ³⁸As it was in the days of the flood, they were eating and drinking, marrying and giving in marriage, until the day Noah entered the ark. ³⁹They did not know until the flood came and they were all drowned. Even so the coming of the Son of Man will be. ⁴⁰Then two men will be in a field; one will be taken and one will be left. ⁴¹Two women will be grinding at a mill; one will be taken and one will be left. ⁴²Watch therefore, because you do not know what day the Lord is coming. ⁴³But know this, if the master of the house had known in what part of the night the thief was coming, he would have watched and not allowed his house to be broken into. ⁴⁴Therefore, you must also be ready, because you do not know the hour when the Son of Man is coming.

The Faithful Servant (Lk 12:41–48)

⁴⁵"Who is a faithful and wise servant? He whom the Lord sets over his household to

---

24:29 Quotation from Isaiah 13:10. Compare Isaiah 34:4; Joel 2:10, 30–31; Doctrine and Covenants 29:14; 34:9; 45:42. **24:30** Allusion to Daniel 7:13. Compare Matthew 26:64; Doctrine and Covenants 45:16, 44. **24:31** These messengers could also be the angels of heaven. **24:32** On the *fig tree*, see Matthew 21:19–21; Doctrine and Covenant 45:63. **24:33** Doctrine and Covenants 110:16 quotes this verse. **24:34** Jesus drew the disciples' attention to an immediate fulfillment of these prophecies, which has caused some concern for believers who question what Jesus meant by *this generation*. The JST version (= Joseph Smith—Matthew 1:34) specifies that Jesus was speaking of the time of the disciples: *Verily, I say unto you, this generation, in which these things shall be shown forth, shall not pass away until all I have told you shall be fulfilled.* Alluded to in Doctrine and Covenants 45:21. **24:36** Some manuscripts omit *nor the Son*, but the phrase appears also in Mark 13:32, and the manuscripts supporting the phrase are earlier and better. See Doctrine and Covenants 39:21; 49:7. **24:37–39** For the story of Noah, see Genesis 6–7. **24:38** See Matthew 22:30, where Jesus similarly speaks of marrying and giving in marriage. The phrase appears to refer to the celebration associated with marriage and giving a son or daughter in marriage (compare Matthew 22:30). **24:42** Quoted in Doctrine and Covenants 133:11. **24:43** Quoted in Doctrine and Covenants 104:86. **24:44** Echoed in Doctrine and Covenants 51:20. **24:45** Alluded to in Doctrine and Covenants 51:19; 72:4.

give the other servants food at the right time. [46]Blessed is that servant who, when his Lord comes, finds him so doing. [47]Truly I say to you that he will put him in charge over all his belongings. [48]If that wicked servant says in his heart, 'My Lord delays his coming,' [49]and begins to beat his fellow servants and to eat and drink with the drunken, [50]then the Lord of that servant will come in a day that he does not expect him and in an hour that he does not know [51]and will cut him off and will establish his part with the hypocrites, and there will be weeping and grinding of teeth.

THE PARABLE OF THE TEN MAIDENS

25 [1]"Then the kingdom of heaven will be like ten maidens, each of whom took her own lamp and came to meet the bridegroom. [2]Five of them were unwise, and five were wise. [3]The unwise took their lamps but did not take additional oil with them; [4]the wise took containers of oil with their lamps. [5]While the bridegroom de-layed, they dozed and fell asleep. [6]In the middle of the night a cry went out, 'The bridegroom is here; go out to meet him!' [7]Then all the maidens awoke and prepared their own lamps. [8]And the unwise said to the wise, 'Give us some of your oil because our lamps have burned out.' [9]The wise answered, 'No, there may not be enough for you and us, but rather go to the sellers and buy for yourselves.' [10]When they went away to buy oil, the bridegroom and those who were ready went with him to the marriage feast, and the door was closed. [11]Later the other maidens came, saying, 'Lord, Lord, open the door for us.' [12]But he answered them, 'Truly I say to you, I do not know you.' [13]Be watchful, therefore, because you do not know the day or the hour.

THE PARABLE OF THE TALENTS
(LK 19:11–27)

[14]"It is just like a man who went abroad to summon his own servants, and he gave to them his wealth. [15]And to one he gave five talents, and to one two talents, and

---

24:48 The idea of the delay of the coming of the Lord is mentioned in Mark 9:1; 13:30. Alluded to in Doctrine and Covenants 45:26. **24:50** Compare Mormon 8:26–32. **24:51** The meaning may also be *cut him in pieces* instead of *cut him off*. Mark's ending to the sermon is different (Mark 13:33–37).

25:1 This chapter continues the discourse from chapter 24. The translation of the Greek word *parthenos* as *virgin* is permissible, but it places a strong emphasis on sexuality when the emphasis should be on age and being unmarried. The ten *maidens* are young maidens, some of whom had failed to prepare beforehand. Some later manuscripts say that the maidens came to *meet the bridegroom and bride*, although this reading appears to be a later tradition added to the story. These three parables in this chapter depict events associated with judgment and the coming of the Son of Man. **25:3, 8** Herodian-period oil lamps are typically quite small, and an extra container of oil would be needed to refill them if they were lit for too long. **25:5** The sleeping maidens echo the sleeping disciples in Gethsemane (Matthew 26:40). **25:6** A midnight wedding is unusual, and more importantly, it is unexpected, which is one of the dominant themes of the parable. This image is used in Doctrine and Covenants 133:10. **25:10** The Doctrine and Covenants engages the themes of this parable in several places (33:17; 45:56; 65:3; 88:92; 133:10, 19). **25:13** Compare Doctrine and Covenants 133:11. Second Nephi 25:13 mentions only three days in the tomb and not three nights also (compare Matthew 12:40). **25:14** The word *wealth* is the same as *belongings* in Matthew 24:47. **25:14–30** Luke knew of a significantly different form of this parable (Luke 19:11–27). **25:15** A talent was a unit of measurement that varied over time, and a Roman talent weighed approximately seventy pounds. Monetarily, it was the equivalent of six thousand denarii. A talent could be measured in either gold or silver. This parable is likely the origin of the idea that a *talent* is a skill or gift that a person possesses. Ether 12:35 speaks of a talent being taken away. See Doctrine and Covenants 60:2, 13; 82:18.

to one he gave one talent, each according to his own ability, and then he departed. [16]The one who was given five talents went off immediately and traded with them and earned five more talents. [17]Likewise, the one who had two talents earned another two talents. [18]The one who had one talent went out and dug in the earth and hid the money of his master. [19]After a long time, the master of those servants came to settle accounts with them. [20]The one with five talents came and brought the other five talents, saying, 'Lord, you gave me five talents, and I have earned another five talents.' [21]His master said to him, 'Well done, good and faithful servant. You were faithful in small things; I will appoint you over many things. Come into the joy of your lord.' [22]The servant who had two talents came and said, 'Lord, you gave me two talents, and I have earned another two talents.' [23]His master said to him, 'Well done, good and faithful servant. You were faithful over small things; I will appoint you over many things. Come into the joy of your lord.' [24]The servant who had one talent came and said, 'Lord, I knew that you were a harsh man, reaping where you did not sow and gathering where you did not throw grain. [25]I was afraid and went and hid your talent in the earth, and now behold, you have your talent.' [26]His master answered him, 'You wicked and lazy servant; you knew that I reap where I did not sow and gather where I did not throw grain. [27]It was better for you to take my money and give it to the lenders, and when I came I would have received what was mine with interest. [28]Take away from

him the one talent and give it to the one who has ten. [29]To the one who has shall be given more and in abundance, and to the one who does not have, it will be taken from that person. [30]Throw the unprofitable servant into the outer darkness, where there will be weeping and grinding of teeth.'

THE PARABLE OF THE SHEEP AND GOATS

[31]"When the Son of Man comes in his glory and all the angels with him, then he will sit upon his throne of glory. [32]And he will gather before him all the nations, and he will separate them one from another, just as a shepherd separates the sheep from the goats. [33]And he will place the sheep on his right and the goats on his left. [34]Then the king will say to those on his right, 'Come, blessed of my Father and inherit the kingdom prepared for you from the foundation of the world. [35]I was hungry and you gave to me something to eat, I was thirsty and you gave me a drink, a stranger and you took me in, [36]naked and you gave me clothing, sick and you looked after me, in prison and you came to me.' [37]Then the righteous will answer him, 'Lord, when did we see you hungry and give you food, or when did we see you thirsty and give you a drink? [38]When did we see you a stranger and take you in, or naked and clothe you? [39]When did we see you sick or thrown in prison and come to you?' [40]And the king answered them, 'Truly I say to you, as you have done this to one of the least of my brothers or sisters, you have done it to me.' [41]Then to those on his left he will say, 'Go

25:18 The servant hid the *silver* of his lord, indicating that the talents in the parable are silver. **25:19** The settling of accounts with the servants implies judgment. **25:21, 23** Doctrine and Covenants 117:10 alludes to these verses (compare Doctrine and Covenants 51:19; 52:13). **25:25** Alluded to in Doctrine and Covenants 60:2, 13. **25:28–29** Echoed in Ether 12:35. **25:29** Compare 2 Nephi 28:30; Doctrine and Covenants 60:3. **25:31** Similar language is used to describe God in 1 Nephi 1:8. **25:34** Compare 1 Nephi 10:18; Enos 1:27; Ether 4:19. **25:35** *Stranger* is used in the sense of a *foreigner*. **25:38** See 3 Nephi 24:5. **25:40** Quoted in Doctrine and Covenants 42:38. **25:41** Compare Mosiah 26:27 and Doctrine and Covenants 29:28 (compare 2 Nephi 9:16; Doctrine and Covenants 76:44).

away from me, cursed, into the everlasting fire that was prepared for the devil and his angels. ⁴²I was hungry and you did not give me something to eat. I was thirsty and you did not give me a drink, ⁴³a stranger and you did not take me in, naked and you did not clothe me, sick and thrown in prison and you did not visit me.' ⁴⁴Then they will answer, 'Lord, when did we see you hungry, thirsty, a stranger, naked, or sick or thrown in prison and we did not care for you?' ⁴⁵Then he will answer them, 'Truly I say to you, as you have not done it to one of the least of these, you have not done it to me.' ⁴⁶These will depart into eternal punishment, and the righteous into eternal life."

THE PLOT TO KILL JESUS
(MK 14:1–2; LK 22:1–2)

26 ¹And it came to pass when Jesus had finished these sayings, he said to his disciples, ²"You know that after two days it will be Passover, and the Son of Man will be handed over to be crucified." ³Then the chief priests and elders of the people gathered together in the courtyard of the high priest Caiaphas, ⁴and they planned to arrest Jesus through deceit and kill him. ⁵But they said, "Not during the feast so that there is not a riot among the people."

JESUS IS ANOINTED AT BETHANY
(MK 14:3–9; LK 7:36–50; JN 12:1–8)

⁶Jesus was in Bethany in the house of Simon the leper, ⁷and a woman came to him having an alabaster jar of expensive perfume, and she poured it on his head while he was eating. ⁸When the disciples saw it, they were displeased and said, "Why such waste? ⁹This could have been sold for a large sum of money and given to the poor." ¹⁰Jesus understood this, and he said to them, "Why do you trouble the woman? She has done a good thing for me. ¹¹You always have the poor with you, but you will not always have me. ¹²She anointed my body with this oil to prepare me for burial. ¹³Truly I say to you that wherever this gospel is declared in all the world, what she has done will be told as a memorial to her."

JUDAS BETRAYS JESUS (MK 14:10–11; LK 22:3–6; JN 13:2)

¹⁴Then one of the twelve, Judas Iscariot, went to the chief priests ¹⁵and said, "What will you give me to deliver him to you?" They agreed with him for thirty silver

---

25:46 On *eternal punishment*, see Mosiah 2:33; Doctrine and Covenants 19:11; 29:28; 76:44.

26:1 Compare 3 Nephi 27:33. **26:2** Matthew's account takes on a historical tone when it reports that *after two days it will be Passover*. While Jesus is teaching his disciples, a conspiracy to arrest him takes place (26:3). Matthew's sources inform the reader that the plot was hatched in Caiaphas's home. **26:3** The courtyard here refers to the uncovered area at the center of a Roman-period home. Joseph Caiaphas was high priest from 18 CE until 36 CE. **26:5** The warning to avoid killing Jesus during the feast is an argument for haste rather than delay. **26:6** On Bethany, see note on Matthew 21:17. **26:7** Jesus is anointed in preparation for his burial, thereby making him the Anointed One, or Messiah (see verse 12). **26:9** The disciples speak of selling the expensive perfume and giving the proceeds to the poor as a way to please Jesus. The story implies that similar acts of charity had been done in the past. **26:13** This saying indicates either that the woman was known to them or that she became famous among Christian communities after Jesus's death. In the Gospel of John, she is identified as Mary, the sister of Martha (John 12:1–8). The term *gospel* also appears in the Book of Mormon with a similar meaning (1 Nephi 10:11). **26:15** *Thirty silver coins* probably represent Roman denarii, approximately a week of pay for a day laborer. Some later manuscripts indicate that these were staters, and thus the sum would be four times the amount than if they were only denarii. Exodus 21:32 notes that the price

coins. [16]From that moment he sought for an opportunity to hand him over.

PREPARATION FOR THE PASSOVER (MK 14:12–16; LK 22:7–13)

[17]On the first day of Unleavened Bread, the disciples came to Jesus and said, "Where do you want us to eat the Passover?" [18]He said, "Go to the city to a certain individual and say to him, 'The teacher says, My time is close. I will observe the Passover with my disciples at your house.'" [19]The disciples did as Jesus appointed them, and they prepared the Passover.

PASSOVER AND BETRAYAL FORETOLD (MK 14:12–21; LK 22:14–23)

[20]When it was evening, he reclined to eat with the twelve. [21]And while they were eating, he said, "Truly I say to you that one of you will betray me." [22]And they were very sorrowful and began to say to him one by one, "Is it I, Lord?" [23]He answered, "He who has dipped his hand with me in the dish will betray me. [24]The Son of Man must go as it is written concerning him, but woe to that man who betrays the Son of Man. It would be better if that man had not been born." [25]Judas, who betrayed him, said, "Is it I, Rabbi?" He said to him, "You said so."

THE SACRAMENT (MK 14:22–25; LK 22:15–20)

[26]While they were eating, Jesus took some bread and blessed and broke it, and gave it to the disciples and said, "Take, eat, this is my body." [27]And taking a cup, he blessed it and gave it to them, saying, "Drink from it, all of you, [28]for this is my blood of the covenant, which I have poured out for many for the forgiveness of sins. [29]I say to you that I will not drink of the fruit of the vine until that day when I drink it new with you in the kingdom of my Father." [30]After singing a hymn, they went to the Mount of Olives.

---

of a male slave was thirty silver shekels, but Jesus was not being sold as a slave. The similarity was inadvertent and coincidental. Jesus was not sold as a slave, and the money that exchanged hands was the price of betrayal. **26:17** *The first day of unleavened bread.* The timing of the Last Supper has been the center of debate for centuries because of its implications for determining the date of Jesus's death. Matthew, Mark, and Luke date the crucifixion to the Jewish month Nisan 15. John dates the crucifixion to Nisan 14 (John 18:28), although the sources all agree that Jesus was crucified on Friday (only the calendar date is different in the Gospels). Matthew's note here puts the Last Supper on Thursday evening on Nisan 15, the first day of Passover when the meal was eaten. Jesus was crucified on Friday, which was still Nisan 15 according to the Jewish manner of reckoning days from evening to evening. See note on Mark 14:12. **26:18** Compare 3 Nephi 17:1. **26:21** Jesus has frequently spoken of being *handed over* or *betrayed*, but now he identifies one of the disciples as being responsible. **26:24** The Greek verb *betrays* is passive, but an English active construction reflects the clarity of Jesus's prophecy better. **26:25** Judas here breaks Jesus's command from Matthew 23:7–8 not to call one another "Rabbi," although Jesus may have permitted the disciples to do so to him. **26:27** With the Passover meal being completed, Jesus then offers them the third or fourth cup of the Passover. Matthew's wording is clear that Jesus has celebrated a traditional Passover feast. He took *some* of the unleavened bread (verse 26), and he took the final cup, which in the first century may have been the third or fourth cup of the celebration. He instills the bread and wine with new meaning in a covenant context. See 3 Nephi 18:1–13. **26:28** Jesus speaks of a covenant in the context of celebrating the old covenant (Passover) using language from Exodus 24:8 and inserting the word *my*. Both look forward to deliverance through blood. Compare Jeremiah 31:31, which promises a new covenant. Some manuscripts add *new* before *covenant*, but the manuscripts that do so are later and less reliable. **26:29** Alluded to in Doctrine and Covenants 27:5. **26:30** Given the Passover context, the disciples sang the *Hallel* (Psalms 113–18), a traditional feature of Passover.

PETER'S DENIAL FORETOLD (MK 14:27–31; LK 22:31–34; JN 13:36–39)

[31]Then Jesus said to them, "All of you will stumble on this night because of me, for it is written, '*I will strike the shepherd, and the sheep of the flock will be scattered.*' [32]After I am risen, I will go before you into Galilee." [33]Peter said to him, "Everyone may stumble because of you, but I will never stumble." [34]Jesus said to him, "Truly I say to you that on this night, before the rooster crows, you will deny me three times." [35]Peter said to him, "Even if I must die with you, I will not deny you." All the disciples likewise said the same thing.

JESUS PRAYS IN GETHSEMANE (MK 14:32–42; LK 22:39–46; JN 18:1)

[36]Then Jesus came with his disciples to a place called Gethsemane, and he said to his disciples, "Sit here while I go over there that I may pray." [37]And he took Peter and the two sons of Zebedee, and he began to be sorrowful and troubled. [38]Then Jesus said to them, "My soul is sorrowful to the point of death. Remain here and be watchful with me." [39]And he went a little way farther, and fell on his face and prayed, saying, "My Father, if it is possible, let this cup pass from me. Nevertheless, not as I want but as you desire." [40]And he came to the disciples and found them sleeping, and he said to Peter, "Were you not strong enough to watch with me one hour? [41]Be watchful and pray that you may not enter into temptation: the spirit is willing but the flesh is weak." [42]Again, a second time, he went and prayed, saying, "My Father,

if this cup cannot be taken away unless I drink from it, your will be done." [43]And he came again and found them sleeping, for their eyes were heavy. [44]And he went from them and prayed again a third time the same words. [45]Then he came to the disciples and said to them, "Sleep for the time that remains and rest; the hour approaches that the Son of Man will be betrayed into the hands of sinners. [46]Rise up, and let us go. The one who betrays me approaches."

THE ARREST (MK 14:43–52; LK 22:47–53; JN 18:2–12)

[47]And while he spoke, Judas, one of the twelve, came and a great crowd with him from the chief priests and elders of the people carrying swords and sticks. [48]And the one who betrayed him gave them a sign, saying, "The one whom I kiss is he; arrest him." [49]And he came to Jesus right away and said, "Greetings, Rabbi," and he kissed him. [50]Jesus said to him, "Friend, do what you are here to do." Then they came and laid hands on Jesus and arrested him. [51]And one of those with Jesus stretched out his hand and drew his sword and struck the servant of the high priest so that he cut off his ear. [52]Then Jesus said to him, "Put away your sword in its place, for all who take the sword will die by the sword. [53]Do you think that I am not able to call to my Father and he will provide me more than twelve legions of angels right now? [54]How will the scriptures be fulfilled that say it must be so?" [55]In that hour Jesus said to the crowd, "You come with swords and sticks to take me like a bandit? But each day I was seated in the temple teaching, and you did not

---

26:31 Quotation from Zechariah 13:7. **26:36** *Gethsemane* means an *olive oil press*. **26:38** Perhaps an allusion to Psalm 42:5, 11. **26:39** This cup is a verbal echo of the cup of the Last Supper. This seems to directly reflect the cup of the supper. Mosiah 15:7 offers the most detailed commentary on the ideas found in this verse. **26:41** Echoed in 3 Nephi 18:18. **26:45** This verse is echoed in Alma 7:9. **26:45–46** Matthew's telling of the events following Jesus's prayer in Gethsemane implies that some time had passed during which Jesus encouraged the disciples to rest and then later asked them to rise and meet Judas. **26:47** *Swords* can also be rendered as *knives*. **26:53** A Roman legion had between three thousand and six thousand soldiers.

arrest me. [56]All this has happened so that the writings of the prophets might be fulfilled." Then all of the disciples departed and left him.

JESUS INTERROGATED (MK 14:53–65; LK 22:54–72; JN 18:13–24)

[57]The ones who arrested Jesus led him to Caiaphas the high priest, where the scribes and elders were gathered. [58]But Peter followed him from afar, up to the courtyard of the high priest, and he came inside and sat with the servants to see the end. [59]The chief priests and the entire Sanhedrin sought false witnesses against Jesus that they might put him to death. [60]But they found none even though many false witnesses came forward. Later, two came forward and [61]said, "This man said, 'I am able to destroy the temple of God and to rebuild it in three days.'" [62]The high priest stood and said to him, "Will you not respond? What is this that they witness against you?" [63]But Jesus was silent. And the high priest said to him, "I direct you under oath by the living God that you tell us if you are the Christ, the Son of God." [64]Jesus said to him, "You said so. Nevertheless, I say to you that from this point on, 'You will see the Son of Man *sitting on the right hand* of power and *coming on the clouds of heaven.*'" [65]Then the high priest tore his cloak and said, "He speaks blasphemy. What need do we still have for witnesses? Look, now you have heard the blasphemy. [66]What do you think?" They answered and said, "He is worthy of death." [67]Then they spit on his face and struck him, and others slapped him, [68]saying, "Prophesy to us, Christ. Who struck you?"

PETER DENIES JESUS (MK 14:66–72; LK 22:56–62; JN 18:25–27)

[69]But Peter sat outside in the courtyard, and a servant girl came to him and said, "You were with Jesus the Galilean." [70]But he denied it in front of them all and said, "I do not know what you mean." [71]He went outside the courtyard, and another maiden saw him and said to those nearby, "This man was with Jesus of Nazareth." [72]And again he denied it with an oath, "I do not know the man." [73]A little while later those standing nearby said to Peter, "Surely you are one of them, because your accent reveals you." [74]Then he started to curse, invoking an oath, "I do not know the man." And immediately the rooster crowed. [75]And Peter remembered the words of Jesus, "Before the rooster crows, you will deny me three times." And he departed and mourned deeply.

JESUS BEFORE PILATE (MK 15:1–5; LK 23:1–5; JN 18:28–38)

27 [1]When it was morning, all the chief priests and elders of the people took counsel against Jesus in order to put him to death. [2]And they bound him and led him away and delivered him to Pilate the governor.

26:56 See note on Matthew 1:22–23. **26:57** These same individuals were previously gathered at the courtyard of Caiaphas's home, so the reader assumes they were waiting there expecting Jesus to be brought to them. **26:58** Peter entered through the gates of the home of Caiaphas, and he watched the interrogation of Jesus from a short distance. **26:59** The Sanhedrin was a body of Jewish elders gathered to judge religious matters. Jerusalem's Sanhedrin was one of several. See note on Matthew 5:22. **26:61** See Matthew 24:1–3. **26:64** Echo of Psalm 110:1 and Daniel 7:13. **26:65** The punishment for blasphemy was stoning (Leviticus 24:13–16). **26:67** Second Nephi 19:9 describes these actions (see also Isaiah 9:9; Matthew 27:30). **26:71** Peter has left Caiaphas's home.

27:2 Pilate was the fifth Roman prefect to govern Judea (26–36 CE). The Gospels depict him as a manipulated and manipulating leader. Matthew calls him a *governor*, but his actual office was that of prefect.

The Death of Judas Iscariot

³Then Judas, who betrayed him, saw that Jesus had been condemned, and he repented and returned the thirty silver coins to the chief priests and elders, saying, ⁴"I have sinned because I betrayed innocent blood." They responded, "What does that matter to us? See to your own affairs." ⁵And he threw down the silver coins in the temple and departed, and then he went and hanged himself. ⁶The chief priests took the money and said, "It is not lawful to put this into the treasury since it is blood money." ⁷Then they took counsel and purchased with the money the potter's field for the burial of foreigners. ⁸Therefore, that field was called the Field of Blood until this day. ⁹Then the word was fulfilled through the prophet Jeremiah, saying, *"They took the thirty silver coins, the price of him on whom a price had been set by the sons of Israel,* ¹⁰*and they gave them for the potter's field, as the Lord commanded me."*

Jesus before Pilate (Mk 15:1–5; Lk 23:1–5; Jn 18:28–38)

¹¹Then Jesus stood before the governor, and the governor asked him, saying, "Are you the King of the Jews?" Jesus said, "You say so." ¹²And when he was accused by the chief priests and elders, he did not answer. ¹³Then Pilate said to him, "Do you not hear how many charges they bring against you?" ¹⁴But he did not answer, not even a word, so that the governor was greatly amazed.

Pilate Delivers Jesus to Be Crucified (Mk 15:6–15; Lk 23:17–25; Jn 18:39–40; 19:16)

¹⁵The governor at the feast was accustomed to release one prisoner whom the crowd chose. ¹⁶At that time they had a notorious prisoner named Barabbas. ¹⁷And when they were gathered, Pilate said to them, "Which one do you want me to release to you, Barabbas or Jesus the one called Christ?" ¹⁸(He knew that they had handed him over because of envy.) ¹⁹When he sat on the judgment seat, his wife sent word to him, saying, "Do not involve yourself with that just man, for I have suffered much today in a dream about him." ²⁰But the chief priests and elders persuaded the crowds so that they would ask for Barabbas and have Jesus killed. ²¹The governor asked them, "Which of the two should I release to you?" And they said, "Barabbas!" ²²And Pilate said to them, "What should I do with Jesus called the Christ?" They all said, "Let him be crucified!" ²³He replied, "Why, what evil has he done?" But they shouted loudly, saying, "Let him be crucified!"

²⁴When Pilate saw that what he said had no effect, but rather a riot began, he took water and washed his hands in front of the crowd, saying, "I am free from this blood. You see this through." ²⁵And all the crowd answered, "May his blood be on us and our children." ²⁶Then he released to them Barabbas and handed Jesus over to be scourged and then crucified.

27:3 For the *thirty pieces of silver*, see the note on Matthew 26:15. **27:4** The meaning of the phrase rendered here as *See to your own* is uncertain. It is a future tense verb that lacks an object. The meaning of the Greek favors the idea that Judas was told to see to his own problem of having betrayed Jesus. The sense may also be that the chief priests and scribes were indicating to Judas that he would yet see the result of his actions. **27:5** Compare Acts 1:18–19. Luke knew of a different account of Judas's death. The accounts in Matthew and Acts are harmonized in the Joseph Smith Translation. **27:9–10** Quotation from Zechariah 11:12–13 and Jeremiah 32:6–10. **27:16** Some later manuscripts note that the prisoner's name was Jesus Barabbas. Mark 15:7 (Luke 23:19) notes that he was a political revolutionary, a label sometimes mistakenly translated as *thief*. **27:24** See note on 27:4, where Matthew again uses the vague description *you will see*, which given the context is translated here as *you see this through*.

SOLDIERS MOCK JESUS
(MK 15:16–20; JN 19:2–3)

²⁷Then the soldiers of the governor took Jesus to the Praetorium, and they gathered around all the cohort of soldiers. ²⁸And they stripped him of his clothes and put on him a red robe, ²⁹and after braiding a crown of thorns, they put it on his head and a reed scepter in his right hand, and they fell on their knees before him and mocked him, saying, "Greetings, King of the Jews." ³⁰And they spit on him and took the scepter and hit him on the head. ³¹And when they finished mocking him, they took the robe from him and put on him his own clothes, and then they led him away to crucify him.

THE CRUCIFIXION (MK 15:21–32; LK 23:32–43; JN 19:17B–27)

³²As they went out, they found a man named Simon of Cyrene, whom they compelled to carry his cross. ³³When they came to the place called Golgotha, or the Place of the Skull, ³⁴they gave him wine mixed with myrrh to drink, but he tasted it and would not drink. ³⁵After they crucified him, *they divided his cloak by casting lots.* ³⁶And they sat down there and watched him, ³⁷and they placed above his head his written accusation, "This is Jesus, the King of the Jews."

³⁸Two bandits were crucified with him, one on the right and one on the left. ³⁹Those that passed by mocked him, shaking their heads ⁴⁰and saying, "You who can destroy the temple in three days and rebuild it, save yourself. If you are the Son of God, come down from the cross." ⁴¹Likewise, the chief priests with the scribes and elders were mocking him, saying, ⁴²"He saved others, but he is not able to save himself. If he is the king of Israel, let him now come down from the cross and we will believe in him. ⁴³*He trusts in God; now let God deliver him if he wants to do so,* because he said, 'I am the Son of God.'" ⁴⁴With the same words, the bandits who were crucified with him abused him.

THE DEATH OF JESUS (MK 15:33–41; LK 23:44–49; JN 19:28–30)

⁴⁵From the sixth hour it was dark on all the land until the ninth hour. ⁴⁶Around the ninth hour, Jesus shouted in a loud voice, saying, "*Eli, Eli, lema sabachthani,* which means, *My God, My God, why have you abandoned me?*" ⁴⁷Some of those standing there heard him and said, "This man calls for Elijah." ⁴⁸And immediately one of them ran and filled a sponge with vinegar and put it upon a reed and gave it to him to drink. ⁴⁹But the others said, "Wait, let us see if Elijah comes to save him." ⁵⁰Then Jesus again shouted in a loud voice, and

---

27:27 The reference to the Praetorium would indicate that they were in the residential palace of Pilate, a palace that may have been built by Herod the Great. The historical record has done little to clarify whose palace this belonged to. The *cohort* in this verse would refer to three to five hundred soldiers. **27:29** First Nephi 1:19 may allude to the mocking of Jesus in describing Lehi being mocked (compare Jeremiah 38:19). **27:30** This verse is echoed in Alma 14:7. **27:33** *Golgotha* means *place of a skull.* **27:35** Quotation from Psalm 22:18. **27:37** The inscription on the placard indicates the official charge against Jesus. **27:38** See Isaiah 53:12. **27:43** Allusion to Psalm 22:8. **27:44** The Joseph Smith Translation reads *One of the thieves also, which were crucified with him, cast the same in his teeth. But the other rebuked him, saying, Dost thou not fear God, seeing thou art under the same condemnation; and this man is just and hath not sinned; and he cried unto the Lord, that he would save him. And the Lord said unto him, This day thou shalt be with me in Paradise.* **27:46** Compare Psalm 22:1 (also verses 35 and 43). Psalm 22 shapes much of the story. *Eli* is the singular of *Elim* (meaning Gods), and *Elohim* is the plural of *'eloah* (meaning *God Almighty*). **27:48** The *vinegar* or *sour wine* given to Jesus was a cheap, diluted vinegar wine that was commonly drunk by soldiers and the poor. **27:50** The Joseph Smith Translation reads *it is finished, thy will is done.*

he released his spirit. ⁵¹And the veil of the temple was torn from the top to the bottom in two pieces, and the earth shook, and the rocks broke apart. ⁵²And the graves were opened, and the bodies of many of the saints who had passed away arose, ⁵³and they came out of the tombs after his resurrection and entered the holy city and appeared to many. ⁵⁴But the centurion and those with him who were guarding Jesus, when they saw the earthquake and what happened, they were very afraid and said, "Truly this was God's Son." ⁵⁵There were many women who watched from afar, who had followed Jesus from Galilee and had cared for him, ⁵⁶one of whom was Mary Magdalene, and Mary the mother of Jacob and Joseph, and the mother of the sons of Zebedee.

THE BURIAL (MK 15:42–47; LK 23:50–56; JN 19:38–42)

⁵⁷When evening came, a rich man from Arimathea came, named Joseph, who was also a disciple of Jesus. ⁵⁸This man came to Pilate and inquired about the body of Jesus. Then Pilate ordered that it be given to him. ⁵⁹And Joseph took the body and wrapped it in clean linen, ⁶⁰and he placed it in his own new tomb, which he had hewn from rock, and he placed a large stone at the entrance of the tomb, and he departed.

⁶¹There sitting in front of the tomb were Mary Magdalene and the other Mary.

THE GUARD AT THE TOMB

⁶²The next day, after the day of preparation, the chief priests and Pharisees gathered to Pilate and ⁶³said, "Sir, we remember that the deceiver said while still alive, 'After three days I will rise again.' ⁶⁴Order the tomb to be guarded until the third day so that his disciples do not come and steal him and tell the people, 'He has risen from the dead,' and the last deceit will be worse than the first." ⁶⁵Pilate said to them, "You have a guard; go and secure it as well as you know how to." ⁶⁶Then they departed with the guard and made the tomb secure by sealing the stone.

THE RESURRECTION (MK 16:1–8; LK 24:1–12; JN 20:1–13)

28 ¹After the Sabbath, toward dawn of the first day of the week, Mary Magdalene and the other Mary went to see the tomb. ²And there was a great earthquake, and an angel of the Lord came down from heaven and rolled back the stone and then sat on it. ³His face was like lightning and his clothing as white as snow. ⁴And as a result of fear, the guards trembled and fell down like corpses. ⁵The angel said to the women, "Do not fear;

27:51 Alluded to in Helaman 10:8; 3 Nephi 8:17–18. **27:52** Echoed in Doctrine and Covenants 88:97. **27:52–53** Alluded to in Helaman 14:25. **27:55** *Cared for* can refer specifically to the action of serving his temporal needs. **27:57** Compare Mark 15:43–45; Luke 23:50; John 19:38. **27:59** Joseph is observing Deuteronomy 21:22–23. **27:62** Matthew is unclear where Mark is explicit: *When evening came, since it was the day of preparation, that is the day before the Sabbath* (Mark 15:42). Matthew's *next day* refers to Friday before the Sabbath at sundown, but it is the next day after the Last Supper (Thursday). **27:65** The final phrase is unclear in Greek, and Pilate tells them to *guard as they know.*

28:1 *The first day of the week* would be Sunday. The Sabbath had ended the evening before on Saturday at sundown. Modern Christians celebrate the day of the resurrection instead of the ancient Jewish Sabbath (Saturday), but early Christians celebrated both the Jewish and Christian Sabbaths, thus recognizing both Saturday and Sunday as holy days. **28:3** The angel looks like the glorified Lord on the Mount of Transfiguration (Matthew 17:2; 2 Peter 1:16). **28:4** The *guards* were those assigned to guard the tomb from mischief. **28:5** The angel was sent to deliver a message and departed after delivering it to Mary Magdalene and the "other Mary," who was likely the mother of Jacob and John.

I know that you seek Jesus the crucified, ⁶but he is not here, for he is risen, as he said. Come, see the place where the Lord lay, ⁷and then go quickly and tell his disciples that he has been raised from the dead, and he goes before you into Galilee, where you will see him. Behold, I have told you." ⁸And they departed quickly from the tomb with fear and great joy, and they ran to tell his disciples, ⁹and while they went to tell his disciples, Jesus met them and said, "Greetings." So the women drew near and held his feet tightly and worshipped him. ¹⁰Then Jesus said to them, "Do not fear, but go and tell my brothers and sisters that they may go to Galilee, and they will see me there."

REPORT ON THE EMPTY TOMB

¹¹And while they went, some of the guard went to the city and declared to the chief priests all that had happened. ¹²And they gathered together the elders and took counsel, and they gave a great deal of money to the guards, ¹³saying, "You must report, 'His disciples came by night and stole him while we were asleep.' ¹⁴If the governor hears this, we will persuade him and keep you free from worry." ¹⁵They took the money and did as they had been instructed. And this story spread among the Jews until this day.

THE GREAT COMMISSION
(MK 16:14–18)

¹⁶The twelve disciples went to Galilee to the mountain that Jesus had shown to them, ¹⁷and when they saw him they knelt before him, but some doubted. ¹⁸And Jesus came to them and said, "All power in heaven and earth has been given to me. ¹⁹Go forward, making disciples of all nations and baptizing them in the name of the Father and the Son and the Holy Spirit, ²⁰teaching them to observe all things that I have commanded you, and behold, I am with you always, until the end of time."

28:7 Compare Mosiah 3:10. **28:11–15** Matthew alone knew of rumors regarding reports of bribery among the guards who were commanded to keep watch over the tomb. **28:17** The Greek could also mean *they all doubted*. **28:18** *All power* echoes Daniel 7:13–14. **28:18–19** Jesus delivers to his disciples in Galilee the *Great Commission*, or the command to take the gospel to all nations and to baptize all those who believe. Matthew's account of the resurrection is brief and leaves off the accounts of those who touched Jesus or dined with him. Matthew is looking forward to the age when a church would be organized to remember Jesus. Alluded to in Doctrine and Covenants 93:17. **28:19** Compare 2 Nephi 31:21; 3 Nephi 11:25; Doctrine and Covenants 24:8; 100:12; 105:41; Moses 7:11, which reflect the wording of the *Great Commission*. Instructions on baptism are found in Doctrine and Covenants 20:73. Jesus, in commanding his disciples to teach *all nations*, uses a verb that refers to making them become *disciples*. **28:20** Compare Mosiah 4:7. Compare Doctrine and Covenants 24:8; 62:9.

THE GOSPEL OF MARK

WHO WAS MARK?

Since at least the second century CE and possibly earlier, Christians believed that the Gospel of Mark was written by someone who was a close follower of, and possibly even a translator for, Peter. The tradition was passed on by an early Christian historian named Papias, whose writings have been lost except for quotations of them preserved in a fourth-century writer named Eusebius. Several of the writings of Eusebius have survived, one in the form of his book titled *Ecclesiastical History* (2.15; 3.30; 6.14). The tradition that Mark received his information about Jesus from Peter is not so strong as to remove all doubt, but it also seems unlikely that anyone would invent such a tradition when it could easily be said that Peter wrote it himself.

The New Testament preserves the account of a man with the Roman double name John Mark, who traveled with Paul (Acts 12:12, 25; 13:5, 13; 15:37–40). Paul directly mentions a traveling companion who was also named Mark (Colossians 4:10; Philemon 1:24; 2 Timothy 4:11). And 1 Peter 5:13 mentions in passing a "son" of Peter named Mark. It would simplify matters greatly if all of these references were about the same person: the companion of Paul's who offended Paul on the first mission (Acts 15:37–38), later reconciled with Paul (Philemon 1:24), and then later assisted Peter in Rome (1 Peter 5:13). But such a simplification overlooks a number of historical issues that are not easily solved. To make matters worse, the name Mark (Latin *Marcus*) was extremely common, and just as there are several women named Mary in the New Testament, it would not be surprising that several persons named Mark worked as missionaries in the early church.

So who was Mark? He was a believer in Jesus Christ who gained his information about the events and sayings of Jesus's life from early witnesses like Peter, or at least that is the most secure tradition to survive. He probably had experience teaching the gospel message to Gentiles, and he possibly saw firsthand some of the friction that existed between ethnic Jews and Gentiles who had come to accept Jesus as Lord and Messiah. Mark alone preserved the names of people like Alexander and Rufus (Mark 15:21), who were the children of Simon of Cyrene. Some scholars have seen in the preservation of these names an eyewitness source that remembered specific individuals who interacted with Jesus personally.

Mark also did not personally know the story well enough, nor was he so interested in history that he paused to set the story in its correct order. He told the story quickly, and later authors like Matthew and Luke who used his Gospel as a source for their own writing adapted its order and telling of events. Some might view this negatively, but the rawness with which Mark tells the story might represent his passion in retelling it. The story moves quickly and inexorably toward the crucifixion. Sixty percent of the verses in Mark begin with *and*, and many begin with *immediately*. Mark was in a hurry to get to the point of the story: the crucifixion and empty tomb.

The Second Gospel also presents a unique view of the disciples who struggle to understand Jesus. They are at times slow to comprehend, they argue among themselves, and they fail to heal a young boy. This feature is not the focus of Mark's Gospel, but it rhetorically encourages readers to see themselves as the struggling disciples who come to understand. For example, after failing to bring bread with them, the disciples became confused about the meaning of one of Jesus's teachings, which elicits a direct question to them: "Do you not yet understand?" (Mark 8:21). During the arrest, the disciples "abandoned him and fled" (Mark 14:50). That is not to say that these stories exclusively define discipleship in Mark, even though the stories of their misunderstanding are numerous (4:41; 6:45–52; 8:31–33; 9:32–34, etc.). Instead, Jesus's disciples are human, influenced by misunderstanding and prone to understand later than expected. Whether this represents Peter's influence in telling the story or his own is now lost to us. This is just one of the important reasons why it matters who Mark was and what his sources were that enabled him to write his Gospel account.

THE MANUSCRIPTS

Surprisingly, only two early papyri exist for the Gospel of Mark, and they are both quite fragmentary and tell us little about the original text. The Second Gospel is constructed largely on the fourth-century Greek copies of the New Testament known as Codex Sinaiticus and Vaticanus, both of which are thought to be textually less corrupted than other witnesses. For the most part, the gospel text is secure, with only its ending in question (see note on Mark 16:9). The manuscripts indicate that the ending of Mark's Gospel was either much shorter than has been passed down in translations or was corrupted and lost and then later restored by Christian scribes. With so many textual variations for the ending of the Gospel after verse 8, it is impossible to determine precisely how Mark originally ended his story. Additionally, several verses that were included in older translations are now thought to be later additions.

Another concern when thinking about the manuscripts of the Second Gospel is the almost certain fact that Mark was the first Gospel to survive. His account was used extensively by Matthew and Luke, although they freely altered its order and wording. Seeing Mark in this way helps the modern reader appreciate that Mark's primitive retelling gave way to more complete versions in which the great sermons were added (Matthew) or the historical order became a point of focus (Luke). Mark also seems to report the sayings of Jesus in the context of the miracles, but for the most part he did not include them for the sole purpose of their inherent value as independent sayings. This may indicate that Jesus's actions were for Mark more important than Jesus's teachings. Later authors offered a different balance in this regard.

Returning to Papias, early Christians believed that Mark wrote his Gospel in Rome to Romans. This would account for a number of Latin words in his Gospel like *legion*,

Praetorium, flagellum, and others. But these words may have been broadly known across the empire, which has caused some scholars to suggest that the Second Gospel was composed in Syria. The answers to these questions are not simply of academic interest, but instead they are vitally important because they have the potential to tell us why this author wrote, which community was large enough to need a written account of Jesus's life, and where the missionary message had spread.

STRUCTURE AND ORGANIZATION

We cannot know with certainty the reasons Mark employed certain mechanisms in writing, nor can we know with certainty why he wrote. In light of that caution, a few features seem to define his account. Mark wrote in a brief, choppy style, with missing antecedents, verbs that were conjugated incorrectly, incorrect historical details, and personal insights into the life of Jesus. Mark's brief style is purposeful and intentional as he moved the story toward its culmination. He also inserted into the story something referred to today as the *Messianic Secret*, a title that describes Jesus's instructions to those who were healed to not declare him to be the Messiah (see note on Mark 1:34). Especially in Mark, Jesus sought to delay the announcement of his messiahship, and Mark sought out those sayings and stories that preserved this aspect of Jesus's ministry.

According to Mark, the story of Jesus's life can be divided into four segments: the early ministry of miracles, the Galilean ministry (Capernaum and mounting opposition), traveling toward Jerusalem (preparation for death and declaration that Jesus is the Messiah), and entry into Jerusalem (culmination of the opposition). The sayings of Jesus fit into these segments haphazardly.

The Second Gospel can also be read in a single sitting, in two hours or less, and scholars now consider it possible that the entire Gospel was read in church services, perhaps even performed in dramatic voice for early Christians. But Mark also omits telling the story of Jesus's birth and his mortal parents, Joseph and Mary. These two details, when combined, suggest that the early church centered their belief on the Messiah, who healed with a consistent focus on his mission to atone for the sins of humanity. Mark tells us that early Christians were intensely interested in the *story* of Jesus's life and that later they became more engaged in the *meaning* of Jesus's life (see the introduction to the Gospel of John). ⸙

JOHN THE BAPTIST (MT 3:1–12; LK 3:1–18; JN 1:19–23)

1 ¹The beginning of the gospel of Jesus Christ, the Son of God, ²as it is written by Isaiah the prophet, *"Behold, I send my messenger before you, who will prepare your way for you, ³the voice declaring in the wilderness, 'Make ready the way of the Lord, make his pathways straight.'"*

⁴John the Baptist was in the wilderness declaring a baptism of repentance for the forgiveness of sins, ⁵and all the land of Judea came to him and all the inhabitants of Jerusalem, and they were baptized by him in the Jordan River, acknowledging their sins. ⁶John was dressed in camel hair and wore a leather belt around his waist, and he ate locusts and wild honey. ⁷And he taught saying, "One stronger than I comes after me, and I am not fit to untie his sandals. ⁸I baptize you in water, but he will baptize you in the Holy Spirit."

THE BAPTISM OF JESUS (MT 3:13–17; LK 3:21–22; JN 1:29–34)

⁹And it came to pass in those days that Jesus came from Nazareth of Galilee and was baptized in the Jordan River by John. ¹⁰And immediately after coming out of the water, Jesus saw the heavens part and the Spirit like a dove descending on him. ¹¹And a voice came from heaven, "You are my beloved Son; in you I am pleased."

The original title of the Second Gospel was *The Gospel according to Mark*, and early Christians widely accepted that the author of the Second Gospel was John Mark, who is mentioned several times in the book of Acts (12:12, 25; 13:5, 14; 15:37–40). A person named Mark is mentioned in some of Paul's letters (Colossians 4:12; Philemon 1:24; 2 Timothy 4:11), and he may be the same person as the John Mark mentioned in Acts. John (Johannon) was his Hebrew name, and his Roman name was Mark (*Marcus*), and therefore it is possible that Paul would use only the Roman name, as he often did for himself. The author of the Gospel does not claim to have known Jesus personally or to have been one of his followers during Jesus's lifetime, and early Christians believed that he drew on the teachings of Peter as a source for information about Jesus.

1:1 Some manuscripts omit *the Son of God* at the end of the verse. Mark begins abruptly with the beginning of the good news, or the *gospel*, a setting that is loosely framed on Isaiah 61:1. He is the only author to specifically refer to his story as a *gospel*. Mark draws attention to Jesus as the *Son of God* (see Psalm 2:7). The *gospel of Jesus Christ* is reflected similarly in 2 Nephi 30:5. The phrase *the beginning* may intentionally allude to Genesis 1:1. **1:2** The quotation is from Isaiah 40:3 with echoes of Exodus 23:20 and Malachi 3:1. The phrase *prepare your way* is echoed in 1 Nephi 3:7. **1:4** Enos 1:2 speaks of a *remission of sins* in a similar way. Compare Mosiah 18:7–8 for repentance as a gateway to baptism. Mark alone refers to John as *John the baptizer*, whereas the other Gospel authors refer to him as *John the Baptist*. The latter has been adopted for the translation because the difference in meaning between the two is minimal. **1:5** The phrase *acknowledging their sins* is often translated as *confessing their sins*. The verb is used in wills and legal contracts and conveys the idea of openly declaring and acknowledging a given set of conditions, which in this case is an acknowledgment that certain actions are considered sinful. **1:6** Jews were permitted to eat locusts according to the law of Moses (Leviticus 11:22). John the Baptist's dress and diet recall Elijah's manner of living (2 Kings 1:8). **1:9–11** Mark omits any reference to Jesus's birth and parentage and instead begins with the baptism. The early stories, including the parting of the heavens, signal a new age (Isaiah 64:1; Ezekiel 1:1). Compare 2 Nephi 31:4; Doctrine and Covenants 112:31. **1:10** Compare 1 Nephi 11:27. **1:11** See Isaiah 42:1; Genesis 22:12, 16. An echo of 2 Samuel 7:14 and Psalm 2:7.

THE TEMPTATION OF JESUS
(MT 4:1–11; LK 4:1–13)

¹²And right away the Spirit drove him into the desert, ¹³and he was tempted by Satan in the desert for forty days, and he was with the wild animals, and angels ministered to him.

THE EARLY GALILEAN MINISTRY
(MT 4:12–17; LK 4:14–15; JN 4:1–3, 43–46A)

¹⁴After John was arrested, Jesus came to Galilee and declared the gospel of God, ¹⁵saying, "The time is fulfilled and the kingdom of God draws near. Repent and believe in the gospel."

JESUS CALLS HIS FIRST DISCIPLES
(MT 4:18–22; LK 5:1–11; JN 1:35–51)

¹⁶And he traveled by the Sea of Galilee and saw Simon and Andrew the brother of Simon throwing their nets into the lake because they were fishermen. ¹⁷Jesus said to them, "Follow me, and I will make you fishermen of men and women." ¹⁸And right away they left their nets and followed him. ¹⁹And he went a little way from there and saw Jacob the son of Zebedee and John his brother, and they were in their boat mending their nets. ²⁰And he called them right away. And they left their father, Zebedee, in the boat with the servants and followed after him.

HEALING OF A MAN WITH AN UNCLEAN SPIRIT (LK 4:31–37)

²¹And they came to Capernaum, and right away he went into the synagogue on the Sabbath and taught. ²²And they were surprised at his teaching because he taught them with power and not as the scribes. ²³There was in their synagogue a man with an unclean spirit, and he cried out, ²⁴"What do you intend to do to us, Jesus of Nazareth? Have you come to destroy us? I know who you are, the Holy One of God!" ²⁵And Jesus rebuked him, "Be silent, and come out of him." ²⁶And the unclean spirit convulsed him and shouted in a loud voice as he came out of him. ²⁷And they were all so amazed that they discussed it among themselves, saying, "What is this, a new teaching? With power he commands the

---

1:12 Mark places little emphasis on the idea of a tempted and tried Messiah. He includes only two verses on this subject (compare Matthew 4:1–11; Luke 4:1–13). See Alma 7:11; Isaiah 53:4–5. **1:13** Mark is unclear whether these messengers are heavenly angels or simple messengers, and the Greek word can mean either a heavenly or human messenger. See note on Matthew 16:27. This is Mark's first use of the concept of *ministering*. The Greek verb forms the basis of the English noun *deacon*. Mark adds *wild animals* to the story of the temptation of Jesus, a possible allusion to Isaiah 34:14; Jeremiah 50:39; Daniel 5:21. **1:14** John the Baptist in Mark is *handed over* or *betrayed* rather than arrested. The verb may have been meant to foreshadow Jesus's being *handed over* (the same verb is used in Mark 14:41). Mark places John's arrest immediately preceding Jesus's public ministry. Matthew tells of the arrest much later in his account (Matthew 14:1–12), but Mark returns to the subject again later (Mark 6:17–29). Some manuscripts have *the gospel of the kingdom of God*, but this reading is not likely to be original. **1:15** John is clear that Jesus teaches the gospel of God rather than his own personal message. Mark prefers the *kingdom of God* instead of the *kingdom of heaven*, as in the Gospel of Matthew. **1:16** Jesus begins his early Galilean ministry, which will end in Mark 3:12. **1:20** Mark prefers to describe following Jesus as *following after him*. Mark insinuates that Jacob and John were wealthy, a conclusion that is made obvious by his note about servants being in the boat. **1:21** Mark says that Jesus went into the synagogue on the *Sabbaths*. He may have intended that as a reference to multiple trips to the synagogue, although the plural form is common. See map for Matthew 4:13. **1:22** This is how Matthew ends the first chapter of the Sermon on the Mount. **1:23** *Their synagogue* shows that the author did not view himself as a member of the Capernaum synagogue.

unclean spirits, and they listen to him." [28]And his fame went immediately around all the region around Galilee.

HEALING OF PETER'S MOTHER-IN-LAW (MT 8:14–17; LK 4:38–41)

[29]Immediately after he left the synagogue, they came to the house of Simon and Andrew, with Jacob and John. [30]Simon's mother-in-law lay ill with a fever, and immediately they told him about her. [31]And he came and took her by the hand and lifted her up, and the fever left her, and she ministered to them. [32]The same evening at sundown, they brought to him all that were sick or possessed with demons, [33]and the entire town gathered around the doorway. [34]And he healed many who were sick with various ailments, and he cast out many demons, but he did not allow the demons to speak, because they knew him.

JESUS DEPARTS FROM CAPERNAUM (LK 4:42–44)

[35]Early in the morning before it was day, he rose and departed to a deserted place, and there he prayed. [36]And Simon with the others looked for him, [37]and when they found him they said to him, "Everyone is looking for you." [38]And he replied, "Let us go to the neighboring towns, that I may teach there, for this is what I came to do." [39]And he came and taught in their synagogues and in all Galilee, and he cast out demons.

HEALING OF A MAN WITH LEPROSY (MT 8:1–4; LK 5:12–16)

[40]And a man with leprosy came begging him and kneeling in front of him, asking, "If you will, you can cleanse me." [41]And he was moved with compassion, and he extended his hand and touched him and said, "I want to do this. Be clean!" [42]And immediately the leprosy left him and he was clean. [43]And he warned him, and he sent him away at once. [44]And he said to him, "See that you tell no one, but show yourself to the priest and offer for your cleansing what was commanded by Moses as a witness to them." [45]But he departed and began to declare it openly and to spread the word, so that Jesus was not able to enter a town openly, but he was out in deserted places, and they came to him from all directions.

HEALING OF A PARALYZED MAN (MT 9:1–8; LK 5:17–26; JN 5:8–9A)

2 [1]And he returned to Capernaum after some days, and it was reported that he was at home. [2]And many gathered so that there was no room, not even in front of the door, and he taught them the word. [3]And some came, bringing to him a paralyzed man, carried by four of them. [4]But

---

1:30 Paul also noted that Simon Peter was married (1 Corinthians 9:5). **1:32** The importance of *sundown* is that the Sabbath had passed and Jesus can now work freely. **1:34** Mark, more than the other Gospels, reports that Jesus frequently told people to not proclaim or make him known. This phenomenon is known as the *Messianic Secret*, and Jesus on occasion encouraged people to delay proclaiming him until it was the right time to do so (see Mark 1:44–45; 7:36; 8:29–30). Mark may have seen this as fulfillment of the saying recorded in Mark 4:11. **1:35** Mark frequently notes that Jesus liked to retire to uninhabited, or *deserted*, places (see Mark 1:45; 6:31, 32, 35). **1:40** Anciently, those with leprosy were banished (2 Kings 7:3–10). Little is known about how they were culturally accepted or ostracized in the first century CE. The Gospels do not portray them as living in separate communities.

2:1 The natural meaning of the phrase that he was *at home* is that Jesus was in his own home in Capernaum. Mark reports five significant stories of conflict in rapid succession between Jesus and his countrymen (see Mark 2:1–12, 13–17, 18–22, 23–28; 3:1–6). They are presented in this early sequence to help establish a theme of hostility toward Jesus. **2:4** The image is of a thatched-style roof and not a

they could not get near him because of the crowd, so they uncovered the roof where he was and dug through it and let down the bed on which the paralyzed man lay. [5]When Jesus saw their faith, he said to the paralyzed man, "Son, your sins are forgiven." [6]There were some scribes sitting there debating this in their hearts. [7]"Why does this man speak blasphemy? Who is able to forgive sins but God alone?" [8]And immediately Jesus knew in his spirit that they debated this among themselves, and he said to them, "Why do you debate these things in your hearts? [9]Which is easier to say to the paralyzed man, 'Your sins are forgiven,' or to say, 'Arise, take up your bed and walk'? [10]But so that you know that the Son of Man has power on earth to forgive sins," he said to the paralyzed man, [11]"I say to you, arise, take your bed, and return to your home." [12]And he arose immediately and took his bed and departed in front of them all so that all were amazed and gave glory to God, saying, "We have never seen anything like this!"

THE CALL OF LEVI (MT 9:9–13; LK 5:27–32)

[13]And he went out again near the sea, and the entire crowd gathered to him, and he taught them. [14]And as he walked by he saw Levi the son of Alphaeus sitting at the tax office, and he said to him, "Follow me." And he arose and followed him. [15]And as he reclined at dinner in Levi's house, many tax collectors and sinners were reclining with Jesus and his disciples because many of them followed him. [16]And the scribes of the Pharisees saw that he dined with sinners and tax collectors, and they said to his disciples, "Why does he eat with tax collectors and sinners?" [17]When Jesus heard it, he said to them, "The healthy do not need a physician, but only those who are ill. I did not come to call the righteous but sinners."

A QUESTION ABOUT FASTING (MT 9:14–17; LK 5:33–39)

[18]The disciples of John and the Pharisees were fasting, and they came to him and said, "Why do the disciples of John and the disciples of the Pharisees fast, but your disciples do not fast?" [19]And Jesus said to them, "Can the guests of the bridegroom fast while the bridegroom is with them? While they have the bridegroom with them they are not able to fast. [20]The days will come when the bridegroom will be taken from them, and then in that day

---

Roman tile roof. Mark's account reflects a typical Jewish home of the period, whereas Luke mentions roof tiles that were typical of a Roman home (Luke 5:19). **2:7** For *blasphemy*, see Leviticus 24:15–16. **2:10** This is the first *Son of Man* saying (see Daniel 7:13). See Mark 2:28; 8:31, 38; 9:9, 12, 31. **2:14** Unlike Matthew, he is named *Levi the son of Alphaeus*. Some scholars have suggested that Alphaeus and Cleopas (also spelled *Clopas*) are the same person. The change in spelling may be the result of different ways to render the Hebrew name into Greek. Some early Christians also thought Alphaeus and Clopas were the same person (see John 19:25; Luke 24:13–27). It is unlikely that Levi and Matthew are the same person, and Matthew and Mark knew of different traditions regarding the name of the disciple sitting at the tax booth. Tax collectors were mostly despised, although it is not clear if there was equal disdain for Roman and Jewish tax collectors. Levi may have collected taxes for one of the Herodians. **2:15** The image of Jesus reclining with the unclean was controversial because Jesus accepted social outcasts and undesirable people into his company. In Luke, this celebration is hosted by Levi (see Luke 5:29), and while Mark does not specifically mention the name Levi, the Greek construction makes it clear that it was Levi's home. **2:17** Compare Moroni 8:8. **2:18** Mark's grammar is unclear regarding who asked the question of Jesus. The most likely solution is that some of the disciples of John or the Pharisees asked. Mark says only that *they* asked. Some Jews fasted twice a week in Jesus's day. **2:19** An allusion to Isaiah 62:4–5.

they will fast. ²¹No one sews a new piece of cloth on an old garment, and if he does the new piece of cloth lifts up at the edges and the tear is made worse. ²²Nor does anyone put new wine in old wineskins. If he does, the wine will burst the skins, and the wine is lost and so are the skins. But they put new wine in new wineskins."

THE SON OF MAN IS LORD OF THE SABBATH (MT 12:1–8; LK 6:1–5)

²³On a Sabbath he went through the fields of grain, and as they went his disciples began to pluck heads of wheat. ²⁴And the Pharisees said to him, "Look, why do they do what is not lawful on the Sabbath?" ²⁵And he said to them, "Have you never read what David did when he and those with him were in need and hungry? ²⁶How he entered the house of God when Abiathar was high priest and ate the bread of the presence, which is not lawful for anyone except for the priests to eat, and he also gave it to those who were with him." ²⁷And he said to them, "The Sabbath was made for men and women, not humankind for the Sabbath. ²⁸The Son of Man is Lord of the Sabbath."

HEALING OF A MAN WITH A WITHERED HAND (MT 12:9–14; LK 6:6–11)

3 ¹And he entered the synagogue again, and there was a man who had a withered hand. ²And they watched him to see if he would heal him on the Sabbath, that they might accuse him. ³He said to the man with the withered hand, "Come here among us." ⁴And he said to them, "Is it lawful to do a good thing or a bad thing on the Sabbath, to save life or to kill?" But they remained silent. ⁵And he looked on them in anger, grieved for the hardness of their hearts, and he said to the man, "Stretch out your hand." And he extended his hand, and it was restored to its former state. ⁶And the Pharisees went out immediately and conspired with the Herodians how they might destroy him.

EARLY MIRACLES (MT 4:23–25; LK 6:17–19)

⁷Jesus departed with his disciples to the sea, and a great crowd followed him from Galilee, Judea, ⁸Jerusalem, and Idumea and across the Jordan River and from around

---

2:22 Matthew adds *and both are preserved* to this saying (Matthew 9:17). Matthew's different version of the saying implies that both the old (the law of Moses) and the new (the gospel of Jesus Christ) are preserved. **2:24** See notes on Matthew 12:1–8. The question of legality may revolve around differing interpretations of Deuteronomy 5:12–15. **2:26** Mark appears to have made a mistake here. The priest in question was Ahimelech and not his son Abiathar (see 1 Samuel 21:1–6). Both Matthew and Luke omit the reference to Abiathar (Matthew 12:4; Luke 6:4), suggesting that they too knew the high priest was Ahimelech. It is uncertain whether the attribution to Abiathar can be traced to Mark, his sources, or possibly Jesus. Directions for the *bread of the presence* are found in Leviticus 24:5–9.

3:1 Mark's *again* may be intended to convey the idea that Jesus often frequented the synagogue. **3:2** Their reason for watching Jesus appears to be malicious (compare Luke 14:1). **3:4** Jesus's question implies that the healing of the withered hand is equivalent to saving a life. There is no specific command against doing good on the Sabbath, and the question he has posed revolves around the interpretation of the command to keep the Sabbath day holy. **3:5** Mark is the only evangelist to report that Jesus grew angry. His anger is a result of the unwillingness of his enemies to answer his question in verse 4. Alluded to in 1 Nephi 2:18; 7:8; 15:4. **3:6** For the Herodians, see Matthew 22:16. They were probably supporters of the Herodian family, or they were employed by the Herodian family. **3:8** Jesus's fame has at this point spread beyond Judea and Galilee into predominantly Gentile regions (compare Matthew 4:25). *Idumea* is southwest of Judea and is the same as the Old Testament *Edom*. Herod the Great was from the region of Idumea.

Tyre and Sidon. A great multitude heard the things he had done, and they came to him. ⁹And he told his disciples that they should prepare a boat for him because of the crowd so that they would not crush him. ¹⁰Because he healed so many, all who had afflictions threw themselves on him in order to touch him. ¹¹When the unclean spirits saw him, they threw themselves in front of him and cried out, "You are the Son of God." ¹²And he warned them many times that they should not make him known.

JESUS CALLS THE TWELVE (MT 10:1–4; LK 6:12–16)

¹³And he went up a mountain and called to him those whom he had chosen, and they went to him. ¹⁴And he called twelve, whom he called apostles, to be with him, and he sent them out to teach ¹⁵and to have power to cast out demons. ¹⁶So he called twelve, Simon whom he named Peter, ¹⁷and Jacob the son of Zebedee and John the brother of Jacob, whom he named Boanerges, which means "sons of thunder," ¹⁸and Andrew, Philip, Bartholomew, Matthew, Thomas, Jacob son of Alphaeus, Thaddeus, Simon the Canaanite, ¹⁹and Judas Iscariot, who betrayed him.

BEELZEBUL (MT 12:22–37; LK 11:14–28)

Then he went home, ²⁰and a crowd gathered so that he could not even eat bread. ²¹When his family heard it, they went out

---

3:13–6:6 This constitutes the second major section of Mark, containing the parables, healings, and the calling of the twelve. **3:14** *Whom he called apostles* is missing from some manuscripts, but it is supported in some early witnesses. The verb of *calling* in Greek is the typical verb *to do*. Mark may have intended the meaning to be *established*, *appointed*, or *set apart*, and older translations preferred the word *ordained*. Mark refers to them as apostles only here in this verse. Elsewhere they are Jesus's disciples, or students. **3:16** *So he called twelve* is lacking in some manuscripts, but it is likely original. *Peter* is the Greek trans-

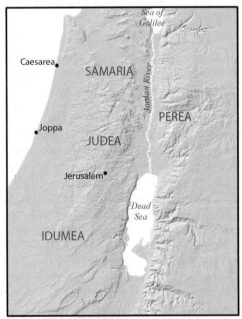

lation of the Aramaic *Cephas*, both of which mean *a stone*. **3:16–19** There are variations in the names and order of the twelve disciples. See Matthew 10:2–4; Luke 6:14–16; John 1:40–49; 21:2; Acts 1:13. **3:17** The term *sons of thunder*, or *Boanerges*, is a transliteration of a Hebrew nickname that refers to their zeal in teaching or the power of their teaching. **3:18** The meaning of *Canaanite* is somewhat obscure but could mean *zeal* or even *zealot* (compare Luke 6:15). **3:19** Scholars often suggest that *Iscariot* is a placename denoting Judas's town of origin, but its precise meaning remains uncertain. **3:21** Mark says *when those who were by him* went to rescue him. *Those who were by him* could refer to his friends, his family, or his disciples and is here rendered as his family members. Matthew and Luke omit the reference to him being *out of his mind*. **3:21–22** Mark's account is slightly different from Matthew's.

The Regions around Jerusalem
Map by Cassie Howe, ThinkSpatial, BYU Geography

to take him, because people were saying, "He is out of his mind." ²²And the scribes who came from Jerusalem said, "He is possessed by Beelzebul" and "By the prince of the demons he casts out demons." ²³And he called to them and spoke to them in parables saying, "How is Satan able to cast out Satan? ²⁴If a kingdom is divided against itself, that kingdom cannot stand. ²⁵And if a house is divided against itself, that house cannot stand. ²⁶And if Satan rises against himself and is divided, he cannot stand, but will come to an end. ²⁷But no one can enter the house of a strong man and rob his house unless he first binds the strong man, and then he may rob his house. ²⁸Truly I say to you that all sins will be forgiven to men and women, and all blasphemies that they speak. ²⁹But whoever blasphemes the Holy Spirit will never have forgiveness, but has committed an eternal sin." ³⁰(Because they said, "He has an unclean spirit.")

THE FAMILY OF JESUS (MT 12:46–50; LK 8:19–21)

³¹Then his mother and his brothers came and stood outside, and they sent to him and called him. ³²And a crowd was seated around him, and they said to him, "Your mother and brothers and sisters are outside looking for you." ³³And he answered them, "Who is my mother, and who are my brothers?" ³⁴And he looked around at those seated by him and said, "Behold, my mother and my brothers! ³⁵Whoever does the will of God is my brother and sister and mother."

THE PARABLE OF THE SOWER (MT 13:1–9; LK 8:4–8)

4 ¹He began to teach again by the sea, and a large crowd gathered to him, so he got into a boat and sat by the lake while the entire crowd was in front of him near the shore of the lake. ²And he taught them many things in parables, and he said to them in his teaching, ³"Listen, a sower went out to sow. ⁴As he sowed, some seed fell by the side of the road, and the birds came and ate it. ⁵Other seed fell on rocky soil where there was not much earth, and immediately it sprouted because there was not much soil. ⁶And the sun rose and it was scorched, and because it did not have roots it withered. ⁷And other seed fell on thorns, and the thorns grew and choked it, and it did not produce fruit, ⁸but other

---

The scribes accuse Jesus when they see that he is *beside himself*, or literally *out of his mind*, thus giving them a reason to assume that he is possessed by Beelzebul. Compare Matthew 12:22–24; Luke 11:14–15. **3:22** For the meaning of *Beelzebul*, see Matthew 9:34. **3:23** For the Old Testament use of parables, see Ezekiel 17:2. Speaking in parables is part of the prophetic tradition of delivering the oracles of God, and often they present messages of condemnation. **3:25** *A house divided*, given Mark's context, could imply that Jesus's family was divided on the issue of Jesus being the Christ (compare John 7:3–5). **3:29** Doctrine and Covenants 132:27 comments on the meaning of this verse (compare Matthew 12:31). **3:30** Mark's aside here offers an explanation of why Jesus spoke about blaspheming against the Holy Spirit. **3:31** Joseph is absent from the family, as he also is in Mark 6:3. One possibility may be that Joseph had passed away by this time, but this must remain a conjecture. **3:32** Many of the best manuscripts omit *and sisters*, but it is present in verse 35, thus likely prompting some scribes to add it here. The term *brothers* in this context refers to Jesus's siblings broadly. Jesus had sisters (see Mark 6:3). **3:35** The addition of *sister* here implies that there were women sitting in the house with Jesus who may have been disciples of the Lord.

4:1–9 *The parable of the sower* is interpreted in 4:10–20. In this chapter, Mark joins the parables about seed (see 4:26–29; 30–34). **4:3–8** Mark uses singular verbs to describe the seeds, whereas Matthew viewed seeds as a plural concept. **4:4** Some manuscripts add *of the air* to refer to the birds, a likely harmonization to Luke 8:5. **4:6** Compare Alma 32:38. **4:8** *A hundredfold* may be an allusion to Genesis 26:12.

seed fell on good earth and produced fruit, and it grew and increased and yielded thirtyfold, sixtyfold, and a hundredfold." [9]And he said to them, "Whoever has ears to hear, let that person hear."

THE REASON FOR TEACHING IN PARABLES (MT 13:10–17; LK 8:9–10)

[10]When he was alone, those that were there with the twelve asked him about the parables. [11]And he said to them, "To you is given the mystery of the kingdom of God, but to those outside the kingdom it is all in parables [12]so that *'they may see but not perceive, and may hear but not understand, so that they do not turn and receive forgiveness.'*"

THE PARABLE OF THE SOWER EXPLAINED (MT 13:18–23; LK 8:11–15)

[13]And he said to them, "Do you not understand this parable? How will you understand any parable? [14]The sower sows the word. [15]The ones where the word was sown on the road are those who hear, and immediately Satan comes and takes the word that was sown in them. [16]The ones sown on the rocky ground are the ones that hear the word and immediately receive it with joy, [17]but they do not have root in themselves and they last for a while. Then trial and persecution come because of the word, and they stumble immediately. [18]And the ones who are sown among thorns, these are the ones who hear the word, [19]and the cares of the world and the deceit of riches and the want of other things enter and choke the word, and it becomes unfruitful. [20]And the ones that are sown on the good earth, these hear the word and receive it and bring forth fruit, some thirtyfold, some sixtyfold, and some a hundredfold."

A LAMP UNDER A BASKET (LK 8:16–18)

[21]And he said to them, "Is a lamp brought to be placed under a basket, or under a bed and not on a stand? [22]There is nothing hidden that will not be revealed, nor anything secret that will not come to light. [23]Whoever has ears to hear, let that person hear." [24]And he said to them, "Consider what you hear. With the measurement that you use, it will be measured to you, and more will be added to you. [25]Whoever has, more

---

4:10 Other followers are with the twelve when they ask about the meaning of the parable. Compare Matthew 13:10. **4:11** The verb *is given* is lacking in the Greek text and must be supplied. It is supplied here based on the parallel passage in Matthew 13:11. *Those outside the kingdom* lacks a finite verb, and thus Mark leaves it unclear whether this is a current or future reality. Mark does little to develop the theme of knowing the *mysteries* of the gospel (compare Alma 12:9; 26:22; 37:4; Doctrine and Covenants 42:65). The singular here points to a secret rite or a secret teaching that the believing will learn. Matthew (13:11) uses a plural noun, possibly in reference to the many insights gained through belief. **4:12** *So that they do not turn* reflects the Hebrew idea of repentance, which is to change one's direction or course. The Greek concept would be to change one's mind or way of thinking. Quotation from Isaiah 6:9–10. **4:13** Sometimes the disciples lack understanding in the Gospel of Mark (see Mark 6:52; 8:17, 21). In portraying them in this way, Mark may have intended the disciples to represent believers who also lack understanding and clarity regarding the meaning of Jesus's teachings. **4:17** *Stumble* can also be translated as *are offended*. **4:19** The *care of the world* in Greek is the *care of the age*. For Jesus, this *age* is a negative concept. Matthew uses a different phrase, *this generation*, to convey a similar idea that the generation of Jesus's day could expect a coming judgment (Matthew 12:41–42, 45). The idea of *the age* expands the reach of the condemnation to include larger societal concerns as indicated through the word *cares*, which can also be translated as *worries*, *concerns*, and *anxieties*. **4:25** Alluded to in Doctrine and Covenants 60:3.

will be given to him, and whoever does not have, it will be taken from him even what he has."

THE PARABLE OF THE GROWING SEED

²⁶And he said, "The kingdom of God is like a man who cast seed on the ground, ²⁷and he sleeps and rises night and day, and the seed sprouts and grows, but he does not know how. ²⁸The earth bears fruit by itself, first the stalk, later the head, then the full grain of wheat in the head. ²⁹When the wheat is ripe, he puts in the sickle because the time of the harvest has come."

THE PARABLE OF THE MUSTARD SEED (MT 13:31–32; LK 13:18–19)

³⁰He asked, "What is the kingdom of God like, or with what parable may we compare it? ³¹It is like a mustard seed, which when it is sown in the earth, it is the smallest of all the seeds of the earth, ³²but when it is sown, it sprouts and becomes greater than any of the plants, and it grows great branches, so that the birds of heaven are able to rest under its shade."

TEACHING IN PARABLES (MT 13:34–35)

³³And with these many parables he taught them the word, as much as they were able to hear. ³⁴He did not speak to them without a parable, but alone to his disciples he explained everything.

THE STILLING OF THE STORM (MT 8:23–27; LK 8:22–25)

³⁵He said to them on that same day when it was evening, "Let us go across to the other side." ³⁶And after he left the crowd, they took him with them in the boat, just as he was. And there were other boats with him. ³⁷And a great windstorm arose, and the waves battered the boat so that it was being filled with water, ³⁸and he was in the stern sleeping on a pillow, and they woke him and said to him, "Teacher, does it not matter to you that we are about to be destroyed?" ³⁹And he arose and rebuked the wind and said to the lake, "Silence, be still!" And the wind ceased, and there was a great calm. ⁴⁰And he said to them, "Why are you fearful? Have you no faith?" ⁴¹And they were very afraid, and they said to one another, "Who is this that even the wind and the lake obey him?"

HEALING OF A MAN AT GADARA/ GERASA (MT 8:28–34; LK 8:26–39)

5 ¹And they crossed to the other side of the lake to the land of the Gerasenes. ²And he climbed out of the boat, and immediately a man from the tombs with an

---

4:26–29 This parable is unique to Mark. **4:38** Mark alone notes that Jesus slept on a *pillow* or *cushion*, perhaps to intensify the contrast between the storm and Jesus sleeping calmly and unafraid. **4:39** Echoed in 1 Nephi 18:21. **4:40** The theme of the disciples feeling fear is common in the Gospel of Mark (see 5:36; 6:50; 9:6, 32; 10:32; 16:8).

5:1 The placement of the story in *Gerasa* (also Luke 8:26; modern Jerash) has been difficult to explain. The town was approximately thirty-five miles southeast of the Sea of Galilee, and it was much too far for the pigs to have run into the sea. Matthew places the event in Gadara, which is much closer to the Sea of Galilee (Matthew 8:28), but still some distance from the sea. A number of different readings in Greek manuscripts make the problem of which town even more confusing because scribes corrected the Gospels so they reflected the names of cities that were closer to the sea. Later Christians also suggested that the event took place in Kursi, which is located very close to the shores of the Sea of Galilee. Despite the problems associated with determining the exact town, all three Gospels note that it was in the *land of* or the *country of* or *region of*, and hence the town names are themselves approximations of the location of the event. Matthew 8:30 notes that the pigs were *far from them*.

unclean spirit met him. ³The man lived among the tombs, and no one was able to bind him, not even with chains. ⁴He had been bound many times with chains and restraints, but the chains were pulled to pieces by him and the restraints broken, and no one was able to subdue him. ⁵He was always in the tombs and on the mountains, day and night crying out and cutting himself with stones. ⁶When he saw Jesus from afar, he ran and knelt before him, ⁷and he cried out in a loud voice, "What do you want with me, Jesus, Son of the Most High God? I command you by God, do not torment me!" ⁸For Jesus had said to him, "Depart from the man, you unclean spirit!" ⁹And Jesus asked him, "What is your name?" And he said, "My name is Legion, because we are many." ¹⁰And he begged him repeatedly that he would not send them out of the region. ¹¹There was in that place a large herd of swine feeding on the mountain, ¹²and they called to Jesus, "Send us into the swine so that we may be in them." ¹³And he permitted them. And the unclean spirits departed and entered into the swine, and the herd rushed down the steep hill to the lake, numbering about two thousand, and they were drowned in the lake.

¹⁴And those who fed them fled and reported it in the town and in the fields, and they came to see what had taken place. ¹⁵And they came to Jesus, and they saw the man possessed, who had the legion, sitting, clothed, and in his right mind, and they were afraid. ¹⁶And those who saw it explained to them how it took place concerning the man possessed and concerning the swine. ¹⁷And they began to ask him to depart from their region. ¹⁸And as he entered a boat, the man who had been possessed called to him that he might go with him, ¹⁹but Jesus did not permit him. He said to him, "Go to your home and to your family, and tell them what the Lord has done for you and how he had mercy on you." ²⁰And he departed and began to teach in the Decapolis what Jesus had done for him, and they were all amazed.

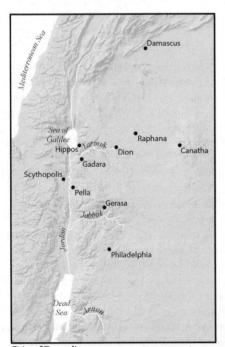

Cities of Decapolis
Map by Brandon Whitney, ThinkSpatial, BYU Geography

5:7 The Greek reads *the Highest God*, but English has adopted the archaic *the Most High God* as a title. Compare 1 Nephi 11:6. **5:9** The word *legion* is a Latin term designating a division within the Roman army. Mark also uses the Latin words *praetorium* (the governor's palace or command center of a fort, 15:16), *denarion* (denarius 6:37), *quadrans* (a small copper coin, 12:42), and *fragello* (the verb of scourging, 15:15). These Latin words may indicate that Mark's audience spoke Latin or was familiar with common Latin terms. **5:11** The presence of pigs in the story points to a Gentile community. **5:17** Little is done to explain the reasons for the destruction of property in the story, but here the negative reaction implies that some were offended by the loss. **5:19** Echoed in 1 Nephi 7:11. **5:20** The positioning of this story provides a foundation for the spread of the gospel into the Greek-speaking Decapolis.

JAIRUS'S DAUGHTER AND A WOMAN HEALED (MT 9:18–26; LK 8:40–56)

²¹And Jesus passed over again in the boat to the other side, and a large crowd met him, and he was near the lake. ²²And Jairus, one of the leaders of the synagogue came to him, and when he saw Jesus he fell at his feet ²³and begged him, "My daughter is near death. Come and lay your hands on her that she may be healed and live." ²⁴And Jesus went with him, and a large crowd followed him, and they pressed him on all sides.

²⁵There was a woman who had been bleeding for twelve years, ²⁶and she had suffered many things by physicians, and she had spent all that she had, but she had not been healed but had become worse. ²⁷She heard about Jesus and came up behind him in the crowd and touched his clothing, ²⁸for she said, "If I can touch his clothing, I will be healed." ²⁹And immediately the source of her bleeding stopped, and she felt in her body that she had been healed of her illness. ³⁰Jesus immediately knew in himself that power had gone from him, and he turned to the crowd and said, "Who touched my clothing?" ³¹His disciples said to him, "Look at the crowd that is pressing you on all sides, and yet you say, 'Who touched me?'" ³²And he looked around to see who had done this. ³³But the woman was afraid and trembled because she knew what had been done to her, and she came and fell down in front of him and told him the entire truth. ³⁴He said to her, "Daughter, your faith has saved you. Depart in peace and be healed from your illness."

³⁵While he was speaking, some from the ruler of the synagogue's home came and said, "Your daughter is dead. Why trouble the teacher any longer?" ³⁶Jesus disregarded what they said and said to the ruler of the synagogue, "Do not fear, but believe only." ³⁷And he permitted no one to follow him except for Peter, Jacob, and John the brother of Jacob. ³⁸And they came into the house of the ruler of the synagogue, and he saw the mourning for the deceased, with people wailing and lamenting greatly. ³⁹And he entered and said to them, "Why do you mourn and wail? The child is not dead but is sleeping." ⁴⁰And they derided him, but he threw them out, and he took the father of the child and the mother with him and those who were with him and went in where the child was. ⁴¹And he took the hand of the child and said to

---

5:22 Jairus is a leader of a synagogue in the Galilee, but his precise duties and the location of his synagogue are unknown. The name *Jairus* is biblical in origin (Numbers 32:41). **5:25** The woman would have been considered unclean according to Leviticus 15. **5:26** Mark notes the common criticism of physicians in his day, namely, that patients were worse off for having undergone treatment. Physicians were often slaves or servants of wealthy households (Colossians 4:14). **5:27** Mark does not record what part of Jesus's clothing the woman touched, but Matthew and Luke specify that it was the fringe of his cloak (Matthew 9:20; Luke 8:44). For Mark's audience, the *tallit* may have been beyond their cultural experience to understand (compare Numbers 15:37–40; Deuteronomy 22:12). **5:30** Jesus knew that *power had gone from him*. In this story, Jesus recognizes that *dynamis*, translated as *power*, has left him. In this context, *dynamis* means something like *inherent goodness, power,* and *influence*. *Touched* represents the Greek word *fastened* or *held on to*, but in this setting she appears to have grabbed his clothing for a moment and then let go and was no longer holding on to it. **5:34** Jesus addressed the woman as *daughter*, which, even though she was probably not much younger than Jesus, was a means of showing respect and parental concern. **5:40** Jesus permits only the parents and Peter, Jacob, and John to witness the raising of the young girl. Luke's wording suggests that the disciples mocked Jesus on this occasion (Luke 8:51–53). **5:41** Mark records the Aramaic words of Jesus and then provides a direct translation of them. Similarly, he also records an Aramaic word of Jesus in Mark 7:34 and 14:36. It is unclear why on this occasion the

her, "Talitha koum," which means "Little girl, I say to you, arise." [42]And immediately the young girl arose and walked around (she was twelve years old), and they were immediately overcome with amazement. [43]And he warned them that no one should know about this, and he told them that she should be given something to eat.

REJECTION OF JESUS AT NAZARETH (MT 13:52–58; LK 4:16–30)

6 [1]And he left that place and went to his own region, and his disciples followed him. [2]When it was the Sabbath, he began to teach in the synagogue. And many who heard him were amazed and said, "Where did he get these things? And what is this wisdom given to him? And what miracles are done by his hands! [3]Is this not the carpenter, the son of Mary and brother of Jacob, Jose, Judah, and Simon? His sisters, are they not with us?" And they were offended because of him. [4]And Jesus said to them, "A prophet is not without honor except in his own hometown, and among his own relatives, and in his own house." [5]And he was not able to do any miracles there except for a few on whom he laid hands and healed them. [6]And he was amazed because of their lack of faith. And he went around the villages teaching.

SENDING OUT THE TWELVE (MT 10:5–15; LK 9:1–6)

[7]And he called twelve, and he began to send them two by two, and he gave them power over unclean spirits. [8]And he commanded them that they should take nothing on the way except a staff, but no bag, bread, or coins in their belts, [9]and to wear sandals and not put on two tunics. [10]He said to them, "Wherever you enter a house, stay there until you depart from that place. [11]And if a place will not receive you or listen to you, as you depart from that place shake the dust from the bottom of your feet as a witness against them." [12]And they went out and declared that all should repent. [13]And they cast out many demons, and they anointed with oil many who were ill, and they healed them.

---

actual words, instead of providing them in a Greek translation only, were so important.

6:1 Even though it is unstated here, Jesus's *own region* would be Nazareth (see Mark 1:9). Luke 4:16 specifically mentions Nazareth. **6:3** Jesus's siblings are also named in Matthew 13:55, although they are listed in a different order. Jose is a shortened from of *Joseph*, and some manuscripts spell out the name, while the majority spell it *Josetos*. The implication of the plural *sisters* is that Jesus had at least two sisters. Joseph's absence may indicate that he was no longer living (see Mark 3:31). Mark calls Jesus a carpenter, and Matthew calls him the son of a carpenter (Matthew 13:55). **6:4** The negative form of this saying can be confusing, but Jesus here laments that prophets are honored except among countrymen and family members. Mark's word for the miracles, *dynameis*, can be interpreted as *acts of power* (see note on Mark 5:30). John 4:44 also records this saying. **6:6–8:21** This section represents Jesus's ministry outside Galilee. **6:7** *Two by two* is an allusion to Deuteronomy 17:6 (compare Doctrine and Covenants 60:8; 62:5). This allusion to judgment is carried out in the command for the disciples to dust their feet as a *witness against them* (6:11). Acts 13:51 records an instance of this practice (compare Doctrine and Covenants 60:15). For the *twelve*, see 1 Nephi 11:29. **6:8–9** The emphasis on traveling without a *bag* or *coins* may indicate that the duration of the teaching mission was short, but it also may have served to help them focus on the power of the word, which was able to feed them literally (see Matthew 10:10). **6:11** Some later manuscripts add at the end of this verse *Truly I say to you, it will be more tolerable for Sodom and Gomorrah in the day of judgment than for that city.* Compare Doctrine and Covenants 75:20–22. **6:12** Mark's wording is abbreviated, and the subject of the verb *repent* is lacking. A more literal translation would be *And they went out and declared that they might repent.* The practice of anointing with oil (verse 13) is mentioned only here and in Luke 7:46 (where it is done as a sign of welcome) and James 5:14.

THE DEATH OF JOHN THE BAPTIST (MT 14:1–12; LK 3:19–20; 9:7–9)

[14]King Herod heard this because Jesus's name had become known. Some said, "John the Baptist was raised from the dead, and because of this the miracles are at work in him." [15]Others said, "He is Elijah," and others said, "He is a prophet, like one of the past prophets." [16]And Herod heard this and said, "John whom I beheaded has been raised."

[17]Herod himself had sent men and had John arrested and bound in prison because of Herodias, the wife of Philip his brother, because Herod had married her. [18]For John said, "It is not lawful to have your brother's wife." [19]And Herodias held a grudge against him and wanted to kill him, but she was not able to [20]because Herod feared John, knowing that he was a righteous and holy man, and he protected John. When he heard John, he was confused, but he listened to him gladly. [21]And a favorable day came that Herod made a feast for his birthday for his nobles and military officers and leading men of Galilee. [22]And his daughter Herodias came and danced and pleased Herod and his guests. And the king said to the young girl, "Ask me for whatever you want, and I will give it to you." [23]And he swore to her, "Whatever you ask, I will give it to you, even half of my kingdom." [24]And she went out and said to her mother, "What shall I ask for?" She said, "The head of John the Baptist." [25]She went immediately and with haste to the king and asked, saying, "I want you to give me the head of John the Baptist on a platter right now." [26]And the king was very sad, but because of the oaths and his dinner guests he did not want to refuse her request. [27]And immediately the king sent an executioner and ordered that his head be brought, and he beheaded John in prison, [28]and he brought the head on a platter and gave it to the young girl, and she gave it to her mother. [29]And when his disciples heard, they came and took his body and laid it in a tomb.

FEEDING THE FIVE THOUSAND (MT 14:13–21; LK 9:10–17; JN 6:1–15)

[30]And the apostles gathered to Jesus, and they told him everything they had done and taught. [31]And he said to them, "Come to a secluded place with me and rest for a little while." For many were coming and going, and they had no time to eat.

6:14 Herod Antipas (died after 39 CE) never held the title of *King*; rather, he was the tetrarch of Galilee (see note on Matthew 14:1). *Jesus's* is lacking in Greek. **6:15** On the return of Elijah, see Malachi 4:5; on the return of Jeremiah, see 2 Esdras 2:18. *Like one of the past prophets* may be an allusion to Deuteronomy 18:15, 18. **6:17** Mark noted earlier that Jesus's public ministry did not begin until John had been imprisoned (1:14), which is being retold at this point of Jesus's ministry. *Because he married her* refers to Herod Antipas's marriage to Herodias. **6:18** John's denunciation of Antipas's marriage drew on the precedent of Leviticus 18:16. **6:19** Mark draws attention to Herodias's personal grudge against John the Baptist. Matthew places more emphasis on Antipas's concern with his own image (Matthew 14:5, 9). Furthermore, Mark draws attention to the urgency of the request to kill John by noting her words, *I want you to give me right now* (6:25). **6:20** *Protected him* implies that Antipas held him captive in prison, but Mark does not use the typical verb of guarding a prisoner. **6:21** Mark notes that some of Antipas's guests were *chiliarchs*, or *military officers*. This term is used to denote someone of considerable rank in the Roman army, perhaps a military tribune or a commander of a thousand foot soldiers. **6:22** Mark notes that Herod's daughter *Herodias* came and danced. This appears to be a historical error because it was Herodias's daughter Salome that danced (compare Matthew 14:6). **6:27** *John* is lacking in Greek. **6:31** The wording indicates a deserted place or a region that was sparsely inhabited.

³²And they departed in a boat to a deserted place by themselves. ³³But many saw them leaving and recognized them, and they ran there on foot from all the towns and arrived there before them. ³⁴And as he disembarked, he saw a great crowd, and he was moved with compassion for them because they were as sheep without a shepherd, and he began to teach them many things. ³⁵And it was late already, and the disciples came to him and said, "This is a deserted place, and it is already late. ³⁶Send them away that they may go around to the fields and villages and purchase something to eat for themselves." ³⁷And he answered, "Give them something to eat." And they said to him, "Should we go and buy two hundred silver coins, or denarii, worth of bread that we may give them to eat?" ³⁸And he asked, "How much bread do you have? Go and see." And when they found out, they said, "Five loaves and two fish." ³⁹And he commanded them to sit in groups on the green grass. ⁴⁰So they sat down in groups by hundreds and fifties. ⁴¹And he took the five loaves and the two fish, and he looked toward heaven and blessed them and broke the bread and gave it to his disciples so that they might set it before the people, and the two fish he divided for all of them. ⁴²And all of them ate and were filled. ⁴³They gathered up twelve baskets full of broken bread and fish. ⁴⁴Those who ate bread were five thousand men.

JESUS WALKS ON WATER
(MT 14:22–33; JN 6:16–21)

⁴⁵And right away he made his disciples enter a boat and cross over to the other side toward Bethsaida while he dismissed the crowd. ⁴⁶And he left them and went to a mountain to pray. ⁴⁷When it was evening, the ship was in the middle of the sea, and he was alone on the land. ⁴⁸And he saw them straining at the oars in the driving wind. It was after three in the morning, and he came to them walking on the sea, and he wanted to pass by them. ⁴⁹When they saw him walking on the sea, they thought it was a ghost, and they cried out. ⁵⁰And they all saw him and were troubled, but immediately he spoke with them, "Cheer up; it is I. Do not be afraid." ⁵¹And he entered the boat, and the wind ceased. And they were completely astounded ⁵²because they did not comprehend the miracle of the loaves, but their hearts were hard.

HEALING IN GENNESARET
(MT 14:34–36; JN 6:22–25)

⁵³And they passed over and came to the land of Gennesaret and disembarked at the shore. ⁵⁴And when they got out of the boat, immediately they recognized him, ⁵⁵and they ran throughout that entire region and began to bring to him on beds those who were ill, wherever they heard he was. ⁵⁶And wherever he entered a village or a town or fields, they set before him those who were sick in the marketplaces, and

---

6:40 The organization into companies is modeled on Exodus 18:21, 25 (compare Mosiah 18:18). **6:41** The sacramental imagery is clearly implied. **6:45** Bethsaida is located on the north shore of the Sea of Galilee. See map for Matthew 11:21. **6:48** Mark notes that it was the *fourth watch*, which would indicate a time very early in the morning, between 3:00 and 6:00 a.m. This would also mean that Jesus had spent the better part of the night alone, probably in prayer. The idea of Jesus wanting to pass the disciples by may be an allusion to God *passing in front* of Moses (Exodus 33:22). **6:50** Mark and John omit any reference to Peter walking on water (Matthew 14:22–33; John 6:16–24). Jesus says literally, *I am* (compare Exodus 3:13–15). **6:52** Mark says only *they did not comprehend the bread*. **6:53** The region of Gennesaret is located on the northwestern shore of the Sea of Galilee near Tiberias. **6:56** Here the ill seek to touch the *tallit*, or *fringes*, of Jesus's clothing. Compare Mark 5:27.

they called on him that they might touch the fringe of his clothing, and as many who touched him were healed.

EATING WITH UNWASHED HANDS (MT 15:1–20; LK 6:39; 11:37–41)

7 ¹The Pharisees with some of the scribes from Jerusalem gathered to him, ²and they saw some of his disciples eating bread with unclean hands, that is, unwashed hands. ³(Because the Pharisees and all the Jews, if they do not wash their hands thoroughly, will not eat, following the tradition of the elders. ⁴And if something comes from the market, if they do not wash it they do not eat it, and many things they follow: washing of cups, pots, and bronze vessels.) ⁵And the Pharisees and scribes asked him, "Why do your disciples transgress the tradition of the elders when they eat bread with unwashed hands?" ⁶He said to them, "Well did Isaiah prophesy concerning you hypocrites, as it is written, '*This people honor me with their lips, but their heart is far from me;* ⁷*in vain they worship me, teaching as truth the traditions of men.*' ⁸You depart from the commandments of God and follow the tradition of men."

⁹And he said to them, "You disregard the commandments of God in order to establish your tradition. ¹⁰Moses said, '*Honor your father and your mother*' and '*Whoever speaks evil of his father or mother must surely die.*' ¹¹But you say if a man says to his father or mother, 'Whatever you may profit from me, it is Corban' (which is a gift given to God), ¹²then you no longer permit him to do anything for his father or mother, ¹³but you set aside the word of God for your tradition that you handed down, and you also do many similar things."

¹⁴And he called to him a crowd again and said, "Listen to me, all of you, and understand: ¹⁵There is nothing outside a man that enters into him that is able to make him unclean, but the things that exit a man, those make him unclean." ¹⁶[[If anyone has ears to hear, let that person hear.]]

¹⁷Then he entered the house away from the crowd, and his disciples asked him about the parable. ¹⁸And he said to them, "Are you also without understanding? Do you not know that nothing entering a man can make him unclean? ¹⁹Because it does not enter his heart, but into his stomach, and then it exits into the sewer?" (Thus,

---

7:4 Some manuscripts add *beds* to the list of things that must be washed to remain ritually pure, but the better and earliest manuscripts omit the word. The Greek verb *to baptize* is used for both the washing of the body and the washing of cups, etc., and is here rendered as *if they do not wash it.* Some manuscripts read *if they do not wash themselves.* See Leviticus 15:11. The Book of Mormon does not mention the kosher standards or ritual impurity (see Alma 5:57; 7:13; Ether 9:18; Moroni 10:30). Compare Psalms 69:28; 109:13; 2 Corinthians 6:17; James 1:17. **7:6–7** Quotation from Isaiah 29:13 (compare Matthew 15:7–9). **7:8** A few later manuscripts add to the end of this verse the phrase *the washing of pitchers, cups, and many other such things.* **7:10** Quotation from Exodus 20:12; 21:17; Leviticus 20:9; Deuteronomy 5:16. **7:11** The word *Corban*, also spelled *Qorban*, is a transliterated Hebrew noun from Leviticus 2:1, 4, 12, 14 and is translated by Mark to mean *a gift.* See note on Matthew 15:5. **7:15** Jesus's words are sharply critical of the idea of kosher foods, or foods that were accepted as clean or unclean. Matthew's version of the same saying is less critical of the kosher standards and likely reflects the concerns and interests of his Jewish audience (see Matthew 15:17–18). Mark goes further and adds the personal interpretation *Thus, he declared all foods clean* (verse 19), which Matthew omits. Leviticus 15 discusses what defiles the body. **7:16** The majority of manuscripts omit this verse, and it is likely not original. **7:19** The final sentence is a comment by Mark drawing attention to what he saw as the end of the designation of clean and unclean foods. The question of kosher foods was raised at the first recorded conference of the early church (see Acts 15:20–21), where they decided that limited kosher requirements

he declared all foods clean.) ²⁰And he said, "That which comes out of a man, that defiles him. ²¹But from within, the human heart issues forth wicked thoughts, immoral behaviors, theft, murder, ²²adultery, greed, wickedness, deceit, excess, envy, slander, arrogance, and reckless behavior. ²³All these evil things come from within, and they defile a person."

THE SYROPHOENECIAN WOMAN'S DAUGHTER (MT 15:21–28)

²⁴And he arose and went to the region of Tyre and Sidon, and he entered a house and did not want to be known, but he could not be hidden. ²⁵A woman soon heard about him, and her daughter had an unclean spirit, and she came and fell at his feet. ²⁶The woman was a Greek, of Syrophoenecian origin. And she asked him if he would cast out the demon from her daughter. ²⁷And he said to her, "Allow the children to be filled first, for it is not appropriate to take the children's bread and to cast it to the dogs." ²⁸She responded, "Yes, Lord, but the dogs under the table eat the children's crumbs." ²⁹Then he said

to her, "Because of this saying you may depart. The demon has left your daughter." ³⁰And she went to her house and found her daughter lying on a couch and the demon gone away.

HEALING OF A DEAF PERSON (MT 15:29–31)

³¹And again he went away from the region of Tyre and came near Sidon to the Sea of Galilee through the region of the Decapolis. ³²And they brought to him a deaf man who stuttered, and they asked him to put his hands upon the man. ³³And he took him away from the crowd by himself, and he put his fingers in his ears and after spitting, he touched his tongue. ³⁴And he looked up toward heaven and groaned and said to him, "Ephphatha," which means, "Be opened." ³⁵And immediately his ears were opened, and his tongue was released and he spoke plainly. ³⁶And Jesus commanded them that they should tell no one, but the more he commanded them, the more zealously they proclaimed it. ³⁷And they were astonished beyond measure, saying, "He has done all

---

should remain in place such as the avoidance of eating undercooked meat, or as Jacob expressed it, they should avoid *blood* (Acts 15:20). It is uncertain if unclean food is the meaning of the references in Alma 5:57 and Moroni 10:30. **7:21** *Immoral behaviors* is a translation of the Greek word *porneiai* (compare Matthew 5:32), and in this context it refers to sexual deviancy or immoral behavior. **7:22** *Reckless behavior* can also be rendered as *thoughtless behavior* or general *foolishness*. The emphasis is on the idea of acting without thinking first. **7:24** Some manuscripts lack *Sidon*. The Joseph Smith Translation says *and would that no man should come unto him. But he could not deny them, for he had compassion upon all men.* **7:26** Mark describes this woman as a Phoenician from Syria, rather than from North Africa, and as a *Greek*. He was seeking to emphasize that she was a Gentile. **7:27** Jesus offers a culturally informed rebuke of the Gentile woman and her request for Jesus to heal her daughter. Jesus uses the word *dog* in a diminutive form, perhaps *household dog* or even *little dog*, but the fact remains that he broadly describes her request as taking the food from the children and giving it to the dogs. Mark does nothing to help the reader understand the reason for such strong language. Compare 1 Samuel 17:43 for the word *dog* used disparagingly. The Joseph Smith Translation says *children of the kingdom.* **7:31** The route of travel depicted here can only be described as meandering or wandering. **7:33** Little can be said with confidence regarding the use of saliva in a healing miracle or regarding the other unusual features of this miracle. The story is unique to Mark, and Matthew and Luke chose not to add it to their accounts, but the reason they omitted it is not known. **7:34** The Aramaic word is pronounced *Effathah* with an aspirated *h* as the concluding consonant. **7:37** Allusion to Isaiah 35:5–6. The miracles described in this verse are promised to the faithful in Doctrine and Covenants 35:9.

things well; he makes the deaf hear and the mute to speak."

FEEDING OF THE FOUR THOUSAND (MT 15:32–39)

8 ¹And in those days there was a large crowd, and they had nothing to eat, and he called his disciples and said to them, ²"I have compassion for the crowd because they have already stayed with me for three days, and they have nothing to eat. ³If I send them away to their homes fasting, they will faint on the way. And some of them have come from far away." ⁴And his disciples answered him, "How can a person feed them with bread while in this deserted place?" ⁵And he questioned them, "How many loaves do you have?" And they replied, "Seven." ⁶Then he commanded the crowd to sit on the ground, and he took the seven loaves and blessed them and broke them, and gave them to his disciples so that they might serve them to the people. And they served the crowd. ⁷And they had some small fish, and he blessed them and commanded that they be served to the crowd. ⁸And they ate and were filled, and they gathered seven baskets full of broken bread and fish. ⁹And there were about four thousand people. Then he sent them away. ¹⁰And immediately he got in the boat with his disciples and came to the region of Dalmanutha.

THE SIGNS OF THE TIMES (MT 16:1–4; LK 12:54–56)

¹¹And the Pharisees came and began to question him, seeking a sign from heaven to test him. ¹²And he groaned in his spirit and said, "Why does this generation seek for a sign? Truly I say to you, no sign will be given to this generation." ¹³And he left them and got into the boat again and crossed to the other side.

THE YEAST OF THE PHARISEES (MT 16:5–12; LK 12:1)

¹⁴But they forgot to take bread, and they had only one loaf with them in the boat. ¹⁵And he admonished them, saying, "Beware and be attentive to the yeast of the Pharisees and the yeast of Herod." ¹⁶And they discussed this among themselves because they had no bread. ¹⁷And he knew it and said to them, "Why do you discuss the fact that you have no bread? Do you not know and understand? Are your hearts hardened? ¹⁸*Having eyes, do you not see, and having ears, do you not hear?* Do you not remember ¹⁹the five loaves I broke for the five thousand and how many baskets full you gathered up? And they said to him, "Twelve." ²⁰"Or the seven loaves for the four thousand, how many baskets full did you gather up?" And they replied, "Seven." ²¹Then he said to them, "Do you not understand yet?"

8:10 The location of Dalmanutha is unknown, and in the parallel passage in Matthew the location is referred to as *Magadan*, a similarly unknown location (Matthew 15:39). Some copyists of the Gospel of Matthew thought that *Magadan* was *Magdala* on the northwestern side of the Sea of Galilee and thus the town of Mary Magdalene. **8:15** Only Mark records the warning about the *yeast of Herod* (compare Matthew 16:6). This would likely be a reference to the actions and deeds of Herod Antipas, but it could be a general warning regarding the entire Herodian family (see note on Matthew 22:16). **8:18** Quotation from Jeremiah 5:21. **8:21** None of the Gospel authors insinuates that there was something to be understood in the numbers of the baskets of bread. Instead, the message appears to be one of abundance and meeting the needs of his followers sufficiently. The context in Mark further suggests that Jesus asked this question because the disciples had been wondering about not having brought sufficient bread with them, and Jesus's answer implies that he would provide for them as he had in the past.

A BLIND MAN HEALED AT BETHSAIDA

²²And they went to Bethsaida, and they brought to him a blind person, and they asked Jesus to touch him. ²³And he took the blind person by the hand, and he took him outside the village and spit on his eyes; then he put his hands on him and asked him, "Do you see anything?" ²⁴He looked around and said, "I see men, as trees, walking around." ²⁵Then he again put his hands on his eyes. And he looked with care, and he was restored to health, and he saw all things clearly. ²⁶And he sent him to his house, saying, "Do not go into the village."

PETER'S DECLARATION AT CAESAREA PHILIPPI (MT 16:13–20; LK 9:18–22; JN 6:67–71)

²⁷Jesus and his disciples went to the villages of Caesarea Philippi, and on the way he asked his disciples, "Who do people say that I am?" ²⁸They said, "Some say John the Baptist, and others Elijah, and others one of the prophets." ²⁹And he asked them, "Who do you say that I am?" Peter answered him, "You are the Christ." ³⁰And he warned them that they should not tell anyone about him.

JESUS FORETELLS HIS DEATH AND RESURRECTION (MT 16:21–23; LK 9:22)

³¹And he began to teach them that the Son of Man should suffer many things and be rejected by the elders, chief priests, and scribes and be killed and after three days rise again. ³²And he was speaking openly. But Peter took him and began to rebuke him. ³³He turned and looked at his disciples and rebuked Peter, saying, "Get behind me, Satan, because you do not think about the things of God but rather the things of man."

TAKING UP A CROSS (MT 16:24–28; LK 9:23–27)

³⁴And he called a crowd to him with his disciples and said to them, "If anyone desires to follow after me, let that person deny himself and take up a cross and follow me. ³⁵Whoever wants to save his life will lose it, and whoever loses his life on account of me and the gospel will save it. ³⁶What will it profit a person to gain the

---

8:22 *Bethsaida* is located on the northeastern shore of the Sea of Galilee. Jesus may have fed the four thousand there (Mark 6:32; Luke 9:10), and some of Jesus's disciples came from Bethsaida (John 1:44; 12:21). **8:23** A similar miracle is recorded in John 9:6. **8:23–26** This is the only double healing told in the Gospels, and the other Gospels omit the story entirely. It stands in stark contrast to the other miracles because Jesus seemingly heals the man twice, the first time using saliva and the second time through laying his hands on the man. **8:27–10:52** This section of Mark focuses on the coming suffering of Jesus. **8:27** Caesarea Philippi was the capital of Philip's government (see note on Matthew 16:13). The city was located at the base of Mount Hermon, which is the likely site of the Mount of Transfiguration (Mark 9:2). The city had a mixed population of Jews, Greeks, and Romans and was lavishly populated with temples to Roman and Greek deities. **8:28** On the return of *Elijah*, see Malachi 4:5. Mark does not specify which prophet, but 2 Esdras 2:18, an apocryphal text, promises the return of Jeremiah. **8:29** Peter declares Jesus to be the *Messiah*, here translated into the Greek word for Messiah, *Christ*. Matthew adds *the Son of the living God* (Matthew 16:16). **8:30** Mark does not mention the promise of the keys of the kingdom (Matthew 16:19; Doctrine and Covenants 90:2). **8:33** Jesus's rebuke of Peter is fundamentally different in Matthew. Here Peter is rebuked for worrying about mundane considerations rather than Jesus's coming trial. In Matthew, Jesus alludes to the fact that Peter is attempting to cause Jesus to stumble (Matthew 16:23), hinting that Peter's questioning had tempted Jesus to choose another way. Jesus's discourse on saving and losing life offers perspective on the necessity of Jesus's impending death (Mark 8:34–37).

whole world but lose his life? ³⁷Or what will a person give in exchange for his life? ³⁸Whoever is ashamed of me and my words in this adulterous and sinful generation, the Son of Man will be ashamed of that person when he comes in the glory of his Father with his holy angels."

9 ¹He said to them, "Truly I say to you that there are some here who will not taste death until they see the kingdom of God come in power."

THE MOUNT OF TRANSFIGURATION (MT 17:1–8; LK 9:28–36)

²After six days, Jesus took Peter, Jacob, and John and brought them to a high mountain by themselves, and they were alone. And he was transfigured before them. ³And his clothing became shining white, such a white as no one on earth could make it. ⁴And Elijah with Moses appeared to them, and they were speak-

ing with Jesus. ⁵Then Peter said to Jesus, "Rabbi, it is good for us to be here. Let us make three booths, one for you, one for Moses, and one for Elijah." ⁶(For he did not know what he might say, because they were greatly afraid.) ⁷Then a cloud overshadowed them, and there was a voice from the cloud: "This is my beloved Son; hear him!" ⁸Suddenly they looked around, but they did not see anyone anymore, but only Jesus with them.

THE COMING OF ELIJAH (MT 17:9–13)

⁹As they descended from the mountain, Jesus commanded them not to tell anyone what they had seen until the Son of Man arose from the dead. ¹⁰And they kept this to themselves, wondering what the rising from the dead meant. ¹¹And they questioned him, "Why do the scribes say that Elijah must come first?" ¹²He answered

---

8:37 The Joseph Smith Translation adds *Therefore deny yourselves of these, and be not ashamed of me.*
8:38 *Ashamed* translates a Greek word that can also mean *disgraced* but not necessarily *embarrassed*. A possible allusion to Daniel 7:13–14. The Joseph Smith Translation adds this sentence at the end of the verse: *And they shall not have part in that resurrection when he cometh. For verily I say unto you, that he shall come; and he that layeth down his life for my sake and the gospel's, shall come with him, and shall be clothed with his glory, in the cloud, on the right hand of the Son of man.*

9:1 This verse belongs to the end of the preceding chapter. It was part of the discourse at Caesarea Philippi (compare Matthew 16:28; Luke 9:27), and the verse is included in this chapter by mistake. **9:2–3** Mark notes both a physical change to Jesus and to his clothing (see Matthew 17:2). Luke notes that the disciples were praying when Jesus was transfigured (Luke 9:29), and some copyists added this phrase to Mark's account. Compare Exodus 24:12. **9:4** The Joseph Smith Translation of Mark 9:4 adds John the Baptist to the appearance by Elijah and Moses (compare Doctrine and Covenants 138:45). For the deaths of Moses and Elijah, see Deuteronomy 34:4–6; 2 Kings 2:9–12. **9:5** Peter uses the respectful term *rabbi* to address Jesus, a word that means simply *my master* or even *my teacher* (see John 20:16). Peter's offer to build three *booths* or tabernacles has led to the conclusion that this experience took place near the time of the Feast of Sukkot or the Feast of Tabernacles. The feast took place between late September and early October and celebrated the annual harvest (Exodus 34:22) and the exodus of the people of Israel when they traveled in tents to the promised land (Leviticus 23:42–43). **9:9** The previous commands to not make Jesus known publicly are to end soon. **9:11–12** The disciples' question asked simply about the return of Elijah as promised in Malachi 4:5–6, a teaching that the scribes had promoted. Jesus's response expanded the context of the question by adding that Elijah *must come first and restore all things*, a teaching that is not preserved in Malachi (compare Matthew 17:11). The word *restore* can also mean to *establish to its former state*, and in this context Jesus seems to allude to the future establishment of the children of Israel to their former glory and grandeur (see also Sirach 48:10). The restoration of all things will also include the coming of a despised or rejected Son of Man, an allusion to Isaiah 53:3.

them, "Elijah must come first and restore all things. And why is it written that the Son of Man should suffer many things and be despised? ¹³But I say to you that Elijah has come, and they did to him as they wanted, even as it is written about him."

A BOY IS HEALED (MT 17:14–21; LK 9:37–43A)

¹⁴When they came to the disciples, they saw a large crowd with some scribes questioning them. ¹⁵And right away, after the entire crowd saw him, they were amazed, and they ran toward him and greeted him. ¹⁶And he asked them, "What are you discussing with them?" ¹⁷One from the crowd answered him, "Teacher, I have brought to you my son, who has a spirit that makes him unable to speak. ¹⁸Whenever it seizes him, it tears him, and he foams at the mouth and grinds his teeth, and he is wasting away. I asked your disciples to cast it out, but they were not able to do it." ¹⁹And he replied, "Oh, faithless generation, how long will I be with you? How long will I endure you? Bring him to me." ²⁰And he brought him to Jesus, and when the spirit saw him it immediately shook him, and he fell to the ground foaming at the mouth and rolling around. ²¹And he asked the boy's father, "How long has it been like this for him?" And he said, "From childhood. ²²Many times it throws him into fire or water that it might kill him. But if you are able, help us and have compassion on us." ²³And Jesus said to him, "If you are

able? All things are possible for the one who believes." ²⁴Right away the father of the child cried out, "I believe. Help my unbelief." ²⁵When Jesus saw that a crowd came running together, he rebuked the unclean spirit, "Mute and deaf spirit, I command you—come out of him and never return to him." ²⁶After crying out and convulsing, it went out, and the boy was like a corpse so that many said, "He is dead." ²⁷But Jesus took his hand and lifted him up, and he stood. ²⁸When he entered the house his disciples asked him privately, "Why were we not able to cast it out?" ²⁹And he said to them, "This kind cannot be cast out except in prayer and fasting."

JESUS FORETELLS HIS PASSION AGAIN (MT 17:22–23; LK 9:43B–45)

³⁰He departed from that place and passed through Galilee because he did not want anyone to know. ³¹He taught his disciples and said to them, "The Son of Man will be betrayed into the hands of men, and they will kill him, and he will rise again after three days." ³²But they did not understand his words, and they were afraid to question him.

ON GREATNESS (MT 18:1–5; LK 9:46–48)

³³And he came to Capernaum, and he was in the house, asking them, "What were you discussing on the way?" ³⁴But they were silent because on the way they discussed

---

9:13 Older translations used an English transliteration to render the Hebrew proper name *Elijah*. Owing to differences of pronunciation, Greek speakers pronounced the name *Elijah* as *Elias*. In all cases in the New Testament, the name *Elijah* stands behind the transliteration *Elias*. The Joseph Smith Translation engages this idea of an Elijah who would restore all things and the coming of Elijah promised in Malachi 4:5–6. It appears that the Joseph Smith Translation seeks to expand the two comings of Elijah depicted in this chapter in verses 12–13: the one who will come and restore all things (referred to as Elijah) and the one who has come (referred to as Elias). See Doctrine and Covenants 138:45–46. **9:14–29** Mark's account of this story is much more detailed than Matthew's (17:14–21). **9:20** The Greek lacks the word *Jesus*. **9:24** The father's declaration is that he both has faith and lacks faith simultaneously. **9:29** Some early manuscripts lack *and fasting*, but the evidence for its inclusion is equally good.

with one another who is greater. ³⁵And he sat down and called the twelve and said to them, "If anyone wants to be first, let that person be last and a servant of all." ³⁶And he took a child and sat him in their midst, and he embraced him and said to them, ³⁷"Whoever among you receives this little child in my name receives me, and whoever receives me does not receive me but receives him who sent me."

THE OTHER HEALER (LK 9:49–50)

³⁸John said to him, "Teacher, we saw a certain individual cast out demons in your name, but we forbade him because he did not follow us." ³⁹Jesus said, "Do not forbid him, for no one who does a miracle in my name will soon thereafter be able to speak evil about me. ⁴⁰For he who is not against us is for us. ⁴¹For whoever gives a drink of water in my name, because you are Christ's, truly I say to you, he will not lose his reward.

CAUSING OTHERS TO STUMBLE (MT 18:6–9)

⁴²"And whoever causes one of the little ones who believe in me to stumble, it is better for him if a millstone were hung around his neck and he were thrown into the sea. ⁴³And if your hand causes you to stumble, cut if off, for it is better for you to go through life maimed than having two hands to go to hell to the unquenchable fire. ⁴⁵And if your foot causes you to stumble, cut it off, for it is better to go through life maimed than having two feet to be cast into hell. ⁴⁷And if your eye causes you to stumble, pluck it out, for it is better for you to enter the kingdom of God with one eye than having two eyes to be cast into hell, ⁴⁸*where their worm does not die and the fire is not quenched.* ⁴⁹Everyone will be salted with fire. ⁵⁰Salt is good, but if the salt has become flavorless, in what way will you season it? Have salt in yourselves, and be at peace with one another."

INSTRUCTIONS ABOUT DIVORCE (MT 19:1–12)

10 ¹And he arose and departed from that place to the region of Judea to the other side of the Jordan River, and again a crowd gathered to him, and as he had been accustomed to do, he taught them. ²And some Pharisees came to him and asked in order to tempt him, "Is it

---

9:36–37 Modern conceptions of being like a child are different from ancient ones. Children were powerless, without a voice in social settings, meek and lowly, and they were viewed as simple. **9:38** This unnamed healer is not mentioned elsewhere in the Gospels and was perhaps one of the seventy disciples who were sent out (Luke 10:1–7). **9:40** Compare Numbers 11:29. The Joseph Smith Translation interprets this as standing on our own and not on our brother's words. **9:42** A millstone used in grinding wheat could easily weigh over one hundred pounds. Compare Doctrine and Covenants 121:22. **9:43** Greek *Gehenna* for *hell.* **9:43–46** These verses are alluded to in Doctrine and Covenants 76:44. **9:44, 46** These verses are omitted in the best manuscripts and are unlikely to be original to the Gospel of Mark. They are identical to verse 48, *Where the worm does not die, and the fire is not quenched.* **9:47** See note on 9:43. **9:48** Quotation from Isaiah 66:24. This saying outside the context of Isaiah 66 makes little sense, but in the context of Isaiah it speaks of the apocalyptic destruction that will come on all nations. **9:49** This verse exists in several different versions, and some manuscripts add *and every sacrifice will be salted with salt.* The translation provided here has the best textual support. The saying is an allusion to Leviticus 2:13, Ezekiel 43:24, and the idea that people now replace the animal sacrifices required in the law of Moses and that as such they would necessarily need to be salted like the animal sacrifices. There may be an allusion to Isaiah 66:20.

10:1 The regions described in these verses were sparsely populated. **10:2** The question about divorce is centered on the interpretation of Deuteronomy 24:1. The Pharisees had assumed that Jesus would

lawful for a man to divorce his wife?" ³He answered them, "What did Moses command you?" ⁴They said, "Moses permitted a certificate of divorce and to dismiss her." ⁵But Jesus said to them, "Because of the hardness of your hearts, he wrote to you this commandment. ⁶But from the beginning of creation, '*God made them male and female*; ⁷*and on this account a man shall leave his father and mother and be joined to his wife.* ⁸*And the two will be one flesh.*' They are no longer two but one flesh. ⁹What God has therefore joined together, let no one divide."

¹⁰In the house, his disciples questioned him again about this. ¹¹He said to them, "Whoever divorces his wife and marries another, he commits adultery against her. ¹²And if a woman divorces her husband and marries another, then she commits adultery."

JESUS BLESSES LITTLE CHILDREN
(MT 19:13–15; LK 18:15–17)

¹³People brought to him young children so that he would touch them, but the disciples rebuked them. ¹⁴When Jesus saw it, he was displeased and said to them, "Let the children come to me and do not forbid them, for the kingdom of God belongs to such. ¹⁵Truly I say to you, whoever does not receive the kingdom of God as a child will not enter it." ¹⁶And he embraced them in his arms, and having put his hands upon them, he blessed them.

THE RICH YOUNG MAN
(MT 19:16–30; LK 18:18–30)

¹⁷And while he was leaving on his way, a man ran up and knelt in front of him and asked, "Good teacher, what must I do to inherit eternal life?" ¹⁸Jesus said to him, "Why do you call me good? No one is good but God only. ¹⁹You know the commandments, '*Do not murder; do not commit adultery; do not steal; do not bear false witness; do not defraud; honor your father and mother.*'" ²⁰And he said to him, "Teacher, I have observed all these things from my youth." ²¹Jesus looked at him and loved him and said, "You lack one thing: go and sell what you have and give to the

---

contradict popular interpretations about permissible divorce. The region near the Jordan River was perhaps the same area where John the Baptist taught, and the Pharisees may have been attempting to entrap Jesus into condemning Antipas's marriages. Paul teaches similarly about divorce (1 Corinthians 7:10–11). **10:4** Reference to Deuteronomy 24:1, 3. **10:6–8** Quotations from Genesis 1:27; 2:24; 5:2 (compare Doctrine and Covenants 49:16). Some manuscripts lack the subject *God* and simply report *he*. **10:7** Some manuscripts omit *and be joined to his wife*, but there is also good textual support for the phrase. **10:12** A woman could not divorce her husband according to Jewish law, but she could according to Roman law. Mark may have included this part of the saying because of his Gentile audience. **10:13** Mark uses an unspecified *they*. Grammatically, the disciples would be the ones who brought the children to Jesus, but since the disciples are the ones who rebuked those who brought the children, it must refer to someone else, which is reflected in the translation through the generic *people*. **10:16** The laying on of hands recalls a blessing of healing (see Mark 6:5; 8:23). **10:18** Jesus's answer, that God alone is good, has provided fodder for controversy through the ages. Trinitarians, those who believe in a triune deity, find this verse particularly thorny because Jesus appears to distance his own goodness and identity from God's. Therefore, some have concluded that Jesus has declared that he is not God in this verse. Jesus's response quotes from the *Shema*, the central prayer that Jews recite in the morning and evening contained in Deuteronomy 6:5. Jesus's response, therefore, calls attention to the questioner's relationship to God and defines that relationship as one built on the commandments and through prayer. Jesus nowhere denies his own, personal goodness, but in this instance he taught the uniqueness of God the Father. **10:19** Quotation from Exodus 20:12–16 and Deuteronomy 5:16–20 (*do not defraud*). **10:21** Mark alone adds that Jesus *loved him*. Compare Luke 3:11; Mosiah 4:24–26.

poor, and then you will have treasure in heaven, and come and follow me." ²²But he was sad upon hearing that teaching, and he went away sorrowful, for he had many possessions.

²³And Jesus looked around and said to his disciples, "How difficult it will be for those who have riches to enter the kingdom of God!" ²⁴The disciples were alarmed at his words, and Jesus said again, "Children, how hard it is to enter the kingdom of God! ²⁵It is easier for a camel to pass through a needle's eye than for a rich man to enter the kingdom of God." ²⁶And they were astonished beyond comparison and said to themselves, "Then who can be saved?" ²⁷Jesus looked at them and said, "For humankind it is impossible, but not for God: all things are possible for God." ²⁸Peter began to say, "We have left everything and have followed you!" ²⁹Jesus said to him, "Truly I say to you, there is no one who has left a house, or brothers, or sisters, or mother, or father, or children, or fields for my sake or for the gospel ³⁰who will not receive, with persecution, a hundredfold now in this age houses, brothers, sisters, mothers, children, fields, and in the age to come eternal life. ³¹Many who are first will be last, and many who are last will be first."

JESUS FORETELLS HIS DEATH A THIRD TIME (MT 20:17–19; LK 18:31–34)

³²And they were on the way going up to Jerusalem, and Jesus went ahead of them, and they were amazed, and those who followed were afraid. And he took the twelve again and began to tell them the things that were about to happen to him. ³³"Behold, we will go up to Jerusalem, and the Son of Man will be delivered to the chief priests and scribes, and they will condemn him to death, and they will deliver him to the Gentiles, ³⁴and they will mock him and spit on him and scourge him and kill him, and after three days he will rise again."

THE REQUEST OF JACOB AND JOHN (MT 20:20–28; LK 22:24–27)

³⁵And Jacob and John, the sons of Zebedee, approached him and said, "Teacher, we desire that whatever we ask you that you will do it for us." ³⁶He asked them,

---

10:22–23 Jesus's teachings following the man's departure draw attention to the difficulty for the rich to sell everything, but those words do not imply that the man rejected the counsel he received. Compare Mosiah 4:23; Doctrine and Covenants 56:16. **10:24** That the disciples were alarmed suggests either that some were wealthy or that they affiliated with some who were wealthy. Some manuscripts read *how hard it is for those who trust in riches*, thus softening and limiting Jesus's otherwise strong statement to the rich only. **10:25** See note on Matthew 19:24. Jesus's reference to the eye of a sewing needle and a camel passing through it caught the disciples by surprise (verse 26). **10:26** The disciples' question, *who can be saved*, implies that the definition of who was rich included many or even all of them. The question could also imply that they were concerned that the poor would enter before them, and they would somehow be precluded from entering. **10:27** The Joseph Smith Translation adds *With men that trust in riches, it is impossible, but not impossible with men who trust in God, and leave all things for my sake.* **10:28** Peter's question relies on a basic clarification of whether *leaving* everything is the same as *selling* everything. **10:30** An allusion to Genesis 26:12. *In this time* can also be rendered as *in the right time* or *in due time*. **10:33–34** Luke places more emphasis on Gentile involvement in the condemnation and death of Jesus, whereas Matthew and Mark carefully note that Jesus would be condemned to death by the chief priests and scribes (Matthew 20:18–19). **10:35** The name *James* does not appear in the New Testament, and all persons who bear that name in modern translations were formally named Jacob in their lifetimes. The origin of the shift from *Jacob* to *James* appears to be the Latin translation of the New Testament, which changed the name *Jacob* in Greek to *Jacobus* in Latin. Owing to verbal shifts in the language,

"What do you desire that I might do for you?" ³⁷They said to him, "Allow us that we may sit one on your right and one on your left in your glory." ³⁸Jesus said to them, "You do not know what you ask for. Are you able to drink the cup that I drink, or to be baptized with the baptism with which I am baptized?" ³⁹They said to him, "We are able." But Jesus said to them, "The cup that I drink you will also drink, and the baptism that I am baptized with you will also experience, ⁴⁰but to sit on my right or on my left is not mine to give, but it is for those for whom it has been prepared."

⁴¹The ten heard this and began to be displeased with Jacob and John. ⁴²Jesus called them and said to them, "You know that those who seem to rule the Gentiles have power over them, and their great ones have authority over them. ⁴³But it is not so among you. Whoever desires to be great among you will be your servant, ⁴⁴and whoever desires to be first among you will be a slave to all, ⁴⁵for the Son of Man did not come to be served but to serve, and to give his life as a sacrifice for many."

THE HEALING OF BARTIMAEUS (MT 20:29–34; LK 18:35–43)

⁴⁶And they came to Jericho, and as he departed from Jericho with his disciples and a substantial crowd, Bartimaeus the blind, the son of Timaeus, was sitting by the road begging. ⁴⁷And he heard that Jesus of Nazareth was there, and he began to cry out, "Jesus, Son of David, have mercy on me!" ⁴⁸And many ordered him to be silent, but he cried out more, "Son of David, have mercy on me!" ⁴⁹And Jesus stood and said, "Call him." And they called the blind man, saying to him, "Cheer up, come; he calls you." ⁵⁰And he threw off his cloak and arose and came to Jesus. ⁵¹And Jesus asked him, "What do you desire that I would do?" The blind man said to him, "Rabbouni, that I may see." ⁵²Jesus said to him, "Go, your faith has healed you." And immediately he saw again, and he followed him along the way.

THE TRIUMPHAL ENTRY (MT 21:1–11; LK 19:28–40; JN 12:12–19)

11 ¹He drew near Jerusalem to Bethphage and Bethany at the Mount of Olives, and he sent two of his disciples

---

Jacobus was later rendered as *Jacomus* and then through French in a shortened form to *James*. Jesus's teaching on being first contains the injunction that the disciple should be the *servant*, or *deacon*, of all. **10:38** The cup foreshadows the cup of Gethsemane (Mark 14:36). See also Psalm 11:6; Isaiah 51:22. **10:43** The greatest Christian will be the *servant*, or *deacon*, of all. **10:45** The idea that Christ gave his life as a *sacrifice for many* or a *ransom for many* is developed by Paul in Romans 3:23–25. **10:46** *Bartimaeus* means the *son of Timai* in Aramaic. **10:47–48** For *Son of David*, see Psalm 89:3–4; compare Alma 36:18. **10:51** *Rabbouni* was a more respectful term than *rabbi*. The same form is used in John 20:16. **10:52** Echoed in Enos 1:8; Alma 18:14.

11:1 Bethphage was located on the road between Jericho and Jerusalem, but the precise location remains unknown. **11:1–13:37** This section records Jesus's ministry in Jerusalem.

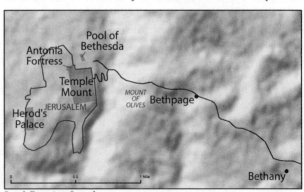

Jesus's Entry into Jerusalem
Map by Cassie Howe and Ryan Shields, ThinkSpatial, BYU Geography

²and told them, "Go to the village in front of you, and immediately upon entering you will find a colt tied up, on which no one has sat; untie it and bring it. ³And if anyone says to you, 'What are you doing?' say, 'The Lord has need of it, and he will send it back here immediately.'" ⁴And they went and found a colt tied near the door, outside near the road, and they untied it. ⁵And certain people standing there said to them, "What are you doing, untying the colt?" ⁶They told them exactly what Jesus said, and they allowed them to go. ⁷And they brought the colt to Jesus and placed their clothes on it, and he sat on it. ⁸And many put their clothes along the road, while others cut down branches from the fields and placed them along the way. ⁹And they went before him and after him and cried out, "*Hosanna! Blessed is the one who comes in the name of the Lord.* ¹⁰Blessed is the coming kingdom of our father David; Hosanna in the highest." ¹¹And he entered Jerusalem and came to the temple, and after he looked around at everything, he saw it was already evening, and he returned to Bethany with the twelve.

CURSING A FIG TREE
(MT 21:18–19)

¹²The next day they came from Bethany, and he was hungry. ¹³And he saw a fig tree from afar with leaves, and he went to see if perhaps he would find some fruit on it, but he came and found nothing except leaves because it was not the time for figs, ¹⁴and Jesus said to it, "Let no one ever eat fruit from you again." And his disciples heard it.

CLEANSING THE TEMPLE
(MT 21:12–17; LK 19:28–40; JN 2:14–22)

¹⁵And they came to Jerusalem, and he entered the temple and began to cast out the sellers and merchants in the temple, and he overturned the tables of the money changers and the seats of those who sold doves. ¹⁶And he did not permit anyone to carry anything through the temple. ¹⁷And he taught them, "Is it not written that '*My house will be called a house of prayer for all nations*?' But you have made it *a den of bandits*?" ¹⁸When the chief priests and the scribes heard this, they sought how they could destroy him, but they feared him because all the crowd was deeply impressed by his teaching. ¹⁹And when it was evening, he went out of the city.

MEANING OF THE FIG TREE
(MT 21:20–22)

²⁰When they passed by early in the morning, they saw the fig tree withered at the roots, ²¹and Peter remembered and said to him, "Rabbi, behold, the fig tree you cursed has withered." ²²Jesus answered them, "Have faith in God. ²³Truly I say to you that whoever says to this mountain, 'Be taken up and cast into the sea,' and does not doubt in his heart but believes what he speaks will come to pass, it will happen. ²⁴Therefore, I say this to you, everything that you ask for in prayer,

---

11:2 Compare Zechariah 9:9. **11:9** Quotation from Psalm 118:25. *Hosanna* means *Save now!* **11:10** This part of the crowd's acclamation of belief is spontaneous and not a quotation of scripture. **11:13** Passover was too early to harvest ripe figs, which would not be ripe until early summer. In Matthew 21:19, the fig tree withers at once, but in Mark the fig tree withers the next day (see also verse 20). **11:15** Mark places the day of the cleansing of the temple one day later than Matthew (21:12–13) and Luke (19:45–46) do. **11:17** Quotation from Isaiah 56:7 and Jeremiah 7:11. Mark's version includes Isaiah's phrase *for all nations*, which expands the context to include Gentiles (compare Matthew 21:13; Luke 19:46). **11:20–25** These verses provide the context for understanding the cursing of the fig tree (11:12–14).

believing that you will receive, it will be yours. ²⁵Whenever you pray standing, forgive so that if you have anything against anyone, your Father who is in the heavens may forgive you of your misdeeds. [[²⁶But if you do not forgive, then your Father in heaven will not forgive your misdeeds.]]"

THE QUESTION ABOUT AUTHORITY (MT 21:23–27; LK 20:1–8)

²⁷And they came again to Jerusalem, and while he was walking around in the temple the chief priests and scribes and elders came to him, ²⁸and they said to him, "By what authority do you do these things, and who gave you this authority to do them?" ²⁹Jesus said to them, "I will ask you one question, and if you answer me, I will tell you by what authority I do these things. ³⁰The baptism of John, was it from heaven or from man? Answer me." ³¹So they discussed it among themselves, saying, "If we say, 'From heaven,' he will say, 'Then why did you not believe him?' ³²But if we say, 'From man'"—they were afraid of the crowd because they all believed that John was a prophet. ³³And they answered Jesus, "We do not know." And Jesus said to them, "Neither do I tell you by what authority I do these things."

THE PARABLE OF THE WICKED TENANTS (MT 21:33–46; LK 20:9–19)

12 ¹And he began to speak to them in parables, saying, "A man planted a vineyard, and he built a fence around it, and dug a winepress, and constructed a tower, and rented it to farmers, and then he went away. ²And he sent a servant to the farmers at harvest time to get some of the fruit of the vineyard. ³But they seized him and beat him and sent him back empty-handed. ⁴And he sent another servant to them, and they injured his head and treated him shamefully. ⁵And he sent another servant, and they killed him. And he sent many others, some of whom they beat and others they killed. ⁶Having one son who was beloved, he sent him to them last, saying, 'They will reverence my son.' ⁷But those farmers said to one another, 'This is the heir; come, let us kill him, and we will receive the inheritance.' ⁸And they seized him and killed him and threw him out of the vineyard. ⁹What will the lord of the vineyard do? He will come and destroy the farmers, and give the vineyard to others. ¹⁰Have you not read this scripture: 'The stone that the builders rejected, this has become the head cornerstone; ¹¹this was the

---

11:25 Mark does not use the typical word for *sins* and instead uses a word that implies not moral sin but *failure, lies, deviations*, and *misdeeds*. Mosiah 26:31 expands the directive to forgive to include neighbors (compare Matthew 6:15). **11:26** This verse is missing from the best manuscripts and is likely not original to Mark. It was probably added through harmonization to Matthew 6:15. **11:27–28** The scribes and chief priests ask Jesus about the source of his *authority*, but they more frequently ask about the legality of Jesus's actions in accordance with their understanding of the law of Moses (Mark 2:24; 10:2; 12:14). **11:28** The word translated as *authority* also means *power, ability, permission*, or *freedom to choose to do something*. **11:31** Matthew 3:7 indicates that Pharisees and Sadducees went to see John baptize, but here some leading Jews claim they had rejected John. The Gospel of John treats a similar question of whether any Pharisees had believed, although in John it is a question of belief in Jesus (John 7:48). Acts 15:5 indicates that some Pharisees did accept Jesus. The evidence for acceptance and rejection of John and Jesus by their contemporaries is mixed, and both drew large crowds as well as a vocal opposition, but none of the Gospels portray the opposition to them as unanimous. **11:31–32** Their debate is whether John was *from heaven* or *from man*. Their debate mirrors the question concerning Jesus's authority and whether it was from heaven or man.

12:1 The parable is built on the imagery and teachings of Isaiah 5:1–7. **12:9** This saying is spoken by Jesus's enemies in Matthew 21:40–41. **12:10** Quotation from Psalm 118:22. Jacob 4:15 also comments

Lord's doing, and it is amazing in our eyes'?" ¹²And they sought to arrest him, but they feared the crowd because they knew that he told the parable about them, and they left and went away.

A QUESTION ABOUT TAXES
(MT 22:15–22; LK 20:20–26)

¹³And they sent to him some of the Pharisees and Herodians so that they would catch him in his talk. ¹⁴And they came and said to him, "Teacher, we know that you are truthful and that you do not pander to anyone, nor do you show partiality, but you teach the way of God in truth. Is it lawful to pay to Caesar the poll tax or not? Do we give or not give?" ¹⁵And when he knew their hypocrisy, he said to them, "Why do you test me? Bring me a coin that I may see it." ¹⁶And they brought one. And he said to them, "Whose image and inscription is this?" And they answered, "Caesar's." ¹⁷Jesus said to them, "Give to Caesar the things of Caesar and to God the things of God." And they were astonished at him.

A QUESTION ABOUT THE RESURRECTION
(MT 22:23–33; LK 20:27–40)

¹⁸Then came to him the Sadducees, who say there is no resurrection, and they asked him, ¹⁹"Teacher, Moses wrote to us that *'If a brother dies, and leaves a wife and has no child, that the brother shall marry the widow and raise children to his brother.'* ²⁰There were seven brothers, and the first married a wife, and he died without having children, ²¹and the second married her, and died without having children, and the third did the same, ²²and the seventh also did not have children. Last of all the woman died. ²³In the resurrection, whose wife will she be, because the seven each married her?" ²⁴Jesus said to them, "Is this not why you are mistaken, because you do not understand the scriptures nor the power of God? ²⁵When the dead arise, they neither marry nor are given in marriage, but they are as the angels in heaven. ²⁶But concerning the dead that rise again, do you not understand in the book of Moses, when at the bush, how God spoke to him, *'I am the God of Abraham and the God of Isaac and the God of Jacob'*? ²⁷He is not a God of dead men but a God of the living, and you are very wrong!"

---

on the rejected stone. The words *cornerstone* and *capstone* are indistinguishable in Greek. **12:13** Only Mark mentions the *Herodians* as being present on this occasion. For the Herodians, see note on Matthew 22:16. **12:14** The poll tax was not an optional or voluntary tax but a census-based tax that all adult males were required to pay. Tiberius was the Roman emperor (died 37 CE), and the coin likely bore his image. Their attempt to entrap Jesus is based on populist anger at Roman taxation policies and rejection of Roman authority to tax. **12:18** Mark here comments on the beliefs of the Sadducees, who were a priestly group that collaborated with the Romans and provided the chief priests for temple services. Caiaphas was likely a Sadducee, as was his father-in-law, Annas. They rejected the oral interpretation of the Torah that the Pharisees had developed and denied that there was a resurrection, although such a belief contradicts Isaiah 26:19. **12:19** Quotation from Deuteronomy 25:5. The practice of levirate marriages, in which a living brother was required to marry his deceased brother's widow in the event that the brother died without children, is used as a theoretical criticism of resurrection. The Sadducees seem to suppose that there was no reasonable answer to their riddle, and therefore the idea of a resurrection was equally absurd to them. **12:24** Jesus asked them if they understood *what is written*, which in this instance has been translated as *the scriptures*. **12:26** Quotation from Exodus 3:6. **12:27** Only Mark preserves the direct rebuke at the end of the verse.

THE GREATEST COMMANDMENT (MT 22:34–40; LK 10:25–28)

28Then one of the scribes came to him when he heard them disputing, and he saw that he answered them well, and he asked Jesus, "What commandment is the most important?" 29Jesus answered, "The first is *'Hear, Israel; the Lord our God is one,'* 30and *'You shall love the Lord your God with all your heart and all your soul and with all your mind and with all your might.'* 31The second is *'You shall love your neighbor as yourself.'* There is no other commandment greater than these." 32The scribe said to him, "Teacher, you speak the truth that *he is one* and *there is no one other than him.* 33And *to love him with all the heart and with all the mind and with all the strength,* and *to love one's neighbor as oneself,* this is much more than all burnt offerings and sacrifices." 34 When Jesus saw that he answered wisely, he said to him, "You are not far from the kingdom of God." And no one dared to question him further.

THE QUESTION ABOUT DAVID'S SON (MT 22:41–46; LK 20:41–44)

35Then Jesus taught in the temple and said, "How do the scribes say that the Christ is the son of David? 36For David himself said in the Holy Spirit, *'The Lord said to my Lord, sit on my right until I place your enemies under your feet.'* 37If David himself called him 'Lord,' how then is he his son?" And a large crowd gladly listened to him.

DENUNCIATION OF THE SCRIBES AND PHARISEES (MT 23:1–36; LK 11:39–54)

38In his teaching he said, "Beware of the scribes who walk around in long robes and love greetings in the marketplaces 39and to have the first seats in the synagogues and the first couches at dinner, 40who devour the houses of widows and for show make long prayers. These will receive the greater judgment."

THE WIDOW'S OFFERING (LK 21:1–4)

41He sat down opposite the treasury and watched how the crowds put coins into the treasury, and many rich people also contributed much. 42Then a poor widow came and put in two copper coins, which is equal to a quadrans. 43And he called his disciples near to him, and he said to them, "Truly I say to you that this poor widow has put in more than all those who are contributing to the treasury, 44for they contribute out of their abundance, but she out of her poverty has contributed everything she had, even what she had to live on."

12:29–30 Quotation from Deuteronomy 6:4–5 and Joshua 22:5. Deuteronomy 6:4 is the opening line of the *Shema* (see note on Mark 10:18). *Mind* can also be translated as *thought.* **12:31** Quotation from Leviticus 19:18. **12:32** Quotation from Deuteronomy 4:35. **12:33** The question of which is greater, the commandment to love God or to offer sacrifice, seems to lie at the heart of Jesus's message. The scribe in verse 32 is *not far from the kingdom of God* when he summarizes Jesus's answer as advocating that loving God and neighbor are the foundational pillars of a righteous life instead of animal sacrifice and burnt offerings. **12:36** Quotation from Psalm 110:1. **12:38–40** Mark records a much shorter condemnation of the scribes than that of Matthew regarding the Pharisees (compare Matthew 23:1–36). **12:40** Compare Isaiah 10:1–2. **12:42** The woman offered two small copper coins called *lepta* (singular *lepton*). Two of these coins was equal to a Latin *quadrans*, a bronze coin that was one fourth of an *as* (a larger Roman bronze coin that was in greater circulation). Mark's audience is familiar with the *quadrans* (a Roman coin) but apparently not a *lepton* (a Judean coin).

THE DESTRUCTION OF THE TEMPLE FORETOLD (MT 24:1–8; LK 21:5–11)

13 ¹And when Jesus left the temple, one of his disciples said to him, "Teacher, look what magnificent stones and buildings!" ²And Jesus said to him, "Do you see these great buildings? There will not remain here a stone upon another stone that will not be thrown down."

³And he sat on the Mount of Olives opposite the temple, and Peter, Jacob, John, and Andrew asked him alone, ⁴"Tell us when these things will be, and what is the sign when all these things will be fulfilled?" ⁵Jesus began to say to them, "Beware that no one leads you astray. ⁶Many will come in my name, saying, 'I am he,' and they will lead many astray. ⁷When you hear of wars and rumors of war, do not be troubled: this thing must be, but it is not the end. ⁸Nation will rise against nation, and kingdom against kingdom, there will be earthquakes in many places, and there will be famines; these are the beginning of the birth pains.

PERSECUTIONS FORETOLD (MT 10:17–22; 24:9–14; LK 21:12–19)

⁹"Be watchful for yourselves: they will hand you over to councils, and you will be beaten in synagogues. You will stand before governors and kings for my sake in order to bear testimony to them. ¹⁰And the gospel will first be declared to all nations. ¹¹And when they arrest you to hand you over for punishment, do not worry what you will say, but say whatever is given to you in that hour, for it will not be you speaking but the Holy Spirit. ¹²A brother will hand over a brother to death, and a father his child, and children will rise up against parents and put them to death. ¹³And you will be hated by all because of my name. But whoever remains patiently, the same will be saved.

THE DESOLATING SACRILEGE (MT 24:15–28; LK 21:20–24)

¹⁴"When you see the desolating sacrilege standing where it should not (let the reader understand), then let those in Judea flee to the mountains. ¹⁵Let him who is on

---

13:1–37 The Olivet Discourse (see Matthew 24:1–55; Luke 21:5–38; Joseph Smith—Matthew 1:1–55). **13:2** Prophecies relating to the destruction of Jerusalem are found in Micah 3:12 and Jeremiah 26:18. Compare Doctrine and Covenants 45:20. **13:3** For the significance of the Mount of Olives and the Messiah, see Zechariah 14:4. Mark alone names the disciples who asked this question of Jesus. **13:6** The declaration *I am he* is meant as the declaration *I am the Christ*. It is a reference to the divine name of Exodus 3:14. **13:8** Echo of Isaiah 19:2 and 2 Chronicles 15:6. Mark notes only *places*. **13:9** The word translated as *councils* is *sanhedrins*. The plural conveys the idea that persecution will spread to small villages and towns. **13:9–13** These verses are unique to Mark's version of the discourse. **13:10** The sense of the verb is that the gospel will need to be declared first in all nations before the remaining events can take place. **13:11** The phrase *hand you over* can also mean *betray* (Mark 1:14; 14:41). Alluded to in Doctrine and Covenants 84:85 (compare Matthew 10:19). **13:12** Echo of Micah 7:6. **13:13** Mark seems to intend the idea *whoever patiently remains steadfast in my name*, but the Greek is abbreviated and not precisely clear. Second Nephi 31:14–15, 20 engages the idea of enduring to the end. Compare Matthew 10:22; Alma 32:13. **13:14** For the desolating sacrilege, see Daniel 9:27; 11:31; 12:11. Older translations preferred to translate this as the *abomination of desolation* or the *abomination that makes desolate*. Jews have long held that one of the desolating sacrileges was the defilement of the temple by Antiochus IV Epiphanes (168 BCE), which provided the impetus for the Maccabean revolt. Here Jesus alludes to another desolating sacrilege that will come. Some scholars have proposed that this second event was the destruction of the temple by the Roman army in 70 CE. **13:15–18** These verses predict that those who see the desolating sacrilege will need to move with haste, and they are encouraged to avoid any delay in their flight to the

the roof not go down or enter to take anything from his house. ¹⁶Let him who is in the field not turn back to take his clothes. ¹⁷Woe to those who are pregnant and nursing in those days. ¹⁸Pray that it does not come in winter. ¹⁹There will tribulation in those days that has not been since the beginning of God's creation until now and never will be again. ²⁰If the Lord does not shorten those days, no one would be saved, but because of the elect whom he chose, he has shortened those days. ²¹And then if anyone says to you, 'Behold, the Christ, he is there,' or 'Look, he is there,' do not believe it. ²²There will arise false Christs and false prophets, and they will perform signs and miracles in order to lead the elect astray if they are able. ²³Beware, I have told you all things beforehand.

THE COMING OF THE SON OF MAN (MT 24:29–31; LK 21:25–28)

²⁴"But in those days after the tribulation, *the sun will be darkened, and the moon will not give its light,* ²⁵*and the stars will fall from heaven, and the powers in heaven will be shaken.* ²⁶Then you will see *the Son of Man coming in the clouds* with great power and glory. ²⁷And then he will send the angels, and they will gather his elect from the four winds, from the ends of the earth to the ends of heaven.

THE MEANING OF THE FIG TREE (MT 24:32–36; LK 21:29–33)

²⁸"From the fig tree, learn this parable. When the branch becomes tender and it puts forth leaves, you know that summer is near. ²⁹So it is with you: when you see these things being accomplished, you will know that it is near, even at the doors. ³⁰Truly I say to you that this generation will not pass away before all these things occur. ³¹Heaven and earth will pass away, but my words will not pass away.

THE NEED TO BE WATCHFUL (MT 24:36–44; LK 12:35–48; 21:34–38)

³²"Concerning that day and hour, no one knows it, not the angels in heaven nor the Son, but only the Father. ³³Be watchful and attentive; you do not know when it is time, ³⁴like a man who left his house and gave authority to his servants, to each his own work, and he commanded the doorkeeper to keep watch. ³⁵Watch, therefore—you do not know when the owner of the house will come, late or in the middle of the night, or when the rooster crows, or early in the morning—³⁶so that he does not come suddenly and find you asleep. ³⁷What I say to you, I say to all: Be watchful!"

Lord's holy place (see Matthew 24:15; Doctrine and Covenants 45:32). **13:20** For the idea of Israel as a *chosen* people, see Isaiah 65:9. **13:24** Compare Doctrine and Covenants 34:9, which quotes this verse. **13:24–25** Allusion to Isaiah 13:10; 34:4; Joel 2:10. Compare Doctrine and Covenants 34:9. **13:26** Allusion to Daniel 7:13. **13:27** Allusion to Zechariah 2:10 and Deuteronomy 30:4. **13:28** Doctrine and Covenants 35:16; 45:37 comment on the meaning of this parable. **13:30** Matthew, Mark, and Luke are unanimous in reporting that Jesus declared that the calamities foretold would be fulfilled in *this generation* (Matthew 24:34; Luke 21:32). The Joseph Smith Translation of Matthew places the fulfillment of some of these events in the days of the disciples and some of them as yet to be fulfilled in the future (compare Joseph Smith—Matthew 1:21–55). Scholars have struggled to make sense of the meaning of *this generation* and whether Jesus was indicating that the fulfillment of these things would take place in the lives of the disciples or in the future. **13:31** Allusion to Isaiah 40:8; 51:6. **13:33–37** The theme of being watchful and attentive is sometimes referred to as the delay of the Lord's coming, and a number of New Testament teachings warn against falling asleep or failing to watch for the Lord's return (see Matthew 25:5; 1 Corinthians 15:16–18; 1 Thessalonians 5:6).

THE PLOT TO KILL JESUS
(MT 26:1–5; LK 22:1–2)

14 ¹It was two days before the Passover and Feast of Unleavened Bread, and the chief priests and scribes sought a way to arrest him by deceit and kill him. ²For they said, "Not during the feast so that there will not be a riot."

JESUS IS ANOINTED AT BETHANY
(MT 26:6–13; LK 7:36–50; JN 12:1–8)

³He was in Bethany at the house of Simon the leper reclining to eat, and a woman came to him who had an alabaster jar of ointment, pure nard, that was very expensive, and having broken the alabaster jar, she poured it on his head. ⁴But some were displeased among them and said to one another, "Why was this ointment wasted in this manner? ⁵This could have been sold for more than three hundred silver coins and given to the poor." And they rebuked her. ⁶But Jesus said, "Leave her alone. Why do you trouble her? She has done a good work for me. ⁷You will always have the poor with you, and whenever you desire you can do good for them, but you will not always have me. ⁸She has done what she could: she anointed my body in preparation for my burial. ⁹Truly I say to you, wherever the gospel is declared in all the world, what she has done will be told in memory of her."

JUDAS BETRAYS JESUS (MT 26:14–16; LK 22:3–6)

¹⁰And Judas Iscariot, one of the twelve, went to the chief priests in order to deliver him to them. ¹¹When they heard it, they were glad and promised to give him money. And he sought how he could deliver him at the right time.

PREPARATION FOR THE PASSOVER
(MT 26:17–19; LK 22:7–13)

¹²It was the first day of the Feast of Unleavened Bread, when the Passover lamb is sacrificed, and his disciples said to him, "Where do you want to go that we may prepare a place to eat the Passover meal?" ¹³And he sent two of his disciples and said to them, "Go into the city, and a man carrying a water jug will meet you: follow him. ¹⁴Wherever he enters, say to the master of the house, 'The teacher asks, Where is my guest room that I may

---

14:1–16:8 The final section of Mark, which details the Last Supper, arrest, trial, crucifixion, and the empty tomb. **14:1** Mark does not note the precise day of the week, but he does draw attention to the fact that they were still in Bethany two days before Passover (14:3). **14:2** Despite the objection to not arrest Jesus during Passover, they arrest him on the evening of the first day of the celebration. **14:3** *Nard*, or *spikenard*, was a costly perfume derived from a plant that grew in India. Some Roman recipes called for the addition of nard. **14:5** Determining the value of the perfume is difficult because of changes in the value of the *denarius* over time. It would have been worth approximately two month's pay for an average day laborer. Following the standard of pay in Jesus's parables, where the average worker earned a denarius for a day's work, this would be equivalent to approximately one and a half year's worth of pay. **14:7** An allusion to Deuteronomy 15:11. **14:8** Jesus teaches his disciples that the anointing of his body with perfume was done as a means of looking forward to his burial. **14:12** The first day of the Feast of Unleavened Bread falls on Nisan 15. By noting that the Passover lambs were sacrificed, Mark has clarified his intent that the day was Nisan 14. There has been a significant amount of confusion regarding the date of the Last Supper celebrated by Jesus and whether it was a Passover meal. The Passover lamb was to be sacrificed on Nisan 14 and eaten after sundown and therefore on Nisan 15 (Exodus 12:18). According to Mark, the Last Supper took place on the first day of the feast (Nisan 14) in the evening (see Matthew 26:17; Luke 22:7). John, however, places the meal before Passover, and therefore it was not a Passover meal, but an ordinary meal enjoyed by Jesus on the eve of his death (John 13:1). Furthermore,

eat the Passover meal with my disciples?' ¹⁵And he will show you a large, second-floor room furnished and ready. Prepare it for us." ¹⁶And the disciples departed and came to the city and immediately found it as he had told them, and they prepared the Passover meal.

PASSOVER AND BETRAYAL FORE-TOLD (MT 26:20–25; LK 22:21–23)

¹⁷When it was evening, he came with the twelve. ¹⁸While they were reclined and eating, Jesus said, "Truly I say to you that one of you will betray me, one who eats with me." ¹⁹They began to be sad and to say to him one by one, "Is it I?" ²⁰He said to them, "One of the twelve who dips with me in the dish. ²¹Because the Son of Man must go as it is written about him, but woe to that man by whom the Son of Man is betrayed: it would be better for that man if he had not been born."

THE SACRAMENT (MT 26:21–25; LK 22:14–20)

²²While they were eating, he took some bread and blessed it and broke it and gave it to them and said, "Take it; this is my body." ²³And taking a cup, he blessed it and gave it to them, and they all drank from it. ²⁴And he said to them, "This is my blood of the covenant, which has been poured out for many. ²⁵Truly I say to you that I will not drink again of the fruit of the vine until that day when I drink it new in the king-dom of God." ²⁶After they sang, they went to the Mount of Olives.

PETER'S DENIAL FORETOLD (MT 26:30–35; LK 22:31–38; JN 13:36–38)

²⁷And Jesus said to them, "All of you will stumble, because it is written, '*I will strike the shepherd, and the sheep will be scattered.*' ²⁸But after I am raised, I will go before you to Galilee." ²⁹But Peter said to him, "Even if all stumble, I will not." ³⁰Jesus said to him, "Truly I say to you that on this very night before the rooster crows twice, you will deny me three times." ³¹And he re-sponded emphatically, "If I am required to die with you, I will still not deny you." And they all said the same thing.

John 18:28 notes that the day of the crucifixion is also a day when the priests did not want to be defiled so that they could eat the Passover presumably later that day, and therefore Jesus was crucified at about the same time the Passover lambs were being sacrificed in the temple (John 19:14). That Jesus celebra-ted a last meal with his disciples on the eve of his death is indisputable, but whether it was a Passover meal is impossible to know given the differences in the sources. It is clear, based on references to the beginning of the Sabbath, that Jesus was crucified on Friday, but the calendar date was either Nisan 14 or 15. **14:15** *Furnished* here means strewn with pillows or carpets on which they could recline and dine. **14:22** The practice of breaking the bread and blessing it is reminiscent of the feeding of the five thousand (Mark 6:41). **14:25** An interpretation of this verse is given in Doctrine and Covenants 27:5. **14:26** The hymn would have been the Hallel Psalms (Psalms 113–18). **14:27** Quotation from Zechariah 13:7. **14:28** The Joseph Smith Translation adds to the end of this verse *And he said unto Judas Iscariot, what thou doest, do quickly; but beware of innocent blood. Nevertheless, Judas Iscariot, even one of the twelve, went unto the chief priests to betray Jesus unto them; for he turned away from him, and was offended because of his words. And when the chief priests heard of him, they were glad, and promised to give him money; and he sought how he might conveniently betray Jesus.* **14:30** Mark records that the rooster will crow twice, while Matthew (26:34, 74–75), Luke (22:34, 60–61), and John (13:38; 18:27) note that the rooster will crow after Peter denied knowing Jesus.

JESUS PRAYS IN GETHSEMANE (MT 26:36–46; LK 22:39–46; JN 18:1)

³²And he came to a place called Gethsemane, and he said to his disciples, "Sit here while I pray." ³³And he took Peter, Jacob, and John with him, and he began to be amazed and troubled. ³⁴And he said to them, "My soul is sorrowful to the point of death. Stay here and be watchful." ³⁵And he went a little way and fell on the ground and prayed that if it were possible that the hour would pass by him. ³⁶And he said, "Abba, Father, all things are possible for you; take this cup from me. Not as I desire, but as you desire." ³⁷And he came and found them sleeping, and he said to Peter, "Simon, why are you sleeping? Are you not strong enough to watch for one hour? ³⁸Watch and pray that you do not enter temptation: the spirit is willing but the flesh is weak." ³⁹And again he went and prayed, saying the same words. ⁴⁰And again he came and found them sleeping, for their eyes were heavy, and they did not know what to say to him. ⁴¹And he came to them the third time and said to them, "Are you still sleeping and resting? It is enough! The hour has arrived. Behold, the Son of Man is betrayed into the hands of sinners. ⁴²Rise and let us go; the one who betrays me approaches."

THE ARREST (MT 26:47–56; LK 22:47–53; JN 18:2–12)

⁴³And immediately, while he was still speaking, Judas, one of the twelve, approached and with him a great crowd with swords and sticks, from the chief priests, scribes, and elders. ⁴⁴And the betrayer had given them a sign saying, "Whomever I kiss, he is the one; arrest him and lead him away under guard." ⁴⁵And he came immediately and drew near to Jesus and said, "Rabbi," and he kissed him. ⁴⁶And they laid their hands on him and arrested him. ⁴⁷One of those standing there drew a sword and struck the servant of the high priest and cut off his ear. ⁴⁸Jesus said to them, "You come out to take me with swords and sticks as a bandit, ⁴⁹but every day I was with you in the temple teaching, and you did not arrest me. But let the scriptures be fulfilled." ⁵⁰And they abandoned him and fled. ⁵¹And there was a young man following him who had put a linen sheet around his naked body, and they grabbed him, ⁵²but he left the linen sheet and fled from them naked.

JESUS INTERROGATED (MT 26:57–68; LK 22:54–71; JN 18:13–24)

⁵³And they led Jesus to the high priest, and all of the chief priests, elders, and scribes gathered around him. ⁵⁴And Peter followed him from a distance until he was inside

---

14:32 The Joseph Smith Translation of this verse reads *And they came to a place which was named Gethsemane, which was a garden; and the disciples began to be sore amazed, and to be very heavy, and to complain in their hearts, wondering if this be the Messiah. And Jesus, knowing their hearts, he said to his disciples, Sit you here while I shall pray.* **14:33** Jesus's emotions may have been *distress* and *anguish*, but Mark uses a verb that also means *wonder* or *amazement*. **14:36** *Abba* is an Aramaic word for *Father* and was also used by Paul (Romans 8:15; Galatians 4:6), perhaps as a means of recalling this prayer. *This cup* may be an echo of the cup of Mark 14:23. **14:38** Alluded to in Doctrine and Covenants 31:12 (compare Matthew 26:41; Luke 22:46). **14:44** *Under guard* conveys the idea that Jesus was not allowed to escape. **14:47** The servant of the chief priest is probably Caiaphas's servant. Caiaphas was high priest during the trial of Jesus and held the position from 18 CE to 36/37 CE. **14:48** Jesus asks if they intend to take him *as a bandit*. He earlier accused them of being *bandits* (Mark 11:17–18). **14:51–52** The identity of the young man who fled from the arrest may represent an eyewitness source known only to the author of the Gospel of Mark.

the courtyard of the high priest, and he was sitting with the guards and warming himself by the fire. ⁵⁵And the chief priests and the entire Sanhedrin sought evidence against Jesus to put him to death, but they found none. ⁵⁶For many witnessed falsely against him, but their testimonies were not alike. ⁵⁷And some stood and bore this false witness against him: ⁵⁸"We have heard him say, 'I will destroy the temple built with hands, and I will build a new one without hands in three days'" ⁵⁹But their testimony did not agree either. ⁶⁰And the high priest stood among them and questioned Jesus, "Do you answer nothing? What is this that they witness against you?" ⁶¹But he was silent and answered nothing. Again, the high priest questioned him, "Are you the Christ, the Son of the Blessed?" ⁶²Jesus said, "I am, and you will see *the Son of Man seated on the right hand of power and coming with the clouds of heaven.*" ⁶³And the high priest tore his clothes and said, "What need do we still have for witnesses? ⁶⁴You have heard blasphemy. How does it appear to you?" They all judged him to be worthy of death. ⁶⁵And some began to spit on him and to cover his face and hit him, and they said to him, "Prophesy!" And the guards took him and also struck him.

PETER DENIES JESUS (MT 26:69–75; LK 22:56–62; JN 18:25–27)

⁶⁶When Peter was in the courtyard below, one of the servant girls of the high priest came, ⁶⁷and she saw Peter warming himself, and she looked at him and said, "You were with Jesus of Nazareth." ⁶⁸And he denied it saying, "I do not know nor do I understand what you are talking about." And he went outside into the forecourt. ⁶⁹And the servant girl saw him and began again to say to those standing there, "This man is one of them." ⁷⁰And he denied it again. After a short time, those standing there again said to Peter, "Truly you are one of them, for you are a Galilean." ⁷¹He began to curse himself and to swear, "I do not know this man of whom you speak." ⁷²And immediately the rooster crowed a second time, and Peter remembered the words that Jesus said to him, "Before the rooster crows twice, you will deny me three times." And he broke down and wept.

JESUS BEFORE PILATE (MT 27:1–2, 11–14; LK 23:1–5; JN 18:28–38)

15 ¹Right away, early in the morning, the chief priests with the elders and scribes and the entire Sanhedrin gathered for a council, and they bound Jesus and led him away and delivered him to Pilate. ²And Pilate questioned him, "Are you the King of the Jews?" He answered, "You say so." ³And the chief priests accused him of many things. ⁴And Pilate questioned him again, "Do you have nothing to say? Look at how much they accuse you!" ⁵But Jesus did not answer, so that Pilate wondered.

14:55 Mark notes that the *entire Sanhedrin* met to interrogate and condemn Jesus. Such a meeting of the entire council would have given the gathering an aura of legality, although the Gospels are fairly unanimous that the actions taken during the interrogation were mob oriented. **14:56–57** An allusion to Deuteronomy 19:15. **14:62** Jesus's answer is built on Psalm 110:1 and Daniel 7:13–14. Echoed in Doctrine and Covenants 49:6. **14:64** For the law of Moses command on blasphemy, see Leviticus 24:16. **14:68** Some manuscripts add to the end of the verse *and the rooster crowed.* Mark may have constructed the story as a means of showing that Peter was reminded partway through his denials that Jesus had foretold what he would do (see also 14:72, where the rooster crows a *second time*).

15:1 Mark notes that the chief priests, elders, and scribes acted *right away* rather than simply early in the morning, giving the story a sense of quick movement toward the crucifixion. Pilate was the highest-ranking civil officer in Judea, where he served as *prefect* of Judea (26–36 CE). **15:2** Pilate's question implies that Jesus was accused of treason.

PILATE DELIVERS JESUS TO BE CRUCIFIED (MT 27:15–26; LK 23:17–25; JN 18:39–19:16)

⁶According to custom, Pilate released to them one prisoner during the feast, whomever they asked for. ⁷There was a man named Barabbas, among the bandits in prison, who in the insurrection had committed murder. ⁸And the crowd arose and began to ask Pilate to do for them according to custom. ⁹Pilate asked them, "Do you want me to release to you the King of the Jews?" ¹⁰(For he knew that the chief priests had delivered him out of envy.) ¹¹But the chief priests stirred up the crowd so that he might release Barabbas to them. ¹²Pilate said to them again, "What do you want me to do with the man you call the King of the Jews?" ¹³They again cried out, "Crucify him!" ¹⁴Pilate responded, "Why, what evil has he done?" But they cried out more, "Crucify him!" ¹⁵Pilate wanted to please the crowd, so he released Barabbas to them, and after he scourged Jesus, he gave Jesus over to be crucified.

SOLDIERS MOCK JESUS (MT 27:27–31; JN 19:2–3)

¹⁶The guards led him inside the courtyard, which is the Praetorium, and they called together the entire cohort. ¹⁷And they clothed him in purple, and after weaving a crown of thorns together, they put it on him. ¹⁸And they began to greet him, "Hail, King of the Jews!" ¹⁹And they hit him on the head with a scepter repeatedly and spit on him, and they knelt down before him. ²⁰And after they had mocked him, they removed the purple robe and placed on him his own clothing. And they led him out to crucify him.

THE CRUCIFIXION (MT 27:45–56; LK 23:32–43; JN 19:17B–27)

²¹And they pressed into service a man walking by, Simon of Cyrene, who was coming from the field (he was the father of Alexander and Rufus), so that he would carry his cross. ²²And they carried him to the place called Golgotha, which means the "Place of the Skull." ²³And they gave him wine mixed with myrrh, but he did not take it. ²⁴And they crucified him and divided his clothing, casting lots to determine what each would take.

15:7 Mark is clear that the prisoners are *bandits or political revolutionaries* and not simply thieves. Barabbas participated in *the insurrection*, but Mark does not provide details of the event in question. **15:11–15** Despite Pilate's recognition that the actions against Jesus were a result of envy, Pilate was still easily manipulated in the trial of Jesus. Historically, Pilate was described as a person who was insensitive to Jewish customs and at the same time willing to provoke Jews (Josephus, *Jewish War* 2.9.2–4; Philo, *On the Embassy of Gaius* 38.299–305). **15:16** The *Praetorium* may refer to Pilate's residential palace, but it could also refer to a Herodian palace. The sources are unclear regarding the precise location of the *Praetorium*. The *entire garrison* would consist of two to six hundred foot soldiers. **15:21** The notice that Simon was the father of Alexander and Rufus (perhaps the same person mentioned in Romans 16:13, but uncertain) may have been included in the story because the two sons were known by name to Jesus's followers. Simon was required to carry the topmost part of the cross, to which the arms were fastened. The upright or vertically positioned poles used in crucifixion would have already been fixed in the ground. **15:22** Only Mark notes that they carried Jesus to Golgotha (Matthew 27:33; Luke 23:33). John notes that Jesus carried his own cross to the site of the crucifixion (John 19:17). **15:23** A possible allusion to Proverbs 31:6. **15:24** An allusion to Psalm 22:18. **15:25** Mark gives the time of the crucifixion as *about the third hour*, or approximately 9:00 a.m.

²⁵It was about the nine in the morning when they crucified him. ²⁶And the inscription of his charge was written, "The King of the Jews." ²⁷And two bandits were crucified with him, one on his right and one on his left. [[²⁸And the scripture was fulfilled that says, "*And with the lawless ones he was numbered.*"]] ²⁹Those who passed by slandered him and shook their heads and said, "Woe to you who can destroy the temple and build it in three days. ³⁰Save yourself and come down from the cross." ³¹Likewise the chief priests with the scribes mocked him among themselves, saying, "He saved others, but he cannot save himself. ³²Christ, the King of Israel, come down now from the cross, and we will see and believe!" And those who were crucified with him also mocked him.

THE DEATH OF JESUS (MT 27:45–56; LK 23:44–49; JN 19:28–30)

³³It was noon, and there was darkness over the whole land until three in the afternoon. ³⁴And around three in the afternoon, Jesus cried out in a loud voice, "*Eloi, Eloi, lema sabachthani,*" which means, "*My God, my God, why have you abandoned me?*" ³⁵Some of those standing by heard him and said,

"He calls for Elijah!" ³⁶One of them ran and filled a sponge with sour wine, and putting it on a reed, he gave it to him to drink saying, "Let us see if Elijah will come and take him down." ³⁷But Jesus uttered a loud cry and breathed his last breath. ³⁸And the veil of the temple was torn in two from top to bottom. ³⁹When the centurion who was standing opposite him saw that he breathed his last breath, he said, "Truly this man was the Son of God." ⁴⁰There were also women who watched from a distance, among whom were Mary Magdalene, Mary the mother of Jacob the younger and Jose, and Salome. ⁴¹They followed him in Galilee and provided for him, and many other women who traveled with him to Jerusalem were there as well.

THE BURIAL (MT 27:57–61; LK 23:50–56; JN 19:38–42)

⁴²When it was evening, because it was the day of preparation, which is the day before the Sabbath, ⁴³Joseph of Arimathea, a notable officer who himself was also looking for the kingdom of God, came and boldly went to Pilate and asked for the body of Jesus. ⁴⁴Pilate was surprised that he was already dead, and he called the centurion

---

15:26–27 That Jesus was crucified between two *bandits* or *political revolutionaries* (see also the note on 15:7) suggests that Jesus was crucified for acting against Roman interests and governance. That act may be described in modern terms as *treason*, and the charge against him that he was the *King of the Jews* confirms that there were political overtones in the charges against him. **15:28** This verse is missing in the majority of early manuscripts. It was likely added on the evidence of the parallel in Luke 22:37. Quotation from Isaiah 53:12. **15:34** Quotation from Psalm 22:1. **15:36** A possible allusion to Psalm 69:21. **15:38** The veil of the temple was torn so that everyone could see into the *Holy of Holies*, or at least could figuratively see inside the holiest part of the temple. **15:40** *Mary the mother of Jacob the younger and Jose* would be Jesus's mother (see Mark 6:3), and Mark describes her in an unexpected fashion if this Mary is indeed the same person as Jesus's mother. **15:41** The women *provided for him*, meaning that they served him as *deacons* would do. This would include attending to his physical needs and looking after his welfare. **15:42** This would indicate that Jesus was crucified on Friday before the Sabbath began at sundown on Friday evening. **15:43** *A notable officer* is unclear in Greek, and the reference could refer to a civic administrator or perhaps even a member of a Sanhedrin. Luke 23:50–51 notes that Joseph was a member of the Judean council. *Arimathea* is the town of *Ramathaim*, which is rendered as *Arimathea* in the Greek translation of the Old Testament (referred to as the Septuagint or LXX) in 1 Samuel 1:1. **15:44** The note that Jesus had been *dead for long* may indicate an attempt to respond to rumors about whether Jesus was really dead at the time of his burial. The centurion confirms that Jesus was dead (15:45).

and asked him if Jesus had been dead for long. ⁴⁵And when he knew from the centurion that Jesus was dead, he gave the body to Joseph. ⁴⁶And he brought fine linen, and after taking him down, he wrapped him in linen and laid him in a tomb that had been hewn out of rock, and he rolled a stone in front of the door of the tomb. ⁴⁷Mary Magdalene and Mary the mother of Jose saw where he was laid.

THE RESURRECTION (MT 28:1–10; LK 24:1–12; JN 20:1–13)

16 ¹When the Sabbath had passed, Mary Magdalene, and Mary the mother of Jacob, and Salome brought spices in order that they might come and anoint him. ²And early in the morning, on the first day of the week, they came to the tomb at the rising of the sun, ³and they said to one another, "Who will move the stone away from the door of the tomb?" ⁴And they looked and saw that the stone had been moved, for it was very large. ⁵And they entered the tomb and saw a young man sitting on the right side, wearing a long white robe, and they were amazed. ⁶And he said to them, "Do not be alarmed. You seek Jesus of Nazareth, who was crucified. He has risen, and he is not here. Behold,

the place where they laid him. ⁷But go, tell his disciples and Peter that he goes before you to Galilee; there you will see him, just as he told you." ⁸And they left and fled from the tomb, for they were trembling and amazement had seized them, and they did not tell anyone anything, because they were afraid.

THE LONGER ENDING OF MARK

JESUS APPEARS TO MARY MAGDALENE (MT 28:9–10; JN 20:14–18)

⁹When he arose early on the first day of the week, he appeared first to Mary Magdalene, out of whom he had cast seven demons. ¹⁰Then she went out and told those who had been with him, while they were mourning and weeping, ¹¹and when they heard that he was alive and was seen by her, they did not believe it.

JESUS APPEARS TO TWO DISCIPLES (LK 24:13–35)

¹²After these things, he appeared in another form to two of them as they went into the countryside. ¹³And they went and told the rest, but they did not believe them.

16:1 *When the Sabbath had passed* indicates only that it was Saturday evening after sundown. The following verse points the reader to the fact that it was Sunday morning because it was *early in the morning, on the first day of the week.* The women disciples had come to *anoint* or *prepare* Jesus in preparation for his burial. **16:5** The *young man* is wearing a *long white robe*, which would have been physically different from the type of clothing worn by Jesus and his contemporaries. This type of clothing was worn by kings and royals. The Joseph Smith Translation says *two angels.* **16:6–8** This is Mark's point of emphasis in the account of the resurrection: *He has risen.* The women disciples immediately spread this good news to the disciples who were to meet with Jesus in Galilee. The Gospel of Mark likely ended at verse 8 originally, although a number of different endings have been preserved in different manuscripts. **16:9** The manuscript sources for the longer ending of Mark are quite late and much less reliable than those that end with verse 8. The longer ending may have been the result of scribes attempting to harmonize the Second Gospel with the other Gospel accounts of the resurrection. Some less trustworthy manuscripts add the following after verse 8, but they omit the longer ending (verses 9–20): *But they reported briefly to Peter and those with him all that they had been told. And after this, Jesus himself sent out by means of them, from east to west, the sacred and imperishable proclamation of eternal salvation.*

THE GREAT COMMISSION
(MT 28:16–20)

¹⁴Afterward, as they were dining, he appeared to the eleven, and he chastised them for their unbelief and their hardness of heart because they did not believe those who had seen him after he had risen. ¹⁵And he said to them, "Go to all the world and declare the gospel to all creation. ¹⁶Those who believe and are baptized will be saved, and those who do not believe will be condemned. ¹⁷Signs will accompany those who believe. In my name they will cast out demons, and they will speak in new languages, ¹⁸they will pick up serpents, and if they drink any poisonous thing, it will not hurt them; they will lay their hands on the sick, and they will recover."

THE ASCENSION (LK 24:50–52)

¹⁹Then the Lord Jesus, after speaking to them, ascended to heaven and sat on the right hand of God. ²⁰And they went out and preached everywhere, the Lord working with them and confirming the word through the signs that followed. Amen.

16:15 The injunction to take the gospel *to all the world* is echoed in Doctrine and Covenants 18:28; 58:64; 68:6, 8–9; 84:62; 112:28–29. Compare Mormon 9:22. **16:15–18** These verses are alluded to in Mormon 9:22–24 and partially in Mormon 9:24; Ether 4:18. **16:16** Compare 3 Nephi 11:33–34; Mormon 9:23; Doctrine and Covenants 68:9–10. **16:17** Echoed in Doctrine and Covenants 24:13; 84:65; 124:98.

THE GOSPEL OF LUKE

WHO WAS LUKE?

As with the other Gospels, the Third Gospel was written by an anonymous author whose identity has been passed down through early Christian writers who lived in the generations after the apostles. According to tradition, Paul's traveling companion named Luke wrote a two-part work, Luke–Acts, to a patron named Theophilus near the time of Paul's death. That traveling companion was a physician (Colossians 4:14), and he seems to have come to believe in the gospel message and come into contact with several eyewitnesses to Jesus's ministry.

The evidence for the authorship of the Third Gospel is the following: (1) Stylistic similarities between the Gospel and book of Acts strongly suggest that the same person wrote both. (2) The author of Acts may signal his own personal involvement in some events from the lifetime of Paul through the use of the first-person plural *we* (16:10–17; 20:5–15; 21:1–18; 27:1–28:16). (3) Both the Gospel and Acts are dedicated to the same person (Theophilus) with similar interests and intent. (4) The book of Acts refers to a former treatise, which is almost certainly the Gospel of Luke. Given these evidences, it is reasonable to conclude that a traveling companion of Paul was involved in the writing of the Gospel of Luke and that he wrote it with the intent to further the spread of the gospel message.

The question of when Luke wrote is more straightforward, with a few key pieces of evidence guiding the discussion. Paul is still alive at the end of Acts, and Paul's death is widely thought to have occurred under Nero's reign (died 9 June 68 CE). Assuming that Paul was still alive when Luke wrote, then it may be possible to suggest that the Gospel of Luke was written before 68 CE. But Luke also drew heavily from Mark's Gospel, and therefore if Mark's Gospel was written sometime in the 60s CE, then Luke must have had access to it and then enough time to compose his own account. To offer a date more specifically would be to force the evidence in ways that are limiting for the discussion.

From the foregoing discussion, a clearer picture of Luke emerges. A traveling companion of Paul accepted the message of the resurrection of Jesus Christ, and he agreed to travel with Paul in the region around Troas and Philippi. That companion was probably named Luke, the name of a physician who is mentioned in several of Paul's letters. Luke

traveled to Jerusalem and came into contact with a generation of living eyewitnesses and probably written sources as well, and he availed himself of those sources when he wrote. Luke shows clear signs of seeing the gospel story through Paul's eyes, and he emphasized the place of women in the church, the plight of the poor, and the universal message of salvation that reached beyond Judea and Galilee. He told the gospel as a self-interested believer who promoted the vantage point of his missionary friend while maintaining Greek standards of writing history.

THE MANUSCRIPTS

For the most part, the Gospel of Luke's manuscript tradition is like that of the other Gospels. A few important papyrus witnesses help confirm the overall accuracy of the fourth-century Greek codices Sinaiticus and Vaticanus. Major sections of Luke are preserved in a third-century codex (Chester Beatty papyrus 45) and in a potentially second-century papyrus (Bodmer XIV). These early papyrus witnesses help establish the fact that some passages in Luke may have been added later or potentially revised over time (see notes on Luke 22:43–44), but they also help confirm the overall integrity of the Gospel of Luke.

The Bodmer papyrus calls this the *Gospel according to Luke*, thus offering a very early textual witness to Luke as author (compare Irenaeus, *Adv. haer.* 3.1.1; Tertullian, *Adv. Marcionem* 4.2.2). Even though the manuscripts of Luke are strong and preserve a fairly cohesive text, none of the manuscripts preserve Luke–Acts as a two-part text. Undoubtedly, Luke wrote the Gospel first and then Acts, probably on two separate papyrus rolls. It is unclear how or when the Gospel of John came between them, and unfortunately none of the surviving manuscripts present Luke's original intent of a two-part work that told the story of Jesus's life followed by a reception history of the gospel message throughout the eastern Roman Empire.

STRUCTURE AND ORGANIZATION

One of the most obvious organizing features of the Third Gospel is the shift in the narrative that takes place at Luke 9:51, when Jesus begins to unequivocally move toward Jerusalem and the completion of his mission. This two-part narrative structure develops into a purpose-driven effort that seeks to promote mission and calling over major life moments or discourses. In this telling of the story, Jesus encounters a series of rejections (Luke 4:14–30; 6:1–11), he performs miracles, and then he is transfigured before three of his disciples (Luke 9:28–36). These experiences prepare Jesus to look toward Jerusalem and to prepare his disciples for his departure. One might think of Luke's retelling as episodic, dramatic, and almost cinematic.

Luke drew on sources in telling the story this way, and he quoted from Mark and another lost source dubbed simply "Q" by scholars (from German *Quelle*, or source). The latter source was a collection of sayings of Jesus that circulated orally, although some scholars think it was a written document. One clue that Luke drew from these sources is that he tells nearly a dozen stories two times. These stories are called the Lukan doublets. The reason that these doublets occur is that Luke told the story once using Mark's version of the story and once through another source like "Q." For example, Luke twice records the saying of placing a lamp under a basket (Luke 8:16; 11:33). The first reflects Mark 4:21, and the second reflects the wording of Matthew 5:15. The point is not to criticize Luke's practice in writing but to show that he carefully drew on sources, and rather than

harmonizing his accounts, he was inclined to include redundant information when he was unsure whether the two accounts spoke of the same event.

Luke also followed the order of the Gospel of Mark for the most part, although there are several places where Luke reshaped the order of Mark. The assumption is that Luke rearranged Mark's Gospel when he had another source that was more credible or more closely associated with an eyewitness. The source may have been the hypothetical "Q" document, in which Matthew and Luke placed great emphasis, or it may have been personal contact with eyewitnesses. In any case, Luke's structure and organizational procedure is not literary but instead historical. He appears to have reviewed his sources, accepted one as more authoritative, and then presented the story according to his own interests.

It may also be that Luke 1–2 are entirely the work of Luke, who seems to have formally begun his Gospel account in Luke 3:1–2. The two preliminary chapters add depth to the story, much in the same way that Matthew added chapters 1–2 to his account to help readers understand events associated with Jesus's birth. Luke 3:1–2 broadly parallels Mark 1:1, indicating that Luke felt he had something original to contribute to the telling of the Gospel story. This would also help explain why Luke at times includes Mary's thoughts or feelings (Luke 2:19). ॐ

INTRODUCTION (MT 1:1; MK 1:1)

1 [1]Inasmuch as many have set forth in order an account of the things that have been accomplished among us, [2]just as they who were eyewitnesses and ministers of the word passed them on to us from the beginning, [3]it seemed good to me, having an accurate understanding of all things from the first days, to write to you in order, noble Theophilus, [4]that you might know with certainty the things about which you were instructed.

THE PROMISE OF JOHN'S BIRTH

[5]It came to pass in the days of Herod, king of Judea, that there was a priest whose name was Zechariah, from the division of Abijah, and his wife was from the daughters of Aaron, and her name was Elizabeth. [6]They were both righteous before God, walking in all the commandments and ordinances of the Lord, and they were blameless. [7]They had no child because Elizabeth was not able to have children, and both were advanced in years. [8]And it came to pass that as he served as priest, in the administration of his duty before God, [9]according to the custom of the priesthood, his lot was to enter the temple of the Lord and to burn incense. [10]And the whole congregation prayed outside at the hour of incense. [11]And an angel of the Lord appeared to him, standing on the right of the altar of incense. [12]And when Zechariah saw it, he was troubled and fear came upon him. [13]But the angel said to him, "Do not fear, Zechariah, because your prayer was heard, and your wife Elizabeth will have a son, and you will call his name John. [14]And you

---

1:1 Luke asserts that others have written before him and that he wishes to set *in order* the events that have transpired among the followers of Jesus. He therefore begins with an acknowledged historical interest, although the wording he uses does not mean that he is promoting his account as being written in precise historical order. The Joseph Smith Translation begins *As I am a messenger of Jesus Christ, and knowing that . . .* **1:1–2:52** These stories are unique to Luke and reflect his interests in recovering the voices of Mary and Elizabeth and their parts in the retelling of Jesus's birth. **1:2** Luke knew some disciples and followers of Jesus from the eyewitness generation, but he was not himself an eyewitness, as he notes here. **1:3** *Theophilus* may be the proper name of the person who commissioned Luke to write, but it may also be intended generically as *a friend of God*, which represents the meaning of the Greek words used to compose the name *Theophilus*. **1:4** *Instructed* represents the translation of the Greek verb *katechethes*, from which English derives the *catechesis*. Many Christians use this term to refer to instruction in the beliefs and tenets of Christianity. **1:5** For a note on Herod the king (died 5/4 BCE), see Matthew 2:1. David divided the priestly families into twenty-four divisions in order to organize their service in the temple. The order of service was determined by lot (1 Chronicles 24:5), and the division of Abijah is noted in 1 Chronicles 24:10. *Daughters of Aaron* further emphasizes that Elizabeth was of priestly lineage. **1:5–6** Luke places special emphasis on their priestly heritage and their obedience to the law of Moses (*they were both righteous before God*). **1:6** The word translated as *ordinances* is *righteousness* and refers to the directives of the Law that lead a person to righteousness. Alluded to in Doctrine and Covenants 136:4. **1:7** A possible parallel to Sarah's age in Genesis 17:17. **1:9** This is the first occurrence of the word *priesthood* in Luke, and the word is an abstract noun built on the word for *priest*. It therefore refers to the things that a *Jewish priest* was required to do in his service in the temple. The word occurs only here in the Gospels and in Hebrews 7:5, 11–12, 24 and 1 Peter 2:5, 9. Having been chosen by lot to burn incense, Zechariah fulfilled the requirements set forth in Exodus 30:7–9. This lot was special, perhaps even coveted because it put the priest in close proximity to the veil of the temple as the priest helped facilitate the ascension of the prayers of God's people (Psalm 141:2). **1:10** In Acts 3:1, Peter and John likely enter the temple at this same hour. For the role of incense in prayer, see Psalm 141:2. **1:13, 17** Commentary on this verse can be found in Doctrine and Covenants 27:7.

will feel joy and gladness, and many will rejoice in his birth. ¹⁵He will be great before the Lord, and he will not drink wine or strong drink, and he will be filled with the Holy Spirit from the time of being in his mother's womb, ¹⁶and he will turn many of the children of Israel to the Lord their God. ¹⁷He will go before the Lord in the spirit and power of Elijah, to turn the hearts of the fathers to the children and the disobedient to the wisdom of the righteous, to prepare the way of the Lord for a people who are prepared." ¹⁸And Zechariah said to the angel, "How will I know this? I am elderly, and my wife is advanced in years." ¹⁹The angel answered him, "I am Gabriel, who stands before God, and I was sent to speak to you and to declare this good news to you. ²⁰You will be silent, and you will not be able to speak until these things come to pass because you did not believe my words, which will be fulfilled at their right time."

²¹And the people waited for Zechariah, and they were surprised that he delayed in the temple. ²²When he came out he was not able to speak to them, and they realized that he had seen a vision in the temple because he signaled to them and could not speak. ²³And when the days of his service were ended, he returned to his own home. ²⁴After those days his wife, Elizabeth, conceived, and for five months she hid herself, saying, ²⁵"The Lord has done this to me in the days in which he looked on me favorably to take away my disgrace among my people."

THE ANNUNCIATION OF JESUS'S BIRTH

²⁶In the sixth month of her pregnancy, the angel Gabriel was sent from God to a town in Galilee called Nazareth, ²⁷to a virgin promised to a man named Joseph from the house of David, and the name of the virgin was Mary. ²⁸And he came to her and said, "Greetings, favored daughter; the Lord is with you." ²⁹But she was troubled upon hearing his words, and she wondered at what type of greeting this might be. ³⁰And the angel said to her, "Do not fear, Mary; you have found grace with God. ³¹You will conceive and bear a son and you will name him Jesus. ³²He will be

---

1:15 The statement that he will not drink wine or strong drink is a quotation from Numbers 6:3 and Leviticus 10:9. It recalls the lifestyle of Samuel (1 Samuel 1:11). Alluded to in Doctrine and Covenants 84:27. **1:16–17** This is Luke's first allusion to Isaiah 40:3. **1:17** The spirit and power of Elijah echoes Malachi 4:5–6. **1:19** The mention of Gabriel recalls Daniel 9:21. See also Doctrine and Covenants 128:21. **1:24** Luke is the only evangelist to quote the words of Elizabeth. Elizabeth's words may echo Genesis 30:23. Compare Isaiah 4:1. **1:25** Elizabeth's inability to have children contrasts with the promises of Genesis 17:6 (see also Psalm 127:3; Leviticus 26:9), and hence it was viewed as a disgrace to be unable to bear children. **1:26** This was the sixth month of Elizabeth's pregnancy, although the Greek says simply *in the sixth month*, and Luke is structuring the narrative around the months of her pregnancy (see 1:24 *five months* and 1:36 *the sixth month*). For Gabriel, see Daniel 8:15–16. This verse and the one following it are echoed in 1 Nephi 11:13, 20. **1:27** The precise translation of the verb describing Joseph and Mary's relationship is problematic today because of differing marriage customs. *Engaged* or *promised* most closely approximates their status. They were not officially married. They were, however, planning for their marriage, and a dowry had been exchanged or promised. The translation of the word *parthenos* as *virgin* is possible, but Luke's account focuses on the fact that Mary does not have a husband and not on the question of chastity. Mary was clearly chaste, but the story in Luke emphasizes her ability to hear the word of the Lord and to accept God's will in her life. Thus, *young woman* is also an accurate translation of *parthenos*. Luke spells her name *Mariam*. **1:28** A number of manuscripts add *blessed are you among women* to the end of this verse. It appears to be a later addition. **1:29** Mary here wonders about the type of greeting and whether it is from God.

great, and he will be called the Son of the Most High, and the Lord God will give him the throne of David his father. ³³And he will rule the house of Jacob for eternity, and there will be no end to his kingdom." ³⁴And Mary said to the angel, "How will this be when I do not have a husband?" ³⁵The angel answered, "The Holy Spirit will come on you, and the power of the Most High will overshadow you. Therefore, the child that will be born will be holy, and he will be called the Son of God. ³⁶And Elizabeth, your relative, has also conceived a son in her old age, and this is her sixth month of pregnancy, and she was called barren. ³⁷But with God nothing is impossible." ³⁸And Mary said, "Behold, I am the servant of the Lord. Let it happen to me according to your word." And the angel left her.

MARY'S VISIT TO ELIZABETH

³⁹Mary arose in those days and went with haste to the hill country, to a town in Judea, ⁴⁰and she entered the house of Zechariah, and she greeted Elizabeth. ⁴¹And it happened that as Elizabeth heard Mary's greeting, the baby in her womb leaped, and Elizabeth was filled with the Holy Spirit. ⁴²And she declared in a loud voice and said, "You are blessed among women, and the child in your womb is blessed. ⁴³Why has this happened to me that the mother of my Lord would come to me? ⁴⁴When the sound of your greeting was in my ears, the baby in my womb leaped in joy. ⁴⁵Blessed is she who believes that what was spoken to her by the Lord will be fulfilled."

⁴⁶And Mary said,

"My soul magnifies the Lord,
⁴⁷and my spirit rejoices in God my Savior,
⁴⁸because he has looked on the humble position of his servant.
Behold, all generations will call me blessed.
⁴⁹For he who is mighty has done great things to me,
and holy is his name.
⁵⁰And his mercy from generation to generation
is on those who fear him.
⁵¹He has acted in power with his arm,
and he scattered the proud by the thoughts of their hearts.
⁵²He brought down the mighty from their thrones,
and lifted up the lowly;
⁵³he filled the hungry with good,
and the rich he sent away empty.
⁵⁴He helped his servant Israel,
to remember mercy,
⁵⁵as he said to our fathers,
to Abraham and his descendants for eternity."

1:33 *No end to his kingdom* echoes the promise of Isaiah 9:7. **1:34** Mary asks literally, *How will this be when I do not know a man?* **1:35** See 1 Nephi 11:18–20; Alma 7:10. **1:36** *Relative* refers to a near relative, including an aunt, a cousin, or possibly someone more remote. The implication is that Mary would be of the house of Levi, but elsewhere Paul notes that Jesus was descended through David (Romans 1:3). The genealogies of Matthew and Luke both report Joseph's lineage (Matthew 1:1–17; Luke 3:23–38). **1:37** A second possible allusion to Sarah (see Genesis 18:14). **1:39** The *hill country* may refer to Hebron (see Joshua 21:11). **1:46–55** This passage, written in a loose poetic style, is known as *Mary's Song of Praise*, or *The Magnificat*. It may intentionally parallel Hannah's prayer (see 1 Samuel 2:1–10).

⁵⁶And Mary remained with her for three months, and then she returned to her own home.

THE BIRTH OF JOHN THE BAPTIST

⁵⁷Then the time came for Elizabeth's delivery, and she bore a son. ⁵⁸And when her neighbors and relatives heard that the Lord had shown his great mercy to her, they rejoiced with her. ⁵⁹And it came to pass that on the eighth day they came to circumcise the boy, and they intended to call him by the name of his father, Zechariah, ⁶⁰but his mother answered them, "No, he will be called John." ⁶¹And they said to her, "None of your relatives are called by this name." ⁶²And they signaled to his father regarding what he would call him. ⁶³And he took a writing tablet and wrote, "His name is John," and they all wondered. ⁶⁴And right away his mouth was opened, and his tongue released, and he spoke, praising God. ⁶⁵And fear fell upon all their neighbors, and these words were declared all around the hill country of Judea. ⁶⁶All who heard them pondered them in their hearts, saying, "What will this child be then?" because the hand of the Lord was with him. ⁶⁷And Zechariah his father was filled with the Holy Spirit, and he prophesied,

⁶⁸"Blessed is the Lord, the God of Israel,
  because he looked on and brought
  redemption to his people,

⁶⁹and he did raise a *horn of salvation* to us
  in the house of David his servant,
⁷⁰as he spoke through the mouth of his holy prophets from ancient times,
    ⁷¹that we would be saved from our
    enemies and from the hands of all
    who despise us.
⁷²He has shown mercy to our ancestors
    and remembered his holy covenant.
⁷³He swore an oath to our father Abraham to enable us,
    ⁷⁴after being delivered from the
    hands of our enemies, to serve
    him without fear ⁷⁵in holiness and
    righteousness before him all the
    days of our lives.
⁷⁶And you, child, you will be called a prophet of the Most High,
    and you will go before the Lord to
    prepare his ways,
⁷⁷to give us knowledge of salvation to his people
    for the forgiveness of sins
⁷⁸through the tender mercy of our God
    when the day dawns on us from
    on high
⁷⁹to give light to those sitting in darkness and the shadow of death,
    to guide our feet in the way of
    peace."

⁸⁰And the child grew and was strong in his spirit, and he was in the desert until the day of his appearance to Israel.

1:56 By Luke's calculation, Mary would have been with Elizabeth during her ninth month of pregnancy, but according to Luke's sequence (Luke 1:57), Mary departed before John the Baptist was born. **1:59** The commandment of circumcision is set forth in Genesis 17:12; 21:4. Echoed in 2 Nephi 3:15. **1:69** Quotation from Psalm 18:2. **1:70** Echoed in Alma 7:25. **1:76** Zechariah's prophecy alludes to Isaiah 40:3 and Malachi 3:1. **1:78** *Tender mercy* is an allusion to the Psalms (see, for example, Psalms 40:11; 51:1; 69:16).

THE BIRTH OF JESUS (MT 1:18–25)

2 ¹And it came to pass in those days that a decree went out from Caesar Augustus that all the world should be enrolled, ²and this census was first given when Cyrenius was governor of Syria. ³And all went to be enrolled, each to their own city, ⁴and Joseph went up from Nazareth to Judea to the city of David, which is called Bethlehem, because he was from the house and lineage of David, ⁵to be registered with Mary, his promised spouse, who was pregnant at the time. ⁶And while they were there, the days for her delivery arrived, ⁷and she bore her firstborn son, and she wrapped him in swaddling clothes and laid him in a manger, because there was no room for them in the guest chamber.

THE SHEPHERDS

⁸And there were shepherds in that same region in the field keeping watch over their sheep at night, ⁹and an angel of the Lord stood above them and the glory of the Lord shone around them, and they were very afraid. ¹⁰But the angel said to them, "Do not fear; I bring you good news of great joy for all people, ¹¹because your Savior, who is Christ the Lord, is born this day in the city of David. ¹²And this will be a sign to you: you will find the baby swaddled and lying in a manger." ¹³And suddenly there was with the angel a heavenly army, praising God and saying, ¹⁴"Glory to God in the highest, and on the earth peace to men and women with whom he is pleased."

¹⁵When the angels went away into heaven, the shepherds said to one another, "Let us go to Bethlehem and see this thing that has happened, which the Lord has made known to us." ¹⁶And they hurried and came to Mary and Joseph and found the baby lying in a manger. ¹⁷When they saw him, they reported to them what

---

2:1 Augustus ruled from 27 BCE until his death on 19 August 14 CE. As Luke notes, Augustus ordered a census to be taken in order for taxes to be collected. If Acts 5:37 refers to the same census, then it was interpreted by some Jews to be a controversial action. The Joseph Smith Translation says *all his empire*. **2:2** Luke notes that the census, or *enrollment*, was carried out under *Cyrenius*. This Cyrenius is probably Publius Suplicius Quirinius, the Roman governor of Syria. That census took place in 6 CE, roughly ten years after the death of Herod the Great (died circa March 4 BCE). Our historical sources do not permit certainty on the issue of whether Luke associated the birth of Jesus with the wrong governor of Syria or whether there was an earlier census at the time of Jesus's birth. Quintilius Varus was the governor of Syria at the time of Jesus's birth. Some scholars postulate that the census took a number of years to be completed and was only finalized in Cyrenius's day. **2:4** *David's city* was located south of Jerusalem (see 1 Samuel 16:1, where Jesse, David's father, is mentioned in connection with the city of David). **2:5** Luke's wording may mean that Joseph and Mary were not married when they traveled to Bethlehem for the census. Some later scribes attempted to correct this so that the text reads *to his betrothed wife*. **2:7** The word translated as *manger* refers to the crib where animals were fed or their stalls where they slept. **2:9** The same language is used to describe the revelatory reception of Doctrine and Covenants 76:19. **2:10** Alluded to in Mosiah 3:3; Doctrine and Covenants 31:3. **2:11** A *Savior . . . who is Christ* implies political and religious deliverance. *Savior* was at times used to refer to the Ptolemaic emperors, and *Christ* is the Greek translation of the word *Messiah*, also a deliverer (see Isaiah 43:3). **2:12** An echo of Isaiah 7:14. **2:14** *A heavenly army* translates a word that is commonly used to describe a group of soldiers or celestial constellations. The Greek text has only *men* and not *men and women*. There is a textual variation for the phrase *with whom he is pleased*. Some good manuscripts have *goodwill among people* instead.

they had been told concerning this child. [18]And everyone who heard it wondered about the things the shepherds told them. [19]But Mary treasured all these things and pondered them in her heart. [20]And the shepherds returned, giving glory and praising God for all the things they had heard and seen, just as it had been told to them.

JESUS'S PRESENTATION AT THE TEMPLE

[21]When eight days were completed, it was time to circumcise him, and he was called Jesus, the name that was given by the angel while he was in the womb. [22]When the days came for their purification, according to the law of Moses, they took him to Jerusalem in order to present him to the Lord, [23]as it was written in the Law of the Lord, that "*every firstborn male will be called holy to the Lord*," [24]and to offer a sacrifice according to that which is said in the Law of the Lord, "*a pair of turtledoves or two pigeons*."

[25]There was a man in Jerusalem whose name was Simeon: he was righteous and devout, and he looked forward to the consolation of Israel, and the Holy Spirit was on him. [26]It had been revealed to him by the Holy Spirit that he would not see death until he had seen the Messiah of the Lord. [27]And he came in the Spirit to the temple, and when the parents brought the child Jesus in order to do for him according to the custom of the Law, [28]he lifted him up in his arms and praised God, saying,

> [29]"Lord, now let your servant depart
> > in peace according to your word,
> [30]because I have seen with my eyes
> your salvation,
> > [31]which you have prepared in
> > the presence of all people,
> [32]a light for revelation to the Gentiles
> > and for the glory of your people
> > Israel."

[33]And his father and mother were amazed at what was said concerning him, [34]and Simeon blessed them and said to Mary, his mother, "Behold, this child is set for the fall and rising again of many in Israel and for a sign to be spoken against [35]so that the thoughts of many hearts may be revealed, and your own soul will be pierced by a sword."

[36]There was a prophetess named Anna, a daughter of Phanuel, from the tribe of Asher, she was also of a great age, having lived with her husband for seven years after her marriage, [37]and then as a widow until she was eighty-four years old. She did not depart from the temple, worshipping in fasting and prayer night and day. [38]In that very hour she came up and

---

2:19 Mary *treasures* the events of the birth (see also Luke 2:35, 51). **2:21** See note on Luke 1:59. **2:22** The requirements for Mary's purification are set forth in Leviticus 12:2–8. Because Luke wrote *their purification* instead of *her purification*, scribes attempted to correct this so that it referred only to Mary's required purification. The best and earliest manuscripts have *their*. **2:23** Quotation from Exodus 13:2. **2:24** Quotation from Leviticus 12:8 (see also Leviticus 5:11). **2:25** The word *consolation* may be an echo of Isaiah 40:1, 61:2. The word means *comfort, consoling*, and *reconciliation*. Luke may have intended it here as a foreshadowing of the consolation that took place in Acts 15:31. **2:26** The Greek text reads *the Lord's Christ*. **2:27** Guidelines for the ransom offering are set forth in Numbers 18:15–16. **2:29–32** These verses are referred to as the *Nunc Dimittis*, the Latin translation of *now let your servant depart*, or more literally *now you are sending me away*. **2:29** Luke uses a different word for *Lord* in this verse, one that can also be translated as *Master*. **2:31** A possible allusion to Isaiah 25:1–7. **2:34** A possible allusion to Isaiah 8:14–15 and 11:10–12. **2:36** Anna is a *prophetess* (compare Acts 21:9). **2:38** Anna speaks of the *redemption* or *ransom* of Jerusalem, whereas Simeon speaks of *consolation*. The word that Anna uses refers more specifically to forgiveness of sin.

began praising God and speaking of him to all who were looking for the redemption of Jerusalem.

THE MOVE TO NAZARETH (MT 2:19–23)

³⁹And when they had finished all things according to the Law of the Lord, they returned to Galilee, to their own town, Nazareth. ⁴⁰The young boy grew and became strong, and he was filled with wisdom, and the grace of God was on him.

JESUS IN THE TEMPLE

⁴¹And his parents went annually to Jerusalem for the Feast of the Passover. ⁴²And when he was twelve years old, they went up according to custom. ⁴³When the feast ended, as they were returning, the boy Jesus remained in Jerusalem and his parents did not know it. ⁴⁴They thought he was among their company of travelers, and they went a day's journey and then looked for him among their relatives and acquaintances, ⁴⁵and when they did not find him, they returned to Jerusalem in order to look for him there. ⁴⁶After three days they found him in the temple, sitting among the teachers, listening to them, and asking them questions. ⁴⁷All who heard him wondered at his understanding and answers. ⁴⁸And when they saw him, they were amazed, and his mother said to him, "Child, why did you do this to us? Your father and I have been anxiously looking for you." ⁴⁹But he said to them, "Why did you search for me? Did you not know that I must be in my Father's house?" ⁵⁰And they did not understand the saying that he spoke to them, ⁵¹and he returned with them and came to Nazareth, and he was obedient to them. But his mother kept all these sayings in her heart. ⁵²And Jesus grew in wisdom and in stature and in favor with God and people.

JOHN THE BAPTIST (MT 3:1–12; MK 1:1–8; JN 1:19–28)

3 ¹In the fifteenth year of the reign of Tiberius Caesar (when Pontius Pilate was governor in Judea and Herod was tetrarch of Galilee, his brother Philip was tetrarch of Ituraea and Trachonitis, and Lysanias was

---

2:41 Luke may allude to the requirement set forth in Exodus 23:17. **2:42** Luke implies that it was customary or even expected for families to travel to Jerusalem for the Passover. **2:46** The Joseph Smith Translation reads *and they were hearing him, and asking him questions.* **2:49** Jesus's response suggests that they had not looked for him in the temple and that if they had, they would have found him quickly.

Greek uses an idiom to convey Jesus's response to his parents that older translations rendered as *I must be about my Father's business.* Today scholars recognize it as a call to receive instruction in the house of the Lord, i.e., the temple. **2:50** Compare Mosiah 27:12. **2:52** The wording suggests that Jesus got along well with God and with those who knew him.

3:1 The *fifteenth year of Tiberius Caesar* is rather difficult to calculate because Tiberius ruled jointly with Augustus starting in 12 CE, and then as sole emperor in 14 CE.

The Regions of Abilene, Ituraea, and Trachonitis
Map by Cassie Howe and Ryan Shields, ThinkSpatial, BYU Geography

tetrarch of Abilene, [2]Annas and Caiaphas being high priests), the word of God came to John, son of Zechariah, in the desert. [3]And he went into all the region of the Jordan River, declaring a baptism of repentance for the forgiveness of sins. [4]As it is written in the book of the words of Isaiah the prophet, *"A voice shouting in the desert, prepare the way of the Lord, make his paths straight.* [5]*Every valley will be filled, and every mountain and hill will be made low, and the crooked way will be made straight, and the rough ways will be made smooth,* [6]*and all flesh will see the salvation of God."* [7]He said to the crowd that came to be baptized by him, "You offspring of snakes, who has warned you to flee from the coming wrath? [8]Bear fruits worthy of repentance, and do not begin to say to yourselves, 'We have Abraham for a father,' because I say that God is able from these stones to bring forth children to Abraham. [9]Already the ax lies at the root of the trees, and every tree that does not bear good fruit will be cut down and thrown in the fire."

[10]And the crowds asked him, "What then should we do?" [11]He answered them, "Whoever has two tunics, let that person give to someone who has none, and whoever has food must do likewise." [12]And tax collectors came to be baptized, and they said to him, "Teacher, what should we do?" [13]He said to them, "Collect no more than you are allotted." [14]Some soldiers asked him, "And us, what should we do?" He said to them, "Do not extort money or make false accusation, and be satisfied with your earnings."

[15]The people were filled with interest and were wondering in their hearts concerning John and whether or not he might be the Christ. [16]John answered them all, "I baptize you in water, but the one who is coming is greater than I.

If Luke meant the first date, which scholars often favor, then the date would be 26/27 CE. If he intended the latter date, when Tiberius was sole ruler, then the date would be 28/29 CE. Also, *fifteen years* is probably to be counted inclusively, but that is also uncertain. The date range thus falls between 26 CE and 29 CE. Herod Antipas was the tetrarch of Galilee. Pilate ruled Judea from 26 CE until 36 CE. **3:2** *Annas and Caiaphas*. Joseph Caiaphas served as high priest from 18 CE until 36 CE. Annas served from 6 CE until 15 CE. The Roman prefect Valerius Gratus was responsible for appointing Caiaphas. **3:4** The Joseph Smith Translation of this verse reads *As it is written in the book of the prophet Esaias, and these are the words, saying, The voice of one crying in the wilderness, Prepare ye the way of the Lord, and make his paths straight. For behold, and lo, he shall come as it is written in the book of the prophets, to take away the sins of the world, and to bring salvation unto the heathen nations; to gather together those who are lost, which are of the sheepfold of Israel; yea, even her dispersed and afflicted; and also to prepare the way, and make possible the preaching of the gospel unto the Gentiles. And to be a light unto all who sit in darkness, unto the uttermost parts of the earth; to bring to pass the resurrection from the dead, and to ascend up on high, to dwell on the right hand of the Father, until the fulness of time, and the law and the testimony shall be sealed, and the keys of the kingdom shall be delivered up again unto the Father; to administer justice unto all; to come down in judgment upon all, and to convince all the ungodly of their ungodly deeds, which they have committed; and all this is in the day that he shall come, for it is a day of power.* **3:4–6** Quotation from Isaiah 40:3–5. Only Luke quotes verses 4–5. **3:5** Alluded to in 1 Nephi 17:46. **3:6** The idea of *seeing salvation* is echoed in Mosiah 15:31. **3:7** See Matthew 3:7; 12:34; 23:33; Doctrine and Covenants 121:23. **3:8** Luke's wording is slightly different; he writes, *Do not begin to say* instead of *Do not think to say*. Luke's account may correct Matthew's somewhat awkward *think to say*. **3:9** Compare Doctrine and Covenants 97:7. **3:11** *Tunics* refers to the piece of clothing worn underneath a cloak and directly touching the skin. *Tunics* varied in length, and many were short and worn above the knee. **3:12–14** These verses are unique to Luke, and they expand John's circle of listeners. **3:16** The word translated as *greater* can also mean *stronger, more powerful*, and *mightier*.

I am not worthy to untie the strap of his sandals. He will baptize you in the Holy Spirit and fire. [17]His winnowing fork is in his hand, and he will clean his threshing floor, and he will gather the wheat to his granary, and the chaff he will burn with unquenchable fire." [18]And he declared the gospel to the people, exhorting them in many other things.

JOHN THE BAPTIST ARRESTED (MT 14:3–4; MK 6:17–18)

[19]But Herod the tetrarch, who had been rebuked by him concerning Herodias, the wife of his brother Philip, and because of all the evil things Herod had done, [20]he added to all those things by confining John in prison.

THE BAPTISM OF JESUS (MT 3:13–17; MK 1:9–11; JN 1:29–34)

[21]And it came to pass, when all the people were baptized, Jesus was also baptized. While Jesus prayed, the heavens were opened, [22]and the Holy Spirit descended on him in bodily form, like a dove, and there was a voice from heaven, "You are my beloved Son; in you I am well pleased."

THE GENEALOGY OF JESUS (MT 1:1–17)

[23]And Jesus was beginning to be about thirty years old, being the son (as was supposed) of Joseph, the son of Heli, [24]the son of Matthat, the son of Levi, the son of Melchi, the son of Jannai, the son of Joseph, [25]the son of Mattathias, the son of Amos, the son of Nahum, the son of Esli, the son of Naggai, [26]the son of Maath, the son of Mattathias, the son of Semein, the son of Josech, the son of Joda, [27]the son of Joanan, the son of Rhesa, the son of Zerubbabel, the son of Shealtiel, the son of Neri, [28]the son of Melchi, the son of Addi, the son of Cosam, the son of Elmadam, the son of Er, [29]the son of Joshua, the son of Eliezer, the son of Jorim, the son of Matthat, the son of Levi, [30]the son of Simeon, the son of Judah, the son of Joseph, the son of Jonam, the son of Eliakim, [31]the son of Melea, the son of Menna, the son of Mattatha, the son of Nathan, the son of David, [32]the son of Jesse, the son of Obed, the son of Boaz, the son of Sala, the son of Nahshon, [33]the son of Amminadab, the son of Admin, the son of Arni, the son of Hezron, the son of Perez, the son of Judah, [34]the son of Jacob, the son of Isaac, the son of Abraham, the son of Terah, the son of Nahor, [35]the son of Serug, the son of Reu, the son of Peleg, the son of Eber, the son of Shelah, [36]the son of Cainan, the son of Arphaxad, the son of Shem, the son of Noah, the son of Lamech, [37]the son of Methuselah, the son of Enoch, the son of Jared, the son of Mahalaleel, the son of Cainan, [38]the

---

3:19 This is Herod Antipas, who ruled from 4 BCE until 39 CE. He was commonly known as Antipas, and he ruled the area west of the Sea of Galilee and Perea to the west of the River Jordan. *By him* refers to John the Baptist's rebuke of Herod Antipas (see note on Matthew 14:1 and Mark 6:17, 19). **3:22** Luke's wording makes it clear that the Holy Spirit descended softly, as a dove would land, and that Jesus experienced a physical or bodily presence of the Holy Spirit. Luke's wording differs from the other Gospels in his description (Matthew 3:16; Mark 1:10, John 1:32). Also, the voice from heaven is directed to Jesus using the second person singular. A significant textual variant occurs for this passage, and instead of *You are my beloved Son; in you I am well pleased*, some later manuscripts note that the Father said, *You are my Son, and I have begotten you on this day* (compare Psalm 2:7). The better manuscripts record the passage as it is translated herein. Compare 2 Nephi 31:8. **3:23** Jesus was about *thirty years old*, but Luke is imprecise in his estimation. **3:23–31** Many of the names from Joseph's genealogy are not recorded in any other known sources. Luke's genealogy may intentionally promote the idea of a common ancestor for all humanity, and therefore he traces Jesus's lineage to Adam.

son of Enos, the son of Seth, the son of Adam, the son of God.

THE TEMPTATION OF JESUS
(MT 4:1–11; MK 1:12–13)

4 ¹Jesus, full of the Holy Spirit, returned from the Jordan River and while in the Spirit was led into the desert, ²where he was tempted for forty days by the devil. He did not eat anything in those days, and when those days ended, he was hungry. ³The devil said to him, "If you are the Son of God, command this stone to become bread." ⁴And Jesus answered him, "It is written, '*One does not live on bread alone.*'"

⁵And he led Jesus up and showed him all the kingdoms of the world in a single moment. ⁶And the devil said to him, "I will give you all this authority and their glory, because it has been given to me, and I give it to whomever I wish. ⁷If you then will bow down before me, it will all be yours." ⁸Jesus answered him, "It is written, '*You shall worship the Lord your God, and you shall serve him alone.*'"

⁹And he led him to Jerusalem and had him stand on the pinnacle of the temple and said to him, "If you are the Son of God, throw yourself down from here. ¹⁰For it is written, '*He will command his angels concerning you, to protect you,*' ¹¹and '*they will lift you up in their hands so that you do not strike your foot against a stone.*'"

¹²And Jesus answered him, "It is said, '*You shall not test the Lord your God.*'" ¹³When the devil had ended every temptation, he departed from him until it was an opportune time. *whea? what?*

THE EARLY GALILEAN MINISTRY
(MT 4:12–17; MK 1:14–15; JN 4:1–3, 43–46A)

¹⁴And Jesus returned in the power of the Spirit to Galilee, and a report of him spread through the entire region. ¹⁵And he began to teach in their synagogues, being praised by all.

REJECTION OF JESUS AT NAZARETH (MT 13:53–58; MK 6:1–6)

¹⁶And he came to Nazareth, where he had been raised, and he came to the synagogue, according to his usual practice on the Sabbath day, and he stood up to read. ¹⁷And the book of the prophet Isaiah was given to him, and he unrolled the scroll and found the place where it was written, ¹⁸"*The Spirit of the Lord is upon me, because he has anointed me to preach the good news to the poor. He has sent me to declare release to the captives, and the restoring of sight to the blind, to deliver the captives,* ¹⁹*and to declare the acceptable year of the Lord.*" ²⁰And when he had rolled up the scroll, he gave it back to the attendant and then sat down, and the eyes of all those in the synagogue were looking at him. ²¹And he began to say to them, "Today this scripture is fulfilled

---

4:2 Luke explicitly notes that Jesus did *not eat anything*. Matthew signals a similar meaning with *fasted forty days and forty nights* (Matthew 4:2). Compare Exodus 34:28; 1 Kings 19:8. **4:4** Quotation from Deuteronomy 8:3. **4:5** The meaning of *a single moment* is not the same as *all at once*, but rather *in an instant*. The Joseph Smith Translation reads *And the spirit taketh him*. **4:8** Quotation from Deuteronomy 6:13. **4:9** The Joseph Smith Translation reads *And the spirit brought him*. **4:10–11** Quotation from Psalm 91:11–12. **4:12** Quotation from Deuteronomy 6:16. Matthew notes that this saying *is written*, but Luke's version appears to trace it to the oral tradition (*it is said*). **4:15** Luke speaks of *their synagogues*, indicating that he did not likely attend those synagogues and that he saw himself as an outsider. **4:18–19** Quotation from Isaiah 58:6; 61:1–2a (LXX; see also Isaiah 42:7). The quotation characterizes Jesus's ministry to the poor or foreshadows their release from oppression. **4:19** This is a *Jubilee year* (see Leviticus 25:10; Isaiah 61:2). Compare Doctrine and Covenants 93:51.

while you hear it." ²²And everyone testified concerning him, and they were amazed at the kind words that came from his mouth, and they said, "Is this not the son of Joseph?" ²³And he said to them, "Surely you will tell me this proverb, 'Physician, heal yourself. The things we have heard that were done in Capernaum, do them likewise in your own country.'" ²⁴And he said, "Truly I say to you that no prophet is acceptable in his own country. ²⁵But in truth I tell you that there were many widows in Israel in the days of Elijah, when heaven was shut for three and a half years, when there was a great famine over all the land. ²⁶And Elijah was sent to none of them except to a woman who was a widow at Zarephath in Sidon. ²⁷And there were many with leprosy in Israel when Elisha was prophet, but no one was cleansed except Naaman the Syrian."

²⁸When they heard this, everyone in the synagogue was filled with anger, ²⁹and they stood and threw him out of the town, and led him to the edge of a hill on which their town was built, so that they might cast him down from there. ³⁰But he passed through their midst and went away.

HEALING OF A MAN WITH AN UNCLEAN SPIRIT (MK 1:21–28)

³¹And he went down to Capernaum, a town of Galilee, and he was teaching them on the Sabbath. ³²And they were filled with astonishment at his teaching because his word was with authority. ³³There was in the synagogue a man with an unclean spirit, and he cried out in a loud voice, ³⁴"Get away! What do you want with us, Jesus of Nazareth? Have you come to destroy us? I know who you are, the Holy One of God." ³⁵But Jesus rebuked him, saying, "Be silent and come out of him." After it threw him down in their midst, the demon came out of him, but it did not hurt him. ³⁶And they were amazed, all of them, and they discussed this with one another, saying, "What is this teaching? He casts out unclean spirits with authority and power, and they depart!" ³⁷And a report concerning him went through every place of the surrounding region.

HEALING OF PETER'S MOTHER-IN-LAW (MT 8:14–17; MK 1:29–34)

³⁸But he arose from the synagogue and entered the house of Simon, and Simon's mother-in-law was ill with a high fever, and they asked him about her. ³⁹And he stood over her and rebuked the fever, and it left her. And immediately she stood and began to serve them.

⁴⁰When the sun set, everyone who had any sick with illnesses brought them to him, and he laid his hands on each one of them, and he healed them. ⁴¹And demons came out of many, crying out, "You are the Son of God!" And he rebuked them, and

---

4:24 Luke's account of the rejection in Nazareth may foreshadow a shift in the ministry to Capernaum and other towns and villages in Galilee (see Luke 4:31). **4:25** Reference to 1 Kings 17:1–16. **4:26** Zarephath (also spelled Sarepta) is located on the coast between Tyre and Sidon and was originally a Phoenician city (see Obadiah 1:20). **4:27** For the story of Naaman the Syrian, see 2 Kings 5:1–14. **4:29–30** Their actions appear to draw on Deuteronomy 13:9–10 as a precedent. **4:30** Luke offers no explanation as to what diffused the hostility against Jesus, and yet he ascribes no miracle to his delivery or departure. **4:34** On *The Holy One of God*, see Habakkuk 1:12; Isaiah 48:17. The demon cries out, *What is it to you and us?*, which means something like *What do we have in common?* **4:38** Peter was not a disciple, according to Luke, when this miracle took place (see Luke 5:1–11). **4:39** The verb describing her ministering or serving is founded on the same root as the noun for a deacon. **4:41** Jesus forbids the demons to declare him to be the Son of God (see also Luke 5:14; 8:28). In Luke, Jesus does not forbid believers to declare him to be the Christ or Son of God. Some later Greek manuscripts have *the Christ, the Son of God*, but the earlier and better manuscripts preserve the text as it is translated here.

he forbade them to speak, because they knew that he was the Christ.

JESUS DEPARTS FROM CAPERNAUM (MK 1:35–39)

⁴²When it was day, he departed to a deserted place, and the crowds sought for him, and they came and would have prevented him from leaving. ⁴³But he said to them, "I must proclaim the good news of the kingdom of God to other towns because I was sent for this purpose." ⁴⁴And then he taught in the synagogues of Judea.

JESUS CALLS HIS FIRST DISCIPLES (MT 4:18–22; MK 1:16–20)

5 ¹And it came to pass that as he stood near the shore of Lake Gennesaret, he was pressed on by a crowd who sought to hear the word of God. ²And he saw two boats near the shore, but the fishermen had departed and were washing their nets. ³And he entered one of the boats, which was Simon's, and he asked him to push back a little way from the land, and he sat down and taught the crowds from the boat.

⁴When he stopped speaking, he said to Simon, "Push out into the deep and lower your nets for a catch." ⁵Simon answered, "Master, we worked the entire night, and we have not caught anything. But according to your word, I will let down the nets." ⁶When they had done this, they caught a great haul of fish, and their nets were about to burst. ⁷And they called to their companions in the other boats to come and assist them. And they came and filled both of the boats, so that they began to sink. ⁸When Simon Peter saw this, he fell down at Jesus's knees and said, "Depart from me, because I am a sinful man, Lord." ⁹For he was amazed, as were all those who were with him, at the catch of fish that they had hauled in, ¹⁰as were Jacob and John the sons of Zebedee, who were partners with Simon. And Jesus said to Simon, "Do not fear; from now on you will be a fisherman of men and women." ¹¹And after they had brought their boats to land, they left everything and followed him.

HEALING OF A MAN WITH LEPROSY (MT 8:1–4; MK 1:40–45)

¹²He was in one of the towns, and a man covered with leprosy saw Jesus, and he fell on his face and begged Jesus, saying, "Lord, if you desire, you can make me clean." ¹³And Jesus stretched out his hand and touched him, saying, "I want this. Be made clean." And immediately the leprosy departed from him. ¹⁴And he commanded him not to tell anyone, saying, "Depart and show yourself to the priest and bring an offering for your cleansing as Moses

---

4:43 Acts 3:26 reflects on Jesus being *sent* to do the work of God. **4:44** Some manuscripts indicate that Jesus taught in the *synagogues of Galilee*.

5:1 Lake Gennesaret is the Sea of Galilee, and the Gospel authors sometimes referred to it using this regional designation (compare Matthew 14:34; Mark 6:53). **5:3** Luke indicates that Simon owns his own boat, thus implying a certain financial status not implied in the parallel accounts of Matthew and Mark (Matthew 4:18–22; Mark 1:16–20). **5:5** One manuscript notes that Simon began his response by saying *Teacher*. **5:10** The Greek has only *men*. A possible allusion to Jeremiah 16:16. **5:11** The translation *they left everything* implies that they left their employment, homes, belongings, and even families to follow Jesus. The Greek wording does not imply that this was a requirement, but it implies that they did it by choice. **5:12** *Covered with leprosy* seems to be an attempt to distinguish between mild skin diseases and a major skin ailment (see Leviticus 13–14) **5:13** The Greek lacks *Jesus*, but it is clear from the context that Jesus stretched forth his hand to touch the man in order to heal him. **5:14** The laws governing a healing from leprosy are found in Leviticus 14:10–20. Jesus here encourages the man to observe the statutes set forth in the law of Moses.

directed, for a testimony to them." ¹⁵But the news about him spread more, and great crowds gathered to hear and to be healed from their illnesses. ¹⁶And he departed into a deserted place and prayed.

HEALING OF A PARALYZED MAN
(MT 9:1–8; MK 2:1–12; JN 5:8–9A)

¹⁷And it came to pass that on one of the days when he taught, there were Pharisees and teachers of the Law sitting there, and they came from every town of Galilee and Judea and from Jerusalem, and the power of the Lord was with him to heal. ¹⁸Some men came and brought to him a man on a mattress who was paralyzed and they sought to bring him in and to place him before Jesus. ¹⁹But they were not able to find a way to bring him in because of the crowd, and having climbed onto the roof, they let him down through the roof tiles on the mattress, and he was in their midst in front of Jesus. ²⁰And when he saw their faith, he said, "Friend, your sins are forgiven you." ²¹Then the Pharisees and scribes began to debate this, saying, "Who is this that speaks blasphemy? Who is able to forgive sins but God only?" ²²When Jesus knew about their debate, he answered them, "Why do you debate this in your hearts? ²³Is it easier to say, 'Your sins are forgiven,' or to say, 'Arise and walk?' ²⁴But so that you may know that the Son of Man has power on the earth to forgive sins (he

said to the paralyzed man), I say to you, arise and carry your mattress and return to your house." ²⁵And right away he stood up in front of them, and he picked up the mattress on which he had been lying and went to his house and gave glory to God. ²⁶And amazement took hold of all of them, and they gave glory to God, and they were filled with fear and said, "We have seen remarkable things today."

THE CALL OF MATTHEW/LEVI
(MT 9:9–13; MK 2:13–17)

²⁷After this he went out and saw a tax collector named Levi sitting at a tax booth, and he said to him, "Follow me." ²⁸And he left everything and stood and followed him. ²⁹And Levi made a great celebration for him in his house, and there was a great crowd of tax collectors and others who were reclining at dinner with them. ³⁰The Pharisees and their scribes complained to his disciples, saying, "Why do you eat and drink with tax collectors and sinners?" ³¹And Jesus answered them, "The healthy have no need of a physician, but those who are ill do. ³²I did not come to call the righteous but the sinners to repentance."

A QUESTION ABOUT FASTING
(MT 9:14–17; MK 2:18–22)

³³They said to him, "The disciples of John fast often and pray, like disciples of the

---

5:16 Luke provides little indication of why Jesus departed to pray, unless it was because the man who was healed *spread the word* concerning him (verse 15). **5:17** Other manuscripts read *to heal them* instead of *with him to heal*. **5:18** Mark uses a different word to describe the man's bed or mattress, which indicated it was more substantial and cumbersome to carry (see Mark 2:4). **5:19** Luke alone notes that the roof had tiles, and therefore he imagines a Roman period home. Mark's account imagines a more modest home typical of a Galilean village (Mark 2:4). **5:21** *Blasphemy*, as used in this context, implies that Jesus assumed a power attributed exclusively to God. Compare Jacob 7:7; Jarom 1:5; Alma 30:30. **5:24** An allusion to Daniel 7:13–14. **5:26** Luke records the sentiment of the crowd by writing, *We have seen remarkable things*. The word translated as *remarkable* can also mean *paradoxical* or *unexpected*. **5:27** On Levi/Matthew, see Matthew 9:9 and Mark 2:14. Only Matthew calls this disciple *Matthew*. Tax collectors appear in prominent positions in Luke (3:12; 5:29–30; 7:29, etc.). **5:29** The celebration takes place at Levi's home (compare Matthew 9:10, where Matthew is ambiguous on this issue). **5:30** Some translations use the word *publicans* for *tax collectors*. **5:33** The subject of *John's disciples* is familiar to the

Pharisees do, but your disciples eat and drink." ³⁴Jesus said to them, "You cannot make the wedding guests fast while the bridegroom is with them, can you? ³⁵But the days will come when the bridegroom will be taken from them; then they will fast in those days." ³⁶And he told them a parable: "No one takes new cloth and puts it on an old piece of clothing; if so, the new cloth is then torn and the piece from the new cloth will not match the old clothing. ³⁷No one puts new wine into old wineskins; if so, the new wine will burst the skins and the wine will be spilled, and the skins will be ruined. ³⁸New wine must be put into new wineskins. ³⁹And no one desires new wine after drinking aged wine, for he says, 'The old is good.'"

THE SON OF MAN IS LORD OF THE SABBATH (MT 12:1–8; MK 2:23–28)

6 ¹And it came to pass on the Sabbath that as he went through the wheat fields, his disciples were picking wheat, rubbing it in their hands, and eating it. ²Then some of the Pharisees said, "Why do you do what is not lawful on the Sab-

bath?" ³Jesus answered them, "Have you not read what David did when he was hungry, including those that were with him? ⁴How he went into the house of God and took the Bread of the Presence and ate it and gave it to those with him, which is not lawful to eat except for the priests?" ⁵And he said to them, "The Son of Man is the Lord of the Sabbath."

HEALING OF A MAN WITH A WITHERED HAND (MT 12:9–14; MK 3:1–6)

⁶And it came to pass on another Sabbath that he entered the synagogue and taught, and there was a man there with a withered right hand. ⁷The scribes and the Pharisees were watching him to see whether he would heal on the Sabbath so that they might find an accusation against him. ⁸But he knew their reasoning, and he said to the man with the withered hand, "Rise and stand among us," and he got up and stood. ⁹Then Jesus said to them, "I will ask you a question: Is it lawful to do good on the Sabbath or to do evil? To save life or to kill?" ¹⁰And he looked around at all of them, and he said to him, "Stretch out your hand."

---

audience. In Matthew, John's disciples come to Jesus and ask a question (Matthew 9:14), and some early and good manuscripts of the Gospel of Luke turn this verse into a question. It does appear that the question's form, however, was created through harmonization to Matthew's account. Compare Alma 6:6. **5:33–39** This discussion took place at the meal in Levi's home, and Jesus here discourses on the tensions between the old and the new, perhaps addressing the challenge directly facing them in accepting Jesus despite their objections regarding his actions (Luke 5:21, 30). **5:38** An allusion to Joshua 9:13. **5:39** Some manuscripts read *the old is better*, but the evidence for *good* is more widely attested. Some late manuscripts omit this verse, probably in an effort to harmonize the account to Matthew, who does not include this saying.

6:1 Some manuscripts read *on the second Sabbath after the first*. That phrase appears here and nowhere else, and therefore its meaning remains unclear. Luke may have intended that the reader count a series of Sabbaths in order, with the first being unmentioned. It could have been the second Sabbath after Passover, and therefore closer to the Day of Pentecost. However, that conclusion must remain conjectural. The conflict described here and in Matthew 12:1 reflects a debate on the meaning of Deuteronomy 23:25 and Exodus 34:21. **6:2** *Certain of the Pharisees* correctly notes that not all Pharisees held to such a stringent view of the commandment not to work on the Sabbath. **6:3–4** See 1 Samuel 21:1–6. **6:4** *The Bread of the Presence* (see Exodus 25:35; Leviticus 24:9). **6:8** *But he knew their reasoning* can mean that Jesus knew their thoughts, but it may also indicate that he became aware of their reasoning through overhearing their discussion or through other means.

And he did so and his hand was restored to health. ¹¹And they were filled with anger, and they discussed among themselves what they might do to Jesus.

JESUS CALLS THE TWELVE
(MT 10:1–4; MK 3:13–19)

¹²And it came to pass in those days that he went out to a mountain in order to pray, and he spent the night in prayer to God. ¹³And when it was day, he called his disciples and chose twelve from among them, whom he called apostles. ¹⁴Simon, whom he also called Peter, and Andrew his brother, Jacob and John, Philip, Bartholomew, ¹⁵Matthew, Thomas, Jacob son of Alphaeus, Simon called the Zealot, ¹⁶Judas son of James, and Judas Iscariot, who became a betrayer.

EARLY MIRACLES
(MT 4:23–25; MK 3:7–12)

¹⁷And he came down with them and stood on a level spot, with a crowd of his disciples and a large group of people from all Judea and Jerusalem and from Tyre and Sidon near the seashore. ¹⁸They came to hear him and to be healed of their illnesses, and those troubled by unclean spirits were healed. ¹⁹And the whole crowd sought to touch him because power went from him, and he healed everyone.

THE SERMON ON THE PLAIN

²⁰And he lifted up his eyes to his disciples and said, "Blessed are you poor, because yours is the kingdom of God. ²¹Blessed are you who hunger now, because you will be filled. Blessed are you who mourn now, because you will laugh. ²²Blessed are you when people hate you and when they reject you and insult you and throw your name around as evil on account of the Son of Man! ²³Rejoice in that day and leap for joy; behold, your reward is great in heaven, for their ancestors did these things to the prophets.

²⁴"Woe to you who are rich, because you have received your comfort. ²⁵Woe to you who are full now, because you will be hungry. Woe to you who laugh now, because you will mourn and weep. ²⁶Woe to you when all people speak well of you, for their ancestors did these things to the false prophets.

²⁷"But I say to you who listen: love your enemies, do good to those who hate you, ²⁸speak well of those who curse you, pray for those who insult you. ²⁹If anyone smites you on the cheek, turn the other cheek to him also, and do not withhold your shirt from him who takes away your

---

6:13 The call of the twelve precedes the delivery of the Sermon on the Plain (6:17) and may intentionally present the newly called disciples with the content of their preaching. This is the first reference to the disciples being called apostles in Luke. The phrase *whom he called apostles* in Greek refers to their role as *missionaries*, or *those who are sent*. The word is not used as a formal title in this instance but signals to the reader that they are being sent out on a mission. The word *apostles* is found only in Matthew 10:2; Mark 3:14; 6:30; Luke 9:10; 11:49; 17:5; 22:14; 24:10 in the Gospels. 6:15 Simon was called a *Zealot*, meaning he or his family was associated with a political or nationalist movement. 6:17 Luke recognizes that there are numerous disciples outside the twelve who were chosen. 6:17–49 It is unclear whether Jesus gave two similar sermons, the Sermon on the Mount (Matthew 5:1–7:29) and the Sermon on the Plain (6:17–49). The two sermons share a significant amount of content, although they are structured differently and each has a number of unique teachings. 6:17–18 Some modern translations divide these two verses differently and end verse 17 with the word *illnesses*. 6:20 In Luke's version of the Beatitudes, the directives are written in the second-person plural *you*. 6:22 Compare 1 Peter 4:14. 6:24–26 The *woes* are unique to Luke's Gospel. 6:29 *Takes away your coat.* This refers to the outermost article of clothing, or *cloak*. The *shirt* (i.e., *tunic*) is the inner article of clothing directly touching the skin.

coat. ³⁰And to everyone who asks of you, give; and from him who takes away your things, do not ask for them back again.

³¹"And whatever you wish that people would do to you, do likewise. ³²And if you love those who love you, what grace is in you? For even sinners love those who love them. ³³If you do good to those who do good to you, what grace is in you? For sinners do the same. ³⁴If you lend to those because you hope to receive something back, what grace is in you? For sinners lend to sinners that they may receive back as much. ³⁵But love your enemies, do good, lend while hoping for nothing in return, and your reward will be great, and you will be children of the Most High, because he is gracious to the ungrateful and wicked.

³⁶"Be merciful even as your Father in heaven is merciful. ³⁷Do not judge that you may not be judged, and condemn not that you may not be condemned. Forgive, and you will be forgiven. ³⁸Give, and it will be given to you. A good measure, pressed down, shaken together, and running over, will be given in your lap. For with what measure you use, it will be measured to you again."

³⁹And he spoke to them in a parable: "Is a blind person able to lead a blind person? Will not both of them fall into a pit? ⁴⁰A disciple is not above his teacher, but everyone who is fully trained is like his teacher.

⁴¹"Why do you look at the splinter in your brother's eye but do not consider the log that is in your own eye? ⁴²How are you able to say to your brother, 'Let me take the splinter out of your eye,' but you do not see the log in your own eye? Hypocrite, first take out the log from your own eye, and then you will see clearly to remove the splinter from your brother's eye.

⁴³"A good tree cannot make bad fruit, nor can a bad tree make good fruit. ⁴⁴For each tree is known by its fruit, for they do not gather figs from thorn bushes, nor grapes from bramble bushes. ⁴⁵The good person brings forth good from the treasury of the heart, and the evil person brings forth evil treasures from the heart. From the fullness of the heart the mouth speaks.

⁴⁶"Why do you call me, 'Lord, Lord,' and do not what I say? ⁴⁷Everyone who comes to me and listens to my words and does them, I will tell you what he is like. ⁴⁸He is a like a man who builds a house, who dug deep and laid its foundation on rock. And when the flood came, the rivers ran against the house but could not move it because it was well built. ⁴⁹The person who hears my words but does not do them is like a man who built a house on the ground without a foundation. When the rivers ran against it, it immediately fell, and the fall of that house was great."

THE CENTURION'S SON IS HEALED (MT 8:5–13; JN 4:46B–54)

7 ¹When he had completed all his teachings in the hearing of the people, he entered Capernaum. ²And a centurion's servant, who was very important to him,

---

6:31 This verse is sometimes referred to as the *Golden Rule*. See Leviticus 19:18 (compare Matthew 7:12; 3 Nephi 14:12). **6:36** An allusion to Deuteronomy 4:31. **6:38** The imagery is that of a harvest, in which the chaff or damaged fruit is culled and the better fruits are preserved. **6:39** See Matthew 15:14; John 3:19; Helaman 13:29. **6:46** This verse anticipates Luke 13:25. **6:49** Matthew notes that the unwise builder built on the sand, whereas Luke's version implies that the foundation is placed directly on top of the soil without any thought of digging (see Matthew 7:26; compare 2 Nephi 28:28; 3 Nephi 11:40).

7:1 *Teachings* can also be translated as *sayings*, but in this context Luke refers to the teachings of chapter 6 that had recently ended. **7:2** A *centurion* was a Roman military officer who commanded a hundred soldiers. Luke uses a different word to describe the *centurion's* servant/son than the one used by Matthew. The word used in this verse clearly demarcates him as a household servant. The word used in Matthew 8:6 can indicate a son or a servant. The description of his value also clarifies that Luke thought this boy

was ill and was about to die. ³When the centurion heard about Jesus, he sent some elders of the Jews to him, asking him to come and heal his servant. ⁴When they came to Jesus, they encouraged him earnestly, saying, "He is worthy to have you do this for him. ⁵He loves our nation, and he built a synagogue for us." ⁶So Jesus went with them. But when they were near the house, the centurion sent friends and said to Jesus, "Lord, do not be troubled, for I am not worthy for you to enter under my roof. ⁷Therefore, I did not presume to be worthy to come to you, but say the word and my servant will be healed. ⁸For I am a man placed under authority, having soldiers under me, and I say to one, 'Go,' and he goes, and to another, 'Come,' and he comes, and to my servant, 'Do this,' and he does it." ⁹When Jesus heard this, he marveled at him, and he turned to the crowd that had gathered and said, "I tell you, I have not found such faith in Israel." ¹⁰And those who were sent returned to the house and found the servant healed.

HEALING OF THE WIDOW'S SON AT NAIN

¹¹And it came to pass that soon afterward he came to a town called Nain, and his disciples and a large crowd went with him. ¹²As he drew near to the gate of the village, a man who had died was being carried out, the only son of his mother, and she was a widow, and a large crowd from that town was with her. ¹³The Lord saw her and had compassion on her and said, "Do not weep." ¹⁴And he approached and touched the bier, and those who carried it stood still, and he said, "Young man, I say to you, arise!" ¹⁵And the dead man sat up and began to speak, and Jesus gave him to his mother. ¹⁶And fear took hold of them all, and they gave glory to God, saying, "A great prophet has arisen among us," and "God has looked on his people." ¹⁷An account of this spread through all Judea and in all the surrounding region.

JOHN'S DISCIPLES VISIT JESUS (MT 11:1–6)

¹⁸And the disciples of John told him about all these things, and John called two of his disciples ¹⁹and sent them to the Lord, saying, "Are you the coming one, or should we look for another?" ²⁰When the men came to him, they said, "John the Baptist sent us to you, asking, 'Are you the coming one, or should we look for another?'" ²¹In that hour he healed many from illness and plagues and unclean spirits, and he restored sight to many who were blind. ²²And he answered them, "Go and tell John what you have seen and heard: 'The blind see again, the lame walk, those with leprosy are cleansed, the deaf hear, the dead are

---

was a servant, although Luke also uses the same word as Matthew later in the story (Luke 7:7). John clearly refers to him as a son (John 4:47). **7:3** Luke's mention of the *elders of the Jews* indicates that the centurion was close to them or knew them. The request to have the elders solicit Jesus's help is unusual in the Gospels. **7:4** Luke uses a circumlocution to convey the idea of the centurion's worthiness. Luke writes, *He is worthy to have you do this for him.* **7:6** Compare Acts 10:28. **7:9** Compare Mark 6:6, where Jesus is also *astonished*. Jesus judges the centurion according to his faith, offering a subtle contrast to the judgment of worthiness (verse 6). **7:11** Nain is located about six miles southeast of Nazareth and near Mount Tabor. Some manuscripts read *the next day* in place of *soon afterward*. The story has many similarities to Elijah (1 Kings 17). **7:14** *Touching the bier* would have violated the directives set forth in Numbers 19:11, 16. **7:15** *And he gave him to his mother* is a literal translation (Jesus is added to clarify the pronouns), and the phrase quotes 1 Kings 17:23, thus solidifying an Elijah parallel. **7:18–19** Some translations place this phrase as part of verse 19: *And John called two of his disciples.* **7:19** The biblical source of their question may be Zechariah 9:9. **7:21** Mosiah 3:6 offers a nuanced view of casting out evil spirits. **7:22** Allusion to Isaiah 61:1. A quotation of the Isaiah passage is found in 2 Nephi 27:29.

raised, and the poor have the good news taught to them.' ²³And blessed is the person who is not scandalized by me."

JESUS DECLARES JOHN TO BE ELIJAH (MT 11:7–19)

²⁴When the messengers of John departed, he began to say to the crowds concerning John, "What did you go out into the desert to see? A reed shaken by the wind? ²⁵What did you go out to see? A man dressed in soft clothing? Behold, those who wear soft clothing live in luxury and are in the houses of kings! ²⁶But what did you go out to see? A prophet? Yes, I tell you he was much more than a prophet. ²⁷This is the one of whom it was written, 'Behold, I send my messenger before my face, who shall prepare the way before you.' ²⁸I say to you, there is not a greater prophet than John the Baptist among those born of women, but he who is least in the kingdom of God is greater than he is." ²⁹(When all the people heard this, and the tax collectors as well, they gave glory to God, having been baptized with the baptism of John. ³⁰But the Pharisees and lawyers rejected the counsel of God for themselves and would not be baptized by him.)

³¹"What shall I compare the people of this generation to, and what are they like? ³²They are like children sitting in the marketplace, who call one another and say,

'We piped to you and you did not dance, we lamented and you did not weep.' ³³For John the Baptist came neither eating bread nor drinking wine, and you say, 'He has a demon.' ³⁴The Son of Man came eating and drinking, and you say, 'Look, a drunk and a glutton, a friend of tax collectors and sinners.' ³⁵Wisdom is justified by all her children."

JESUS IS ANOINTED AT BETHANY (MT 26:6–13; MK 14:3–9; JN 12:1–8)

³⁶A certain Pharisee asked him if he could eat with him, and he entered the house of the Pharisee and reclined to eat. ³⁷And a woman in the town, who was a sinner, knew that he reclined to eat in the house of the Pharisee. She had an alabaster jar of ointment, ³⁸and she stood behind him near his feet, and while weeping she began to wet his feet with tears, and with the hair of her head she wiped them, and she kissed his feet and anointed them with the ointment. ³⁹But the Pharisee who called him, when he saw this, he said to himself, "If he were a prophet, he would have known who and what type of woman touched him, because she is a sinner." ⁴⁰Jesus answered him, "Simon, I have something to say to you." And he replied, "Teacher, speak." ⁴¹"A certain creditor had two debtors; one owed five hundred denarii, and

---

7:23 The word *scandalized* can also mean *stumbled* or *tripped up*. **7:24** Luke uses the word *angels* to refer to John's disciples. The word can mean both a heavenly *angel* and a human *messenger*. **7:25** John's clothing is used to contrast the clothing of the wealthy (compare Luke 3:11). **7:27** Quotation from Malachi 3:1 and Exodus 23:20. **7:29–30** This editorial comment by the author summarizes the reception that Jesus and John had received up to this point of the story. **7:33** Fasting and avoiding drinking wine drew attention to John and his disciples. **7:36** First-century diners reclined while eating, and here Luke notes that Jesus *reclined*, thus placing him in the posture of eating. Luke reports this story much earlier in the ministry than Matthew (26:6–13) and Mark (14:3–9) do. Luke does not place the event in Bethany. The invitation extended to Jesus to dine with this Pharisee in his home shows acceptance of Jesus. **7:38** See Genesis 18:4. In the Book of Mormon and Doctrine and Covenants, *anointing* is often associated with royal anointing (Ether 9:4; Doctrine and Covenants 109:80). **7:39** There may have been some concern that when the woman touched Jesus, he was rendered unclean by the act of being touched by a sinful person (Leviticus 5:1–5). **7:40–43** This parable is unique to Luke. **7:41** The two debts, fifty and five hundred denarii, are both noteworthy. The lesser debt approximates a month of wages, whereas the greater

the other owed fifty. [42]When they could not pay it back, he forgave both. Which one of them loved him more?" [43]Simon answered, "I suppose that the one to whom he forgave more." He said to him, "You judge correctly." [44]And he turned toward the woman and said to Simon, "Do you see this woman? When I entered your house, you did not give me water for my feet, but this woman wet my feet with her tears, and with her hair she wiped them. [45]You did not kiss me, but since I came in she has not stopped kissing my feet. [46]You did not anoint my head with oil, but she anointed my feet with ointment. [47]For this reason I say to you, her many sins have been forgiven because she loved much, but the one who is forgiven of little loves little." [48]And he said to her, "Your sins are forgiven." [49]Those dining with him began to say to themselves, "Who is this who even forgives sins?" [50]But he said to the woman, "Your faith has saved you; depart in peace."

FEMALE FOLLOWERS

8 [1]And it came to pass that he went through the towns and villages, declaring and teaching the good news of the kingdom of God with the twelve, [2]and some women were with him who had been healed from evil spirits and illnesses: Mary called Magdalene, from whom seven demons had gone out; [3]and Joanna the wife of Chuza, Herod's steward; Susanna; and many others, who served them from their own resources.

THE PARABLE OF THE SOWER
(MT 13:1–9; MK 4:1–9)

[4]When a large crowd gathered and people from town after town came to him, he said in a parable, [5]"A sower went out to sow his seed. And as he sowed, some fell along the way and was trampled upon, and the birds of heaven ate it. [6]And other seed fell on rock, and when it sprouted it withered because it had no moisture. [7]And other seed fell among thorns, and the thorns grew and choked it. [8]And other seed fell on good ground, and it grew and produced fruit, a hundredfold." When he said this, he declared, "Whoever has ears to hear, let that person hear."

THE REASON FOR
TEACHING IN PARABLES
(MT 13:10–17; MK 4:10–12)

[9]Then his disciples asked him what the parable meant. [10]And he said, "To you it is given to know the mysteries of the kingdom of God, but to others parables are given so that '*seeing they may not see, and hearing they may not understand.*'

THE PARABLE OF THE
SOWER EXPLAINED
(MT 13:18–23; MK 4:13–20)

[11]"This is the parable: The seed is the word of God. [12]The ones on the way are those who have heard, but then the devil comes and takes the word from their hearts so that they may not believe and be saved. [13]Those on the rocks are those who when they hear, they receive the word with joy, but they have no roots. They believe for a

---

is much closer to a year's wages. **7:42** Similar language of forgiveness is found in 1 Nephi 7:21. **7:50** The language of being *saved* often accompanies the miracles in Luke (8:36, 48; 17:19; 18:42).

8:3 Little is known about Joanna and Susanna, but they do appear in the resurrection account (Luke 23:49, 55; 24:10). The intent of *who served him from their own resources* conveys the idea of financial support to Jesus and his disciples. Nothing more is known of *Chuza*, although he was likely a political appointee of Herod Antipas. **8:10** Quotation from Isaiah 6:9. The Isaiah reference draws attention to the fact that some teachings can be divisive. Compare Alma 26:22; Doctrine and Covenants 42:65. **8:12** The noun *devil* is derived from the verb *to slander*, and the noun indicates *the one who slanders*.

time, but during a time of trial they fall away. [14]The ones who fell among thorns, these are the ones who hear, but as they go forward, they are choked by anxieties and riches and pleasures of life, and they do not produce fruit. [15]The ones in good ground, these are the ones who when they hear the word, retain it in a good and upright heart, and they bear fruit in patience.

A LAMP UNDER A BASKET (MK 4:21–25)

[16]"No one who lights a lamp hides it under a pot or under a mattress, but places it on a lampstand so that those who enter may see the light. [17]Nothing is secret that will not become manifest, nor hidden away that will not be known and become manifest. [18]See how you listen, for whoever has, more will be given to that person, and whoever has not, even what that person seems to have will be taken."

THE FAMILY OF JESUS (MT 12:46–50; MK 3:31–35)

[19]His mother and brothers came to him, but they were not able to get near him because of the crowd. [20]And it was reported to him, "Your mother and brothers are standing outside, wishing to see you." [21]He answered them, "My mother and my brothers are those who hear the word of God and do it."

THE STILLING OF THE STORM (MT 8:23–37; MK 4:35–41)

[22]And it came to pass that one day he entered a boat with his disciples, and he said to them, "Let us cross over to the other side of the lake." And they set out, [23]but as they were sailing he fell asleep, and a windstorm arose on the lake, and the boat was filling up and they were in danger. [24]Then they approached him and woke him, saying, "Master, Master, we are about to perish." He arose and rebuked the wind and the raging water, and they ceased and there was calm. [25]And he said to them, "Where is your faith?" But they were afraid and wondered, saying to one another, "Who is this that he commands the winds and water, and they obey him?"

HEALING OF A MAN AT GADARA/ GERASA (MT 8:28–34; MK 5:1–20)

[26]And they sailed to the region of the Gerasenes, which is opposite Galilee. [27]And he went forth on the land, and a certain man from the town met him. That man was possessed by demons, and for a long time he had been unclothed; neither did he reside in a house, but among the tombs. [28]When he saw Jesus, he cried out and fell down before him and in a loud voice said, "What do I have to do with you, Jesus, Son of the Most High God? I beg you, do not trouble me." [29]For Jesus had commanded the unclean spirit to come out of the man (many times it had taken hold of him, and he was bound with chains and bonds and was under guard, but he broke the bonds, and he was driven by the demon into deserted regions). [30]But Jesus asked him, "What is your name?" And he said, "Legion" (because there were many demons in him). [31]And they begged him that he might not expel them to depart

---

8:18 Compare Doctrine and Covenants 1:33. **8:19** Jesus redefines family as those who obey his teachings. See Matthew 12:50; Mark 3:35. **8:22** Luke is aware that Jesus spoke of the Sea of Galilee as a lake, thus offering a more accurate description of it. **8:26** Some manuscripts read *Gadarenes* or *Gergasenes*. Luke's account of this story offers little that would clarify the precise location where the event took place. See the note for Matthew 8:23–34. *Opposite Galilee* would likely refer to the southeast region of the Sea of Galilee near the Decapolis. **8:29** The individual who was possessed responded to Jesus only after Jesus had already rebuked the spirits that possessed him. **8:30** *Legion* is a technical term designating a detachment of the Roman army between four and six thousand soldiers. **8:31** *Abyss* indicates a pit or hole that has no bottom.

into the abyss. ³²There was a large herd of pigs feeding on the mountain, and the demons asked him that he might permit them to enter the swine. And he permitted them. ³³And the demons left the man and entered the pigs, and the herd rushed down the hillside to the lake and was drowned.

³⁴Those who fed the pigs saw what had happened and fled and told it in the town and in the fields. ³⁵Then they came to see what had happened, and they came to Jesus and found the man from whom the demons had been cast out sitting at the feet of Jesus, clothed and in his right mind. And they were afraid. ³⁶And those who saw it reported how the man who was possessed by demons had been healed. ³⁷And the entire multitude of the region of the Gadarenes asked Jesus to depart from them, because they felt great fear. So he entered a boat and departed. ³⁸But the man from whom the demons had been cast out begged him that he might be with him, but Jesus sent him away, saying, ³⁹"Return to your house, and declare what things God has done." And he went away and declared in the entire town what things Jesus had done for him.

JAIRUS'S DAUGHTER AND A WOMAN HEALED
(MT 9:18–26; MK 5:21–43)

⁴⁰When Jesus returned, the crowd received him because they were waiting for him. ⁴¹And a man came whose name was Jairus, who was a leader of the synagogue. And he fell at the feet of Jesus and called on him to come to his house ⁴²because his only daughter, who was about twelve years old, was dying. And as he departed, the multitude pressed on him. ⁴³And a woman, hemorrhaging for twelve years, who had spent all her earnings on physicians, but none were able to heal her, ⁴⁴came up behind him and touched the fringe of his clothing, and immediately her hemorrhaging stopped. ⁴⁵Then Jesus said, "Who touched me?" All denied it, but Peter said, "Master, the crowd presses you and surrounds you." ⁴⁶But Jesus said, "Someone touched me, for I know that power departed from me." ⁴⁷When the woman saw that she was no longer hidden, she came trembling and fell down in front of him, and in front of them all she told the reason why she touched him and how she had been immediately healed. ⁴⁸And he said to her, "Daughter, your faith has healed you; depart in peace."

⁴⁹While he was still speaking, someone from the leader of the synagogue's house came and said, "Your daughter has died. Do not bother the teacher." ⁵⁰When Jesus heard this, he answered, "Do not fear, but believe only, and she will be healed." ⁵¹Then he came to the house, and he permitted no one to enter except for Peter, Jacob, and John and the father and mother of the child. ⁵²And they all wept and mourned for her. But he said, "Do not weep, for she is not dead but sleeping." ⁵³And they laughed at him because they knew she was dead. ⁵⁴And he took her by the hand and called to her, "Child, arise!" ⁵⁵And her spirit returned to her, and she arose immediately, and he instructed them

---

8:32 Compare Deuteronomy 14:8. **8:36** The meaning could also be *had been saved.* **8:39** Here the healing miracle is proclaimed openly to encourage others to accept Jesus. **8:43** Some manuscripts lack *who had spent all her earnings on physicians,* and the evidence for it is of a mixed quality. If original, it represents Luke's criticism of the physicians of his day, and similar wording is found in Mark 5:31. Bleeding would have made one unclean (Leviticus 15:25–30). **8:48, 50** Jesus again uses the phrase *your faith has saved you,* where a verb of healing was also possible (see 8:36). **8:52** Luke says literally that they were *striking themselves.* **8:53** Some translations rendered the laughing episode as *laughed him to scorn,* a phrase that appears in the Book of Mormon (Alma 26:23, but compare Nehemiah 2:19). **8:54** Some late manuscripts note that Jesus *threw them out.* **8:55** The act of giving her food appears to have the intent

to give her something to eat. ⁵⁶Her parents were astonished, but he commanded them to not tell anyone what had happened.

SENDING OUT THE TWELVE
(MT 10:5–15; MK 9:7–13)

9 ¹And he called the twelve and gave them power and authority over all demons and to heal illnesses, ²and he sent them out to proclaim the kingdom of God and to heal the sick, ³and he said to them, "Take nothing on the way, neither a staff, nor a wallet, nor bread, nor money, nor two coats. ⁴Whatever house you enter, remain there and then depart, ⁵and whoever does not receive you, when you leave that town, shake the dust from your feet as a testimony against them." ⁶They went out and passed through the villages, proclaiming the good news and healing everywhere.

HEROD'S CONFUSION
(MT 14:1–2; MK 6:14–16)

⁷When Herod the tetrarch heard all the things that had been done, he was confused because it was declared by some that John the Baptist had been raised from the dead, ⁸and by some that Elijah had appeared, and by others that one of the ancient prophets had risen. ⁹But Herod said, "I have beheaded John. Who is this that I hear these things about?" And he sought to see him.

FEEDING THE FIVE THOUSAND
(MT 14:13–21; MK 6:30–44; JN 6:1–15)

¹⁰And the apostles returned and declared to him the things they had done. And he took them and departed to a town called Bethsaida to be alone. ¹¹When the crowds knew it, they followed him. And he received them and spoke to them about the kingdom of God, and he healed those who needed healing. ¹²But the day began to end, and the twelve came to him and said, "Send the crowd away, that they may go into the surrounding villages and fields and lodge and find food, because we are in a deserted place." ¹³And he said to them, "Give them something to eat." But they responded, "We have no more than five loaves and two fish, unless we depart so that we may purchase food for the entire multitude." ¹⁴(There were about five thousand men.) He said to his disciples, "Have them sit in groups of fifty each." ¹⁵And they did so, and everyone sat down. ¹⁶And he took the five loaves and the two fish, and he looked to heaven and blessed them and broke them and gave them to the disciples to set before the crowd. ¹⁷And they ate, and everyone was filled, and

---

of confirming to those assembled that she was genuinely alive again.

9:1 The granting of *power and authority* to heal is mentioned here for the first time. The phrase can be used in a secular sense as well as a religious sense (see Luke 20:20). These two terms are often used in connection with priesthood power and authority (Mosiah 18:17; Helaman 5:18; 3 Nephi 7:17; Doctrine and Covenants 107:18, 20, 24). Only Luke uses the phrase in the Gospels (4:36; 20:20). **9:2** The disciples are *sent out* to proclaim the kingdom of God. The Greek verb for this action is *apostellein* and conveys the idea of sending someone out with a purpose. The disciples will at times be described as *apostles* or as *those who are sent out*. **9:3** Mark 6:8 allows for a staff. By commanding the disciples not to take with them items necessary for traveling, he has forced the disciples to rely on the generosity of the people in the Galilean villages. **9:5** Compare Doctrine and Covenants 24:15; 75:20. **9:6** *Villages* would imply Galilee. **9:7** This is Herod Antipas (see notes on Matthew 2:1; 14:1). **9:9** This is the only notice in Luke that Herod had beheaded John, and thus it signals that Luke assumed his readers would know this story. **9:10** Bethsaida is situated on the northern shore of the Sea of Galilee. Philip, Andrew, and Peter were from Bethsaida, according to John 1:44; 12:21. **9:14** Calling on the multitude to sit in groups of fifty may recall Exodus 18:21, 25.

they gathered up twelve baskets of what remained of the broken bread.

PETER'S DECLARATION AT CAESAREA PHILIPPI (MT 16:13–20; MK 8:27–30; JN 6:67–71)

18And it came to pass that as he prayed alone, his disciples were with him, and he asked them, saying, "Who do the crowds say I am?" 19They answered, "John the Baptist, others say Elijah, but others that one of the ancient prophets has risen." 20He said to them, "Who do you say that I am?" Peter answered, "The Christ of God." 21And he commanded them not to tell this to anyone. 22And he said, "The Son of Man must suffer many things and be judged by the elders and chief priests and scribes and be killed, and be raised on the third day."

TAKING UP A CROSS (MT 16:24–48; MK 8:34–9:1)

23And he said to them all, "If anyone desires to follow after me, let him deny himself and take up his cross daily and follow me. 24For whoever desires to save his life will lose it, and whoever loses his life for my sake, he will save it. 25What does it profit a man if he gains the whole world but loses or damages himself? 26Whoever is ashamed of me and my words, the Son of Man will be ashamed of him when he comes in his Father's glory and the glory of the holy angels. 27I say to you, truly there are some of those standing here who will not taste death until they see the kingdom of God."

THE MOUNT OF TRANSFIGURATION (MT 17:1–9; MK 9:2–8)

28And it came to pass that about eight days later he took Peter, John, and Jacob and went up to a mountain to pray. 29And it came to pass that while he was praying, the appearance of his face was changed, and his clothing was shining white. 30And two men were with him, Moses and Elijah, 31who appeared in glory and spoke of his journey that he was about to complete in Jerusalem. 32But Peter and those with him were weighed down in sleep, and when they woke, they saw his glory and two men standing with him. 33And it came to pass, when they departed from him, Peter not knowing what to say, said to Jesus, "Master, it is good for us to be here, and let us make three booths, one for you, one for Moses, and one for Elijah." 34After he said this, a cloud appeared and overshadowed them, and they were afraid of entering into the cloud. 35And a voice came out of the cloud, saying, "This is my beloved Son, my Chosen One; hear him!" 36And when the voice ended, Jesus was found alone, and they were silent, and they told no one in those days what they had seen.

A BOY IS HEALED (MT 17:14–21; MK 9:14–29)

37And it came to pass that on the next day, after they came down from the mount, a

---

9:18 This story is situated in or near Caesarea Philippi in the other Gospels (Matthew 16:13–23; Mark 8:27–33). Luke does not mention a specific place, but Peter's declaration that Jesus is the *Christ* is the focal point of the story. **9:23** Luke's account includes the adverb *daily* to the saying, thus heightening the expectation the faithful will suffer tribulation (see Matthew 16:24). **9:28** The Doctrine and Covenants contains several clarifications about this event (Doctrine and Covenants 63:21; 138:45). Matthew 17:1 places this event six days later, whereas Luke mentions that it was *eight days*. **9:29** The angels at Jesus's tomb are described similarly (24:4). **9:31** Only Luke mentions that they spoke to him about his journey to Jerusalem. **9:32** That they are overcome with sleep suggests that Jesus prayed for some time before the appearance of Moses and Elijah. **9:35** The directive *hear him* may allude to Deuteronomy 18:15. Some later manuscripts lack *Chosen One*. Second Nephi 31:11 calls on believers to follow the *Beloved Son*.

large crowd gathered to him. [38]And a man from the crowd cried, "Teacher, I beg you to look upon my son, because he is my only child. [39]And a spirit seizes him, and he cries out suddenly, and it tears him, and he foams at the mouth, and it hardly ever leaves him, and it breaks him down. [40]I asked your disciples that they might cast it out, but they were not able to." [41]Jesus answered, "Oh, faithless and perverse generation, how long will I be with you, and endure you? Bring your son here." [42]And as he approached, the demon tore him, and he convulsed, but Jesus commanded the unclean spirit, and the boy was healed, and he returned him to his father. [43]But they were all amazed at the greatness of God.

JESUS FORETELLS HIS PASSION AGAIN (MT 17:22–23; MK 9:30–32)

While they were amazed at all of the things which Jesus did, he said to his disciples, [44]"Pay attention to these words, for the Son of Man is about to be betrayed into the hands of men." [45]But they did not understand this, and it was hidden from them that they might not understand it, and they were afraid to ask him about this teaching.

ON GREATNESS (MT 18:1–5; MK 9:33–37)

[46]A debate came up among them regarding who among them might be greater.

[47]When Jesus knew their concerns, he took a child and set him near himself. [48]And he said to them, "Whoever receives this child in my name receives me, and whoever receives me receives him who sent me. For the least among you all is great."

THE OTHER HEALER (MK 9:38–41)

[49]John answered, "Teacher, we saw a certain man casting out demons in your name, and we forbade him because he did not follow with us." [50]Jesus said to them, "Do not forbid him; whoever is not against you is with you."

A SAMARITAN VILLAGE REJECTS JESUS

[51]And when the days of his ascension were fulfilled, he turned his face to go to Jerusalem. [52]And he sent messengers before him, and after they had departed, they entered a village of the Samaritans in order to prepare for him. [53]But they did not receive him, because he was prepared to go to Jerusalem. [54]When his disciples Jacob and John saw it, they said, "Lord, do you want us *to call down fire from heaven to destroy them*?" [55]But he turned and rebuked them, [56]and then they went to another village.

FOXES HAVE HOLES (MT 8:18–22)

[57]While they traveled along the road, someone said to him, "I will follow you wherever you go." [58]Jesus said to him,

---

9:40 Compare Mark 9:28–29. **9:42** See 1 Nephi 11:31. **9:44** The Greek says literally *put your ears to these words*. **9:46–48** Luke's version of the dispute among the disciples concerning who was greater lessens the subsequent friction that developed among the twelve (Matthew 18:1–5; Mark 9:33–37). **9:47** The wording, *their concerns*, implies that Jesus knew what they were thinking without having heard them speak about this concern. **9:51–19:29** This verse begins one of the central sections of Luke, and it describes Jesus's long and arduous journey to Jerusalem, where he will be crucified. **9:52** These messengers are referred to as *angels*. **9:52–53** Compare Doctrine and Covenants 24:15; 75:19–20. **9:54** The question relies on the language of 2 Kings 1:10, 12, and some manuscripts add *as Elijah did*. Jews often rejected Samaritan claims to being Israelites (compare John 4:9). **9:55–56** A few inferior manuscripts expand these verses following Jesus's rebuke by adding the saying *You do not know what spirit you are of, for the Son of Man did not come to destroy human lives but to save them*. **9:57–62** Luke appears to have grouped several different events into a single encounter that focuses on the cost of being a disciple

"Foxes have holes, and the birds of heaven have nests, but the Son of Man does not have a place to lay his head." [59]To another he said, "Follow me." But he responded, "Lord, first let me go and bury my father." [60]He said to him, "Let the dead bury their dead, but you, go and declare the kingdom of God." [61]Another said, "I will follow you, Lord, but first let me return and bid farewell to those in my house." [62]Jesus said to him, "No one who has placed his hand on the plough and then looks back is fit for the kingdom of God."

THE MISSION OF THE SEVENTY

10 [1]After this, the Lord also appointed seventy, and he sent them two by two before him into every town and place where he was about to go. [2]And he said to them, "The harvest is great, but the workers are few. Request that the lord of the harvest may send workers to his harvest. [3]Be on your way. Behold, I send you as sheep among wolves. [4]Do not carry a bag, nor a wallet, nor sandals, and greet no one on the way. [5]Whenever you enter a house, first say, 'Peace be on this house.' [6]And if a peace-loving person is there, your peace will rest on him; but if not, it will come back to you. [7]Remain in that house, eating and drinking what they provide, for the worker is worthy of his wage. Do not go from house to house. [8]And whatever town you enter and they receive you, eat the things placed in front of you. [9]Heal the sick in that place and say to them, 'The kingdom of God has come near to you.' [10]And whatever city you enter and they do not receive you, when you have gone into the streets say, [11]'The dust that has clung to our feet from your town, we shake it off against you. But know this, the kingdom of God has come near you.' [12]I say to you that in that day, it will be more tolerable for Sodom than it will be for that town.

WOES ON GALILEAN CITIES
(MT 11:20–24)

[13]"Woe to you, Chorazin; woe to you, Bethsaida. If the miracles that were done in you were done in Tyre and Sidon, they would have repented a long time ago, sitting in sackcloth and ashes. [14]It will be more tolerable in the judgment for Tyre and Sidon than for you. [15]And you, Capernaum, will you be exalted to heaven? No, you will be brought down to Hades. [16]Whoever listens to you listens to me, and whoever rejects you rejects me. And whoever rejects me rejects him who sent me."

---

of Jesus. The theme that brings these sayings together is that the Son of Man has no fixed home where he can sleep.

10:1 Several manuscripts have *seventy-two* instead of *seventy*, but the problem of which number is original is difficult to solve because equally good manuscripts support both readings. See Exodus 24:1–9 on Moses's call of seventy elders. Their mission parallels that of the twelve (Luke 9:1–6). Genesis 10–11 lists seventy nations descended from Noah, and the Septuagint version of Genesis 10–11 lists seventy-two. Luke is the only New Testament author to mention the call of the seventy. **10:2** *Harvest* is a metaphor for the gathering of Israel; see Jeremiah 2:3 (compare Matthew 9:38; Alma 26:7). **10:7** Alluded to in Doctrine and Covenants 84:79; 106:3. **10:12** See Genesis 19:24–28. Compare Doctrine and Covenants 75:21–22. **10:13** Chorazin is located a short distance from the northern shore of the Sea of Galilee. The town was known as a site for olive processing. Bethsaida sat on the shore, but today its precise location is disputed. Tyre and Sidon were on the Mediterranean coast to the north of Galilee. The latter two cities were inhabited predominantly by Gentiles. Jesus speaks of *works of power*, which is rendered here as *miracles*. Second Nephi 10:4 paraphrases a portion of this verse (compare Matthew 11:21). **10:15** Capernaum was located on the northern shore of the Sea of Galilee, and it functioned as a center of operations for Jesus and his disciples. The town stood near some of the most productive fishing grounds on the Sea of Galilee.

THE RETURN OF THE SEVENTY

¹⁷And the seventy returned with joy, saying, "Lord, even the demons were subject to us in your name." ¹⁸He said to them, "I saw Satan as lightning falling from heaven. ¹⁹I give you power to tread on snakes and scorpions and over all the power of the enemy, and nothing will hurt you. ²⁰But do not rejoice that the spirits are subject to you, but rejoice that your names are written in the heavens."

²¹In that hour Jesus rejoiced in the Holy Spirit and said, "I praise you, Father, Lord of heaven and earth, that you have hidden these things from the wise and learned, and you have revealed them to babies. Yes, Father, because this was pleasing before you. ²²All things were given to me by my Father, and no one knows who the Son is except the Father, and who the Father is except the Son, and to whomever the Son desires to reveal him."

²³And he turned to the disciples and said to them privately, "Blessed are the eyes that see what you see! ²⁴I say to you that many prophets and kings wanted to see what you see, but they did not see, and to hear what you hear, but they did not hear."

THE PARABLE OF THE GOOD SAMARITAN

²⁵A certain lawyer stood, tempting him and saying, "Teacher, what can I do to inherit eternal life?" ²⁶He said to him, "What is written in the Law? How do you read it?" ²⁷He answered, *"Love the Lord your God with all your heart and with all your soul and with all your strength and with all your understanding,* and *love your neighbor as yourself."* ²⁸Jesus said to him, "You answered correctly; do this and you will live."

²⁹But desiring to justify himself, he said to Jesus, "Who is my neighbor?" ³⁰Jesus responded and said, "A certain man went down from Jerusalem to Jericho, and he fell among bandits, who stripped him and beat him, and they departed, leaving him half dead. ³¹By chance a certain priest went down that way, and when he saw him he passed by on the opposite side. ³²Likewise, a Levite was near the place, and when he saw him he passed by on the opposite side. ³³But a certain Samaritan went on the way and came to him and saw him and was moved with compassion. ³⁴He came near and bound up his wounds and poured in oil and wine, and he put him on his animal and led him to an inn and cared for him. ³⁵The next day he gave two denarii to the innkeeper and said, "Care for him, and whatever you might spend for him I will repay it to you when I return." ³⁶Which of these three seems to you to have become a neighbor to him who fell among bandits?" ³⁷He said to Jesus, "The one who showed kindness to him." Then Jesus said to him, "Depart and do likewise."

MARY AND MARTHA

³⁸While they were on their way, they came to a certain village, and a woman named Martha received him into her house. ³⁹And she had a sister called Mary, who sat down to hear at the feet of the Lord and listened to his word. ⁴⁰But Martha was busy with

---

10:17 Some manuscripts read *seventy-two* (compare note for Luke 10:1). **10:18–19** An allusion to Isaiah 14:12 and possibly Psalm 91:13. Compare 2 Nephi 2:17. **10:20** Alluded to in Doctrine and Covenants 50:30. **10:27** Quotation from Deuteronomy 6:5 and Leviticus 19:18. **10:29–37** This parable is unique to Luke. **10:30** The road to Jericho descends quite dramatically, and it was noted for its dangers. **10:32** For a description of the duties and responsibilities of the *Levites*, see Numbers 3. Compare John 1:19. **10:33** For a similarly positive view of the Samaritans, see Luke 17:16. **10:39** *Mary of Bethany* is named *Mariam* in Luke. The different spellings of the name were quite common in the first century. **10:40** Martha was busy serving, an action described as *diakonia*, or in the capacity of a deacon or deaconess. Such a description indicates that she was likely preparing or serving food. The actions of a deacon

serving; she came and stood by and said, "Lord, do you not care that my sister left me alone to serve? Tell her to help me." [41]The Lord answered, "Martha, Martha, you are anxious and worried about many things, [42]but one thing is needed, and Mary has chosen the part that will not be taken from her."

OFFERINGS AND PRAYER
(MT 6:1–15)

11 [1]He was in a certain place praying, and when he stopped, one of his disciples said to him, "Lord, teach us to pray as John taught his disciples." [2]He said to them, "When you pray, say, 'Father, let your name be holy, let your kingdom come, [3]give us our daily bread each day, [4]and forgive us of our sins, for we forgive everyone indebted to us, and do not lead us into temptation.'" [5]And he said to them, "Suppose one of you has a friend and you go to him in the middle of the night and say to him, 'Friend, lend me three loaves of bread [6]because a friend of mine came to me from the road and I do not have anything to set before him.' [7]And he responds from within, 'Do not cause trouble for me, the door is already locked, and my children are with me in bed, and I am not able to get up and give you anything.' [8]I say to you, even if he does not rise and give him anything because he is a friend, yet because of his insistence he will arise and give him what he needs. [9]I say to you, ask and it will be given to you, seek and you will find, knock and it will be opened to you. [10]Everyone who asks receives, and everyone who seeks finds, and everyone who knocks has it opened to them. [11]Which of you as a father, if your son asks for a fish, gives him a snake instead of a fish? [12]Or if he asks for an egg, will give him a scorpion? [13]If you, then, who are evil, know how to give good gifts to your children, how much more will your Father in heaven give the Holy Spirit to those who ask him?"

BEELZEBUL
(MT 12:22–32; MK 3:22–30)

[14]And he cast out a demon, and it could not speak, and when the demon left the man he began speaking, and the crowd was astonished. [15]But some of them said, "He casts out demons by Beelzebul, the ruler of the demons." [16]But others tried him and sought a sign from heaven from him. [17]But when he knew their thoughts, he said to them, "Every kingdom divided against itself is ruined, and a house divided falls. [18]If Satan is divided against himself, how will his kingdom stand? You say that I cast out demons by Beelzebul. [19]If I cast out demons by Beelzebul, by whom do your sons cast them out? Because of this they will be your judges. [20]If I cast out demons by the finger of God, then the kingdom of God has come upon you. [21]When an armed, strong man guards his courtyard, his belongings are safe. [22]But when someone stronger than he comes, he conquers him, and he takes away his armor in which he trusted, and he gives away the spoils. [23]Whoever is not with

---

or deaconess became the model for service among Christians (see Luke 8:2–3; Acts 9:36–39).

11:2 Some good manuscripts add to the end of the verse *on earth as it is in heaven*. The words *Let your name be holy* may reflect the admonition of Psalm 145:21. **11:3** *Daily bread* may reflect the Israelite exodus and the provision of manna on a daily basis. **11:4** *Temptation* can equally be translated as *trial*. Some manuscripts add *but deliver us from evil*. The textual support for this addition is quite good, but the texts that omit it are older and of a better quality. **11:5–8** This parable is unique to Luke. **11:11** Mosiah 4:14 teaches a similar principle about hearing the needs of children. **11:14** For *Beelzebul* in the Old Testament, see 2 Kings 1:2–6. The title is here applied to Satan, or the devil. **11:16** The request to perform a sign may be an allusion to Elijah (1 Kings 18:20–46). **11:20** Compare Exodus 8:19. Matthew 12:28 has the *Spirit of God* instead of the *finger of God*.

me is against me, and whoever does not gather with me scatters. ²⁴When the unclean spirit departs from a person, it travels through arid places seeking rest, but it finds none. Then it says, 'I will return to my house where I came from.' ²⁵When it comes back, it finds it cleaned and furnished. ²⁶Then it goes and takes seven other spirits more wicked than it, and they live there, and the end state of the man is worse than the first."

²⁷And it came to pass that after he said these things, a woman from the crowd raised her voice and said to him, "Blessed is the womb that bore you and the breasts that nursed you." ²⁸But he said, "Rather, blessed are those who hear the word of God and keep it!"

DENUNCIATION OF THE SCRIBES AND PHARISEES
(MT 23:1–36; MK 12:38–40)

²⁹When the crowds were increasing, he began to speak, "This generation is a wicked generation. It seeks for a sign, but a sign will not be given to it except for the sign of Jonah. ³⁰Just as Jonah was a sign to the Ninevites, even so the Son of Man will be a sign to this generation. ³¹The queen of the South will rise up in judgment with the people of this generation and condemn it because she came from the ends of the world to hear the wisdom of Solomon, and behold, someone greater than Solomon is here. ³²The people of Nineveh will rise up with the people of this generation and condemn it because they repented as a result of the preaching of Jonah, and behold, something greater than Jonah is here.

³³"No one who lights a lamp places it in a cellar or under a basket but on a lampstand so that those who enter may see the light. ³⁴Your eye is the light of the body. When your eye is healthy, your entire body is full of light, but when it is wicked, your entire body is full of darkness. ³⁵Contemplate whether the light in you is darkness. ³⁶If your entire body is full of light, without any portion of darkness, it will be full of light like when a lamp gives you light with its rays."

³⁷While he spoke, a Pharisee invited him to eat with him. And he entered and dined with him. ³⁸When the Pharisee saw that he did not first wash before dinner, he was amazed. ³⁹But the Lord said to him, "Now, you Pharisees cleanse the outside of the cup and the plate, but inwardly you are full of robbery and wickedness. ⁴⁰Fools! Did not the one who made the outside also make the inside? ⁴¹But the things that are inside you, give them as offerings, and then everything will be clean to you.

⁴²"Woe to you Pharisees, because you tithe mint and rue and every herb, but you pass by on judgment and the love of God. You should have done these things and not have neglected the others. ⁴³Woe to you Pharisees, because you love the first seats in the synagogues and greetings in the marketplace. ⁴⁴Woe to you, because you are like unmarked graves, and people walk on top of them and do not know it."

⁴⁵A lawyer responded to him, "Teacher, in saying these things you also offended us." ⁴⁶But he said, "Woe to you lawyers, because you burden people with loads that are difficult to bear, but you will not lift

---

11:30 Jesus here seems to emphasize the teachings of Jonah, or Jonah himself, as the sign that would be given. Jonah was sent to the Ninevites as a sign that they were being called to repentance, and they were perhaps unaware of his miraculous delivery from the belly of the whale. Jonah is a type of the prophet who calls the wicked to repentance (see verse 32). **11:31** The *queen of the South* is the queen of Sheba (1 Kings 10:1–13). **11:34** Alluded to in Doctrine and Covenants 88:67. **11:38** *Wash* is in Greek *baptize himself*, but in this context it refers only to the washing of hands. The Pharisees are surprised that Jesus rejects this common practice. **11:44** This act of walking on top of an unmarked grave would have rendered a person unclean (Leviticus 21:11; Numbers 19:11–22).

your finger to help them. ⁴⁷Woe to you, because you build the tombs of the prophets, but your ancestors killed them. ⁴⁸You are witnesses and approve of the works of your ancestors, because they killed them and you build their tombs. ⁴⁹Because of this the wisdom of God said, 'I will send them prophets and apostles, and some of them they will kill and persecute.' ⁵⁰The blood of all the prophets that has been poured out from the foundation of the world will be charged to this generation, ⁵¹from the blood of Abel to the blood of Zechariah, who died between the altar and the sanctuary. Yes, I say to you, it will be charged to this generation. ⁵²Woe to you lawyers, because you have taken away the key of knowledge, but you did not enter in, and you hindered those who were entering." ⁵³He left that place, and the scribes and Pharisees began to be terribly hostile to him and to provoke him in many things, ⁵⁴and they waited for him to catch him in his words.

The Yeast of the Pharisees (MT 16:5–12; MK 8:14–21)

12 ¹At that time, a crowd of thousands gathered so that they pressed on one another, and he began to say to his disciples first, "Beware of the yeast of the Pharisees, which is hypocrisy.

Do Not Fear (MT 10:26–33)

²"Nothing is concealed that will not be revealed, and nothing is hidden that will not be known. ³Therefore, what you said in the dark will be heard in the light, and what you speak in private rooms will be declared upon the rooftops. ⁴I say to you, my friends, do not fear those who kill the body but afterward no longer have any power. ⁵I will show you whom to fear: fear the one who, after killing you, has authority to cast you into hell. Yes, I say to you, fear that person. ⁶Are not five sparrows sold for two copper coins? But not one of them is forgotten before God. ⁷But even every hair of your head is numbered. Do not fear; you are more valued than many sparrows. ⁸I say to you, everyone who confesses me before men, the Son of Man will confess him before the angels of God. ⁹Whoever denies me before men will be denied before the angels of God. ¹⁰Everyone who speaks a word against the Son of Man, it will be forgiven, but whoever blasphemes the Holy Spirit will not be forgiven. ¹¹When they bring you to the synagogues and the rulers and the authorities, do not worry about how you will respond or what you should say. ¹²For the Holy Spirit will teach you in that hour what you should say."

11:51 See Genesis 4:1–12; 2 Chronicles 24:19–22. **11:52** *Taken away the key of knowledge* could refer to the idea that their interpretations of scripture obscured the meaning of those texts.

12:1 The mention of the *yeast of the Pharisees* may have Passover connotations (see Exodus 12:14–20). During Passover, bread was eaten that had not been made with yeast or leaven. **12:5** The word *hell* translates from the Greek word *Gehenna*, which refers to the small valley on the southern slope of Mount Zion in Jerusalem where some of the kings of Judah offered child sacrifices (2 Kings 23; Jeremiah 7:31; 19:2–6), and later generations may have used it as a place to burn rubbish. **12:6** The coins mentioned here are *asses*, sometimes referred to in the plural as *assaria*. One of these coins was worth about one-sixteenth of a denarius. **12:9** The Joseph Smith Translation reads for this verse *But he who denieth me before men shall be denied before the angels of God. Now his disciples knew that he said this, because they had spoken evil against him before the people; for they were afraid to confess him before men. And they reasoned among themselves, saying, He knoweth our hearts, and he speaketh to our condemnation, and we shall not be forgiven.* **12:10** Compare Doctrine and Covenants 105:15.

THE PARABLE OF THE RICH FOOL

[13]Someone from the crowd said to him, "Teacher, tell my brother to divide our inheritance with me." [14]Jesus said to him, "Man, who set me as a judge and arbitrator over you?" [15]He said to them, "Watch and beware of all types of greed, because a person's life is more than the quantity of his possessions." [16]He told them a parable, saying, "The land of a certain rich man produced well, [17]and he thought to himself, 'What will I do, because I have nowhere to store my fruit?' [18]And he said, 'I will do this: I will tear down my barns and build larger ones, and I will gather in them all my grain and goods. [19]I will tell my soul, "Soul, you have many goods placed in storage for many years; relax, eat, drink, and be merry!"' [20]But God said to him, 'Fool! On this night your life will be taken back from you, and the things that you stored, whose will they be?' [21]Thus it is for those who store treasure for themselves but are not rich toward God."

ON DISCIPLESHIP (MK 6:19–34)

[22]And he said to his disciples, "Therefore I say to you, do not worry about your life, what you will eat, or for your body, about what you will wear. [23]For there is more to life than food and more to the body than clothing. [24]Consider the ravens: they do not sow or reap, they do not have a storehouse or barn, but God feeds them. You are more valuable than the birds! [25]Are any of you able, by worrying, to add an hour to your lifetime? [26]If you are not able to do the smallest thing, why do you worry about the rest? [27]Consider the lilies: how they grow, neither do they work or spin, but I say to you that Solomon in all his glory was not clothed like one of them. [28]If God clothes the grass of the field that lives today but is cast into the oven tomorrow, how much more will he clothe you who are of little faith! [29]Do not seek out what you will eat or what you will drink, and do not continue to worry. [30]The nations of the world seek after all these things, but your Father knows that you need them. [31]But seek his kingdom, and these things will be given to you. [32]Do not fear, little flock, because your Father in heaven willingly gives the kingdom to you. [33]Sell your possessions and give alms and make for yourselves bags that do not wear out, an unfailing treasure in heaven, where a thief cannot draw near and a moth does not destroy. [34]For where your treasure is, there your heart will be also.

THE NEED TO BE WATCHFUL (MT 24:42–51; MK 13:32–37)

[35]"Be dressed and ready, and have your lamps burning. [36]Be like the ones who are

---

12:13 Laws regarding inheritance are found in Genesis 48:6; Numbers 36:6–9; Deuteronomy 21:15–17. Compare Acts 20:32; Doctrine and Covenants 38:20. *Our* is lacking in Greek, but the questioner and brother clearly have a claim to the inheritance. **12:13–21** This parable is unique to Luke. **12:19** See 1 Corinthians 15:32. Echoed in 2 Nephi 28:7. **12:20** Compare Jeremiah 17:11. **12:24** *Ravens* are considered unclean (Leviticus 11:13–15; Deuteronomy 14:11–14), but God still feeds them (Psalm 147:9). **12:27** Compare Doctrine and Covenants 84:80–94. **12:30** *The nations of the world* refers to the Gentiles, and the noun *nations* can refer specifically to Gentiles. In this instance, the context *of the world* indicates that this is a political designation. Alluded to in Doctrine and Covenants 84:83. **12:31** Compare Jacob 2:18 for a similar injunction. **12:32** Doctrine and Covenants 6:34; 29:5; 35:27. **12:34** Second Nephi 9:30 offers commentary on the concepts of this verse (compare Matthew 6:21). **12:35** Allusion to Exodus 12:11. The original context of the passage from Exodus describes being prepared for the Passover. The same may be implied here. Jesus is encouraging believers to be ready for his return, when he will dine with them again. **12:36** The word translated as *master* is also the same word used elsewhere for the Lord (Greek *kyrios*).

prepared for their master to return from the wedding feast, and when he comes and knocks they open to him immediately. [37]Blessed are those servants who, when the master comes, he finds them attentive. Truly I say to you, he will buckle his belt and will make them recline to eat, and he will come and serve them. [38]And if he comes in the second or third watch and finds them so, blessed are those servants. [39]Know this, that if the master of the house had known in what hour the thief was coming, he would not have allowed his house to be robbed. [40]And you should also be ready, because the Son of Man comes in an hour that you do not know."

[41]Peter said, "Lord, did you speak this parable to us or to everyone?" [42]And the Lord said, "Who is a faithful and wise master, whom the Lord will set over his household, to give an allowance of food at the right time? [43]Blessed is that servant whom his master shall find so doing when he comes. [44]Truly I say to you, he will place him over all his belongings. [45]But if that servant says in his heart, 'My master delays his arrival,' and then he begins to beat the male and female servants and to eat and drink and to get drunk, [46]then the master of that servant will come in a day and hour that he does not know or look for him, and he will cut him off, and he will place him with the unfaithful. [47]That servant who knew his master's will but did not prepare for him or do his will shall be beaten severely. [48]But the one who did not know the master's will and did what deserved a beating will be beaten little. To everyone to whom much is given, much will be required, and to whom much has been entrusted, more will be asked.

THE COST OF DISCIPLESHIP (MT 10:34–36)

[49]"I came to cast fire on the earth, and what I wish is that it were already on fire. [50]I have a baptism to be baptized with, and I feel distressed until it is completed. [51]Do you think that I came to bring peace to the earth? No, I say to you, but rather division. [52]For there will now be five divided in a house: three against two, and two against three. [53]Father will be divided against son, and son against father, mother against daughter, and *daughter against mother*, mother-in-law against daughter-in-law, *and daughter-in-law against mother-in-law*."

[54]He also said to the crowd, "When you see a cloud rising from the west, immediately you say, 'The rain is coming.' And then it happens. [55]When you see the south wind blowing, you say, 'The heat comes.' And it happens. [56]Hypocrites! You know how to understand the appearance of the earth and sky, but you do not understand the current time. [57]Why do you not judge by yourselves what is right? [58]As you are departing with your accuser to the judge, while on the way make an effort to settle with him, because he may drag you before the judge, and the judge may deliver you to the officer, and the officer may throw you into prison. [59]I say to you, you will never depart from there until you have paid the last coin."

12:37 The master of the house will *serve them* in the capacity of a deacon (compare Isaiah 25:6). **12:39** Some manuscripts add *he would have watched* before *he would not have allowed*. **12:40** Compare Revelation 3:3. **12:42** Compare Doctrine and Covenants 78:22; 101:61; 104:75; 136:27. **12:45** Compare Matthew 24:48; 3 Nephi 29:2. **12:47–48** This parable is unique to Luke. **12:48** Quoted in Doctrine and Covenants 82:3. Echoed in 2 Nephi 28:8. **12:50** *Baptism* is used as a metaphor to describe suffering and trial. **12:51** The theme of *division* is common in the Book of Mormon; compare 2 Nephi 30:10; Mosiah 19:2; 4 Nephi 1:35. **12:53** Quotation from Micah 7:6. **12:56** *Hypocrites* are defined as those who misinterpret the meaning of the signs. **12:59** For the value of the *coin* (= *a lepton*), see Mark 12:41–44 and Luke 21:1–4. Two *lepta* were equivalent to a *quadrans* (see Matthew 5:26).

THE PARABLE OF THE BARREN FIG TREE

13 [1]There were some people there at that time who told him about the Galileans whose blood Pilate mixed with their sacrifices. [2]And he answered them, "Do you think that these Galileans were worse sinners than all other Galileans because they experienced these things? [3]I say to you, no. But if you do not all repent, you will likewise be destroyed. [4]Or the eighteen on whom the tower of Siloam fell and killed, do you think that they became worse offenders than all people living in Jerusalem? [5]I say to you, no. But if you do not repent, you will all likewise be destroyed."

[6]He spoke this parable, "A farmer had a fig tree planted in his orchard, and he came looking for fruit on it, but he did not find any. [7]And he said to the orchard worker, 'Look, for three years I came looking for fruit on this fig tree, and I have found none. Cut it down. Why should it render the ground useless?' [8]But he answered him, 'Leave it alone, master, this year also, so that I may dig around it and fertilize it. [9]It may indeed bear fruit, and if not, then you can cut it down.'"

JESUS HEALS A WOMAN ON THE SABBATH

[10]And he taught in one of the synagogues on the Sabbath. [11]And there was a woman who had a spirit of affliction for eighteen years, and she was bent over completely and was not able to straighten her back at all. [12]When Jesus saw her, he called her near and said to her, "Woman, you are freed from your affliction." [13]And he laid his hands on her, and immediately she stood upright and glorified God. [14]The ruler of the synagogue answered, because he was displeased that Jesus healed on the Sabbath, and said to the crowd, "There are six days during which one ought to work: during these, then, come and be healed and not on the Sabbath day." [15]Jesus answered him, "Hypocrites, do not each of you on the Sabbath untie his cow or ass from the stable and lead it away to water? [16]But this one, being a daughter of Abraham, whom Satan bound for eighteen years, should she not be loosed from this bondage on the Sabbath day?" [17]When he said this, all of his enemies were ashamed, and the entire crowd rejoiced at the glorious things that were done by him.

THE PARABLE OF THE MUSTARD SEED (MT 13:31–32; MK 4:30–32)

[18]And he said, "What is the kingdom of God like? And to what shall I compare it? [19]It is like a mustard seed that a man took and cast into his garden, and it grew, and then it became a great tree and the birds of the heavens nested in its branches."

THE PARABLE OF THE LEAVEN (MT 13:33)

[20]Again he said, "What is the kingdom of God like? [21]It is like yeast that a woman took and mixed in three portions of dough until all was leavened."

THE NARROW DOOR

[22]And he passed through the towns and villages, teaching and making his journey to Jerusalem. [23]A certain person said to him, "Lord, are there few who are saved?"

13:1 Luke alone records this story, the details of which are now lost. Historical sources do note that Pilate, on occasion, acted violently against Jews and Samaritans. **13:1–9** This parable is unique to Luke. **13:3, 5** A portion of these verses is alluded to in 2 Nephi 30:1; Helaman 7:28. **13:4** This story is known only through Luke's mention of it. The name *Siloam* indicates that the tower was in Jerusalem. **13:8** The act of *fertilizing* the tree is described as adding manure. **13:16** *Daughter of Abraham* appears to evoke empathy for the woman since she is also a daughter of the covenant.

But he said to them, [24]"Seek to enter in through the narrow doorway, because many, I say to you, will try to go in but will not be able to do so. [25]When the master of the house has risen and shut the door, you will stand outside and begin to knock at the door, saying, 'Lord, open up to us.' And he will answer them, 'I do not know you, where you are from.' [26]Then you will begin to say, 'We dined with you, and we drank with you, and you taught us in our streets.' [27]And he will say to you, '*I do not know where you come from. Depart from me, all you who are wrongdoers.*' [28]There will be weeping and grinding of teeth there when you see Abraham and Isaac and Jacob and all the prophets in the kingdom of God, and you will be thrown out. [29]They will come from the east and west and from the north and south, and they will sit down in the kingdom of God. [30]Indeed, the last will be first, and the first will be last."

A WARNING TO HEROD

[31]At that time some Pharisees came and said to him, "Depart and be on your way, because Herod wishes to kill you." [32]And he said to them, "Go and tell that fox, behold, I cast out demons and heal today and tomorrow, but the third day I will finish my work. [33]But I must continue today, tomorrow, and the day following because it is not possible for a prophet to be killed outside Jerusalem.

JESUS'S LAMENT OVER JERUSALEM (MT 23:37–39)

[34]"Jerusalem, Jerusalem, who kills the prophets and stones those who were sent to you, how often I desired to gather together your children as a hen gathers her brood under her wings, but you would not. [35]Behold, your house is desolate. I say to you, you will not see me until you say, '*Blessed is he who comes in the name of the Lord.*'"

JESUS HEALS A MAN ON THE SABBATH

14 [1]And it came to pass that he entered the house of a ruler of the Pharisees on a Sabbath to eat bread, and they were watching him. [2]And there was a man in front of him who had severe swelling. [3]And Jesus said to the lawyers and Pharisees, "Is it lawful to heal on the Sabbath or not?" [4]But they were silent. And he took him and healed him and sent him away. [5]And he said to them, "Which of you, having a child or cow that has fallen into a well, will not immediately lift him out on the Sabbath day?" [6]And they were not able to respond to this.

ON HUMILITY

[7]And he spoke a parable to those who were gathered, drawing attention to how they chose the prominent seats. He said to them, [8]"When you are invited by anyone

---

13:24 Although the doorway is defined as *narrow*, the Lord forbids entrance because he did not know them, and not because the doorway is too narrow for entry (verse 25). **13:27** Quotation from Psalm 6:8. **13:29** The act of *sitting down* described in this verse is the act of reclining to eat. The note regarding the gathering from all directions probably implies the gathering of Gentiles. Compare Psalm 107:3; 3 Nephi 20:13; Doctrine and Covenants 42:63; 44:1; 125:4. **13:30** Compare Ether 13:12. **13:31** Only Luke records this friendly warning from the Pharisees, who appear in this instance to be attempting to help Jesus. **13:32** *Go tell that fox* plays on a negative stereotype of craftiness and lack of power to confront Jesus directly (see Song of Solomon 2:15). Mosiah 3:10 similarly views the raising of Jesus on the *third day* in positive terms. **13:35** Quotation from Psalm 118:26.

14:2 Many translations describe the man's condition as *dropsy*. The Greek word implies the swelling of the tissues. **14:5** Some manuscripts read *a cow or a donkey* instead of *a child or cow*. **14:8** The act of *sitting* in this and the following verses describes *reclining to eat*.

to a marriage, do not sit in the prominent seat lest someone more distinguished than you is invited by him. ⁹When the person who invited you enters, he will say, 'Give this place to him,' and you will be ashamed to take the lowest place. ¹⁰But when you are called, after you enter, sit in the lowest place so that when he who invited you comes, he will say to you, 'Friend, come up higher.' Then you will have honor in front of all those sitting with you. ¹¹For everyone who exalts himself will be humbled, and whoever humbles himself will be exalted."

¹²And he also said to the man who invited him, "When you prepare a meal or a feast, do not call your friends or your brothers and sisters or your relatives or your rich neighbors, lest they invite you in return and you are therefore repaid. ¹³But when you prepare a feast, invite the poor, the disabled, the maimed, and the blind, ¹⁴and you will be blessed because they cannot repay you, for you will be repaid in the resurrection of the righteous."

THE PARABLE OF THE WEDDING FEAST (MT 22:1–14)

¹⁵And one of those sitting with him, when he heard this, said to him, "Blessed is the person who will eat bread in the kingdom of God!" ¹⁶But Jesus said to him, "A man prepared a great feast, and he invited many, ¹⁷and he sent his servant at the hour of the feast to tell those who were invited,

'Come, because it is ready now.' ¹⁸And they began each one of them to make excuses. The first said to him, 'I have purchased a field, and I must go and see it. I ask you, allow me to be excused.' ¹⁹And another said, 'I have purchased five yoke of oxen, and I go to approve them. I ask you, allow me to be excused.' ²⁰And another said, 'I have married a woman, and because of this I am not able to come.' ²¹And the servant went and told his master this. Then the master of the house was angry and said to his servant, 'Go quickly into the streets and alleys of the city, to the poor and disabled, to the blind and maimed, and bring them here.' ²²And the servant said, 'Master, it has been done as you commanded, and there is still room.' ²³And the master said to the servant, 'Go into the highways and hedges and persuade them to come, so that my house is full. ²⁴For I say to you that none of those invited to my feast will taste it.'"

THE COST OF DISCIPLESHIP (MT 10:37–38)

²⁵A large crowd came to him, and he turned and said to them, ²⁶"If anyone comes to me and does not hate his own father and mother and wife and children and brothers and sisters and even his own life, he is not able to be my disciple. ²⁷Whoever does not bear his own cross and come after me is not able to be my disciple. ²⁸Who among you while wanting

---

14:10 Perhaps an allusion to Proverbs 25:6–7. **14:11** This verse is quoted differently in Doctrine and Covenants 101:42 (compare Doctrine and Covenants 112:3). **14:14** Here Jesus speaks of the *resurrection of the righteous*. The insinuation is that such acts would earn a person a place in that resurrection. Verse 15 follows this by praising those who achieve a place in the resurrection of the righteous. **14:18–20** The excuses for not attending are similar to those of Deuteronomy 20:5–8. **14:21** Compare Leviticus 21:16–24. **14:23** When the master invites those out on the *highways and hedges*, the implication is that the new guests are outside of Israel and possibly Gentiles. **14:26** The Joseph Smith Translation clarifies *or in other words, is afraid to lay down his life for my sake*. **14:27** *Come after me* implies following Jesus after he has departed and left them. **14:28** *Counting the cost* and *bearing his own cross* (verse 27) both imply that discipleship will be burdensome and costly to those who follow Jesus. Some of the negative insinuations may arise from the nearness of Jesus's impending death and an increasing sense of being required to offer himself to fulfill God's will.

to build a tower does not first sit down and count the cost to see whether he has enough to complete it? ²⁹Otherwise, when he sets his foundation and is not able to finish it, those watching will mock him, ³⁰saying, 'This man began to build, and he was not able to finish it.' ³¹Or what king who goes against another king to engage in battle will not first sit down and consult whether he is able with ten thousand men to meet twenty thousand coming against him? ³²And if he cannot succeed, having sent an embassy when he is yet a long way off, does he ask for peace? ³³Thus, every one of you who does not forsake all that he has is not able to be my disciple. ³⁴Salt is good, but if the salt has become flavorless, in what way will it be seasoned? ³⁵It is not useful for the land or manure pile, but they throw it away. Whoever has ears to hear, let that person hear."

THE PARABLE OF THE LOST SHEEP
(MT 18:12–14)

15 ¹Then all the tax collectors and sinners drew near him to listen. ²And both the Pharisees and scribes complained, saying, "This man accepts sinners and eats with them." ³He spoke to them this parable, saying, ⁴"What man among you having one hundred sheep and loses one of them does not leave behind the ninety-nine in the desert and go after the lost one until he finds it? ⁵When he finds it, he places it on his shoulders, rejoicing. ⁶And when he comes to the house, he calls his friends and neighbors, saying to them,

'Rejoice with me, because I have found my lost sheep.' ⁷I say to you that there will be more joy in heaven over one repentant sinner than over the ninety-nine righteous who do not need to repent.

THE PARABLE OF THE LOST COIN

⁸"What woman who has ten silver coins, if she loses one, does not light a lamp and sweep the house and search carefully until she finds it? ⁹When she finds it, she says to her friends and neighbors, 'Rejoice with me, because I have found the coin that was lost. ¹⁰Thus, I say to you, that there will be rejoicing before the angels of God when one sinner repents."

THE PARABLE OF THE PRODIGAL SONS

¹¹And he said, "A man had two sons, ¹²and the younger son said to his father, 'Father, give me my portion of the inheritance that will belong to me.' And he divided his assets between them. ¹³Not many days later, the younger son gathered everything he had together, and he went away to a distant region, and there he wasted his substance in careless living. ¹⁴After he spent everything, there was a great famine in that region, and he began to be in need. ¹⁵And he went away and joined himself to one of the citizens of that region, and he sent him into the fields to feed the pigs. ¹⁶And he wanted to fill himself from the carob pods that the pigs were eating, but no one gave him anything. ¹⁷Then he came to himself

---

15:1 The three parables of this chapter all treat the topic of things that are lost but are subsequently found. **15:2** The question of eating with *sinners* raises the issue of becoming unclean through contact with someone who is unclean. In the Book of Mormon, *uncleanness* becomes a description of spiritual sin (see 1 Nephi 10:21). **15:8–10** This parable is unique to Luke. **15:11** This parable is often referred to as the parable of the *prodigal son*, but the behavior of the two sons is equally criticized: one for wandering and spending his inheritance, and the other for hardheartedness and being judgmental. **15:11–32** This parable is unique to Luke. **15:13** The younger son wasted his money, but the parable does not specify how. Later the older brother will imply certain sinful actions (verse 30). **15:16** *Carob pods* are from the pea family, and their seeds were commonly consumed, but in a dried and ground form or when they were newly ripe. Eating with pigs is more alarming than eating carob pods. **15:17–19** These verses may suggest the proper

and said, 'How many of my father's hired servants have an abundance of bread, but I am dying with hunger here! [18]I will arise and go to my Father, and I will say to him, 'Father, I have sinned against heaven and against you. [19]I am no longer worthy to be called your son. Make me like one of your hired servants.' [20]And he arose and came to his father. When he was yet a long way from home, his father saw him and had compassion on him, and he ran and hugged him and kissed him. [21]The son said to him, 'Father, I have sinned against heaven and against you. I am no longer worthy to be called your son.' [22]But the father said to his servants, 'Quickly, bring out the best robe and put it on him, and place a ring on his hand and sandals under his feet, [23]and bring the fatted calf and butcher it, that we may eat and be merry, [24]because this son of mine was dead, and he lives again; he was lost, but he is found.' And they began to be merry. [25]But his older son was in the field, and as he came near to the house, he heard music and dancing, [26]and he called one of the servants, and he asked what this meant. [27]And he said to him, 'Your brother arrived, and your father killed the fatted calf because he received him back safe and healthy.' [28]He was angry and refused to go in, and therefore his father came out and entreated him. [29]And he answered his father, 'Look, I have served you like a slave for many years, and never have I transgressed your command, but you never gave me a young goat that I might cele-

brate with my friends, [30]but when your son came, the one who consumed his living with prostitutes, you butchered a fatted calf.' [31]But he said to him, 'Son, you are always with me, and everything that is mine is yours. [32]It was appropriate to celebrate and rejoice because this brother of yours was dead, but he is alive; he was lost, but he is found.'"

THE PARABLE OF
THE UNJUST STEWARD

16 [1]He said to his disciples, "A rich man had a steward, and the man heard accusations that the steward was wasting his goods. [2]And he called and said to him, 'What is this that I hear about you? Surrender the management of your account, for you are no longer able to serve.' [3]But the steward said to himself, 'What will I do, because my master is taking away the stewardship from me? I am not able to dig, and I am ashamed to beg. [4]I know what I will do so that when I am removed from this position people will receive me into their homes.' [5]And he called each one of the debtors of his master and said to the first, 'How much do you owe to my master?' [6]And he said, 'One hundred measures of olive oil.' But he said to him, 'Take your bill and sit down and quickly write fifty.' [7]Then he said to another, 'How much do you owe?' And he said, 'One hundred measures of grain.' He said to him, 'Take your bill and sit down and quickly write eighty.' [8]And the master commended the

---

beginning of the process of repentance, namely, a realization of having gone astray. **15:23** Compare 1 Samuel 28:24. **15:27** The servant reports that the father was happy to hear of his son's health, thus emphasizing his paternal role in looking out for his son's welfare. **15:28** *Entreat* can also mean *admonish* or *comfort*. **15:29** The older son emphasizes his *service* to his father, but not his love. **15:32** *Appropriate*, in this context, can also mean *necessary*, *fitting*, or *prudent*.

16:1 The verb of wasting his master's goods is the same as that used of the younger son in Luke 15:13. **16:1–12** This parable is unique to Luke. **16:2** Alluded to in Doctrine and Covenants 69:5; 70:4; 72:3. **16:6** The measures are in *baths*, which are equivalent to about 8 gallons each (about 32 liters). This was an extremely large debt of over 800 gallons. **16:7** The precise amount of this measure is difficult to determine, and each measure was equivalent to 10–12 bushels (just under 400 liters). **16:8** For *children of the light*, see John 12:36.

dishonest steward because he acted prudently. For the children of this age are wiser in dealing with their generation than are the children of light. ⁹I say to you, make friends for yourselves by means of unrighteous wealth, so that when it fails they will receive you into eternal habitations.

¹⁰"The one who is faithful in the little things is also faithful in much, and the one who is dishonest in little things is also unrighteous in much. ¹¹If you have not been trustworthy in unrighteous riches, who will trust you in true riches? ¹²And if you have not been trustworthy with another's property, who will give you property of your own? ¹³No servant can serve two masters, for either he will hate the one and love the other or he will heed one and despise the other. You cannot serve God and riches."

TEACHINGS ABOUT
THE PHARISEES

¹⁴When the Pharisees, who loved money, heard all this, they ridiculed him. ¹⁵And he said to them, "You declare yourselves to be righteous before men, but God knows your hearts. What is lofty among humankind is an abomination before God. ¹⁶The Law and the Prophets were until John, but since then the good news of the kingdom of God is taught, and everyone is urged into it. ¹⁷It is easier for heaven and earth to pass away than for the smallest portion of a letter of the Law to fail. ¹⁸Everyone who divorces his spouse and marries another commits adultery, and whoever marries the divorced spouse commits adultery.

THE RICH MAN AND LAZARUS

¹⁹"There was a rich man, and he dressed in purple and fine linen, and he dined lavishly every day. ²⁰There was a poor man named Lazarus, who lay near his gates and he was covered in sores. ²¹And he desired to be filled from the crumbs that fell from the rich man's table, and even the dogs came and licked his sores. ²²And it came to pass that the poor person died and was carried away by the angels into the arms of Abraham, and the rich person died and was buried. ²³And in hell he lifted up his eyes while in torment and saw Abraham a long way off and Lazarus in his arms. ²⁴And he called out and said, 'Father Abraham, have mercy on me and send Lazarus so that he may dip the tip of his finger in water so that he may cool my tongue because I am in agony in these flames.' ²⁵But Abraham said, 'Child, remember that you received

---

16:9 There is some dispute regarding the precise meaning of the Aramaic word *mammon*, translated here as *wealth*. Riches or wealth are the most widely agreed-on meanings. Alluded to in Doctrine and Covenants 82:22. **16:11, 13** See note on verse 9. **16:16** From the context it is not certain whether the phrase *and everyone is urged into it* is to be taken critically or favorably. The verb can be translated in a negative sense as *is forced into it* but also in a positive sense, *since the period of the Law and Prophets has ended, now everyone is forced to choose the kingdom of God.* There is no verb in the first part of the sentence, so it may be rendered *the Law and the Prophets until John*. *Law* and *Prophets* are capitalized because they refer technically to divisions of the Old Testament. **16:17** The Joseph Smith Translation reads *And why teach ye the law, and deny that which is written; and condemn him who the Father hath sent to fulfill the law, that you might all be redeemed? O fools! For you have said in your hearts, There is no God. And you pervert the right way; and the kingdom of heaven suffereth violence of you; and you persecute the meek; and in your violence you seek to destroy the kingdom; and ye take the children of the kingdom by force.* **16:19–31** Compare Doctrine and Covenants 56:14–20. This parable is unique to Luke. **16:20** *Lazarus* is the only named individual in Jesus's parables. **16:22** *Arms of Abraham* can also be translated as *Abraham's embrace.* Some translations refer to this as *Abraham's bosom.* It is not a place but the state of being welcomed by Abraham. **16:23** *Hell* is the translation of the Greek *Hades*. Here it is a place of burning-hot torment.

good things in your life, and Lazarus received bad things. Now he is comforted and you are in agony. ²⁶And apart from all this, a great chasm is fixed between us and you so that those who wish to go from here to you are not able to do so, neither can someone pass from you to us.' ²⁷But he said, 'I beg you, Father, that you will send him to my father's house, ²⁸for I have five brothers, so that he may warn them, that they might not come to this place of torment.' ²⁹Abraham said, 'They have Moses and the Prophets; let them hear them.' ³⁰But he said, 'No, Father Abraham, but if someone from the dead goes to them they will repent.' ³¹And he replied, 'If they do not listen to Moses and the Prophets, then they will not be persuaded if someone rises from the dead.'"

UNPROFITABLE SERVANTS

17 ¹And he said to his disciples, "It is impossible for offenses not to come, but woe to that person through whom they come. ²It is better for that person if a millstone is hung around his neck and that person is cast into the sea than for that person to cause one of these little ones to stumble. ³Pay attention to yourselves. If your brother sins, rebuke him, and if he re-

pents, forgive him. ⁴And if he sins against you seven times in a day, and if he turns to you seven times and says, 'I repent,' you must forgive him."

⁵And the apostles said to the Lord, "Increase our faith." ⁶The Lord responded, "If you have the faith of a mustard seed, you will say to this mulberry tree, 'Be uprooted and planted in the sea,' and it would obey you.

⁷"Will anyone among you who has a servant plowing or caring for sheep, when he comes from the field, say to him, 'Come and dine right away'? ⁸Instead, will the master not say to him, 'Prepare something and I will dine, and dress yourself for the occasion to serve me while I eat and drink, and afterward you will eat and drink'? ⁹Does he thank the servant because he did what he was commanded to do? ¹⁰So it is for you: when you do all things that you are commanded, you should say, 'We are useless servants; we have accomplished only what we were supposed to do.'"

JESUS HEALS TEN WITH LEPROSY

¹¹And it came to pass that as he traveled to Jerusalem, he passed through the region between Samaria and Galilee. ¹²And

---

16:26 See 1 Nephi 12:18. **16:29–31** Quoted in Doctrine and Covenants 45:37–38. **16:31** The conclusion of the parable equates living and dead witnesses in their power to convert. See Mormon 8:26; Moroni 10:27.

17:1 *Offenses* is the equivalent of the Greek word *stumbling blocks*, which refers to the mechanism in a trap that springs the trap. It refers generally to anything that trips a person or causes a person to stumble. **17:1–2** The context of the first two verses appears to be offending little children, which is implied in the phrase *little ones*, but it could also refer to the disciples. **17:2** A millstone could easily weigh several hundred pounds. Alluded to in Doctrine and Covenants 121:22. **17:3** Greek uses *brother* in a generic sense of *brothers and sisters*. In this verse, *brother* has been retained because of the singular verbs. The focus is on the individual, whether a brother or sister. **17:4** Doctrine and Covenants 98:40 alludes to this verse. **17:5** Luke refers to the disciples as *apostles* or *missionaries* more than any other Gospel writer does (Luke 6:13; 9:10; 11:49; 22:14; 24:10). By comparison, the Gospel of John does not use that term, and the Book of Acts uses it more frequently (thirty times) than all of the Gospels combined. **17:10** The context appears to be an encouragement to be humble, and some of the language of this verse also appears in Mosiah 2:21; 22:4. **17:11** This would be the region to the south and west of the Sea of Galilee. This region would put him near Nazareth, but the precise location is not mentioned. **17:12** *They stood at some distance*, which enabled them to speak to Jesus but not render him unclean according to the law of Moses (see verse 14).

after he entered a certain village, ten men who had leprosy met him, and they stood at some distance. [13]And they raised their voices and said, "Jesus, master, have mercy on us." [14]When he saw them he said, "Go and show yourselves to the priests." And it came to pass that as they went they were healed. [15]But one of them, when he saw that he was healed, turned back and with a loud voice glorified God, [16]and he fell on his face at Jesus's feet and thanked him. And he was a Samaritan. [17]Jesus asked, "Were not ten healed?" Where are the nine? [18]Did none of them except this foreigner return and give glory to God?" [19]And Jesus said to him, "Rise and be on your way. Your faith has healed you."

THE COMING OF
THE KINGDOM OF GOD

[20]When he was questioned by the Pharisees about when the kingdom of God was coming, he answered them, "The kingdom of God will not come by means of observation, [21]nor will they say, 'Behold, here, or there.' For the kingdom of God is within you." [22]Then he said to his disciples, "The days will come when you will desire to see one of the days of the Son of Man, and you will not see it. [23]And they will say to you, 'Look, there,' or 'Look, here.' Do not go or pursue it. [24]For as lightning flashes and lights up one part of sky to the other, even so the Son of Man will be in his day. [25]But first he must suffer many things and be rejected by this generation. [26]As it was in the days of Noah, even so will it be in the days of the Son of Man. [27]They were eating and drinking and marrying and giving in marriage until the day Noah entered into the ark. Then the flood came and destroyed them all. [28]Likewise, as it was in the day of Lot, they were eating and drinking and buying and selling and planting and building, [29]but on the day that Lot departed from Sodom, it rained fire and sulfur from heaven and destroyed them all. [30]That is how it will be in the day the Son of Man is revealed. [31]In that day, whoever is on the housetop and his belongings are in the house, he must not come down and take them. And whoever is in the field, likewise let him not turn back. [32]Remember Lot's wife. [33]Whoever seeks to protect his life will lose it, and whoever seeks to lose his life will preserve it. [34]I say to you, on that night there will be two on a bed; the one will be taken and the other left. [35]There will be two grinding grain together; one will be taken and the other left. [[[36]Two will be in the field; one will be taken and the other left."]] [37]And they answered him, "Where, Lord?" And he said to them, "Where the body is, there will the vultures be gathered."

17:14 Compare Leviticus 13:2–8; 14:2–3. **17:16** John mentions the Samaritans more than the other Gospel authors do (see John 4:5–7, 39–40; 8:48). Luke is largely favorable toward them (compare Luke 10:25–37). **17:19** The Greek can also mean *saved you* instead of *healed you*. **17:21** Although the coming of the *kingdom of God* typically refers to an event, here it is a place inside of the believer. The kingdom comes with a person. A possible allusion to Ezekiel 36:27. **17:26** For the story of Noah, see Genesis 6:1–7:7. Those days were characterized by careful preparation by Noah, who found favor in the sight of God. **17:27** *Giving in marriage* refers to the act of *giving away someone* in a marriage, a role usually assumed by the parents. **17:28** Compare Genesis 19:1–25. **17:29** Compare Genesis 19:24. **17:32** Allusion to Genesis 19:26. **17:36** This verse is omitted in the majority of New Testament manuscripts and is not likely to be original. **17:37** The disciples wonder where those who are taken will go. Luke uses the term *eagles* where *vultures* would be expected. The Joseph Smith Translation for this verse reads *And they answered and said unto him, Where, Lord, shall they be taken? And he said unto them, Wheresoever the body is gathered; or, in other words, whithersoever the saints are gathered, thither will the eagles be gathered together, or thither will the remainder be gathered together. This he spake signifying the gathering of his saints;*

THE PARABLE OF THE WIDOW

18 ¹He told them a parable concerning how they ought to pray always and not lose heart, ²saying, "There was a judge in a certain city who did not fear God, and he did not respect people. ³But there was a widow in that city who kept coming to him, saying, 'Give me justice against my adversary.' ⁴And he refused for a while, but after this he said to himself, 'I do not fear God, nor do I respect people, ⁵but because this widow keeps troubling me, I will give her justice so that she will not wear me down by continually coming to me.'" ⁶The Lord said, "Listen to what the unjust judge says. ⁷Will God not administer justice to his chosen who cry to him night and day? Will he delay long in helping them? ⁸I say to you that he will give justice to them quickly. But will he find faith on the earth when the Son of Man comes?"

THE PHARISEE AND THE TAX COLLECTOR

⁹And he told this parable to some of them who trusted in themselves that they were righteous but despised others: ¹⁰"Two men went up to the temple to pray; one was a Pharisee and the other a tax collector. ¹¹The Pharisee stood by himself and prayed these words: 'God, I thank you that I am not like other men, extortioners, unjust, adulterers, or like this tax collector. ¹²I fast twice in the week; I pay tithes on all things that I receive.' ¹³But the tax collector stood at a distance and did not want to lift his eyes toward heaven, but he struck his breast, saying, 'God, be merciful to me, a sinner.' ¹⁴I say to you that this man went to his home being justified rather than the Pharisee, for everyone who exalts himself will be humbled, and whoever humbles himself will be exalted."

JESUS BLESSES LITTLE CHILDREN (MT 19:13–15; MK 10:13–16)

¹⁵And people brought infants to him that he might touch them, and when the disciples saw it they began to rebuke them. ¹⁶But Jesus called for them and said, "Permit the children to come to me and do not stop them, for the kingdom of God is made of such. ¹⁷Truly I say to you, whoever does not receive the kingdom of God as a little child will never enter into it."

THE RICH YOUNG MAN (MT 19:16–30; MK 10:17–31)

¹⁸And a certain ruler asked him, "Good teacher, what can I do that I may inherit eternal life?" ¹⁹Jesus said to him, "Why do you call me good? No one is good but

---

and of angels descending and gathering the remainder unto them; the one from the bed, the other from the grinding, and the other from the field, withersoever he listeth. For verily there shall be new heavens and a new earth, wherein dwelleth righteousness. And there shall be no unclean thing; for the earth becoming old, even as a garment, having waxed in corruption, wherefore it vanisheth away, and the footstool remaineth sanctified, cleansed from all sin.

18:1 Compare 2 Nephi 32:9. **18:1–8** The parable and comments on it treat the topic of endurance in prayer. Jesus indirectly confronts the issue of praying without receiving an answer. This parable is unique to Luke. Compare the interpretation of this parable in Doctrine and Covenants 101:81–92. **18:7** Compare 2 Peter 2:9. **18:11** This verse has similar language to the Zoramite prayer (Alma 31:15–18; 38:14). **18:12** The Pharisee defines his righteousness as being the result of specific actions. **18:13** Compare Psalms 41:4; 73:8. **18:14** The Greek notes only *that one* in place of *the Pharisee.* **18:15** *Infants* can also be translated as *babies.* **18:16** The idea is that the kingdom of God is composed *of such,* namely little children, or that the kingdom belongs to them. **18:19** *No one is good but God alone* may refer to the idea that God is the source of all good (James 1:17). Christians have long debated whether Jesus here intended to deny that he was God. Verse 22 offers some clarification because in it Jesus directs the rich

God alone. ²⁰You know the commandments. '*Do not commit adultery; do not murder; do not steal; do not bear false witness; honor your father and your mother.*' ²¹But he responded, "I have obeyed all these things since my youth." ²²When Jesus heard this he said to him, "One thing remains. Sell everything that you have and give it to the poor, and then you will have treasure in heaven. Then come and follow me." ²³When he heard these things, he became very sad, for he was exceptionally rich. ²⁴When Jesus saw that he became sad; he said, "How difficult it will be for those who are rich to enter into the kingdom of God! ²⁵It is easier for a camel to pass through a needle's eye than for a rich person to enter into the kingdom of God." ²⁶Those who heard it said, "Who, then, can be saved?" ²⁷He said, "The things that are impossible for humanity are possible with God." ²⁸But Peter said, "We have left our possessions to follow you." ²⁹Jesus said to them, "Truly I say to you that there is no one who has left a house or spouse or siblings or parents or children for the sake of the kingdom of God ³⁰who will not receive back many times more in due time and eternal life in the age to come."

JESUS FORETELLS HIS DEATH A THIRD TIME (MT 20:17–19; MK 10:32–34)

³¹And he took the twelve and said to them, "We are going up to Jerusalem, and every thing concerning the Son of Man will be fulfilled as it is written by the prophets. ³²For he will be betrayed to Gentiles, and he will be mocked and insulted and spit on. ³³And after they have scourged him, they will kill him, and on the third day he will rise again." ³⁴But they did not understand these things, and the saying was hidden from them, and they did not comprehend what he said.

THE HEALING OF BARTIMAEUS (MT 20:29–34; MK 10:46–52)

³⁵And it came to pass that as he drew near to Jericho, a blind person was sitting by the road begging. ³⁶And when he heard the multitude passing by, he asked what it might be, ³⁷and they brought him word that Jesus of Nazareth was passing by, ³⁸and he cried out, saying, "Jesus, Son of David, have mercy on me." ³⁹And those who went before him rebuked him so that he would be silent, but he called out more loudly, "Son of David, have mercy on me." ⁴⁰And Jesus stopped and called to him to be brought to him, and when he came near Jesus asked him, ⁴¹"What do you want me to do for you?" He answered, "Lord, that I may see." ⁴²And Jesus said to him, "Receive your sight; your faith has saved you." ⁴³And he immediately received his sight, and he followed him and glorified God, and all the people who saw it gave praise to God.

---

man to *follow me*, thus making Jesus the focus of the message. **18:20** Quotation from Exodus 20:12–16; Deuteronomy 5:16–20. **18:25** *A camel passing through a needle's eye* was a common metaphor for doing the impossible. It heightens the contrast with God, who can do all things (verse 27). **18:27** The Joseph Smith Translation reads *It is impossible for them who trust in riches to enter into the kingdom of God; but he who forsaketh the things which are of this world, it is possible with God, that he should enter in.* **18:29** *Siblings* in Greek is *brothers*, the generic term used for both male and female siblings. **18:30** The idea that one will receive many more *parents*, *brothers*, or *children* implies a vibrant and dynamic community of believers. **18:33** Compare Hosea 6:2. **18:38** Jesus is declared to be the *Son of David* as he prepared to enter Jerusalem. *Son of David* is a favorite phrase of Matthew (see Matthew 1:1; 12:23; 15:22). **18:42** Here *saved* is used in the sense of *healed* (7:50; 8:36, 48; 17:19). The gift of sight may intentionally signal the fulfillment of Isaiah 61:1.

ZACCHAEUS

19 ¹And he entered and then passed through Jericho, ²and there was a man named Zacchaeus, who was a chief tax collector, and he was rich. ³And he sought to see Jesus, but he was not able to see over the crowd because he was short. ⁴And he ran ahead and climbed a sycamore tree so that he could see him because Jesus was about to pass by there. ⁵And as he came to that place, Jesus looked up and said to him, "Zacchaeus, climb down quickly because today I must stay in your house." ⁶And he hurried and climbed down, and he welcomed him while rejoicing. ⁷And when the people saw this, they all murmured, saying, "He went in to be a guest with a man who is a sinner." ⁸But Zacchaeus stood and said to the Lord, "Behold, Lord, half of my belongings I give to the poor, and if I have cheated anyone in anything, I give it back fourfold." ⁹Jesus said to him, "Today, salvation has come to this house because even he is a son of Abraham. ¹⁰For the Son of Man came to seek out and to save the lost."

THE PARABLE OF THE POUNDS
(MT 25:14–30)

¹¹While they listened to these things, he taught a parable because he was near Jerusalem, and because they thought that the kingdom of God was about to appear immediately. ¹²Therefore he said, "A nobleman went off to a distant region to receive a kingdom for himself and then to return. ¹³And he called his ten servants and gave them ten pounds and said to each of them, 'Carry on in business until I come.' ¹⁴But his citizens hated him, and they sent an embassy after him, saying, 'We do not want this person to rule over us.' ¹⁵When he returned from receiving the kingdom, he ordered those servants, the ones to whom he gave the money, to be summoned to him so that he might know what each had done in business. ¹⁶And it came to pass that the first said, 'Lord, your pound earned ten pounds.' ¹⁷And he said to him, 'Well done, good servant. Because you were faithful in a small thing, you will have authority over ten cities.' ¹⁸And the second came and said, 'Your pound earned five pounds.' ¹⁹He said to this one, 'You will be over five cities.' ²⁰And the other came and said, 'Lord, behold your pound, which I stored in a napkin. ²¹I was afraid of you because you are an austere man; you take what you did not deposit, and you harvest what you did not plant.' ²²And he said to him, 'From your mouth I will judge you, wicked servant. You knew that I was an austere man, taking what I did not deposit, and harvesting what I did not plant. ²³Why did you not put my money in the bank, and upon my return I would have collected it with interest?' ²⁴And he said to those who stood nearby, 'Take from him the pound and give it to the one who has ten pounds.' ²⁵And he said to him, 'Lord, he has ten pounds already.' ²⁶'I say to you that to everyone that has, more will be given, and from those who do not have, even what they have will be taken from them. ²⁷But as for my enemies, who did not want me to rule over them, bring them here and kill them in front of me.'"

19:2 The Hebrew form of the name was *Zakkai* (Ezra 2:9). **19:8** Zacchaeus followed the directive set forth in Exodus 22:1; Numbers 5:7; 2 Samuel 12:6. **19:9** The recognition that Zacchaeus was a *son of Abraham* identifies him as an Israelite. **19:13** A *pound*, or mina, is a unit of weight and was equal to about three months' worth of wages for an average laborer. Earlier it was worth seventy silver coins, drachmae or denarii, but in the Roman period its value had increased to a hundred drachmae. Matthew uses a much greater sum in his version of the parable (see Matthew 25:15). **19:23** Collecting interest on loans was mostly forbidden (Deuteronomy 23:20). The parable may intentionally engage the theme of obeying the Law while overlooking weightier matters.

THE TRIUMPHAL ENTRY (MT 21:1–9; MK 11:1–10; JN 12:12–19)

²⁸And after he said this, he went ahead of them journeying up to Jerusalem. ²⁹And it came to pass that as he drew near to Bethphage and Bethany to the mount called Olivet, he sent two of his disciples, ³⁰saying, "Go into the village opposite us, and when you enter it you will find a colt tied on which no one has ever sat. Untie it and bring it. ³¹And if anyone asks you, 'Why are you untying it?' tell them this, 'The Lord needs it.'" ³²Those who were sent went and found it just as he told them. ³³And while they were untying the colt, the owners said to them, "Why are you untying the colt?" ³⁴And they responded, "The Lord needs it." ³⁵And they led the colt to Jesus, and they placed their clothing on it, and they set Jesus on it. ³⁶And as he went, they spread their clothing in the road. ³⁷As he drew near at the descent of the Mount of Olives, the entire crowd of disciples began rejoicing, and they praised God with a loud voice for all the miracles they had seen, ³⁸saying, "*Blessed is the king who comes in the name of the Lord*: peace in heaven and glory in the highest." ³⁹And some of the Pharisees from the crowd said to him, "Teacher, rebuke your disciples." ⁴⁰And he answered, "I say to you, if they were silent, the stones would cry out."

JESUS WEEPS FOR JERUSALEM

⁴¹And as he drew near, he saw the city, and he wept for it, ⁴²saying, "If you had known on this day the things that create peace! But they are hidden from your eyes! ⁴³Because the days will come upon you when your enemies will build a ramp around you, and they will encircle you, and press you on every side. ⁴⁴And they will bring you down, you and your children with you, and they will not leave a stone on another stone because you did not know the time of your visitation from God."

CLEANSING THE TEMPLE (MT 21:12–13; MK 11:15–17; JN 2:13–17)

⁴⁵And he entered the temple and began to throw out the sellers, ⁴⁶saying to them, "It is written, '*My house will be a house a prayer,*' but you have made it *a den of bandits.*" ⁴⁷And he taught them each day in the temple. But the chief priests and scribes, and also the leaders of the people, sought to destroy him. ⁴⁸But they did not find a way to do it, for all the people were captivated by what they heard.

THE QUESTION ABOUT AUTHORITY (MT 21:23–27; MK 11:27–33)

20 ¹And it came to pass on one of the days that he taught the people in the temple and proclaimed the good news, and the chief priests, scribes, and elders

---

19:28 Jesus has finally arrived in Jerusalem (see Luke 9:51). **19:29** *Bethphage* and *Bethany* were located east of Jerusalem on the slopes of the Mount of Olives. The precise location of *Bethphage* remains unknown. **19:30** Reference to Zechariah 9:9. **19:36** Compare 2 Kings 9:13. **19:37** *Miracles* can also be translated in this example as *works of power*. **19:38** Quotation from Psalm 118:26. Some of this language is reflected in Doctrine and Covenants 19:37; 36:3; 39:19 (compare Job 1:21; Psalm 113:2; Daniel 2:20). **19:40** Allusion to Habakkuk 2:11. **19:43** This prophetic reminder envisions the siege ramp built by the Roman emperor Titus's army when they sacked Jerusalem in 70 CE. **19:45** Matthew's description of the event is more detailed (Matthew 21:12). **19:46** Quotation from Isaiah 56:7 and Jeremiah 7:11. **19:48** The phrase *a way to do it* could also be rendered as *anything they could do*. Luke's phrase suggested they deliberated how they might kill Jesus, but they were unable to find a means to achieve that goal.

20:1 These teachings would have taken place in the courtyard of the temple.

came to him. [2]And they said to him, "Tell us by what authority you do these things. Who gave you this authority?" [3]He answered and said to them, "I will ask you one question. Tell me, [4]the baptism of John, was it from heaven or from people?" [5]And they discussed it with one another, saying, "If we say, 'From heaven,' he will say, 'Why did you not believe him?' [6]If we say, 'From people,' all the people will stone us because they are persuaded that John was a prophet." [7]And they answered that they did not know where it came from. [8]Jesus said to them, "Nor do I tell you by what authority I do these things."

THE PARABLE OF THE WICKED TENANTS
(MT 21:33–46; MK 12:1–12)

[9]And he began to speak this parable to the multitude, "A man planted a vineyard, and he rented it to farmers, and went away for a long time, [10]and at harvest time he sent a servant to the farmers so that they would give him some of the fruit of the vineyard. But the farmers beat him and sent him away empty-handed. [11]And he sent another servant, but they also beat him and insulted him and sent him away empty-handed. [12]And he sent a third, and this one they even wounded and cast out. [13]The lord of the vineyard said, 'What can I do? I will send my beloved son, and perhaps they will show him respect.' [14]When the farmers saw him, they discussed it among themselves, saying, 'This is the heir. Let us kill him so that the inheritance will be ours.' [15]And they threw him out of the vineyard and killed him. Therefore, what will the lord of the vineyard do to them? [16]He will come and destroy those farmers, and will rent the vineyard to others." And when they heard this, they said, "Let it not be so." [17]But he looked at them and said, "What is this that has been written, '*The stone that the builders rejected, this became the cornerstone*'? [18]Everyone who falls on this stone will be broken, and when it falls on anyone, it will crush that person. [19]And the scribes and chief priests sought to arrest him in that hour, but they feared the people, for they knew that he told this parable against them.

A QUESTION ABOUT TAXES
(MT 22:15–22; MK 12:13–17)

[20]And they watched him and sent out people to spy on him, pretending to be righteous so that they might catch him in his word and so that they could hand him over to the rule and authority of the governor. [21]And they questioned him, saying, "Teacher, we know that you speak and teach uprightly, and you do not look on people with partiality, but in truth you teach the word of God. [22]Is it lawful to pay tax to Caesar or not?" [23]But he knew their craftiness, and he said to them, [24]"Show

---

20:2 The question of authority has many potential implications, and with Pharisees and Sadducees asking the question, they may have wanted to know if he aligned with one of these groups. The word *authority* also means *strength, power,* or *liberty*. **20:4** Jesus's question regarding *the baptism of John* implies a connection between the two and their *authority*. **20:9** Compare Isaiah 5:1–7. **20:16** Jesus answers his own question, which causes a strong reaction from those who had listened to the parable. **20:17** Quotation from Psalm 118:22. **20:18** The stone that crushes conveys the idea that Jesus and his teachings will be troubling to many people, causing some to stumble. Not everyone will have the stone fall on them, nor will they fall on the stone. **20:20** The account of spies being sent to trap Jesus in his words is unique to Luke and may offer a foreshadowing of Judas Iscariot. The spies are literally said *to pretend to be righteous*, which has been translated into *to spy on him*. **20:21** The Greek text literally reads *you do not receive a face* in place of *you do not look on people with partiality*. The passage may be an allusion to Deuteronomy 1:17. **20:22** This would be the census-based tax, or poll tax. See note in Matthew 17:24. **20:24** A *denarius* was worth *ten Roman asses,* or *assaria* (see Luke 12:6).

me a denarius. Whose image and inscription is on it?" And they said, "Caesar's." ²⁵So he said to them, "Give back to Caesar what is Caesar's and to God the things of God." ²⁶And they were not able to trap him in his word before the multitude, and they were amazed at his answer and became silent.

A QUESTION ABOUT THE RESURRECTION (MT 22:23–33; MK 12:18–27)

²⁷And some Sadducees, who deny that there is a resurrection, came to him and questioned him, ²⁸saying, "Teacher, Moses wrote to us, '*If a man dies and is married, and he dies without children, his brother must marry his spouse and raise children to his brother.*' ²⁹There were seven brothers, and the first married and died without children. ³⁰The second likewise, ³¹and the third married her, and also the seventh. They left no children, and they all died. ³²Last of all, the woman died. ³³Whose wife will she be in the resurrection? For all seven married her."

³⁴And Jesus said to them, "The people of this age marry and are given in marriage, ³⁵but those who are worthy to obtain that age and the resurrection from the dead will not marry, nor are they given in marriage. ³⁶For they can no longer die, because they are like the angels. They are the children of God, like children of the resurrection. ³⁷But that the dead rise,

even Moses showed it in the story about the bush, since he calls the Lord '*the God of Abraham, the God of Isaac, and the God of Jacob.*' ³⁸He is not a God of the dead, but of the living, for they all live in him." ³⁹Some of the scribes responded and said, "Teacher, you spoke well." ⁴⁰And no one dared to ask him a question.

THE QUESTION ABOUT DAVID'S SON (MT 22:41–46; MK 12:35–37)

⁴¹And he said to them, "Why do they say that Christ is the son of David? ⁴²For David said in the book of Psalms, '*The Lord said to my lord, sit on my right hand* ⁴³*until I make your enemies your footstool.*' ⁴⁴If David called him 'Lord,' how is he his son?"

DENUNCIATION OF THE SCRIBES

⁴⁵After everyone in the crowd heard it, he said to his disciples, ⁴⁶"Beware of the scribes, who desire to walk around in long robes, and they love greetings in the markets and the first seats in the synagogues and the first seats at feasts. ⁴⁷They devour the houses of widows, and they make long prayers for the sake of appearance. These will receive the greater judgment."

THE WIDOW'S OFFERING (MK 12:41–44)

21 ¹And he looked up and saw some rich men casting their offerings into the treasury. ²Then he saw a certain

---

20:25 Compare Doctrine and Covenants 63:26. **20:27** The statement that the Sadducees denied the *resurrection* cannot be proved from Sadducean texts and documents. They read passages such as Isaiah 26:19 and Psalm 16:10 differently than their peers did. This was because they accepted only the five books of Moses (the Torah) as legally binding in religious matters. The word *resurrection* appears more frequently in the Book of Mormon (eighty-one times) than in any other book of scripture. **20:28** The Greek says specifically *raise up seed to his brother*. The legal precedent is Deuteronomy 25:5–6 (quotation from verse 5). **20:37** Quotation from Exodus 3:6. **20:42–43** Quotation from Psalm 110:1. **20:44** Jesus's question, which has no obvious answer, may be a subtle critique of the idea of a messianic *Son of David* to describe the *Christ* or *Messiah*. **20:45–47** Luke's account of the denunciation of the scribes is short and similar to Mark's (Mark 12:38–40). Matthew's is much longer and more provocative (Matthew 23:1–36).

21:1 The offering being made on this occasion appears to have been a voluntary offering. **21:2** Two *lepta*

poor widow cast in two copper coins, ³and he said, "Truly I say to you that this poor widow has offered more than all of them. ⁴For all of them cast their offerings from their abundance, but she from her poverty offered her entire living."

THE DESTRUCTION OF THE TEMPLE FORETOLD
(MT 24:1–8; MK 13:1–8)

⁵While some were speaking concerning the temple and its beautiful stones and offerings, he said ⁶"In the days to come, these things that you see will be thrown down so that no stone will be left on another."

⁷And they questioned him, "Teacher, when will these things be, and what will be the sign when these things are about to take place?" ⁸He said, "Watch but do not be deceived, for many will come in my name, saying, 'I am' and 'The time approaches.' Do not follow after them.

⁹"When you hear of wars and instability, do not be terrified, for these things must take place first, but the end is not immediate." ¹⁰Then he said to them, "Nation will rise against nation, and kingdom against kingdom. ¹¹There will be large earthquakes, and in various places famines and plagues, and there will be dreadful things and great signs from heaven.

PERSECUTION FORETOLD
(MT 10:16–25; 24:9–14; MK 13:9–13)

¹²"Before this, they will place their hands on you and persecute you and deliver you up to synagogues and prisons and bring you before kings and governors for my name's sake. ¹³It will be a time for you to testify. ¹⁴Decide in your hearts not to prepare your defense beforehand, ¹⁵for I will give you a voice and wisdom so that all who oppose you will not be able to refute or resist you. ¹⁶You will be betrayed by parents and siblings and relatives and friends, and they will put some of you to death. ¹⁷And you will be hated by everyone because of my name. ¹⁸And not a hair from your head will be destroyed. ¹⁹By endurance you will gain your lives.

THE DESOLATING SACRILEGE
(MT 24:15–22; MK 13:14–23)

²⁰"When you see Jerusalem encircled by armies, then know that its desolation is near. ²¹Then let those who are in Judea flee to the mountains and those in the city depart; and those in the fields, let them not enter the city, ²²because those are days of punishment in order to fulfill all things that were written. ²³Woe to those who are pregnant and who are nursing in those days, for there will be great distress on the land and wrath on this people. ²⁴And they will fall by the edge of the sword, and they will be led captive into all

---

was equivalent to a *quadrans* (see Mark 12:41–44). Eighty *lepta* was equivalent to a denarius. **21:7** The crowd asks Jesus to explain future events as a *teacher* and not as a prophet. The friendly use of the title *teacher* demonstrates acceptance of what he was explaining to them. **21:8** *I am* is an overt claim meaning *I am the Christ* or *I am the Messiah*. **21:9** See Doctrine and Covenants 45:26. **21:12** The persecutions are both Jewish in origin (*synagogues*) and Roman (*prisons* and *kings*). **21:15** The saints will be strengthened so that they can testify against those who wish to harm them. **21:16** Greek uses the generic *brothers* to refer to both *brothers and sisters* in this passage, and therefore the word *siblings* more closely approximates the meaning. **21:19** *Lives* can also mean *souls* depending on context. Here it is unclear whether the emphasis is on living a life of constant or patient endurance or whether it is a reference to peace of soul. Quoted in Doctrine and Covenants 101:38. **21:20** Compare Daniel 9:26–27, which shares a significant amount of vocabulary with these verses. **21:21** Perhaps passages such as Zechariah 14:5 were in mind with the counsel to flee to the mountains. **21:24** See Doctrine and Covenants 45:25, 30.

nations, and Jerusalem will be trampled by nations until the times of the nations are fulfilled.

THE COMING OF THE SON OF MAN (MT 24:29–31; MK 13:24–27)

²⁵"And there will be signs in the sun and moon and stars and distress of nations in disarray on the earth because of the roaring of the sea and the waves, ²⁶people fainting because of fear and the expectation of what is coming upon the world, for *the powers of the heavens will be shaken.* ²⁷And then they will see *the Son of Man coming in a cloud* with great power and glory. ²⁸When these things begin to take place, rise up and lift up your heads because your deliverance draws near."

THE MEANING OF THE FIG TREE (MT 24:32–36; MK 13:28–31)

²⁹And he told them a parable, "Look at the fig tree and all the trees; ³⁰when they put out leaves, you see and know that the summer is already near. ³¹Likewise for you, when you see these things taking place, you will know that the kingdom of God is near. ³²Truly I say to you that this generation will not pass away until all things are fulfilled. ³³The heavens and the earth will pass away, but my words will not pass away.

THE NEED TO BE WATCHFUL (MT 24:43–51; MK 13:33–37)

³⁴"Watch yourselves so that your hearts are not weighed down in a stupor and in drunkenness and in the anxieties of this life, and then that day comes suddenly on you as a trap. ³⁵It will come on everyone living on the face of the whole earth. ³⁶But watch in every season, praying that you will be strong enough to flee all these things that are about to take place and to stand before the Son of Man."

³⁷He was in the temple teaching each day, and he departed at night and lodged on the Mount of Olives. ³⁸And all the people came to him early in the morning to hear him in the temple.

THE PLOT TO KILL JESUS (MT 26:1–5; MK 14:1–2)

22 ¹The Feast of Unleavened Bread, which is called the Passover, drew near. ²And the chief priests and scribes sought how they might kill Jesus, but they feared the people. ³Then Satan entered Judas called Iscariot, who was one of the number of the twelve. ⁴And he went and spoke with the chief priests and officers how he might deliver him to them. ⁵And they rejoiced and promised to give him money. ⁶And he agreed, and he sought a

---

21:25 Compare Joel 2:30–32; Doctrine and Covenants 45:42 (see Matthew 24:29; the Joseph Smith Translation changes the verse in Matthew so that it represents the shift toward discussing modern calamities). **21:26** Quotation from Isaiah 34:4. **21:27** Quotation from Daniel 7:13 (compare Matthew 24:30; 1 Nephi 11:28; Doctrine and Covenants 34:7). **21:28** Alluded to in Doctrine and Covenants 35:26. **21:32** This verse may cause some concern to readers because it indicates that the signs of the times will all be fulfilled in the days of the disciples, or in the days of *this generation*. Those signs were fulfilled in the days of the disciples but may also portend a future fulfillment (see Joseph Smith—Matthew 1:19–21).

22:4 Luke is not specific regarding the *officers* mentioned here. They may have been civil magistrates, or even temple guards. The word can imply army officers, temple police, or officers of the governor. **22:5** Matthew (26:15) may have seen an echo of Zechariah 11:12–13 in the price, which Luke does not mention. **22:6** Luke's wording insinuates that Judas sought an opportunity to deliver Jesus into the hands of his enemies at a time when there were no crowds. Luke is the only author to add this detail to the story of Judas's betrayal.

good time to betray Jesus to them when there was no crowd.

PREPARATION FOR THE PASSOVER (MT 26:17–20; MK 14:12–17)

[7]The day of Unleavened Bread came on which the Paschal lamb must be sacrificed. [8]And he sent Peter and John, saying, "Go and prepare for us the Passover in order that we may eat." [9]They asked him, "Where do you want us to prepare it?" [10]He said to them, "When you enter the city, a man carrying a pitcher of water will greet you. Follow him to the house he enters. [11]And you will say to the owner of the house, 'The teacher says to you, Where is the guest room where I may eat the Passover with my disciples?' [12]He will show you a large, furnished upstairs room. Prepare it there." [13]And they went and found it as he had told them, and they prepared the Passover.

THE SACRAMENT (MT 26:26–29; MK 14:22–25)

[14]And when the hour came, he reclined to eat with the apostles, [15]and he said to them, "I earnestly desired to eat this Passover with you before I suffer. [16]I tell you that I will not eat it again until it is fulfilled in the kingdom of God." [17]And he took a cup, and after he had blessed it he said, "Take this and distribute it to each other. [18]For I say to you that from now on I will not drink the fruit of the vine until the kingdom of God comes." [19]And he took bread and blessed it, and after breaking it he gave it to his disciples, saying, "This is my body that has been given for you. Do this in order to remember me." [20]And likewise he took the cup after they had dined, saying, "This cup is the new covenant in my blood, which has been poured out for you. [21]But the hand of him who delivers me is with me at the table. [22]Because the Son of Man goes as it has been determined, but woe to that man by whom he is betrayed." [23]And they began to question one another who it might be among them who was about to do this.

THE REQUEST OF JACOB AND JOHN (MT 20:24–28; MK 10:41–45)

[24]And there was contention among them regarding who among them was greater.

22:7 This would be the day of preparation, Nisan 14. The events that are described here (verses 7–13) appear to happen in the daytime. At sundown the new day would begin, and hence it would be Nisan 15. A further confusion arises from the fact that *unleavened bread* was eaten all seven days of Passover (Exodus 12:15). **22:8** Passover was a celebration of deliverance from Egypt, and families shared in the celebrations. It is likely that the families of the disciples and others were in attendance at this meal. **22:9** The question implies that they had limited personal contacts in Jerusalem. The story implies that there was some personal connection between the owner of the room and Jesus, who is referred to simply as the *teacher* (verse 11). **22:14** The phrase *the twelve apostles* occurs here, in Matthew 10:2 and Revelation 21:14, and frequently in the Book of Mormon (compare 1 Nephi 11:36). **22:14–23** The institution of the sacrament is reported here. The New Testament does not use the name *the sacrament*, but see Mormon 9:29. **22:15** Jesus here declares unequivocally that they are eating a Passover meal. This is one of the primary differences between Matthew, Mark, and Luke (the synoptic Gospels) and John. In John 13:1–2 this same meal is eaten before the Passover meals were typically eaten. **22:16** The subject *it* is ambiguous but logically refers to *Passover* in verse 15. It is unclear how the *Passover* will be fulfilled, but perhaps the intended meaning is that it will no longer be celebrated until Jesus comes again. **22:18** Compare Doctrine and Covenants 27:5. **22:19** The symbols of bread and wine (verse 17) are taken from the Passover meal and given new meaning. **22:20** There are two different cups in Luke's account, one that was used in the institution of the sacrament and the other that symbolized the *new covenant*. This verse is a clear allusion to Jeremiah 31:31–34. **22:21** See Psalm 41:9. **22:24–30** Mark and Matthew

²⁵But he said to them, "The kings of the nations act as lords over them, and those who exercise authority over them are called benefactors. ²⁶You are not like that, but let the greatest among you be like the youngest, and the leader like the one who serves. ²⁷Who is greater, the one who reclines to eat or the one who serves? Is it not the one who reclines to eat? I am in your midst as one who serves. ²⁸You are the ones who have stayed with me in my trials. ²⁹I covenant with you, even as my Father covenanted with me, a kingdom ³⁰so that you will eat and drink at my table in my kingdom, and you will sit on thrones judging the twelve tribes of Israel.

PETER'S DENIAL FORETOLD
(MT 26:30–35; MK 14:27–31; JN 13:36–38)

³¹"Simon, Simon, behold, Satan sought for you that he might sift you like wheat, ³²but I have prayed for you so that your faith may not fail, and when you have returned, strengthen your brothers and sisters." ³³He answered him, "Lord, I am ready to go to prison and to death with you." ³⁴Jesus said, "I say to you, Peter, the rooster will not crow today until you have denied that you

know me three times." ³⁵And he said to them, "I have sent you without a wallet or bag or sandals, and did you lack anything? They responded, "Nothing." ³⁶He said to them, "But now let whoever has a wallet take it and whoever has a bag do likewise, but whoever does not have a sword, let that person sell his cloak and buy a sword. ³⁷I say to you that this is written to be fulfilled in me, 'And he was numbered with the sinners,' for what is said concerning me is being fulfilled." ³⁸And they said, "Lord, here are two swords!" And he responded, "It is enough."

JESUS PRAYS IN GETHSEMANE
(MT 26:36–46; MK 14:32–42; JN 18:1)

³⁹And he went out according to his custom to the Mount of Olives, and the disciples followed him. ⁴⁰When they reached the place, he said to them, "Pray that you do not fall into temptation." ⁴¹And he went away from them about a stone's throw, and he kneeled and prayed, ⁴²saying, "Father, if you are willing, take this cup from me, but not my will but yours be done. [[⁴³And there appeared an angel from heaven strengthening him, ⁴⁴and he was in agony,

relate this story much earlier in their accounts (Matthew 20:20–28; Mark 10:35–45). In this context, it highlights misunderstandings among the disciples on the eve of Jesus's death. **22:25** *The nations* can also be translated as *the Gentiles.* **22:26** *Like the one who serves* is in Greek *like a deacon.* Jesus extolls those who serve in the capacity of deacons. The deacon serves in contrast to the wealthy who take care of their subjects as *benefactors.* **22:28** *Trials* can also be translated as *temptations* (the same word appears in Luke 22:40, 46). Mosiah 15:5 speaks of the temptation of Christ in greater detail. **22:29** Some manuscripts have *appoint you a covenant,* but the likely original reading is the one given here. **22:30** Compare Matthew 19:28; 1 Nephi 12:9; Mormon 3:18–19. **22:31** Jesus here tells Peter that Satan desires to try all of the disciples and not him alone. Satan's actions are here interpreted as directed against Peter. Compare Alma 37:15. **22:32** *When you have returned* reflects a Hebrew concept of the verb *repent* and is likely the intended meaning here. It probably prefigures Peter's denial and subsequent return to steady faith. Greek uses *brothers* generically to refer to *brothers* and *sisters.* **22:34** Only Luke clarifies that Peter's denial was with respect to knowing Jesus. **22:37** *Sinners* also means *lawless.* Quotation from Isaiah 53:12. **22:38** The meaning of this verse is unclear but seems to mean that Jesus declared *two swords* to be enough for their coming struggles. **22:40** Doctrine and Covenants 10:5 possibly alludes to the imagery of this verse. **22:43–44** These two verses are greatly disputed, and a number of important ancient manuscripts omit them. Other early and important manuscripts include these verses. Given the current evidence, it is unlikely that the question of their omission or inclusion can be resolved.

and he prayed more intently, and his sweat became as if it were large drops of blood falling to the ground.]] ⁴⁵After he rose from the prayer, he came to his disciples, and he found them sleeping as a result of sorrow, ⁴⁶and he said to them, "Why do you sleep? Arise and pray so that you do not fall into temptation."

THE ARREST (MT 26:47–56; MK 14:43–52; JN 18:2–12)

⁴⁷While he was speaking, suddenly a crowd gathered, and the one called Judas, who was one of the twelve, was leading them, and he drew near to Jesus to kiss him. ⁴⁸But Jesus said to him, "Judas, are you about to betray the Son of Man with a kiss?" ⁴⁹When those that were with him saw what was about to happen, they said to him, "Lord, shall we fight with a sword?" ⁵⁰And one of them smote the high priest's servant and cut off his right ear. ⁵¹But Jesus said, "No more of this!" And he touched his ear and healed him. ⁵²Jesus said to the chief priests, officers of the temple, and the elders who were gathered to take him, "Did you come out with swords and clubs as though I were a bandit? ⁵³Each day I was with you in the temple, and you did not arrest me. But this is your hour and the power of darkness."

JESUS INTERROGATED (MT 26:57–68; MK 14:53–65; JN 18:13–24)

⁵⁴Then they took him and led him to the high priest's house, but Peter followed from a distance. ⁵⁵And they started a fire in the middle of the courtyard, and they sat down together, and Peter sat among them. ⁵⁶But a servant saw him sitting near the fire, and she looked at him and said, "He was with him." ⁵⁷But he denied it, "I do not know him, woman." ⁵⁸Shortly after, another saw him and said, "You are also one of them!" But Peter said, "Man, I am not!" ⁵⁹And about an hour later another insisted, "Certainly this man was with him, for he is from Galilee!" ⁶⁰But Peter said, "Man, I do not know what you say." And immediately while he was speaking he heard a rooster crow. ⁶¹And the Lord turned and looked at Peter, and Peter remembered the word of the Lord as he told him, "Before a rooster crows today you will deny me three times." ⁶²And he went out and wept bitterly.

⁶³And the men who held Jesus mocked and beat him, ⁶⁴and after they blindfolded him they questioned him, saying, "Prophesy to us. Who struck you?" ⁶⁵And they said many other things to him while insulting him. ⁶⁶And as it began to be day, the council of the elders of the people gathered, both the chief priest and scribes, and they led him up to their council ⁶⁷and said, "If you are the Christ, tell us." But he answered them, "If I tell you, you will not believe. ⁶⁸And if I question you, you

---

However, the evidence is strong enough to suggest that they may be original to Luke's Gospel but were perhaps omitted over doctrinal concerns. Mosiah 3:7 seems to have these verses in mind (compare Doctrine and Covenants 19:16–19). **22:45** *As a result of sorrow*, a unique phrase added by Luke, implies that the disciples shared in Jesus's anguish. **22:50** John identifies the servant as Malchus (John 18:10). **22:52** Here Luke designates them as *officers of the temple*. The word *bandit* implies a political revolutionary. **22:53** Compare Colossians 1:13. **22:54** Even though they travel to Caiaphas's personal residence, the gathering of leaders may have met there for other formal decisions and councils. **22:60** Mark 14:70 notes that Peter's accent gives him away as a Galilean. **22:66** *Sanhedrin* implies that the governing body of elders acted in unison against Jesus, even though many of the events of the arrest and interrogation seem to be descriptions of mob activity. **22:67–68** Compare Jeremiah 38:15.

will not answer. [69]From now on *the Son of Man will be seated on the right hand* of the power of God." [70]But they all said, "Are you, therefore, the Son of God? He said to them, "You say that I am." [71]And they said, "Why do we still need a witness, for we have heard from his own mouth."

JESUS BEFORE PILATE (MT 27:1–2, 11–14; MK 15:1–5; JN 18:28–38)

23 [1]After they rose, the entire group led him to Pilate. [2]And they began to accuse him, saying, "We found this man leading the nation astray and forbidding paying taxes to Caesar and saying that he is Christ, a king." [3]So Pilate asked him, "Are you the king of the Jews?" He answered, "You say so." [4]Then Pilate said to the chief priests and the crowd, "I find no fault in this man." [5]But they were insistent, saying, "He stirs up the people, teaching all of Judea, beginning in Galilee to this place."

JESUS BEFORE HEROD ANTIPAS

[6]When Pilate heard this, he asked if the man was a Galilean. [7]When he knew that he was from the jurisdiction of Herod, he sent him to Herod, who was in Jerusalem at that time. [8]When Herod saw Jesus, he was very glad, for he had wanted to see him for a long time because he had heard many things about him and he hoped to see a miracle performed by him. [9]Herod questioned him extensively, but Jesus did not answer him. [10]And the chief priests and scribes stood against him and ac-

cused him, [11]and Herod with his soldiers treated him shamefully and mocked him, and they dressed him in fine clothing and sent him back to Pilate. [12]And Pilate and Herod became friends with one another on that day, for previously there was animosity between them.

PILATE DECLARES JESUS TO BE INNOCENT

[13]Pilate called together the chief priests and rulers of the people [14]and said to them, "You brought me this man as though he led the people astray, and I have examined him before you and have found no fault in this man regarding the charges you brought against him. [15]Neither did Herod, for he sent him back to us, and he has done nothing worthy of death. [16]Therefore, I will have him scourged and will release him."

PILATE DELIVERS JESUS TO BE CRUCIFIED (MT 27:15–23; MK 15:6–14; JN 18:29–40; 19:16)

[[[17]For it was necessary for him to release one person at every feast.]] [18]And the whole multitude cried out, "Take him! Release Barabbas to us!" [19]He had been cast into prison because of murder and sedition in the city. [20]Again Pilate, wishing to set Jesus free, spoke to them. [21]But they shouted, "Crucify, crucify him!" [22]But he said to them the third time, "Why? What evil has he done? I found nothing worthy of death in him. I will scourge him and then release him." [23]But they insisted, and

---

22:69 Quotation from Psalm 110:1; Daniel 7:13.

23:1 *Pilate* was prefect of Judea (26–36 CE). **23:2** The accusations made against Jesus are political in nature, as this verse clearly indicates. **23:3** Pilate's question views Jesus as a direct threat to Roman governance in the region. **23:5** Compare John 18:36, 38. **23:7** *Herod Antipas* (died after 39 CE), who ruled as tetrarch in Galilee and Perea, was called on to assess the question of jurisdiction over Jesus. **23:9** *Extensively* is in Greek *in many words* (compare Alma 14:18). **23:11** This is the same type of robe worn by the bride of the Lamb in Revelation 19:8. **23:12** The new friendship between *Pilate* and *Herod* underlines the fact that the trial of Jesus also had political motivations. **23:17** The textual evidence for this verse is relatively weak, and the better manuscripts omit it. It appears that scribes added it to Luke based on Matthew 27:15 and Mark 15:6.

in a loud voice they demanded that he be crucified, and their vocal demands prevailed. ²⁴So Pilate decided to fulfill their request. ²⁵And he released the man who was thrown into prison for murder and sedition because they asked for him, but he delivered Jesus according to their will.

SIMON OF CYRENE (MT 27:31–32; MK 15:20–21; JN 19:17)

²⁶And as they led him away, they seized Simon of Cyrene, who was coming in from his field, and they placed the cross on him to carry it behind Jesus. ²⁷A large multitude of people followed him, and also women who mourned and lamented for him. ²⁸But Jesus turned and said to them, "Daughters of Jerusalem, do not weep for me, but weep for yourselves and for your children, ²⁹because the days will surely come in which they will say, 'Blessed are the childless and the wombs that never bore children and the breasts that never nursed.' ³⁰Then they will begin *to say to the mountains, 'Fall upon us!' And to the hills, 'Cover us!'* ³¹For if they do these things to a green tree, what will happen to a dry one?"

THE CRUCIFIXION (MT 27:33–44; MK 15:22–32; JN 19:17–27)

³²And they led away two other criminals to be crucified with him. ³³And they came to the place called "The Skull," and they cru-cified him there with the criminals, one on his left and one on his right. [[³⁴But Jesus said, "Father, forgive them, for they do not know what they are doing."]] Then they *cast lots to divide his clothing.* ³⁵And the people stood and watched, and the rulers ridiculed him, saying, "He saved others; if this is the Messiah of God, his chosen one, let him save himself." ³⁶The soldiers mocked him, approaching him and offering sour wine to him ³⁷and saying, "If you are the king of the Jews, save yourself." ³⁸And it was written above him, "This is the King of the Jews."

³⁹One of the criminals hanging next to him insulted him, saying, "Are you not the Messiah? Save yourself and us." ⁴⁰The other responded and rebuked him, "Do you not fear God because you are under the same condemnation? ⁴¹We received the rewards of our actions, and indeed justly, but this man has done nothing wrong." ⁴²And he said, "Jesus, remember me when you enter into your kingdom." ⁴³And he said to him, "Truly I say to you that this day you will be with me in paradise."

THE DEATH OF JESUS (MT 27:45–56; MK 15:33–41; JN 19:25–30)

⁴⁴And at about noon, darkness came upon the whole land until three in the afternoon ⁴⁵because the sun was darkened, and the veil of the temple was torn in two. ⁴⁶Then Jesus shouted in a loud voice, "*Father,*

23:24 Despite his objections (verses 15–16), Pilate accepts their demands. **23:26** Simon was from *Cyrene*, a town located on the north coast of Africa in Libya. **23:30** Quotation from Hosea 10:8. **23:31** The saying is delivered as a proverb, but no source has been identified for it. Its meaning remains elusive. The Joseph Smith Translation adds a comment to this verse to apply the reference to the *dry one* to the destruction of the Gentiles. **23:32** The implication is not that Jesus was being referred to as a criminal but that he was crucified with two men who were themselves criminals. **23:34** Quotation from Psalm 22:18. The portion of this verse set off in double brackets may not have been original. Some early and good manuscripts omit it, but it also has some significant textual support. **22:35** *The Messiah of God* or *God's Messiah* is in Greek *God's Christ*. **23:36** *Sour wine* was a common drink among Roman soldiers (see Psalm 69:21). **23:39** This verse has given rise to the idea that the two bandits were tied to the cross instead of nailed. **23:43** In the LXX, Genesis 2:8 refers to Eden as the *Garden of Paradise*. See 2 Nephi 9:13; Alma 40:12, 14; 4 Nephi 1:14; Moroni 10:34. **23:44** Compare Joel 2:10. **23:46** Quotation from Psalm 31:5.

into your hands I place my spirit." After saying this, he died. ⁴⁷When the centurion saw what happened, he glorified God, saying, "Truly this was a righteous man." ⁴⁸When all the crowds had gathered to see this, they saw what had taken place, and they returned home striking their breasts. ⁴⁹And everyone who knew him stood at a distance, and the women who followed him from Galilee watched these things.

THE BURIAL (MT 27:57–61; MK 16:42–47; JN 19:38–42)

⁵⁰And a man named Joseph, who was a member of the council, a good and righteous man ⁵¹(but he did not consent to their decision and action), he was from the Jewish town of Arimathea, and he looked for the kingdom of God. ⁵²He went to Pilate and requested the body of Jesus. ⁵³Then he took it down and wrapped it in linen and placed it in a tomb cut from stone where no one had been placed yet. ⁵⁴And it was the day of preparation, and the Sabbath was approaching. ⁵⁵And the women who came with him from Galilee followed, and they saw the tomb and how his body was placed in it. ⁵⁶Then they returned and prepared the spices and ointments, and on the Sabbath they rested according to the commandment.

THE RESURRECTION (MT 28:1–10; MK 16:1–8; JN 20:1–13)

24 ¹On the first day of the week, early near dawn, the women came to the tomb and brought with them the spices they had prepared. ²They found the stone had been rolled away from the tomb, ³and they entered, but they did not find the body of the Lord Jesus. ⁴And it came to pass that while they were perplexed about this, two men in resplendent clothing stood by them. ⁵And they were afraid and bowed their faces toward the ground, and the men said to them, "Why do you seek the living among the dead? ⁶He is not here, but he has risen. Remember how he told you while he was still in Galilee ⁷that the Son of Man must be delivered into the hands of sinful men and be crucified and on the third day rise again?" ⁸Then they remembered his words. ⁹And they returned from the tomb and reported all these things to the eleven and to all the others. ¹⁰And it was Mary Magdalene, Joanna, Mary of Jacob, and the other women with them who told these things to the apostles. ¹¹But these words appeared to them as idle talk, and they did not believe them. ¹²And Peter stood and ran to the tomb, and when he stooped down he saw the strips of linen, and he departed, wondering to himself what had taken place.

23:49 Compare 8:2–3 for a description of Jesus's female followers from Galilee. **23:52** Joseph is following the command from Deuteronomy 21:22–23 not to allow Jesus's body to remain on the cross overnight. **23:54** Jesus was killed on the day before the *Sabbath*, and therefore on Friday. **23:56** The *spices and ointments* were used to prepare the body for burial.

24:1 The first day of the week is Sunday, early in the morning. They prepared spices and ointments to anoint the body of Jesus for burial. Compare John 19:39–40. **24:2** These stones were typically quite large, and some were rolled using a log or branch to act as a lever. **24:4** The Joseph Smith Translation says *two angels*. **24:5** *The living* is singular and hence *the living one* is also possible. **24:7** See Luke 9:22. **24:10** The first witnesses to the empty tomb were all women. Mary Magdalene is mentioned in all four Gospels as being in the group of women followers who went to the tomb. In John 20:16–18, she is the first to see the resurrected Lord. **24:12** This would be the winding strips used to wrap the body of Jesus.

JESUS APPEARS TO TWO DISCIPLES (MK 16:12–13)

¹³And two of them went on that day to a village named Emmaus, about sixty stadia from Jerusalem, ¹⁴and they discussed with one another all these things that had taken place. ¹⁵And it came to pass that while they were discussing and reasoning together, Jesus himself approached and began to walk with them. ¹⁶But their eyes were kept from recognizing him. ¹⁷And he said to them, "What are these words that you are debating with one another?" And they stood, looking sad. ¹⁸Then the one named Cleopas answered him, "Are you the only stranger in Jerusalem who does not know what has taken place in these days?" ¹⁹And he said to them, "What things?" They responded, "The things regarding Jesus of Nazareth, a man who was a prophet powerful in word and deed before God and all the people, ²⁰and how our chief priests and rulers handed him over to be condemned to death, and they crucified him. ²¹But we hoped that he was the one who would redeem Israel. But besides all this, today is the third day since these things happened. ²²And some of the women among us surprised us when they went to the tomb early this morning, ²³and after they did not find his body, they came and reported that they had seen a vision of angels, who said that he is alive. ²⁴Then some of those with us went to the tomb and found it just as the women said, but they did not see him." ²⁵So he said to them, "Fools and slow of heart to believe all that the prophets have spoken! ²⁶Was it not necessary for the Christ to suffer these things and then enter into his glory?" ²⁷And he began with Moses and all the prophets, and he explained to them the things about himself in all the scriptures.

²⁸And they drew near to the village that they were traveling to, and he acted as though he would travel further. ²⁹But they urged him, saying, "Stay with us, for it is near evening, and the day is almost ended." And he entered to stay with them. ³⁰And it came to pass while reclining with them, he took the bread and blessed it and broke it and gave it to them. ³¹And their eyes were opened, and they recognized him, but he was no longer visible to them. ³²And they said to one another, "Did our hearts not burn within us as he spoke to us on the way, and as he opened to us the scriptures?"

³³And they stood in that same hour and returned to Jerusalem and found the eleven and those with them gathered together, ³⁴saying, "The Lord was indeed resurrected, and he has appeared to Simon." ³⁵Then they explained what occurred on the way and how he was made known to them while breaking the bread.

JESUS APPEARS TO HIS DISCIPLES IN JERUSALEM (JN 20:19–23)

³⁶While they were saying these things, Jesus himself stood among them and said, "Peace be with you." ³⁷But they were amazed and fearful because they thought they had seen a spirit. ³⁸And he said to

---

24:13 A stadia is about 600 feet/180 meters and thus about seven miles from Jerusalem. **24:13–35** Luke tells the account of the witnesses on the road to Emmaus in more detail than the other Gospel authors do. There may have been some link between him and these two witnesses, but Luke only identifies one of them. **24:19** Jesus is called a *prophet*, and perhaps Deuteronomy 18:15–18 is intended. **24:21** Their hope that Jesus would *redeem* Israel was lost when Jesus died. This may indicate that they had hoped for a Messiah who would deliver them from political subjection. **24:27** The calling to explain or expound (the verb used by the King James Version) was promised to Oliver Cowdery, Emma Smith, Joseph Smith, Sidney Rigdon, and others (Doctrine and Covenants 24:5, 9; 25:7; 97:5; 100:11). **24:32** An allusion to Psalm 39:3. **24:34** Luke does not report this appearance (compare 1 Corinthians 15:5).

them, "Why are you afraid? And why do you deliberate in your hearts? [39]Look at my hands and my feet, that I am he. Touch me and see, because a spirit does not have flesh and bones as you see that I have." [40]After he said this, he showed them his hands and feet. [41]While they still did not believe because of their joy and amazement, he said to them, "Do you have something to eat here?" [42]They gave him a portion of cooked fish, [43]and he took it and ate it in front of them.

[44]And he said to them, "These are my words that I spoke to you while I was still with you, that all things concerning me must be fulfilled that are written in the law of Moses and the Prophets and the Psalms." [45]Then he opened to their minds the meaning of the scriptures, [46]and he said to them, "As it is written, the Christ would suffer and be resurrected from the dead on the third day, [47]and repentance for the remission of sins would be proclaimed in his name to all nations, beginning at Jerusalem. [48]You are witnesses of these things. [49]And I am sending the promised blessing of my Father upon you. Stay in the city of Jerusalem until you are clothed with power from on high."

THE ASCENSION (MK 16:19–20)

[50]Then he led them out as far as Bethany, and he lifted up his hands and blessed them. [51]And it came to pass that after he blessed them, he departed from them and was lifted up to heaven. [52]And they knelt before him and then returned to Jerusalem with great joy. [53]And they were always in the temple praising God.

24:39 The encouragement to touch his body serves as a witness of the reality of a physical resurrection. Doctrine and Covenants 129:2 quotes this verse and offers commentary. **24:42** Eating demonstrates that Jesus has a physical body after the resurrection. In Luke 8:55, Jesus commanded the parents of a young girl who had been raised from the dead to give her food as a way of demonstrating life and vitality. This account may emphasize the physical nature of Jesus's body in order to settle disputes among some early Christians who felt that Jesus was resurrected in a spirit body. **24:49** The promise that Jesus will come and clothe his followers remains enigmatic and is not mentioned in the other Gospel accounts. Compare Doctrine and Covenants 38:32, 38; 95:8–9; 105:33. Some scholars see an allusion to Jeremiah 31:31. **24:51** A fuller account of this is given in Acts 1:3–11.

THE GOSPEL OF JOHN

WHO WAS JOHN?

As in the other Gospels, the author of the Gospel of John never mentions himself by name directly. In the stories that are retold in the Fourth Gospel, an unnamed disciple sees and experiences the life of Jesus personally and uniquely. He was a follower of John the Baptist (John 1:35–39), and he became a follower of Jesus after hearing John's testimony. During Jesus's final week of life, the unnamed disciple grew more prominent in the story, perhaps suggesting that his witness was shaped by the events of the final week. He sat next to Jesus at the Last Supper (John 13:21–30), he may have watched the trial of Jesus with Peter (John 18:15–18), he visited Jesus during the crucifixion (John 19:26–27), he was among the first to visit the empty tomb (John 20:2–10), and he dined with Jesus after the resurrection (John 21:7–20). The author was reluctant to name himself, although he clearly told of his involvement in the story. Tradition has connected John the son of Zebedee with the author of the Gospel, although some early Christians like Irenaeus (died 202 CE) thought another disciple named John was responsible for writing the Gospel, but for the most part the tradition has been fairly stable that John the early disciple wrote it.

The Greek of the Fourth Gospel and writing style can be described as simple and perhaps the work of a non-native Greek speaker. Beginning with the opening lines, it quickly becomes apparent that John was not writing a historical record of Jesus's life (John 20:30) but rather a reflection on the meaning of Jesus's life (John 20:31). Stories and events from Jesus's life were chosen for a specific purpose and interest. Also, the author writes from the vantage point of a completed resurrection (John 2:17–22; 20:9), and the story is also intentionally reflective about what events mean. It also seems to be the case that the author ended the work at chapter 20 and then later added an epilogue to the work (John 21) to clarify the fate of the apostle Peter. The final chapter treats the topic of the fallout from Peter's denial of Jesus during the last week of Jesus's life, and it also provides new details about a prophecy concerning Peter's death.

THE MANUSCRIPTS

Interestingly, the Gospels of Matthew and John have more surviving copies than those of Mark and Luke. This may have been happenstance, but it also may signal that the two apostolic Gospels (Matthew and John) were more widely read and distributed. One of the earliest New Testament manuscripts to survive, a small fragment of papyrus not larger than a credit card, contains a fragment from John 18. But the manuscripts do not tell us anything more about the author, about how the books of 1–3 John and Revelation relate to the author of the Gospel, or anything else about his life after the close of the Gospels.

STRUCTURE AND ORGANIZATION

One method of dividing the Gospel of John has been to suggest that it is a two-part work divided nearly equally into a "book of signs" (1:1–12:50) and a "book of glory" (13:1–20:31). Although this is only one possible means of structuring the Fourth Gospel, it does effectively draw attention to the fact that a large portion of the book is dedicated to the march toward crucifixion. John 13–17 represent an extended discourse that Jesus gave to his disciples after the Last Supper was completed, and it has no parallel in the other Gospels. Also, there is no account of Gethsemane in the Fourth Gospel, suggesting that John intentionally omitted retelling that story. One reason may be that in Gethsemane, Jesus's full humanity was on display: he cried out, he pled, and he bled from every pore. An author wishing to highlight the exaltation of Jesus may have wished not to draw attention to that fact.

John preserves a very different set of events compared to the synoptic Gospels, with the result that over 90 percent of his material is unique. Among this material are several noteworthy contributions to the understanding of Christ and his ministry. For example, John 3–4 are the only passages where Christ teaches an individual in an extensive personal encounter. Both encounters share the theme of elusiveness and rebuke (Nicodemus in chapter 3, the Samaritan woman at the well in chapter 4). John openly acknowledges Jesus's divinity as not only the Son of God but also as a God and as Jehovah in several passages. In the prologue hymn (1:1–18), Jesus is God alongside God the Father, and he identifies himself as Jehovah in John 8:58, which also raises the consistent theme that Jesus's countrymen felt that he spoke blasphemy. Several of the major discourses introduce new themes to the Gospel stories such as the symbolic connection between his death and Passover sacrifices (the Bread of Life sermon, John 6), and teachings about the role of the Holy Spirit (John 14). ☞

THE PROLOGUE HYMN

1 ¹In the beginning was the Word, and the Word was with God, and the Word was God. ²Thus, he was in the beginning with God. ³All things were created through him, and without him nothing was created. What was created ⁴in him was life, and the life was the light of humanity. ⁵And the light shines in the darkness, but the darkness does not comprehend it.

⁶There was a man, sent by God, whose name was John. ⁷He came as a witness in order to testify of the light so that all might believe through him. ⁸He was not the light, but he came to witness to the light, ⁹the true light that lightens all humanity—those who come into the world. ¹⁰He was in the world, and the world was created through him, but the world did not know him. ¹¹He came to his own, but his own did not comprehend him. ¹²And to all who receive him, to those who believe in his name, he gave them power to become the children of God, ¹³who were born not from blood, nor the will of the flesh, nor the will of man, but from God.

¹⁴And the Word became flesh and lived among us in a body, and we saw his glory,

---

1:1 The author models the beginning of the Gospel on Genesis 1:1. The Word existed before the creation, and therefore he was not created. This verse may prefigure John 10:30, *I and the Father are one* (the King James Version follows an inferior manuscript tradition *I and my Father are one*). Mosiah 15:2 contains what is the closest Restoration scriptural parallel to the opening verses of the Gospel of John (but compare also Genesis 1). In Mosiah 15, Abinadi presents aspects of Christ's identity as both the Father and Son. John describes the relationship between the two, and therefore he presents a statement of purpose. Alluded to in Doctrine and Covenants 93:7–8. The Joseph Smith Translation titles this *The Testimony of St. John* and begins *In the beginning was the gospel preached through the Son. And the gospel was the Word, and the Word was with the Son, and the Son was with God, and the Son was of God.* **1:1–5** The opening verses are written in poetic style, and they are interrupted by the introduction of verse 6. Scholarship on these verses has suggested that they were originally a Christian hymn to Christ that have been adapted by the author of the Fourth Gospel. John 1:1–18 constitutes what is often called the Prologue Hymn or the Hymn to the Logos (Word). **1:2** Alluded to in Doctrine and Covenants 93:21. **1:2–3** These verses contain similar language to the description of Jesus Christ's appearing in 3 Nephi 9:15, 18. **1:3** Alluded to in Doctrine and Covenants 93:10. **1:3–4** Many modern translations punctuate the Greek differently so that the verse could read *All things were created through him, and without him nothing was made that was made.* The parallelism of the preceding verses suggests a shorter sense unit, which is reflected in this translation. Doctrine and Covenants 93:10 quotes these verses. **1:4** Perhaps an allusion to Genesis 3:20. Eve was the mother of all that was alive, and now Jesus as the Word is the life of humanity. Compare Mosiah 16:9; 3 Nephi 9:18; 11:11. Alluded to in Doctrine and Covenants 93:9. **1:5** This verse is quoted in a new context and with new meaning in Doctrine and Covenants 88:49. Compare Doctrine and Covenants 6:21; 10:57–58; 11:11; 34:1–3; 39:2; 45:7, 29. **1:6–8** Like the other Evangelists, John the Baptist is the teacher who brings the believing to Jesus. John's account emphasizes that John the Baptist was not himself *the light* but a witness of it. **1:9** Quoted in Doctrine and Covenants 93:2 (compare Doctrine and Covenants 84:46). **1:11** In Greek, *His own* refers to *his own family, city, country,* or *people.* Compare 3 Nephi 9:16. **1:11–12** Quoted in Doctrine and Covenants 11:29–30. **1:12** *Power* is the primary meaning of the noun, but it can also mean *right, authority,* or *honor.* Compare 3 Nephi 9:17, which alludes to this verse. Alluded to in Doctrine and Covenants 11:30; 34:3; 39:4; 42:52; 66:1. **1:13** Alluded to in Doctrine and Covenants 63:10. **1:14** The author refers to the dwelling of the Logos among us as *taking a tabernacle*, a possible reference to the tabernacles built during the Feast of Tabernacles, or more literally that the Word lived in a mortal tabernacle. Similar wording is expressed in 1 Nephi 15:13; 2 Nephi 2:6; 25:12–14; Mosiah 3:5; Alma 5:48; 9:26; Doctrine and Covenants 66:12; 76:23; 93:11.

which is the glory of an Only Begotten of the Father, who is full of grace and truth. [15]John testified of him and declared, "This was him of whom I said, 'He who comes after me is greater than me because he existed before me.'" [16]And from his fullness we have all received grace in place of grace. [17]The Law was given through Moses, and grace and truth began as a result of Jesus Christ. [18]No one has ever seen God. The Only Begotten God, who is in the embrace of the Father, he has declared him.

JOHN THE BAPTIST (MT 3:1-17; MK 1:1-11; LK 3:1-22)

[19]This was the testimony of John, when the Jews from Jerusalem sent priests and Levites to him. And they asked him, "Who are you?" [20]He declared and did not deny, but declared, "I am not the Christ." [21]And they asked him, "Who are you, then? Are you Elijah?" And he said, "I am not." "Are you the prophet?" And he answered, "No." [22]Then they said to him, "Who are you, that we may give an answer to those who sent us, what do you say about yourself?" [23]He said, "*I am the voice shouting in the desert, 'Prepare the way of the Lord,'*" as spoken by the prophet Isaiah. [24]And they were sent from the Pharisees, [25]and they asked him, "Why do you baptize if you are not the Christ nor Elijah nor the prophet?" [26]John answered them, "I baptize in water. One among you, whom you do not know, [27]he comes after me, and I am not worthy to untie the latch of his sandal." [28]These things took place in Bethany, across the Jordan River, where John was baptizing.

[29]The next day he saw Jesus come to him, and he said, "Behold, the Lamb of God who takes away the sin of the world. [30]This is the one about whom I said, 'After me comes a man who is greater than me, because he existed before me.' [31]I did

---

1:16 Quoted in Doctrine and Covenants 93:12. The Joseph Smith Translation says *And as many as believe on his name shall receive of his fullness. And of his fullness have all we received, even immortality and eternal life through his grace.* **1:17** The Joseph Smith Translation says *For the law was given through Moses, but life and truth came through Jesus Christ. For the law was after a carnal commandment, to the administration of death; but the gospel was after the power of an endless life, through Jesus Christ, the only begotten Son, who is in the bosom of the Father.* **1:18** *He has declared him* renders the Greek accurately but ambiguously in English. Here *Christ declared the Father*, which John notes is necessary as a result that *no one has ever seen God.* Compare Joseph Smith—History 1:17. Some manuscripts read *the Only Begotten Son*. The better reading, based on the manuscript evidence, is *the Only Begotten God*. Compare Doctrine and Covenants 67:11; 76:13, 25, 39; Moses 7:24. The Joseph Smith Translation for this verse reads *And no man hath seen God at any time except he hath borne record of the Son, for except it is through him no man can be saved.* **1:21** *Are you Elijah?* Greek spells the Hebrew name *Elijah* as *Elias*, which is the way the name is rendered in older translations. See Malachi 4:5 for the coming of *Elijah*. **1:23** John declares that he is the fulfillment of Isaiah 40:3, which he quotes. **1:25** The *prophet* is a reference to Deuteronomy 18:15–18 (see Acts 3:22–23; 1 Nephi 22:20). **1:26–29** Compare 1 Nephi 10:7–10. **1:27** The Joseph Smith Translation adds *or whose place I am not able to fill: for he shall baptize, not only with water, but with fire, and with the Holy Ghost.* **1:28** A number of inferior Greek manuscripts read *Bethabara* in the place of *Bethany*. First Nephi 10:9 also reads *Bethabara*. The location of *Bethabara*, which means a *crossing* or *ford*, remains unknown, as does the precise location of *Bethany*. The manuscript evidence supports the reading *Bethany*, and the precise location and physical relationship of *Bethany-Bethabara* must await further discoveries. For Bethabara, see Joshua 15:6, 61; 18:22; Judges 7:24. **1:29** *The next day* refers to the day after an embassy went to John the Baptist. The first chapters report a three-day sequence of events (John 1:19; 1:35; 2:1). *The Lamb of God* is mentioned frequently in the Book of Mormon (for example, in 1 Nephi 10:10; 11:21; 2 Nephi 31:4) but only twice in the New Testament (see John 1:36). Jesus as the Lamb is mentioned frequently in the book of Revelation.

not know him, but so that he might be revealed to Israel I came baptizing with water." [32]And John declared, saying, "I saw the Spirit descending like a dove from heaven and remaining upon him. [33]I did not know him, but he who sent me to baptize in water, he said to me, 'Upon whom you see the Spirit descending and remaining on him, this is the one who baptizes in the Holy Spirit.' [34]I have seen and have testified that this is the Son of God."

EARLY DISCIPLES CALLED

[35]The next day, John stood again with two of his disciples, [36]and he saw Jesus walking by and said, "Behold, the Lamb of God!" [37]When the two disciples heard him, they followed Jesus. [38]Jesus turned and saw them following and said, "What do you seek?" They said to him, "Rabbi," (which means 'Teacher'), "Where are you staying?" [39]He said to them, "Come and see." And they went and saw where he was staying, and they stayed with him that day, and it was about four in the afternoon. [40]Andrew, Simon Peter's brother, was one of the two disciples who heard John speak and followed Jesus. [41]He first found his own brother, Simon, and said to him, "We have found the Messiah" (which means "Christ"). [42]He brought him to Jesus, and when Jesus saw him he said, "You are Simon, the son of Jonah, but you will be called Cephas" (which means "Peter").

[43]The next day he decided to go to Galilee. And he found Philip, and Jesus said to him, "Follow me." [44]Now Philip was from Bethsaida, the town of Andrew and Peter. [45]Philip found Nathanael and said to him, "We have found the one about whom Moses wrote in the Law and the Prophets, Jesus the son of Joseph from Nazareth." [46]And Nathanael replied, "Is it possible for anything good to come from Nazareth?" But Philip responded, "Come and see." [47]When Jesus saw Nathanael coming to him, he said about him, "Look, an Israelite *in whom there is no deceit.*" [48]Nathanael responded, "How do you know me?" Jesus answered him, "Before Philip called you, I saw you underneath the fig tree." [49]Nathanael responded, "Rabbi, you are the Son of God, you are the King of Israel!" [50]Jesus responded to him, "Do you believe because I said to you that I saw you underneath the fig tree? You will see greater things than these." [51]And he said to him, "Truly, truly, I say to you that you

---

1:32 First Nephi 11:27 also speaks of God or the Spirit descending from heaven. Doctrine and Covenants 93:15 offers important commentary on this verse. **1:34** Some manuscripts read *God's chosen* instead of *Son of God*, but *Son of God* is the more likely reading. First Nephi 11:7, 32 offers a similar testimony to the *Son of God*. Echoed in Doctrine and Covenants 93:14. **1:36** The symbol of Jesus as a lamb is used frequently in the Fourth Gospel and the book of Revelation (John 1:29, 36; Revelation 5:6, 8, 12–13, etc.). **1:38** The two disciples refer to Jesus as *Rabbi*, a respectful term for a *teacher*. Echoed in Alma 18:13. **1:40** The Greek has only *and followed him*. **1:42** *Which means Peter* may be the author's way of saying *which means rock*. Here, *Peter* functions as an explanation of the Aramaic word *Cephas* and not as the name Peter. Simon was likely known as *Cephas* among the disciples who spoke Aramaic, but as the Gospel message spread, his Latin name *Peter* (built from the Greek *petros* meaning "a stone") began to gain prominence. Peter's father's name is traditionally rendered as *Jonah*, but the typical transliteration into English would be John. **1:42** The disciple Philip is different from the deacon named Philip in Acts 6:5. **1:44** See map for Matthew 11:21. **1:45** Some scholars have suggested that Bartholomew is the same person as Nathanael, but such a connection is historically unlikely. The differences in the lists of the twelve disciples may indicate that some of the early disciples died or fell away (see John 6:66; Acts 1:13). **1:46** Nathanael's criticism of Nazareth may have arisen out of the concern that the Messiah would not come from Nazareth, but Bethlehem. **1:47** An allusion to Psalm 32:2. Quoted in Doctrine and Covenants 41:11. **1:51** Quotation of Genesis 28:12. Compare 1 Nephi 11:30.

will see heaven opened and *the angels of God descending and ascending* on the Son of Man."

The Wedding of Cana

2 ¹On the third day there was a marriage in Cana of Galilee, and Jesus's mother was there. ²And Jesus and his disciples were invited to the wedding. ³When the wine ran out, Jesus's mother said to him, "They have no wine." ⁴And Jesus replied to her, "Woman, what does that matter to you and me? My time has not yet come." ⁵His mother said to the servants, "Do whatever he tells you." ⁶There were six stone water vessels standing there for washing according to Jewish practice, each holding two or three measures of liquid. ⁷And Jesus said to them, "Fill the vessels with water." And they filled them up. ⁸Then he said to them, "Now draw some out and take it to the master of the feast." So, they took it. ⁹When the master of the feast tasted it, the water changed to wine (he did not know where it came from, but the servants who drew out the water knew); he called the bridegroom ¹⁰and said to him, "Every man serves the good wine first, and after they are drunk, then he serves the weak wine, but you have kept the good wine until now." ¹¹Jesus did this, the first of the miracles, in Cana of Galilee, and he revealed his glory, and his disciples believed in him. ¹²After this he went down to Capernaum with his mother, brothers and sisters, and his disciples, and stayed there a short time.

Jesus Cleanses the Temple
(Mt 21:12–17; Mk 11:15–19; Lk 19:45–48)

¹³And it was near the Passover of the Jews, and Jesus went up to Jerusalem. ¹⁴And in the temple he found those who sell oxen, sheep, and doves, and the money changers were sitting there. ¹⁵And after he made a whip of cords, he drove them all from the temple, both the sheep and oxen, and he dumped out the coins of the money changers and overturned their tables. ¹⁶And to those who sold doves, he said,

---

2:1 See Joshua 19:28, which also refers to *Cana* (spelled Kanah). **2:2** Jesus, his mother, and disciples were invited to the wedding, thus making it likely that this was the marriage of a near relative. **2:4** Jesus frequently speaks of his *hour* or *time* (see John 4:21, 23; 5:25; 12:23, 27; 17:1, etc.). The force of Jesus's response *woman* is difficult to translate without implying condescension in English. The response is typical, but somewhat more formal than one would expect in the setting of a wedding, or between a mother and son. See Matthew 15:28; Luke 13:12. **2:5** *Servants* here are deacons in Greek. **2:6** A Greek *measure* was equal to about ten gallons/thirty-five liters, indicating that each could have held up to thirty gallons of liquid. The purifying or washing mentioned in this verse is similarly referred to in Matthew 15:2. **2:11** John refers to the *miracles of Jesus* as signs instead of miracles. John's choice of word interprets the miracles as enabling readers to believe in Jesus. First Nephi 19:13 speaks of signs in a similar way. There are seven miracles in the Gospel of John, not including the miracle of the resurrection. See 2:1–11; 4:46–54; 5:1–15; 6:5–14; 6:16–24; 9:1–7; 11:1–45. These seven miracles lead the reader to believe in Jesus, and they are literally signs of Jesus's divinity. **2:12** John uses *brothers* to refer to Jesus's mortal brothers (see John 7:3, 5) and *disciples* to refer to the twelve, indicating that he was aware that Jesus had siblings. Jesus also had sisters (Mark 6:3). **2:13** Three Passovers are mentioned in John (2:13; 6:4; 11:55). A fourth may be referred to in the unnamed feast in John 5:1. **2:13–17** John places the cleansing of the temple at the beginning of Jesus's ministry, whereas the other Evangelists place the event at the time of the triumphal entry (Matthew 21:12; Mark 11:15; Luke 19:45). It remains impossible to determine whether there were two separate events, one at the beginning of the ministry and one at the end, or whether the same event is described as having occurred at different times. John alone mentions sheep and oxen, the whip, and the scattering of the coins. **2:16** An allusion to Zechariah 14:21, where the mundane has been made holy in the temple and where there will no longer be traders there.

"Take these things from this place. Do not make my Father's house a marketplace." [17]His disciples remembered that it is written, *"Zeal for your house will consume me."*

[18]Therefore, the Jews responded to him, "Because you do these things, what sign do you show us?" [19]Jesus answered them, "Destroy this temple and I will raise it up again in three days." [20]Then the Jews said, "This temple has been under construction for forty-six years, and you will raise it up in three days?" [21]But he said this concerning the temple of his body. [22]Therefore, when he was raised from the dead, his disciples remembered that he said this, and they believed the scripture and the word which Jesus had told them.

[23]When he was in Jerusalem during the Feast of Passover, many believed in his name after they saw the miracles that he did. [24]But Jesus did not entrust himself to them because he knew all people, [25]because he did not need anyone to testify about man, and because he knew what was in humans.

NICODEMUS

3 [1]There was a man from the Pharisees named Nicodemus, a ruler of the Jews. [2]He came to Jesus at night and said to him, "Rabbi, we know that you are a teacher who has come from God, for no one would be able to do these miracles that you do if God were not with him." [3]Jesus answered him, "Truly, truly, I say to you, if a person is not born from on high, that person is not able to see the kingdom of God." [4]Nicodemus said to him, "How is a person able to be born while being old? Can a person enter his mother's womb a second time and be born?" [5]Jesus answered, "Truly, truly, I say to you, unless a person is born of water and Spirit, that person cannot enter the kingdom of God. [6]That which is born of flesh is flesh, and that which is born from the Spirit is spirit. [7]Do not be amazed that I said to you, 'You must be born from on high.' [8]The wind blows where it desires, and you hear its sound, but you do not know where it goes or where it leads to, even so it is for all who are born from the Spirit." [9]Nicodemus responded to him, "How can these things be?" [10]Jesus answered and said, "Are you a teacher in Israel and you do not know these things? [11]Truly, truly, I say to you that we speak about what we know, and we testify about what we have seen, and you do not accept our testimony. [12]If I had told you about earthly things and you

---

2:17 Quotation from Psalm 69:9. Psalm 69 contains a past tense form of the verb *consume*, whereas it is a future tense here. **2:20** Herod the Great began rebuilding the temple during the eighteenth (= 19 BCE) year of his rule. The major reconstruction effort was finished in less than ten years, but work continued on the site through the middle of the first century CE. The *forty-sixth year* would be 27–28 CE. Josephus also mentions this building project (*Antiquities* 15.11.380). **2:21** This may be an allusion to the future age when there would be no temple. Instead, the believers will have God and the Lamb of God in their presence (Revelation 21:22). **2:22** John does not clarify which scripture is in mind here, but verse 17 probably refers to Psalm 69:9.

3:1 John refers to Nicodemus simply as an *archon*, a term that indicates he held some institutional authority, perhaps in the local synagogue or even in the Jerusalem Sanhedrin. **3:2** The text says only *he came to him at night*. Much has been said about this night visit, but it may have been a pragmatic decision to speak to Jesus alone, or feasibly because the Sabbath had passed. **3:3** The Gospel of John prefers the word *signs*, here translated as *miracles*. See John 2:11. Some translations prefer *born again* because Nicodemus's question implies a second birth. See 3:31, which uses the same Greek word for *from above*. **3:5** Echoed in Doctrine and Covenants 5:16 and expanded in Moses 6:59. **3:7** Alluded to in Mosiah 27:25; Alma 7:14. **3:11** *You do not accept* is plural, referring not just to Nicodemus, but probably to Pharisees generally. **3:12** The passage could also be translated as *things upon the earth* and *things in the heavens*.

did not believe, how would you believe if I told you about heavenly things? [13]No one has ascended into heaven except the Son of Man, who descended from heaven. [14]Just as Moses lifted up the serpent in the desert, even so must the Son of Man be lifted up [15]so that whoever believes in him might have an eternal life.

[16]"For this is how God loved the world: he gave his Only Begotten Son so that all who believe in him will not perish but have eternal life. [17]For God did not send his Son to judge the world, but that the world would be saved through him. [18]Whoever believes in him is not judged, but whoever does not believe in him is already judged because that person has not believed in the name of the Only Begotten Son of God. [19]And this is the judgment: the light has come into the world, but humanity loved the darkness more than the light, for their works were wicked. [20]Everyone who performs wicked actions hates the light and does not come to the light so that their actions will not be exposed. [21]He who acts in truth comes to the light so that his actions are revealed, that his actions have been performed in God."

JOHN THE BAPTIST'S DISCIPLES

[22]After these things, Jesus and his disciples came to the land of Judea, and he baptized alongside them and remained there. [23]John was baptizing in Aenon near Salem because there was plentiful water there, and people came and were baptized. [24](For John was not yet cast into prison.)

[25]There was a debate among the disciples of John and a Jew regarding purification. [26]And he came to John and said to him, "Rabbi, the one who was with you across the Jordan River, the one who you testified about, he is baptizing and everyone goes to him." [27]John answered, "A person is not able to receive anything unless it has been given to him from heaven. [28]You yourselves bear witness that I said, 'I am not the Christ, but I am sent before him.' [29]Whoever has the bride is the groom. The friend of the groom, the one who stands and hears him, rejoices greatly because of the voice of the groom. Therefore, my joy is full. [30]He must increase, but I must decrease.

[31]"He who comes from above is above all, he who is from the earth is of the earth and speaks of earthly things. The one who comes from heaven is above all. [32]He testifies regarding what he has seen and heard,

---

3:13 An allusion to Deuteronomy 30:12. Some inferior manuscripts add *who is in heaven* in reference to the *Son of Man*. **3:14** An allusion to Numbers 21:9. Compare Helaman 8:14. **3:15** Some interpreters note that the quotation of Jesus's discourse to Nicodemus ends at verse 15; others argue that it concludes with verse 21. The discourse takes a dramatic change in tone at verse 16. **3:16** Quoted in Doctrine and Covenants 34:3. **3:18** The Greek verbs are singular in this verse. **3:19** *Wicked* represents here a life of wicked works or evil actions. The word can also mean diseased or troubled, but the Fourth Gospel uses the word in the sense of wicked deeds. An interpretation of this verse is given in Doctrine and Covenants 10:21 (compare Doctrine and Covenants 29:45). **3:21** English prefers to have a noun follow *God* so that the verse would read *in God's name*. The sense is that a person performs actions with God in mind, or with an eye on God. See John 19:39 for Nicodemus's involvement with caring for the body of Jesus after the crucifixion. **3:23** The location of *Aenon near Salem* is unknown. **3:25** Some manuscripts describe the debate as taking place between the disciples of John and the *Jews* rather than a single *Jew*. **3:31–36** John has not indicated a change in speaker, and therefore the logical assumption is that these are the words of John the Baptist. Some scholars, however, argue that it is a continuation of Jesus's words to Nicodemus, which ended in verse 21. **3:32** Jesus testifies of the things that he has seen and heard, thus providing a substantive basis for the things that he has taught. Seeing and hearing provide the foundation of his witness.

and no one receives his testimony. ³³Whoever accepts his testimony sets his seal that God is true. ³⁴Therefore, the one whom God sent speaks the words of God, for he gave the Spirit without measure. ³⁵The Father loves the Son, and he has handed over all things to him. ³⁶Whoever believes in the Son has eternal life, but whoever rejects the Son will not see life, but the wrath of God resides on him."

THE WOMAN OF SAMARIA
(MT 4:12–17; MK 1:14–15; LK 4:14–15)

4 ¹When Jesus learned that the Pharisees heard that Jesus made a greater number of disciples and baptized more than John ²(although Jesus did not baptize, but his disciples did), ³he departed from Judea and came again to Galilee, ⁴but he had to travel through Samaria. ⁵Therefore, he came to a town of the Samaritans called Sychar, neighboring the region that Jacob gave to his son Joseph. ⁶Jacob's well was there, and Jesus was tired from the journey, and he sat upon the well. It was about noon.

⁷A Samaritan woman came to draw water. Jesus said to her, "Give me something to drink." ⁸For his disciples had departed to the town so that they might purchase food. ⁹Therefore, the Samaritan woman said to him, "How can you, being a Jew, ask a drink of me, who is a Samaritan woman? (For Jews do not have anything

---

3:33 The concept of *setting a seal* is to seal a document by a personal signature or to place a mark upon something so that it represents acceptance of the terms of a contract. **3:34** *Without measure* may anticipate the outpouring of the Spirit on Pentecost (Acts 2:1).

4:1–2 The Joseph Smith Translation says *When therefore the Pharisees had heard that Jesus made and baptized more disciples than John, they sought more diligently some means that they might put him to death; for many received John as a prophet, but they believed not on Jesus.* **4:1–3** Jesus's popularity was increasing, which caused a reaction from the Pharisees. John's wording implies that the increase in the number of disciples was of greater concern than the fact that Jesus and his disciples were baptizing. A number of early and good Greek manuscripts read *the Lord* in place of *Jesus,* in the first instance in this verse, but the evidence seems to support *Jesus* as the original. **4:2** The parenthetical insertion by the author contradicts what was stated in John 3:22. The Joseph Smith Translation for this verse reads *Though he himself baptized not so many as his disciples, for he suffered them for an example, preferring one another.* **4:4** It is unclear why Jesus had to travel through Samaria, but the implication is that he was facing hostility and rejection in Judea. The typical route from Judea to Galilee would circumvent Samaria. **4:5** Compare Acts 7:16. Jacob's well was in Shechem, but Sychar may have been a village near Shechem. **4:9** The complex relationship between Jews and Samaritans was marked with hostility and mutual condemnation. The Samaritans were a mixture of native Israelites, some of whom had been deported to Assyria in 722 BCE, and colonists who had been relocated in the region by the Assyrians and Babylonians. The Samaritans claimed Israelite heritage, and they built a temple on Mount Gerizim in Samaria (see 2 Kings 17:24), although it had been destroyed by New Testament times.

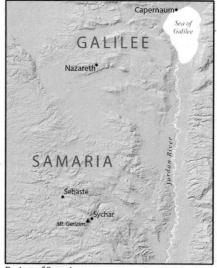

Regions of Samaria
Map by Cassie Howe, ThinkSpatial, BYU Geography

in common with Samaritans). [10]Jesus responded to her, "If you knew the gift of God and who it is who said to you, 'Give me something to drink,' you would have asked him and he would have given you living water." [11]She said to him, "Sir, you have nothing to draw water with, and the well is deep. From what source do you have living water? [12]Are you greater than our father Jacob, who gave us the well, and he drank from it, as did his sons and animals?" [13]Jesus responded to her, "Everyone who drinks from this water will thirst again, [14]but everyone who drinks the water that I give will never thirst, and the water that I give will be in him a well of water springing up to eternal life." [15]The woman said to him, "Sir, give me this water, that I may not thirst or have to come to this place to draw water." [16]He said to her, "Go and call your husband and come here." [17]The woman responded, "I do not have a husband." Jesus said to her, "You have said correctly, 'I do not have a husband.' [18]You have had five husbands, and now the one you are with is not your husband. You have told the truth in this regard." [19]The woman said to him, "Sir, I see that you are a prophet. [20]Our fathers worshiped on this mountain, but you say that Jerusalem is the place where people should worship."

[21]Jesus said to her, "Believe me, woman, the hour will come when neither on this mountain nor in Jerusalem will you worship the Father. [22]You have not understood what you worship; we have understood what we worship because salvation is from the Jews. [23]But the hour comes, and it is now, that the true worshippers will kneel before the Father in spirit and truth, for the Father is seeking such people to worship him. [24]God is spirit, and those who worship him should do so in spirit and truth." [25]The woman said to him, "I know that the Messiah comes, who is called Christ. When he comes, he will make known all things to us." [26]Jesus said to her, "I am the Christ who speaks to you."

[27]His disciples came upon this, and they were amazed that he spoke with a woman, but no one said, "What do you want?" or "Why are you speaking with her?" [28]Then she left her water jar, and the woman went into the town and said to the people, [29]"Come, see a man who told me everything that I have ever done. Can this be the Christ?" [30]They went out of the town and came to him.

[31]In the meantime, the disciples were saying to him, "Rabbi, eat." [32]But he said to them, "I have food to eat that you do not know about." [33]Therefore, the disci-

---

4:10 Compare Jeremiah 2:13; 1 Nephi 11:25. **4:11** Calling Jesus *Sir* is a term of respect used in public, but in other instances it is translated as *Lord* when in reference to Jesus as *the Lord*. **4:14** Alma 32:41 and Doctrine and Covenants 63:23 allude to this verse. **4:22** The Samaritans accepted the five books of Moses (the Pentateuch) and a version of Joshua, but they rejected the Prophets and other writings of the Old Testament. Jesus's statement here may have specifically had in mind the understanding of God that results from reading the words of the prophets only. **4:23–24** Alma 34:38 expands the meaning of these verses (compare Alma 43:10). **4:24** The statement *God is spirit* is made in reference to the nature of God, who is to be worshipped in the spirit (verse 23) and who is a spiritual being. The statement need not be taken as an assertion that God is only a spiritual being but that his work is a spiritual effort to save humanity. The Joseph Smith Translation for this verse reads, *For unto such hath God promised his Spirit: and they who worship him must worship in spirit and in truth.* **4:25** *Who is called Christ* is probably a parenthetical explanation by the author. **4:26** When Jesus responds, he states simply, *I am he who speaks to you.* The phrase *I am* is understood to be a declaration that Jesus is the Christ following the woman's assertion, *I know that the Messiah comes, who is called the Christ.* The phrase *I am* could also imply *I am Jehovah* (see John 8:58), but here it is taken as an affirmative response to her probing faith (compare Exodus 3:14).

ples said to one another, "Did someone give him something to eat?" ³⁴Jesus said to them, "My food is that I may do the will of him who sent me, and that I may complete his work. ³⁵Do not say, 'There are still four months, and then the harvest comes.' I say to you, lift up your eyes, and see that the fields are already white for harvest. ³⁶The one who harvests receives wages and gathers fruit for eternal life in order that the sower and harvester may celebrate together. ³⁷For the teaching is true in this regard, 'One sows, and another harvests.' ³⁸I sent you to harvest what you did not work for, others have worked, and you have received the benefits of their labor."

³⁹Many Samaritans out of that town believed in him because of the word of the woman, who testified, "He told me everything that I have ever done." ⁴⁰When the Samaritans came to him, they asked him to stay with them, and he stayed there two days. ⁴¹And many more believed because of his teaching. ⁴²They said to the woman, "It is no longer because of what you said that we believe, for we have heard for ourselves, and we know that this is truly the Savior of the world."

JESUS HEALS AN OFFICIAL'S SON
(MT 8:5–13; LK 7:1–10)

⁴³After two days, he departed to Galilee. ⁴⁴(Jesus testified that a prophet has no honor in his own country.) ⁴⁵Therefore, he came to Galilee, and the Galileans received him because they had seen all that he did in Jerusalem at the feast, for they also went to the feast. ⁴⁶And he came again to Cana of Galilee, where he made the water into wine. And there was a certain government official in Capernaum whose son was ill. ⁴⁷When he heard that Jesus came from Judea to Galilee, he went to him and asked him whether he would come and heal his son, for he was about to die. ⁴⁸Then Jesus said to him, "If you do not see a sign, you do not believe." ⁴⁹The official said to Jesus, "Lord, come before my child dies." ⁵⁰Jesus said to him, "Go, your son will live." The man believed the word that Jesus said to him and he departed. ⁵¹While he departed, his servants met him and said to him that his son lives. ⁵²Therefore, he enquired about the hour in which he began to recover, and they told him, "Yesterday, at one in the afternoon the fever left him." ⁵³Then the father knew that it was in that hour that Jesus said to him, "Your son will live," and he believed together with his entire household. ⁵⁴This was the second sign that Jesus did after coming from Judea to Galilee.

A HEALING ON THE SABBATH

5 ¹After these things there was a Jewish feast and Jesus went up to Jerusalem.

4:35 *Four months and then the harvest comes* would place this encounter in the winter. The wheat harvest occurred in April–May. *Four months* would indicate that the seed had not yet been sown into the ground (compare verse 37). Compare Leviticus 26:16. Harvest language drawn from this verse appears in the Doctrine and Covenants 4:4; 11:3; 12:3; 14:3; 31:4; 33:3, 7. **4:42** Echoed in 1 Nephi 10:4. **4:44** It is unclear why John mentions that Jesus was rejected in his own town, and perhaps this explains why he went to Cana and not Nazareth. This parenthetical statement may be an allusion to Jesus's later rejection in Galilee. **4:45** The believing *Galileans* were Jews who believed in Jesus because of what they had seen him do in Jerusalem. **4:46** Compare Matthew 8:5–13; Luke 7:1–10. In John's account the boy who is healed is referred to as a *son* (also verses 50 and 53). **4:48** Compare 1 Nephi 11:7.

5:1 This unnamed feast draws Jesus to Jerusalem, suggesting it is one of the major pilgrimage feasts (Passover, Pentecost, and Tabernacles). John 7:2 takes place at the Feast of Tabernacles, which is the next major feast following Pentecost, but John 6:4 notes that the Passover was near. The most likely situation is that 5:1 refers to Pentecost. John does not distinguish between Pharisees or Sadducees, but only loosely describes the opposition Jesus faces as deriving from Jews. This is not an indication that Jesus faced

²There is in Jerusalem by the Sheep Gate a pool which is called Bethesda in Aramaic which has five colonnades. ³Among the colonnades lay a multitude of sick, blind, lame, and paralyzed individuals. ⁵There was a certain man there who had been disabled for thirty-eight years. ⁶When Jesus saw him lying there and knew that he had already been there a long time, he asked him, "Do you desire to be healed?" ⁷The sick man answered him, "Sir, I have no one to put me in the pool when the water is moved. While I am going, another steps in before me." ⁸Jesus said to him, "Get up, and take your bed and walk!" ⁹Immediately the man was healthy, and he took his bed and walked. (That day was the Sabbath.)

¹⁰Therefore, the Jews said to the man who had been healed, "It is the Sabbath, and it is not lawful for you to carry your bed." ¹¹But he answered them, "He who made me healthy, he told me, 'Take your bed and walk.'" ¹²They asked him, "Who is the man who told you, 'Take your bed and walk?'" ¹³The man who was healed did not know who it was, for Jesus had departed because there was a crowd in the place where he was. ¹⁴After this Jesus found him in the temple and said to him, "You are healthy now; sin no more so that

nothing worse happens to you." ¹⁵The man departed and told the Jews that it was Jesus who healed him. ¹⁶And because he did these things on the Sabbath, the Jews harassed Jesus.

¹⁷But Jesus responded to them, "My Father works until now, and I am working." ¹⁸Therefore, because of this, the Jews sought to kill him even more, because he was not only breaking the Sabbath, but he was also calling God his own Father, making himself equal with God.

THE SON DOES WHAT THE FATHER DOES

¹⁹Therefore, Jesus answered them, "Truly, truly, I say to you, the Son does nothing by himself, but only what he sees the Father doing. For what he does, the Son does likewise. ²⁰For the Father loves the Son, and he shows him all things that he does, and he will show him greater works than these, so that you will wonder. ²¹As the Father raises the dead and gives them life, even so the Son gives life to those whom he will. ²²The Father judges no one, but he has given all judgment to the Son, ²³so that all may honor the Son just as they honor the Father. Whoever does not honor the Son does not honor the Father who sent

---

widespread opposition from all Jews but only that a select group who objected to his actions on the Sabbath opposed him.**5:2** Some manuscripts spell the name *Bethzatha* or *Bethsaida*. The *Sheep Gate* and its construction are discussed in Nehemiah 3:1, 32; 12:39. Archaeological work at the site has revealed a shrine to the pagan healing deity Asclepius, thus helping explain the strong pagan healing elements in this story. **5:3** *Waiting for the moving of the water* is added by some late and inferior Greek manuscripts to the end of this verse. The addition is unlikely to be original to the Fourth Gospel. **5:4** Some inferior manuscripts add a verse that is confidently not original to the Gospel of John. That verse reads (with variations), *For an angel of the Lord went down at a certain time to the pool and moved the water. Whoever was first to step in after the moving of the water was made healthy.* **5:8** The *bed* is more likely a portable mattress, perhaps made of straw. **5:9** Compare Jeremiah 17:21. **5:10** *The Jews* refers to Jewish leaders, perhaps Pharisees. **5:13** The verb translated as *departed* can also mean *escaped*. **5:14** Jesus's words do not connect sin and sickness but that sinning results in a state that is worse than being physically ill. **5:15** The Book of Mormon's usage of the term *the Jews* closely approximates that of the Gospel of John (compare John 5:18; 6:41; 7:1; 1 Nephi 10:2; 13:23; 2 Nephi 30:2–4, etc.). This usage is similar to other biblical texts that view *the Jews* as a foreign people (see Ezra 4:12; Nehemiah 1:2; Esther 9:25–28). **5:18** For the regulations regarding blasphemy, see Leviticus 24:14, 16. **5:19** John's *therefore* signals that Jesus was unwilling to permit their criticisms to go unchallenged.

him. [24]Truly, truly, I say to you that the one who hears my word and believes in him who sent me has eternal life, and he will not be judged but will pass from death to life.

[25]"Truly, truly, I say to you that the hour comes and is now here when the dead will hear the voice of the Son of God, and those who hear it will live. [26]Just as the Father has life in himself, even so he has granted the Son to have life in himself. [27]He gave authority to him to execute judgment because he is the Son of Man. [28]Do not be amazed at this because the hour comes in which all who are in the graves will hear his voice, [29]and they will come out, those who have done good to the resurrection of life, and those who have practiced evil to the resurrection of condemnation. [30]I am not able to do anything by myself. As I hear, even so I judge, and my judgment is just because I do not seek my own will but the will of him who sent me.

WITNESSES TO JESUS

[31]"If I testify concerning myself, my witness is not true. [32]There is another who testifies concerning me, and I know that the witness he gives concerning me is true. [33]You sought out John, and he testified of the truth. [34]I do not accept human testimony, but I say these things that you may be saved. [35]He was a burning and bright lamp, and you wanted to rejoice for an hour in his light. [36]I have a testimony greater than John's. For the works that the Father gave me to accomplish, the works that I am doing, they testify of me and that the Father sent me. [37]The Father who sent me, he has testified concerning me. You have never heard his voice, nor have you seen his image, [38]and you do not have his word abiding in you, because you do not believe the one whom he sent.

[39]"You search the scriptures because you think that you have eternal life in them, and yet it is they that testify concerning me, [40]but you do not desire to come to me that you may have life. [41]I do not accept praise from men, [42]but I know that you do not have the love of God in you. [43]I have come in the name of my Father, and you did not receive me. If another comes in his own name, you will receive him. [44]How are you able to believe when you accept praise from one another, and do not seek for the glory that is only of God? [45]Do not think that I will accuse you before the Father. Moses, on whom you have placed your hope, is your accuser. [46]Therefore, if you believed Moses, you would believe me because he wrote about me. [47]If you do not believe that which is written, how will you believe in my teachings?"

FEEDING OF THE FIVE THOUSAND (MT 14:13–21; MK 6:30–44; LK 9:10–17)

6 [1]After this Jesus went across the Sea of Galilee, which is also called the Sea of Tiberias. [2]And a large crowd followed him because they saw the miracles that he did for the sick. [3]Then Jesus went up a mountain, and there he sat with his disciples. [4]It was near the Passover, the Jewish feast. [5]Then Jesus lifted up his eyes and saw that

---

5:25 Doctrine and Covenants 76:16 echoes this verse. **5:29** Compare this verse to Helaman 12:26. This verse also provided inspiration for the revelation of Doctrine and Covenants 76 as Joseph Smith worked at translating the Bible. Alluded to in Mosiah 16:11; 3 Nephi 26:5. **5:32** *I know* is preserved in the majority of manuscripts, but one early and important Greek manuscript reads *you know*. **5:39** Jesus's criticism of scripture searching implies that his audience relied too heavily on the written word instead of accepting the living voice of John the Baptist. The mood is indicative and not imperative, and Jesus did not instruct his readers to *search the scriptures*, but instead he criticized them directly for searching but not understanding. **5:46** Perhaps Deuteronomy 18:18, 22 is in mind here (compare 1 Nephi 22:20–21). **5:47** *My teachings* can also be rendered as *my words*.

a large crowd came to him, and he said to Philip, "Where may we buy bread so that they may eat?" 6(This he said testing him, for he knew what he was about to do.) 7Philip answered him, "Two hundred silver coins worth of bread would be insufficient even if each of them took a little." 8One of his disciples, Andrew, the brother of Simon Peter, said to him, 9"There is a boy here who has five barley loaves and two fish, but what does this amount to for so many?" 10Jesus said, "Make the people sit down." (There was a great deal of grass in that place). Therefore the people sat down, and the number was about five thousand. 11Jesus took the bread and after he blessed it, he gave it those who were seated. Likewise, with the fish, as much as they wanted. 12When they were full, he said to his disciples, "Gather up the leftover food, so that it is not wasted." 13Therefore, they gathered them up and filled twelve baskets with leftovers from the five barley loaves which were left by those who had eaten. 14When the people saw the miracle that was done, they said to one another, "This is truly *the prophet who comes into the world*." 15When Jesus knew that they intended to come and take him so that they might make him a king, he departed again to a mountain alone.

JESUS WALKS ON WATER
(MT 14:22–33; MK 6:45–52)

16When it was evening, his disciples went down to the sea 17and entered a boat and began to cross over the lake to Capernaum. It was already dark, and Jesus had not come to them. 18The lake was rough because a great wind was blowing. 19Therefore they rowed about twenty-five or thirty stadia, when they saw Jesus walking on the lake and coming near the boat, and they were afraid. 20But he said to them, "Do not be afraid, it is I." 21Therefore, they wanted to take him into the boat, and immediately the boat was at the land where they were going.

THE BREAD OF LIFE
(MT 14:34–36; MK 6:53–56)

22The next day, the crowd was standing on the other side of the sea, and they saw that there was only one boat there, and they saw that Jesus had not entered into the boat with his disciples but that the disciples had departed alone. 23But other boats from Tiberias came near the place where they had eaten the bread after the Lord had blessed it. 24Therefore, when the crowd saw that Jesus was not there and neither were his disciples, they entered boats and came to Capernaum seeking Jesus.

25And they found him across the sea, and they said to him, "Rabbi, when did you come here?" 26Jesus answered them, "Truly, truly, I say to you, you seek me not because you saw the miracles, but because you ate the bread and were satisfied. 27Work not for food that perishes, but for food that lasts for eternal life, which the Son of Man will give you. For God the Fa-

---

6:6 The verb of testing or trying is the same one used in Matthew's and Luke's accounts of the temptations, and Jesus tests his disciples quite early in the ministry. While the English *temptation* carries with it negative implications, the word is neutral in this setting. **6:7** *Two hundred silver coins*, or denarii, would purchase a significant amount of bread and perhaps offers an estimate of what it would cost to feed such a large crowd. **6:10, 14** The Greek uses *men*, which represents men, women, and children in this setting. Green grass is indicative of springtime in the region before the summer heat dried out the grass. **6:14** Allusion to Deuteronomy 18:15. **6:15** The effort to take Jesus and make him a king probably rests on their understanding of him as the Messiah. **6:19** A stadia is about 600 feet/180 meters. The disciples were therefore approximately in the middle of the Sea of Galilee. **6:23** The *boats from Tiberias* suggests that the city of Tiberias was a center for commerce and shipping on the Sea of Galilee. None of the Gospels report that Jesus entered Tiberias, despite its being the largest city on the Sea of Galilee.

ther has placed his seal on him." ²⁸Therefore, they said to him, "What may we do that we may perform the works of God?" ²⁹Jesus answered them, "This is the work of God, that you believe in the one whom he sent." ³⁰Then they said to him, "Then what miracle do you do that we may see it and believe you? What work do you perform? ³¹Our ancestors ate manna in the desert, just as it is written, '*Bread from heaven he gave them to eat.*'" ³²Therefore, Jesus said to them, "Truly, truly, I say to you, Moses did not give you bread from heaven, but my Father gives you the true bread from heaven. ³³For the bread of God is the one who comes down from heaven and gives life to the world." ³⁴Then they said to him, "Lord, always give us this bread."

³⁵Jesus said to them, "I am the bread of life. The one who comes to me will never be hungry, and the one who believes in me will never suffer thirst. ³⁶But I say to you that you have seen me and you do not believe. ³⁷All that the Father gives me will come to me, and whoever comes to me I will never send that person away. ³⁸Because of this, I have come down from heaven, not to do my own will, but the will of him who sent me. ³⁹This is the will of him who sent me, that I should not lose one person he has given to me, but should raise them up at the last day. ⁴⁰This is the will of my Father, that all who see the Son and believe in him will have eternal life, and I will raise him in the last day."

⁴¹Therefore, the Jews complained about him because he said, "I am the bread that has come down from heaven," ⁴²and they said, "Is this not Jesus, the son of Joseph? Do we not know his father and mother? How can he say now, 'I have come down from heaven?'" ⁴³Jesus answered, "Do not complain to one another. ⁴⁴No one is able to come to me unless he is drawn by the Father who sent me, and I will raise him at the last day. ⁴⁵It is written in the prophets, '*They will all be taught by God.*' All who have heard and learned from the Father come to me. ⁴⁶No one has seen the Father, except the one who is from God—he has seen the Father. ⁴⁷Truly, truly, I say to you, whoever believes has eternal life. ⁴⁸I am the bread of life. ⁴⁹Your ancestors ate manna in the desert and died. ⁵⁰This is the bread that comes from heaven so that whoever may eat it will not die. ⁵¹I am the living bread that came down from heaven, whoever eats of this bread will live forever, and the bread that I give for the life of the world is my flesh."

⁵²The Jews therefore disputed with one another, saying, "How is he able to give his flesh to us to eat?" ⁵³Jesus responded to them, "Truly, truly, I say to you, unless you eat the flesh of the Son of Man and drink his blood, you do not have life in you. ⁵⁴Whoever consumes my flesh and drinks my blood has eternal life, and I will raise him at the last day. ⁵⁵For my flesh is true food, and my blood is true drink. ⁵⁶Whoever consumes my flesh and drinks

---

6:30 Jesus's opponents ask for a *sign*. This word can also mean a *miracle*. **6:31** Quotation of Psalm 78:24. **6:33** Perhaps an allusion to John 1:14. **6:37** Jesus's promise that *whoever comes to me I will never send that person away* may intentionally contrast the Jews who were willing to cast out people from the synagogues for breaking Jewish laws and customs. **6:40, 44, 54** Alluded to in Alma 22:18. **6:44** The sense of the phrase *unless he is drawn by the Father* is difficult to render. The verb is active in Greek and conveys the sense that the Father *brings, draws,* or *enables* a believer to do something. The Joseph Smith Translation says *No man doeth the will of my Father who hath sent me. And this is the will of him who hath sent me, that ye receive the Son; for the Father beareth record of him; and he who receiveth the testimony, and doeth the will of him who sent me, I will raise up in the resurrection of the just.* **6:45** Quotation from Isaiah 54:13 (compare Jeremiah 31:34). **6:46** Perhaps an allusion to John 1:18. **6:54** The verb *consumes* can also be rendered as *gnaws* or *chews*. It describes the action of an animal eating.

my blood abides in me, and I in him. ⁵⁷Just as the living Father sent me, even I live through the Father, and whoever consumes me, he will live because of me. ⁵⁸This is the bread that came down from heaven, not like your ancestors ate and died. Whoever consumes this bread will live forever." ⁵⁹He said these things while teaching in the synagogue in Capernaum.

CONCERN AMONG THE DISCIPLES (MT 16:13–20; MK 8:27–30; LK 9:18–22)

⁶⁰When they heard this, many of his disciples said, "This is a difficult teaching, who is able to listen to it?" ⁶¹But when Jesus knew that the disciples complained about this, he said, "Does this offend you? ⁶²What if you see the Son of Man ascending to where he was before? ⁶³The Spirit is what gives life: the flesh is no help at all. The words that I have spoken to you are spirit and life. ⁶⁴But there are some among you who do not believe" (for Jesus already knew from the beginning that there were some who did not believe and who would betray him). ⁶⁵And he said, "Because of this I told you that no one is able to come to me unless it is granted to him from the Father."

⁶⁶After this many of his disciples departed and no longer walked with him. ⁶⁷Then Jesus said to the twelve, "Do you also desire to depart?" ⁶⁸Simon Peter answered him, "Lord, to whom would we go? You have the words of eternal life, ⁶⁹and we have come to believe and to know that you are the Holy One of God." ⁷⁰Jesus responded, "Did I not choose you, the twelve, and one of you is a devil?" ⁷¹(He spoke of Judas, the son of Simon Iscariot, one of the twelve, because he was about to betray him.)

JESUS'S SIBLINGS DO NOT BELIEVE

7 ¹After this Jesus traveled in Galilee, for he did not wish to walk in Judea because the Jews sought to kill him. ²The Jewish Feast of Tabernacles was near; ³therefore, his brothers said to him, "Depart from here and go to Judea so that your disciples may see the works that you do. ⁴For no one works in secret and then seeks to be public. If you do these things, show yourself to the world." ⁵(For not even his brothers believed in him.) ⁶Then

---

6:61 The idea that *Jesus knew* implies that he knew of their concerns separately from hearing the disciples voice those concerns. Jesus's question can also be rendered *Does this cause you to stumble?* **6:66** Some of the disciples of the Lord stopped following him because his sayings were too difficult to understand and accept. **6:67** Despite some of his disciples stumbling, the twelve remained firm. Peter's answer (6:68) does not explain the meaning of Jesus's teachings from this chapter but asserts a patient trust in Jesus as Lord and Savior. **6:69** The phrase *the Holy One of God* is preserved in a number of different textual variations. Some later manuscripts add *the Christ, the Holy One of the Living God*, but the phrase as translated here is the most likely to be original. *One of you is a devil* implies that there is more than one devil. *Judas* is designated as *the devil*, the opponent of Jesus.

7:1 This story marks the end of Jesus's ministry in Galilee, and it begins to narrate a sequence of events that leads up to Jesus's death during Passover, approximately six months after the events told in this chapter took place. **7:1, 11, 13** *The Jews* clearly refers to the Jewish leaders who oppose Jesus. The Feast of Tabernacles took place near the end of September. The two short hymns of thanksgiving found in Isaiah 12:1–6 help provide some context for the spirit of celebration felt at the Feast of Tabernacles. **7:3** *His brothers,* see Mark 6:3 and Matthew 13:55. John does not name the siblings of Jesus, which has led some to interpret this passage as a reference to brothers in the church. Such a usage would be anachronistic during Jesus's earthly ministry. **7:5** Jesus's brothers do not believe his teachings, thus also making it obvious that these are Jesus's mortal siblings.

Jesus said to them, "It is not my time yet, but it is always the right time for you. ⁷The world is not able to hate you, but it hates me, because I testify about it, that its works are evil. ⁸You go up to the feast. I am not going to this feast, because my time is not fully here." ⁹After he said this, he stayed in Galilee.

FEAST OF TABERNACLES

¹⁰After his brothers went to the feast, then he went, not openly but in secret. ¹¹Then the Jews sought him at the feast, asking, "Where is he?" ¹²And there was much murmuring about him in the crowd, and some said, "He is a good man," but others said, "No, he leads the people astray." ¹³But no one spoke openly about him for fear of the Jews.

¹⁴Now, in the middle of the feast, Jesus went up to the temple and taught. ¹⁵And the Jews were amazed, saying, "How does he know how to read, not having learned?" ¹⁶Jesus replied to them, "My teaching is not mine but his who sent me. ¹⁷If anyone desires to do God's will, he will know about my teaching, whether it is of God or whether I speak on my own behalf. ¹⁸He who speaks on his own behalf seeks his own glory, but the one who seeks the

glory of him who sent him, he is true and there is no unrighteousness in him. ¹⁹Did Moses not give you the Law? And yet none of you keep the Law. Why do you seek to kill me?" ²⁰The crowd answered him, "You have a demon. Who seeks to kill you?" ²¹Jesus responded to them, "I have done one work and you are all amazed. ²²Moses gave you circumcision (not that it is from Moses but from the fathers), and you circumcise a man on the Sabbath. ²³If a male child receives circumcision on the Sabbath so that the law of Moses might not be broken, why are you angry with me because I healed a man on the Sabbath? ²⁴Do not judge according to appearance, but make righteous judgments."

IS THIS THE CHRIST?

²⁵Then certain of those from Jerusalem said, "Is this not the one they seek to kill? ²⁶And here he is speaking openly, and they say nothing to him. Perhaps the rulers truly know that he is the Christ? ²⁷But we know where he is from. When Christ comes, no one will know where he is from." ²⁸Then Jesus cried out while teaching in the temple, "You know me, and you know where I am from. I have not come on my own behalf, but he who sent me is true. You

---

7:8 *I am not going* may look forward to Jesus ascending to heaven. Here, Jesus literally says *I am not going up yet.* 7:12 The question of whether or not Jesus is *good* misses the larger issue of whether he is the Son of God and Savior. The verse also implies that there was a strong division among the people about Jesus. 7:15 Given the usage of the term *the Jews* in this story, these individuals were likely treating Jesus with contempt, and their assessment of his ability to read may have been derisive. This statement need not be taken as an indication that Jesus had never learned to read but only that he had not done so in Judea under their tutelage. 7:16 *My teaching* is sometimes translated as *my doctrine.* The word translated as *teaching* means *instruction, what is taught,* or the *meaning of what is taught.* Doctrine has come to mean a binding set of teachings, and here Jesus appears to be referring to the corpus of his teachings, but he does not imply that those teachings are yet binding. He is responding to the criticisms that he seems unlearned. See Isaiah 11:2. 7:19 See also John 8:17. 7:20 Some translations prefer *devil* in place of *demon.* The Greek indicates an *evil spirit.* 7:22 See Genesis 17:9–13 for the commandment to circumcise. The issue that Jesus has drawn attention to is the practice of circumcising male infants at eight days old even if the eighth day fell on the Sabbath. 7:24 The Joseph Smith Translation changes *appearances* to *your traditions.* 7:26 Some translations render the final phrase as a sentence, *Can the rulers truly know that he is the Christ? Christ* in this verse is intended as the equivalent of *Messiah. Rulers* refers to religious leaders and not government officials.

do not know him. ²⁹I know him because I am of him and he sent me." ³⁰Then they sought to apprehend him, but no one laid a hand on him because his hour had not arrived. ³¹Many from the crowd believed in him and said, "When Christ comes, will he do more miracles than this man has done?"

ATTEMPT TO ARREST JESUS

³²The Pharisees heard that the crowd complained about him, and the chief priests and Pharisees sent officers that they might arrest him. ³³Therefore, Jesus said, "I am yet with you a little while, and then I go to him who sent me. ³⁴You will seek for me and not find me, and where I am you will not be able to come." ³⁵Then the Jews said to him, "Where does he intend to go that we will not be able to find him? Does he intend to go to the Greek Diaspora and to teach the Greeks? ³⁶What is this word that he said, 'You will seek for me and not find me,' and 'Where I am you will not be able to come?'"

LIVING WATER

³⁷On the last day of the feast, the great day, Jesus stood and declared, saying, "If anyone thirsts, let that person come to me, ³⁸and let the person who believes in me drink. As the scripture says, '*Rivers of living water will flow out of his heart.*'" ³⁹(This he said concerning the Spirit that those who believe in him were about to receive. For the Spirit had not been given because Jesus was not yet glorified.)

IS THIS THE PROPHET?

⁴⁰Some from the crowd heard this saying and said, "This is truly the prophet." ⁴¹Others said, "This is the Christ." But some responded, "Does the Christ come from Galilee? ⁴²Does the scripture not say that the Christ comes from the seed of David and from Bethlehem, the city of David?" ⁴³There was a division in the crowd about him. ⁴⁴Some of them wanted to arrest him, but no one laid a hand on him.

7:31 *Miracles* can also be translated as *signs*. The age of the Messiah would see many miracles (Isaiah 35:4–10). **7:32** The Greek notes that they complained about *these things*, but it does not indicate what those things are. The *officers* in this verse are the *servants* of the chief priests, and they were likely carrying out orders rather than acting in an official capacity. **7:34** Echoed in Doctrine and Covenants 29:29. **7:35** The crowd questions whether Jesus will go to diaspora Jews, or Jews who live outside Judea and Galilee. The diaspora generally describes all Jews who do not live in the Jewish homeland. The crowd also wonders whether Jesus would teach Greeks as well. **7:37** The *great day* was the eighth day of the feast (Leviticus 23:36). The theme of water is important in the following verses and may draw upon the context of the Feast of Tabernacles, wherein a priest carried water from the pool of Siloam into the temple. **7:38** The quotation is not from a single source, but from several (Isaiah 43:19; 44:3; Joel 2:23; Zechariah 14:8, 16–17; Psalm 36:8–9). The Greek uses the word *bosom*, *belly*, or *naval* for the *heart*. The implication seems to be that the rivers of water will flow from the seat of emotion. Following *believe in me* some manuscripts add *let that person come to me, and let that person who believes in me drink. As the scriptures say.* **7:39** The promises of Joel 2:28 are probably in mind, and not a general lack of the gift of the Holy Spirit. This verse may look forward to the outpouring of the Spirit that would take place on the day of Pentecost (Acts 2:1–13). Some later manuscripts and one early one add the idea that the *Spirit was given*, whereas the original reading appears to be that the *Spirit was not yet present* or the *Spirit was not yet in existence.* **7:40** See Deuteronomy 18:15–18. **7:42** See Micah 5:2; Psalm 89:3–4 for the source of the allusion in this verse (compare 2 Samuel 7:12–14).

FOLLOW UP ON
THE ATTEMPTED ARREST

⁴⁵Then the officers returned to the chief priests and Pharisees, who asked them, "Why did you not bring him?" ⁴⁶The officers answered, "Never has any man talked like this." ⁴⁷The Pharisees responded, "Have you also been deceived? ⁴⁸Have any of the leaders of the Pharisees believed in him? ⁴⁹But this crowd, which does not know the Law, is cursed." ⁵⁰Nicodemus, who had gone to him previously and who was one of them, said, ⁵¹"Does our Law judge a man if it has not first listened to him and known what he does?" ⁵²They responded to him, "Are you also from Galilee? Search and see that no prophet arises from Galilee." [[⁵³And each returned to his own house.

THE WOMAN
CAUGHT IN ADULTERY

8 ¹But Jesus departed to the Mount of Olives. ²At dawn he was again in the temple, and all the people came to him, and he sat down and taught them. ³The scribes and Pharisees brought a woman, having been caught in adultery, and when they set her in their midst, ⁴they said to him, "Teacher, this woman was caught in the very act of adultery. ⁵In our Law, Moses commanded that such should be stoned. Therefore, what do you say?" ⁶They said this to trap him, so that they might have something with which to accuse him. But Jesus bent forward and wrote on the ground with his finger. ⁷But as they continued to ask him, he stood up and said to them, "Whoever is without sin among you, let him cast a stone at her first." ⁸And again he bent down and wrote on the ground. ⁹When they heard this, beginning with the older men, they left one by one. And Jesus was left alone with the woman being in front of him. ¹⁰Jesus stood and said to her, "Woman, where are they? Does no one condemn you?" ¹¹She said, "No one, Lord." Jesus said, "Neither do I condemn you. Depart, and from now on sin no more."]]

THE LIGHT OF THE WORLD

¹²Then Jesus spoke to them again, saying, "I am the light of the world. Whoever follows me will never walk in darkness but

---

7:45 The implication seems to be that they wanted Jesus brought to them. **7:50** John affirms that Nicodemus became a defender of Jesus. **7:52** Some translations prefer *no prophet arises from Galilee*. Jonah was from Galilee (2 Kings 14:25). At least one early manuscript notes that Jesus said *the prophet* does not come from Galilee, indicating that the prophet like Moses (Deuteronomy 18:15–18) does not come from that region. **7:53** The earliest manuscripts of the New Testament omit this verse and John 8:1–11. Some manuscripts place the story of the woman caught in adultery at John 7:36, after John 21:25, or after Luke 21:38. The story appears to have strong external support that it originated with Jesus, but it may not have originally been placed here in the Gospel of John or even to have been written by the author of the Fourth Gospel. It is placed in double brackets to indicate that it has questionable textual support, but it is included in the text because it has a reasonable likelihood of describing a historical event from the life of Jesus.

8:1 This verse is meant to contrast Jesus's actions with the people mentioned in 7:53 who each went to their own home. **8:3** For the law of Moses guidelines on infidelity, see Numbers 5:11–31. **8:5** On stoning, see Leviticus 20:10–16 (compare John 8:59). The scribes and Pharisees appear to be omitting any condemnation of the male who was also caught in adultery, contrary to Leviticus 20:10. **8:11** Alluded to in Doctrine and Covenants 6:35; 24:2. The Joseph Smith Translation adds *And the women glorified God from that hour, and believed on his name.* **8:12** The temple was brightly lit during the Feast of Tabernacles, and Jesus here draws upon the theme of light. Compare Mosiah 16:9; 3 Nephi 11:11; Doctrine and Covenants 10:70; 11:28; 12:9; 39:2; 45:7.

will have the light of life." [13]Therefore the Pharisees said to him, "You testify of yourself: your witness is untrue." [14]Jesus responded to them, "Even if I testify concerning myself, my witness is true, because I know where I came from and where I am going. You do not know where I came from nor where I am going. [15]You judge according to the outward appearance: I do not judge anyone. [16]And if I judge, my judgment is true, because I am not alone in judgment, but the Father who sent me is with me. [17]In your Law it is written that *the witness of two is true.* [18]I am the one who testifies of myself and the Father who sent me testifies of me." [19]Then they said to him, "Where is your Father?" Jesus answered, "You do not know me or my Father. If you knew me, you would know my Father also." [20](He spoke these words while teaching near the treasury of the temple. But no one arrested him because his hour had not arrived.)

I AM FROM ABOVE

[21]Then he said to them again, "I am going away and you will seek for me, but you will die in your sin. Where I am going, you will not be able to come." [22]Then the Jews said, "Perhaps he is going to kill himself, because he said, 'Where I am going you will not be able to come.'" [23]And he said to them, "You are from below, I am from above. You are of this world, I am not from this world. [24]I said to you that you will die in your sins. If you do not believe that I am, you will die in your sins." [25]Then they said to him, "Who are you?" Jesus said to them, "What I told you at the beginning. [26]I have many things to say and judge about you, but he who sent me is true. The things that I have heard from him, I speak these things to the world." [27](They did not understand what he said to them about the Father.) [28]Jesus said to them, "When you have lifted up the Son of Man, then you will know that I am and that I do not work on my own, but I say the things the Father taught me. [29]He who sent me is with me. He did not leave me alone because I always do the things that are pleasing to him." [30]After he said these things, many believed in him.

JESUS DECLARES, *I AM*

[31]Then Jesus said to those Jews who had believed in him, "If you abide in my word, you are truly my disciples. [32]And you will know the truth, and the truth will set you free." [33]They responded to him, "We are the children of Abraham, and we have never been slaves to anyone. How can you say, 'You will be free?'" [34]Jesus answered them, "Truly, truly, I say to you that everyone who commits sin is a slave of sin. [35]The servant does not stay in the house forever. The son stays in the house forever. [36]Therefore, if the Son makes you free, then you will be free indeed. [37]I know that you are Abraham's descendants. But you seek to kill me, because my word does not have place in you. [38]I declare what I have

---

8:13 John 5:31 may be intended. **8:15** The verb specifically means *judge* versus *condemn*, which was used in John 8:10–11. When Jesus states that he does not judge, it is clear that he means something other than the fact that he never judges. The next verse indicates that he does judge (verse 16). He seems to be clarifying that he does not judge as his opponents judge others. **8:16** *Is with me* is not directly attested in the Greek, but this is the implied meaning of Jesus declaring that the Father assists him in judgment. **8:17** On other occasions, Jesus speaks of *our law* or simply *the law*. Allusion to Deuteronomy 17:6. **8:21** This verse is echoed in Mosiah 15:26 and may in turn be an allusion to Ezekiel 3:18–20. **8:23** Echoed in Doctrine and Covenants 63:59. **8:24** The implication of *believing I am* is that Jesus is the Messiah (compare Exodus 3:14). **8:32–33** Judea and Galilee were subject to Roman rule during this time, and while they were not slaves, they were subject to Roman law and edicts. **8:35** Perhaps an allusion to Genesis 21:10–14. **8:38** Some manuscripts read *of your father*, which would indicate that

seen in the presence of my Father. Even so, you should do what you have heard of the Father."

³⁹They answered him, "Our father is Abraham." Jesus said to them, "If you are children of Abraham, you would be doing the works of Abraham. ⁴⁰But now you seek to kill me, a man who has told you the truth that I heard from God. This is not what Abraham did. ⁴¹You do the works of your father." They said to him, "We were not born of fornication. We have one Father only, God." ⁴²Jesus said to them, "If God were your Father, you would love me, for I came from God and I am here. I did not come on my own behalf, but he sent me. ⁴³Why do you not understand what I say? Because you are not able to hear my word. ⁴⁴You are from your father the devil, and your desire is to do the will of your father. He was a murderer from the beginning, and he does not stand in truth, because truth is not in him. When he tells a lie, he speaks of his own authority because he is a liar and the father of lies. ⁴⁵But because I speak the truth, you do not believe me. ⁴⁶Who among you convicts me of sin? If I speak truth, why do you not believe me? ⁴⁷Whoever is from God listens to the words of God. For this reason, you do not listen, because you are not of God."

⁴⁸The Jews answered him, "Do we speak well in saying that you are a Samaritan and are possessed by a demon?" ⁴⁹Jesus re-sponded, "I am not possessed by a demon, but I honor my Father, and you dishonor me. ⁵⁰I do not seek my own glory. There is one who seeks it and who judges. ⁵¹Tru-ly, truly, I say to you, if anyone obeys my word, he will never see death." ⁵²Then the Jews said to him, "Now we know that you are possessed by a demon. Abraham and the prophets died, and you say, 'If anyone obeys my word, he will not taste death forever.' ⁵³Are you greater than our father Abraham, who is dead? And the prophets died also. Who do you claim to be?" ⁵⁴Jesus responded, "If I glory in myself, my glory is nothing. My Father glorifies me, about whom you say, 'He is our God.' ⁵⁵You do not know him, but I know him, and if I told you I did not know him, I would be a liar like you, but I know him and I obey his word. ⁵⁶Your father Abraham was glad that he might see my day, and he saw it and rejoiced." ⁵⁷Then the Jews said to him, "You are not fifty years old yet and you have seen Abraham?" ⁵⁸Jesus said to them, "Truly, truly, I say to you, before Abraham was, I am." ⁵⁹Then they picked up stones that they might throw them at him, but Jesus hid himself and he left the temple.

A MAN BORN BLIND

9 ¹As Jesus passed by, he saw a man who was blind since birth. ²And his disci-ples asked him, "Rabbi, who sinned that caused him to be born blind, this man or

---

Jesus was speaking of their father the devil. The earlier and better manuscripts omit the pronoun *your*, indicating that Jesus spoke of *God the Father*. **8:41** *Fornication* is the Greek *porneia*, which is a general term for sexual impropriety. See Matthew 5:32. This may have been a popular criticism of the virgin birth of Jesus. **8:48** The accusation found in this verse is probably in mind in Mosiah 3:9 (compare John 10:20). **8:58** It is unclear why Jesus's statement triggered such a violent reaction. He had said earlier in the discourse *I am*. The statement *I am* is taken by Jesus's opponents as a declaration that Jesus was Jeho-vah (see Exodus 3:14) or that he had pronounced the divine name YHWH. **8:59** The act of picking up stones to throw at Jesus should not be understood as an act of stoning but as murder because there had been no trial, witnesses, or legal process. Some inferior manuscripts add to the end of this verse *passing among them and thus passed by*.

9:2 Jesus's disciples have not been mentioned as being with him since John 6:66, when some disciples became disaffected. The disciples' question implies premortal sin, or that by virtue of being in his moth-er's womb, the baby participated in the sins of the parents.

his parents?" ³Jesus answered, "Neither this man nor his parents sinned, but he was born blind in order that the works of God might be shown in him. ⁴We must do the works of him who sent me while it is day. The night comes and then no one is able to work. ⁵While in the world, I am the light of the world." ⁶After he said this, he spat upon the ground and made mud from the spittle, and he anointed the man's eyes with the mud. ⁷And he said to him, "Go and wash in the Pool of Siloam" (which means "Sent"). Then he went, washed, and he returned seeing.

⁸The neighbors and those who saw him before when he was begging said, "Is not this the one who sat and begged?" ⁹Others said, "This is him." Still others said, "It is not, but it is someone like him." The man kept saying, "I am the one." ¹⁰Then they said to him, "How were your eyes opened?" ¹¹He responded, "The man called Jesus made mud and anointed my eyes and he said to me, 'Go to the Pool of Siloam and wash.' Then I went and washed and I received my sight." ¹²And they said to him, "Where is he?" And he responded, "I do not know."

PHARISEES INTERROGATE THE BLIND MAN

¹³They led the man who was formerly blind to the Pharisees. ¹⁴And it was the Sabbath day when Jesus made mud and opened his eyes. ¹⁵Again the Pharisees asked him how he received sight. And he said, "He put mud on my eyes, and I washed, and I see." ¹⁶Then some of the Pharisees said,

"This man is not of God, because he did not obey the Sabbath." Others said, "How is a man who is a sinner able to do these miracles?" And there was a schism among them. ¹⁷Therefore, they said to the blind man again, "What do you say concerning the man who opened your eyes?" He answered, "He is a prophet." ¹⁸But the Jews did not believe him that he was blind and received sight until they called the parents of the man who received sight. ¹⁹And they asked them, "Is this your son, who you say was born blind? How does he see now?" ²⁰Then his parents answered, "We know that this is our son, and that he was born blind. ²¹But we do not know how he is able to see now, nor who opened his eyes. Ask him, he is of a suitable age, he speaks for himself." ²²(His parents said these things because they feared the Jews, for the Jews had already determined that if anyone declared him to be the Christ, he would be cast out of the synagogue. ²³Because of this, his parents said, "He is of a suitable age; ask him.")

²⁴Then for a second time they called the man who was blind and said to him, "Give glory to God. We know that this man is a sinner." ²⁵He answered them, "Whether he is a sinner, I do not know. What I know is that I was blind and now I see." ²⁶They said to him, "What did he do to you? How did he open your eyes?" ²⁷He answered them, "I have told you already, and you did not listen. Do you want to hear it again? Do you want to become his disciples?" ²⁸And they heaped abuse on him and said, "You are his disciple, but we are the disciples of

---

9:5 The language of this verse is interwoven into Mosiah 16:9. **9:6** The emphasis in the story might be on the necessity of *anointing* rather than on the making of clay from spittle. Compare Moses 6:35–36, where Enoch anoints his own eyes with clay, washes them, and subsequently sees spiritual things. **9:7** A possible allusion to Naaman (2 Kings 5:10–13). The pool of Siloam was located at the southern tip of Jerusalem near the place where the Kidron and Tyropoeon valleys met. The Gihon spring emptied into it. **9:16** The designation that *some* spoke up signals that there was a division among the Pharisees regarding how to interpret Sabbath observance. **9:22** The family was concerned about excommunication from their local synagogue. The practice of excommunication varied, and individuals could be banished for a week, a month, or permanently, depending on the infraction.

Moses. ²⁹We know that God spoke to Moses, but we do not know where this man is from." ³⁰The man answered them, "This is a wonder that you do not know where he is from, and yet he caused me to see. ³¹We know that God does not listen to sinners, but if anyone is a worshipper of God and does his will, God listens to him. ³²Since the beginning, it has not been heard that someone opened the eyes of a man born blind. ³³If he were not of God, he could do nothing." ³⁴They responded, "You were born entirely in sin, and then you teach us?" And they threw him out.

THE BLIND MAN BELIEVES

³⁵Jesus heard that they threw him out, and he found him and said, "Do you believe in the Son of Man?" ³⁶He answered, "Who is he, sir, that I might believe in him?" ³⁷Jesus said to him, "You have seen him, and the one speaking with you is he." ³⁸He said, "I believe, Lord." And he worshipped him. ³⁹And Jesus said, "In judgment, I came into the world, so that those who do not see will see and those who see will be blind." ⁴⁰When some of the Pharisees who were with him heard this, they said to him, "Are we also blind?" ⁴¹Jesus said to them,

"If you were blind, then you would have no sin. Now that you say, 'We see,' your sin remains."

THE GOOD SHEPHERD

10 ¹"Truly, truly, I say to you, whoever does not enter through the door to the sheepfold but climbs up from another way is a thief and robber, ²but he who enters through the door is the shepherd of the sheep. ³The doorkeeper opens to him, and the sheep hear his voice, and he calls his own sheep by name, and he leads them out. ⁴When he has brought out all his own sheep, he goes in front of them, and the sheep follow him because they know his voice. ⁵They will not follow a stranger, but they will flee from him because they do not know the voice of strangers." ⁶Jesus told them this parable, but they did not understand what he said to them.

⁷Jesus spoke to them again, "Truly, truly, I say to you that I am the gate for the sheep. ⁸All who came before me were thieves and robbers, but the sheep did not listen to them. ⁹I am the door. If anyone enters through me, he will be saved, and he will enter and exit and will find pasture. ¹⁰The thief does not come except to steal,

---

9:29 Compare Exodus 33:11. **9:31** Isaiah 1:15 confirms the idea that God does not hear sinners. **9:35** Their actions contrast Jesus's in John 6:37. **9:38–39** This verse and the opening words of verse 39 *Jesus said* are omitted in several early and important Greek manuscripts, but the omission may have been the result of a copying error, and therefore they have been included in the translation. **9:39** Perhaps an allusion to Isaiah 42:7.

10:1 John uses the Greek *lestes* to mean a simple robber and not a political revolutionary, although the primary meaning of that term is a political insurrectionist (Matthew 27:38; Luke 23:19). **10:3** The idea is that the shepherd leads the sheep from their protective enclosure to pasture. See Ezekiel 34:2–15. **10:3, 11–14** The meaning of these verses is expanded in Alma 5:37–38. **10:6** John uses a different word for *parable* or *proverb* than the synoptic Gospels (Matthew, Mark, and Luke), but there appears to be no substantive difference in meaning in this instance. **10:7** A possible allusion to Psalm 118:19–21. **10:8** The precise meaning is unclear because Jesus speaks of *all*. In other places, he speaks positively of the prophets. Here he may have intended those who had come before him more recently, but that would also likely include John the Baptist (see Acts 5:36–37). Some manuscripts omit the words *all who came before me*, but the original reading is the one translated here. Later scribes appear to have emended the text in an attempt to make sense of Jesus's condemnation of prophets. The Joseph Smith Translation reads *All that ever came before me who testified not of me are thieves and robbers, but the sheep did not hear them.* **10:9, 16, and 27** are combined in 1 Nephi 22:25.

kill, and ruin. I came in order that they may have life and have it abundantly.

[11]"I am the good shepherd. The good shepherd lays down his life for the sheep. [12]He who is a servant and not a shepherd, who is not with his own sheep, sees the wolf coming and abandons the sheep and flees. And the wolf seizes them and scatters them; [13]because he is a servant and he does not care for the sheep, he runs away.

[14]"I am the good shepherd, and I know my own, and my own know me; [15]just as the Father knows me, even I know the Father, and I lay my life down for the sheep. [16]And I have other sheep that are not of this sheepfold, and I must lead them too and they will hear my voice so that there will be one flock and one shepherd.

[17]"This is why the Father loves me, because I lay down my life so that I may take it again. [18]No one takes it from me, but I lay it down on my own. I have authority to lay it down, and I have authority to take it back again. I have received this commandment of my Father."

[19]There was again a schism among the Jews because of these words. [20]Many of them said, "He is possessed by a demon and is out of his mind. Why do you listen to him?" [21]Others said, "These are not the words of someone possessed by a demon. Can a demon open the eyes of the blind?"

JESUS REJECTED AT THE FEAST

[22]The Feast of Dedication arrived in Jerusalem, and it was winter. [23]And Jesus walked in the colonnade of Solomon in the temple. [24]The Jews encircled him and said, "How long will you keep us in suspense? If you are the Christ, tell us clearly." [25]Jesus answered them, "I told you and you do not believe. The works that I do in the name of my Father, these testify about me. [26]But you do not believe, because you are not among my sheep. [27]My sheep hear my voice, and I know them and they follow me. [28]And I give them eternal life and forever they will not perish, and no one will seize them from my hand. [29]My Father who gave them to me is greater than all, and no one is able to seize them from his hand. [30]I and the Father are one."

[31]The Jews took up stones again to stone him. [32]Jesus responded to them, "I

10:11 The sense that the *good shepherd* lays down his life may imply that the shepherd places his life in danger for the sheep and not necessarily dies for the sheep (see John 13:37; 15:13). Shepherding imagery is prevalent in the Old Testament (see Numbers 27:16–17). Moses (Isaiah 63:11) and God are described as shepherds (Genesis 48:15; 49:24; Psalms 23:1; 28:9; 77:20; 78:52; 80:1; Isaiah 40:11; Ezekiel 34:2–31). **10:12** 4 Ezra 5:18, a pseudepigraphical writing, speaks of shepherds who abandon their flocks, which may indicate that this was a common theme of the day. **10:13** *He runs away* is lacking in several important and early Greek manuscripts, but it greatly clarifies the criticism of the hired servant and helps improve the clarity of the English translation. **10:16** This reference would also include Gentiles and Samaritans (compare 3 Nephi 15:17, 21–22). See also 1 Nephi 22:25; Doctrine and Covenants 10:59. **10:17** The meaning of this verse is expanded in 2 Nephi 2:8. **10:21** See Psalm 146:8. **10:22** This is the Feast of Hanukkah or rededication of the temple that celebrated the Maccabean victory over the Syrians, who profaned the temple in 167–164 BCE. **10:23** The Stoa or Portico built by Solomon was located on the perimeter of the outer courtyard of the temple, and Herod retained it when he rebuilt the temple. The portico on the east side was specifically thought to have been constructed by Solomon. It appears to have been an informal place for conversation and teaching. **10:30** The Greek can also be translated as *I and the Father are in one*. The noun *one* is neuter in Greek, meaning that Jesus was not declaring that they were the same person but of the same essence, purpose, and mission. Some have argued that Latter-day Saints who hold the view that Jesus and the Father are distinct beings who are united in purpose deny the divinity of Jesus Christ. Jesus, however, is clearly presenting himself as the shepherd of the Father's flock and thus unified in the mission of the Father; he is also the divine Son of God. Compare 3 Nephi 20:35. **10:31** See Leviticus 24:14–16.

have shown you many good works from my Father. For which of these works do you stone me?" ³³The Jews answered him, "We do not stone you for a good work, but for blasphemy, because you are a man and claim to be God." ³⁴Jesus answered them, "Is it not written in your Law, '*I said, you are gods*'? ³⁵If he called them gods to whom the word of God came and the scripture cannot be broken, ³⁶do you say of the one whom the Father consecrated and sent into the world, 'You speak blasphemy,' because I said, 'I am the Son of God?' ³⁷If I do not do the works of my Father, do not believe me. ³⁸If I do them, even if you do not believe me, believe the works, that you may know and understand that the Father is in me and I am in the Father." ³⁹Then they sought to arrest him again, but he escaped from their hands.

⁴⁰And he went again across the Jordan River to the place where John first baptized and he stayed there. ⁴¹And many came to him and they said, "John did no miracle, but everything that John said concerning him is true." ⁴²And many there believed in him.

THE DEATH OF LAZARUS

11 ¹A certain man was ill, Lazarus from Bethany, from the village of Mary and Martha, her sister. ²(It was Mary who anointed the Lord with ointment and dried his feet with her hair. Her brother Lazarus was ill.) ³Therefore, the sisters sent to Jesus, saying, "Lord, the one whom you love is ill." ⁴When Jesus heard this, he said, "This illness will not lead to his death, but for the glory of God, so that the Son of God will be glorified through it." ⁵Jesus loved Martha and her sister and Lazarus. ⁶When he heard that Lazarus was sick, then he stayed in that place for two more days.

⁷Then afterwards he said to the disciples, "Let us go to Judea again." ⁸The disciples said to him, "Rabbi, the Jews now seek to stone you, and yet you are going there again?" ⁹Jesus answered, "Are there not twelve hours in the day? If someone walks in the day, he does not stumble, because he sees the light of the world. ¹⁰If someone walks at night, he stumbles, because the light is not in him." ¹¹He said this and afterwards said to them, "Our friend Lazarus has fallen asleep, but I go that I may wake him." ¹²The disciples said to him, "Lord, if he has fallen asleep, he will be well." ¹³But Jesus had spoken about his death, but they thought that he spoke of resting in sleep. ¹⁴Then Jesus said to them clearly, "Lazarus is dead, ¹⁵and I am glad for you that I was not there, that you may believe. But let us go to him." ¹⁶Then Thomas, who is called Didymus, said to

---

10:34 Quotation from Psalm 82:6, which Jesus refers to as the law. **10:35** Echoed in Doctrine and Covenants 42:30; 78:11; 82:11. **10:36** Jesus again states that he is *consecrated* in John 17:19.

11:1 See map for Mark 11:1. **11:2** Mary of Bethany anointed Jesus's feet. Luke 7:37 and Matthew 26:7 describe another event wherein an unnamed woman anointed Jesus's feet. Luke refers to her as a sinner, but Matthew omits that reference. It is possible that there were two separate anointing events. **11:3** The phraseology of this verse suggests that Jesus knew Mary, Martha, and Lazarus well, but the Gospels report few details of their relationship apart from the healing told in John 11 (see also verse 5) and the encounter in Luke 10:38–42. **11:4** This verse signals the transition between the signs that lead to the reader to believe that Jesus is the Christ and the beginning of the experiences that will lead to his glorification. **11:6** John's description of Jesus's actions suggest that Jesus wanted Lazarus to die before he went to help him. **11:8** See John 10:31. **11:11–12** For sleep as a metaphor for death, see 1 Corinthians 15:18, which uses sleep to describe death and is translated that way in some older translations. **11:12** The sense of the verb *he will be well* can also mean that *he will recover* or *he will be healed*. **11:15** *That you may believe* shows that the disciples were still growing in their understanding of Jesus. **11:16** *Didymus* is the Greek word for a twin, whereas *Thomas* is the Hebrew word for a twin. Thomas assumes that a

his fellow disciples, "Let us go so that we may die with him."

I AM THE RESURRECTION AND THE LIFE

[17]Then Jesus came and found that Lazarus had already been in the tomb for four days. [18]Bethany was near Jerusalem, about fifteen stadia away. [19] Many Jews came to Martha and Mary to console them concerning their brother. [20]Then Martha, when she heard that Jesus was coming, met him, but Mary sat in the house. [21]And Martha said to Jesus, "Lord, if you were here, my brother would not have died. [22]But I know that even now if you ask God for something, God will give it to you." [23]Jesus said to her, "Your brother will rise again." [24]Martha said to him, "I know that he will rise again in the resurrection on the last day." [25]Jesus said to her, "I am the resurrection and the life. Whoever believes in me, even if he is dead, will live. [26]All who live and believe in me will never die. Do you believe this?" [27]She answered, "Yes, Lord. I believe that you are the Christ, the Son of God, the one who comes into the world."

JESUS RAISES LAZARUS FROM DEATH

[28]And after she said this, she went and privately called Mary her sister, saying, "The teacher is here and calls for you." [29]When she heard this, she arose quickly and came to him. [30]But Jesus had not yet entered the village, but he was still in the place where Martha had met him. [31]Then the Jews who were with her in the house who were consoling her, when they saw that Mary arose quickly and left, they followed her, thinking that she went to the tomb to mourn there. [32]Then when Mary came to where Jesus was, she saw him and fell at his feet and said to him, "Lord, if you were here, my brother would not have died." [33]When Jesus saw her crying, and the Jews gathered with her crying, he was troubled and moved in spirit, [34]and he said, "Where have you placed him?" They said to him, "Lord, come and see." [35]And Jesus wept. [36]Then said the Jews, "Look how he loved him." [37]Some of them said, "This is the one who opened the eyes of the blind man, could he not have made it so that Lazarus did not die?"

[38]Then Jesus was again troubled as he came to the tomb. (It was a cave, and a stone was placed in front of it.) [39]Jesus said, "Remove the stone." Martha, the sister of him who had died said, "Lord, there is already a stench, for he has been dead for four days." [40]Jesus responded, "Did I not say to you that if you believe, you would see the glory of God?" [41]Then they removed the stone. And Jesus lifted up his eyes and said, "Father, I am glad that you have heard me. [42]I knew that you always hear me, but because of the crowd I said this, that they may believe that you sent me." [43]After he said this, he cried with a loud voice, "Lazarus, come out!" [44]The man who had died came forth, and his hands and feet were bound with linen cloth, and his face was bound with a cloth.

---

return trip to Jerusalem will certainly result in their deaths. Jesus is ready to lay down his life for his friend (John 10:11). **11:17** Jesus was across the Jordan River when he learned of Lazarus's death (John 10:40), and the note that Lazarus had been in the tomb for four days serves to heighten the sense that Jesus delayed in coming to him (verse 6) and that he had to travel some distance to arrive in Bethany. **11:18** Bethany is about 1.5 miles/2.5 kilometers from Jerusalem. **11:20** Compare Luke 10:40. **11:33** *Troubled* represents a concept that is difficult to translate into English. The Greek word means *indignant* or *moved with profound emotion*. An undertone of the idea is *anger*. **11:37** The Greek has only *he* in place of *Lazarus*. **11:43** A possible allusion to John 5:25. The grave clothes must be removed for Lazarus to be free to walk. Jesus, on the other hand, was not bound in grave clothes after the resurrection.

Jesus said to them, "Unwrap him, and let him go."

CAIAPHAS SEEKS TO KILL JESUS

⁴⁵Then many of the Jews, who came to Mary, when they saw what was done, believed in him. ⁴⁶Some of them went to the Pharisees and told them what Jesus had done. ⁴⁷Then the chief priests and Pharisees gathered in council and said, "What shall we do, because this man does many miracles? ⁴⁸If we leave him to continue like this, everyone will believe in him, and the Romans will come and take this place and our nation." ⁴⁹One of them, Caiaphas, who was high priest that year, said to them, "You know nothing at all! ⁵⁰You do not understand that it is better that one man might die for the people than for the entire nation to be destroyed." ⁵¹(He did not say this on his own, but being high priest that year, he prophesied that Jesus was about to die for the nation, ⁵²and not for the nation alone but to gather the children of God in one who are scattered abroad.) ⁵³Then from that day they planned how they might kill him.

⁵⁴Then Jesus no longer walked openly among the Jews but went from there to a place near the desert, to the village called Ephraim, and there he stayed with his disciples. ⁵⁵And the Jewish Feast of Passover was near, and many from the region went to Jerusalem for the Passover in order to purify themselves. ⁵⁶Therefore, they sought for Jesus and said to one another as they stood in the temple, "What do you think? Will he not come for the feast?" ⁵⁷The chief priests and Pharisees gave a command that if anyone knew where he was, he should let them know so that they might arrest him.

JESUS IS ANOINTED AT BETHANY (MT 26:6–13; MK 14:3–9; LK 7:36–50)

12 ¹Then Jesus, six days before Passover, came to Bethany, where Lazarus lived, whom Jesus raised from the dead. ²So they made a dinner for him there, and Martha served, and Lazarus was one of those who dined with him. ³Then Mary took a pound of costly ointment of pure nard and anointed Jesus's feet and wiped his feet with her hair. And the house was filled with the aroma of the ointment. ⁴But one of his disciples, Judas Iscariot, who was about to betray him, said, ⁵"Why was this ointment not sold for three hundred silver coins and given to the poor?" ⁶He said this not because he cared for the poor, but because he was a thief. And because he had the money bag he took what was put into it. ⁷Then Jesus said, "Let her be, she did this for the day of my burial. ⁸You always have the poor with you, but you do not always have me with you."

11:47 This is a gathering of the Sanhedrin, a governing body of Jewish priests and elders. The word *Sanhedrin* (translated as *council*) occurs only in this verse in John. **11:48** *This place* refers to the temple. **11:49** Caiaphas's tenure of service is alluded to (contrast Exodus 40:15). Under Roman occupation, the governor appointed the high priest, but according to Jewish law it was a lifetime position. **11:50** Compare the similar statement in 1 Nephi 4:13. **11:54** The location of *Ephraim* is uncertain, but it was possibly near Bethel (see 2 Samuel 13:23).

12:2 Martha acts as *deacon* at the dinner, a model of service for later *deacons* in the church. **12:3** The *pound* mentioned here is just under twelve ounces (or approximately 325 grams). *Nard* was burned on the altar of incense and was also incorporated into some recipes of wealthy Romans. **12:5** In Jesus's parables, day laborers earned one silver coin, or denarius, for a day of labor. Documentary evidence suggests that actual pay was much higher and could range between three and eight denarii for a day's work. Even at the highest pay, the cost of this ointment was well over a month's wages, and at the lowest pay it was well over a year's wages. **12:7** Jesus was also anointed at his death (Luke 23:56).

THE PLOT TO KILL LAZARUS

⁹When the large crowd from Judea learned that he was there, they came not because of Jesus only but so that they might see Lazarus, whom he raised from the dead. ¹⁰So the chief priests counseled how they might kill Lazarus ¹¹because many Judeans went away and believed in Jesus because of him.

THE TRIUMPHAL ENTRY (MT 21:1–9; MK 11:1–10; LK 19:28–40)

¹²The next day a large crowd came to the feast, and they heard that Jesus was coming to Jerusalem. ¹³They took palm fronds and went out to meet him, and they cried out, "*Hosanna, blessed is he who comes in the name of the Lord,* even the King of Israel!" ¹⁴And Jesus found a young donkey and sat upon it, just as it is written, ¹⁵"*Do not fear, daughter of Zion; behold, your king comes, sitting upon a donkey's colt!*" ¹⁶His disciples did not understand these things at first, but when Jesus was glorified, then they remembered that these things were written about him and that these things had been done to him. ¹⁷The crowd that was with him continually bore witness, the one that was with him when he called Lazarus from the tomb and raised him from the dead. ¹⁸This is why the crowd went to meet him, because they heard he had performed a miracle. ¹⁹Then the Pharisees said to one another, "Do you see that you gain nothing? Behold, the world has gone after him."

GREEKS DESIRE TO SEE JESUS

²⁰There were certain Greeks who went up to the feast that they might worship. ²¹Then these individuals came to Philip, who was from Bethsaida of Galilee, and asked, "Sir, we wish to see Jesus." ²²Philip came and told Andrew, and Andrew and Philip came and told Jesus. ²³Jesus answered them, "The hour has come when the Son of Man is glorified. ²⁴Truly, truly, I say to you that unless a kernel of wheat falls into the earth and dies, it remains alone. But if it dies, then it bears much fruit. ²⁵Whoever loves his life will lose it, and whoever hates his life in this world will preserve it in the life to come. ²⁶Whoever serves me must follow me, and where I am, my servant will be there. If anyone serves me, the Father will honor him.

JESUS FORETELLS HIS DEATH

²⁷"Now my soul is troubled, and what might I say? 'Father, save me from this hour'? But for this very reason I came to this hour. ²⁸Father, glorify your name." Then came a voice from heaven, "I have glorified it and will glorify it again." ²⁹So the crowd that was standing there heard it and said it was thunder, but others said,

---

12:12 *The next day* would be Sunday (see verse 1). **12:13** Quotation from Psalm 118:25–26. See Leviticus 23:40 for the use of palm fronds at the Feast of Tabernacles. **12:15** Quotation from Zephaniah 3:16 and Zechariah 9:9. **12:18** *Miracle* can also be translated as *sign*. **12:19** The declaration of the Pharisees is probably intentionally ironic. In the previous chapter, Caiaphas lamented that if too many followed Jesus, then the Romans would come and destroy the nation. **12:21** *Sir* is translated instead of Lord. The Greek word *kyrios* (sir or lord) is a polite term of respect but can also refer to *the Lord*. **12:23** The questioning in verse 21 triggers Jesus to respond that the hour of the Son of Man has arrived. Their request to *see* implies that everyone will be able to see the glory of the Son of Man, including Greeks. **12:25** The sense of *preserve* is also to *protect* or *guard*. **12:26** This verse lays out the idealized service of the *deacon*, who *serves* and *follows*. The word *servant* and the act of *service* are built upon the noun and verb *deacon* in Greek. **12:27** *Now my soul is troubled* is a quotation from Psalm 6:4. *Soul* as used here can also mean *life*. The quotation also includes the phrase *save me*. This verse appears to be a reference to Jesus's suffering in Gethsemane.

"An angel has spoken to him." ³⁰Jesus responded, "This voice was for you but not for me. ³¹Now is the judgment of this world; now the ruler of this world will be thrown out. ³²When I am lifted up from the earth, I will draw all people to me." ³³(He said this signifying by what death he would die.)

³⁴Then the crowd answered him, "We have heard from the Law that *the Christ remains forever*, and how do you say that 'The Son of Man will be lifted up?' Who is this Son of Man?" ³⁵So Jesus said to them, "The light is with you still a little longer. Walk while you have the light so that darkness does not take hold of you. The one who walks in darkness does not know where he goes. ³⁶While you have the light, believe in the light, that you may be children of light."

PROPHECIES REGARDING JESUS

Jesus said these things, and he left and hid from them. ³⁷He had done so many signs in front of them, yet they did not believe in him ³⁸so that the word of the prophet Isaiah might be fulfilled which says, "*Lord, who has believed our message, and to whom has the arm of the Lord been revealed?*" ³⁹Because of this, they were not able to believe, for Isaiah again said, ⁴⁰"*He has blinded their eyes, and he has hardened their heart, that they might not see with their eyes and understand with their heart and turn, that I might heal them.*" ⁴¹Isaiah

said these things because he saw his glory and he spoke about him. ⁴²Even so, many of the rulers believed in him, but because of the Pharisees they did not declare it so that they were not thrown out of the synagogue. ⁴³For they loved the glory of men more than the glory of God.

THE FATHER SENT ME

⁴⁴Jesus cried out, "Whoever believes in me does not believe in me but in him who sent me. ⁴⁵And whoever sees me sees him who sent me. ⁴⁶I have come into the world as light, that all who believe in me might not remain in darkness. ⁴⁷And if anyone listens to my words and does not keep them, I do not judge him. I did not come that I might judge the world but that I might save the world. ⁴⁸The one who rejects me and does not receive my words has a judge. The word that I have spoken, that will judge him in the last day ⁴⁹because I have not spoken on my own behalf but on behalf of the Father who sent me. He gave me a commandment regarding what I would say and speak. ⁵⁰I know that his commandment is eternal life. What I tell you I tell you just as the Father told me."

JESUS WASHES THE FEET OF THE DISCIPLES

13 ¹Before the feast of the Passover, Jesus saw that his hour had arrived to depart from this world to the Father,

---

12:31 *The ruler of this world* is Satan (compare John 14:30; 16:11; 2 Corinthians 4:4; Ephesians 2:2; 6:12). **12:32** Second Nephi 26:24 expands the meaning of this verse (compare 3 Nephi 27:14). **12:34** This question is probably included in the story to help early Christian believers understand the relationship of the *Christ* and the *Son of Man*. That Christ would live forever, see Isaiah 9:6–7; Psalm 89:3–4. **12:36** Alluded to in Doctrine and Covenants 106:5. **12:38** Quotation from Isaiah 53:1. **12:39** The statement that *because of this they were not able to believe*, appears to build upon the idea that Isaiah had prophesied of them and therefore their unbelief had been foretold. John's wording, however, does imply that they *were not able to believe* even had they wanted to do so. **12:40** See Isaiah 6:9–10; 1 Nephi 12:17; Doctrine and Covenants 112:13. **12:42** The word translated as *synagogue* is a plural noun intended as a singular concept.

13:1–2 John's description of the Last Supper omits reference to it being a Passover dinner (Matthew 26:17–19; Mark 14:12–16; Luke 22:7–13). In John, the Passover dinner would have been eaten while

having loved his own who were in the world—he loved them to the end. ²And after dinner, the devil had already entered into the heart of Judas, son of Simon Iscariot, that he should betray him. ³Jesus knew that the Father had given all things into his hands and that he had come from God and was going to God. ⁴He arose from dinner and set aside his outer clothing and took a towel and tied it around himself. ⁵Then he poured water in a basin and began to wash and dry the feet of the disciples with the towel tied around him. ⁶Then he came to Simon Peter, who said to him, "Lord, are you going to wash my feet?" ⁷Jesus answered, "What I do to you, you do not know yet, but you will understand after these things." ⁸Peter said to him, "You will never wash my feet." Jesus responded, "If I do not wash you, then you have no inheritance with me." ⁹Simon Peter said to him, "Lord, then not my feet only but also my hands and head." ¹⁰Jesus replied, "He who has been washed does not need to wash further except for his feet, but he is completely clean, and you are clean, but not all of you." ¹¹(For he knew who was about to betray him. This is why he said, "Not all of you are clean.")

¹²When he had washed their feet, he put on his outer clothing and reclined again and said to them, "Do you know what I have done to you? ¹³You call me, 'Teacher' and 'Lord,' and you speak correctly, for I am. ¹⁴If therefore I, your Lord and teacher, have washed your feet, you ought to wash each other's feet. ¹⁵For I have given you an example that, just as I have done, you should also do as I have done. ¹⁶Truly, truly, I say to you, a slave is not greater than his master, nor an apostle greater than him who sent him. ¹⁷If you know these things, you are blessed if you do them.

¹⁸"I do not speak to you all. I know whom I have chosen, but so that the scripture might be fulfilled, '*He who eats bread with me, lifts up his heel against me.*' ¹⁹From this point on, I will tell you before it happens so that you will believe it when it happens and believe that I am. ²⁰Truly, truly, I say to you, whoever receives the one I send receives me, and whoever receives me receives the one who sent me."

ONE OF YOU WILL BETRAY ME

²¹Jesus said these things and was troubled in spirit and testified, "Truly, truly, I say to you that one of you will betray me." ²²The disciples began to look at one another in doubt concerning whom he spoke. ²³There was one of his disciples, the one whom he loved, reclining to eat at Jesus's

---

Jesus was hanging on the cross. The discrepancy regarding the type of meal Jesus celebrated with his disciples does not overshadow the emphasis that the gospels place on describing a private and intimate meal on the eve of Jesus's death, where Jesus predicted his betrayal and where he taught his disciples. **13:2** *The devil entered the heart of Judas* is an idiom and not a physical description of the devil being able to physically enter Judas's mind or heart. **13:4** The *towel* spoken of here is a linen cloth, the type that was used by field workers as aprons. Jesus would have removed his tunic and cloak, and thus he would have been dressed like a slave in a loincloth or underclothing (compare John 19:24). **13:5** The *basin* here is specifically mentioned as being a basin for washing. See Luke 7:44; 1 Samuel 25:41 for another example of washing someone else's feet. Compare Doctrine and Covenants 88:137–41. **13:10** This verse is addressed to the body of disciples and not to Peter alone. Jews ritually bathed in a *mikvah* before the major feasts. Jesus may allude to this practice here, where the disciples had already bathed prior to Passover. Echoed in Doctrine and Covenants 38:10. **13:16** *Apostle* may be used in a generic sense here, as *one who is sent* or *messenger*. **13:18** Quotation from Psalm 41:9 (compare 2 Samuel 15–17). **13:19** Jesus says *I am*, but the meaning may be *I am he* and not a pronouncement of divinity (Exodus 3:14). **13:20** Echoed in Doctrine and Covenants 39:5; 84:36–37. **13:23** The Greek says literally *the one reclining on Jesus's breast*. The position of the diners who were reclined

side. ²⁴So Simon Peter nodded to him to ask concerning whom he spoke. ²⁵Then the one reclining in front of Jesus asked him, "Lord, who is it?" ²⁶Jesus answered, "It is the one to whom I shall give this piece of bread after I have dipped it." So he dipped the bread and gave it to Judas, son of Simon Iscariot. ²⁷And after he took the bread, Satan entered into him. Then Jesus said to him, "What you are going to do, do it quickly." ²⁸No one at the meal knew why Jesus said this to Judas. ²⁹Some thought that because Judas had the money bag that Jesus said to him, "Go and buy what we need for the feast," or that he might give something to the poor. ³⁰After he took the piece of bread, he departed immediately, and it was night.

JESUS'S NEW COMMANDMENT

³¹When he departed, Jesus said, "Now the Son of Man is glorified, and God is glorified in him. ³²If God is glorified in him, God will also glorify him in himself, and he will immediately glorify him. ³³Little children, I am still with you yet for a little while. You will seek for me; just as I said to the Jews I say to you now, 'Where I am going you will not be able to come.' ³⁴A new commandment I give to you, that you love one another; just as I have loved you, you will also love one another. ³⁵In this way, everyone will know that you are my disciples, if you have love for one another."

PETER'S DENIAL FORETOLD (MT 26:30–35; MK 14:26–31; LK 22:31–34)

³⁶Simon Peter said, "Lord, where are you going?" Jesus answered, "Where I am going you will not be able to follow me now, but you will follow me later." ³⁷Peter said to him, "Lord, why am I not able to follow you now? I will lay down my life for you." ³⁸Jesus answered, "You will lay down your life for me? Truly, truly, I say to you, the rooster will not crow before you will deny me three times.

I AM THE WAY

14 ¹"Do not be troubled in your hearts; believe in God, and believe also in me. ²In my Father's house there are many rooms. If it were not so, I would have told you. I am going to prepare a place for you. ³And if I go and prepare a place for you, I will come again and bring you to me so that you may also be where I am. ⁴You know the way to where I am going."

---

while eating makes this a description of the person reclining directly in front of Jesus. It need not describe the situation of him lying on Jesus. **13:27** For Satan's influence on Judas, see Luke 22:3. **13:29** It appears from this passage that Jesus was in the habit of giving money to the poor. This may have been why Judas thought the expensive nard should have been sold and the money given to the poor (see John 12:3–6). **13:31** John does not specify where Jesus departed to, but 13:6; 14:1–4; 16:5 all discuss the theme of Jesus's departure. The suggestion is that Jesus intended to leave the city of Jerusalem. This verse may also indicate that the following discourses, chapters 14–17 were delivered while the disciples walked through the city. **13:32** A reference to John 8:21–22. **13:34** The new commandment was also an old commandment (Leviticus 19:18), but it is now expanded to include loving one another.

14:1–17:26 John alone reports these discourses given after the Last Supper and to the disciples. **14:1** The end of the verse could also be translated as *Do you believe in God? Believe in me.* **14:2** Some translations prefer the word *mansions* (originally used by Tyndale) instead of *rooms*. The word *mansion* has taken on a dramatically different meaning in the last century, but it originally referred to a house where travelers stayed while on the road. The idea in Greek is that of a temporary resting place or way station. The Greek word used here means *single rooms*, probably referring to a room within a larger structure, or places to *stop and rest*. Compare Enos 1:27; Ether 12:32, 34, 37. An interpretation of this verse is given in Doctrine and Covenants 98:18.

⁵Thomas said to him, "Lord, we do not know the way to where you going. How can we know the way?" ⁶Jesus answered, "I am the way, the truth, and the life. No one comes to the Father unless it is through me. ⁷If you have known me, you will know my Father also, and from this point on you know him and have seen him."

⁸Philip said, "Lord, show us the Father, and it is enough for us." ⁹Jesus replied, "Philip, have I been with you so long, and yet you have not known me? The one who has seen me has seen the Father. How can you say, 'Show us the Father?' ¹⁰Do you not believe that I am in the Father and the Father is in me? What I say to you I do not speak on my own behalf, but the Father who abides in me does his works. ¹¹Believe me that I am in the Father and the Father is in me. But if not, believe through the works themselves. ¹²Truly, truly, I say to you, whoever believes in me will do the works that I do, and he will do greater works than these because I am going to the Father. ¹³And whatever you ask in my name, I will do it so that the Father may be glorified in the Son. ¹⁴If you ask me in my name, I will do it.

THE COMFORTER

¹⁵"If you love me, you will keep my commandments. ¹⁶I will ask the Father, and he will send you another Comforter to be with you forever—¹⁷the Spirit of truth, which the world is not able to receive, because it does not see him or know him. You know him because he abides in you and will be with you. ¹⁸I will not leave you as orphans; I will come to you. ¹⁹In a little while the world will not see me, but you will see me; because I live, you will also live. ²⁰In those days you will know that I am in my Father and you are in me, and I am in you. ²¹He who has my commandments and obeys them, he is the one who loves me. Whoever loves me will be loved by my Father, and I will love him, and I will show myself to him."

²²Judas, not Iscariot, said to him, "Lord, how is it that you will show yourself to us but not to the world?" ²³Jesus answered, "If anyone loves me, he will obey my word and my Father will love him, and we will come to him, and we will make our residence with him. ²⁴The one who does not love me does not obey my words. The word that you hear is not from me but from my Father who sent me.

²⁵"I have spoken these things while I reside with you. ²⁶The Comforter, the Holy Spirit, whom the Father will send in my name, he will teach you all things and will bring all things that I have said to you to your remembrance. ²⁷I leave peace with you; I give my peace to you. I do not give it as the world gives it. Do not let your

---

14:7 Some manuscripts read *If you had known me, you would have known.* **14:8** Philip's question was similar to Moses's (Exodus 33:18). **14:10** Jesus's tone may be critical here because he had explicitly challenged his opponents to understand this basic principle (John 10:38). **14:11** Compare 3 Nephi 9:15; Doctrine and Covenants 93:3, 20. **14:13** Alluded to in Moroni 7:26. **14:14** Some later manuscripts omit the word *me*. Given the manuscript evidence, the verse most likely included *me*. **14:15** Quoted in Doctrine and Covenants 124:87 (compare Doctrine and Covenants 29:12; 42:29; 46:9). **14:16** The word translated as *Comforter* is *paracletos*, and it means *advocate, counselor,* or *helper.* It is commonly understood to be a description of the Holy Spirit (see John 14:26; 15:26; 16:7). Compare Doctrine and Covenants 88:3. **14:17** It is unclear whether *Spirit of truth* is a definition of the *Comforter* mentioned in verse 16 or whether Jesus intended to refer generally to the *spirit of truth*. The translation reflects the idea that *Spirit of truth* further defines the *Comforter*, but it is possible that Jesus was instructing his disciples to listen to the *spirit of truth*. **14:20** Similar ideas are taught in Doctrine and Covenants 50:43; Moses 6:34. **14:22** For *Judas*, see Luke 6:16. Echoed in Ether 12:32. **14:23** See Doctrine and Covenants 130:3. **14:26** Second Nephi 32:5 echoes this verse but changes the verb of teaching to *show*.

hearts be troubled nor afraid. ²⁸You heard me say to you, 'I am going away, and I am coming back to you.' If you have loved me, you would rejoice that I am going to the Father because the Father is greater than I am. ²⁹And now I have told you before it happens so that you will believe when it happens. ³⁰No longer will I speak much with you, for the ruler of this world is coming, and he has no power over me. ³¹But that the world may know that I love the Father, I act just as the Father commanded me. Rise and let us go from here.

I AM THE TRUE VINE

15 ¹"I am the true vine, and my Father is the caretaker. ²Every branch that does not bear fruit in me, he takes away, and every one that bears fruit he prunes that it may bear more fruit. ³You are already clean because of the word I have spoken to you. ⁴Abide in me, even as I in you. Just as a branch cannot bear fruit by itself if it does not live on the vine, even so you cannot if you do not abide in me. ⁵I am the vine; you are the branches. Whoever abides in me even as I abide in him bears much fruit because without me he is able to do nothing. ⁶If anyone does not abide in me, he is cast out as a branch and

withers, and they are gathered, thrown into the fire, and burned. ⁷If you abide in me and my words abide in you, whatever you desire to ask for, it will be done for you. ⁸My Father is glorified in this way, that you bring forth much fruit and are my disciples. ⁹Just as the Father loved me, even so I have loved you. Abide in my love. ¹⁰If you obey my commandments, you will abide in my love, just as I have obeyed my Father's commandments and I abide in his love. ¹¹I have told you these things that my joy may be in you and that your joy may be complete.

¹²"This is my commandment, that you love one another as I have loved you. ¹³No one has greater love than this, that one lays down his life for his friends. ¹⁴If you do the things that I have commanded you, you are my friends. ¹⁵No longer do I call you servants because the servant does not know what his master does. I have called you friends because everything that I have heard from my Father, I have made it known to you. ¹⁶You did not choose me, but I have chosen you, and I appointed you so that you may go out and bear fruit, fruit that remains, so that whatever you ask the Father in my name, he will give

---

14:28 Possibly an allusion to John 13:33. **14:30** *Authority over me* is also possible. Quoted in Doctrine and Covenants 127:11.

15:1 Compare Isaiah 5:1–7 (also Jeremiah 2:21; 6:9; 8:13; Hosea 10:1; 2 Nephi 15:7; Jacob 5:3) for the idea of Israel as a vineyard. First Nephi 15:15 also teaches about the *true vine*. **15:1–4** These verses may contain a subtle critique of Judas Iscariot. **15:2** The verb for *pruning* means *to cleanse*. The same verb is used in verse 3, and it may be that the meaning of *to prune* is implied in verse 3. **15:3** This verse contains an echo of John 13:10, when Jesus washed the disciples' feet, thus further hinting that Judas Iscariot was in view in these verses. **15:4** *Even so you cannot unless you abide in me* is abbreviated and should read *even so you cannot bear fruit unless you abide in me*. **15:7** Compare Moroni 7:26 for a similar promise. **15:10** Here Jesus speaks of *my commandments*, but in 15:12 (also verse 17) Jesus gives only one commandment. Doctrine and Covenants 46:9 may echo this verse. **15:13** Second Nephi 26:24 and Ether 12:33 may allude to this verse in describing Christ laying down his life, also using the language of John 12:32 (also John 3:16). **15:15** Jesus had earlier called them servants (John 13:16; Luke 17:10). Mosiah (2:21) spoke of the plight of the faithful in being viewed as unprofitable servants. **15:16** The disciples are *chosen*, a theme that is also developed in Ephesians 1:4. The twelve disciples serve as examples to the faithful believer. *Established* can also mean *ordained* (compare 1 Nephi 14:25). Echoed in Doctrine and Covenants 88:64; 101:27.

it to you. [17]These things I command you, that you love one another.

THE WORLD HATES JESUS

[18]"If the world hates you, know that it hated me first. [19]If you are of the world, the world loves its own. But because you are not of the world, I have chosen you out of the world, and because of this the world hates you. [20]Remember the word that I have spoken to you, 'A servant is not greater than his lord.' If they persecuted me, they will persecute you. If they obeyed my word, they will obey yours. [21]But they will do all these things to you because of my name because they do not know who sent me. [22]If I did not come and speak to them, they would not be guilty of sin, but now they have no excuse for their sin. [23]The one who hates me hates my Father. [24]If I did not do the works among them which no one else has done, they would not be guilty of sin, but now they have seen me and hated both me and my Father. [25]But so that the word that is written in their Law might be fulfilled, '*They hated me without a cause.*' [26]When the Comforter comes, the Spirit of truth who comes from the Father that I will send to you from the Father, he will testify concerning me. [27]You will also testify because you have been with me from the beginning.

16 [1]"I have spoken these things to you so that you will not be offended. [2]They will put you out of the synagogues, but the hour will come when whoever kills you will think he is offering service unto God. [3]They will do these things because they have not known the Father nor me. [4]But I have told you these things so that when their hour comes you will remember that I told you about them. I did not tell you these things from the beginning because I was with you. [5]But now I am going to him who sent me, and none of you are asking me, 'Where are you going?' [6]But because I have told you these things, sadness has filled your heart. [7]But I tell you the truth, it is to your advantage that I am going away. For if I do not go away, the Comforter will not come to you, but if I go, I will send him to you. [8]When he comes, he will convict the world for sins, righteousness, and judgment—[9]for sins because they do not believe in me, [10]for righteousness because I am going to the Father and you no longer see me, [11]and for judgment because the ruler of this world is condemned.

THE SPIRIT OF TRUTH

[12]"I have yet many things to tell you, but you are not able to bear them yet. [13]When he comes, the Spirit of truth, he will guide you in all truth, for he does not speak of himself, but whatever he hears he speaks, and he will proclaim things to come. [14]He will glorify me because he will receive from me and proclaim it to you. [15]Everything the Father has is mine; because of this I

15:20 Jesus refers to his own teaching in John 13:16. **15:25** Quotation from Psalm 35:19 or 69:4.

16:1 *Offended* in Greek is also *to stumble.* The allusion may again be to Judas Iscariot (see John 15:1–4; for others who stumbled over Jesus's words, see John 6:61). **16:2** Excommunication or banishment from the synagogue may have been based on the practice described in Ezra 10:8. **16:6** The disciples are *sad* that Jesus is leaving them. This is one of the few times that John has recorded personal emotion by Jesus and his disciples. **16:8** *Convict* could also be to *prove the world wrong.* **16:11** Compare John 3:19–20. The *ruler of this world* is Satan (see note on John 12:31). **16:12** Jesus promises to reveal more to his disciples after his death and resurrection. Echoed in Doctrine and Covenants 50:40. **16:13** The Holy Spirit is a *guide* to truth. Jesus's words here emphasize the Spirit's guiding influence, allowing the person the choice to follow. A similar promise is made in 3 Nephi 18:20. Compare Doctrine and Covenants 101:27. The idea of the *Spirit of truth* is used to describe the Holy Spirit (Doctrine and Covenants 50:17–21; 93:11), Christ (Doctrine and Covenants 93:9, 26), and believers (Doctrine and Covenants 93:23). **16:15** Compare

tell you that he receives from me and proclaims it to you.

JOY IN FOLLOWING CHRIST

[16]"In a little while you will no longer see me, and in a little while you will see me again." [17]Therefore, some of the disciples said to one another, "What is this which he says to us, 'In a little while you will no longer see me, and in a little while you will see me again?'" [18]Then they were saying, "What is this, 'a little while'? We do not know what he means." [19]Jesus knew they wanted to ask him, so he said to them, "Were you discussing with one another about what I said concerning this, 'In a little while you will no longer see me, and in a little while you will see me again'? [20]Truly, truly, I say to you that you will cry and mourn, and the world will rejoice. You will be filled with grief, but your grief will become joy for you. [21]When she is giving birth, a woman has pain because her hour has come, but when she gives birth to a child she no longer remembers the trial because of the joy that a child has been born into the world. [22]Therefore, now you have pain, but *I will see you again, and your hearts will rejoice, and no one will take your joy from you.* [23]In that day you will ask me for nothing. Truly, truly, I say to you, whatever you ask the Father in my name, he will give it to you. [24]Until now you have asked for nothing in my name. Ask and you will receive so that your joy will be full.

JESUS SPEAKS CLEARLY

[25]"I have spoken these things to you in similes. The hour comes when I will no longer speak to you in similes, but I will openly proclaim the Father to you. [26]In that day, you will ask in my name, and I do not say to you that I will ask the Father on your behalf. [27]The Father himself loves you because you have loved me and have believed that I came from God. [28]I came from the Father and I have entered the world. I am leaving the world, and I go to the Father."

[29]The disciples said to him, "Look, now you are speaking clearly, and you no longer speak in similes. [30]Now we know that you know all things and you do not need anyone to question you. For this reason we believe that you have come from God." [31]Jesus answered, "You believe now? [32]The hour is coming and has come when you will be scattered, each to his own home, and you will leave me alone because the Father is with me. [33]I have told you these things that you might have peace in me. In the world you have trial, but cheer up; I am victorious over the world!"

THE GREAT INTERCESSORY PRAYER

17 [1]Jesus said these things and lifted his eyes up to heaven and said, "Father, the hour has come. Glorify your Son so that your Son may glorify you. [2]Just as you have given him authority over all

---

John 6:39; 13:3; Doctrine and Covenants 27:14. **16:16** Jesus speaks of the nearness of the resurrection, perhaps to soften the grief caused by his departure (see John 16:6). An interpretation of this verse is given in Doctrine and Covenants 84:119. **16:21** *The joy that a child* literally means *the joy that a human.* Alluded to in Doctrine and Covenants 136:35. **16:22** An allusion to Isaiah 66:14. **16:25** Jesus's teachings in parables are viewed as obscuring the true meaning of those teachings. **16:28** The Fourth Gospel began with a hymn of Jesus's descent to earth, and now Jesus signals his return to the Father. **16:32** *His own home* could also be rendered *his own family* or even *his own belongings.* The word *home* is absent in the Greek text. **16:33** *Trial* is a singular noun with a plural meaning in this setting, perhaps in the sense of *continual trial. Suffering* and *tribulation* are also possible meanings. Alluded to in Doctrine and Covenants 50:41.

17:1 This entire chapter records a direct prayer that Jesus offered to the Father, making it the longest

flesh, even so he may give an eternal life to all whom you have given him. ³This is eternal life, that they may know you, the only true God, and Jesus Christ, whom you have sent. ⁴I have glorified you on the earth by completing the work that you gave me to do. ⁵And now glorify me with your presence, Father, with the glory that I had with you before the world.

⁶"I have made your name obvious to the men and women whom you gave to me from the world. They were yours, and you have given them to me, and they have obeyed your word. ⁷Now they know everything that you have given me is from you. ⁸Because I have given them the words you gave me, and they have received them and they know truly that I have come from you, and they have believed that you sent me. ⁹I ask on their behalf; I do not ask for the world, but for the ones you have given me, because they are yours. ¹⁰All that are mine are yours, and yours are mine, and I am glorified in them. ¹¹I am no longer in the world, but they are in the world, and I am coming to you. Holy Father, protect them in your name, which you have given me, that they may be one as we are one. ¹²While I was with them, I protected them in your name—those that you gave me—and I have guarded them, and I have lost none of them except the son of destruction, that the scripture may be fulfilled.

¹³But now I come to you, and I say these things in the world that my joy may be fulfilled in them. ¹⁴I have given them your word, and the world hated them because they are not from the world, just as I am not from the world. ¹⁵I do not ask that you take them from the world, but so that you will protect them from evil. ¹⁶They are not from the world, just as I am not from the world. ¹⁷Consecrate them in truth; your word is truth. ¹⁸Just as you have sent me into the world, even so I have sent them into the world. ¹⁹And for them I have consecrated myself, that they may also be sanctified in truth.

²⁰"I do not ask for them alone but also for those who will believe, through their word, in me, ²¹that all may be one, as you, Father, are in me and I am in you, that they may be one in us, so that the world may believe that you sent me. ²²I have given them the glory that you gave to me, that they may be one as we are. ²³I am in them as you are in me so that they may be perfected in one, that the world may know that you sent me and loved them as you have loved me. ²⁴Father, I desire that the ones you have given me may be with me where I am, that they may see my glory, which you have given me, because you loved me before the foundation of the world. ²⁵Righteous Father, the world does not know you, but I know you, and these

---

prayer in the New Testament (compare 3 Nephi 19:22–23, 29). Jesus looked toward heaven when he prayed (John 11:41). Jesus's time has come (compare John 7:6). Some manuscripts read *the Son* instead of *your Son*. This verse is alluded to in 3 Nephi 9:15. **17:3** John rarely uses the title *Jesus Christ* (compare John 1:17 for the other usage in the Fourth Gospel). The concept of eternal life expressed in this verse is alluded to in 1 Nephi 14:7; 2 Nephi 9:39; Doctrine and Covenants 19:7–12; 81:6; 88:4; Moses 6:59. **17:5** Compare Philippians 2:6. Jesus clearly asserts his own preexistence with God. **17:6** Echoed in 3 Nephi 19:20. Greek uses *men* generically to refer to *men* and *women*. **17:9–10** Alluded to in 3 Nephi 19:29. **17:12** The one who is lost is Judas Iscariot, who is literally referred to as the one who is destined for destruction. A possible allusion to Psalm 41:9. Alluded to in 3 Nephi 27:30; Doctrine and Covenants 50:42. **17:15** The end of the verse may also refer to *the evil one* instead of *evil* generally. **17:17** *Consecrate* can also mean *make them holy* or *sanctify*. *Consecrate* more closely follows the meaning of the word as it is used in verse 19. **17:19** Jesus *consecrates* himself as God consecrated the priests in Exodus 40:13. **17:20–22** Alluded to in 3 Nephi 19:23. **17:21** Alluded to in Doctrine and Covenants 35:2. **17:25** The abbreviated structure of the Greek makes the final clause of the sentence unclear. Jesus contrasts his

ones know that you sent me. ²⁶I made your name known to them, and I will continue to make it known so that the love with which you loved me may be in them, and I may be in them."

JESUS IS ARRESTED AND BETRAYED (MT 26:47–56; MK 14:43–52; LK 22:47–53)

18 ¹After Jesus said these things, he went with his disciples across the Kidron Valley where there was a garden into which Jesus and his disciples entered. ²Judas, who betrayed him, knew the place, because Jesus often met there with his disciples. ³Then Judas took a detachment of soldiers, and some officers from the chief priests and Pharisees, and they went there with torches, lanterns, and weapons. ⁴Then Jesus, who knew everything that was happening to him, came forward and said, "Whom do you seek?" ⁵They answered, "Jesus of Nazareth." He said to them, "I am he." Judas, who betrayed him, stood with them. ⁶When he said to them, "I am he," they pulled back and fell

upon the ground. ⁷Again, he asked them, "Whom do you seek?" They said, "Jesus of Nazareth." ⁸Jesus answered, "I told you that I am he. If you seek me, let these men leave." ⁹This was to fulfill the word that he had spoken, "Of those whom you gave me, I have not lost one." ¹⁰Then Simon Peter, having a sword, drew it out and struck the servant of the high priest and cut off his right ear; the servant's name was Malchus. ¹¹Then Jesus said to Peter, "Put away your sword into its sheath. Will I not drink the cup that my Father gave me?"

JESUS BEFORE CAIAPHAS AND ANNAS (MT 26:57–68; MK 14:53–65; LK 22:54–71)

¹²Then the detachment of soldiers, the captain, and the officers of the Jews arrested Jesus and bound him. ¹³And they led him to Annas first, for he was the father-in-law of Caiaphas, who was high priest in that year. ¹⁴(It was Caiaphas who had counseled the Jews that it was to their advantage that one man should die for the people.)

---

knowledge of the Father with the world's lack of knowledge. Jesus's disciples, like him, know the Father.

18:1 Much of the Kidron Valley, directly east of the temple, is filled with tombs, both ancient and modern. The small valley is properly classified as a wadi, wherein a stream ran after heavy rainfall. Neither John, nor the synoptic Gospels refer to a *Garden of Gethsemane*. John refers to a garden, or more properly an orchard/vineyard, and the synoptics refer to an *olive press* (*Gethsemane* in Aramaic). If the different sources are combined, then the resulting idea is an orchard/vineyard with an olive press. Compare Matthew 26:36; Mark 14:32. **18:3** The presence of weapons among the arresting party highlights Roman involvement. The weapons mentioned here are not simply sticks and clubs (see Matthew 26:47), but swords or weapons of war. The lanterns may have been intended to assist the search party in looking into the many caves in the region. John mentions that a *cohort* of soldiers was there, probably under the direction of the *chiliarch* (verse 12, a commander of a thousand foot soldiers). A *cohort* would consist of up to six hundred men if the entire *cohort* came to arrest Jesus. John is the only author to mention *Pharisees* during the arrest. **18:5** The Greek is ambiguous and could mean *I am he* or simply *I am*. Those who react to this statement by falling down clearly understood the latter meaning (compare Exodus 3:14). Jesus is called *Jesus the Nazarene*, which could mean *Jesus of Nazareth* as it is translated here (compare Matthew 2:23). **18:9** This is a reference to John 6:39 and 17:12. **18:10** The naming of the servant, *Malchus*, may suggest the author is drawing upon eyewitness testimony in telling this event. **18:11** The presence of a sheath intimates that the sword was not hidden but visible to the arresting party. **18:12** The *captain* in this verse is a Roman *chiliarch*. **18:13** Elsewhere, John refers to Caiaphas as the high priest during Jesus's lifetime (John 11:49). John is the only Gospel to record the visit to *Annas*, who was previously a high priest (6–15 CE). **18:14** A reference to John 11:49–51.

PETER DENIES JESUS (MT 26:69–75; MK 14:66–72; LK 22:56–62)

¹⁵Simon Peter followed Jesus, and so did another disciple. That other disciple was known to the high priest, and he entered with Jesus into the courtyard of the high priest. ¹⁶But Peter stood outside in front of the door. Then the disciple who was known to the high priest came and spoke to the servant girl who guarded the door and brought Peter inside. ¹⁷The servant girl at the door said to Peter, "Are you not one of this man's disciples?" He replied, "I am not." ¹⁸The servants and officers had built a charcoal fire, and they stood around it warming themselves because it was cold. Peter also stood with them and warmed himself.

CAIAPHAS QUESTIONS JESUS

¹⁹Then the high priest questioned Jesus about his disciples and his teaching. ²⁰Jesus responded, "I have spoken clearly to the world. I have always taught in synagogues or in the temple, where all the Jewish people gather together, and I have said nothing in secret. ²¹Why are you asking me? Ask those who have heard what I said. They know what I have said." ²²When Jesus said this, one of the officers standing nearby struck Jesus and said, "Do you answer the high priest in this way?" ²³Jesus answered, "If I have spoken incorrectly, testify of the wrong, but if I have spoken correctly, why do you strike me?" ²⁴Then Annas tied and sent him to Caiaphas the high priest.

PETER DENIES JESUS AGAIN (MT 26:69–75; MK 14:66–72; LK 22:56–62)

²⁵Simon Peter stood outside warming himself. So they said to him, "Are you not one of his disciples?" He denied it: "I am not." ²⁶One of the servants of the high priest, a relative of the man whose ear Peter had cut off, said, "Did I not see you with him in the garden?" ²⁷Again, Peter denied it, and immediately the rooster crowed.

JESUS DELIVERED TO PILATE (MT 27:1–2, 11–26; MK 15:1–15; LK 23:1–5, 17–25)

²⁸Then they led Jesus from Caiaphas to the Praetorium, and it was early in the morning. They themselves did not enter into the Praetorium, so that they would not be defiled but could eat the Passover. ²⁹Then Pilate went outside to them and said, "What accusation do you bring against this man?" ³⁰They answered, "If he were not a criminal, we would not have handed him over to you." ³¹Then Pilate said to them, "Take him and judge him according to your law." The Jews responded to him, "It is not lawful for us to kill anyone." ³²(This was

---

18:15 *The courtyard of the high priest* is an abbreviated reference to the high priest's home. The *other disciple* who entered the home is traditionally thought to be John the Beloved. However, the unnamed disciple in this story is a friend of the high priest and was also known in Annas's home, thus suggesting that the unnamed disciple was at least partially complicit in the events that transpired. **18:21** There may be a subtle play on the idea of asking those who have *heard* or *listened* to Jesus's teachings, which, in part, defines Jesus's disciples. **18:27** The crowing of the rooster also signals that day is approaching and that a significant amount of time has passed wherein Jesus was interrogated. Some scholars have argued that this rooster's crow may refer technically to the sounding of the trumpet at the end of the third watch of the night, or three a.m. **18:28–29** The *Praetorium* is the house of the governor or *praetor*. This would logically be Pilate's dwelling in Jerusalem. Acts 23:35 notes that Pilate's official residence was at Caesarea. This has led some to suppose that John is referring to the Antonia Fortress or to Herod Antipas's residence in the city of Jerusalem. Although the exact source of their concern for being unclean is unclear, those who are unclean must celebrate the feast a month later (Numbers 9:10–11). **18:31** Despite the

to fulfill the word Jesus had spoken concerning what type of death he was going to die.)

³³Then Pilate entered the Praetorium and called Jesus and asked him, "Are you the King of the Jews?" ³⁴Jesus answered, "Do you say this of your own accord, or did others tell this to you about me?" ³⁵Pilate responded, "Am I a Jew? Your people and your chief priests handed you over to me. What have you done?" ³⁶Jesus answered, "My kingdom is not of this world. If my kingdom were of this world, my servants would be fighting so that I would not be handed over to the Jews. But my kingdom is not from here." ³⁷Then Pilate said to him, "Are you a king?" Jesus answered, "You say that I am a king. I was born for this reason, and for this reason I came into the world, so that I might testify of the truth. Everyone who is of the truth hears my voice." ³⁸Pilate asked him, "What is truth?"

When he said this, he went out again to the Jews and said to them, "I find no guilt in him. ³⁹But there is a custom among you that I release to you one person during the Passover. Do you want me to release to you the King of the Jews?" ⁴⁰They cried out again, saying, "Not this man, but Barabbas!" (Barabbas was a revolutionary.)

19 ¹Then Pilate took Jesus and had him scourged. ²And the soldiers braided a crown of thorns and placed it upon his head and they put a purple robe on him. ³And they came to him and said, "Greetings, King of the Jews!" And they struck him repeatedly. ⁴And Pilate went out again and said to them, "I am bringing him out to you so that you may know that I find no guilt in him." ⁵Then Jesus came out, bearing the crown of thorns and the purple robe. And Pilate said to them, "Behold the man!"

⁶When the chief priests and officers saw him they cried out, "Crucify him! Crucify him!" Pilate responded, "Take him and crucify him. I find no guilt in him." ⁷The Jews responded to him, "We have a Law, and according to our Law he ought to die because he claimed to be the Son of God." ⁸When Pilate heard this, he was more afraid, ⁹and he entered into the Praetorium again and said to Jesus, "Where are you from?" But Jesus did not answer him. ¹⁰Then Pilate said to him, "Why do you not speak to me? Do you not know that I have power to release you or to crucify you?" ¹¹Jesus answered him, "You would

---

prohibition of Jews taking the life of a prisoner, Herod Antipas killed Jacob the son of Zebedee (Acts 12:1) and a group of Jews acted together in the stoning of Stephen (Acts 6). **18:36** *Servants* can also be translated as *officers*, and most commonly it means *attendants*. **18:40** John refers to Barabbas as a *political revolutionary*, which could mean a thief or bandit, but the term more commonly meant a guerilla fighter (Josephus, *Jewish War* 2.13.3–3).

19:1 An echo of Isaiah 50:6. Some individuals died as a result of scourging. Scourging associated with crucifixion took two forms: a severe beating or flogging and scourging. Scourging was done with a whip into which glass, bone, or metal fragments had been sewn. **19:2** The crown of thorns has become, through Christian art, an emblem of torture, and often Jesus is depicted as bleeding from the thorns that pierced his head. The crown may also have been intended to mimic depictions of kings who have the rays of the sun radiating from their heads. **19:2, 5** Purple is the color of wealth and specifically the Roman emperor. Matthew reports that it was a red robe (Matthew 27:28). **19:5** Probably an intentional allusion to Zechariah 6:12. **19:6** Pilate's directive to take Jesus and crucify him is beyond the legal authority of the Jewish authorities (see John 18:31). **19:7** Leviticus 24:16 is the law under consideration. **19:9** The question *Where are you from?* may have been an inquiry about jurisdiction and whether or not Jesus was from Nazareth and thus under the jurisdiction of Herod Antipas. **19:11** This may refer to Judas Iscariot or the high priest, both of whom handed Jesus over.

have no power over me unless it had been given to you from above. Because of this, the one who handed me over to you is guilty of the greater sin."

¹²From that point on, Pilate sought to release him. But the Jews cried out, saying, "If you release him, you are not a friend of Caesar. Everyone who claims to be a king speaks against Caesar." ¹³When Pilate heard these words, he led Jesus outside and sat down upon the judgment seat, which place is called the Stone Pavement ("Gabbatha" in Aramaic. ¹⁴It was the day of preparation for the Passover, about noon). He said to the Jews, "Behold your King!" ¹⁵Then they cried out, "Away with him! Away with him! Crucify him!" Pilate asked, "Shall I crucify your king?" The chief priests responded, "We have no king except Caesar!" ¹⁶Then he handed him over to be crucified.

THE CRUCIFIXION (MT 27:33–37; MK 15:22–26; LK 23:33–34)

Then they took Jesus. ¹⁷And he went out, bearing his own cross to a place called The Place of the Skull ("Golgotha" as it is called in Aramaic). ¹⁸They crucified him there, and with him two others, one on either side with Jesus in the middle. ¹⁹Pilate had an inscription written and placed upon the cross. It read, "Jesus of Nazareth, the King of the Jews." ²⁰Many Jews read this inscription because the place where

Jesus was crucified was near the city. And it was written in Aramaic, Latin, and Greek. ²¹Then the chief priests of the Jews said to Pilate, "Do not write 'The King of the Jews,' but that 'This man said, I am the King of the Jews.'" ²²Pilate responded, "What I have written, I have written."

²³Then the soldiers who crucified Jesus took his clothes and divided them in four, one part for each soldier. And his tunic, it was seamless, woven from a single piece from the top to bottom, ²⁴so they said to one another, "Let us not tear it apart, but cast lots for it to determine whose it will be." This was to fulfill the scripture that says, "*They divided my garments among them, and they cast lots for my clothing.*" Then the soldiers did these things.

²⁵The mother of Jesus and his mother's sister, Mary the wife of Clopas, and Mary Magdalene stood by the cross. ²⁶When Jesus saw his mother and the disciple whom he loved standing by, he said to his mother, "Woman, behold your son!" ²⁷Then he said to the disciple, "Behold your mother!" From that hour, the disciple took her to his own home.

JESUS DIES (MT 27:45–54; MK 15:33–39; LK 23:44–48)

²⁸After this, Jesus knew that all things were already fulfilled, and in order to fulfill the scripture he said, "*I thirst.*" ²⁹A jar of sour wine stood nearby, so they put a sponge

---

19:13 *The Stone Pavement* was possibly located in the Antonia Fortress, although its location has never been confidently identified. The Greek word *lithostroton* refers to a mosaic floor into which precious stones were also laid. **19:14** The *day of preparation* is mentioned in all four Gospels (Matthew 27:62; Mark 15:42; Luke 23:54). The difference in the Gospel of John is that this was the day of preparation for the Sabbath and also the day of preparation for the Passover. The next day would be both the beginning of Passover and the Sabbath (John 19:31). **19:17** Simon of Cyrene carries the cross in the other Gospels (Matthew 27:32; Mark 15:21; Luke 23:26). The place is called *Golgotha*, but Luke gives its Latin translation as *Calvary* (Luke 23:33). **19:19** *Jesus of Nazareth* in Greek is *Jesus the Nazarene*. **19:23** The *tunic* that was divided among the soldiers was worn underneath the outer garment. **19:24** Quotation from Psalm 22:18. **19:25** The Greek is not clear whether there were three or four women at the cross. Certainly, Jesus's mother and Mary Magdalene were present, but whether Mary, the wife of Clopas and Jesus's aunt, were one and the same remains ambiguous. **19:26** *Woman, behold your Son!* is also possible. **19:28** Quotation from Psalm 69:21 (see also Psalm 22:15). **19:29** *Sour wine* was a cheap wine drunk by soldiers and the poor.

soaked in sour wine on a hyssop branch and lifted it to his mouth. ³⁰When Jesus took the sour wine, he said, "It is finished!" Then he bowed his head and gave up his spirit.

³¹Then, because it was the day of preparation, that the bodies might not remain upon the cross during the Sabbath (that Sabbath was especially important), the Jews asked Pilate to have the victim's legs broken and to have the bodies taken down. ³²Then the soldiers came and broke the legs of the first man and of the other man who had been crucified with him. ³³But when they came to Jesus, they saw that he was already dead, and they did not break his legs. ³⁴But one of the soldiers pierced his side with a spear, and blood and water came out immediately. ³⁵The one who saw it testified, and his testimony is true, and he knows that he speaks the truth, that you may also believe. ³⁶These things took place that the scripture may be fulfilled, "*None of his bones will be broken.*" ³⁷And again another scripture, "*They will look on him whom they have pierced.*"

JESUS IS BURIED (MT 27:57–61; MK 15:42–47; LK 23:50–56)

³⁸After these things, Joseph of Arimathea, who was a secret disciple of Jesus because of his fear of the Jews, asked Pilate that he might take the body of Jesus. And Pilate permitted it, and he came and took his body. ³⁹And Nicodemus, who came to him first at night, came also carrying a mixture of myrrh and aloes, about a hundred pounds. ⁴⁰Then they took the body of Jesus and wrapped it in linen cloths with spices, just as it is the custom of the Jews. ⁴¹In the place where he was crucified there was a garden, and in the garden there was a new tomb in which no one had been laid. ⁴²Because it was the Jewish day of preparation, and since the tomb was nearby, they laid Jesus there.

THE DISCOVERY OF THE EMPTY TOMB (MT 28:1–10; MK 16:1–8; LK 24:1–12)

20 ¹On the first day of the week, Mary Magdalene came early to the tomb, and it was still dark, and she saw that the stone had been taken away from the entrance, ²so she ran to Simon Peter and to the other disciple whom Jesus loved and told them, "They have taken the Lord from the tomb, and we do not know where they have placed him." ³Then Peter and the other disciple went to the tomb. ⁴And the two ran together, and the other disciple ran more quickly than Peter, and he came first to the tomb. ⁵And when he saw the linen clothes lying there, he did not enter. ⁶Then

---

19:31 The Sabbath was approaching at sundown and the leaders were interested in removing the bodies of the deceased before the Sabbath started at sundown (see Deuteronomy 21:22–23; Joshua 8:29). Earlier translations referred to this as a *high day* or *high Sabbath*. The Greek says that it was an *especially important* or *great Sabbath* because the beginning of Passover fell on the Sabbath. **19:36** Quotation from Exodus 12:46; Numbers 9:12; Psalm 34:20. **19:37** Quotation from Zechariah 12:10. **19:39** This was about seventy-five pounds (= 34 kg) in weight according to modern measures of weight. This would have been far more than was needed to care for the body of Jesus. **19:40** John envisions wrapping Jesus's body with strips of linen cloth, whereas Matthew, Mark, and Luke imply that a large sheet was used (Matthew 27:59; Mark 15:46; Luke 23:53).

20:1 John refers to this as the *first day of the Sabbaths*. The phrase is not perfectly clear, but *early* signifies in the morning, and the *first day* signals that it is Sunday morning. *From the entrance* is not recorded by the author but is supplied to clarify the meaning of the passage. Tombs of the sort described in the gospels typically had a large stone sealing the entrance. The Joseph Smith Translation adds *two angels sitting thereon*. **20:2** *We* signifies that other unnamed women were with Mary at the tomb. **20:5–6** The different reactions of the beloved disciple and Peter upon seeing Jesus's grave clothes are noted, but not

Simon Peter came following behind him, and he entered the tomb and saw the linen clothes lying there ⁷and the cloth which had been upon his head was not with the linen cloths but lying apart, folded up in another place. ⁸Then the other disciple, who came first to the tomb, entered and saw and he believed. ⁹(For they did not yet understand the scripture that said he must rise from the dead.) ¹⁰Then the disciples again went away to their homes.

JESUS AND MARY MAGDALENE
(MT 28:9–10; MK 16:9–11)

¹¹But Mary stood in front of the tomb weeping, and as she wept she bent down to look into the tomb, ¹²and she saw two angels in white, sitting, one near the head and the other near the feet where the body of Jesus had been placed. ¹³And they said to her, "Woman, why do you weep?" She said to them, "They have taken away my Lord, and I do not know where they have placed him." ¹⁴After she said this, she turned around and saw Jesus standing, but she did not know that it was Jesus. ¹⁵Jesus said to her, "Woman, why do you weep? Whom do you seek?" She thought he was the gardener, and she said to him, "Sir, if you have taken him, tell me where you have placed him, and I will take him away." ¹⁶Jesus said to her, "Mary!" She turned and said to him in Aramaic, "Rabbouni" (which means "Teacher"). ¹⁷Jesus

said to her, "Do not hold me back, for I have not yet ascended to the Father. Go to my brothers and sisters and tell them. 'I am ascending to my Father and your Father, to my God and your God.'" ¹⁸Mary Magdalene came and told the disciples, "I have seen the Lord!" And she told them what he said to her.

JESUS APPEARS TO THE TEN
(LK 24:36–43)

¹⁹It was the evening of that first day of the week, and the doors were closed where the disciples were because of a fear of the Jews. Jesus came and stood among them and said, "Peace be with you!" ²⁰After he said this, he showed them his hands and his side, and the disciples rejoiced upon seeing the Lord. ²¹Then Jesus said to them again, "Peace be with you! Just as the Father sent me, even so I send you." ²²And after he said this, he breathed on them and said, "Receive the Holy Spirit. ²³If you forgive the sins of anyone, they are forgiven, and if you retain anyone's sins, they are retained."

JESUS APPEARS TO THOMAS

²⁴Thomas, one of the twelve, who is called Didymus, was not with them when Jesus came. ²⁵Therefore, the other disciples told him, "We have seen the Lord." But he said, "If I do not see the marks of the nails in his hands, and put my finger into the mark of

---

interpreted by the author. **20:7** *Folded up in another place* is in Greek *folded up in one place*. The author's intent is clear in trying to point out that the grave clothes were laid in one part of the tomb but that the facial cloth had been treated differently and was placed in a different part of the tomb. **20:9** See Isaiah 53:10–12; Psalm 16:10; Jonah 1:17. John does not quote the words of the scripture that he had in mind. **20:15** *Sir* in Greek can also be translated as *Lord*. In this context, Mary was being polite, and therefore *sir* is warranted. **20:16** Mary speaks Aramaic (*Rabbouni*, or *My Teacher*) to Jesus. **20:17** This is the first time in John that Jesus has unquestionably referred to the disciples as *brothers*. The term translated as *brothers* refers to *brothers* and *sisters*. The Joseph Smith Translation says *Hold me not*. **20:20** Jesus foretold this (John 16:22). **20:22** Compare Genesis 2:7. This is a possible allusion to breathing on them the breath of life. **20:23** The language of forgiving and retaining sins in Greek is *to let go, to disregard, to permit*, or *to allow*. The retaining of sins is conveyed through the Greek verb, *to have power over, to retain*, or *to keep carefully*. **20:25, 27** Similar language is used to describe the Nephite experience (3 Nephi 11:14; see also John 20:25).

the nails, and place my hand in his side, I will never believe." [26]After eight days, the disciples were again inside, and Thomas was with them. Even though the doors were closed, Jesus came and stood among them and said, "Peace be with you!" [27]Then he said to Thomas, "Bring your finger and look at my hands. Bring your hand and put it in my side, and do not continue to be unbelieving, but believe." [28]Thomas responded, "My Lord and my God." [29]Jesus said to him, "Do you believe because you have seen me? Blessed are those who do not see, but believe."

THE PURPOSE OF THIS BOOK

[30]Jesus did many other signs in the presence of his disciples, which are not written in this book, [31]but these things are written so that you may believe that Jesus is the Christ, the Son of God, and that by believing you will have life in his name.

JESUS APPEARS IN GALILEE

21 [1]After this, Jesus appeared again to his disciples on the Sea of Tiberias, and he appeared in this way. [2]Simon Peter, Thomas called Didymus, Nathanael from Cana of Galilee, the sons of Zebedee, and two other disciples of his were together. [3]Simon Peter said to them, "I am going fishing." They replied, "We are coming with you." And they went and entered into a boat, and in that night they caught nothing. [4]When it was early in the morning, Jesus stood on the shore, but the disciples did not know that it was Jesus. [5]Then Jesus said to them, "Children, do you have anything to eat?" They answered him, "No." [6]He said to them, "Throw your net on the right side of the ship, and you will find some." Then they threw it and they were not able to haul it in because of the number of fish. [7]Therefore, the disciple whom Jesus loved said to Peter, "It is the Lord." When Simon Peter heard that it was the Lord, he put on his cloak, for he had nothing on underneath it, and he dove into the sea. [8]But the other disciples came in the boat, dragging the net full of fish, for they were not far from the land, but they were about one hundred yards away. [9]When they came to the land, they saw a charcoal fire and a fish lying on it and bread. [10]Jesus said to them, "Bring some of the fish you caught now." [11]Then Simon Peter went and pulled up the net to land, full of large fish—one hundred fifty-three—and even though there were so many, the net was

---

20:28 This is the first time that one of the disciples has unequivocally declared Jesus to be God. **20:31** John has conceived of his Gospel as a book with a distinct purpose, which he indicates here. The phrase *that you may believe* has a textual variant, which makes it difficult to determine the original text at this point. John may have written it in a way that it would be translated as *that you may continue to believe* or following a different textual variant, *that you may come to believe.* First Nephi 13:26 envisions the gospel of Jesus Christ going forth by the hand of the twelve apostles, similar to how John has declared his purpose in writing.

21:1 Because the author appears to have ended his book with John 20:31 and because the appearances of Jesus recorded in this chapter appear later and are outside of Jerusalem, many scholars assert that this chapter was added as a postscript, perhaps in an attempt to address new or growing concerns. The Sea of Tiberias is also known as the Sea of Galilee. **21:2** Nathanael is mentioned again in the story after a long hiatus (John 1:46–49). He is here included with the disciples, but he may not have been a member of the twelve. He is only known in the Gospel of John, and he is never specifically mentioned as belonging to the twelve during the mortal ministry of Jesus. **21:7** Peter may have been wearing an apron and not completely naked. A similar type of apron was worn when Jesus washed the disciples' feet (John 13:4). **21:8** Greek *two hundred cubits* or about one hundred yards or meters. The translation reflects a more familiar term of measurement rather than the unfamiliar measurement of a *cubit.*

not torn. [12]Jesus said to them, "Come and dine." But none of the disciples dared ask him, "Who are you?" because they knew it was the Lord. [13]Jesus came and took the bread and gave it to them, and likewise with the fish. [14]This was the third time that Jesus appeared to the disciples after he was raised from the dead.

FEED MY SHEEP

[15]When they had dined, Jesus said to Simon Peter, "Simon, son of Jonah, do you love me more than these?" He said to him, "Yes, Lord, you know that I love you." Jesus said to him, "Feed my lambs." [16]He said to him a second time, "Simon, son of Jonah, do you love me?" He said to him, "Yes, Lord, you know that I love you." Jesus said to him, "Feed my sheep." [17]Jesus said to him the third time, "Simon, son of Jonah, do you love me?" Peter was saddened because Jesus said to him the third time, 'Do you love me?' and said to him, "Lord, you know all things, you know that I love you." Jesus replied, "Feed my sheep. [18]Truly, truly, I say to you that when you were young, you dressed yourself and walked wherever you wanted. When you are old, you will stretch out your hands, and others will bind you and carry you where you do not want to go." [19]He said this indicating by what death he would glorify God. After this he said to him, "Follow me."

THE FATE OF THE BELOVED DISCIPLE

[20]Peter turned around and saw the disciple whom Jesus loved following (the one who reclined next to him during dinner and said, "Lord, who is it who will betray you?"). [21]When Peter saw him, he said to Jesus, "Lord, what about him?" [22]Jesus answered, "If I want him to remain until I come, what does that matter to you? Follow me." [23]Then this saying that this disciple would not die went out among the brothers and sisters. But Jesus did not say to him that he would not die, but "If I want him to remain until I come, what does that matter to you?"

POSTSCRIPT BY JOHN'S FOLLOWERS

[24]This is the disciple who testifies and wrote these things, and we know that his testimony is true. [25]There are many things that Jesus did, which if they were each written, I suppose that the world itself would not have space for the books that would be written.

21:15 Some manuscripts refer to Peter as *Peter, the son of John. These* probably refers to the implements of the fishing industry. **21:15–17** Peter's affirmation of his love for Jesus is paralleled by his three denials (John 18:15–18, 25–27). **21:18–19** Peter's death is foretold. The insinuation is that Peter will be tied up and possibly crucified (see 1 Peter 4:16). **21:22–23** The fate of the beloved disciple is described (compare 3 Nephi 28:4–6; Doctrine and Covenants 7:1–6). **21:23** The Greek uses *brothers* in a generic sense to refer to the believers in Christ. **21:24** The account shifts to describing the author of the Gospel in the third person, and the final verses appear to be a postscript by another author. **21:25** Echoed in 3 Nephi 26:6.

THE ACTS OF THE APOSTLES

AUTHOR

The book of Acts is the second part in a two-part work that exists separately from the Gospel of Luke in its purpose. Acts tells the story of the growth of the early church, and its goal is to document the importance of Paul's ministry. As stated in the opening lines, the book is dedicated to an otherwise unknown individual named Theophilus (1:1), who likely sponsored the writing of the book, thus making him the consumer and Luke the interested producer. Similar to the Gospel of Luke, Acts is written in educated Greek, revealing that its author had received some formal training, although not advanced. The author originally envisioned two individual books, and the length of those books was determined by the length of a papyrus scroll. He may have intended to write more, but from the outset his ability to write the story of Jesus and Paul was limited by the physical reality that papyrus scrolls were available only in fairly standard lengths.

The story of Acts moves quickly to Paul, who is introduced into the story in 7:58 as a persecutor of the church named Saul. From that point forward, Paul, or Saul, quickly takes over the narrative, and from chapter 16 onward he dominates the narrative. Although it remains a matter of debate, Luke may have intended that his readers understand that he was an eyewitness to some of the events in Paul's life, and while Paul was traveling in Macedonia, Luke begins telling the story in the first-person plural "we," suggesting he was present for certain events (see, for example, 16:10). Regardless of whether Luke was personally in attendance, it demonstrates how important the eyewitness tradition was for Luke, a feature that was also prominent in the early part of his account of Jesus's life.

PURPOSE OF WRITING

Because Acts is such a substantial book, it is impossible to provide a single description of the book's purpose. Instead, the following themes were important to Luke. Woven within the story is the consistent thread made up of the problems associated with circumcision, a practice that had both cultural and religious significance. Christian Jews

believed that all Christian men should undergo circumcision at the time of conversion or baptism, which became a major stumbling block for the conversion of Gentiles. The discussion resulted in a general conference of the church, where the matter was publicly resolved (Acts 15:1–29), but the issues discussed at that conference continued to create problems for missionaries working in Gentile communities.

Luke also frames Paul's mission into three major journeys, one with Barnabas and then two where Paul's companions vary. The missions do not focus on reporting the number of baptisms or even the success that the missionaries experienced, but rather Luke seems more interested in telling the foundation narratives for the beginning of preaching the gospel in the cities of Macedonia, the Roman province of Asia, and Greece. The stories are full of conflict, affliction, and trial. A final point of emphasis in the story is the bleak picture left at the end of Luke's account, where Paul is arrested due to inner-church intrigue and then helpless to be rescued from false charges. The story continually flirts with Paul being released, both through miraculous means or otherwise, but eventually the Roman juridical process takes over and Paul is brought up on spurious charges, only to rely on the Jewish community in Rome for assistance (28:17–22). The story is one of contrasts of faith and setback, triumph and trial. By the end, it is certain that Luke was retelling the story of a hero.

CONNECTION TO LATTER-DAY SAINT BELIEFS

Acts provides several precedents for practice and procedure in the organization of the church as well as describing in broad terms the experiences that new members will have. Because Acts provides the only account of an apostle being replaced in the early church, this text is used as evidence for the necessity of having a quorum of twelve "witnesses" (1:22) at the head of the church and that if an apostle dies, he is to be replaced through a process of revelation in order to preserve the correct number of quorum members. Acts deliberates what is unique about the witness of an apostle and comes to the conclusion that an apostle must be a witness to the resurrection.

Acts also shows the importance of continued and expansive missionary work in the early church. The success of the missionaries became the lifeblood of the church that was struggling to overcome the cultural pressures of its origins within Judaism. The book begins with Jesus's command to teach all people (1:8), and the fulfillment of this injunction starts at Pentecost, with the apostles teaching Jews, Samaritans, and Gentiles throughout the narrative. The Church of Jesus Christ of Latter-day Saints is also fundamentally a missionary church, having inherited the legacy of proselyting from the early church. ᧙

INTRODUCTION

1 ¹In the former book, Theophilus, I wrote about all that Jesus began to do and teach ²until the day he was taken up after giving instructions through the Holy Spirit to the apostles whom he had chosen. ³After his suffering, he presented himself to them to be alive by many evidences. He was seen by them during a forty-day period, and he spoke to them about the kingdom of God. ⁴While he dined with them, he declared to them, "Do not depart from Jerusalem, but wait for what my Father promised, which you heard about from me, ⁵for John baptized in water, but you will be immersed in the Holy Spirit not many days from now."

THE ASCENSION OF JESUS

⁶Therefore, when they had gathered together, they asked him, "Lord, is this the time when you will restore the kingdom to Israel?" ⁷He answered them, "It is not for you to know the times or seasons that the Father has established by his own authority. ⁸But you will receive power when the Holy Spirit has come upon you, and you will be my witnesses in Jerusalem and in all Judea, Samaria, and until the ends of the earth." ⁹After he said this, while they were watching, he was lifted up and a cloud hid him from their sight. ¹⁰And while they were looking up to heaven as he departed, behold, two men in white robes stood by them. ¹¹And they said, "Men of Galilee, why do you stand looking up to heaven? This same Jesus, who has been taken up from you into heaven, will also return in the same way that you saw him ascend to heaven."

MATTHIAS CHOSEN AS THE NEW APOSTLE

¹²Then they returned from the mount called Olivet, which is a Sabbath day's journey from Jerusalem. ¹³And when they entered the city, they went to the upstairs room where they were staying. Peter, John, Jacob, Andrew, Philip, Thomas,

---

The book of Acts was probably originally titled The Acts of the Apostles, although the early manuscripts preserve a number of slightly different titles. Many of the later manuscripts emphasize the word *apostles*, referring to them as the *holy apostles*, and the two earliest copies contain no title at all.

1:1 *The former book* refers to the Gospel of Luke. Acts was intentionally written as the second part of a two-part series. The *apostles whom he had chosen* designates the twelve to distinguish them from the other apostles (1 Corinthians 15:7). The word *apostle* is often used generically to refer to *a missionary*, the primary meaning of the Greek word. *Theophilus* is mentioned also in Luke 1:3. **1:3** The evidences spoken of are those mentioned in Luke 24:31, 36–51. Doctrine and Covenants 97:14 offers a similar promise to missionaries in this day and age. Compare Mosiah 18:18 for the concepts of authority and being ordained to preach. **1:4** In Greek, *dined* can also mean *to spend the night with*, *to stay with*, or *to meet with*. There is no context that would clarify which meaning Luke intended, but following Luke 24, it is clear that the event took place in Jerusalem privately with the disciples, and therefore the meaning appears to reflect an intimate gathering. **1:4** *What my Father promised* is interpreted in Doctrine and Covenants 95:8–10. **1:5** The verbs *baptized* and *immersed* are the same in Greek. **1:6** The question implies that they looked for the restoration of Israel as an independent nation. **1:10** The two men in white are probably the same two messengers from Luke 24:4 (compare Luke 9:30–31). **1:11** All surviving eleven disciples were from Galilee. **1:12** Given the description of the location of Jesus's ascension while in the presence of the disciples, it is likely that Luke is describing the village of Bethany. *A Sabbath day's journey* would be approximately a half mile. This length was determined by the rabbis to be 2,000 cubits, or about 3,000 feet (914 meters). The discussion of what constituted a Sabbath journey, according to the *Jewish Encyclopedia*, arose from commentary on Exodus 16:29. This term is different than the one used to describe the room in Luke 22:12 and likely indicates that they were staying in a different part of the city. **1:13** *Where they were staying* can also

Bartholomew, Matthew, Jacob the son of Alpheus, Simon the Zealot, and Judas the son of Jacob were there. ¹⁴All of them continued in prayer with one mind, together with the women, Mary the mother of Jesus, and his brothers.

¹⁵In those days, Peter stood in their midst and said to the believers (there was a gathering of about one hundred twenty people), ¹⁶"Brothers and sisters, the scripture had to be fulfilled which the Holy Spirit spoke through the mouth of David concerning Judas, who became the guide for those who arrested Jesus—¹⁷for he was counted among us, and he was accorded his portion of this ministry. ¹⁸(This man purchased a field with the gains of wickedness, and, falling headlong, he burst open in the middle, and his bowels fell out. ¹⁹This was known by all who lived in Jerusalem, so that the field was called in their language, *Hakeldama*, which is the 'Field of Blood.') ²⁰For it is written in the book of Psalms, '*Let his house become deserted, and let there be no one to live in it,*' and '*Let another take his stewardship.*' ²¹Therefore, one of the men who has walked with us

all the time that the Lord Jesus went in and out among us, ²²beginning from the baptism of John until the day that he was taken from us, one of them must become a witness of his resurrection with us." ²³And they proposed two, Joseph called Barsabbas, who was also called Justus, and Matthias. ²⁴Then they prayed, "Lord, you know the hearts of all people. Show us which of these two you have chosen ²⁵to take the place of this ministry and apostleship of Judas, who followed his own path and fell away." ²⁶And they cast lots, and the lot fell to Matthias, and he was counted with the eleven apostles.

THE HOLY SPIRIT ON THE DAY OF PENTECOST

2 ¹When the day of Pentecost arrived, they were all together in one place. ²And there was suddenly a sound from heaven like a rushing wind, and it filled the whole house where they were seated. ³Tongues like fire appeared to them and were divided among them and rested on each one of them. ⁴And they were all filled with the Holy Spirit, and they began to

---

mean *where they were living*. The names of the disciples are the same as those mentioned in Luke 6:14–16 with the omission of Judas Iscariot. **1:14** For the brothers, see John 7:1–5. Jacob, one of Jesus's brothers, is later mentioned in Acts 15:13; 21:18. **1:15** The better Greek manuscripts read *brothers* in place of *believers* to mean brothers and sisters. Some inferior manuscript read *disciples*. **1:16** Greek uses *men, brothers* in place of *brothers and sisters*, but Luke mentions in the previous verse that it was a mixed audience of men and women. **1:17** The Greek *this service as deacons* is translated as *this ministry*. **1:18–19** These verses represent an editorializing comment by Luke. **1:19** *Their language* is Aramaic. **1:20** Quotations from Psalms 69:25; 109:8b. **1:21** The important distinction of how to choose the person from among the disciples who would fill Judas's stewardship is based on the idea that the new disciple would have literally *traveled with, accompanied*, or *walked with us*. *Walked with us* seems to best convey the idea of commitment to following Jesus. **1:22** The Greek wording suggests that the person to be chosen would need to become a witness of the resurrection but that he had not already physically witnessed Jesus's resurrected body. **1:23** Some late and inferior manuscripts shift the plural to a singular to emphasize Peter's role in making the decision to consider Barsabbas and Matthias. Joseph Barsabbas was his Jewish name, and Justin was his Roman name.

2:1 *The day of Pentecost* was celebrated fifty days after Passover (see Leviticus 23:15–21; Deuteronomy 16:9–12). **2:3** The meaning of *tongues like fire appeared to them and were divided among them* is unclear in Greek. The Greek reads literally *divided tongues like fire*, but *divided* likely refers to the distribution of the tongues of fire among the group so that each person received the gift, a gift that spread among them like fire. A similar gift is referred to in Doctrine and Covenants 109:36.

speak in other languages as the Spirit gave them the ability to speak.

⁵Among the Jews visiting Jerusalem, there were devout men and women from all nations under heaven. ⁶When the sound occurred, a crowd gathered, and they were confused because each one heard the disciples speaking in their own language. ⁷They were completely amazed and said, "Are not the ones who are speaking all Galileans? ⁸And how are we each able to hear in our own native language? ⁹Parthians, Medes, Elamites, those living in Mesopotamia, Judea, Cappadocia, Pontus, and Asia, ¹⁰Phrygia, Pamphylia, Egypt, the part of Libya near Cyrene, and visitors from Rome, ¹¹both Jews and proselytes, Cretans, Arabs—we each hear them in our own language speaking about the great works of God." ¹²And they were amazed and confused, and they said to one another, "What does this mean?" ¹³But others mocked them, saying, "They are full of new wine."

PETER'S FIRST ADDRESS

¹⁴But Peter stood with the eleven and lifted up his voice and declared to them, "People of Judea, and all those living in Jerusalem, let this be known to you and listen to my words. ¹⁵For they are not drunk as you say, for it is only nine in the morning, ¹⁶but this is what was spoken of by the prophet Joel, ¹⁷'In the last days, *it will be,*' God declares, *'that I will bestow my Spirit upon all flesh, and your sons and daughters will prophesy, and your children will see visions, and your elderly will dream dreams,* ¹⁸*and even upon my male and female servants in those days I will bestow my Spirit*' and they will prophesy. ¹⁹*'And I will give miracles from heaven*

2:5 Greek uses *men* to describe the *men and women* living in Jerusalem. Echoed in Doctrine and Covenants 64:42. **2:7** *They were completely amazed* comes from the Greek *they were amazed and astonished.* **2:8** The Greek says literally *how is it that each of us hears,* but the sense is better conveyed in English by *how are we each able to hear.* The question is not about one's ability to hear, but rather about the process by which each hears the spoken word in their native language. **2:9** This refers to the Roman province of *Asia* specifically (today western Turkey). **2:9–11** Many of the cities that became the focus of Paul's later missionary journeys are included in this list, but some are not mentioned (Macedonia and Greece). **2:11** A *proselyte* was an individual who was literally a newcomer to the Jewish faith, and hence it describes a convert. **2:14** Greek uses *men* here instead of *people,* but *all those living in Jerusalem* makes it obvious that Peter was speaking to *men and women.* This is one of five speeches that Peter gave in Acts (3:12–26; 4:8–12; 10:34–47; 11:5–17). **2:15** *Nine in the morning* is the third hour of the day. **2:17–21** Quotation from LXX Joel 2:28–32a. The introduction *In the last days* was added by Peter to provide a new context for the fulfillment of Joel's proph-

ecy. **2:18** *Male and female servants* refer to slaves or household servants, and therefore the promise is extended to all social classes. Peter adds that these servants will *prophesy,* which is an addition to Joel's prophecy (2:29). **2:19** First Nephi 22:18 resembles Joel 2:30, but the wording of Nephi's prophecy is closer to that of Acts and the LXX text. Echoed in Doctrine and Covenants 45:41.

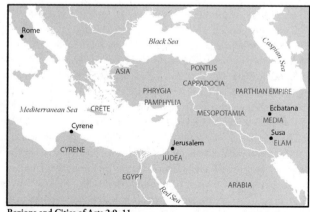

Regions and Cities of Acts 2:9–11
Map by Brandon Whitney, ThinkSpatial, BYU Geography

*above and signs from the earth below, blood,
fire, and a vapor of smoke.* [20] *The sun will be
darkened and the moon turned to blood before the great and wonderful day of the Lord
comes.* [21] *And then everyone who calls upon
the name of the Lord will be saved.'*

[22] "Fellow Israelites, listen to these
words; Jesus of Nazareth, a man attested
to you by God through miracles, wonders, and signs, which God performed
through him in your midst as you yourselves know—[23] this man, who was handed over to you by the ordained will and
foreknowledge of God, you crucified
by the hands of lawless men. [24] But God
raised him again, having released him
from the pains of death because it was
not possible for him to be held by death's
power. [25] David speaks concerning him, *'I
always saw the Lord in front of me because
he is on my right hand so that I will not be
shaken.* [26] *Therefore, my heart was glad and
my tongue rejoiced, and even my flesh will
live in hope* [27] *because you will not abandon my soul in hell, nor will you let your
Holy One experience corruption.* [28] *You
have made known to me the paths of life;
you will fill me with rejoicing with your
presence.'*

[29] "Brothers and sisters, I may tell you
confidently about our ancestor David,
that he died and was buried and his tomb
is with us to this day, [30] because he was a
prophet and he knew that God *had promised him with an oath to place one of his descendants upon his throne;* [31] by foreseeing
this, David spoke about the resurrection
of Christ, because *he was not abandoned to
hell, nor did his flesh experience corruption.*
[32] God resurrected this Jesus, and we are all
witnesses of him. [33] Therefore, being lifted up to the right hand of God and having received from the Father the promise
of the Holy Spirit, he has demonstrated
what you both see and hear. [34] David did
not ascend to heaven, but he himself says,
*'The Lord said to my Lord, Sit at my right
hand* [35] *until I make your enemies your footstool.'* [36] Therefore, let all the house of Israel know with certainty that God made
this Jesus whom you crucified both Lord
and Messiah."

THE FIRST CONVERTS

[37] When they heard this, they were troubled in heart and said to Peter and the other apostles, "What should we do, brothers?" [38] Peter answered them, "Repent, and
be baptized, each one of you in the name

2:21 Helaman 14:8; Doctrine and Covenants 100:17 allude to Acts 2:21. **2:22** Compare Hebrews 2:4;
2 Nephi 26:13. **2:23** God's plan is a prominent feature of the Book of Mormon (introduction; Jarom
1:2; Alma 24:14; 42:5; compare Moses 6:62). Acts later refers to God's plan (Acts 4:28). The word *ordained* refers to the idea of *being established, set up,* or *placed in order.* God's will is established according
to a plan, and therefore it is *ordained.* **2:25–28** Quotation from Psalm 16:8–11. **2:27** Peter refers to Hades specifically, which has been translated by the more familiar term *hell.* **2:29** Greek uses *brothers* only,
but it is used in a general sense to refer to the Israelites in attendance at the celebration of Pentecost. **2:30**
Reference to Psalm 132:11. Peter's logic is that David has died, and therefore the Psalm cannot refer to
him personally but must refer to Jesus, particularly the promise that he would not *experience corruption*
(verse 27). The presence of David's tomb testifies that he was not speaking of himself. **2:31** An explanation of Psalm 16:10. **2:33** An explanation of Psalm 110:1 (quoted in verses 34–35). Here the promise of
the Father, noted in Acts 1:4–5, is partially fulfilled for the early saints. **2:34–35** Quotation from Psalm
110:1 (compare Luke 20:41–44). **2:36** *Messiah* in English better conveys the Old Testament expectation
of an anointed one who would deliver Israel. The Greek uses *Christ,* which is the Greek translation of
the Hebrew word *Messiah,* and also the title *Lord.* **2:38** This is the first instance in the New Testament to
speak of *the gift of the Holy Spirit* or *Holy Ghost.* The phrase appears in the Book of Mormon (e.g., 2 Nephi 28:26; Jacob 6:8) and frequently in the Doctrine and Covenants (18:41; 33:11; 49:14; 55:3; 68:25).

of Jesus Christ for the forgiveness of your sins, and you will receive the gift of the Holy Spirit. ³⁹For the promise is for you and your children and for all who live far away and for everyone whom the Lord God calls to him." ⁴⁰And he testified with many other words and encouraged them, saying, "Save yourselves from this corrupt generation!" ⁴¹Those who accepted his teaching were baptized, and about three thousand people were added that day.

⁴²They dedicated themselves to the apostles' teaching and community, to breaking bread, and to prayer. ⁴³And reverent fear came upon them all because many wonders and signs were done by the apostles. ⁴⁴All who believed were together, and they shared all things in common, ⁴⁵and they sold their property and belongings and distributed the proceeds to all, to anyone that had a need. ⁴⁶And they gathered daily in the temple, and they broke bread from house to house, eating their food with gladness and humble hearts, ⁴⁷praising God and having the favor of all the people. And daily the Lord added those who were being saved to their number.

PETER PERFORMS A MIRACLE

3 ¹Peter and John went up to the temple at the hour of prayer, at three in the afternoon, ²and a man who was lame from birth was being carried in. He was placed daily in front of the gate called "the Beautiful Gate" so that he could beg for money from those people entering the temple. ³When he saw Peter and John about to enter the temple, he asked them for money. ⁴Peter, with John, looked directly at him and said, "Look at us." ⁵And he looked directly at them, expecting to receive something from them. ⁶But Peter said, "I have no silver or gold, but what I do have I will give to you. In the name of Jesus Christ of Nazareth, stand up and walk!" ⁷Then he took him by the right hand and lifted him up, and right away his feet and ankles were made strong. ⁸He stood up quickly and walked around, and then he entered with them into the temple, walking, jumping, and praising God. ⁹And all the people saw him walking and praising God, ¹⁰and they knew him because he usually sat and begged for money at the Beautiful Gate of the temple, and they were filled with wonder and awe at what happened to him.

PETER'S SECOND ADDRESS

¹¹While the man was holding on to Peter and John, all the people, greatly amazed, ran to them in the covered colonnade called Solomon's Portico. ¹²When Peter saw it, he responded to the people, "Men and women of Israel, why are you amazed at this? Why do you look at us so intently, as if we made him walk by our own power or godliness? ¹³*The God of Abraham, and Isaac, and Jacob,* the God of our ancestors, glorified his

---

2:39 There is no verb associated with *far away*, and therefore *live* has been supplied because the reference appears to be to those living in distant lands. Perhaps an allusion to Isaiah 57:19. **2:40** Alluded to in Doctrine and Covenants 36:6. **2:43** The Greek notes only that *fear* came upon them, but in this context their fear is inspired through righteous actions and following the apostles. **2:44** Alluded to in 3 Nephi 26:19. **2:47** *Having the favor* is *having grace* in Greek.

3:1 The Greek *at the ninth hour* is three o'clock in the afternoon. Peter and John went to the temple for one of the daily calls to prayer, thus implying that they were still observing Jewish customs and practices. **3:2** *The Beautiful Gate* was either the eastern gate, called the Shushan Gate, or the gate leading into the court of women, called the Nicanor Gate. **3:11** The temple in Jerusalem contained several covered walkways, one of which was attributed to Solomon. The colonnaded walkway attributed to Solomon was located on the east side of the temple. **3:12, 17** Given the location in the temple (see note for 3:11), men and women would have been present. Greek uses the generic *men* to describe a mixed audience of men and women. **3:13** Quotation from Exodus 3:6. On Pilate's decision to let Jesus

servant Jesus, whom you handed over and denied before Pilate when he had decided to release him. ¹⁴But you denied the Holy and Righteous One, and you asked for a man who was a murderer to be released to you. ¹⁵You killed the author of life, whom God raised from the dead, and we are witnesses to this. ¹⁶And faith in his name has made him strong, this man whom you see and know. And the faith that is through Jesus has given him perfect health in your sight. ¹⁷And now, brothers and sisters, I know that you acted in ignorance just as your leaders did. ¹⁸But the things that God declared beforehand by the mouth of all the prophets, that his Christ would suffer, have thus been fulfilled. ¹⁹Therefore, repent and return so that your sins may be washed away ²⁰so that the times of refreshing may come from the presence of the Lord and that he may send to you the appointed one, Christ Jesus, ²¹whom heaven must receive until the times when all things are restored, which God declared through the mouths of his holy prophets from past ages. ²²Moses said, '*The Lord God will raise up a prophet for you like me from among your brothers, and you shall listen to him in everything that he tells you. ²³And it will be that everyone who does not listen to that prophet will be destroyed from the people.*' ²⁴And all the prophets from Samuel and those who came after him, they likewise spoke of and declared these days. ²⁵You are the children of the prophets and the children of the covenant that God made with your ancestors when he said to Abraham, '*And in your offspring all the nations of the earth will be blessed.*' ²⁶God raised up his servant first and sent him to you to bless you by turning each one of you from your wickedness."

PETER AND JOHN ARRESTED

4 ¹While Peter and John were speaking to the people, the priests, the captain of the temple, and the Sadducees came up to them quickly, ²and they were angry because they taught the multitude and declared the resurrection of the dead in Jesus. ³So they laid hands on them and took them into custody until the next day because it was already late. ⁴But many who heard the word believed, and the number of men was about five thousand.

⁵And it happened on the next day that their rulers, elders, and scribes gathered in Jerusalem, ⁶and Annas the high priest,

---

go, see Luke 23:13–16. **3:16** *In your sight* can also be rendered *in full view of you all*. **3:19** The washing away of sins in this verse describes the acts of *covering, blotting out with paint,* or *washing off.* Some translations break verses 19–21 differently, but this translation follows the Greek text. **3:20** *Refreshing* describes the act of *a cooling* or *a refreshing breeze.* Therefore, *the times of refreshing* refer to a moment of relief. **3:21** *The times when all things are restored* builds upon a verb meaning *to set up, establish,* and *build up.* It refers to the full establishment of God's kingdom on the earth. Compare 1 Nephi 3:20; Doctrine and Covenants 27:6; 86:10. **3:22–23** Quotation from Deuteronomy 18:15, 19 and Leviticus 23:29. First Nephi 10:4 and 22:20 quote the same prophecy from Deuteronomy, but Nephi's wording is closer to Acts than Deuteronomy (compare Acts 7:37). The word *brothers* has been retained instead of rendering it as *brothers and sisters* to retain the sense of the Hebrew prophecy. Moroni quoted these verses to Joseph Smith (though the wording is not recorded), stating that they were *soon to be* (Joseph Smith—History 1:40). **3:23–24** Compare 3 Nephi 20:23–24. **3:25** Quotation from Genesis 22:18 (see also Genesis 26:4). Third Nephi 20:25–26 paraphrases this verse and also 3:26; compare 1 Nephi 15:18; 22:9.

4:1 The Greek text mentions only *them,* but Peter and John are certainly the ones speaking. The Sadducees held the majority of positions in the Jerusalem Sanhedrin, and the high priests during Jesus's lifetime were Sadducees. **4:4** Luke uses a different word here to denote only the men, indicating that the size of the crowd was likely much larger if women and children were added to the number. **4:6** Technically,

and Caiaphas, John, Alexander, and all who were from the family of the high priest were there. [7]And they stood them in their midst and questioned them, "By what power or by what name did you do this?" [8]Then Peter, being filled with the Holy Spirit, said to them, "Rulers of the people and elders, [9]if we are being questioned today about a good work done for a man who was ill—by what means he was healed—[10]let it be known to all of you and all the people of Israel that in the name of Jesus Christ of Nazareth, whom you crucified, whom God raised from the dead, this man stands healthy before you. [11]*This is the stone which was rejected* by you *the builders, that has become the cornerstone.* [12]And there is no salvation by anyone else, nor is there another name under heaven that has been given to men and women by which we must be saved."

[13]After they saw the courage of Peter and John and discovered that they were uneducated and common, they were amazed and recognized them as companions of Jesus. [14]And when they saw the man standing with them who was healed, they had nothing to say against it. [15]But after they had ordered them to leave the council, they began to discuss with one another, [16]saying, "What can we do with these men? Because it is obvious to all who live in Jerusalem that a mighty miracle has been done through them, and we cannot deny it. [17]But so that this matter does not spread further among the people, let us warn them not to speak any longer in this name to anyone." [18]So they summoned them and ordered them not to speak nor to teach any longer in the name of Jesus. [19]But Peter and John responded to them, "Whether it is right before God to listen to you or to God, you decide. [20]For we cannot avoid speaking about what we have seen and heard." [21]After they threatened them, they let them go because they could not determine how to punish them because of the people who were all praising God for what had happened. [22]For the man was over forty years old on whom this sign of healing had been performed.

THE PRAYER OF JESUS'S FOLLOWERS

[23]When they were released, they went to the other followers and told them what the chief priests and elders said to them. [24]When they heard it, they raised up their voice to God in one accord and said, "Lord, you made the heaven and the earth and the sea and everything in them, [25]who by our ancestor, your servant David, said by the Holy Spirit, *'Why do the nations behave arrogantly, and the people devise empty plans?* [26]*The kings of the earth stood and the rulers gathered in one place against the Lord and his Christ.'* [27]For Herod and Pontius Pilate with the Gentiles and the people

---

Caiaphas (18–36 CE) was the high priest during Jesus's lifetime and during the events described here. Luke seems to be referring to Annas as *the high priest* out of respect for the fact that Annas had held that office previously (6–15 CE). **4:11** Peter quotes Psalm 118:22 but adds *by you* to the psalm in order to make the point that people in his audience were partially responsible for the fulfillment of the prophecy. The same passage from Psalms is quoted in Matthew 21:42 in the context of the triumphal entry. **4:12** Compare 2 Nephi 25:20; 31:21; Mosiah 3:17; 5:8. Alluded to in Doctrine and Covenants 18:23. **4:13** The implication is that Jesus was also *uneducated and common.* The meaning is not that they were unable to read or write but that they had had no formal training, which became obvious under questioning. **4:15** *The council* is the Sanhedrin in Greek. It does not, however, refer to a place or building but a gathering where a council is held to determine the fate of Peter and John. **4:24** The idea that they prayed in unity is also described in Acts 1:14. They prayed to the *Lord* or literally to the *Master.* *Lord* is used in the translation to reflect the relationship of servant and Lord of the servant. **4:25b–26** Quotation from Psalm 2:1–2. **4:27** Those praying refer to Jesus as the *servant* of God using a word

of Israel were truly gathered together in this city against your holy servant Jesus, whom you anointed [28]to do whatever your hand and your will had predetermined to happen. [29]And now, Lord, observe their threats and grant to your servants to speak your word with great courage [30]while you extend your hand to heal and signs and wonders are done through the name of your holy servant Jesus." [31]And after they prayed, the place where they were gathered was shaken, and all were filled with the Holy Spirit, and they spoke the word of God with courage.

HAVING ALL THINGS IN COMMON

[32]And the whole gathering of believers was of one heart and soul, and no one said that any of his belongings were his own, but they had everything in common. [33]In great power the apostles gave their witness of the resurrection of the Lord Jesus, and great grace was upon all of them. [34]For there was no one who needed anything among them, for those who owned land or houses sold them and brought the proceeds from the sales [35]and placed them at the apostles' feet. And it was distributed to each as anyone had a need. [36]Joseph, by the apostles called Barnabas, which means "a

son of comfort," was a Levite and a native of Cyprus, [37]and after he sold his field he brought the money and laid it at the feet of the apostles.

ANANIAS AND SAPPHIRA

5 [1]A man named Ananias with Sapphira, his wife, sold their property, [2]and he retained part of the money with his wife's knowledge. And he brought only a part of the proceeds and laid it at the feet of the apostles. [3]But Peter said, "Ananias, why did Satan fill your heart to lie to the Holy Spirit and retain part of the money from the sale of the land? [4]While it remained in your possession, was it not your own? And after it was sold, was the money not at your disposal? Why have you devised this thing in your heart? You have not lied to people but to God." [5]After Ananias heard these words, he fell down and died, and great fear came upon everyone who heard about it. [6]So the young men arose and wrapped him up, and took him out and buried him.

[7]It came to pass after three hours, his wife came in, but she did not know what had happened. [8]Peter said to her, "Tell me, were you paid this amount for the land?" And she said, "Yes, that much." [9]But Peter responded to her, "Why have you both

---

that describes a typical household servant or even a *child of God*. **4:30** See Moroni 8:3 following the language of the King James Bible. **4:31** Perhaps an allusion to Exodus 19:18. **4:34** The ideal of meeting the needs of all the poor is set forth in Deuteronomy 15:4 (see also Alma 1:27; Doctrine and Covenants 38:35; 44:6; 52:40). **4:36** Levites were responsible for carrying out the daily sacrifices in the temple and also for the sacrifices performed at the annual festivals. *Cyprus* is located off the southern coast of Turkey. Barnabas belonged to a diaspora community living there.

5:1 Luke notes only that they *sold property*, which could refer to land or their belongings. Verse 3 indicates that a piece of property was sold, but this verse may refer to the liquidation of all their assets. A more accurate transliteration of the name *Ananias* would be Hananiah. **5:3** Peter asks about *Satan filling your heart*, implying that Satan has influence over one's heart. As the seat of emotion in the New Testament, this description of Satan's control or power promotes the idea that Satan has influenced their actions, but not that he has control over their hearts literally. *Satan* and *devil* are used interchangeably in the New Testament, but the noun *Satan* is used only twice in Acts (26:18). **5:8** Luke summarizes Peter's question to Sapphira when he notes that Peter asks *were you paid so much for the land?* The Greek implies that Peter asked her about a specific amount for which the land or property was sold. **5:9** The Greek verb *to test* has the double meaning of *to tempt*.

agreed to test the Spirit of the Lord? Behold, the feet of those who buried your husband are at the door, and they will carry you out. [10]She immediately fell down at his feet and died. When the young men entered, they found her dead, and they carried her out and buried her by her husband. [11]And great fear seized the entire church and all who heard these things.

EARLY APOSTOLIC MIRACLES

[12]Now, many signs and wonders were done among the people by the hands of the apostles, and they were all together in Solomon's Portico. [13]And none of the others dared to associate with them, but the people held them in high esteem. [14]More than before, believers were added to the Lord, crowds of men and women, [15]so that they even carried the sick into the main streets and placed them on cushions and mats so that when Peter went by, his shadow might fall upon some of them. [16]A large crowd from the towns around Jerusalem gathered and brought the sick and those tormented by unclean spirits, and they were all healed.

PERSECUTION OF THE APOSTLES

[17]But the high priest stood and all those with him who were of the sect of the Sadducees, and they were filled with jealousy. [18]And they laid hands on the apostles and threw them into the public prison. [19]But at night an angel of the Lord opened the doors of the prison and led them out and said, [20]"Go and stand in the temple and teach the people all the words of this life." [21]After they heard this, they entered the temple at dawn and taught.

When the high priest and those who were with him arrived, they summoned the Sanhedrin and the entire body of the elders of Israel, and they sent word to the jail to have the apostles brought out. [22]But when the officers arrived, they did not find them in the prison, so they returned and reported, [23]saying, "We found the jail locked securely and the guards standing in front of the doors, but when we opened them we found no one inside." [24]When the officer of the temple and the chief priests heard these words, they were confused about them and wondered what this could mean. [25]Then someone arrived and told them, "Look, the men who were in the prison are standing in the temple and teaching the people!" [26]Then the officer went with the temple police and

---

5:11 This is the first time that Luke has referred to the early Christian community as a *church*. The word *church* refers to an assembly of people who are gathered for a shared purpose. The word appears most frequently in Acts and 1 Corinthians but in only two verses in the Gospels (Matthew 16:18; 18:17). **5:12** See note on Acts 3:11. Given the location in *Solomon's Portico*, the *signs and wonders* done by the apostles were public miracles and not among the community of saints exclusively. **5:17** Luke's intent in mentioning that those who stood with the *high priest* were *Sadducees* is unclear. Many translations take it as a parenthetical explanation, but it is also possible that Luke was signaling that not everyone stood with the high priest in his decision, namely, the Pharisees. Pharisees were present, see Acts 5:34. In Greek, *jealousy* is a type of religiously motivated hatred or fervor. Sometimes it is translated in its more positive aspect as zeal. **5:20** The Greek text says simply *tell the people*, but English usage prefers to describe this as a teaching moment. **5:21** The description of the convening of the Sanhedrin is somewhat unclear in Greek. The meaning can be that Caiaphas summoned a council that included the *elders* and others, but it appears to represent an official gathering, and hence *Sanhedrin* is the more appropriate translation. Luke mentions besides the *elders* that the *sons of Israel* were at the council. The meaning appears to be that the entire council was summoned to interrogate the apostles. **5:26** The *officers* here can also be attendants or servants. The same Greek word is used for both.

brought them, but without violence, because they were afraid of the people who might stone them.

²⁷When they brought them, they stood them in front of the council, and the high priest questioned them, ²⁸saying, "We gave you strict orders not to teach in this name, and yet you have filled Jerusalem with your teaching, and you intend to bring this man's blood upon us." ²⁹Peter and the apostles answered, "We must obey God rather than man! ³⁰The God of our ancestors raised up Jesus, whom you had killed by hanging him on a tree. ³¹God exalted him on his right hand as Leader and Savior, to give repentance to Israel and forgiveness of sins. ³²And we are witnesses to these things, and so is the Holy Spirit, which God gave to those who obey him."

³³When they heard this, they were enraged and wanted to kill them. ³⁴But a Pharisee in the council named Gamaliel, a teacher of the Law who was respected by all the people, stood and ordered that the men be put outside for a little while. ³⁵And he said to them, "Fellow Israelites, be careful about what you are going to do to these men. ³⁶For some time ago, Theudas rose up and declared himself to be someone, to whom a number of men, about four hundred, joined themselves. He was killed, and all who followed him were scattered and came to nothing. ³⁷After him, Judas the Galilean arose in the days of the census and got people to follow him. He also died, and all who followed him were scattered. ³⁸And now I say to you, stand apart from these men and let them be, because if this plan and work is from people, then it will fail, ³⁹but if it is from God, you will not be able to overthrow them, and you may be found to be fighting against God." They were convinced by him. ⁴⁰And they called the apostles, and they had them beaten, and they ordered them not to speak in the name of Jesus, and they released them. ⁴¹Then they departed from the council, rejoicing because they were considered worthy to suffer dishonor for his name. ⁴²And they were in the temple every day, and from house to house they did not stop teaching and proclaiming Jesus as the Christ.

SEVEN CALLED TO SERVE AS DEACONS

6 ¹In those days, when the number of disciples was growing, the Hellenists complained against the Hebrews because their widows were being neglected in the daily distribution of food. ²So the twelve called together the body of disciples and

---

5:28 Some early manuscripts turn this verse into a question (*Did we not give you strict orders?*), but the better manuscripts preserve it as it is translated here. **5:29** An allusion to Acts 4:19. **5:30** The reference to *hanging him on a tree* uses the language of Deuteronomy 21:23 and is not a revision of Luke's earlier description of the cross (Luke 23:26, 32–33). **5:31** *Leader* can be translated as *Prince* in some contexts, but the fundamental meaning is that of someone who leads a group as their representative. **5:34** This same *Gamaliel* was probably Paul's teacher (Acts 22:3). **5:36** The rebellion of *Theudas* is noted by the Jewish historian Josephus (*Antiquities* 20:97–98). The event took place ca. 44 CE. **5:37** This is the same *census* mentioned in Luke 2:1–2, and it took place under Quirinius in 6 CE. **5:40** The beating given to the apostles was probably the forty lashes minus one (Deuteronomy 25:2–3; 2 Corinthians 11:24). **5:41** Many translations favor *for the name*, but the name in question is certainly Jesus's name.

6:1 The *Hellenists* and *Hebrews* in this verse are Greek-speaking Jews and Aramaic-speaking Jews respectively and are also probably divided between those who lived in Jerusalem and those who came from diaspora communities. **6:2** This is an important moment in the history of the church when the apostles realize that they cannot also be deacons *to serve tables*. The apostles literally state that they cannot act like deacons in serving tables. This realization gives rise to the calling of those who would serve as deacons (see verse 3). The verb used to describe the selection of deacons in verse 3 is the verb that

said, "It is not right for us to disregard the word of God to serve tables. ³Therefore, choose from among you, brothers, seven men who are held in high regard, full of the Spirit and wisdom, whom we can appoint to this duty. ⁴But we will devote ourselves to prayer and the service of the word." ⁵And the decision pleased the entire group, and they chose Stephen, a man full of faith and the Holy Spirit, Philip, Prochorus, Nicanor, Timon, Parmenas, and Nicolaus, a proselyte from Antioch. ⁶And they stood before the apostles, and they laid their hands on them and prayed. ⁷And the word of God spread, and the number of disciples increased greatly in Jerusalem, and a large group of priests were obedient to the faith.

ARREST OF STEPHEN

⁸Stephen, full of grace and power, did great wonders and signs among the people. ⁹But some from the synagogue of the Freedmen (as it was called), both Cyrenians, Alexandrians, and those from Cilicia and Asia, stood and argued with Stephen, ¹⁰but they were not able to resist the wisdom and Spirit with which he spoke. ¹¹Then they secretly influenced some men to claim,

"We have heard this man speaking words of blasphemy against Moses and God." ¹²So they stirred up the people, and the elders, and scribes. Then they approached him, and they arrested him and led him to the council. ¹³They put forward false witnesses who said, "This man does not cease to say things against this holy place and the Law. ¹⁴For we have heard him say that Jesus the Nazarene will destroy this place and change the customs that Moses gave to us." ¹⁵All who were sitting in the council stared at him and saw his face like the face of an angel.

STEPHEN'S SPEECH

7 ¹And the high priest said, "Are these things true?" ²Then Stephen replied, "Men, brothers and fathers, listen to me. The God of glory appeared to our father Abraham when he was in Mesopotamia before he lived in Haran ³and said to him, '*Go out from your country and relatives, and go to the land that I will show you.*' ⁴Then he departed from the land of the Chaldeans and dwelt in Haran. He lived there until after his father died, and then God moved him to this land where you now live. ⁵But God did not give it to him as an inheri-

---

would later describe the act of calling a bishop. **6:4** The decision is made that the apostles will still act in service (the Greek noun *deacon*) to the word of God, but the physical needs of the community will be met by the newly called deacons. **6:5** The seven who were chosen all have Greek names. *Nicolas* had converted to Judaism before following Christ. Philip is mentioned in Acts 8:5–13, 26–40; 21:8. **6:7** These *priests* would be Levites like *Zechariah* (Luke 1:5). **6:9** *Freedmen* refers to freed slaves or servants. Asia refers to the Roman province of Asia (modern Turkey). There are two regions represented in these locations, those from North Africa (Cyrene and Alexandria) and the Roman province of Asia (Cilicia and Asia). **6:11–13** The charges made against Stephen are similar to those made against Jesus. **6:12** Luke offers little explanation, but *the people* have changed their views contrary to the message of the disciples (Acts 5:13). **6:13** For the commandment against bearing false witness, see Exodus 20:16. **6:14** Jesus was accused of threatening to destroy the temple (Matthew 26:60–62), but now the accusation has expanded to include neglecting the law of Moses.

7:1 The high priest's question is literally *are these things so?* **7:2, 26** The Greek indicates that this discourse was delivered to a male audience, and therefore *brothers* most accurately captures the meaning. **7:3** Quotation from Genesis 12:1. **7:4** Abraham went to dwell in *Haran*, which is where Abraham and Sarai settled. They had come from Ur of Chaldees (Genesis 11:26–32), which is depicted in Abraham 1:1. The book of Abraham 2:4–6, 15 depicts an eventual move from *Haran* into Canaan. Stephen seems to imply that Abraham moved from *Haran* to the region of Canaan.

tance, not even a foot of ground, and he promised to give it to him as his property and to his children after him even though Abraham did not yet have a child. ⁶God spoke to him in this manner, '*His descendants will be foreigners in a land belonging to others, who will enslave them and mistreat them for four hundred years. ⁷And I will punish the nation that made them serve,*' God said, '*And after that they will come out and worship me in this place.*' ⁸And he gave him the covenant of circumcision, and Abraham became the father of Isaac, and he circumcised him on the eighth day, and Isaac became the father of Jacob, and Jacob became the father of the twelve patriarchs.

⁹"And the patriarchs were jealous of Joseph and sold him into Egypt, but God was with him. ¹⁰And he rescued him from all his trials and gave him grace and wisdom before Pharaoh, king of Egypt, and he established him as a ruler over Egypt and over all his house. ¹¹Then a famine came upon all of Egypt and Canaan, and with it great suffering, and our fathers did not find any food. ¹²When Jacob heard that there was wheat in Egypt, he sent our fathers there on their first visit. ¹³On the second visit, Joseph made himself known to his brothers, and Joseph's family was made known to Pharaoh. ¹⁴So Joseph sent and summoned his father Jacob and all his relatives, seventy-five people in total.

¹⁵And Jacob went down to Egypt, and he died there along with our ancestors, ¹⁶and they were brought back to Shechem and placed in the tomb that Abraham had purchased for a sum of money from the sons of Hamor in Shechem.

¹⁷"Just as the time drew near for God to fulfill the promise made to Abraham, even so the people in Egypt grew in number ¹⁸until *another king ruled in Egypt who did not know Joseph.* ¹⁹He treated our ancestors with deceit, forcing them to abandon their infants so that they would not survive. ²⁰At this time, Moses was born, and he was pleasing to God. For three months he lived in his father's house, ²¹and when he was abandoned, Pharaoh's daughter took him in and raised him as her own son. ²²So Moses was educated in all the wisdom of the Egyptians, and he was powerful in his words and actions.

²³"When he was forty years old, it entered his heart to visit his brothers and sisters, the Israelites. ²⁴When he saw one of them being hurt unjustly, he defended him and avenged the injured man by striking down the Egyptian. ²⁵He thought his countrymen would understand that God was rescuing them through his hand, but they did not understand. ²⁶The next day he saw some of them fighting, and he tried to make peace between them, saying, 'Men, brothers, why are you hurting one

---

7:6 Quotation from Genesis 15:13. Stephen agrees with Genesis that it was *four hundred years*, but Exodus 12:40 notes that the time in Egypt lasted 430 years. The difference in number indicates that there were two different traditions for the time the Israelites spent in Egypt, or perhaps there were textual variants for both passages that indicated different durations. **7:7** Quotation from Genesis 15:14 with an allusion to Exodus 3:12. **7:8** The command to circumcise is found in Genesis 17:11–12. **7:14** The Greek translation of the Old Testament notes that the number was seventy-five, but the Hebrew notes there were only seventy (Genesis 46:27). This passage provides strong evidence that Stephen and Luke relied upon the Greek text. **7:16** This story is told in Genesis 50:2–13. **7:17** *The people* are the Israelites who grew in population before their departure from Egypt. **7:18** Quotation from Exodus 1:8. **7:20** The text literally says that Moses was *beautiful to God*, an interpretation of Exodus 2:2, which notes that Moses was *healthy as a child* or *a pleasing child*. The adjective can mean *beautiful, fair*, and *pleasant*. **7:23** Greek uses *brothers* generically to refer to *brothers and sisters*. Another possible translation in this instance is *relatives*. **7:24** *Injured man* must be supplied to clarify the pronouns in Greek, which uses only *him*. **7:26** *Hurt* in this verse translates the same verb as *hurt unjustly* in verse 24.

another?' ²⁷But the man who was unjustly hurting his brother pushed him aside, saying, '*Who made you a ruler and judge over us?* ²⁸*Do you want to kill me in the same way you killed the Egyptian yesterday?*' ²⁹At this, Moses fled and was a resident alien in the land of Midian, where he also became the father of two sons.

³⁰"After forty years had passed, an angel appeared to him in the desert of Mount Sinai in the flame of a burning bush. ³¹When Moses saw it, he was amazed at the sight, and when he drew near to investigate, there came a voice from the Lord, ³²'*I am the God of your ancestors, the God of Abraham and Isaac and Jacob.*' Moses began to shake and did not dare to look further. ³³But the Lord said to him, '*Remove the sandals from your feet, for the place where you are standing is holy ground.*' ³⁴*I have certainly seen the mistreatment of my people in Egypt, and I have heard their groaning, and I have come down to deliver them. Come now, I will send you into Egypt.* ³⁵This was the same Moses whom they rejected when they said, '*Who made you a ruler and judge?*' God made him a ruler and liberator through the hand of the angel who appeared to him in the bush. ³⁶He led them out and performed wonders and signs in the land of Egypt, at the Red Sea, and in the desert for forty years. ³⁷This is the Moses who said to the Israelites, '*God will raise up for you a prophet like me from among your brothers.*' ³⁸He is the one who was in the congregation in the desert with the angel who spoke to him at Mount Sinai and with our ancestors and who received the living revelations to give to us. ³⁹Our ancestors did not want to obey him, but they pushed him aside, and they turned back to Egypt in their hearts, ⁴⁰saying to Aaron, '*Make gods for us who will lead the way for us. For this Moses, who led us from the land of Egypt, we do not know what has happened to him.*' ⁴¹In those days they made a calf, offered a sacrifice to the idol, and rejoiced in the works of their hands. ⁴²But God turned away from them, and gave them to worship the host of heaven, as it is written in the book of the prophets: '*Did you offer to me, house of Israel, slain animals and sacrifices for forty years in the wilderness?* ⁴³*But you took the tent of Moloch, the star of your god Rephan, and the images that you made to worship, so I will banish you to live in Babylon.*'

⁴⁴"Our ancestors had the tabernacle of testimony in the desert just as God spoke to Moses and commanded him to make it according to the type that Moses had seen. ⁴⁵Our ancestors received it and brought it in with Joshua when they drove out the nations that God removed before our ancestors. The tabernacle was there until the time of David, ⁴⁶who found favor before God, and asked that he might find a permanent place for the house of

---

7:27–28 Quotation from Exodus 2:14. **7:29** *A resident alien* describes a foreigner who lives permanently in another land. **7:30** This event is described in Exodus 3:2. **7:32** Quotation from Exodus 3:6. **7:33–34** Quotation from Exodus 3:5, 7–8, 10. **7:35** Quotation from Exodus 2:14 (see 7:27). **7:37** Quotation from Deuteronomy 18:15. **7:38** The word *congregation* refers to a gathering or assembly of people, and in New Testament times it eventually took on the meaning *church*. The word *revelations* translates a Greek word meaning *stories, wise tales,* and *oracles* (compare Doctrine and Covenants 90:5). **7:40** Quotation from Exodus 32:1, 23. **7:42** *Hosts of heaven* can also mean *stars of heaven*. The act of worshipping the *heavenly hosts* is condemned in Deuteronomy 4:19. *Slain animals and sacrifices* are intentionally redundant as a way of reinforcing the idea that God expected the Israelites to offer sacrifice to him. **7:42–43** Quotation from Amos 5:25–27. **7:43** The *tent of Moloch* refers to the sacred but movable shrine dedicated to the Canaanite deity *Moloch*. *Rephan* was a Canaanite or Egyptian deity. **7:45** This story is told in Joshua 3:14–17. **7:46** Some early manuscripts read *the God of Jacob*, but the earlier and better manuscripts read *house of Jacob*.

Jacob, [47]although Solomon built a house for him. [48]But the Most High does not live in houses made by hands, as the prophet says, [49]"*The heaven is my throne, and the earth is my footstool. What type of house will you build for me, says the Lord, and where is my place of rest?* [50]*Did my hand not make all these things?'*

[51]"You stiff-necked people and uncircumcised of heart and ears. You always resist the Holy Spirit as your ancestors did. [52]Which of the prophets did your fathers not persecute? They killed those who foretold the coming of the Righteous One, of whom you have become his betrayers and murderers, [53]you who received the Law given through angels but did not obey it."

THE STONING OF STEPHEN

[54]When they heard these things, they were enraged in their hearts, and they ground their teeth at him. [55]But being filled with the Holy Spirit, he looked into heaven and saw the glory of God and Jesus standing at the right hand of God, [56]and he said, "Behold, I see the heavens opened and the Son of Man standing at the right hand of God!" [57]They cried out in a loud voice and covered their ears and rushed against him as a group. [58]And they dragged him out of the city, and they began to stone him. And the witnesses laid their cloaks at the feet of a young man named Saul, [59]and they stoned Stephen while he prayed, saying, "Lord, Jesus, receive my spirit!" [60]Then he

fell on his knees and cried out in a loud voice, "Lord, do not count this sin against them!" After he said this, he died. [1]And Saul was in agreement with the decision to kill him.

SAUL'S EARLY PERSECUTION

8 On that day a severe persecution began against the church in Jerusalem, and all, with the exception of the apostles, were forced to flee to the countryside of Judea and Samaria. [2]Some godly men buried Stephen and mourned him loudly. [3]But Saul was devastating the church, entering house after house, carrying off men and women and putting them in prison.

PHILIP TEACHES IN SAMARIA

[4]Those who had been forced to flee traveled around teaching the word. [5]And Philip went to a city of Samaria, and began declaring Christ to them. [6]And the crowd paid close attention to what was said by Philip, listening to and watching the signs that he did. [7]For unclean spirits, after crying out loudly, came out of many who were possessed. And many others who were paralyzed or ill were healed. [8]So there was great joy in that city.

[9]A man named Simon had practiced magic in that city and amazed the people of Samaria, claiming that he was someone great. [10]All of them from the smallest to the greatest said, "This man is called the

---

7:47 *Him* refers to God. **7:49–50** Quotation from Isaiah 66:1–2. **7:51** Compare Helaman 9:21. **7:53** The notion that the Law was given through *angels* would have been a point of debate in Stephen's speech. It may have been based on Deuteronomy 33:2 (LXX) and was likely used to draw attention to the inferiority of the Law that was revealed by *angels* versus the law of the gospel revealed by *the Son of Man* (verse 56). **7:54** For *ground their teeth*, see Matthew 8:12. **7:56** See Daniel 7:13; Psalm 110:1; Luke 22:69; Romans 8:34; Moroni 7:27; 9:26; Doctrine and Covenants 76:23. **7:58** The practice of stoning conforms to Leviticus 24:14. *Cloaks* in this verse refers to their outer article of clothing.

8:1 The departure of Christians from the city did not last forever because a significant group appears to have been there for the council described in Acts 15. **8:5** Some manuscripts note *the city of the Samaritans*, which would indicate their largest or most important city. Philip is one of the seven who was chosen in Acts 6:5. **8:7** This verse explains how the crowd listened to the miracles performed by Philip. **8:10** Luke uses the title *the Great Power of God* as though his audience would be familiar with it.

Great Power of God." ¹¹And the crowd paid close attention to him because for a long time he had amazed them by his magic. ¹²But after they believed Philip, who was proclaiming the good news about the kingdom of God and the name of Jesus Christ, they began to be baptized, both men and women. ¹³Even Simon believed them and was baptized, and he stayed with Philip constantly, and when he saw the signs and great miracles he was amazed.

¹⁴When the apostles in Jerusalem heard that Samaria had accepted the word of God, they sent Peter and John to them. ¹⁵They went down and prayed for them that they would receive the Holy Spirit. ¹⁶(For the Spirit had not come upon any of them, having only been baptized in the name of the Lord Jesus.) ¹⁷Then they placed their hands upon them, and they received the Holy Spirit.

¹⁸When Simon saw that the Spirit was given by the laying on of the apostles' hands, he offered them money, ¹⁹saying, "Give me this power so that whomever I lay my hands upon will receive the Holy Spirit." ²⁰Peter responded to him, "May your money go with you to damnation because you thought you could obtain the gift of God with money! ²¹You have no part or share in this word, for your heart is not right before God. ²²Therefore, repent of this wickedness and pray to the Lord that he may forgive you of the desire of your heart. ²³I see that you are extremely envious and are bound to unrighteousness." ²⁴But Simon answered, "Pray to the Lord for me that nothing of what you have said will come upon me."

²⁵After they had testified and spoken the word of the Lord, they returned to Jerusalem, declaring the word in many villages of the Samaritans.

THE ETHIOPIAN EUNUCH

²⁶An angel of the Lord spoke to Philip, saying, "Get up and travel south on the road that goes down from Jerusalem to Gaza." (This is a deserted road.) ²⁷He arose and departed. And he met an Ethiopian eunuch, a court official of Candace, queen of the Ethiopians, who was in charge of her entire treasury. He came to Jerusalem to worship, ²⁸and he was returning and sitting in his chariot, reading the prophet Isaiah. ²⁹Then the Spirit said to Philip, "Go and meet his chariot." ³⁰Philip ran and heard him reading Isaiah the prophet, so he asked, "Do you understand what you are reading?" ³¹He replied, "How can I unless someone guides me?" So he invited Philip to come up and sit beside him. ³²The passage of scripture that he was reading was this, "*Like a sheep to the slaughter he was led, and like a lamb before the shearer is silent, so he does not open his mouth.* ³³*In his humiliation, justice was denied him.*

It might represent an intentional contrast with the power of God, namely the Holy Spirit, that resides with believers. **8:14** Luke's wording implies that the entire region of Samaria was beginning to accept Philip's teachings and that Philip needed assistance in handling the influx of believers. **8:18** A directive to follow this pattern of laying on of hands is noted in Moroni 2:2–3. **8:21** Doctrine and Covenants 49:2 echoes this verse. **8:22** *Desire* in this context can also mean *intent* or *thought*. **8:23** *Extremely envious* is conveyed through the Greek idiom *gall of bitterness*, and Deuteronomy 29:18–20 describes it. Compare Mosiah 27:29; Mormon 8:31. **8:26** *Travel south* can also mean *around noon*, but Philip is clearly heading south from Jerusalem, and he is told to depart right away. **8:27** The word *Ethiopian*, in Luke's day, referred to anyone with dark or black skin. A *eunuch* is a castrated male who serves the queen in some ancient societies. The law of Moses forbids them from being accepted in Israel (Deuteronomy 23:1), although Philip is willing to offer him baptism. *Candace* is a title and not the specific name of an Ethiopian queen. She was probably the queen of Meroe in Egypt, and thus she was probably a Nubian. If this is correct, then Amanitere (25–41 CE) was the queen mentioned. **8:32–33** Quotation from Isaiah 53:7–8.

Who can describe his posterity? For his life is taken from the earth."

³⁴Then the eunuch responded to Philip, "I pray, tell me about whom does the prophet say this? About himself or about someone else?" ³⁵Philip opened his mouth, and beginning with this scripture he declared to him the good news about Jesus. ³⁶As they went along the road, they came upon some water, and the eunuch said, "Look, some water! What prevents me from being baptized?" ³⁸He ordered the chariot to stop, and both went down in the water, Philip and the eunuch, and Philip baptized him. ³⁹When they came up out of the water, the Spirit of the Lord took Philip away, and the eunuch no longer saw him, but he went on the way rejoicing. ⁴⁰But Philip was found at Azotus, and while he was traveling he declared the good news to all the towns until he came to Caesarea.

SAUL'S CONVERSION

9 ¹But Saul was still breathing out threats and murder against the disciples of the Lord, and he went to the high priest ²and asked him for letters to the Damascus synagogues so that if he found any who were of the Way, men or women, he would bring them to Jerusalem as prisoners. ³While he went, as he drew near to Damascus, a light from heaven suddenly shone around him, ⁴and he fell to the ground and heard a voice saying to him, "Saul, Saul, why are you persecuting me?" ⁵He replied, "Who are you, Lord?" He answered, "I am Jesus whom you persecute. ⁶But arise and go into the city, and you will be told what you should do." ⁷The men who were traveling with him stood there speechless, listening to the voice but not seeing anything. ⁸Saul arose from the ground, and although his eyes were open, he saw nothing. They led him by the hand and brought him to Damascus. ⁹And he spent three days without seeing, and he did not eat or drink.

¹⁰There was a disciple in Damascus named Ananias, and the Lord said to him in a vision, "Ananias." And he replied, "Behold, I am here, Lord." ¹¹The Lord said to him, "Arise, and go to the street called Straight, and in Judas's house look for a man of Tarsus named Saul, for he is praying. ¹²And he has seen in a vision a man named Ananias coming in and placing his hands upon him in order that he may see again." ¹³But Ananias answered,

---

8:37 This translation omits verse 37, which reads *If you believe with all your heart, you may be baptized. And he answered and said, "I believe that Jesus is the Son of God,"* because it is missing in nearly every early and important manuscript. It was certainly not part of the original book of Acts, but it may have been a later attempt to place an official confession of faith into the text. **8:39** Philip's experience parallels that of Elijah (1 King 18:12; 2 Kings 2:16) and Nephi (Helaman 10:16–17). The Joseph Smith Translation reports a similar experience during Jesus's temptations (JST, Matthew 4:5, 8). **8:40** *Azotus* was a city about twenty-two miles north of Gaza. Luke and Paul met Philip and his daughters in Caesarea several years after this incident (Acts 21:8).

9:2 The title *the Way* is the earliest known title describing believers in Christ before the title *Christian* was used. **9:3** Damascus is in Syria, and significantly to the north of Jerusalem. It lies approximately sixty miles north of the Sea of Galilee. Acts depicts the move of the church into Syria quite early. **9:5** Some inferior manuscripts add the statement here at the end of the verse, *It is hard for you to kick against the pricks.* The statement is clearly secondary and was not part of Acts originally, although it is recorded in Acts 26:14. Doctrine and Covenants 121:38 interprets this phrase. **9:7** Acts 22:9 and 26:13 indicate that Paul's companions did not hear the voice of God but that they saw the light. The Joseph Smith Translation harmonizes those accounts to this one. **9:11** *Tarsus* is the capital city of the Roman province of Cilicia. **9:12** *In a vision* is missing in many early and good manuscripts, but the meaning is clearly implied and is therefore included in the translation. **9:13** This is the first time the followers of Jesus are called *saints*.

"Lord, I have heard from many about this man, how he has done many evils to your saints in Jerusalem, ¹⁴and he has authority here from the chief priests to arrest all those who call on your name." ¹⁵The Lord replied to him, "Go, because he is a chosen instrument for me, to bear my name among the Gentiles, kings, and the people of Israel. ¹⁶For I will show him how much he must suffer for my name." ¹⁷Ananias went and came to the house, and laid his hands upon him and said, "Brother Saul, the Lord Jesus, who appeared to you on the way as you came here, sent me so that you may see again and be filled with the Holy Spirit." ¹⁸And right away, like scales falling from his eyes, he saw again, and he arose and was baptized, ¹⁹and he took some food and was strengthened. He was with the disciples in Damascus for several days, ²⁰and immediately he declared Jesus in the synagogues, saying, "He is the Son of God." ²¹All who heard him were amazed and said, "Is this not the man who destroyed those who call on this name in Jerusalem, and who came here to bring them bound to the chief priests?" ²²But Saul grew stronger and confounded the Jews who lived in Damascus, proving that Jesus is the Christ.

SAUL ESCAPES FROM DAMASCUS

²³When some days had passed, the Jews planned to kill him, ²⁴but the plan was known to Saul. And they watched the gate day and night so that they could kill him. ²⁵And the disciples took him at night and let him down through an opening in the wall in a basket.

SAUL VISITS JERUSALEM

²⁶When he arrived in Jerusalem, he tried to join with the disciples, but they all feared him, and they did not believe that he was a disciple. ²⁷But Barnabas took him and led him to the apostles, and he described to them how he saw the Lord on the way and what the Lord told him and how in Damascus he taught boldly in the name of Jesus. ²⁸And he went in and out with them in Jerusalem, and taught boldly in the name of the Lord. ²⁹He was speaking and debating with the Hellenists, but they were trying to kill him. ³⁰When the brothers knew about this, they took him down to Caesarea and sent him to Tarsus. ³¹Then

9:14 *Your name* is Jesus's name (see Acts 4:10–12; 1 Corinthians 1:2). **9:18** Compare to 2 Nephi 30:6. **9:25** Second Corinthians 11:33 describes a window or *opening* in the wall, which is not mentioned in this account. The translation reflects the description of the window opening of 2 Corinthians. The *disciples* mentioned are most likely local Christians and not the twelve disciples of the Lord. **9:26** This experience may be connected to the vision that Paul had that is described in Acts 22:17–21. **9:27** Paul's own account seems to indicate that he met only with Peter and Jacob, Jesus's brother, on this visit, but it is possible that they are describing two differing events (Galatians 1:18–24). **9:29** *Hellenists* are Greek-speaking Jews living in or visiting Jerusalem. **9:31** Saul's departure caused peace.

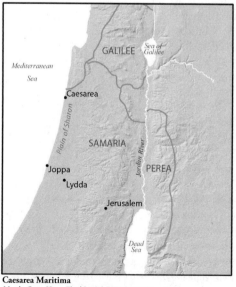

Caesarea Maritima
Map by Cassie Howe, ThinkSpatial, BYU Geography

all the churches in Judea, Galilee, and Samaria had peace and grew, walking in the fear of the Lord and in the comfort of the Holy Spirit, and the church multiplied.

PETER IN LYDDA AND JOPPA

³²And it came to pass that Peter traveled from place to place among them all, and he also went down to the saints who lived in Lydda. ³³He found there a man named Aeneas, who had been bedridden for eight years and who was paralyzed. ³⁴Peter said to him, "Aeneas, Jesus Christ heals you. Arise and make your bed." And he immediately got up. ³⁵All those living in Lydda and Sharon saw him, and they turned to the Lord.

³⁶In Joppa there was a disciple named Tabitha, which means "Dorcas." She was continually doing good works and caring for the poor. ³⁷It happened in those days that she grew ill and died. After washing her body, they placed it in an upstairs room. ³⁸Because Joppa is near Lydda, the disciples heard that Peter was there, so they sent two men to him and asked him, "Please come to us without delay." ³⁹So Peter arose and went with them, and when he arrived they led him to the upstairs room. All the widows stood by Peter and, while weeping, showed him the tunics and other articles of clothing that Dorcas made while she was with them. ⁴⁰But Peter sent them all outside and knelt and prayed and turned toward her body and said, "Tabitha, arise." She opened her eyes, and when she saw Peter she sat up. ⁴¹He gave her his hand and raised her, and then he called the saints and widows and presented her alive. ⁴²This was known throughout all of Joppa, and many believed in the Lord. ⁴³So Peter stayed in Joppa many days with Simon, a tanner.

PETER AND CORNELIUS: GENTILES BELIEVE IN CHRIST

10 ¹There was a man in Caesarea named Cornelius, who was a centurion of what is called the Italian Cohort. ²He was a devout man, who together with all his house feared God, and he gave many offerings to the people and prayed to God continually. ³About three o'clock in the afternoon, he saw in a vision an angel of God coming to him and saying to him, "Cornelius." ⁴He looked at him intently, and in fear he said, "What is it, Lord?" The angel replied to him, "Your prayers and offerings have ascended to God as a memorial. ⁵Now send men to Joppa for a man named Simon, who is called Peter. ⁶He is staying with Simon, a tanner, whose house is near the sea." ⁷After the angel who had spoken to him departed, he called two household servants and a devout soldier from among those who served him, ⁸and after explaining everything to them he sent them to Joppa.

⁹The next day about noon, while they were on their journey and approaching

---

9:34 The precise meaning of *make your bed* is unclear and is probably close to *take care of your bed* by taking it home. **9:36** *Tabitha* and *Dorcas* both mean *gazelle*. She is referred to as a *disciple* using the same noun in its feminine form as that used of Jesus's twelve disciples. **9:39** *Tunics* were articles of clothing worn next to the skin and were the regular daily clothing for most people.

10:1 *The Italian Cohort* was a military unit of the Roman army, and Cornelius commanded a hundred soldiers (the meaning of the title *centurion*). The cohort was stationed in Syria and is known in historical records as the *II Italica*, although it was stationed in the region later than the story described here, and thus Luke may have intended another division of the army. **10:2** The description of Cornelius as *God-fearing* likely indicates that he had followed Judaism but that he had not been circumcised and thereby become a proselyte (see Acts 10:45). In a Roman household, the master of the house would guide and determine the religious practices of everyone in the house, including servants. **10:4** Alluded to in Doctrine and Covenants 112:1. **10:9** The hour is important because it was observed as an hour of prayer for many Jews (Psalm 55:17).

the city, Peter went up on the roof to pray. [10]He was hungry and wanted to eat, but while they were preparing a meal he fell into a trance. [11]And he saw heaven opened and something like a large sheet descending, being let down by its four corners to the ground. [12]In it were all types of four-footed animals and reptiles from the ground and birds of the air. [13]Then a voice came to him, "Peter, rise, kill, and eat!" [14]But Peter said, "Certainly not, Lord, because I have never eaten anything common or unclean." [15]A voice came to him a second time, "What God has cleansed you must not call unclean." [16]This happened three times, and immediately the object was taken into heaven.

[17]As Peter wondered to himself what the vision might mean, the men who were sent by Cornelius arrived. And they enquired at the house of Simon and were standing at the gate. [18]They called out to determine if Simon called Peter was staying there. [19]While Peter was pondering the vision, the Spirit said to him, "Look, three men are looking for you. [20]But arise and go with them without hesitation, for I have sent them." [21]Peter went down to the men and said, "Here I am, the one for whom you are looking. Why have you come?" [22]They replied, "Cornelius, a centurion, a righteous and God-fearing man, praised by the entire Jewish nation, was commanded by a holy angel to summon you to his house and to listen to your message." [23]Then he invited them in and hosted them.

The next day he arose and went with them, and some of the brothers from Joppa traveled with him. [24]The next day he came to Caesarea. Cornelius was waiting for them, and he called his relatives and his close friends together. [25]When Peter entered, Cornelius met him and, falling at his feet, worshipped him. [26]But Peter helped him up and said, "Stand up. I am only a man." [27]And as he talked with him, he entered and found many people gathered together. [28]He said to them, "You know that it is unlawful for a Jew to associate with or visit a Gentile. But God has shown me that I should not call a person unclean or common. [29]Therefore, when I was sent for, I came without objection. Now, may I ask why you summoned me?"

[30]Cornelius replied, "Four days ago at this same hour, at three in the afternoon, I was praying in my house, and suddenly a man in shining clothes stood before me [31]and said, 'Cornelius, your prayer has been heard, and your offerings have been noted before God. [32]Therefore, send to Joppa and summon Simon called Peter, who is staying in the house of Simon the tanner near the sea.' [33]Therefore, I sent for you right away, and you were kind enough

---

10:10 Luke uses a different verb to describe Peter's vision, and hence *trance* is meant to reflect that nuance. The next verse (11) makes it clear that it was a visual experience. **10:12** The mention of *four-footed animals* and *birds* indicates that there were likely clean animals depicted in the vision, while the *reptiles* would be considered unclean for eating. Many of the biblical guidelines for the kosher (kashrut) standards are found in Leviticus 11. **10:14** *Unclean* would have been a sufficient description of foods that were not clean to eat according to the law of Moses. It is unclear what additional emphasis is being made by the mention of *common* foods unless it was to designate those foods that were not expressly forbidden by the law of Moses but that Jews still refused to eat. The implication of this verse is that Peter remained kosher while Jesus was alive. **10:20** Luke's construction *arise* suggests that Peter was possibly praying and pondering on his knees when the men arrived. The angel's counsel to move *without hesitation* reflects Peter's reluctance to eat the animals he had seen in vision. **10:23** Acts 11:12 indicates that there were six men who went with Peter from Joppa. They also became witnesses of the event. **10:24** *Caesarea* is *Caesarea Maritima*. **10:28–29** Peter describes his change in attitude regarding people of other nations.

to come. So now we are all here in the presence of God to listen to everything that the Lord has commanded you to say."

³⁴Then Peter began to open his mouth and say, "I truly understand that God does not show partiality. ³⁵But in all nations, anyone who fears him and does what is right is acceptable to him. ³⁶You know the word that he sent to the people of Israel, declaring the good news—peace through Jesus Christ, who is Lord of all. ³⁷That message spread throughout all Judea, beginning in Galilee with the baptism declared by John. ³⁸Regarding Jesus of Nazareth, whom God anointed with the Holy Spirit and with power, he went around doing good and healing all who were oppressed by the devil, because God was with him. ³⁹We are witnesses of all that he did in the land of Judea and in Jerusalem. They killed him by hanging him on a tree. ⁴⁰And God raised him on the third day and allowed him to be seen, ⁴¹not by all people, but by us who were chosen by God as witnesses. We ate and drank with him after his resurrection from the dead. ⁴²And he commanded us to declare to the people and to testify that he is the one appointed by God as judge of the living and the dead. ⁴³All the prophets testified about him, that everyone who believes in him will have forgiveness of sins through his name."

THE HOLY SPIRIT GIVEN

⁴⁴While Peter was still speaking these words, the Holy Spirit fell upon all those who heard the word. ⁴⁵And the circumcised believers who traveled with Peter were amazed that the gift of the Holy Spirit had been poured out upon the Gentiles. ⁴⁶For they heard them speaking in tongues and praising God. Then Peter replied, ⁴⁷"Can anyone withhold water from these people, who like us have received the Holy Spirit, to be baptized?" ⁴⁸So he ordered them to be baptized in the name of Jesus Christ. Then they asked him to remain for several days.

PETER RETURNS TO JERUSALEM

11 ¹Then the apostles and brothers and sisters who were in Judea heard that the Gentiles had accepted the word of God. ²Then Peter went up to Jerusalem, and the circumcised followers criticized him, ³saying, "You went to uncircumcised men and shared a meal with them." ⁴Peter began to explain it to them in order, saying, ⁵"I was praying in the city of Joppa, and while in a trance I saw a vision of something like a large sheet descending from heaven, being let down by its four corners, and it came to me. ⁶As I looked at it closely, I saw four-footed animals, wild animals, reptiles, and birds of the air. ⁷I heard a voice telling me, 'Arise, Peter, kill

---

10:34 Acts 15:7–11 may allude to this verse and the contents of Peter's vision. This theme is mentioned frequently in Romans 2:11; James 2:1; 1 Peter 1:17. Compare Moroni 8:12; Doctrine and Covenants 38:16. **10:36–37** English usage requires these two verses to be divided differently. The main verb is delayed in Greek until verse 37, but it is included in verse 36 (*you know*). Also, the translation has attempted to smooth out Peter's parenthetical remarks. **10:38** Peter does not refer to possession but rather to *oppression* or *influenced by the devil*. **10:39** Peter describes the crucifixion of Jesus using the language of Deuteronomy 21:23. His testimony is not a revision of the physical method of crucifixion. **10:41** This event is described in Luke 24:36–43. **10:42** Compare Moroni 10:34.

11:1 Greek uses *brothers* generically to refer to *brothers and sisters*. **11:2** The supposed boundaries that existed between *circumcised* and uncircumcised members of the church are largely cultural. The *circumcised* members wished to require circumcision for all adult male members. **11:3** The Greek notes only that Peter *ate with them*, but the issue extends beyond simply eating to welcoming uncircumcised individuals into the church.

and eat.' ⁸But I said, 'Certainly not, Lord, for nothing common or unclean has entered my mouth.' ⁹But the voice responded a second time from heaven, 'What God has cleansed, you must not call unclean.' ¹⁰This happened three times, and everything was taken up into heaven again. ¹¹And right away three men who were sent from Caesarea arrived at the house where we were. ¹²And the Spirit told me to go with them without hesitation. These six brothers went with me, and we came to the man's house. ¹³He reported how he saw an angel in his house, standing and saying, 'Send to Joppa and summon Simon who is called Peter, ¹⁴who will deliver a message to you by which you will be saved together with your entire house.' ¹⁵As I began to speak, the Holy Spirit fell upon them just as it did on us at the beginning. ¹⁶And I remembered the word of the Lord that he said, 'John baptized you in water, but you will be baptized in the Holy Spirit.' ¹⁷Therefore, if God gave them the same gift that he gave us when we believed in the Lord Jesus Christ, who was I to hinder God?" ¹⁸When they heard these things, they were silent. And they gave glory to God, saying, "Then God has given repentance that leads to life even to the Gentiles."

THE CHURCH IN ANTIOCH

¹⁹Then those who had been scattered because of the persecution that happened over Stephen went as far as Phoenicia, Cyprus, and Antioch, speaking the word to no one but Jews. ²⁰But there were some men from Cyprus and Cyrene among them who came to Antioch and began to speak to the Hellenists, proclaiming the good news of Lord Jesus. ²¹And the hand of the Lord was with them, and a great number believed and turned to the Lord. ²²News about them came to the attention of the church in Jerusalem, and they sent Barnabas to Antioch. ²³When he came and saw the grace of God, he rejoiced and called on all of them to remain faithful to the Lord with devoted hearts. ²⁴He was a good man, full of the Holy Spirit and of faith. And a multitude gathered to the Lord. ²⁵Then he went to Tarsus to look for Saul, ²⁶and he found him and brought him to Antioch. For an entire year they met with the church and taught a multitude of people, and the disciples were first called Christians in Antioch.

²⁷In those days, prophets came down from Jerusalem to Antioch. ²⁸One of them named Agabus stood and predicted through the Spirit that a severe famine was about to come on the entire world. (This happened during the reign of Claudius.) ²⁹The disciples decided that each would send relief according to their ability to the brothers and sisters living in Judea, ³⁰which they did by sending it to the elders by the hand of Barnabas and Saul.

11:15 *As it did on us at the beginning* alludes to the outpouring of the Spirit at Pentecost (Acts 2:1–13). **11:18** *Repentance that leads to life even to the Gentiles* is an ethnically charged statement, betraying some surprise that Gentiles have been fully accepted into the church. The *life* spoken of is ambiguous and may refer to eternal life or the abundance of life. **11:19** The early preaching to Gentiles was a divisive topic for early Christians (see Acts 11:2). This is *Antioch* on the Orontes, which became a central location for Saul's early ministry. **11:19–30** These verses describe some of the motivations for beginning the Gentile mission. **11:20** Some manuscripts change *Hellenists* to Greeks. The difference in meaning is slight unless the intent was to convey the idea that the Greeks had no affiliation with Judaism, whereas *Hellenists* would imply an association with Judaism. **11:22** *Came to the attention of* translates the Greek idiom *came to the ears of.* **11:26** Christianity has developed from being the Way (Acts 9:2) to being the gathering of Christians. The name is built from the title *Christ* and means *the ones associated with* or *the followers of Christ.* Compare Alma 46:13–16. **11:28** Historical sources indicate that there was a severe famine around 45–48 CE. Claudius was the Roman emperor between 41–54 CE.

JACOB, SON OF ZEBEDEE, IS KILLED

12 [1]Around that time, King Herod laid his oppressive hands on some who belonged to the church. [2]He had Jacob the brother of John killed by the sword. [3]When he saw that it pleased the Jews, he moved to arrest Peter. (This was during the Feast of Unleavened Bread.) [4]After he had arrested him, he placed him in prison and delivered him to four squads of soldiers to guard him. He wanted to lead him out before the people after the Passover. [5]While Peter was kept in prison, those in the church prayed earnestly to God for him.

PETER'S MIRACULOUS ESCAPE FROM PRISON

[6]On that night when Herod intended to bring him out, Peter was sleeping between two soldiers and was bound with two chains while guards were keeping watch over the prison at the doors. [7]And suddenly an angel of the Lord appeared, and a light brightened the cell. He touched Peter on the side and raised him up, saying, "Get up quickly." And the chains fell from his hands. [8]Then the angel said to him, "Fasten your belt and put on your sandals." And he did so. Then the angel said to him, "Put on your cloak and follow me." [9]And he went out and followed the angel, but he did not know that what was happening with the angel was real: he thought he was seeing a vision. [10]After they had passed by the first and second guard, they came to the iron gate leading into the city, which opened automatically to them, and they went outside and walked along an alley, and the angel left him at once. [11]Then Peter came to himself and said, "Now I know for certain that the Lord has sent his angel and delivered me from the hand of Herod and from everything the Jewish people expected to happen."

[12]When Peter realized this, he went to the house of Mary, the mother of John who is called Mark, where there were many gathered in prayer. [13]When he knocked at the outer gate, a servant girl named Rhoda came to answer. [14]When she recognized Peter's voice, she was overjoyed, but instead of opening the gate she ran and declared that Peter was in front of the gate. [15]But they responded to her, "You are out of your mind." But she insisted that it was him. So they said, "It is his angel." [16]But Peter continued knocking. And when they opened the gate, they saw him and were amazed. [17]He motioned to them with his hand to be silent, and he related to them

12:1 *King Herod* refers to Herod Agrippa I, who died in 44 CE. The event described in these verses, the killing of Jacob, took place in 42 or 43 CE. Agrippa I was quite powerful and ruled a territory similar in size to his grandfather Herod the Great. **12:2** *Jacob* refers to *Jacob* the brother of John, one of the two sons of Zebedee (Matthew 4:21). *By the sword* likely refers to beheading. **12:3** *The Feast of Unleavened Bread* is another name for the Passover, and the death of Jacob recalls the death of Jesus during the same pilgrimage festival. **12:4** Herod may have intended to hold a very public trial and condemn Peter or to have him publicly beaten before a crowd. **12:8** The angel is instructing Peter to change out of his bedclothes and to put on something that he can wear to go outside. The wording suggests that he was putting on his tunic which had a sash or belt. In the verse following, Peter puts on his *cloak*. **12:10** *Automatically* implies that the gate opened of its own accord without any human assistance. **12:11** Compare 1 Nephi 5:8. **12:12** *John Mark* was a traveling companion of Barnabas and Paul and is mentioned in verse 25 and Acts 15:37–39. Scholars often associate him with the person named Mark who wrote the Gospel of Mark. **12:13** Rhoda's name may be included in the story because members of the church knew her at the time when Acts was written. Many of the names in these stories were likely included because people knew them personally. **12:15** *His angel* may refer to the idea that Peter had an angel to protect him and watch over him. A similar idea is expressed in Matthew 18:10. **12:17** This *Jacob*

how the Lord led him out of the prison, and he said, "Tell this to Jacob and the brothers." Then he departed and went to another place.

¹⁸When day came, there was significant commotion among the soldiers about what happened to Peter. ¹⁹When Herod searched and did not find him, he interrogated the guards and ordered that they be put to death. Then he went down from Judea and stayed in Caesarea.

HEROD'S DEATH

²⁰Herod was in a dispute with the people of Tyre and Sidon, so they came to him as a group. And after winning over Blastus, the king's attendant, they sought for peace because their region depended upon the king's land for food. ²¹On the appointed day, Herod put on his royal robes and sat down on the judgment seat and delivered a speech to them. ²²But the people were shouting, "The voice of a god, and not of a man." ²³Immediately an angel of the Lord struck him down because he did not give glory to God, and he was eaten by worms and died.

²⁴But the word of God continued to spread and multiply. ²⁵Barnabas and Saul, after completing their service, returned to Jerusalem, bringing with them John Mark.

BARNABAS AND SAUL SET APART

13 ¹In the church in Antioch there were prophets and teachers: Barnabas; Simeon called Niger; Lucius of Cyrene; Manaen, a close friend of Herod the tetrarch; and Saul. ²While they were serving the Lord and fasting, the Holy Spirit said, "Set apart Barnabas and Saul for me for the work for which I have called them." ³Then after they had fasted, prayed,

---

refers to Jesus's brother, who is mentioned in Matthew 13:55; Mark 6:3. **12:19** Herod's examination of the guards involved questioning and possible beatings. **12:20–23** Herod's untimely death is noted by the Jewish historian Josephus (*Antiquities* 19:343–52). Acts depicts his death as immediate, but Josephus relates that it took place several days after the event described here. Both sources agree that he died as a result of accepting divine honors. Josephus records that Herod wore a robe made of silver thread and that when the sun hit it Herod shone like a divine being, which is why the crowd declared him to be *a god*. **12:24** The phrase *their service* is often translated as *their mission*. The fundamental idea is that of service, and the noun translated as *service* refers to the service of a deacon. Barnabas and Paul *returned to Jerusalem*, likely from delivering relief to the saints described in Acts 11:29–30. Luke's wording seems to prefigure their return at the end of the first mission described in Acts 14:24–28.

13:1–14:28 These chapters constitute Paul's first mission to Cyprus, Galatia, and Pamphylia (modern southern Turkey). Herod Antipas died after 39 CE. **13:1** *Herod* is designated as *the tetrarch*, thus indicating that this is Antipas (died ca. 39 CE and ruled Perea and Galilee). Niger means *black*, and *Cyrene* is in North Africa. **13:3** The *setting apart* of Barnabas and Paul reflects their appointment for a special ministry or calling.

Paul's First Mission
Map by Brandon Whitney, ThinkSpatial, BYU Geography

and laid their hands on them, they sent them off.

MINISTRY IN CYPRUS—
THE FIRST MISSION

[4]Therefore, they were sent by the Holy Spirit, and came to Seleucia, and from there they sailed to Cyprus. [5]When they arrived in Salamis, they taught the word of God in the Jewish synagogues. And they had John as an assistant. [6]When they had traveled across the entire island as far as Paphos, they found a magician, a Jewish false prophet whose name was Bar-Jesus, [7]who was with the proconsul Sergius Paulus, an intelligent man. He summoned Barnabas and Paul and enquired of them to hear the word of God. [8]But Elymas the magician (for that is the translation of his name) opposed them, trying to turn the proconsul from the faith. [9]But Saul, also called Paul, filled with the Holy Spirit, looked intently at him, [10]and said, "You are full of deceit and wickedness, you son of the devil, you enemy of all righteousness. Will you not stop distorting the straight paths of the Lord? [11]Now, look, the hand of the Lord is against you, and you will be blind, unable to see the sun for a time." Immediately mist and darkness came over him, and he sought for someone to lead him by the hand. [12]Then the proconsul saw what happened, and he believed because he wondered at the teaching about the Lord.

PSIDIAN ANTIOCH

[13]Then Paul and those with him set sail from Paphos and came to Perga in Pamphylia, but John left them and returned to Jerusalem. [14]They traveled on from Perga and arrived in Pisidian Antioch, and they entered the synagogue on the Sabbath and sat down. [15]After the reading from the Law and Prophets, the synagogue leaders sent them a message, saying, "Brothers, if there is someone among you who has a word of exhortation for the people, say it." [16]Paul stood and gestured with his hand, saying, "Men of Israel and those who fear God, listen. [17]The God of this people, Israel, chose our fathers and made the people great during their stay in the land of Egypt, and with uplifted arm he led them out. [18]For about forty years he endured them in the wilderness. [19]After he had destroyed seven nations in the land of Canaan, he gave them their land as an inheritance [20]for about four hundred and fifty years. After this he gave them judges until the time of Samuel the prophet. [21]Then they asked for a king, and God gave them Saul, the son of Kish, a man from the tribe of Benjamin,

---

13:5 This is John Mark, who was mentioned in Acts 12:25. Luke uses a word that indicates he was their servant to care for their day-to-day needs. He left the group suddenly and returned to Jerusalem (Acts 13:13). *Salamis* is a city on the eastern side of the island of Cyprus. **13:6** *Paphos* is a city on the western side of the island of Cyprus. **13:7** *Proconsul* is the technical term for the person assigned by the Roman senate to oversee the administration of a province. The precise dates of Sergius Paulus's tenure as proconsul are unknown. **13:8** The meaning of *Elymas* is unknown, although Luke indicates that it is a translation of *Bar-Jesus*, or *son of Jesus*. **13:9** Paul will mostly be known by his Roman name from this point on in Acts, but in some instances he will still use his Hebrew name *Saul* (Acts 22:7, 13; 26:14). **13:10** Compare 1 Nephi 13:27; 22:14; 2 Nephi 28:15; Alma 34:23. **13:12** *Wondered* can also be translated as *was amazed*. The tone is reverential, and therefore *wonder* better reflects what appears to be a softening of the heart. **13:13** *Perga* was a city in the region of Pamphylia near the coast (modern southern Turkey). **13:15** In this instance, *brothers* is the correct translation because there were likely no women in the audience in the synagogue. In some instances, Greek can indicate the presence of a male audience through the phrase *men, brothers*, which is used in this verse. **13:18** Some manuscripts note that he cared for them instead of *endured them*. The differences arise from the Septuagint (LXX) translation of Deuteronomy 1:31, which is echoed in this verse. **13:19** An allusion to Deuteronomy 7:1.

who ruled for forty years. ²²After God removed him, he raised up David for them as king, about whom he testified, '*I have found David the son of Jesse to be a man after my own heart, who will carry out my whole will.*' ²³From this man's descendants, God brought forth a Savior for Israel, Jesus, as he promised. ²⁴John proclaimed a baptism of repentance for all the people of Israel before Jesus arrived. ²⁵While John completed his ministry, he said, 'Who do you think I am? I am not the one. But one is coming after me, and I am not worthy to untie the sandals on his feet.'

²⁶"Brothers, descendants of Abraham's family, and those among you who fear God, word of this salvation has been sent to us. ²⁷For those living in Jerusalem and their rulers did not recognize him or understand the voices of the prophets, which are read every Sabbath. They fulfilled these words by judging him. ²⁸Though they found no cause worthy of death, they asked Pilate to have him killed. ²⁹When they had completed everything that was written about him, they took him down from the tree and placed him in a tomb. ³⁰But God raised him from the dead, ³¹and for many days he appeared to those who accompanied him from Galilee to Jerusalem, who are now his witnesses to the people. ³²And we proclaim to you the good news that was promised to our ancestors, ³³God has fulfilled this promise to us, who are their children, by raising Jesus as it is written in the second psalm, '*You are my Son, today I have begotten you.*' ³⁴But regarding his raising from the dead, no longer to return to decay, God has spoken in this way, '*I will give you the holy promises made to David.*' ³⁵Therefore, in another psalm he said, '*You will not let your Holy One experience corruption.*' ³⁶For David, when he had served the will of God in his own generation, died and was placed next to his fathers, and he experienced corruption. ³⁷But the one whom God raised did not experience corruption. ³⁸Therefore, let it be known to you, brothers, that through this man forgiveness of sins is declared to you. ³⁹By this man, all who believe are set free from everything from which the law of Moses could not set you free. ⁴⁰Therefore, beware that what was spoken about by the prophets does not happen to you, ⁴¹'*Look, you mockers! Be amazed and perish, because I am performing a work in your days, a work that you will never believe unless someone tells it to you.*'"

13:22 This quotation is formed from Psalm 89:20 and 1 Samuel 13:14. **13:25** This account has several similarities to John's account (John 1:19–23). *Ministry* can also mean *course of life, mission,* or *calling.* **13:26** Paul appears to be speaking directly to men. **13:29** *Tree* is a metaphor for the cross, here using the language of Deuteronomy 21:23. **13:31** Paul places significant emphasis on the eyewitnesses, implying that he has heard the testimony of some of them. **13:33** Quotation from Psalm 2:7. **13:34** Quotation from Isaiah 55:3. **13:35** Quotation from Psalm 16:10. **13:35–37** *Corruption* refers to the decay of the physical body. **13:37** Paul is emphasizing the idea that David's prophecy in Psalms cannot refer to David because David was buried and his body decayed. Instead, the prophecy must refer to Jesus, whose body did not decay in a tomb. **13:38–39** These two verses are difficult to translate into English because of some technical vocabulary and a Greek passive construction. *Set free* can also be translated as *justified,* but that language is quite strong. The meaning is closer to *deliver* or *determine that you are righteous.* Paul is discussing the merits of the law of Moses, which cannot enable a person to be free from sin, and Jesus Christ, whose sacrifice can truly render a person free from sin. The division of these two verses also reflects modern practice of dividing the Greek sentences differently. Older translations included much of verse 37 as verse 38. **13:39** The theme that the law of Moses is insufficient to save them is introduced for the first time in this verse (compare Galatians 3:23–29). **13:41** Quotation from Habakkuk 1:5. The same passage from Habakkuk is quoted differently in 3 Nephi 21:9.

⁴²When Paul and Barnabas were departing, they urged them to speak about this message on the next Sabbath. ⁴³After the meeting in the synagogue ended, many of the Jews and God-fearing proselytes, who were speaking with them and encouraging them to remain in the grace of God, followed Paul and Barnabas.

⁴⁴The next Sabbath, nearly everyone in the city gathered to hear the word of the Lord. ⁴⁵When the Jews saw the crowd, they were filled with jealousy, and while slandering, they began to contradict what was said by Paul. ⁴⁶Then Paul and Barnabas spoke boldly, saying, "It was necessary to speak the word of God to you first. We are turning now to the Gentiles because you reject it and you consider yourselves to be unworthy of eternal life. ⁴⁷For this is what the Lord commanded us, '*I have established you as a light to the Gentiles, to bring salvation to the ends of the earth.*'"

⁴⁸When the Gentiles heard this, they rejoiced and gave glory to the word of the Lord, and those who had been appointed to eternal life believed. ⁴⁹And the word of the Lord began to spread through the entire region. ⁵⁰But the Jews incited the pious women who were of high social position and the prominent men of the city. And they stirred up persecution against Paul and Barnabas and threw them out of their region. ⁵¹So they shook the dust from their feet and went to Iconium. ⁵²And the disciples were filled with joy and the Holy Spirit.

ICONIUM

14 ¹And it happened in Iconium that Paul and Barnabas entered into the Jewish synagogue and spoke in such a way that a large group of Jews and Greeks believed. ²But the Jews who would not believe stirred up the Gentiles and poisoned their minds against the brothers. ³Then they stayed there for a long time, speaking boldly about the Lord, who testified to the word of his grace, granting signs and wonders to be done by their hands. ⁴But the people of the city were divided: some were with the Jews, and some with the apostles. ⁵When there was an attempt by some Gentiles, Jews, and their rulers to abuse them and stone them, ⁶Paul and Barnabas learned of it and fled to Lystra and Derbe, cities of Lycaonia, and the surrounding region. ⁷They proclaimed the good news there.

LYSTRA AND DERBE

⁸In Lystra, a man who was not able to use his feet, who had never walked, was sitting. ⁹This man was listening to Paul speaking. And Paul looked at him and saw that he had the faith to be healed. ¹⁰So he said in a loud voice, "Stand upright on your feet." And he jumped up and began

---

13:42 *This message* is plural in Greek, but English usage prefers to describe the discourse as a single message. **13:43** The departure of the *proselytes* and their interest in following the teachings of Paul and Barnabas would indicate that they had left their course of instruction that would lead them to becoming Jews. **13:47** Quotation from Isaiah 49:6. Doctrine and Covenants 86:11 and 133:3 echo this verse. **13:48** Paul's words (*and those who had been appointed to eternal life believed*), imply that only those who had been *appointed* were able to believe. The Greek verb indicates that the appointment to eternal life occurs after one has demonstrated actions, and therefore it is not to be taken as a type of predestination or predetermined action. **13:51** The disciples were commanded to dust off their feet in Matthew 10:14; Luke 9:5.

14:2 *Poisoned their minds* is the Greek idiom *made their souls bitter*. **14:4, 14** Paul and Barnabas are referred to as *apostles* for the first time, drawing upon the general meaning of the term as *missionaries*. **14:6** *Lystra and Derbe* were Greek cities in Lycaonia, where Paul and Barnabas would encounter mostly Greek-speaking people.

walking. ¹¹When the crowd saw what Paul had done, they shouted in the language of the Lycaonians, saying, "The gods have descended among us like humans." ¹²They called Barnabas Zeus, and Paul they called Hermes because he was the lead speaker. ¹³The priest of Zeus, whose temple was just outside the city, brought bulls and garlands to the gates of the city, and together with the crowd he wanted to offer sacrifices to them. ¹⁴When the apostles Barnabas and Paul heard this, they tore their clothes and rushed into the crowd, ¹⁵saying, "Men, why are you doing these things? We are men like you and we are proclaiming the good news to you so that you may turn from these worthless things to the living God, *who made the heaven, the earth, the sea, and all things in them,* ¹⁶who in past generations permitted all nations to pursue their own ways. ¹⁷But he did not leave you without evidence of good works, providing rains from heaven and seasons of bounteous harvest, filling you with food and your hearts with joy." ¹⁸Even with these words, they barely restrained the crowd from sacrificing to them.

¹⁹But Jews came from Antioch and Iconium and persuaded the crowds, and they stoned Paul and dragged him outside the city thinking that he was dead. ²⁰But the disciples gathered around him, and he got up and went into the city. The next day he went with Barnabas to Derbe.

RETURN TRIP TO ANTIOCH

²¹After proclaiming the good news in that city and making many disciples, they returned to Lystra, Iconium, and Antioch. ²²And they strengthened the souls of the disciples, encouraging them to remain in the faith, saying, "We must enter the kingdom of God through many trials." ²³When they had appointed elders for them in each church, with prayer and fasting they entrusted them to the Lord in whom they had believed. ²⁴And they went through Pisidia and came to Pamphylia. ²⁵After speaking the word in Perga, they went down to Attalia. ²⁶From there they set sail for Antioch, where they had been set apart to the grace of God for the work which they had accomplished. ²⁷When they arrived, they gathered the church together and declared all the things that God had done with them and that God had opened a door of faith to the Gentiles. ²⁸And they stayed with the disciples for a long time.

THE JERUSALEM CONFERENCE

15 ¹Some men came down from Judea and taught the brothers, "Unless you are circumcised following the practice

---

14:12 *Zeus* was the chief god in Greek mythology, and *Hermes* was the messenger of the gods. **14:14** The tearing of clothes is an indication that Paul and Barnabas heard something they considered to be blasphemous. Their rejection of having sacrifices made to them is in contrast to Herod's acceptance of divine honors (Acts 12:20–23). **14:15** Quotation from Exodus 20:11. **14:17** Compare Romans 1:20; Alma 30:44. **14:21** *Antioch* is the city in Asia Minor referred to as Psidian Antioch and not Antioch in Syria (see verse 26). **14:22** Paul here begins developing the idea that persecution attends belief. This will become a significant part of his message (1 Corinthians 4:9; Philippians 1:29). **14:23** The appointment of *elders* in the churches follows the pattern of elders in Jewish communities. These elders would have been older members of the congregation who attended to its spiritual needs. **14:26** Paul and Barnabas had been *set apart* to do a specific work, which is now completed. This verse, together with Acts 13:2, establishes the idea of being *set apart* to do the work of God.

15:1–29 These verses describe the first known council meeting of the church in Jerusalem in which the early saints met to discuss matters of religious practice. **15:1** The Jewish saints insisted that Gentile believers observe some requirements of the law of Moses, with a particular emphasis on circumcision (Genesis 17:9–14).

of Moses, you will not be saved." [2]After Paul and Barnabas had a lively debate with them, they appointed Paul and Barnabas and some others from among them to meet with the apostles and elders in Jerusalem about this disagreement. [3]Then they were sent out by the church, and as they traveled through Phoenicia and Samaria they related the conversion of the Gentiles, and they brought great joy to all the brothers and sisters. [4]When they arrived in Jerusalem, they were received by the church, the apostles, and the elders, and they related all things that God had done with them. [5]But some who were from the sect of the Pharisees who believed stood and said, "The Gentiles must be circumcised and ordered to observe the law of Moses."

[6]The apostles and elders gathered to consider this issue. [7]After considerable debate, Peter stood and said to them, "Brothers, you know that some time ago, God made a choice among you and determined that by my mouth the Gentiles might hear the gospel message and believe. [8]God, who knows the heart, has testified to them by giving them the Holy Spirit just as he gave it to us, [9]and he made no distinction between us and them, purifying their hearts by faith. [10]Now, why are you trying God by placing a burden on the neck of the disciples, a burden that neither our ancestors nor we have been able to bear? [11]But by the grace of the Lord Jesus, we believe that we are saved just as they will be saved."

15:2 Luke describes the Jerusalem church as being organized with *apostles and elders*. The early days of the church were characterized by a small number of leaders that were described as missionaries (*apostles*), those who oversaw the ordinances and religious needs of the church (*elders*), and deacons who cared for the physical needs of the members. The parallel to this story appears to be Galatians 2:1–10 (it is possible that Galatians 2:1–10 describes the events of Acts 11:30). **15:3** The Greek text reports only *brothers*, but it is used generically here to describe all believers in Christ. *Conversion* represents the Greek noun *to turn toward*. Accepting the message of Christ is here described as a conversion toward the new faith. This might result from the idea that it describes the actions of Gentiles, who were viewed as leaving their old worldview and beliefs behind and were now *turning toward* a new faith. Such a strong word may not have been used to describe ethnic Jews who began to accept Christ. **15:5** The Greek omits *the Gentiles* and notes only *they*. The requirement set forth by the Pharisees, however, was for the new Gentile converts. **15:6** This verse establishes key precedents for how matters were resolved in the early church. A problem was presented to the leaders in Jerusalem, and two opposing views were presented, both by believing groups in the church. As a result, the *apostles* and *elders* gathered together. The Greek notes literally that they gathered *to see to the matter*. The primary meaning of the verb is that they intended to *look at* and *become acquainted with* the issue at hand. In the following verses, Peter and Jacob (Jesus's younger sibling, see Mark 6:3) address the audience. **15:7** *The gospel message* comes from the Greek *the word of the gospel*. **15:7, 13** Peter appears to have been speaking to an assembly of men only, and hence *brothers*. **15:8** Peter here refers to the outpouring of the Spirit at Pentecost on the Jewish believers as well as the outpouring of the Spirit on Gentile believers (Acts 2:1–4; Acts 13:48–52). **15:9, 11** These verses serve as the basis for the early church's approach to ethnic diversity in preaching the gospel. No limitations were placed on the preaching of the gospel or on who might be accepted in full fellowship. Compare Acts 8:26–39, where Philip teaches the Ethiopian eunuch. *Ethiopian* was understood to refer to someone with black skin. **15:10** *Burden* is literally the wooden yoke placed on draft animals that enabled them to be fitted with a harness to pull wagons or plows. This yoke is mentioned figuratively as a restraint that was difficult to carry. **15:11** This early notion of salvation *by the grace of the Lord Jesus* is an important step in articulating how believers are saved through Jesus. The word *grace* used here means *an act of loving kindness, an act of mercy, a gift from God*, or *something that affords joy and pleasure*. Therefore, the meaning is close to *saved by God's loving act of kindness*.

¹²The whole gathering kept quiet and listened to Barnabas and Paul as they explained all the miraculous signs and wonders that God had done through them among the Gentiles. ¹³When they were silent, Jacob responded, "My brothers, listen to me. ¹⁴Simon has described how at first God sought to choose a people for his name from the Gentiles. ¹⁵The words of the prophets agree with this, as it is written, ¹⁶*After this I will return, and I will build again the fallen tabernacle of David. I will build it again from ruins and restore it* ¹⁷*so that the rest of humanity may seek the Lord and all the Gentiles who are called by my name, says the Lord, who makes things* ¹⁸*known from long ago.'*

¹⁹"Therefore, I determine that we should cause no additional difficulty for the Gentiles who turn to God. ²⁰But we should write to them, telling them to abstain from foods defiled by idols, from sexual impropriety, from what has been strangled, and from blood. ²¹For Moses from generations of old has had those who declare him in every city when he is read in the synagogues each Sabbath."

THE DECISION OF THE CONFERENCE

²²Then the apostles, elders, and the entire church decided to send men chosen from among them to Antioch with Paul and Barnabas, men who were leaders among the brothers, Judas called Barsabbas and Silas, ²³writing by their hand, "*The apostles and elders, your brothers, to the Gentile brothers and sisters in Antioch, Syria, and Cilicia, greetings.* ²⁴*Because we have heard that some whom we did not command went out from among us and confused you with words, troubling your minds,* ²⁵*we have decided unitedly to choose men and send them to you with our beloved Barnabas and Paul,* ²⁶*men who have risked their lives for the name of Lord Jesus Christ.* ²⁷*Therefore, we are sending Judas and Silas to you, who will declare to you the same things in person.* ²⁸*For it seemed good to the Holy Spirit and to us not to place any greater burden on you than these directives:* ²⁹*to abstain from what*

15:13 This is Jacob the brother of Jesus (Matthew 13:55; Mark 6:3). **15:14** Jacob used an Aramaic form of Peter's name (*Simeon*), rendered here using the more familiar *Simon*. **15:16** *Tabernacle* refers to David's kingdom, monarchy, or house in a general sense. **15:16–17** Quotation from Amos 9:11–12. Amos's prophecy is drawn upon to declare the idea that God had always planned on the salvation of Gentiles. **15:17** *The rest of humanity* translates the Greek phrase *the remainder of the people*. **15:18** Allusion to Isaiah 45:21. **15:19** The word translated as *difficulty* can also mean *trouble*. Jacob is declaring circumcision and the full kosher standards to be a *difficulty*. **15:20** *Foods* is not specified in the text, but the issue is the consumption of meat that was sacrificed to a pagan deity where a portion of the animal was offered in sacrifice and the remaining parts were sold in a meat market. Christians could inadvertently purchase meat that was offered as part of a pagan sacrifice, and Jacob condemns consuming such meat. The condemnation of *sexual impropriety* reflects the Greek abstract concept *porneia*, which describes all sexual misconduct. The call to abstain from *what has been strangled* reflects a concern with the way that animals were butchered (Leviticus 17:13–14). Kosher guidelines called for butchering by draining the blood of an animal, and therefore Jacob calls on Gentiles to be aware of the way that animals were butchered before consuming them (Leviticus 3:17). **15:22** *Antioch* in this verse is the one in Syria (not Psidian Antioch). *Silas* is the same person as *Silvanus* (2 Corinthians 1:19; 1 Thessalonians 1:1; 2 Thessalonians 1:1). **15:23** Greek uses the generic *brothers* to refer to *brother and sisters*. **15:23–29** The structure of these verses represents a copy of a private letter sent by the church in Jerusalem to the Gentile members of the church in Antioch, Syria, and Cilicia. They are presented as a quotation of an actual letter. **15:24** The Greek idiom is *troubling your souls*. Some significantly later manuscripts add a phrase to this verse: *telling them to be circumcised and keep the Law*. **15:28** *Directives* translates a Greek word meaning

has been offered in animal sacrifices, from blood, from things strangled, and from sexual impropriety. If you obey these directives, you will do well. Farewell."

³⁰Then when they were dismissed, they went down to Antioch, and after assembling the group, they delivered the letter. ³¹After reading it out loud, the saints rejoiced in its comforting message. ³²Both Judas and Silas, who were both prophets, strengthened and encouraged the brothers and sisters with many words, ³³and after spending some time with them, they were sent off in peace by the brothers to those who sent them. ³⁵But Paul and Barnabas stayed in Antioch and taught, declaring with many others the good news of the word of the Lord.

PAUL AND BARNABAS GO THEIR SEPARATE WAYS

³⁶After a few days, Paul said to Barnabas, "Let us return to visit the brothers and sisters in every town where we declared the word of the Lord and determine how they are." ³⁷But Barnabas wanted to take John called Mark with them. ³⁸And Paul insisted that they not take him with them because he left them in Pamphylia and had not traveled with them in the work. ³⁹There was such a strong disagreement that they separated from one another, and Barnabas took Mark and sailed to Cyprus, ⁴⁰and Paul chose Silas and set out, and after commending the brothers and sisters to the grace of the Lord, ⁴¹he traveled through Syria and Cilicia, strengthening the churches.

TIMOTHY TRAVELS WITH PAUL— PAUL'S SECOND MISSION

16 ¹Paul went down to Derbe and Lystra, and a disciple named Timothy was there, the son of a Jewish woman of faith, but his father was Greek. ²And he was favorably spoken of by the brothers and sisters in Lystra and Iconium. ³Paul wanted Timothy to go with him, and he

necessary things. Compare Paul's discussion of this issue in 1 Corinthians 8:1–11:1. **15:32** Greek uses the generic *brothers* to refer to *brothers and sisters.* **15:34** Some late and inferior manuscripts add a verse here, indicating *But Silas decided to stay with them.* This spurious verse was likely added to make sense of Silas being chosen by Paul because verse 33 implies that Silas had returned to Jerusalem. **15:36** See verse 32 for a note on *brothers.* **15:38** See Acts 13:13 for John Mark's departure. **15:39** See Galatians 2:11–14 for Paul's comments about Barnabas. **15:40** See verse 32 for a note on *brothers.*

16:1 *Timothy* was a consistent traveling companion of Paul's, and later Paul wrote two personal letters to him (1–2 Timothy). Compare 1 Thessalonians 1:1; Philippians 1:1; 2:19–22; Philemon 1:1. His mother's name was Eunice (2 Timothy 1:5). **16:2** Greek uses the generic *brothers* to refer to *brothers and sisters.* **16:3** Paul's decision to have Timothy be circumcised was a result of the consideration that if a person had a Jewish mother, that person was considered to be Jewish and therefore was required to be circumcised. Luke

Paul's Second Mission
Map by Brandon Whitney, ThinkSpatial, BYU Geography

took him and circumcised him because of the Jews who were in those regions, for they all knew that his father was Greek. [4]As they went through the towns, they delivered to them the decrees for the Gentile believers to obey that had been decided upon by the apostles and elders in Jerusalem. [5]Therefore, the churches were strengthened in the faith and were growing in number daily.

PAUL'S VISION OF THE MAN FROM MACEDONIA

[6]They went through the region of Phrygia and Galatia, having been forbidden by the Holy Spirit to speak the word in Asia. [7]Then they came up to Mysia, and they tried to go into Bithynia, but the Spirit of Jesus did not permit them to do so. [8]And they passed through Mysia and came down to Troas. [9]A vision appeared to Paul in the night, and a Macedonian man stood and called to him, saying, "Travel to Macedonia and help us." [10]After he saw the vision, we sought to go into Macedonia right away, determining that

God had called us to declare the good news to them.

LYDIA'S CONVERSION

[11]We set sail from Troas and sailed directly to Samothrace, and the next day to the city of Neapolis [12]and from there to Philippi, which was a leading city of that part of Macedonia and a Roman colony. We stayed in that city for several days. [13]On the Sabbath day we went outside the city gate near a river that we thought to be a place of prayer, and we sat down and began to speak to the women who were assembled. [14]A woman named Lydia, who sold purple cloth from the city of Thyatira and who feared God, listened. The Lord opened her heart to respond to what Paul was saying. [15]After she and her household were baptized, she encouraged us, saying, "If you deem me to be faithful to the Lord, come to my house and stay." And she persuaded us.

---

may have included this story to highlight the differing practices for ethnic Jews who believed and ethnic Gentiles who believed, for whom circumcision would not be required. One of the major questions at the Jerusalem council was to seek a resolution regarding whether ethnic Gentiles needed circumcision. **16:4** This is the first time that Luke has spoken of *dogma*, translated as *decrees*, in Acts. The term represents the legal decisions or decrees of government and hence has a legally binding status for believers. The *decrees* spoken of here are those decided upon in Acts 15:28–29. **16:6** Luke's description of them being *forbidden to speak the word* implies that they were forbidden to teach openly. The regions mentioned in the verse indicate that Paul was traveling northwest. **16:7** Some very late and inferior manuscripts omit *of Jesus*. The *Spirit of Jesus* is used interchangeably with *the Spirit of the Lord*, and it shows that Luke thought of them in similar ways. **16:9** Compare 2 Corinthians 2:12. **16:10** *We sought*: this is the first passage from Acts written in the first-person plural *we*, suggesting that the author of Acts was present when this event took place. At several points in the story, Luke uses *we* or *us* to describe Paul's travels (for example, see Acts 20:5–15; 21:1–18; 27:1–28:16). It may also have been used as a literary device without the intended consequence of telling the reader that Luke was present. **16:12** The designation of *Philippi* as a *Roman colony* signifies that its inhabitants were Roman citizens who likely spoke Latin (and Greek). The colonies had high populations of former soldiers, and under Caesar Augustus the number of Roman citizens living in the colonies was increased. Paul appears to have preferred visiting Roman colonies, perhaps because of their large populations. Corinth and Troas, both second mission cities, were Roman colonies. **16:13** The note that they went out on the *Sabbath* to a place designated for prayers signals a Jewish audience, which in this case was exclusively female. **16:14** *Purple cloth* was expensive to produce. Some markers in the story indicate that Lydia was wealthy.

THE IMPRISONMENT OF PAUL

[16]As we went to the place of prayer, a slave girl met us who had a spirit of divination, and she brought significant wealth to her owners by fortune-telling. [17]She followed Paul and us and cried out, "These men are servants of the Most High God, who proclaim to you the way of salvation." [18]She did this for many days, but Paul began to be annoyed, and after turning around he said to the spirit, "I command you in the name of Jesus Christ to come out of her." And the spirit left at that moment. [19]When her owners saw that the hope for their income was gone, they seized Paul and Silas and took them to the marketplace before the rulers. [20]And they brought them to the magistrates and said, "These men are Jews, and they are troubling our city. [21]They declare customs that are not lawful for us to receive or practice because we are Romans."

[22]And the crowd arose together against them, and the magistrates tore the clothing from Paul and Silas and commanded them to be beaten with sticks. [23]And after receiving many blows, they threw them into prison and gave the jailor an order to securely guard them. [24]When he received this order, he put them in the inner cell and bound their feet.

[25]In the middle of the night, Paul and Silas were praying and singing hymns to God, and the prisoners were listening to them, [26]and suddenly a large earthquake occurred so that the foundations of the prison were shaken, and all the doors were opened, and their bands were undone. [27]And the jailor woke up, and when he saw the prison doors opened, he drew his sword and intended to kill himself because he thought the prisoners had fled. [28]But Paul cried out in a loud voice, "Do not harm yourself, for we are all here." [29]So he asked for a light and went in and fell down at the feet of Paul and Silas, trembling. [30]Then he brought them out and asked, "Sirs, what must I do to be saved?" [31]They answered, "Believe in the Lord Jesus, and you and your house will be saved." [32]And they taught him the word of the Lord and to all who were in his household. [33]He took them in at that hour of the night, and he bathed their wounds, and he and all his family were baptized right away. [34]He brought them into his house and put food in front of them, and he rejoiced with all his household that he believed in God.

[35]When day came, the magistrates sent their officers, saying, "Release those men." [36]And the jailor related these words to Paul, "The magistrates have sent an order that you may be released. Now go out in peace." [37]But Paul responded to them, "They beat us publicly and uncondemned, even though we are Roman citizens, and they threw us into prison; now they want to send us away privately? No, let them come themselves and release us." [38]Then the officers told the magistrates these words, and they were afraid when they heard that they were Romans. [39]And they went and apologized to them and brought them out and asked them repeatedly to leave the city. [40]They left the prison and entered the house of Lydia, and when they saw the brothers and sisters, they comforted them and then departed.

16:16 Her ability to divine and tell fortunes is connected to pagan worship practices. The Greek says literally that she had the spirit of Python, the snake god associated with Delphi. **16:22–23** Paul may have been referring to this event in 2 Corinthians 11:23, 25. **16:31** Paul's encouragement to *believe in the Lord Jesus* lays the foundation for a person who desires to be baptized. Some later manuscripts read *believe in the Lord Jesus Christ*. **16:37** The beating of Paul without a trial was illegal, and Paul was ready to pursue a formal complaint against the magistrates of the city. Paul notes that he was a Roman citizen. As such, he would have had specific rights when he was accused of a crime. Citizens were guaranteed a trial and better treatment than noncitizens. **16:40** Greek uses *brothers* generically to refer to brothers and sisters.

PAUL IN THESSALONICA AND BEROEA

17 [1]After they traveled through Amphipolis and Apollonia, they came to Thessalonica, where there was a Jewish synagogue. [2]As was custom for Paul, he entered the synagogue, and on three Sabbath days he discussed the scriptures with them, [3]explaining and demonstrating that the Messiah had to suffer and to arise again from the dead, saying, "This Jesus is the Messiah, whom I am proclaiming to you." [4]Some of them were convinced and joined Paul and Silas, together with a large group of God-fearing Greeks and a significant number of prominent women. [5]But the Jews were jealous and gathered some rabble from the marketplace, and they formed a mob and initiated a riot in the city. They attacked Jason's house, trying to find Paul and Silas to bring them to the town council. [6]When they did not find them, they dragged Jason and some brothers to the city administrators, shouting, "These men who put the world into commotion have come here too, [7]and Jason has welcomed them. They all oppose Caesar's decrees, saying there is another king who is named Jesus." [8]They stirred up the crowd and the city rulers when they heard these things. [9]And they took a deposit of money from Jason and the others and then released them.

BEROEA

[10]The brothers immediately sent Paul and Silas to Beroea during the night. When they arrived, they went to the Jewish synagogue. [11]They were more receptive than those in Thessalonica, for they willingly received the message, studying the scriptures carefully every day to determine if these things were so. [12]Therefore, many of them believed, and a considerable number of prominent Greek women and men believed. [13]But when the Jews from Thessalonica knew that the word of God was proclaimed by Paul in Beroea, they went there also, inciting and stirring up the crowds. [14]The brothers immediately sent Paul to travel to the sea, but Silas and Timothy remained there. [15]Those who traveled with Paul, led him as far as Athens, and after receiving a command for Silas and Timothy to come to him quickly, they departed.

PAUL PREACHES IN ATHENS

[16]While Paul waited for them in Athens, his spirit was troubled because he saw the city was full of idols. [17]Therefore, he taught the Jews and the God-fearers in the synagogue, and he taught in the marketplace every day with those who happened to be there. [18]And some Epicureans and Stoic philosophers were conferring with him, and some said, "What does this foolish

---

17:2 Echoed in Doctrine and Covenants 68:1. **17:3** The Greek word translated as *Messiah* is *Christos*, usually translated as Christ. Because English speakers tend to understand Christ as a name instead of a title, the translation attempts to reflect the emphasis of the discussion. Those in the synagogue were discussing whether the *Messiah* would need to suffer and be resurrected. **17:4** *God-fearing* is used as a technical term to refer to Gentiles (Greeks) who have agreed to follow the law of Moses but who have remained unwilling to accept circumcision. **17:5** The *town council* was a gathering of prominent citizens in a Greek city that judged civic and other matters relating to citizens living in that city. **17:7** The vague charge of acting against *Caesar's decrees* appears to be a general challenge that Paul was acting against Roman sovereignty. **17:10–11** These cities were on the Via Egnatia, a large and well-traveled Roman road that connected the Adriatic Sea to Byzantium. **17:11** *Receptive* translates a Greek word that means *well-born* or *noble*. The issue here, however, is not birth status but their willingness to accept the teachings of Paul and Silas. Luke may have intended something close to *good-natured*. **17:17** *He taught* can also be translated as *he reasoned* or *he argued*. **17:18** The *Epicureans* were a philosophical school dedicated to the teachings of Epicurus (ca. 300 BCE). They rejected traditional notions about God, the afterlife,

show-off want to say?" Others said, "He seems to be a teacher of foreign deities." (They said this because he proclaimed Jesus and the resurrection.) ¹⁹And they took him and brought him to the Areopagus, saying, "Can we know what this new teaching is that you are offering? ²⁰For you are bringing some strange things for us to hear. Therefore, we want to know what these things mean." ²¹(All the Athenians and the foreigners who lived there spent their time in nothing else except telling or listening to something new.)

²²So Paul stood in the Areopagus and said, "Athenians, I perceive that you are very religious in all things. ²³As I passed through and considered your objects of worship, I found an altar on which had been written 'To the unknown god.' Therefore, what is unknown to you in worship, this I declare to you. ²⁴God, the creator of the world and everything in it, the Lord of heaven and earth, does not live in temples made with hands, ²⁵nor is he served by human hands, as though he needed something, since he gives life and breath to all things and to everyone. ²⁶He also made all people of the human race to live over all the earth from one person, having determined beforehand their set times and the boundaries where they would live ²⁷so that they might seek for God and perhaps feel for him and find him, although he is not far from each one of us. ²⁸For we live in him and move and exist, even as some of your poets have said, 'For we are also his offspring.' ²⁹Therefore, being the children of God, we should not think deity is like gold, silver, stone, or an image made by the skill and imagination of mankind. ³⁰God has overlooked the times of ignorance and now commands all men and women everywhere to repent, ³¹because he set a day on which he intends to judge the world in righteousness, by a man whom he ordained, and he has given an assurance of this to all by raising him from the dead."

³²When they heard about the resurrection of the dead, some mocked, but others said, "We will hear you again on this." ³³So Paul left them, ³⁴but some men joined him and believed, among whom were Dionysus the Areopagite and a woman named Damaris, among others.

PAUL IN CORINTH

18 ¹After these things, Paul departed from Athens and came to Corinth, ²and he met a Jew named Aquila, of Pontus by birth, who recently came from Italy

and punishment. They pursued the ultimate goal of pleasure, which was obtained through modest living and limiting the pursuit of physical desires. The Stoics were founded on the teachings of Zeno (died 270 BCE), and they taught that the ultimate goal of life was the pursuit of virtue. They sought to overcome the natural urge to become enslaved to desires and passions, and instead to pursue a life of balance and virtue. *Foolish show-off* is literally a *seed picker*. **17:19** The *Areopagus* was a council that met in the marketplace to decide religious and cultural matters relating to the city of Athens. A small rocky outcrop near the Parthenon in Athens has been designated as the *Areopagus*, but the word refers to the council, which may have met near the rocky outcrop. **17:22** *Athenians* in Greek is *Men of Athens*. The phrase is used generically to refer to those in attendance at his sermon. **17:26** The *one person* refers to Adam. Some inferior manuscripts read *the blood of one man*. **17:28** This quotation is from the poet Aratus (died ca. 245 BCE) and his work titled the Phaenomena. The phrase beginning *we live in him* is thought to come from the poet Epimenides of Crete. This verse is alluded to in Doctrine and Covenants 45:1. **17:29** *Children of God* can also be translated as *offspring of God*. **17:30** Compare 3 Nephi 11:32. Greek uses the generic *brothers* in place of *brothers and sisters*. **17:31** The word translated as ordained also means *appointed* or *designated*. The *Areopagite* refers to a member of the Areopagus.

18:2 Claudius was the emperor between 41 and 54 CE. Luke notes that Paul *found* Aquila, although the English verb *met* better represents the situation described in this verse. *Pontus* was a Roman province in

with Priscilla, his wife, because Claudius had expelled all the Jews from Rome. Paul came to them ³because they were of the same occupation, and he remained with them and worked. They were tentmakers by trade. ⁴He reasoned in the synagogue every Sabbath, attempting to persuade both the Jews and Greeks.

⁵When Silas and Timothy came down from Macedonia, Paul was occupied with the word, witnessing to the Jews that Jesus is the Christ. ⁶When they opposed and slandered him, he shook out his clothes and said to them, "Your blood is upon your own heads. I am clean. From now on I will go to the Gentiles." ⁷And he departed from there and came to the house of a man named Titius Justus, a man who worshipped God. His house was adjacent to the synagogue. ⁸And Crispus, the leader of the synagogue, believed in the Lord with his entire household, and many among the Corinthians listened and believed and were baptized.

⁹The Lord said to Paul in a night vision, "Do not fear, but continue speaking and do not be silent, ¹⁰because I am with you, and no one will hurt you or do you harm because I have many people in this city." ¹¹And he continued teaching the word of God among them for eighteen months.

PAUL ARRAIGNED BEFORE GALLIO

¹²While Gallio was the proconsul of Achaia, the Jews attacked Paul and brought him to the judgment seat, ¹³saying, "This man is persuading people to worship God contrary to the law." ¹⁴But Paul was about to open his mouth when Gallio said to the Jews, "If this were a matter of a crime or wicked villainy, O Jews, I would have been justified in accepting your complaint. ¹⁵But since it is a debate about a word and names and your law, look into it yourselves. I do not desire to be a judge of these things." ¹⁶And he drove them away from the judgment seat. ¹⁷And they all seized Sosthenes, the ruler of the synagogue, and beat him in front of the judgment seat. But Gallio was not concerned about these things.

PAUL RETURNS TO ANTIOCH IN SYRIA

¹⁸After this, Paul remained for many days in Corinth and then took leave of the

---

Asia Minor on the southern shores of the Black Sea. Claudius's expulsion of Jews from Rome is noted by the Roman historian Suetonius, but the date of the edict is uncertain. See 1 Corinthians 16:19 for further reference to the work of Aquila and Priscilla (in Paul's letters she is called *Prisca*). **18:3** *Tentmakers* would work in canvas and leather and probably canvas awnings and other products for shade in the marketplaces and elsewhere. See 1 Thessalonians 2:9 for Paul's thoughts on working with his own hands. **18:4** *The Greeks* refers to God-fearing Greeks who attended synagogue and accepted many of the tenets of Judaism. **18:5** Some inferior manuscripts read *in the Spirit* in place of *with the word*. **18:6** See Nehemiah 5:13 for a parallel to the shaking off one's clothing as a sign. Doctrine and Covenants 24:15 contains instructions on the practice. Jacob 1:19 greatly expands the meaning of this verse. **18:7** Some good manuscripts omit the name *Titius*, but the manuscript evidence seems to indicate that *Titius* was original. **18:8** Paul baptized Crispus (1 Corinthians 1:14). **18:10** Doctrine and Covenants 100:3 echoes this verse. **18:12** Based on an inscription found at Delphi, Gallio's tenure can be fixed with relative certainty (51–52 CE). Paul was probably arraigned before Gallio in summer to fall of 51 CE. A *proconsul* was responsible for ruling over a Roman province, much like a modern governor. Lucius Junius Gallio Annaeanus was proconsul of Achaia, 51–52 CE. **18:18** The *vow* was a Nazarite vow. Part of the vow required the individual to shave the head and at the conclusion of the vow to once again shave the head and have the hair burned on the altar of the temple (Acts 21:24). Numbers 6:1–21 provides a description of the practice. There remains some question of whether this was a Nazarite vow because Paul was not in Jerusalem when he first shaved his head.

brothers and sisters and sailed for Syria. And Priscilla and Aquila were with him. At Cenchrea he cut his hair, for he had taken a vow. ¹⁹And they came down to Ephesus, and he left them there, but he went into the synagogue and reasoned with the Jews. ²⁰And they asked him to stay longer with them, but he declined. ²¹And he departed, telling them, "I will return to you if God is willing." And he set sail from Ephesus. ²²He arrived at Caesarea, and he went up and greeted the church, and then he went down to Antioch. ²³And he spent some time there and departed and went through the region of Galatia and Phrygia, strengthening all the disciples.

APOLLOS TEACHES IN EPHESUS

²⁴A Jew named Apollos, born in Alexandria, a well-spoken man, capable in the scriptures, went down to Ephesus. ²⁵He had been instructed in the Way of the Lord, and lively in the Spirit he spoke and taught the things about Jesus accurately, although he knew only the baptism of John. ²⁶He began to speak boldly in the synagogue, and Priscilla and Aquila heard him, so they took him aside and explained to him more accurately the Way of God. ²⁷He wanted to travel through Achaia, and the brothers encouraged him and wrote to the disciples to receive him. When he arrived, he greatly helped those who had believed through grace, ²⁸for he refuted the Jews powerfully in public, showing through the scriptures that the Christ is Jesus.

PAUL TRAVELS TO EPHESUS—PAUL'S THIRD MISSION

19 ¹While Apollos was in Corinth, Paul passed through the interior regions and came to Ephesus, where he found some disciples ²and he said to them, "Did you received the Holy Spirit when you believed?" They replied, "We have not even heard that there is a Holy Spirit." ³He said, "Into what were you baptized?" They answered, "Into John's baptism." ⁴Then Paul said, "John baptized with a baptism of repentance, telling the people to believe in the one who followed after him; that is, in Jesus." ⁵When they heard this they were

---

18:21 Some manuscripts add *I must by all means keep this feast that is coming in Jerusalem*, but the manuscripts that support it are late and inferior. **18:22** This verse signals the end of Paul's second major missionary journey. Verse 23 describes events prior to Paul's third major journey, which commences in Acts 19:1. See map. **18:24** Doctrines and Covenants 100:11 may allude to this verse. **18:25–26** *The Way* in these verses refer to Christianity. **18:27** *Through grace* signifies that their faith was received through the gift of God.

19:1 Paul's visit to Ephesus was in response to Apollos's teaching there and Apollos's lack of knowledge about the Holy Spirit. **19:3** When Paul asks *into what were you baptized*, the intent of the question might be better reflected in English as *why were you baptized*. However, Paul may have intended to highlight the fact that they were being baptized *into the Holy Spirit*.

Paul's Third Mission
Map by Brandon Whitney, ThinkSpatial, BYU Geography

baptized in the name of the Lord Jesus, [6]and Paul laid his hands on them, and the Holy Spirit came upon them, and they spoke in tongues and prophesied. [7]There were about twelve of them.

[8]He entered the synagogue and spoke boldly for three months, reasoning and persuading them about the kingdom of God. [9]When some were hardened and refused to believe and spoke evil of the Way before the multitude, he left them and took the disciples with him. So he taught them every day in the lecture hall of Tyrannus. [10]This happened for two years so that all who lived in Asia heard the word of the Lord, both Jews and Greeks.

THE SONS OF SCEVA

[11]God was performing extraordinary miracles by Paul's hands [12]so that when handkerchiefs or aprons that had touched him were brought to the sick, their illnesses left them and the evil spirits departed from them. [13]Some traveling Jewish exorcists called on the name of the Lord for those who were possessed by evil spirits, saying, "I command you by Jesus whom Paul preaches." [14]There were seven sons of a Jewish high priest named Sceva who were doing this. [15]But the evil spirit replied to them, "I know Jesus, and I am acquainted with Paul, but who are you?" [16]The man in whom there was an evil spirit jumped upon sons of Sceva and overpowered them so that they fled from the house naked and wounded. [17]This was known to all the Jews and Greeks who lived in Ephesus, and fear fell upon them, and the name of the Lord Jesus was praised. [18]Many of those who believed came forward, confessing and making their actions known. [19]Many of those who practiced magic gathered their books and burned them publicly. When they added up the price of them, they were worth fifty thousand silver coins. [20]In this way the word of God was increasing in power and prevailed.

[21]When these things were finished, Paul determined to go to Jerusalem after having passed through Macedonia and Achaia, saying, "After I go there, I must also see Rome." [22]He sent two of those serving with him, Timothy and Erastus, to Macedonia, but he stayed for a while in Asia.

THE RIOT IN EPHESUS

[23]It happened at that time that there was a significant commotion about the Way. [24]For a man named Demetrius, a silversmith, made silver replicas of the temple

---

19:9 Luke mentions the *lecture hall of Tyrannus* as though his readers would recognize it. Nothing is known of the lecture hall or of Tyrannus. *The Way* is a technical name for *Christianity*. **19:10** *Asia* refers to the Roman province of Asia located in modern Turkey. **19:12** *Handkerchiefs* were used for wiping away perspiration, and *aprons* were used by servants and workers who worked in the fields and orchards. The latter was a narrow apron used to protect the clothing. **19:18** *Confessing* translates a semi-technical term that means to *declare* or *swear an oath*. The word often appears in legal contracts, and here the persons *confessing* their actions are doing so formally and openly. **19:19** *Fifty thousand silver coins*, or drachmae, represent a considerable amount of money, more than most day laborers would earn for several years of work. A precise cost comparison is difficult to determine because pay varied according to occupation, age, sex, and locale. **19:21** *Paul determined* is a Greek idiom that literally states *Paul proposed in the spirit*. **19:22** For Timothy's visits to Corinth, see 1 Corinthians 4:17; 16:10. Erastus is noted in Romans 16:23. **19:23** *The Way* refers to Christianity, and the group of believers continued to be designated by this term for some time (see Acts 9:2; 11:26; 24:14, 22). It appears that the title *Christian* was slow to catch on. **19:24** *Artemis* (Diana in Roman mythology) was the goddess of the hunt and was worshipped at Ephesus in a temple that was considered to be one of the seven wonders of the ancient world. Very little of the temple has survived, but at one time it was an enormous and impressive structure.

of Artemis, and he brought a significant amount of business to the craftsmen. ²⁵He gathered them together with the workers in similar trades, and said, "Men, you know that our wealth comes by this work. ²⁶And you see and hear that not only in Ephesus but in nearly all of Asia, this Paul has persuaded and turned away a large crowd by saying that the gods made by hands are not gods. ²⁷There is danger that our business will fall into disregard but also that the temple of the great goddess Artemis will be considered to be nothing, and the goddess whom all Asia and the world worship is about to be brought down."

²⁸When they heard this, they were filled with wrath, and they cried out, saying, "Great is Artemis of the Ephesians." ²⁹And the entire city was filled with commotion, and they ran together into the theater, and they seized Gaius and Aristarchus, Macedonians and fellow travelers with Paul. ³⁰When Paul wanted to enter the public assembly, the disciples would not let him. ³¹Some provincial authorities who were his friends, sent a message and called on him to not enter the theater. ³²Some were crying out for one thing, and some for another. For the assembly was confused, and the majority did not understand why they had come together. ³³From among the crowd, the Jews put Alexander forward, and Alexander motioned with his hand and desired to make a speech to the public assembly. ³⁴But when they knew that he was a Jew, they cried out in a single voice for about two hours, "Great is Artemis of the Ephesians!" ³⁵And the city clerk quieted the crowd and said, "Men of Ephesus, who does not know that the city of Ephesus is the guardian of the temple of the great Artemis and of her image that fell from the sky? ³⁶Therefore, because these things are undeniable, you must keep quiet and do nothing rashly. ³⁷For you have brought these men here, and they are not temple robbers nor blasphemers of our goddess. ³⁸If therefore Demetrius and those with him have a complaint against someone, then the courts are open and there are proconsuls. Let them bring charges against one another in that setting. ³⁹If you seek after other matters, it will have to be resolved in the legal assembly. ⁴⁰For we are in danger of being accused of rioting today because there is no reason we can give to account for this commotion." ⁴¹After he said this, he dismissed the gathering.

MACEDONIA AND GREECE

20 ¹After the disturbance ceased, Paul sent for the disciples, and when he

19:25 Conversion to Christianity has financial implications for those who accept the message (see Acts 16:16–21). 19:29 This theater still stands today and holds approximately 25,000 spectators. *Gaius* (Romans 16:23; 1 Corinthians 1:14) and *Aristarchus* (Colossians 4:10; Philemon 1:24) are both known from Paul's other letters. 19:30 Paul wanted to go before the people, but Luke uses a word that implies that Paul wanted to come before the official tribunal that convened to consider the business of the city. It appears that Paul wanted to appeal for a legal remedy to the mob action developing against him and his traveling companions. 19:31 The *provincial authorities* were in charge of public games and other civic events. They had considerable authority in the region. 19:33 Alexander is not referred to as a Christian, and it may be that the crowd has confused Christians and Jews. 19:35 It is uncertain whether men and women were part of the congregation and whether Luke used *men* in this verse to describe both men and women in the crowd. The possibility that this was a formal public assembly suggests that *men* only were in attendance. The *clerk* is literally the city scribe, who recorded the legal documents and city business. 19:38 The city clerk encourages the mob to pursue formal charges against Paul and his fellow travelers and not to act against them as a mob. This restraint was a great blessing to the early traveling missionaries.

20:1 The region of *Macedonia* includes the cities of Thessalonica, Philippi, Amphipolis, and some other areas from his second missionary journey.

had encouraged them and took leave of them, he departed for Macedonia. ²After he went through those parts and encouraged them with many words, he came to Greece, ³where he stayed three months. Because the Jews had developed a plot against him as he was intending to travel to Syria, he decided to return through Macedonia. ⁴And Sopater, son of Pyrrhus from Beroea; Aristarchus and Secundus from Thessalonica; Gaius from Derbe; and Timothy, Tychicus, and Trophimus from Asia accompanied Paul. ⁵They all went ahead and waited for us in Troas. ⁶We set sail from Philippi after the days of Unleavened Bread, and within five days we came to them in Troas, where we stayed for seven days.

⁷On the first day of the week, when we gathered to break bread, Paul began to speak to them, and because he intended to depart the next day, he continued the speech until midnight. ⁸There were many lamps in the upper room where we were meeting. ⁹And a young man named Eutychus was sitting upon a window ledge, and he was weighed down by a deep sleep while Paul continued for a long time.

As sleep overcame him, he fell down from the third story, and he was taken up dead. ¹⁰Paul went down and bent over him, and while embracing Eutychus he said, "Do not be alarmed; his life is in him." ¹¹Then Paul went back upstairs and after breaking bread and having eaten, they talked for a long time, until daylight, and then he departed. ¹²They brought the boy home alive and were profoundly relieved.

MILETUS

¹³We went ahead to the ship and set sail to Assos, intending to take Paul in there, for he had planned it this way. He was intending to go there on foot. ¹⁴When he met us in Assos, we took him in and we went to Mitylene. ¹⁵We set sail from there, and the next day we came to Chios, and the day following we arrived at Samos, and the day after that we arrived in Miletus. ¹⁶For Paul had decided to sail past Ephesus in order to not spend time in Asia, for he was eager to arrive in Jerusalem, if possible, by the day of Pentecost. ¹⁷He sent a message from Miletus to Ephesus, telling the members of the church to meet him. ¹⁸When they met him, he said to them,

---

20:2 This trip into *Greece* was to revisit Corinth as promised in 1 Corinthians 16:6. **20:4** *Tychicus* is also mentioned in Ephesians 6:21, 24; Colossians 4:7, 18; 2 Timothy 4:12; Titus 3:12; *Trophimus* later became the center of a debate (Acts 21:29). *Gaius* is said to be from *Derbe* in Asia Minor, but elsewhere he is called a Macedonian (Acts 19:29). This may signal that two different individuals are intended, since Derbe is not in Macedonia. **20:6** The *Feast of Unleavened Bread* or Passover was held in March or April and its celebration is set forth in Exodus 12:1–20. Paul was attempting to arrive in Jerusalem for Pentecost, which was celebrated fifty days after the conclusion of Passover. **20:7** *The first day of the week* indicates that they were celebrating the day of Jesus's resurrection (Sunday) instead of the Jewish Sabbath (Saturday). They broke bread or celebrated the sacrament (Eucharist). The official shift from Saturday to Sunday worship only begins to occur officially after the books of the New Testament were written. **20:9** *Taken up dead* implies that some of those in attendance ran down to help him after the fall, and when they lifted him from the ground they realized he was dead. English idiom would prefer *they found him dead*. The Greek text notes only that Eutychus was sitting on a window, which was probably an opening cut into the wall, and hence window ledge better describes the situation envisioned in the narrative. **20:13** Luke's intent is to note that an advance party sailed out to meet Paul and bring him by boat to his destination. Paul had previously set out to travel to those locations on foot. **20:15** Some late and inferior manuscripts add another city after Samos that Paul visited called Trogyllium. It is unlikely that this additional city is original to Acts. **20:17** *To meet him* is not indicated in the Greek text, and Luke simply notes that Paul sent a message to the elders in Miletus. **20:18** Paul's note that he *lived with you*

"You know that from the first day in which I arrived in Asia, how I lived with you at all times, [19]serving the Lord with all humility, with tears, and with trials that came upon me through the plots of the Jews, [20]how I did not withhold proclaiming anything that would be helpful and from teaching you in public and house to house, [21]testifying both to the Jews and Greeks about repentance toward God and faith in our Lord Jesus Christ. [22]And now I am going to Jerusalem, compelled by the Spirit, not knowing the things that will come upon me there [23]except that the Holy Spirit witnesses that imprisonment and trials await me in every city. [24]But I do not consider my life worth a single word so that I may finish my race and the ministry that I received from the Lord Jesus, to testify of the good news of the grace of God.

[25]"Now I know that you, among whom I went about declaring the kingdom, will not see my face again. [26]Therefore, I testify to you this day, that I am clean from the blood of all. [27]For I did not cease from proclaiming the entire plan of God to you. [28]Beware for yourselves and for all the flock, over which the Holy Spirit has made you overseers to shepherd the church of God that he purchased through his own blood. [29]I know that after my departure, insatiable wolves will enter in among you, and they will not spare the flock. [30]And among you, men will arise, speaking crooked things to draw away disciples after them. [31]Therefore, watch and remember that for three years, night and day, I did not cease to warn each one of you with tears. [32]And now I entrust you to God and the message of his grace, a message that is able to build

---

or that he *stayed with you* implies that he was in Ephesus for a substantial amount of time. Acts 20:31 indicates that it was a three-year period. **20:19** Luke may have intended the events described in Acts 9:24; 20:3. Paul describes his *service* as the act of serving them in the capacity of a deacon or servant. **20:21** The phraseology of this verse conceptualizes repentance as reconciliation toward God's will and having faith sufficient to believe in Jesus. Some manuscripts omit *Christ*, and, given the textual evidence, it is difficult to determine the original reading. **20:24** *Ministry* can also mean *service*, and the noun refers to the service of a deacon. Paul notes that he has been called to serve as a deacon, but he would also have been considered an apostle because he was sent out to declare the gospel message (*apostle* means *sent*). *Good news* is often translated as *gospel*, but here Paul seems to refer to the message of God's grace and not specifically to the entire gospel message unless he intended to describe the gospel uniquely and inclusively as God's grace. When speaking of the end of his life, Paul reflectively refers to it as a *race*, a word that is normally associated with athletic competitions (compare 2 Timothy 4:7). The word can refer specifically to an *event* or a *task*. **20:26** Compare 2 Nephi 9:44; Mosiah 2:27–28. **20:27** *The entire plan of God* represents God's will for humanity. The word translated as *plan* also refers to the *desires* and *wishes* of God. Given the belief in God's omniscience, God's desires are also fundamentally his plan for the salvation of humanity. **20:28** The word translated as *overseers* later came to refer specifically to the work of *bishops*, and that translation is possible here as well. This verse constitutes the first primary description of the work of bishops or overseers in the church, and the term is used to describe the work of a shepherd. An overseer can describe the work of many different professions, but Paul has used it here to refer to the work of a caring shepherd. A second feature of this verse is that God *purchased [the church] through his own blood*. There are two ways to translate this verse, both equally plausible. It can mean that God purchased the church through the blood of his own (Son, servants, and others) or that Jesus Christ purchased the church through his own blood. **20:29** In Greek, *insatiable* also means *fierce* or *ruinous*. **20:30** *Crooked things* represents a literal translation of the Greek, and many translations favor *perversions*. The word *perversion* has come to have a decidedly sexual connotation, but here it is not used in that way. **20:32** *Made holy* also means *sanctified*. The term is not used in a future context to refer to the existence of the saints among those who are sanctified, but it refers to the earthly kingdom of people who have

up and provide you an inheritance among all who are made holy. ³³I have desired no one's silver, gold, or clothing. ³⁴You know that my hands provided for my needs and the needs of those who were with me. ³⁵I have shown you by all these things that by working in this way we must care for the weak, and remember the words of the Lord Jesus that he said, 'It is more blessed to give than to receive.'"

³⁶After he said these things, he knelt with them all and prayed. ³⁷But they all began to cry freely, and they hugged Paul and kissed him, ³⁸lamenting most of all over the word that he had said, that they would not see his face again. And they accompanied him to the ship.

PAUL TRAVELS TO JERUSALEM

21 ¹After we departed from them, we set sail on a direct course and came to Cos and on the following day to Rhodes and from there to Patara. ²We found a ship departing for Phoenicia, boarded it, and set sail again. ³After we spotted Cyprus and left it behind on the left, we sailed to Syria and came to Tyre because the ship was to be unloaded there. ⁴After finding the disciples, we remained there seven days. Some told Paul through the Spirit not to travel to Jerusalem. ⁵When our days there had passed, we departed on our way, and all of

them with their wives and children accompanied us outside the city. Then we knelt on the beach and prayed. ⁶We said farewell to one another and we entered the ship, and they returned to their own homes.

⁷We sailed from Tyre and arrived at Ptolemais, and we greeted the brothers and sisters and stayed with them one day. ⁸On the next day we departed and came to Caesarea, and we entered the house of Philip the evangelist, who was one of the seven, and we remained with him. ⁹He had four unmarried daughters who prophesied. ¹⁰While staying there for many days, a prophet named Agabus from Judea came down, ¹¹and he came to us and he took Paul's belt and tied his own feet and hands and said, "The Holy Spirit says the following, 'In this way the Jews in Jerusalem will tie up the man to whom this belt belongs, and will deliver him into the hands of Gentiles.'" ¹²When we heard this, we and the local inhabitants begged him not to go to Jerusalem. ¹³Then Paul answered, "What are you doing, crying and breaking my heart? For I am ready not only to be tied up but even to die in Jerusalem for the name of Lord Jesus." ¹⁴He was not persuaded, and so we said no more but only "The will of the Lord be done."

¹⁵After these days, we prepared to go up to Jerusalem. ¹⁶Some of the disciples from

---

been made holy through the *message of his grace*. **20:35** This saying of Jesus is not recorded elsewhere in the Gospels, and it appears that Paul learned of this saying from an oral source (compare Matthew 10:8; Luke 6:38).

21:1 Some early manuscripts read *Patara and Myra*. **21:7** Greek uses *brothers* in a generic way to refer to *brothers and sisters*. **21:8** *Caesarea* refers to Caesarea Maritima, a port city on the Mediterranean coast. See Acts 6:5 for the calling of Philip to serve the Greek widows. For Philip's ministry, see Acts 8:26–40. He is called an *evangelist*, a term that means one who proselytizes or preaches the gospel message. It may have been intended to distinguish him from the apostle of that name who was sent on a mission. Philip's daughters are called *parthenoi*, which often means virgins, but in this case the emphasis appears to be on their marital status. **21:9** Luke does nothing to indicate the content of their prophecies and, given the context of Paul's final journey to Jerusalem, it would appear that they spoke of his coming imprisonment. **21:10** *Agabus* is also mentioned in Acts 11:28. **21:11** Luke's description here closely resembles the betrayal of Jesus into the hands of Gentiles, perhaps intentionally drawing out the idea that Paul was a type of Christ (see Matthew 26:59–61). **21:16** *Early disciple* can also mean a *disciple from the beginning*. Luke's wording could imply that this disciple knew Jesus and followed him, and in the generation in

Caesarea traveled with us also and brought us to the house of Mnason of Cyprus, an early disciple with whom we would stay. [17]When we arrived in Jerusalem, the brothers and sisters greeted us gladly.

PAUL MEETS WITH JACOB

[18]The next day, Paul went in with us to Jacob, and all the elders were there as well. [19]After he greeted them, he explained to them in detail what God had done among the Gentiles through his service. [20]When they heard this, they gave glory to God and said to him, "You see, brother, how many thousands there are among the Jews who have believed, and all are zealous to obey the Law. [21]But they have been informed about you, that you teach all Jews living among the Gentiles to abandon Moses, telling them not to circumcise their children and not to follow the statutes. [22]Therefore, what do we do? Everyone has heard that you have come. [23]So do what we tell you. We have four men who have taken a vow upon themselves. [24]Take them and purify yourself together with them and cover their expenses so that they may have their heads shaved, and everyone will know that what they have been told about you is nothing but that you obey the Law carefully. [25]Regarding the Gentiles who have believed, we have sent them a message, having determined that they should abstain from meat that has been sacrificed to idols, blood, what has been strangled, and sexual impropriety." [26]Then Paul took the men the next day, and together with them he purified himself. And he entered the temple and provided notice of the completion of the days of purification when the sacrifice would be offered on behalf of each of them.

PAUL ARRESTED

[27]When the seven days were almost over, the Jews from Asia saw him in the temple and stirred up the entire crowd, and they seized him [28]and cried out, "Men of Israel, help! This is the man who teaches everyone everywhere against the people of Israel, the Law, and this place! He has even brought Greeks into the temple and has defiled this holy place." [29]For they had seen Trophimus the Ephesian in the city with him, whom they assumed Paul had brought into the temple. [30]The whole city was in commotion, and the people ran together and seized Paul and dragged him from the temple, and the doors were shut immediately. [31]As they were trying to kill him, a message was sent to the commanding officer that all Jerusalem was in confusion. [32]Immediately he took the soldiers and centurions and ran in among them. When they saw the commanding officer and soldiers, they stopped beating Paul.

which Luke was writing, this type of disciple was now a novelty. **21:17** Greek uses *brothers* in a generic way to refer to *brothers and sisters.* **21:18** *The elders* refer to the *elders* of the church, and hence Christian elders. *Jacob* is Jesus's brother (Matthew 13:55; Mark 6:3). **21:21** *Abandon* is in Greek *to apostatize from Moses.* **21:23–24** For details on this vow, see Numbers 6:18–21. Paul's actions constitute a Nazarite vow. **21:24** First Corinthians 9:20 reflects Paul's own views on undergoing this purification ritual reserved exclusively for Jews. **21:25** Compare Acts 15:20, 29 for the decision of the council on these matters. **21:28** The Greek notes only *the people* in place of *people of Israel.* **21:29** This verse may be a parenthetical note by the author. The importance of this verse is profound for understanding the reasons for Paul's arrest. Trophimus (Acts 20:4) was one of the four men whom Paul brought into the temple in order to pay for the completion of their vows. It appears that Luke is signaling to the reader that Paul was mistakenly arrested for bringing Trophimus into the temple and that such a charge was incorrectly levied against Paul. **21:31** *The commanding officer* was technically the chiliarch, a Roman officer who commanded a thousand men (see verses 32–33). In this situation, he commanded a cohort of six hundred soldiers in Jerusalem.

³³Then the commanding officer drew near and arrested him and ordered that he be placed in chains, and he asked who he was and what he had done. ³⁴But some among the crowd shouted one thing and some another. When he was unable to determine the truth because of the riot, he ordered that Paul be brought to the barracks. ³⁵When he came to the steps, he had to be carried by the soldiers because of the violence of the crowd. ³⁶For a crowd of people followed and cried out, "Away with him!"

PAUL SPEAKS PUBLICLY

³⁷Paul was about to be led into the barracks, and he said to the officer in charge, "Am I permitted to say anything to you?" And he replied, "Do you know Greek? ³⁸Are you not the Egyptian who before these days started a riot and led four thousand Sicarii into the desert?" ³⁹But Paul answered, "I am a Jew from Tarsus in Cilicia, a citizen of an important city. I ask you: permit me to speak to the people." ⁴⁰When he had given him a chance to speak, Paul stood upon the steps and motioned with his hand to the people, and there was a profound silence. He spoke to them in the Aramaic language, saying,

PAUL'S PERSONAL DEFENSE AND CONVERSION

22 ¹"Brothers and fathers, listen now to my defense that I present to you." ²When they heard that he spoke in Aramaic, they grew quieter. Then he said, ³"I am a Jew born in Tarsus of Cilicia, educated with strictness under Gamaliel according to the Law of our ancestors, zealous for God just as you are today. ⁴I persecuted this Way to the point of death, binding and delivering men and women to prison, ⁵as the high priest and the entire council of elders will witness about me. I received letters from them written to the brothers in Damascus, and I went there to arrest them and bring them to Jerusalem to be punished. ⁶As I was traveling and approaching Damascus around noon, a great light from heaven appeared suddenly and shone around me. ⁷And I fell to the ground and heard a voice telling me, 'Saul, Saul, why are you persecuting me?' ⁸And I replied, 'Who are you, Lord?' And he said, 'I am Jesus of Nazareth, whom you are persecuting.' ⁹Those who were with me saw the light, but they did not hear the voice speaking to me. ¹⁰And I said, 'What shall I do, Lord?' The Lord said to me, 'Arise and

---

21:36 The phrase *away with him* is reminiscent of the call against Jesus (John 19:15). **21:37** The word *barracks* reflects the physical location where the soldiers were stationed but not necessarily where in the city they were stationed. The Greek word could also mean *headquarters*. The *officer in charge* is the chiliarch. When the commanding officer asked Paul whether he could speak Greek, he was seeking to determine if he had successfully arrested the Egyptian insurrectionist mentioned in verse 38. **21:38** The term *Sicarii* refers to a group of ultranationalists who willingly assassinated Roman and other public figures in their failed attempt to create a Jewish state independent of Rome. The word describes the type of sword they used, called a *sicarius*, which was a short, curved dagger. **21:40** The Greek notes *the Hebrew dialect*, which at this time was Aramaic. *A chance to speak* is not noted specifically in Greek, but Greek uses the idiom *he gave him permission*.

22:1 The Greek indicates that this discourse was delivered to *men*. **22:2** The Greek notes *the Hebrew dialect*, which at this time was Aramaic. **22:3** Gamaliel was a Pharisee and scholar of the Law who taught moderation in dealing with Christians (Acts 5:34–39). **22:4** Paul still refers to Christianity as *the Way* (see Acts 9:2; 18:25–26). **22:5** *Brothers*, instead of *brothers and sisters*, is the correct translation in this instance because it appears that Paul is referring to synagogue leaders who would be male. **22:6** Paul also told his conversion in Acts 9:1–9; 26:9–20. In the account in 9:7, Paul's traveling companions did not see the light, but they heard the voice. **22:7** In retelling this story in Aramaic, Paul used his Hebrew name, *Saul*, instead of his Roman name (Paul).

go to Damascus, and there you will be told all that is appointed for you to do.' ¹¹But since I could not see because of the glory of that light, I was led by the hand of those with me, and I came to Damascus.

¹²"A man named Ananias, a devout believer in the Law and of good reputation of all the Jews lived there. ¹³He came to me and while standing by me said, 'Saul, brother, receive your sight.' At that very hour I received my sight and saw him. ¹⁴And he said, 'The God of our ancestors appointed you to know his will and to see the Righteous One and to hear a voice from his mouth ¹⁵because you will be a witness of him and of all that you have seen and heard. ¹⁶Now, why do you wait? Arise and be baptized and have your sins washed away while calling on his name.'

¹⁷"When I had returned to Jerusalem and while praying in the temple, I fell into a trance ¹⁸and saw him saying to me, 'Hurry and depart from Jerusalem quickly because they will not accept your testimony about me.' ¹⁹I replied, 'Lord, they knew that I imprisoned and beat those who believed in you in synagogue after synagogue. ²⁰And when the blood of your witness Stephen was being poured out, I was standing by and approving of it and watching over the clothing of those who killed him.' ²¹Then he said to me, 'Go, because I will send you far away to the Gentiles.'"

PAUL IS QUESTIONED

²²Up to this point they listened to the message, and then they raised their voices, saying, "Take him from the earth, for he should not be permitted to live!" ²³As they shouted, they tore off their cloaks and threw dust into the air. ²⁴So the commanding officer ordered Paul to be taken back into the barracks. He told them to question Paul by beating him with a whip so that the officer might understand the reason why they were shouting at him in this manner. ²⁵And as Paul was being stretched out for the lashes, Paul said to the centurion standing nearby, "Is it legal to beat a Roman citizen who has not been condemned?" ²⁶When the centurion heard this he went to the commanding officer and told him, saying, "What are you about to do, for this man is a Roman citizen?" ²⁷The commanding officer came and said to him, "Tell me, are you a Roman citizen?" And Paul replied, "Yes." ²⁸The commanding officer responded, "I purchased this citizenship with a large sum of money." But Paul responded, "I was born a citizen." ²⁹Then those who were intending to question him departed from him immediately, and the commanding officer was afraid, knowing that he was a Roman citizen and that he had tied him up.

PAUL'S DEFENSE TO THE SANHEDRIN

³⁰The next day, the officer wanted to know why he was accused by the Jews, and he untied him, and ordered the chief priest and the entire Sanhedrin to gather, and he brought Paul and placed him in front of them.

22:14 *The Righteous One* is a distinctly Jewish way of referring to Jesus, who is considered to be righteous according to the Law. **22:16** The Greek of the end of this verse is not precisely clear, and the act of *calling on his name* may be interpreted as a declaration of a person's faith when being baptized (as translated here) or it can describe the means through which a person is forgiven, through *calling on his name*. Compare Mosiah 4:11 and Doctrine and Covenants 39:10. **22:17** *Trance* represents a different Greek word than is typically used for a vision or dream. Paul indicates that he had a lively spiritual encounter. **22:23** *Cloaks* are the outer article of clothing worn on top of the tunic. **22:24** *The commanding officer* is the chiliarch (Acts 21:32–33). *The barracks* can also refer to their headquarters. **22:25** The Greek text does not use the word *citizen*, but the force of Paul's question is whether a Roman citizen could be beaten without a trial. A *centurion* commands a hundred soldiers. **22:30** The commanding officer followed

23 ¹While looking directly at the council, Paul said, "Brothers, I have lived my life with a clear conscience before God until this day." ²And the high priest Ananias commanded those who stood near him to strike him on the mouth. ³Then Paul said to him, "God is about to strike you, you whitewashed wall. Are you sitting there judging according to the Law, and contrary to the Law you order me to be struck?" ⁴Those who stood nearby said, "Are you insulting God's high priest?" ⁵Paul replied, "I did not know, brothers, that it was the high priest, for it written, '*You shall not speak evil about a ruler of my people.*'"

⁶When Paul knew that one part were Sadducees and the other part were Pharisees, he cried out in the Sanhedrin, "Brothers, I am a Pharisee, a son of Pharisees. I am on trial for a hope in the resurrection of the dead." ⁷When he said this, there was a dispute between the Pharisees and the Sadducees, and the gathering was divided. ⁸For the Sadducees say that there is no resurrection, nor angels, nor spirit, but the Pharisees accept them all. ⁹There was a great cry, and the scribes from the group of Pharisees arose and were contending, "We find nothing wrong with this man. What if a spirit or angel has spoken to him?" ¹⁰When the contention was so great, the commanding officer was afraid that Paul would be torn apart by them, and he ordered the soldiers to go down and take him from them by force and bring him into the barracks. ¹¹The following night, the Lord stood by and said to him, "Cheer up, for just as you have testified of me in Jerusalem, you must also testify of me in Rome."

THE PLOT TO KILL PAUL

¹²When it was day, the Jews made a plot and swore an oath between themselves not to eat or drink until they had killed Paul. ¹³There were more than forty who made this oath. ¹⁴They went to the chief priests and elders and said, "We have agreed by an oath to taste nothing until we have killed Paul. ¹⁵Now then, you and the Sanhedrin must inform the commanding officer to bring him to you as though you intended to examine him more carefully. We are ready to kill him before he comes near here."

¹⁶When the son of Paul's sister heard the plot, he went and entered the barracks and told Paul. ¹⁷Paul called one of the centurions and said, "Take this young man to the commanding officer, for he has a message for him." ¹⁸Then the centurion took him and brought him to the commanding officer and said, "The prisoner named Paul asked me to bring this young man to you because he has something to tell you."

---

standard practice by using a local court to determine the crimes of the accused. The *Sanhedrin* would have considered the issue of religious crimes against Paul.

23:1 *Clear conscience* is in Greek *in all good conscience*. The Sanhedrin was an official council organized to judge religious matters and practice. This verse shares significant wording with King Benjamin's declaration in Mosiah 2:15. **23:1, 6** The discourse was delivered to *men* in the Sanhedrin, and therefore *brothers* is the correct translation. **23:2** Ananias, son of Nebedeus, was high priest 47–52 CE. **23:3** The reference to a *whitewashed wall* may be an allusion to Ezekiel 13:10. If the text intentionally alludes to Ezekiel 13, then the reference to a *whitewashed wall* points to their hypocrisy. This interaction between Paul and the high priest may be following the standard set forth in Deuteronomy 1:16–17. **23:5** Quotation from Exodus 22:28. **23:6** The meaning can also be *for the hope that the dead will be resurrected*. **23:8** According to Paul, the Sadducees denied the existence of the human *spirit*. **23:9** Some inferior manuscripts add to the end of the verse *let us not fight against God*. **23:10** Luke uses a word that describes a *detachment of soldiers*, suggesting an official inquiry. The *barracks* can also refer to their headquarters (also verse 16). The *commanding officer* was the chiliarch (Acts 21:32–33; see also verses 15, and 17–18).

[19]The commanding officer took him by the hand and went off privately and asked, "What is it you have to tell me?" [20]He replied, "The Jews agreed to ask you to bring Paul to the Sanhedrin tomorrow as though they intended to question him more carefully. [21]But do not be persuaded by them, for there are more than forty of them waiting to ambush him. And they have made an oath not to eat or drink until they have killed him, and now they are ready, waiting for your approval." [22]Then the commanding officer sent the young man away, and he ordered him, "Tell no one that you have reported these things to me."

THE LETTER TO FELIX

[23]Then he called two of the centurions and said, "Prepare two hundred soldiers, seventy horsemen, and two hundred spearmen to go to Caesarea by nine o'clock tonight. [24]And provide horses for Paul to ride and bring him safely to Felix the governor." [25]He wrote a letter like this: [26]*"Claudius Lysias to His Excellency Felix, the Governor, greetings. [27]This man was seized by the Jews and was about to be killed by them when I came upon him with a detachment of soldiers and rescued him because I had learned that he was a Roman citizen. [28]I wanted to know the charge for which they had accused him, so I brought him down to their Sanhedrin. [29]I found that he was accused of questioning their Law, but he had no accusation worthy of death or imprisonment. [30]But when the plot against this man was reported to me, I sent him to you right away and ordered that his accusers tell what things they have against him."*

FELIX AND PAUL

[31]Then the soldiers took Paul, according to their orders, and brought him at night to Antipatris. [32]On the next day they let the horsemen go with him, and they returned to the barracks. [33]When they came to Caesarea and delivered the letter to the governor, they also presented Paul to him. [34]After reading the letter, he asked what province he was from, and when he learned Paul was from Cilicia [35]he said, "I will hear your case when your accusers arrive." Then he ordered him to be held in Herod's palace.

THE CHARGES AGAINST PAUL

24 [1]After five days, the high priest Ananias went with some elders and the lawyer Tertullus, and they brought their case against Paul to the governor. [2]When Paul had been summoned, Tertullus began to accuse him, saying, "Most excellent Felix, we have had great peace because of you, and reforms are being made in this nation through your foresight. [3]We accept

---

23:22 *Sent the young man away* is not in the Greek text but is needed in English to clarify the meaning of the sentence. **23:23** The precise definition of the word translated as *spearmen* is unknown. **23:24** Felix, the *Roman governor*, was technically the procurator of the region. Historical sources note the corruption of his tenure, which ended in 58 CE. He was succeeded by Porcius Festus, procurator of Judea 59–62 CE (Acts 24:27). **23:26** Record of *Claudius Lysias's* service has been lost outside of the references to it in Acts. **23:26–30** These verses report a summary or copy of a letter sent from Claudius to Felix, and Luke has preserved several epistolary features of the letter. The signature and closing remarks have been omitted by Luke. **23:27** *Citizen* is omitted in the Greek text but is supplied to make sense of Claudius's treatment of Paul. Claudius presents Felix with a slightly altered description of his actions (Acts 22:24–29). **23:31** This city was located about halfway between Jerusalem and Caesarea. **23:32** *The barracks* can also refer to their headquarters. **23:34** The question about *province* was to determine jurisdiction. **23:35** The Greek text notes specifically that Paul was held at *Herod's praetorium* (built about 56 CE). This word is the same as that used to describe the building where Jesus was interrogated (John 18:28, 33; 19:9).

24:1 Nothing more is known about *Tertullus* other than that he acted as the prosecuting attorney against Paul.

this in every way and everywhere with all gratitude. [4]But in order to not weary you longer, I ask you to briefly listen to us in your customary kindness. [5]For we have found this man to be a plague, one who stirs up all Jews throughout the world, and he is the ringleader of the sect of the Nazarenes, [6]who tried to defile the temple, but we seized him. [8]By examining him yourself, you will be able to determine all these things about what we are accusing him of doing." [9]The Jews also joined in the attack, confirming that these things were so.

PAUL'S DEFENSE

[10]After the governor motioned for him to answer, Paul said, "I know that you have been judge over this people for many years, and so I confidently make my defense. [11]You are able to determine that it has not been more than twelve days since that I went up to worship in Jerusalem. [12]And they did not find me contending with anyone or stirring up a crowd in the temple or in the synagogues or in the city. [13]Neither can they prove to you what they are now accusing me of doing. [14]But I declare this to you, that according to the Way, which they say is a heresy, I worship the God of our ancestors, believing in everything according to the Law and what is written in the Prophets, [15]having a hope in God, a hope that these men accept, that there will be a resurrection of the righteous and unrighteous. [16]This is why I always strive to have a clear conscience toward God and all people. [17]After several years, I came bearing offerings for the poor and to offer sacrifices, [18]which they found me doing, purifying myself in the temple, without a crowd or disturbance. [19]There were some Jews from Asia who should be here before you to accuse me if they have anything against me. [20]Or these men here should relate what crime they found me guilty of when I was standing before the Sanhedrin, [21]unless it was this one thing that I shouted out while I stood among them: it is concerning the resurrection of the dead that I am on trial before you today."

[22]But Felix, having a more accurate understanding of the Way, adjourned the hearing, saying, "When Lysias, the commanding officer, comes down, I will judge your case." [23]Then he ordered the centurion to guard Paul but to permit him some freedom and not to prevent his family and friends from assisting him.

[24]After some days, Felix arrived with Drusilla, his wife who was Jewish, and he sent for Paul and listened to his faith in Christ Jesus. [25]While he spoke about

---

24:5 *Sect* can also be translated as *heresy*, and in later centuries the word was often used to refer to Christian heretical groups. Tertullus is describing the Christians as a Jewish sect with beliefs that went against mainstream ideas and practices. **24:7** Some very late and inferior manuscripts have an added verse here: *We wanted to judge him by our Law, but Lysias, who was the commanding officer, came and took him from us with substantial violence, and he ordered those who accused him to come to you.* It is doubtful that this verse is original to Acts. **24:14** Instead of referring to his faith as a sect (see verse 5), Paul refers to his own faith as *the Way*. **24:15** Paul asserts that his own faith is congruent with his Jewish beliefs and practices. **24:16** This verse influenced the wording of Doctrine and Covenants 135:4. **24:17** Paul's mention of coming to Jerusalem to offer *sacrifices* probably implies his intent to offer a sacrifice in the Jerusalem temple. It is also possible, given the following verse, that he was referring to paying for the Nazarite vows described in Acts 21:23–26. The *offerings for the poor* are a topic of significant discussion in Paul's letters (see 1 Corinthians 16:1–4; Galatians 2:10). **24:23** *Family and friends* is a single word in Greek and can mean either one. Acquaintances is perhaps the closest word in English, but that word can imply friends only. **24:24** *Drusilla* was the daughter of Herod Agrippa I. She may have been aware of Christianity through her connections to the Herodian family. **24:25** The message of Christianity is described as teaching *self-control* or *restraint*. The word implies control over one's emotions and actions.

righteousness, self-control, and the coming judgment, Felix became frightened and said, "Go away for now, and when I have an opportunity I will summon you." ²⁶At the same time, he was hoping that Paul would give him money, so he sent for him often and conferred with him. ²⁷When two years had passed, Felix was succeeded by Porcius Festus, and, wanting to do a favor for the Jews, Felix left Paul in prison.

PAUL APPEALS DIRECTLY TO CAESAR

25 ¹Then three days after Festus arrived in the province, he went up to Jerusalem from Caesarea. ²The chief priests and leading Jews brought charges against Paul, and they encouraged Festus, ³asking for a favor against Paul to summon Paul to Jerusalem because they planned an ambush to kill him while on the way. ⁴Then Festus replied that Paul would remain in Caesarea, and he intended to go there soon. ⁵He said, "So let your authorities go down with me, and if there is anything wrong, they may bring charges against him."

⁶After he stayed among them for no more than eight or ten days, he went down to Caesarea, and the next day he sat on the judgment seat and ordered Paul to be summoned. ⁷When he arrived, the Jews who came down from Jerusalem stood around him, and they brought many weighty charges that they were not able to prove. ⁸Paul gave his defense: "I have not sinned against the Jewish law or the temple or against Caesar." ⁹But Festus wanted

to do a favor for the Jews, and he asked Paul, "Do you want to go up to Jerusalem to be judged by me there concerning these things?" ¹⁰But Paul replied, "I am standing before the judgment seat of Caesar, where I ought to be judged. I have done nothing wrong against the Jews, as you know quite well. ¹¹But if I am wrong and have done something worthy of death, I am not trying to avoid death. But if there is nothing in their charges against me, then no one can hand me over to them. I appeal to Caesar." ¹²Then after speaking with his council, Festus replied, "You have appealed to Caesar, and to Caesar you will go."

FESTUS AND AGRIPPA

¹³When several days had passed, King Agrippa and Bernice went down to Caesarea and greeted Festus. ¹⁴When they had stayed there for many days, Festus set out the matter of Paul, saying, "There is a man left in prison by Felix ¹⁵concerning whom the chief priests and elders of the Jews, while I was in Jerusalem, laid out charges against and sought a sentence against him. ¹⁶I replied to them that that it was not the custom of the Romans to hand over anyone before that person has had an opportunity to meet his accusers face to face and has made a defense concerning the charges put forth. ¹⁷Then, when they came here with me, I did not delay the trial, but the next day I sat on the judgment seat and summoned the man to be brought. ¹⁸When his accusers stood, they brought no accusation of the evil things I

24:26 Many translations prefer to translate *conferred* as *talked*, but Felix appears in the story to be manipulating Paul and trying to gain Paul's trust, and therefore *conferred* better approximates the meaning. **24:27** The emperor Nero recalled Felix for corruption in about 58 CE and sent Festus to take over in Judea. Festus is regarded in historical sources as being a more balanced and careful ruler, but Luke asserts that corruption continued with the case of Paul.

25:8 Paul's defense includes the note that he did not act against *Caesar*, probably alluding to the charge that he had instigated civil unrest in Jerusalem. **25:11** Paul insinuates that the real threat remains with his accusers in Jerusalem. **25:13** King Agrippa II's father is mentioned in Acts 12:1. The family had a history of persecuting Christians. **25:14** Herod Agrippa II ruled from 53 until ca. 92 CE. Julia Bernice, sister of Agrippa II, died after 81 CE.

was expecting. [19]But they had certain disagreements about their own religion with him and concerning a certain Jesus who was dead who Paul asserted was alive. [20]Because I was undecided about how I might look into these matters, I asked if he wanted to go to Jerusalem to be tried there on these matters. [21]But when Paul appealed to remain in custody for the decision of the emperor, I ordered that he be guarded until I could send him to Caesar." [22]So Agrippa said to Festus, "I would like to listen to this man." Festus replied, "Tomorrow you will hear him."

PAUL BEFORE KING AGRIPPA AND BERNICE

[23]Then the next day, Agrippa and Bernice came with a great demonstration, and they entered the reception hall with the commanding officers and leading men of the city. And Festus gave the command, and Paul was brought in. [24]And Festus said, "King Agrippa and all who are present, you see this man about whom the entire multitude of Jews appealed to me, both in Jerusalem and here, shouting that he should not live any longer. [25]But I found he had done nothing worthy of death, and when he appealed to Caesar, I decided to send him. [26]But I have nothing specific to write to my lord about him; therefore,

I have brought him before you all and particularly before you, King Agrippa, so that after we have questioned him I might have something to write about. [27]For it seems unreasonable to me to send a prisoner without indicating the charges against him."

PAUL'S DEFENSE BEFORE AGRIPPA

26 [1]Then Agrippa said to Paul, "You are permitted to speak on your own behalf." Then Paul extended his hand and spoke in his defense. [2]"Regarding all the things I am accused of by the Jews, King Agrippa, I have considered myself blessed that I am about to defend myself in front of you today, [3]especially knowing that you are familiar with all customs and questions relating to Jews. Therefore, I ask you to listen to me patiently. [4]All Jews know my way of life from my youth, a life that from the beginning was spent among my own people and in Jerusalem. [5]They have known since my early life and if they desire to testify, that following the strictest sect of our religion, I lived as a Pharisee. [6]And now, because of my hope in the promise God made to our ancestors, I stand here on trial. [7]Our twelve tribes hope to realize this promise when they serve earnestly night and day. It is for this hope that I am accused by the Jews, King Agrippa. [8]Why

25:19 *Religion* can also mean *worship* or *belief*. Festus saw them as all belonging to one *religion* and made no distinction between Jews and Christians but rather saw it as strife among religious practitioners. **25:21** The emperor at this time was Nero, who ruled 54–68 CE. **25:23** These *commanding officers* were military officers. **25:26** Luke may have included this story, which contains few new details of Paul's trial, to once again assert that Paul had been found innocent of all charges.

26:4 Paul asserts that his life was spent in Jerusalem, but elsewhere he also claims to be from Tarsus in Cilicia. The two statements are not contradictory, but it is unknown whether Paul was born in Tarsus and then spent his later life in Jerusalem or how his time was spent between the two cities (see Acts 21:39). **26:5** In light of Paul's other statements where he refers to being part of *the Way*, Paul's declaration that he belonged to *our religion* implies that he accepted his Jewish religion and followed it in another way, the way that accepted Jesus as the Messiah (compare Acts 9:2). **26:6** The Greek word translated as *promise* may be a play on words. The Greek word *gospel* is *euangelion*, and the word *promise* is *epangelion*. The meaning of the word is an *announcement* or *promise*. **26:7** A similar thought is expressed in Philippians 3:11. Paul alludes to the idea that God has opened a new way to the promise, where he describes the old way as service *both night and day*. The new way involves the eyes, turning from darkness

is it unbelievable to any of you that God raises the dead? [9]Indeed, it seemed to me that I should do many things opposing the name of Jesus of Nazareth, [10]which I did in Jerusalem. I not only imprisoned many of the saints when I received authority from the chief priests, but when they were put to death I gave my vote against them. [11]In every synagogue I punished them often, and I tried to make them blaspheme. Because I was so deeply angry with them, I persecuted them even in foreign cities.

PAUL'S CONVERSION

[12]"While I was doing this, as I was traveling to Damascus with authority and complete power from the chief priests, [13]in the middle of the day, King Agrippa, I saw on the road a light from heaven brighter than the sun, shining around me and those who traveled with me. [14]And when we had all fallen to the ground, I heard a voice speaking to me in Aramaic, 'Saul, Saul, why are you persecuting me? It is hard for you to kick the prod.' [15]And I replied, 'Who are you, Lord?' The Lord said, 'I am Jesus Christ, whom you are persecuting. [16]But rise and stand on your feet, for I have appeared to you in order to appoint you as a servant and witness of the things that you have seen and of those things about which I will appear to you. [17]I will deliver you from your people and from the Gentiles, to whom I am sending you [18]to open their eyes and to turn them from darkness to light and from the power of Satan to God to receive a forgiveness of sins and an inheritance among those who are sanctified by faith in me.'

[19]"Therefore, King Agrippa, I was obedient to the heavenly vision. [20]I taught them to repent and to turn to God, to do works worthy of repentance, first while in Damascus then to those in Jerusalem, to all the region of Judea also, and to the Gentiles. [21]For this reason, the Jews seized me while in the temple, and they attempted to kill me. [22]Therefore, to this day I have had help from God, and so I stand witnessing both to the small and great, saying nothing except what the prophets and Moses said would come to be, [23]that the Christ would suffer and be the first to rise from the dead, to declare the light to our people and the Gentiles."

[24]As he was relating these things in his defense, Festus spoke in a loud voice, saying, "Paul, you are mad! Your considerable learning is driving you out of your mind." [25]But Paul replied, "I am not mad, noble Festus, but I relate these words in truth and reason. [26]For the king knows these things about which I am speaking boldly. For I am convinced that none of these things are hidden from him, for this thing was not done in a corner. [27]Do you believe the

---

to light, and following God (verse 18). **26:10** Paul uses an idiom to describe his vote against the Christians, declaring that he *cast his stone against them.* Black and white stones were used in voting in some judicial settings. **26:13** Greek uses *O King* instead of Agrippa's name, but English usage prefers a direct address to Agrippa. Similar language is used in the description of God in Doctrine and Covenants 110:3; Joseph Smith—History 1:16. First Nephi 1:9 alludes to a portion of this verse. **26:14** That God spoke to Paul in Aramaic is noted only in this account (compare Acts 9:4; 22:7). The word translated as *prod* refers to the sting of an insect, the goad used to prod cattle, or something similar to a spur. Echoed in Doctrine and Covenants 121:38 (compare Acts 9:5). **26:16** Echoed in Doctrine and Covenants 14:8. **26:18** The language of *inheritance* implies a future reward, but the reference to those who are *sanctified in me* has a temporal aspect that is contemporary with Paul's message. Some will accept Paul's teachings, turn to the Lord, be forgiven, and thereby be sanctified. **26:19** The Greek text uses a double negative, *I was not disobedient,* which has been translated as a direct statement of action. **26:20** A similar teaching is found in Matthew 3:8. **26:23** The language of Christ being the *first to rise from the dead* is used in 2 Nephi 2:8. Perhaps an allusion to Isaiah 60:1.

prophets, King Agrippa? I know that you believe." [28]Agrippa said to Paul, "Are you trying to persuade me to be a Christian in such a short time?" [29]But Paul replied, "I pray to God that whether it is a short or long time, that not only you but all those who listen to me today might become even as I am, except for these chains."

[30]Then the king, the governor, and Bernice arose and those who were sitting with them. [31]When they had departed, they spoke to one another, saying, "This man is not doing anything worthy of death or imprisonment." [32]But Agrippa said to Festus, "This man could be set free if he had not appealed to Caesar."

PAUL'S TRIP TO ROME

27 [1]When it was determined that we would sail to Italy, they handed Paul and some other prisoners over to a centurion of the Augustan cohort named Julius. [2]We boarded the ship from Adramyttium, which was about to sail to the ports along the coast of Asia, and went to sea accompanied by Aristarchus, a Macedonian from Thessalonica. [3]The next day we came to Sidon, and Julius treated Paul kindly and permitted him to go to his friends to receive care. [4]We departed from there, and we sailed under lee of Cyprus because the winds were opposing. [5]After we had sailed into the open sea off Cilicia and Pamphylia, we arrived in Myra in Lycia. [6]There the centurion found a ship from Alexandria sailing to Italy, and we boarded it. [7]After we sailed slowly for many days, we arrived with difficulty off Cnidus, but the wind did not permit us to travel further, so we sailed under lee of Crete off Salmone. [8]And with difficulty we traveled along the coast of Crete, and we came to a place named Fair Havens, which was near the city of Lasea.

SHIPWRECKED

[9]Since some time had passed and sailing was already dangerous, because even the fast was already over, Paul advised them, [10]saying to them, "Men, I see that the voyage is going to experience danger and great loss not only for our cargo and the ship, but also for our lives." [11]But the centurion was more convinced by the captain and the ship's owner than by what Paul said. [12]Because the harbor was not suitable to spend the winter in, the majority decided to set sail from there, that perhaps they might arrive in Phoenix, a harbor of Crete facing southwest and northwest, and spend the winter there.

[13]A south wind blew gently, and they thought they had obtained their purpose, so they raised anchor and sailed close to the shore of Crete. [14]Not much later, a violent wind called the Euroclydon blew down from land. [15]When the ship was caught in it, and not being able to sail into the wind, we gave up and we were carried along by it. [16]Then we ran under the lee of a small

---

26:28 *Trying* is added to clarify the Greek. Agrippa questions whether Paul assumes that one can become a Christian in such a short amount of time and after hearing this single discourse. **26:31** Those who question Paul again conclude that he was innocent (see note on Acts 25:26).

27:1 *The Augustan cohort* designates the emperor's own auxiliary troops, but it is unlikely that these are the imperial troops. It may be that this title was used in an honorary fashion. A *cohort* consisted of six hundred soldiers. **27:2** This may be the same person as the *Aristarchus* mentioned in Acts 19:29 (compare Philemon 1:24). **27:4** Paul's group traveled in a way that enabled them to use the island as protection against the wind. **27:7** *Salmone* was a raised point on the northwest corner of Crete. **27:8** *Lasea* was on the south side of Crete, thus indicating that they took the southerly route around Crete. **27:9** The *fast* spoken of here is the Day of Atonement (Yom Kippur), which took place in late September or early October, and therefore the winter winds had begun to arrive and had made sailing dangerous. **27:14** The *Euroclydon* was a northern wind that was described as a hurricane-force wind. **27:16** *The ship's boat* was

island named Clauda, and we were barely able to control the ship's boat. [17]After hoisting it on board, they used supports to undergird the ship, and, fearing that they would run aground in Syrtis, they lowered the sea anchor, thus permitting them to be carried along. [18]The following day, after being battered by the storm, they began unloading the cargo. [19]On the third day, they threw the ship's gear into the sea by hand. [20]But neither sun nor stars appeared for many days, and no small storm was upon us, and all hope of being saved was lost for us.

[21]They were without food for many days, and then Paul stood among them and said, "Men, you should have listened to me and not set out from Crete and thus avoided this damage and loss. [22]And now I advise you to take courage, for there will be no loss of life, but the ship will go down. [23]For last night an angel of the God to whom I belong and worship stood before me and [24]said, 'Do not fear, Paul, you must stand in front of Caesar, and behold, God has granted you the safety of all those sailing with you.' [25]Therefore, take courage, men. I believe that it will be just as I have been told. [26]But we must run aground on some island."

[27]When the fourteenth night arrived, as we were being pushed across the Adriatic Sea, around midnight the sailors suspected that they were approaching land. [28]Then they took a sounding and found it was twenty fathoms deep, and after they had sailed further they took a sounding and found it was fifteen fathoms deep. [29]We were afraid that we would run aground on the rocks, so they let down four anchors from the stern and prayed for day to come. [30]Then the sailors sought to flee from the ship, and as they were lowering the ship's boat into the sea under the pretext that they were putting down anchors from the bow, [31]Paul said to the centurion and the soldiers, "If these men do not remain in the ship, you cannot be saved." [32]Then the soldiers cut the rope of the ship's boat and let it fall away.

[33]When it began to be day, Paul encouraged them to take some food, saying, "Today is the fourteenth day that you have continued in suspense and without food. You have eaten nothing. [34]Therefore, I encourage you to take food. For it is necessary for your deliverance. For not a hair from any of your heads will be lost." [35]After he said these things, he took bread and gave thanks to God in front of them all and broke it and began to eat. [36]So they all took courage and took food themselves. [37](We were in all 276 people on the ship.) [38]After they had eaten and were full, they lightened the ship by throwing the wheat into the sea.

[39]When it was day, they did not recognize the land, but they saw an inlet with a beach where they decided to run the ship aground if they were able to do so. [40]Then they threw off the anchors and left them in the sea, and at the same time they loosened the ropes that tied the rudders. Then they hoisted the foresail in the wind and made for the beach. [41]But they struck a sandbar and ran the ship aground. The bow was stuck and could not be moved, and the stern was being broken into pieces

---

a small rowboat used to go ashore and in emergency situations. **27:17** The precise meaning of the word translated as *sea anchor* is unknown. The word could also refer to the lowering of the mainstay. **27:21** They had lost their desire to eat because of the storm, and later in the story it is clear that there was food on the ship (verse 33). **27:27** A *fathom* was the distance between the fingertips of a person's hands when the arms are outstretched. The first *sounding* put them in about 120 feet (= 36 meters) of water, and the second sounding put them in 90 feet (= 27 meters) of water, thus confirming that they were approaching land. **27:34** The word translated as *deliverance* is the same word that is translated elsewhere as *salvation*. This verse provides good context for how the word was used in other settings.

by the waves. ⁴²It was the soldier's plan to kill the prisoners so that none of them might swim away and escape. ⁴³But the centurion wanted to save Paul and stopped them from carrying out their plan. He ordered those who were able to swim to go overboard first and make it to land. ⁴⁴The remainder were on planks of wood or on pieces of the ship. In this way, all were brought safely to land.

PAUL'S TIME IN MALTA

28 ¹After we were safe, we learned that the island was called Malta. ²The local inhabitants showed us great kindness and built a fire and welcomed us all because it had started to rain and it was cold. ³When Paul had gathered a bundle of wood and placed it on the fire, a venomous snake came out because of the heat and bit his hand. ⁴When they saw the snake hanging from Paul's hand, they said to one another, "Without a doubt this man is a murderer who escaped from the sea, but Justice has not permitted him to live." ⁵Then Paul shook the snake off into the fire, and he suffered no harm. ⁶But they were thinking that he was about to swell or suddenly fall down dead. After they waited for a long time and saw that nothing unusual happened to him, they changed their minds and said that he was a god.

⁷In that place and region there were fields that belonged to the chief official of the island, who was named Publius. He welcomed us and treated us as guests for three days. ⁸It happened that Publius's father was sick in bed, suffering from fever and dysentery. Paul came to him and after praying, he laid his hand on him and healed him. ⁹After this happened, the other people on the island who were ill came to him and were healed. ¹⁰They also honored us greatly, and as we were leaving, they put the things we needed on board.

PAUL ARRIVES IN ROME

¹¹After three months, we set sail on an Alexandrian ship that had wintered on the island and had the Dioscuri on its bow. ¹²We arrived in Syracuse and stayed for three days. ¹³From there we sailed away and arrived at Rhegium, and after one day a south wind arose, and then on the second day we arrived in Puteoli. ¹⁴We found some brothers and sisters there and were invited by them to remain with them for seven days. And in this manner, we came to Rome. ¹⁵The brothers and sisters there, when they heard about us, they came from as far as the Forum of Appius and the Three Taverns to meet us. When Paul saw them, he thanked God and took courage. ¹⁶When we entered Rome, Paul was permitted to stay by himself with the soldier who guarded him.

PAUL SPEAKS TO THE JEWS IN ROME

¹⁷After three days, Paul called the leading Jews together. When they had gathered, he said to them, "Brothers, I have done nothing against our people or the customs of our ancestors. I was handed over as a prisoner from Jerusalem to the Romans. ¹⁸When they had judged my case, they wanted to release me because they found no reason for a death sentence against me.

28:2 The *local inhabitants* translates the Greek word *barbarians*, which refers to people who speak a different language. **28:4** This is the goddess *Justice*. **28:11** The *Dioscurii*, Castor and Pollux, were known as the heavenly twins. They were believed to be the children of Zeus and Leda. **28:14–15** Greek uses the generic *brothers* for *brothers and sisters*. **28:15** The *Three Taverns* was located along the Appian Way south of Rome about thirty miles. *The Forum of Appius* was also located along the Appian Way. **28:17** The setting of this story suggests that this was a gathering of Jewish leaders, and therefore *brothers* is the correct translation (see also verse 21).

[19]But the Jews spoke against this, and I was forced to appeal to Caesar, even though I had no charge against my people. [20]Therefore, for this reason, I have requested to see you and speak to you. It is for the hope of Israel that I am bound by this chain." [21]They responded to him, "We have not received letters about you from Judea, nor have any of the brothers come here to speak or report anything bad about you. [22]We would like to hear from you, what you think, for we know that everywhere this heresy is maligned."

[23]They planned a day to meet with him, and they came to him where he was staying in greater numbers. He testified of the kingdom of God, trying to convince them from morning until evening about Jesus from the law of Moses and the Prophets. [24]And some were convinced by what he said, but others did not believe.

[25]As they were leaving, they disagreed with one another about one word that Paul said, "The Holy Spirit spoke well through the prophet Isaiah about your ancestors, [26]saying, *'Go to this people and say, hearing you hear but you do not understand, and looking you see, but you do not perceive. [27]For the heart of this people has become dull, and they are slow to listen, and they have closed their eyes, so that they might not see with their eyes, and hear with their ears, and understand with their heart, and return that I might heal them.'* [28]Therefore, know that this salvation has been sent from God to the Gentiles, and they will listen."

[30]He stayed there for two years in his own lodgings and received all who went to him, [31]proclaiming the kingdom of God and teaching about the Lord Jesus Christ with all boldness and without limitation.

28:19 Paul was attempting to present himself as positive to his *people* despite having been judged by some Jews. **28:22** The Roman Jews refer to Christianity as a sect. The word refers primarily to a division within a religious movement, one that is not viewed favorably. **28:26–27** Quotation from Isaiah 6:9–10. **28:29** A number of very late and inferior manuscripts add verse 29, which reads *And after he said these things, the Jews departed, and they were arguing among themselves.* **28:31** *Without limitation* probably refers to Paul teaching the gospel message to Jews and Gentiles equally. In other words, there were no ethnic boundaries to his teaching.

ROMANS

AUTHOR

Paul is listed as the sole sender of the letter to the Roman saints, a community that he had not visited previous to writing to them. At the time that Paul wrote, he had many contacts in Rome. Before he sent his letter, he was aware that a community of saints had been established in that city (15:23). Paul implies that the Roman community of Christians was famous (1:8), but he does not indicate why, and the reader is left to wonder if it was a result of size, influence, or the profile of its membership. In writing to them, Paul indicated that he wanted to visit them, but Paul's destination was Spain and not Rome (15:23–25). For reasons that remain unclear, he had determined to go there after completing his third missionary journey in Asia, Macedonia, and Greece. Based on clues in the final chapter, many scholars suggest that Paul wrote this letter while in Corinth (16:1). Prisca and Aquila, Paul's coworkers from Corinth, had returned to Rome, and he greeted them at the close of the letter (16:3). Paul also greeted a variety of other friends and acquaintances, including some that may have been his relatives (16:7, 11) and close personal friends (16:9). The letter is also signed by an otherwise unknown individual named Tertius (16:22), who was responsible for scribing the letter. Several missionary companions are noted at the end of the letter, some of which are also mentioned in Acts: Sosipater, Gaius, and Erastus (16:21, 23; Acts 20:4). Phoebe, a deaconess of the church in Cenchrea (see note on 16:1), appears to be on her way to Rome and may have been the letter carrier.

PURPOSE OF WRITING

Romans is Paul's most theologically rich and developed letter, and it represents a shift in the type of writing that Paul sent to the Christian communities of the Mediterranean basin. This letter signals an interest in describing a foundational statement about belief in Jesus Christ and what it means for the believer to be considered righteous and a full participant in the community of Christian believers. Paul also introduces the audience to an extended conversation about what it means to be justified in the faith of Christ.

One of the focal points of the letter is the concise statement found in 1:16–17 that presents a summary of Paul's gospel teaching, perhaps even a thesis for the letter: "For I

am not ashamed of the gospel, for it is the power of God leading to salvation for every-one who believes, first to the Jew and also the Greek. For the righteousness of God is revealed in the gospel from faith to faith, as it is written, '*The righteous will live by faith.*'" This summary captures the most important points of focus in his teaching—righteous-ness is defined as an act of faith, and God's salvation has been extended to Jews and Gentiles alike. As an ethnic Jew and a missionary to the Gentiles, Paul had continually struggled to make these points clear to his audiences.

Among the consequences of declaring these teachings is that some Christians felt that Paul had abandoned the law of Moses, while others felt that he had not fully embraced the new covenant in Christ. This letter shares Paul's personal expression of struggle in finding balance between the Law and faith: "For I know that nothing good resides in me; that is, in my flesh" (7:18). The argument that Paul fought against the personal desire to sin—and that he used the Law as a means of defining what sin is—is a central point of the letter: "For I do not understand my own actions. For I do not do what I want to do, but I do the thing I hate to do. Now, if I do what I do not want to do, I agree that the Law is good" (7:15–16). Ultimately, he shifted righteousness away from being an ethnic designation toward a concept that arises from the suppression of the urge to sin, which the righteous individual seeks to do constantly.

CONNECTION TO LATTER-DAY SAINT BELIEFS

Latter-day Saints will find in the letter to Romans a source of information about what it means to be justified or considered righteous. For many believers, the word *justified* has come to have a technical meaning that represents a state of existence that is award-ed after a demonstration of a life of faith. The Greek word is more simply formulated and refers to the idea of being made good, righteous, or obedient. Romans presents a confident discussion of what it means to be justified in the faith of Christ, "because all have sinned and fall short of the glory of God" (3:23), thus introducing the concept of deficit. A believer is immediately deficient because of sin, an unavoidable part of human existence. God offers a remedy to that state of deficit: "they are justified freely by his grace through the redemption that is in Jesus Christ" (3:24). The definition of being made righteous arises out an individual's faith in Christ, "For we consider that a person is justified by faith apart from the works of the law" (3:28). The word *faith* is not to be defined too narrowly, as belief only, but it is a word signaling orientation, an orientation to God and Christ.

The Book of Mormon offers a clarification on this concept: "For we labor diligently to write, to persuade our children, and also our brethren, to believe in Christ, and to be reconciled to God; for we know that it is by grace that we are saved, after all we can do" (2 Nephi 25:23). The language is not precisely the same, Paul using the concept of justification and Nephi using the language of reconciliation, but the introduction of "all we can do" furthers Paul's concept to include works done in faith as an explicit part of the process of being righteous. Paul's statement does not exclude works from the for-mulation, and the two different discussions on the topic of individual righteousness are similar in many respects. ❧

INTRODUCTION

1 ¹Paul, a servant of Jesus Christ, called to be an apostle, appointed to the gospel of God, ²which he announced beforehand through his prophets in the holy scriptures, ³regarding his Son who would come as a descendant of David according to the flesh, ⁴who was appointed the Son of God in power according to the Spirit of Holiness by the resurrection from the dead. Jesus Christ our Lord, ⁵through whom we have received grace and apostleship that brings about obedience leading to faith among all the Gentiles on behalf of his name. ⁶And you are among those who are called by Jesus Christ. ⁷To all those who are in Rome, beloved of God, called to be saints: grace to you and peace from God our Father and Jesus Christ our Lord.

PAUL'S PRAYER OF THANKSGIVING

⁸First, I thank my God through Jesus Christ for all of you, because your faith is proclaimed in all the world. ⁹For my witness is God, whom I serve with my soul in the gospel of his Son. I remember you constantly, ¹⁰always asking in my prayers if somehow, by God's will, I may now succeed in visiting you. ¹¹For I desire to see you so that I may give you a spiritual gift in order to strengthen you; ¹²that is, that we may be mutually comforted by one another's faith, both yours and mine. ¹³I do not want you, brothers and sisters, to misunderstand because I planned to come to you many times (and I was hindered until now), that I might have some fruit among you just as I have already done among the rest of the Gentiles. ¹⁴I am a debtor both to Greeks and foreigners and to the wise and foolish. ¹⁵Thus, it is my desire to proclaim the gospel to you in Rome.

1:1 *Servant* can also be translated as *slave*, and the technical meaning of the term would be a bondservant or a free person who serves another willingly but for pay. The *gospel of God* can refer to the *gospel* that *God* has as his own message of salvation, or the *gospel about God*. Both translations are equally possible. **1:3** *Descendant of David* refers to Christ being born into David's family or lineage. **1:4** The *Holy Spirit* is referred to as the *Spirit of Holiness* (only here in the New Testament), and it is unclear whether this is a poetic variation or an intentionally nuanced difference in meaning. *By the resurrection* can be taken as a statement that the resurrection is what resulted in Jesus Christ being appointed the *Son of God*. Such an interpretation overlooks verse 2, where Jesus had been announced many years before the resurrection. Paul's intent appears to be to provide evidence that Jesus was the chosen Son of God. **1:5** *On behalf of his name* reflects God's interest to exalt the name of his Son among the nations. The Joseph Smith Translation adds a phrase indicating one of the duties of an apostle to this verse. The latter portion reads *through obedience, and faith on his name, to preach the gospel among all nations.* **1:6** The translation of this verse provides a vital piece of evidence regarding whether the church in Rome was predominantly Gentile. The verse begins with a relative pronoun that almost certainly refers to the preceding noun *Gentiles* in verse 5, thus encouraging the Gentiles to see themselves as also among the called or chosen. **1:8** This verse provides part of the teaching for praying to *God* the Father through *Jesus Christ*. As it is used here, faith describes an association with the church of Christ and is not a designation of personal belief. This subtle nuance may help describe the faith of those who have stood as a community of believers for Christ in the context of opposition. **1:10** Paul makes his desire known that he wanted to visit Rome for some time, and he appears to be more optimistic that he will now be permitted the opportunity to travel there. **1:11** Compare Doctrine and Covenants 46:11. **1:13** The phrase *I do not want you . . . to misunderstand* signals Paul's emphasis in writing (1 Corinthians 10:1; 12:1; 1 Thessalonians 4:13).

THE THEME OF THE LETTER

[16]For I am not ashamed of the gospel, for it is the power of God leading to salvation for everyone who believes, first to the Jew and also the Greek. [17]For the righteousness of God is revealed in the gospel from faith to faith, as it is written, "*The righteous will live by faith.*"

GOD IS SEEN IN THE CREATION

[18]For the wrath of God is revealed from heaven upon all the ungodly and unrighteous people who suppress the truth in their unrighteousness [19]because what is known about God is obvious to them, for God did make it plain to them. [20]Since the creation of the world, his unseen attributes, namely his eternal power and divine nature, have been clearly understood in the things that have been created. So they are without excuse. [21]Even though they knew God, they did not honor him as God or give thanks to him, but they became futile in their thinking and their ignorant hearts were darkened. [22]They claimed to be wise, but they became fools. [23]They exchanged the glory of the immortal God for an image like a mortal human being or birds or four-footed animals or reptiles.

[24]Therefore, God handed them over to the desires of their heart to uncleanness, to dishonor their bodies with one another, [25]because they exchanged the truth about God for a lie, and they worshiped and served the creation rather than the one who created it, who is praised forever! Amen.

[26]Because of this, God gave them over to dishonorable passions. For their women did exchange the natural use of sex for something unnatural. [27]Likewise, the men also abandoned natural intercourse with women and were inflamed in their desires for one another. Men acting shamefully

---

1:16 A possible allusion to Psalm 119:46; compare Alma 26:35. Echoed in Doctrine and Covenants 68:4. **1:17** Quotation from Habakkuk 2:4 (with differences from the Hebrew and Greek texts). The *righteousness of God* is taken to mean his righteous actions and plan, not a description of God's personal righteousness that was achieved by human standards. **1:18–31** Paul develops in these verses his view of universal salvation for those who have not had the opportunity to hear the word of God for themselves. **1:19** Paul argues that God has sent his wrath upon the ungodly (verse 18), a sign that God exists and works on behalf of his children. Paul seems to be promoting the idea that a punishment attends sin and that this causal connection, sin leading to wrath, is a sign of God's existence (compare 2 Nephi 2:10). **1:20** The word *attributes* is supplied to clarify the meaning of the Greek. *Actions* could work equally well. *Understood* translates a Greek word that fundamentally implies that a person *perceives* God's attributes. *Divine nature* is the very essence of God himself, the essence or substance of his person. **1:21** *Knowing God* in this verse can imply an obvious revelation of his attributes and actions. Paul is arguing that the visible world was the testimony people received and that they failed to recognize that creation itself was testimony enough to know God. First Nephi 2:11 echoes this verse. **1:23** Paul is condemning the practice of Greek and Roman religion to make images of the gods. His own faith tradition, Judaism, resisted making any images of God. **1:24** A possible allusion to Psalm 81:12. **1:24–25** Paul's primary complaint is that people have not seen God as the Creator but have worshipped the creation itself, thus confusing the product with the producer. **1:26–27** These verses have become one of the primary pieces of evidence for the discussion of homosexuality in the New Testament. In Paul's day, pederasty and other abhorrent sexual practices were more common, particularly in accusations made by religious individuals against foreign religious cults. It is therefore unclear that Paul is condemning the practice of homosexuality but instead may be condemning what he perceives to be strange and foreign sexual practices such as pederasty. From such scant evidence, it remains unclear what actions Paul had in mind here, but it is obviously abhorrent to him.

with males, they received in their own persons the due punishment for their error.

28Because they did not see fit to honor God, God handed them over to a degenerate mind, to do what should not to be done. 29They were filled with all kinds of unrighteousness: wickedness, greed, depravity, full of envy, murder, contention, deceit, craftiness, spreading gossip, 30slanderers, haters of God, insolent, prideful, boastful, inventors of evil, disobedient to parents, 31foolish, promise breakers, heartless, and ruthless. 32Although they know God's righteous decree that those who do these things are worthy of death, they not only do these things but delight in those who do them.

RIGHTEOUS JUDGMENT

2 1Therefore, you have no excuse, whoever you are, when you judge someone else. For when you judge another, you condemn yourself because as the judge you are doing the same things. 2We know that the judgment of God against those who do such things is based on truth. 3Do you think, whoever you are, that when you condemn those who do such things while doing them yourself that you will escape the judgment of God? 4Or do you despise the wealth of his kindness, tolerance, and patience and are unaware that the kindness of God leads you to repentance? 5But you are accumulating wrath for the day of wrath and the revelation of the righteous judgment of God because of your stubborn and unrepentant heart. 6For he will recompense each according to his works, 7with eternal life to those who by patience in good works seek glory, honor, and immortality, 8but wrath and anger for those who promote themselves and do not obey the truth but unrighteousness. 9There will be affliction and distress for everyone who does evil, for the Jew first and also the Greek, 10but glory, honor, and peace to all who do good, for the Jew first and also the Greek. 11For there is no partiality with God.

12For all those who sinned without the law will die without the law, and those who have sinned under the law will be judged by the law. 13For it is not those who hear the law who are righteous before God but

---

1:30 *Insolent* is *hubris* in Greek. **1:32** The summary of the list of vices (verses 29–32) concludes with the strongest condemnation of hypocrisy—namely, those who know the decrees of God but who do not live up to them.

2:1, 3 The Greek text reads *Oh man* in place of *whoever you are*. The term is used in a generic way to refer to men and women and signals a shift to a diatribe (verses 1–5), which is a form of discourse that confronts a theoretical opponent. **2:4** Paul appears to equate the opportunity to repent as an act of kindness on the part of God or an act of kindness in providing his Son as a means to repentance. **2:5** *The day of wrath* is the day of judgment, which is here interpreted negatively for those who have earned the wrath of God. Anger is the defining feature of the judgment for those who do not follow God. **2:6** *Recompense* can also be translated as *reward*. The verse is a quotation of Psalm 62:12; Proverbs 24:12. **2:7** *Seek glory* may imply to the modern reader a lack of humility on the part of the seeker. However, Paul is extolling those who seek God's glory. **2:11** Compare Acts 10:34; Ephesians 6:9; Colossians 3:25; Deuteronomy 10:17; Helaman 3:27–28; Moroni 8:12; Doctrine and Covenants 1:35. **2:12** The word *law* has not been capitalized in this instance because it is not clear that Paul is referring to the law of Moses. The term as used in Romans ranges in meaning between *principle, the law of God*, and the *law of the gospel*. Lowercase *law* represents instances in the translation when it is unclear what law he is referring to. **2:13** Paul may have intended *will be made righteous* to imply a sense of *justification*, a translation that is also possible. The question is whether the state of being righteous is a result of being awarded it by God or whether the person becomes righteous through the patient process of obedience.

those who obey the law who will be made righteous. ¹⁴For whenever Gentiles who do not have the law, by nature obey the law, they become a law to themselves, even though they do not have the law. ¹⁵They demonstrate that the work of the law is written in their hearts, while their conscience bears witness and their conflicting thoughts accuse or perhaps excuse them ¹⁶on the day that God judges the hidden things of humanity though Jesus Christ, according to my gospel.

LIVING UNDER THE LAW

¹⁷If you call yourself a Jew and rely upon the Law and boast of your relationship to God ¹⁸and you know his will and approve of its statutes after having been instructed in the Law, ¹⁹and if you are sure that you are a guide for the blind, a light to those in darkness, ²⁰a teacher of the senseless, an instructor of infants, having a type of knowledge and truth in the Law, ²¹then you who teach others, do you not also teach yourself? Do you preach against stealing, but steal? ²²Do you tell others not to commit adultery but you commit adultery? Do you detest idols but rob temples? ²³You

who boast under the Law dishonor God because you break the Law. ²⁴For just as it is written, '*The name of God is slandered among the Gentiles because of you.*'

²⁵For circumcision is beneficial if you obey the Law, but if you break the Law, your circumcision becomes uncircumcision. ²⁶Therefore, if the uncircumcised person obeys the ordinances of the Law, will his uncircumcision not be regarded as circumcision? ²⁷Then the person who is physically uncircumcised but keeps the Law will judge you who have the written Law and circumcision but you break the Law. ²⁸For a person is not a Jew who is one outwardly, nor is circumcision something that is external and physical. ²⁹Instead, a person is a Jew who is one inwardly, and circumcision is from the heart, in the Spirit and not by the written Law. That person receives praise from God and not from people.

JEWISH OBJECTIONS TO CHRISTIAN FAITH

3 ¹Therefore, what advantage does the Jew have, or what is the benefit of circumcision? ²Much in every way. First,

---

2:14 The meaning of this verse remains obscure because of the phrase *by nature*. The Greek may mean that Gentiles by their very nature do not have the law but that Jews do by virtue of their birth. It may also mean that Gentiles do the works of the law because their nature leads them into good works (compare Doctrine and Covenants 84:45). **2:15** Paul's point seems to be that despite the conflicting evidence of their thoughts, which both excuse and accuse them, their conscience, the source of good in a person, will testify to their actions. Paul's teaching is informed by the Greek concept of the conscience, the part of the self that determines morally guided decisions and that today would be referred to as the soul or spirit. **2:18** *Its statutes* refers literally to *what is excellent* in the Law. **2:19** *A guide to the blind* is used metaphorically to describe the teacher who knows her way and can lead her students on carefully. **2:24** Quotation from Isaiah 52:5. Paul is drawing attention in these verses (17–24) to assumptions surrounding the concept of being chosen and elect and how those concepts do not guarantee that a person is righteous. **2:25** Circumcision was first revealed in Genesis 17:10–14. **2:26** *Righteous things of the Law* is also possible in place of *ordinances of the Law*. The first, however, implies that if there are *righteous things of the Law*, then there must also be wicked things in the Law, a conclusion that moves beyond Paul's intent. Paul is drawing upon the idea of the precepts that are good that direct human behavior. **2:27** *Keeps* can also be translated as *fulfills*.

3:2 Many modern translations have preferred to translate the Greek word *logia* as *oracles*. The word as used in this sentence ranges in meaning from God's promises to his people, to the writings given to the prophets and Moses. *Oracle* is a word that can imply revelations or new communications from God,

the Jews were entrusted with the words of God. ³What then? What if some were unfaithful? Does their lack of faith void the faithfulness of God? ⁴Certainly not. Let God be true and every person a liar, just as it is written, "*So that you may be justified in your words and prevail when you are judged.*" ⁵And if your unrighteousness establishes the righteousness of God, what will we say? That God is unrighteous to inflict wrath? (I am speaking in a human way.) ⁶Certainly not. Otherwise, how can God judge the world? ⁷If by means of my lie, the truthfulness of God increases his glory, why am I still being judged to be a sinner? ⁸Why not say, "Let us do evil so that good may come from it"?—just as some slander us by claiming that we say this. Their condemnation is just.

⁹What then? Are we better off? Not by any means. For we have charged that all, both Jews and Greeks, are under sin, ¹⁰just as it is written that "*there is no one who is righteous, not even one;* ¹¹*there is no one who understands; there is no one who seeks for God.* ¹²*All have turned away; together they have become worthless; there is no one who shows kindness, not even one.*" ¹³"*Their throat is an open grave; they deceived with their tongues; the poison of snakes is under their lips.*" ¹⁴"*Their mouths are full of cursing and bitterness.*" ¹⁵"*Their feet are quick to spill blood,* ¹⁶*ruin and misery are in their paths,* ¹⁷*and they have not known the way of peace.*" ¹⁸"*There is no fear of God before their eyes.*" ¹⁹We know everything that the Law says; it speaks to those under the Law so that every mouth may be closed and the entire world may be held accountable to God. ²⁰For by the works of the Law, *no one will be declared to be righteous before God*, for through the Law comes a knowledge of sin.

JUSTIFICATION

²¹Now, the righteousness of God has been disclosed apart from the law, being witnessed to by the Law and the Prophets; ²²namely, the righteousness of God through

---

but here it refers to what the Jewish people were given in the past, and hence *words* best reflects Paul's thoughts. Doctrine and Covenants 90:4–5 speaks of continuing *oracles*. **3:3** *Faithfulness of God* is used here to denote a part of God's fundamental identity. He acts faithfully in all his dealings despite the fact that people do not always act in faith. **3:4** Quotation from Psalm 51:4. **3:7** Paul is not arguing that he is currently being judged to be a sinner but rather that ultimately the sins and misdeeds of people do not decrease the glory of God and instead increase his glory by establishing his constancy (verse 5) and his need to judge the world (verse 6). Paul's goal appears to be the dismantling of the criticism that he has taught things that were against the law of Moses and therefore encourage people to sin (verse 8). These verses (5–8) are an attempt to undermine that logical problem in the arguments of his opponents. **3:10–12** Quotation from Psalm 13:1–3. **3:12** Compare the similar quotation of this passage from Psalms in 2 Nephi 28:11; Moroni 10:25 (with parallels to Psalms 14:3; 53:2–4). **3:13** Quotation from Psalm 5:9; 140:3. **3:14** Quotation from Psalm 10:7. **3:15–17** Quotation from Isaiah 59:7–8 and Proverbs 1:16. **3:18** Quotation from Psalm 36:1. **3:20** An allusion to Psalm 143:2. Paul sets out to provide an explanation of justification based on the setting of a court where God is the judge (see verses 21–31). The idea of justification is clearly informed by the notion of vindication in court. The Joseph Smith Translation reads *For by the law is the knowledge of sin. Therefore by the deeds of the law shall no flesh be justified in his sight.* **3:20–24** The language of these verses is reflected heavily in 2 Nephi 2:5–8 (which draws on John 1:14), where comment is also made upon the meaning of the *works (deeds) of the law.* **3:21** The *Law and the Prophets* refers to two divisions within the Old Testament: the five books of Moses (= the *Law*) and the writings by the prophets. The historical and poetic books are often referred to in this period simply as the Writings. **3:22** *The faith of Jesus Christ* may refer to Jesus's life of faith and perfect offering, or it may be an encouragement to find the disclosure of God's righteousness in the act of believing *in Jesus Christ* or *faith in Jesus Christ.*

the faith of Jesus Christ for all who believe. For there is no distinction, ²³because all have sinned and fall short of the glory of God; ²⁴they are justified freely by his grace through the redemption that is in Jesus Christ, ²⁵whom God put forward on the seat of mercy, through faith in his death. This was to demonstrate his righteousness because in his divine forbearance he had passed over previously committed sins. ²⁶This was to establish his righteousness at the present time so that he would be just and the justifier of the one who has faith in Jesus.

²⁷Therefore, where is boasting? It is excluded. By what law? Of works? No, but by the law of faith. ²⁸For we consider that a person is justified by faith apart from the works of the law. ²⁹Or is God the God of the Jews only? Is he not the God of the Gentiles too? Yes, of the Gentiles too. ³⁰Since God is one and justifies the circumcised by faith and the uncircumcised through faith, ³¹do we then nullify the law through faith? Certainly not, but we uphold the law.

THE FAITH OF ABRAHAM

4 ¹What, then, will we say was gained from Abraham, our ancestor according to the flesh? ²For if Abraham was justified by works, he has something to boast about, but not before God. ³What does the scripture say? *"Abraham believed God, and it was reckoned to him as righteousness."* ⁴The wage for the one who works is not reckoned according to grace but according to an obligation. ⁵The one who does not work but has faith in him who justifies the ungodly, his faith is reckoned as righteousness. ⁶Just as David speaks about the blessedness of the person to whom God reckons righteousness apart from works, ⁷*"Blessed are those who are forgiven, whose sins are covered. ⁸Blessed is the person against whom the Lord will not reckon sin."*

⁹Is this, then, the blessedness for the circumcised, or for the uncircumcised

---

3:24 *Justified* represents the Greek concept of being made righteous, and *freely* translates a word meaning *given as a gift* and hence *undeservedly*. The word *redemption* describes a verb that means *paying a ransom* or *releasing someone from debt*. This verse constitutes one of Paul's most succinct statements on the gift of salvation through Jesus Christ. Compare Doctrine and Covenants 20:30. **3:25** *Faith in his death* is literally *faith in his blood*. Paul speaks specifically of Jesus being put forward on the *seat of mercy*, a technical term referring to the covering or lid of the ark of the covenant where the blood of sacrifice was sprinkled (see Leviticus 16:13–16). This verse may represent an early confessional formula. **3:26** *Faith in Jesus* can also be translated as *faith of Jesus*. The implication is that Paul could be drawing attention to Jesus as an example of faith and that believers should emulate his faith. **3:28** Nephi emphasizes salvation by grace *after all we can do* (2 Nephi 25:23), in contrast to the emphasis Paul places here that justification is achieved *apart from the works of the law*. Nephi's context is clearly the law of Moses (2 Nephi 25:24), but Paul's teaching is not specifically stated in the context of the law of Moses. **3:30** An allusion to Deuteronomy 6:4.

4:2 Paul may have intended *works of the law*, as many translations render the passage, but the Greek text uses only the word *works*. **4:3** Quotation from Genesis 15:6. **4:5** In this formulation, Paul extols belief without work. While placing so much emphasis on the notion of belief, Paul encourages his Gentile audience to feel welcomed into the fellowship of the community through their belief. **4:6** *God reckons* implies a deliberative approach to judgment, which represents closely the meaning of the Greek. *About the blessedness* is in Greek *a blessing*, but the intent of the Greek is that David had spoken of a state of blessedness for those who have been forgiven (verse 7). **4:7–8** Quotation from Psalm 32:1–2. The concept of sin is often based on the idea that sin is lawlessness or iniquity because sin involves breaking or violating the law of Moses. In a sense, sin is a state of lawless existence because a person is no longer guided by God's law. **4:9** Quotation from Genesis 15:6 with differences in wording. The question of

too? For we say, *"Faith was reckoned as righteousness to Abraham."* [10]How was it reckoned to him? Was he circumcised or uncircumcised at the time? He was not circumcised but uncircumcised. [11]And he received the sign of circumcision as a seal of the righteousness of his faith while being uncircumcised in order that he would be the father of all those who believe but were uncircumcised and would thus have righteousness reckoned to them. [12]And he is the father of the circumcised, of those who are not only circumcised but who also walk in the footsteps of the faith of our father Abraham when he was uncircumcised.

THE PROMISE
GIVEN TO ABRAHAM

[13]For the promise given to Abraham and to his descendants that he would inherit the world did not come through the Law but through the righteousness of faith. [14]For if the heirs are those who follow the Law, faith is empty and the promise is void. [15]For the Law brings wrath, but where there is no law, there is no transgression. [16]For this reason it depends on faith, so that the promise is according to grace in order that the promise may be guaranteed to all the descendants, not only those who are under the Law but also those who have the faith of Abraham, who is the father of us all, [17]just as it is written, *"I have made you a father of many nations"*—in the presence of God in whom he believed, who gives life to the dead, and he calls into being the things that do not exist. [18]Who against hope, he believed that he would become *the father of many nations,* according to what he had been told, *"So will your descendants be."* [19]And not being weak in faith, he considered his own body as already dead (for he was about one hundred years old) and the barrenness of Sarah's womb. [20]And he did not lack trust concerning the promise of God, but he grew strong in faith while giving glory to God, [21]being fully convinced that God was able to do what he had promised. [22]Therefore, it was reckoned to him as righteousness. [23]But the words, *"It was reckoned to him,"* were not written for him only, [24]but for us also, to whom it will be reckoned to those who believe in him who raised Jesus our Lord from the dead, [25]who was handed over because of our sins and raised for our justification.

Abraham's state of being blessed draws attention to the possibility that he was blessed prior to observing the commandment of circumcision. In the following verses, Paul will present the conclusion that Abraham was blessed before obeying that covenant (verses 10–12). **4:11** Compare Paul's other statement on this idea (Galatians 3:8). **4:12** The Greek says literally *believe through uncircumcision.* **4:13** The phrase *and to his descendants* extends the promises of Abraham and his children independently of the Law. Paul is suggesting that God's promise has always been extended, in part, separate from the Law. **4:15** *Transgression* reflects a Greek word that emphasizes the act of violating the commandments, whereas *sin* represents the translation of a Greek word that emphasizes the uncleanness resulting in violating the commandments. **4:16** The Joseph Smith Translation changes this verse so that it presents *faith and works* as equally necessary, thus bringing Paul's statement into harmony with the Book of Mormon (2 Nephi 25:23). **4:17** Quotation from Genesis 17:5. **4:18** Quotation from Genesis 15:5; 17:5. The Genesis account refers to the innumerability of Abraham's descendants, which is implied in the quotation. **4:19** Some manuscripts read *He did not consider,* which appears to be a later scribal attempt to extol the faith of Abraham, who was nearly one hundred years old but who did not consider it impossible for him and his wife to bear children. The better and earlier manuscripts omit the negative particle, which is reflected in the translation. Some good manuscripts omit *already,* but the word appears to be original based on its excellent manuscript support. **4:23** An allusion to Genesis 15:6. **4:25** *Our justification* can also be translated as *our being made righteous.*

RECONCILIATION

5 ¹Therefore, because we have been justified by faith, we have peace with God through our Lord Jesus Christ, ²through whom by faith we have achieved access to this grace in which we stand, and we rejoice in the hope of God's glory. ³And not only that, we rejoice in trials, knowing that trial produces endurance, ⁴and endurance produces character, and character produces hope, ⁵and hope does not disappoint us, because God's love has been poured into our hearts through the Holy Spirit, which has been given to us.

⁶For while we were still weak, Christ died at the appointed time for the ungodly. ⁷For rarely will someone die for a righteous person, although for a good person someone might dare to die. ⁸But God demonstrates his love for us, because while we were still sinners Christ died for us. ⁹Therefore, having been much more justified now by his blood, how much more are we saved from wrath through him. ¹⁰For while we were enemies, we were reconciled to God through the death of his Son, how much more are we saved by his life after having been reconciled? ¹¹But not only that, we also rejoice in God through our Lord Jesus Christ, through whom we have now received reconciliation.

DEATH AND SIN

¹²Therefore, just as sin entered the world through one man and death entered through sin and death spread to all people because all sinned, ¹³sin was indeed in the world before the Law was revealed, but sin is not reckoned when there is no law, ¹⁴but death ruled from Adam until Moses, even upon those whose sins were not like the transgression of Adam, who was a type of the one who was to come.

¹⁵But the freely gracious gift is not like the sin. For if many died as the result of the sin of one man, how much more have the grace of God and the gift of grace of that one man, Jesus Christ, abounded for many. ¹⁶The free gift is not like the one person's sin. For judgment as a result of a single transgression led to condemnation, but the free gift following many sins led to justification. ¹⁷For if death ruled through that man because of one transgression, how much more will those who receive an abundance of grace and the gift of righteousness reign in life through the one man, Jesus Christ.

¹⁸Therefore, just as one man's sin led to the condemnation of all people, even so through one man's righteousness came righteousness in their life. ¹⁹For just as through the disobedience of one man many were made sinners, even so through the obedience of one man many will be made righteous. ²⁰But a law entered with the result that sin increased, but where sin

---

5:1 Paul concludes the first major section of the letter and begins a second section, which ends in 8:39. This section focuses on election, righteousness, and justification. Compare 1 Nephi 4:14. **5:3** *Trials* refers also to human suffering and tribulation. Paul reflected earlier in his life on his trials (2 Corinthians 4:17). **5:5** First Nephi 11:22 is similar to this verse. **5:5, 8** The word *love* can in some contexts be translated as *charity*. The phrase *God's love* can refer to his love for us or our love for God. Both are equally possible. **5:10, 11** *Reconcile* is the Greek word that describes atonement, the act of reconciling our sins with God. Some translations prefer the noun *atonement*, but *reconciliation* captures the nuance of the Greek. In Paul's letter we are reconciled by the Son of God, and in 2 Nephi 10:24 we reconcile ourselves. **5:12** *One man* refers to Adam. This teaching is alluded to in 2 Nephi 9:6. **5:13** The ideas in this verse are alluded to in 2 Nephi 2:13. **5:14** Compare Mosiah 3:11. The Joseph Smith Translation adds to the very end of this verse the phrase *For I say that through the offense death reigned over all.* **5:18** The final phrase *came righteousness in their life* is difficult to render into English. The Greek literally states *came righteousness of life.*

increased, grace abounded all the more [21]so that just as sin ruled in death, even so grace might rule through righteousness to eternal life through Jesus Christ our Lord.

RISING WITH CHRIST

6 [1]What will we say, then? Should we remain in sin so that grace may increase? [2]Certainly not. Can we who are dead to sin still live in it? [3]Do you not understand that all of us who were baptized into Christ Jesus were baptized to his death? [4]Therefore, we have been buried with him through baptism into death so that just as Christ was raised from the dead through the glory of the Father, even so we may walk in newness of life.

[5]For if we become united in the figure of his death, we will certainly be united in his resurrection. [6]We know this, that our former self was crucified with him so that the sinful body might be destroyed and so that we would no longer be enslaved to sin. [7]For the one who has died is freed from sin. [8]But if we have died with Christ, we believe that we will live with him. [9]We know that Christ was raised from the dead to die no more; death no longer ruled over him. [10]Regarding the death he died, he died with respect to sin once and for all, but the life he lives, he lives to God. [11]So you must consider yourselves dead to sin and alive with God in Christ Jesus.

[12]Therefore, do not allow sin to rule your mortal body so that you follow its desires. [13]Do not offer the parts of your body to sin as instruments of wickedness, but present yourselves to God as those who are alive from the dead, and your members to God as instruments to be used for righteousness. [14]For sin will not rule over you, for you are not under the Law but under grace.

OUR COMMITMENT TO RIGHTEOUSNESS

[15]What then? Do we sin because we are not under the Law but under grace? Certainly not. [16]Do you not know that if you present yourselves as obedient slaves, you are slaves of the one whom you obey, whether to sin which results in death, or to obedience which results in righteousness? [17]But thanks be to God that although you were formerly slaves to sin, you obeyed the type of teaching to which you were entrusted from the heart [18]and that you were set free from sin and became enslaved to righteousness [19](I am speaking in human terms

---

6:1 According to Paul, if sinning results in God forgiving us and thereby providing us with an act of grace, some may assume then that sinning is a means to allow God to act in the world. Paul rejects this notion entirely. **6:1–11** These verses present a model of Christian behavior based on the idea that we die with Christ when we put off the old and sinful self and begin a new life to God. In this way, Christ's atoning sacrifice is exemplary and a model of the life of faith. **6:15** Paul rejects the notion that the Law defines the reasons for being righteous. Paul sees it as an informed choice to serve God, to accept the calling to be his servant, and to serve through belief and hope in an eternal life (verse 22). **6:16–18** Paul interprets life as competing and contradictory enslavements, to sin or to righteousness. **6:16** The concept of enslavement had both negative and positive aspects in the New Testament. Paul is drawing upon the concept of the bondservant, the one who agrees to serve someone for pay or for position. Compare Ephesians 4:22; Colossians 3:9–10 for the later development of the idea of the *former self*. **6:17** The phrase employed by Paul, *you obeyed from the heart the type of teaching to which you were entrusted*, is cumbersome in English. The intent seems to be *you obeyed with your heart the teachings you were given*, but the Greek has been translated precisely as Paul wrote it. A possible allusion to Isaiah 12:1. **6:19** Paul speaks of the *flesh* as a reason for speaking in a blunt and straightforward manner. Typically the inability to accept new truths is understood to be an issue of the heart or mind, but in this instance it is likely an indicator that he was writing, in part, to a Gentile audience who were not part of the covenant people according to the *flesh*. *Holiness* can also be translated as *sanctification* (also verse 22).

because of the weakness of your flesh). For just as you once presented your members as slaves to impurity and to greater and greater lawlessness, so now present your members as slaves to righteousness, leading to holiness. ²⁰For when you were slaves of sin, you were free from righteousness. ²¹Then what fruit did you produce in the things that you are now ashamed of? For the end of those things is death. ²²But now that you are free from sin and enslaved to God, you produce fruit leading to holiness and its end, an eternal life. ²³For the wages of sin are death, but the gift of God is eternal life in Christ Jesus, our Lord.

THE EXAMPLE OF MARRIAGE

7 ¹Do you not understand, brothers and sisters (for I am speaking to those who know the Law), that the law rules a person for the duration of one's life? ²For a married woman is bound by a law to her husband as long as he is living, but if her husband dies, she is released from her marriage contract. ³Accordingly, she will be called an adulteress if she lives with another man while her husband is living. But if the husband dies, she is free from that law,

and if she marries another man she is not an adulteress.

⁴Likewise, my brothers and sisters, you have died with respect to the Law through the body of Christ so that you belong to another, to him who was raised from the dead, in order that we may bear fruit to God. ⁵While we are in the flesh, our sinful desires aroused by the Law were at work in our members to bear fruit to death. ⁶Now, we have been released from the Law, having died to what controlled us so that we may serve in a new life in the Spirit and not under the old written words.

THE LAW DEFINES SIN

⁷What will we say, then? The Law is sin? Certainly not. But, I would not have known sin without a Law. For I would not have known what it means to covet if the Law had not said, "*Do not covet.*" ⁸But sin, seizing an opportunity through the commandment, worked all kinds of covetousness in me. For apart from the Law, sin is dead. ⁹But I once lived apart from the Law, but after the commandment came, sin revived ¹⁰and I died. And the commandment that promised life brought death to me.

6:20 Paul's argument implies that a person is entirely enslaved to righteousness or sin, a point that is likely made for rhetorical effect because later he presents the idea that the individual is at war with the desires to sin and do good (Romans 7:14–25), thereby indicating that both influences were at work in the individual. **6:23** Compare Alma 5:42.

7:1 Greek uses *brothers* generically to refer to *brothers and sisters.* Paul does not speak of eternal law but seems to be referring to the cessation of human laws like the law of Moses, which he does not see as eternal in nature. **7:2** The Greek says literally *she is released from the law of her husband,* which refers to her contract with him. **7:4** See note on 7:1. **7:5** *Our sinful desires aroused by the Law* refers to the Law's ability to curtail or to specify what constitutes sin, and thereby it *aroused* sin. **7:5–25** These verses were heavily revised in Joseph Smith's translation of the Bible to make them more autobiographical about Paul's own spiritual journey from persecutor to believer. **7:6** Many translations prefer the word *code* to *words,* which makes Paul's reference more obvious to be the law of Moses. Paul's precise intent is not clear, but his argument is that the former writings are no longer binding in the same way that a new life in the Spirit is binding. *Serve* is in this verse the service of a slave or bondservant. **7:7** Quotation from Exodus 20:17; Deuteronomy 5:21. **7:8** This verse strongly implies that by *law* Paul is referring to the law of Moses, but other parts of the discussion are less clear that he is always referring to the law of Moses (see Romans 2:12–16). **7:9** Many commentators have seen in this verse an admission that Paul had at one time not followed his ancestral religion. The Joseph Smith Translation indicates that they reflect Paul's unwillingness to believe in Christ. **7:10** Compare Leviticus 18:5.

[11]For sin seized an opportunity through the commandment and deceived me, and through it I died. [12]So then the Law is holy and the commandment is holy, righteous, and good.

[13]Then did that which is good become death for me? Certainly not. But sin, so that it would be shown to be sin, worked death in me by means of that which is good so that through the commandment sin would become entirely sinful.

FIGHTING THE DESIRE TO SIN

[14]For we know that the Law is spiritual, but I am mortal, sold as a slave to sin. [15]For I do not understand my own actions. For I do not do what I want to do, but I do the thing I hate to do. [16]Now, if I do what I do not want to do, I agree that the Law is good. [17]Then it is no longer me doing it, but the sin residing in me. [18]For I know that nothing good resides in me; that is, in my flesh. For I can desire to do what is right, but I am not able do it. [19]For I do not do the good I desire to do, but the evil I do not want, that is what I do. [20]Now, if I do what I do not want to do, it is no longer me doing it but the sin that resides in me.

[21]So I find it to be a law, that when I desire to do good, evil is also present in me. [22]For I delight in the law of God in my inner self, [23]but I see another law in my members waging war against the law of my mind, making me captive to the law of sin which is in my members. [24]Wretched man that I am! Who will rescue me from this body of death? [25]Thanks be to God through Jesus Christ our Lord. Therefore, I am a slave to the Law of God in my mind, but in my flesh I serve the law of sin.

THE SPIRIT GUIDES

8 [1]Now, there is no condemnation of those who are in Christ Jesus. [2]For the law of the Spirit of life in Christ Jesus has freed you from the law of sin and death.

[3]For God accomplished what the Law was not able to do because it was weakened by the flesh. By sending his own Son in the likeness of sinful flesh and as an offering for sin, he condemned sin in the flesh [4]so that the just requirements of the Law would be fulfilled in us, who do not walk according to the flesh but according to the Spirit. [5]For those who live according to the flesh set their minds upon mortal things, but those who live according to the Spirit set their minds upon spiritual things. [6]A mind set on the flesh is death, but a mind rooted in the Spirit is life and peace, [7]because a mind set on the flesh is hostile to God, for it does not submit to God's law, nor is it able to do so. [8]Those who are in the flesh cannot please God.

[9]You are not in the flesh but in the Spirit if indeed the Spirit of God resides

---

7:14 This verse speaks of the mortal self and its inclination to sin. A similar view is expressed in Mosiah 16:3, 11–12 (compare James 3:15). **7:16** By asserting that Paul conforms his desires to follow the commandments of the Law, he thereby affirms that the Law is good. **7:24** Compare 2 Nephi 4:17.

8:1 Some later manuscripts add at the end of the verse the phrase *who do not walk according to flesh*, and some add the additional note *but according to the Spirit*. These additions are late and appear to be scribal attempts to clarify precisely who would avoid condemnation. The additions seem to imply that scribes knew of people who were *in Christ Jesus* but who still lived after the flesh and not according to the Spirit. A life in Christ enables the believer to be justified, which in turn results in that person not experiencing any *condemnation*. **8:2** Some early manuscripts read *has freed me* in place of *has freed you*. The better reading is *has freed you* based on the available manuscripts. Compare 2 Corinthians 3:17. **8:3** *Weakened by the flesh* alerts us that the law itself is good, but human attempts to live it perfectly have failed. **8:5–8** Paul sets forth the idea that living a spiritually informed and guided life in Christ leads to the fulfillment of the Law. **8:6** Compare 2 Nephi 9:39.

in you. If anyone does not have the Spirit of Christ, this person does not belong to him. [10]If Christ is in you, even though your body is dead because of sin, your spirit is alive because of righteousness. [11]If the Spirit of him who raised Jesus from the dead resides in you, he who raised Jesus from the dead will give life to your mortal bodies through his Spirit who resides in you.

[12]However, brothers and sisters, we are obligated not to the flesh, to live according to the flesh [13](if you live according to the flesh, you will die), but if by the Spirit you put to death the actions of the body, you will live. [14]For all who are led by the Spirit of God, they are the children of God. [15]For you did not receive the spirit of slavery again to cause you to fear, but you received the Spirit of adoption in which we cry out, "Abba, Father." [16]The Spirit itself testifies to our spirit that we are the children of God. [17]And if we are children, then heirs, heirs of God, coheirs with Christ, if indeed we suffer jointly with him so that we may also be glorified with him.

THE GLORY OF THE COMING AGE

[18]For I think that the sufferings of the present age are not worthy to be compared to the glory that will be revealed to us. [19]For the creation waits with eager expectation for the revealing of the children of God, [20]for the creation was subjected to futility not of its own will but because of him who subjected it in hope, [21]because the creation itself will be set free from servitude to corruption to receive the freedom of the glory of the children of God. [22]We know that the entire creation has been groaning in pain until now, [23]but not only it but we ourselves, who have the firstfruits of the Spirit, we also groan in ourselves anticipating our adoption, the redemption of our bodies. [24]We were saved in hope, but hope that is seen is not hope, because who hopes for what he sees? [25]If we do not see what we hope for, we eagerly anticipate with patience.

[26]In a like manner, the Spirit helps our weaknesses, for we do not know what we should pray for, but the Spirit itself intercedes with unspeakable groanings. [27]And he who searches the hearts knows the mind of the Spirit, because the Spirit intercedes on behalf of the saints according to God's will.

[28]We know that all things work together for good for those who love God, who are called according to his purpose, [29]because those whom he knew beforehand he also foreordained to be conformed to the

---

8:10 *Your spirit* can also be translated as *the Spirit*. Paul's precise intent is unclear in speaking of being alive in Christ and saying our *body is dead*, which may imply that he was speaking of our spirits that were still alive. **8:12** Greek uses *brothers* generically to refer to *brothers and sisters*. **8:13** This is Paul's argument for active belief and faith, which cannot be simply passive in its acceptance of Christ and the gospel. A person must work to put to death *the actions of the body*. Compare Colossians 3:5. **8:14** The state of being a child of God is predicated upon being *led by the Spirit*. It is not a universal condition but rather something that a believer becomes (Galatians 4:1–7). **8:15** Compare Mark 14:36. Paul had earlier presented his thoughts about adoption (Galatians 4:5–7). **8:18–25** Paul sets forth the idea that the eventual goal of God's plan was that all would become *the children of God* and that the creation has eagerly awaited the time when the earth's inhabitants would become children. **8:20** *Subjected to futility* implies Paul's awareness that the created world was never sufficient enough to exist independently of God. Genesis 3:17–19 may be the source of the concept of the earth that is *subjected to futility*. **8:21** Paul treats similar themes in 2 Corinthians 5:17; Colossians 1:15. **8:28** *Called* is used here in the sense of *chosen*. The language of this verse is echoed in Doctrine and Covenants 90:24; 100:15. **8:29** See note on 8:2. *Foreordained* can also be translated as *predestined*. Greek does not distinguish between the two words, and Paul draws upon the idea of a foreknowing God who prepared salvation beforehand.

image of his Son in order that he might be the firstborn among many brothers and sisters. [30]And those whom he foreordained he also called. And those whom he called he also justified, and those whom he justified he also glorified.

GOD IS WITH US

[31]What shall we say about these things? If God is for us, who is against us? [32]He who did not spare his own Son but handed him over for all of us, how will he not also graciously give us all things with his Son? [33]Who will bring any charge against God's elect? It is God who justifies. [34]Who will condemn? Christ is the one who died, and more than that he was also raised. He is at the right hand of God, who intercedes on our behalf. [35]Who will separate us from the love of Christ? Trial or calamity or persecution or famine or nakedness or danger or a sword? [36]As it is written, *"For your sake we are being killed all day long; we are regarded as sheep to be slaughtered."* [37]But in all these things, we are more than conquerors through him who loved us. [38]For I am convinced that neither death nor life nor angels nor heavenly rulers nor things that are present nor things to come nor powers [39]nor height nor depth nor anything else in creation will be able to separate us from the love of God in Christ Jesus our Lord.

THE PROMISES TO ISRAEL

9 [1]I speak the truth in Christ; I do not lie. My conscience testifies to me in the Holy Spirit [2]that I have great sorrow and unceasing pain in my heart. [3]For I would pray that I am cursed and cut off from Christ on behalf of my brothers and sisters, my relatives according to the flesh, [4]who are Israelites. To them belong the adoption, the glory, the covenants, the giving of the Law, the temple service, and the promises. [5]To them belong the patriarchs, from whom came the Christ by means of the flesh, who is God over all things, blessed in the eternities, amen.

[6]It is not as though the word of God failed. For not all who belong to Israel are Israelites, [7]nor do all the children belong to Abraham because they are his descendants, but *"Through Isaac your descendants will be called."* [8]That is to say, it is not the children by the flesh who are the children of God, but the children of the promise are considered descendants. [9]For the promise declares this, *"About this time next year I will return, and Sarah will have a son."* [10]Not only that, but when Rebecca had conceived a child by Isaac our father, [11]even

---

8:31 Compare 2 Kings 6:16. **8:32** *With his Son* is in Greek *with him*, but the pronoun has been clarified for the reader. **8:36** Quotation from Psalm 44:22. **8:38** The Greek reads only *rulers*, but *heavenly* has been supplied to clarify that Paul was speaking of angelic intermediaries. Compare 2 Corinthians 2:14. **8:39** Compare 2 Nephi 1:15.

9–11 These chapters constitute the third major doctrinal section of the letter, focusing on what it means to be of the house of Israel. These chapters provide a scriptural basis for the Gentile mission and the concept of adoption. These chapters draw heavily upon passages from the Old Testament. **9:5** *The Christ* has the same meaning as *the Messiah*, and the emphasis is on Jesus coming as the promised Messiah. **9:6–13** Paul sets forth the idea that Israel is not defined by lineage alone or even primarily through lineage but through accepting Christ. This logic helped support the early church's efforts to develop an ethnically diverse missionary effort. Part of Paul's message is that the plan of God exists beyond human reason to explain it because God hated Esau (see verses 10–13) before his birth and loved Isaac. Such obvious unfairness helps Paul draw the conclusion that God exists beyond the realm of human reason. **9:7** Quotation from Genesis 21:12. Paul was attempting to draw attention to the fact that Ishmael and his descendants were excluded from the promises. **9:9** Quotation from Genesis 18:10, 14. **9:10** See Genesis 25:22–23. **9:11–12** These verses are divided differently in some translations, where verse 12

though they were not born, nor had they done anything good or bad, in order that God's purpose according to election might remain, not because of works but because of the one who calls, [12]she was told, "*The older will serve the younger,*" [13]just as it is written, "*I loved Jacob, but I hated Esau.*"

[14]What will we say then? Is there injustice with God? Certainly not. [15]For he says to Moses, "*I will have mercy upon whom I have mercy, and I will have compassion upon whom I have compassion.*" [16]Therefore, it does not depend on desire or exertion but upon God's mercy. [17]For the scripture says to Pharaoh, "*I have raised you up so that I might show my power in you so that my name may be proclaimed in all the earth.*" [18]Therefore, God has mercy upon whom he desires, and he hardens whomever he wants.

GENTILES AND ISRAEL

[19]Therefore, you will say to me, "Then why does he still find fault? For who has resisted his will?" [20]Oh man, who are you to question God? "*Does what is molded say to the shaper, 'Why have you made me like this?'*" [21]Does the potter not have the power over the clay to make out of the same lump, one vessel of beauty and another for ordinary use? [22]But what if God were willing to show his wrath and to make his power known and has endured with great patience the vessels of wrath destined for destruction? [23]And what if he wanted to make the richness of his glory known upon the vessels of mercy that he had prepared beforehand for glory, [24]even us whom he

has called, not from the Jews only but also from the Gentiles? [25]as he said in Hosea, "*I will call those who are not my people, 'My people,' and I will call her who was not loved, 'My beloved.'*" [26]"*And in every place where it was told to them, 'You are not my people,' there they will be called the 'children of the living God.'*" [27]As Isaiah declares concerning Israel, "*Even though the number of the children of Israel are like the sand of the sea, only a remnant will be saved, [28]for the Lord will carry out his sentence upon the earth completely and quickly.*" [29]Just as Isaiah predicted, "*If the Lord of armies had not left us children, we would have been like Sodom and been made like Gomorrah.*"

[30]What will we say then? That the Gentiles who did not pursue righteousness have obtained it—that is, righteousness through faith—[31]but Israel who pursued righteousness that is based upon the Law did not obtain it by fulfilling that Law. [32]Why? Because they did not pursue it by faith but as though it were based on works. They have tripped over the stumbling stone, [33]just as it is written, "*Behold, I am laying in Zion a stone that will cause people to stumble, and a rock that will make them fall, and the one who believes in him will not be ashamed.*"

10 [1]Brothers and sisters, it is the desire of my heart and my prayer to God on their behalf for their salvation. [2]For I testify that they have zeal for God, but it is without knowledge. [3]For while ignoring the righteousness of God and seeking to establish their own righteousness, they did not submit to God's righteousness. [4]For

---

begins with *not because of works.* **9:12** Quotation from Genesis 25:23. **9:13** Quotation from Malachi 1:2–3. **9:15** Quotation from Exodus 33:19. **9:17** Quotation from Exodus 9:16. **9:18** Compare Deuteronomy 2:30. **9:20** Quotation from Isaiah 29:16; 45:9. **9:22** Alluded to in Doctrine and Covenants 76:33. **9:21** Compare Jeremiah 18:1–11. **9:25** Quotation from Hosea 2:23. **9:26** Quotation from Hosea 1:10. **9:27–28** Quotation from LXX Isaiah 10:22–23 with variations from the Hebrew text. **9:28** Alluded to in Doctrine and Covenants 52:11. **9:29** Quotation from Isaiah 1:9. **9:33** Quotation from Isaiah 28:16; 8:14. The phrase *make them fall* can also be translated as *make them be offended.*

10:1 Greek uses *brothers* generically to refer to *brothers and sisters.* The subject of this verse is the wayward Israelites mentioned in 9:32.

Christ is the end of the Law for the purpose of righteousness for all who believe.

SALVATION AVAILABLE TO ALL

[5]For Moses writes about the righteousness which is from the Law, "*The one who does these things will live by them.*" [6]But the righteousness through faith says, "*Do not say in your heart, 'Who will ascend to heaven?'*" (that is, to bring down Christ) [7]or, "*Who will descend into the abyss?*" (that is, to lead Christ out from the dead). [8]But what does it say? "*The word is near you, in your mouth, and in your heart*" (that is, the word of faith that we proclaim). [9]If you confess Jesus is the Lord with your mouth and you believe in your heart that God raised him from the dead, you will be saved. [10]For a person believes with the heart and is righteous and confesses with the mouth for salvation. [11]For the scripture says, "*Everyone who believes in him will not be put to shame.*" [12]For there is no difference between Jew and Greek, for the same Lord is Lord of all, who richly blesses all who call upon him: [13]"*Everyone who calls on the name of the Lord will be saved.*"

[14]How can they call on him in whom they have not believed? And how do they believe in one they have not heard? How do they hear without someone proclaiming him? [15]How can they proclaim the word if they are not sent? Just as it is written, "*How timely is the arrival of those who proclaim the good news.*" [16]But not everyone has obeyed the gospel, for Isaiah says, "*Lord, who has believed our message?*" [17]So faith comes from what is heard, and what is heard comes through the teaching of the word of Christ.

[18]But I say, have they not heard? Indeed, they have, "*Their voice went out to all the earth, and their words to the ends of the world.*" [19]But I say, did Israel not understand? First, Moses says, "*I will make you jealous by those who are not a nation; by a foolish nation I will make you angry.*" [20]Isaiah is bold when he says, "*I was found by those who did not seek for me: I became known to those who did not ask for me.*" [21]To Israel he says, "*All day long I extended my hands to this disobedient and stubborn people.*"

THE OPPORTUNITY FOR THE GENTILES

11 [1]Then I ask, has God rejected his people? Certainly not. For I am an Israelite, a descendant of Abraham, of the tribe of Benjamin. [2]*God has not rejected his*

10:5 Quotation from Leviticus 18:5. **10:6** Quotation from Deuteronomy 9:4; 30:12. **10:7** Quotation from Deuteronomy 30:13. The *abyss* refers to a subterranean realm where the dead reside in torment (compare Luke 8:31). It has a spiritual quality in Mosiah 27:29, and the word does not occur in the Old Testament. **10:8** Quotation from Deuteronomy 30:14. **10:9, 13** The quotation of Joel 2:32 appears to be in view here, and Paul is directing his audience to declare that Jesus is the Lord God. **10:11** Quotation from Isaiah 28:16. **10:13** Quotation from Joel 2:32. **10:15** *The word* is added for clarification. The Greek notes simply, *How can they proclaim unless they are sent?* Quotation from Isaiah 52:7; Nahum 1:15. The word *timely* can also mean *beautiful*, but it appears that Paul is drawing on the former meaning of the word. The phrase *is the arrival* translates the Greek idiom *are the feet*. The Isaiah passage looks to a time when the arrival of those who proclaim the good news will be welcomed fully. **10:16** Quotation from Isaiah 53:1. **10:17** Many translations prefer to render the last phrase as *the preaching of Christ*. This translation recognizes the context of this passage where Paul has been speaking of the proclamation and preaching of Christ. However, the shift to *the word* may intentionally emphasize the power of *the word of Christ* both in its written and taught forms. **10:18** Quotation from Psalm 19:4. **10:19** Quotation from Deuteronomy 32:21. **10:20** Quotation from Isaiah 65:1. **10:21** Quotation from Isaiah 65:2 (compare Jacob 5:47, which also quotes this passage from Isaiah, see also 2 Nephi 28:32; Jacob 6:4).

11:2 Quotation from LXX 1 Samuel 12:22.

people whom he knew beforehand. Do you not know what the scripture says about Elijah, how he entreats God against Israel? ³"*Lord, they have killed your prophets, they have demolished your altars, and I am left alone and they seek my life.*" ⁴But what was the response he received? "*I have kept for myself seven thousand men who have not bowed a knee to Baal.*" ⁵So it is now, there is a remnant chosen by grace. ⁶And if it is by grace, then it is no longer by works; otherwise, grace is no longer grace.

⁷What then? Israel sought for but did not obtain it, but the elect obtained it. The rest were hardened, ⁸just as it is written, "*God gave them a spirit of stupor, eyes that would not see and ears that would not listen until this very day.*" ⁹And David says, "*Let their table become a snare and a trap and a stumbling block and a retribution for them;* ¹⁰*let their eyes be darkened so that they do not see, and make their backs bend forever.*"

SALVATION OF THE GENTILES

¹¹Then I ask, have they stumbled so that they might fall? Certainly not. But salvation has come to the Gentiles by means of their transgression to make Israel jealous. ¹²If their transgression brings riches to the world and their defeat brings riches to the Gentiles, how much more will their full inclusion bring?

¹³I am speaking to you Gentiles inasmuch as I am an apostle to the Gentiles; I magnify my service ¹⁴if somehow I could make my fellow Jews jealous and save some of them. ¹⁵For if their rejection is the reconciliation of the world, what will their acceptance mean but life from the dead? ¹⁶If the first portion of the dough is holy, so is the whole lump, and if the root is holy, so too are the branches.

¹⁷If some of the branches were broken off and you who are a wild olive shoot were grafted in among the others and now share in the richness of the olive tree, ¹⁸do not boast to the other branches. If you do so, remember that you do not sustain the root, but the root sustains you. ¹⁹Then you will say, "Branches were broken off so that I might be grafted in." ²⁰That is right. They were broken off because of their unbelief,

---

11:3 Quotation from 1 Kings 19:10, 14. *Altars* refers to the place where sacrifices were made in the temple. These are the altars of the Lord and not pagan altars. **11:4** Quotation from 1 Kings 19:18. *Baal* was a god of the indigenous people living in the Levant and later came to be applied to a number of false or pagan deities. **11:6** *It* refers to the chosen or elected status of Israel, which Paul argues was done by an act of grace and not in recognition of works. Some early manuscripts add to the end of this verse an explanatory addition, *But if it is of works then it is no longer of grace; otherwise grace is no longer grace.* **11:8** Quotation from Deuteronomy 29:4; Isaiah 29:10. **11:9–10** Quotation from Psalm 69:22–23. The passage from the Psalms mentions three different types of traps: one for birds, one for animals, and one for humans. **11:11** *Israel* is added to clarify the Greek *them*, which can be ambiguous in English. Paul may have found a precedent for these ideas in Isaiah 24:5. **11:12** *Inclusion* is added to clarify the ambiguous Greek *their fullness.* The meaning could also be *their full participation* or *their full acceptance of the gospel.* **11:13** Paul speaks of being an *apostle* or missionary (the primary meaning of the Greek word *apostle*) and that he has glorified his *service.* The noun *service* is the translation of the Greek word meaning *the work of a deacon.* Thus, Paul confirms that his ministry as an apostle was to serve the Gentiles as a deacon would serve them. This teaching is echoed in Jacob 1:19; Doctrine and Covenants 24:3, 9; 66:11. **11:15** *Reconciliation of the world* can also be translated as *atonement of the world.* The suggestion is that by rejecting God's Son, Israel opened a door for the salvation of the Gentiles and therefore the world. **11:16** *The first portion of dough* likely refers to the portion of dough set aside for the creation of the *showbread*, or the *Bread of the Presence*, which was placed in the temple and was to be eaten by the priests. **11:17–24** Many of the principles of olive cultivation and grafting are also found in Jacob 5. Compare Jacob 5:9. The question that led to these two different discourses is similar (see Jacob 4:17).

but you stand in faith. Do not be proud, but fear. ²¹For if God did not spare the natural branches, neither will he spare you. ²²Therefore, notice the kindness and severity of God, severity toward those who have fallen, but God's kindness toward you if you continue in his kindness; otherwise, you will be cut off too. ²³Even they, if they do not remain in their unbelief, will be grafted in, for God has the power to graft them in again. ²⁴For if you were cut off from what is a wild tree by nature and grafted contrary to nature into a cultivated tree, how much more will these, the natural branches, be grafted back into their own olive tree?

ISRAEL WILL TURN TO THE LORD

²⁵I do not want you to be ignorant of this mystery, brothers and sisters, so that you are not conceited. Israel has experienced a partial hardening until the fullness of the Gentiles has entered in. ²⁶And so all Israel will be saved, just as it is written, *"The Deliverer will come out of Zion, and he will turn ungodliness away from Jacob;* ²⁷ *and this will be my covenant with them when I take away their sins."*

²⁸Concerning the gospel, they are enemies for your sake, but concerning the election, they are beloved because of their ancestors. ²⁹For the gifts and calling of God are irrevocable. ³⁰Just as you were previously disobedient to God, now you have received mercy because of their disobedience. ³¹So they have now been disobedient in order that by the mercy that is shown to you, they may also now receive mercy. ³²For God has relegated everyone to disobedience so that he may extend mercy to all. ³³Oh, the depth of his riches, and the wisdom and knowledge of God! How unsearchable are his judgments, and how incomprehensible his ways! ³⁴*"For who has understood the mind of the Lord, or who has been his counselor?"* ³⁵*"Or who has given a gift to him, that God needs to repay him?"* ³⁶For all things are from him and through him and to him. Let glory be to him forever, amen.

OUR LIVING SACRIFICE

12 ¹Therefore, I encourage you, brothers and sisters, by the mercies of God to present your bodies as a living sacrifice, holy and acceptable to God, which is your reasonable service. ²Do not be conformed to this age, but be transformed by the renewing of your mind, so that you determine what the will of God is, what is good, acceptable, and perfect.

³For I say, by the grace given to me, to everyone who is among you not to think more highly of yourself than you ought to

---

11:24 Compare 1 Nephi 15:16. **11:25** Greek uses *brothers* generically to refer to *brothers and sisters*. *Until the fullness of the Gentiles has entered in* refers to the time when the full number of Gentiles have accepted the gospel message. It designates a time when they have all had the opportunity to accept the gospel message. First Nephi 15:13 refers to this concept of the fullness of the Gentiles. **11:26–27** Quotation from Isaiah 59:20–21. The last phrase of verse 27 is a quotation from Isaiah 27:9. The concept of Israel gaining forgiveness is from Zechariah 13–14; compare Doctrine and Covenants 45:19–30, 51–53. **11:31** Some early manuscripts omit the second now in this verse, signaling that scribes attempted to emend the verse to indicate that the Jews would only later receive mercy. **11:34** Quotation from Isaiah 40:13. Compare Jacob 4:8. **11:35** Quotation from Job 41:11. **11:36** Doctrine and Covenants 76:24 draws on the language of this verse.

12:1–15:13 The last major exhortation of the letter is designed to strengthen the Christian community through actions that emulate brotherly affection and care. **12:1** Greek uses *brothers* generically to refer to *brothers and sisters*. Paul presents a new model of temple service that replaces animal sacrifice. The believer is to think in terms of offering their own bodies as holy and acceptable offerings to the Lord that are living as opposed to the dead animals offered as part of temple ritual.

think, but to think with sound judgment, as God has given you each a measure of faith. [4]For just as we have many members in one body and all the members do not have the same function, [5]so too we are many in the body of Christ, and individually we are members serving one another. [6]But we have different gifts according to the grace that is given to us. If it is the gift of prophecy, then the person must use it in proportion to faith. [7]If it is service, then let him serve; if it is teaching, then let him teach; [8]if it is exhortation, then let him exhort; if it is giving, let him give with sincerity; if it is leadership, let him lead with diligence; if it is mercy, let him do so with cheerfulness.

A CHRISTIAN LIFE

[9]Love must be genuine. Abhor what is evil; hold tightly to what is good. [10]In loving one another, do so with sincere affection. Take the lead in honoring one another. [11]Do not be slow in your diligence; be enthusiastic in spirit; serve the Lord. [12]Rejoice in hope; endure suffering; be constant in prayer. [13]Assist in the needs of the saints; pursue hospitality. [14]Bless those who persecute you; bless and do not curse. [15]Rejoice with those who are rejoicing; weep with those who are weeping. [16]Be of the same mind one toward another. Do not be haughty, but give yourself to lowly tasks. Do not

be conceited in your thinking. [17]Do not repay anyone with evil for evil; consider what is good for all people. [18]If it is possible, so far as it depends upon you, live peaceably with all people. [19]Do not avenge yourselves, beloved, but give place for God's wrath, for it is written, *"Vengeance is mine, and I will repay,"* says the Lord. [20]But *"If your enemy is hungry, feed him; if he is thirsty, give him something to drink. For in doing this you will be heaping burning coals on his head."* [21]Do not be overcome by evil, but overcome evil with good.

CIVIC AUTHORITIES

13 [1]Let every person be subject to the governing authorities. For there is no authority except from God, and the authorities that do exist have been appointed by God. [2]Therefore, whoever resists such authority resists what God has appointed, and those who resist them will incur judgment. [3]For the rulers do not create fear for good actions but for evil ones. Do you want to avoid fearing the one who is in authority? Do good and you will receive his approval [4]because he is God's servant for your good. But if you do wrong, be afraid, for he does not bear a sword without a reason. For he is a servant of God who administers wrath on the one who does wrong. [5]Therefore, it is necessary to be in subjection not only to avoid wrath

---

12:4–5 Compare 1 Corinthians 12:12–23. **12:5–11** Compare Moroni 10:8–17. **12:6–7** In describing the first gifts of the Spirit, Paul has described the gifts associated with being a prophet, deacon, and teacher. **12:6–8** This list of the gifts of the Spirit lacks finite verbs so that each phrase is constructed without a main verb. The verb *let him* has been supplied in each case to attempt to clarify Paul's intent. **12:10** Compare Philippians 2:2. **12:14** Compare Matthew 5:11–12. **12:15** Compare Mosiah 18:8. **12:16** Perhaps an allusion to Proverbs 26:12. **12:17** Compare 2 Corinthians 8:21. **12:19** Quotation from Deuteronomy 32:35. Compare Mormon 3:15. **12:20** Quotation from Proverbs 25:21–22.

13:1 A similar injunction is found in Doctrine and Covenants 58:21–22. **13:1–7** Paul issues guidelines for civic obedience, which may have arisen out of a need for Christian communities, particularly in Rome, to be aware of the potential for legal action to be taken against them. Acts describes examples of heated exchanges between local Jewish and Christian communities that may have resulted in civic authorities becoming aware of problems between Jews and Christians. **13:4** *Bear a sword* refers to the administration of justice in situations of wrongdoing. **13:5** According to Paul's statement, civil authorities administer God's wrath.

but also for your conscience. ⁶Because of this you pay taxes, for the authorities are God's servants who are concerned with this very thing. ⁷Pay to everyone what is owed to them, taxes to whom taxes are due, earnings to whom earnings are owed, respect to whom respect is due, honor to whom honor is due.

LOVE ONE ANOTHER

⁸Do not owe anyone anything except to love one another, for the one who loves another has fulfilled the Law. ⁹For it says, *"Do not commit adultery; do not murder; do not steal; do not covet,"* and if there is another commandment, it is summed up in this, *"Love your neighbor as yourself."* ¹⁰Love does no wrong to a neighbor; therefore, love is the fulfillment of the Law.

PUT ON THE LORD

¹¹And you know the time, that the hour has arrived for you to wake from sleep. For salvation is nearer to us now than when we began to believe. ¹²The night has advanced, and the day is drawing near. Then let us cast off the works of darkness and put on the armor of light. ¹³Let us walk in decency as in the daytime, not in riotous extravagance and drunkenness nor in adultery and lust nor in contention and jealousy. ¹⁴But put on the Lord Jesus Christ and take no forethought for the flesh, for its desires.

DO NOT JUDGE

14 ¹Welcome the one who is weak in faith, and do not have heated disputes over opinions. ²One person believes in eating all things, while the weak person eats only vegetables. ³Do not let the one who eats despise the one who does not eat, and the one who abstains from eating must not judge the one who eats all things, for God has welcomed him. ⁴Who are you to act as judge for another person's servant? He stands or falls before his own master. And he will stand, for the Lord is able to make him stand.

⁵One person considers one day to be better than another, while another thinks that all days are alike. Each must be convinced in his own mind. ⁶The one who observes the day does so for the Lord. The one who eats does so for the Lord and gives thanks to God, and the one who does not eat does so for the Lord and gives thanks

---

13:6 Perhaps an allusion to Jesus's teaching in Mark 12:13–17. **13:7** Doctrine and Covenants 134:6 offers valuable commentary on this verse. **13:9** Quotation from Exodus 20:13–15, 17 (Deuteronomy 5:17–19, 21); Leviticus 19:18. **13:9–10** Jesus issued this as a new commandment to his disciples (see John 13:34–35; Leviticus 19:18). **13:12** Perhaps an allusion to Isaiah 59:16–17. **13:13** *Riotous extravagance* can also be translated as *drunken reveling and partying*. The word translated as *adultery* also refers to other forms of sexual impropriety. **13:14** Compare Matthew 6:34.

14:1 There appeared to be infighting and contention arising from differing perspectives on the proper diet for Christians, and Paul encouraged them not to fight over the matter but to find a resolution that was based on love for one's neighbor. **14:2** The division within the Roman branch of the church was one of what foods were considered clean and unclean. The division was not between kosher and nonkosher foods exclusively, but rather it was an issue of eating meat or not (verses 2–3, 22). Paul condemned neither position but encouraged the saints to live with the concern of their brothers and sisters in mind. **14:4** The question about judging *another person's servant* may reflect the idea that all Christians were considered to be God's servants, and Paul is therefore questioning why anyone would judge another person because that person could be a servant of God. **14:5** The issue of which day was better or holier may have arisen from a dispute concerning the day on which to celebrate the Sabbath: the Jewish Sabbath (Saturday) or the day of Christ's resurrection (Sunday). This would explain why Paul says that each was doing so for the Lord (verse 6). A similar concern is expressed in Galatians 4:10.

to God. [7]For none of us lives for himself, and none dies for himself. [8]For if we live, we live for the Lord, and if we die, we die for the Lord. Therefore, whether we live or die, we are the Lord's. [9]For this reason, Christ died and lives again, that he might reign among the dead and the living.

[10]Why do you judge your brother or sister? Or why do you despise your brother or sister? For we will all stand before the judgment seat of God. [11]For it is written, *"As I live, says the Lord, every knee shall bow to me, and every tongue shall confess God."* [12]Therefore, each of us will give an account of himself to God.

DO NOT OFFEND

[13]Therefore, let us not pass judgment upon one another, but rather let us decide to never place a stumbling block or trap in front of a brother or sister. [14]I know and am convinced in the Lord Jesus that there is nothing unclean in itself, but it is unclean for anyone who considers it to be unclean. [15]For if your brother or sister is offended by what you eat, you are no longer walking in love. Do not ruin someone for whom Christ died by your food. [16]So do not let what you regard as good be slandered. [17]For the kingdom of God is not founded upon food and drink but upon righteousness, peace, and joy in the Holy Spirit. [18]For the one who serves Christ in this way is acceptable to God and esteemed by people.

[19]So let us pursue the things that bring peace and the things that build one another up. [20]Do not destroy the work of God for the issue of food. Even though all things are clean, it is wrong to cause anyone to stumble because of what you eat. [21]It is good not to eat meat or drink wine or to do anything that causes your brother or sister to stumble. [22]The faith that you have, keep between yourself and God. Blessed is the one who does not judge himself by what he approves. [23]But whoever has doubts is condemned if he eats, because he does not eat by faith, and everything that is not by faith is sin.

SEEK TO PLEASE OTHERS

15 [1]We who are strong ought to bear the shortcomings of the weak and not to please ourselves. [2]Let each of us please his neighbor for good in order to build him up. [3]For Christ did not seek to please himself, but as it is written, *"The reproaches of those who reproached you fell upon me."* [4]For everything that was written before was written for our instruction so that through patience and comfort of the

---

14:7 A clearer expression of this idea is found in 2 Corinthians 5:15. **14:10** Greek uses *brothers* generically to refer to *brothers and sisters*. **14:11** Quotation from Isaiah 45:23 (also quoted in Philippians 2:10–11). Doctrine and Covenants 76:110 quotes this verse. **14:12** Some early and important witnesses lack *to God*, but other early and important manuscripts contain the prepositional phrase. The meaning seems to be implied even if the words were not originally included, and therefore they have been retained in the translation despite the ambiguous textual tradition. **14:13** See note on 14:10. **14:13–21** Compare 1 Corinthians 8:10. **14:14** Paul's view that food is never inherently unclean of itself would have been controversial for Jewish members who had accepted Christ. These verses represent his attempt to explain the reason behind the kosher guidelines (Leviticus 11). **14:19** The church is an institution for promoting peace and harmony between its members. **14:21** See note on 14:10. Compare 1 Corinthians 8:13. **14:22** The intent appears to be the idea that a person should not make judgments of their own self based on their own exclusive assessments of facts but that they should rely on the Holy Spirit as well.

15:3 Quotation from Psalm 69:9. **15:4** Paul understood that all former scripture led to hope in the current age because it helped him and others see that Christ was the expected Messiah. The idea of *patience* (also *endurance*) and *comfort* encourage the reader to know that seeing the Messiah of the Old Testament was not always immediately obvious. Second Nephi 4:15 offers an additional perspective on scripture.

scriptures we might have hope. ⁵But may the God of patience and comfort grant you to live in such unity with one another and in accordance with Jesus Christ ⁶so that with one voice you may glorify the God and Father of our Lord Jesus Christ.

THE GOSPEL IS OPEN TO EVERYONE

⁷Therefore, welcome one another just as Christ welcomed you into God's glory. ⁸For I say that Christ became a servant to the circumcised for the sake of God's truth in order to confirm the promises given to the patriarchs ⁹and in order that the Gentiles might glorify God for his mercy, just as it is written, "*Therefore, I will confess you among the Gentiles, and sing to your name.*" ¹⁰And again it says, "*Rejoice, O Gentiles, with his people.*" ¹¹And again, "*All you Gentiles, praise the Lord, and let all people praise him.*" ¹²And again, Isaiah says, "*The root of Jesse will come, even he who arises to rule the Gentiles, and upon him will the Gentiles hope.*" ¹³May the God of hope fill you with all joy and peace in believing so that you may increase in hope by the power of the Holy Spirit.

PAUL ACKNOWLEDGES THE WEIGHT OF HIS WORDS

¹⁴I am persuaded, my brothers and sisters, that you yourselves are filled with goodness, full of all knowledge, and able to teach one another. ¹⁵I have written to you more boldly in some instances as a way to remind you, because of the grace that has been given to me by God, ¹⁶to be a minister of Christ Jesus to the Gentiles, serving as a priest for the gospel of God so that the Gentiles might become acceptable, sanctified by the Holy Spirit. ¹⁷Therefore, I have reason to boast in Christ Jesus of the things pertaining to God. ¹⁸For I will not dare to speak of anything except what Christ has done through me to bring the Gentiles to obedience in word and deed ¹⁹by the power of signs and wonders, by the power of the Spirit of God, so that from Jerusalem and all the way around until Illyricum, I have made the gospel of Christ fully known. ²⁰In this way, it is an honor to proclaim the good news where Christ has not been named, that I might not build upon the foundation of another, ²¹but just as it is written, "*Those who have never been told about him will see, and those who have never heard will understand.*"

15:8 Paul seems aware of the criticism that Christ came only to minister to the Jewish people and not to Gentiles, which he defends here as a result of Jesus fulfilling the promises made to the patriarchs (compare Genesis 22:17; 32:12). Paul refers to Christ as a servant or *deacon* (the meaning of the Greek word). Later deacons would model their service on the concept that Christ served others as a *deacon* and that a *deacon* cared for the temporal needs of others, such as serving them at dinner. **15:9** Quotation from Psalm 18:49; 2 Samuel 22:50. **15:10** Quotation from LXX Deuteronomy 32:43. **15:11** Quotation from Psalm 117:1. **15:12** Quotation from Isaiah 11:10. **15:13** First Nephi 10:17 and 13:37 use the phrase *power of the Holy Ghost*, which occurs in this verse. This translation avoids the reference to the Holy Spirit being a *ghost*, which has negative connotations in the modern era. Translations at the time of Joseph Smith frequently referred to the *Holy Ghost*. **15:14** Greek uses *brothers* generically to refer to *brothers and sisters*. **15:16** The wording of this verse is similar to Alma 5:54. The *gospel of God* may also refer to the *gospel about God*—namely, the gospel about God's Son. Paul compares his own service to that of the priests who administered the sacrifices in the temple. This helps draw out the concept that he as priest is offering the Gentiles to God as an acceptable offering to the Lord. **15:19** Nothing is known of Paul's travel to or ministry in *Illyricum*, which today is located in Croatia, Bosnia, Herzegovina, and Montenegro. **15:20** Paul's reason for avoiding working where others had already worked may be reflected in 2 Corinthians 10:15–16. Alluded to in Doctrine and Covenants 52:33. **15:21** Quotation from Isaiah 52:15.

PLANS TO VISIT ROME AND SPAIN

²²This is the reason why I was hindered many times from coming to you: ²³I no longer have any place in these regions now, and because I have desired to come to you for many years ²⁴I hope to see you as I travel to Spain and to be helped by you on my travel there after I have first enjoyed your company for a while. ²⁵But now I am traveling to Jerusalem to minister to the saints. ²⁶For Macedonia and Achaia are pleased to make some offering for the poor among the saints in Jerusalem. ²⁷For they were pleased to do it, and they are indebted to them. For if the Gentiles have come to share in their spiritual blessings, they ought to share in their material things. ²⁸Therefore, after I have finished this and have delivered to them this gift, I will pass by you on the way to Spain. ²⁹I know that when I come to you, I will come in the fullness of Christ's blessing.

³⁰I encourage you, brothers and sisters, through our Lord Jesus Christ and through the love of the Spirit to join with me in your earnest prayers to God on my behalf ³¹so that I may be saved from those who are disobedient in Judea, and that my service in Jerusalem may be acceptable to the saints, ³²so that I may come to you through God's will in joy and be renewed by your company. ³³May the God of peace be with you all, amen.

GREETINGS TO THE SAINTS IN ROME

16 ¹I commend our sister Phoebe to you, a servant of the church in Cenchreae, ²that you may receive her in the Lord in a way that is worthy of the saints and provide her whatever she might need from you. For she has been a benefactor for many, including me.

³Greet Prisca and Aquila, my fellow workers in Christ Jesus, ⁴who risked their own necks for my life, to whom I give thanks, not only I but all the churches of the Gentiles. ⁵And greet the church in their house. Greet my dear friend Epaenetus, who is the first believer in Christ in Asia. ⁶Greet Mary, who has worked hard

---

15:25 This likely indicates the end of Paul's third missionary journey, described briefly in Acts 21:1–17. **15:26** These regions would have included the cities of Philippi, Thessalonica, Beroea (all in Macedonia), and Corinth (Achaia). To provide a monetary collection for the relief of the poor in Jerusalem was a matter that was decided upon at the Jerusalem conference (Galatians 2:10). Paul's third missionary journey was intended to gather the collection and take it back to Jerusalem (see Acts 24:17; 1 Corinthians 16:1–4; 2 Corinthians 9:1–15). **15:26–27** The collection for the poor saints permitted the Gentile and Jewish members of the church to offer mutual support and thanks to one another, thus drawing them closer together. **15:30** Greek uses *brothers* generically to refer to *brothers and sisters*. *Wrestle with me* represents a verb that means to *fight for*, *strive for*, or *agonize over*. **15:31** The *disobedient* may refer to Jews in Jerusalem who had not accepted Christ but who judged Paul for his temple practices (see Acts 21:27–32).

16:1 Phoebe is a *servant* or *deaconess* of the church in Cenchreae. Scholars continue to debate whether this word is used in a technical sense (*deaconess*) or whether it is used broadly (*servant*). Later church tradition was unaware of a calling as a *deaconess*, but such a calling was certainly possible, and Phoebe may have served in the official capacity as a female servant to the branch in Corinth-Cenchreae. The port of Cenchreae was located across the Isthmus of Corinth in the Saronic gulf. **16:3** Paul uses the shortened form of her name (*Prisca*), and Luke uses the full form (*Priscilla*). See Acts 18:2; 1 Corinthians 16:19. **16:5** Some modern translations have shifted to spelling the name *Epenetus*. *Epenaetus* may have been a member of the household of Stephanus (1 Corinthians 16:15) because both are referred to as the first believers in Achaia. *Convert* is also possible as a translation for *believer*, but the word implies a complete departure from one organization into another. It is not certain that they would have called their

for you. [7]Greet Andronicus and Junia, my relatives and fellow prisoners. They are well known to the apostles, and they were in Christ before I was. [8]Greet Ampliatus, my dear friend in the Lord. [9]Greet Urbanus, our fellow worker in Christ, and my dear friend Stachys. [10]Greet Apelles, who is approved in Christ. Greet those who are of the household of Aristobulus. [11]Greet Herodion, my relative. Greet those from the household of Narcissus who are in the Lord. [12]Greet Tryphaena and Tryphosa, laborers in the Lord. Greet Persis, a friend who has worked hard in the Lord. [13]Greet Rufus, chosen in the Lord, and his mother, who is a mother to me also. [14]Greet Asyncritus, Phlegon, Hermes, Patrobas, Hermas, and the brothers and sisters with them. [15]Greet Philologus, Julia, Nereus and his sister, and Olympas, and all the saints who are with them. [16]Greet one another with a holy kiss. All the churches of Christ greet you.

FINAL ENCOURAGEMENT

[17]I encourage you, brothers and sisters, to watch for those who create divisions and scandals contrary to the instruction you received; avoid them. [18]For these are the kind who do not serve our Lord Christ, but they serve their own stomachs, and by smooth talking and kind words they deceive the hearts of the naive. [19]Your obedience is known to all, so that I rejoice for you, but I want you to be wise concerning what is good, and innocent regarding what is evil. [20]The God of peace will quickly crush Satan under his feet. May the grace of the Lord be with you.

[21]My fellow worker, Timothy, greets you, as do Lucius, Jason, and Sosipater, my relatives. [22]I, Tertius, who am writing this letter, greet you in the Lord. [23]Gaius, who is my host and for the whole church, greets you. Erastus, the city treasurer, and our brother Quartus, greet you.

FINAL DOXOLOGY

[25]To him who is able to strengthen you according to my gospel and the proclamation of Jesus Christ, according to the revelation of the mystery that has been kept secret for a long time [26]but is now made known through the writings of the

---

acceptance and belief in Christ a *conversion*. Paul speaks of Judaism as having prefigured the coming of Christ. For example, Paul speaks of being *in Christ* (verse 8), whereas the description *Christian* would be used today. The better manuscripts note that he was from *Asia*, but some inferior ones indicate he was from Achaia. **16:7** *My relatives* can refer to close relatives like an aunt but also to more distant family members like distant cousins, including the possibility that they were from the same region or that they were Jews (Romans 9:3). The name *Junia* can also be the masculine *Junias*, but the name is quite rare outside of the New Testament, and so there is some question regarding the form that is used in this verse. It likely refers to the husband-and-wife team of *Andronicus and Junia*. It is unknown which imprisonment this refers to. **16:11** See note on 16:7. Agrippa I (grandson of Herod the Great) had a brother named *Herodion*, but it seems unlikely that these are the same person. **16:14** Greek uses *brothers* generically to refer to *brothers and sisters*. **16:16** The *holy kiss* mentioned here is that of greeting and friendship, and it became a means of expression of Christian identity. It was likely a kiss on the cheek. **16:17** See note on 16:14. *Scandals* can also be translated as *stumbling blocks*. **16:20** The verb used to describe the *crushing* of Satan is different than that used in the Greek translation of the Old Testament (the LXX or Septuagint) of Genesis 3:15. The action described by Paul is more violent and unequivocal. **16:21** Compare Acts 13:1; 17:5–9; Acts 20:4 for *Lucius*, *Jason*, and *Sosipater* (also spelled *Sopater*). **16:23** *Gaius* is mentioned also in Acts 19:29; 1 Corinthians 1:14, and *Erastus* is mentioned in Acts 19:22; 2 Timothy 4:20. **16:24** Some late and inferior manuscripts add a verse here: *May the grace of our Lord Jesus Christ be with all of you. Amen.* The verse has been omitted in this translation because of its weak textual support. **16:25–27** These three verses appear differently in a number of early and important New Testament manuscripts, and

prophets, according to the command of the eternal God, to him has been made known to all nations to bring about obedi- ence to the faith—[27]to the only wise God, through Jesus Christ, may the glory be forever! Amen.

the evidence is inconclusive regarding where they were originally placed. The options are (1) they were included immediately after 16:23, which has the best manuscript support (2) they were included after 14:23, which has moderately good manuscript support, or (3) they appeared after 15:33, which has the support of one early and very good papyrus manuscript. The language and style of these verses is quite different from that of the letters, and they may have been added by the scribe Tertius, who wrote the letter, or by another scribe, although it is possible that Paul was quoting from an early church statement of faith. These verses form part of the letter called a *doxology*, indicating that the letter or portions of it were used in worship. This may indicate a shift in the way Paul's letters were received in the churches (this is the only Pauline letter to have a final doxology).

1 CORINTHIANS

AUTHOR

Paul is listed as the sender of this letter along with Sosthenes, Paul's traveling companion, and the letter was written after Paul had visited the city on his second missionary journey. After the second missionary journey, Paul returned to Jerusalem and then almost immediately set out on a return trip to Macedonia (Thessalonica and Philippi). When he wrote 1 Corinthians, he had not yet arrived in Macedonia (16:5), but he was intending to return to the region probably in an effort to follow up on concerns about the community in Thessalonica. During that period, Paul wrote a letter indicating to the saints that they should not associate with immoral people (5:9). Chloe, a saint living near Corinth, then wrote a letter indicating that the problems in Corinth were more severe than initially supposed (1:11). Paul had hoped to visit the saints in Corinth, and he also wanted to stay with them for some time (16:6), but he also felt that the work had drawn him to Ephesus (16:8–9).

At the time of writing, Apollos did not want to return to Corinth (16:12), likely as a result of problems that had occurred there. It is unclear why Apollos did not wish to return, but Paul's contact with Apollos was probably a source of information about what was going on with the community there. Also, Paul had met Prisca and Aquila there, who could provide him with information (Acts 18:2; 1 Corinthians 16:19). Because Acts reports that Paul was in Corinth during the proconsulship of Gallio (51–52 CE), Paul's letter to the Corinthians can be dated with greater precision than his other letters. First Corinthians was likely written between 53 and 54 CE.

PURPOSE OF WRITING

This letter has a clear purpose—to respond to the concerns raised in Chloe's letter (1:11) in direct and point-by-point fashion. Chapters 1–4 include introductory material that laid a foundation for Paul's later direct responses to the concerns of Chloe's letter. The specific items of concern were the marriage of a young man to his stepmother (5:1), Christians suing other Christians in pagan courts (6:1), questions about marriage (7:1–40), consuming meat that had been used in pagan sacrifices (8:1), the actions of the

apostles (9:1), head coverings (11:2), meeting etiquette (11:7), spiritual gifts (12:1), and the resurrection (15:1). Paul offered extended answers for each of the questions, and some contain direct quotations from Chloe's letter. Much of the counsel that Paul gave deals with specific concerns of a first-century Christian community that was struggling in their newly found faith.

The letter also shows the works and thought processes of an early Christian apostle. Much of Paul's thinking is evident in the way he used scriptural examples to respond to new problems and challenges. He offers his own opinions at various stages, and he draws upon the teachings of the Lord at other stages. It is also obvious that he was engaging questions for which there had been no previous official response, and he was placed in a position to offer a response that would be binding upon the entire community. Second Corinthians may indicate that his words were received with mixed acceptance and that the challenges facing the Corinthian community continued to develop in new and challenging ways.

Connection to Latter-day Saint Beliefs

The most obvious and important connection to Latter-day Saint beliefs is the single reference to the practice of baptism for the dead (15:29), a practice that appears to have been initiated in some areas of the church and which the Corinthians saints were familiar with. Paul says almost nothing on how baptism for the dead was administered or to what extent the saints practiced it. He brought up the topic to draw attention to the fact that baptizing a living individual for a deceased individual made little sense if there was not a general resurrection for the dead.

Another key connection can be found in the discussion of the importance and priority of charity that is also discussed in Moroni 7 using the language of 1 Corinthians 13. These two passages serve as the foundational source of Latter-day Saint understanding of the characteristics and significance of charity. Other gifts of the Spirit are also reviewed, particularly the gifts of prophecy and tongues. ⅌

OPENING ADDRESS

1 ¹Paul, called to be an apostle of Christ Jesus through the will of God, and Sosthenes our brother ²to the church of God which is in Corinth, to those who are made holy in Christ Jesus, called to be saints, together with all those who call on the name of our Lord Jesus Christ in every place. He is our Lord and theirs. ³Grace to you and peace from God our Father and the Lord Jesus Christ.

THANKSGIVING

⁴I always thank my God for you for the grace of God that was given to you in Christ Jesus, ⁵that in all things you were enriched in him, in all speech and knowledge. ⁶Just as the testimony of Christ was confirmed among you ⁷so that you are not lacking in any spiritual gift while you await the revealing of our Lord Jesus Christ, ⁸who will confirm you until the end without blame in the day of our Lord Jesus Christ. ⁹God is faithful, through whom you were called into the community of his Son, Jesus Christ our Lord.

DIVISIONS AT CORINTH

¹⁰I encourage you, brothers and sisters, through the name of our Lord Jesus Christ, that all of you agree that there are no divisions among you and to be united by the same mind and intent. ¹¹For it has been reported to me, my brothers and sisters, by Chloe's household, that there are rivalries among you. ¹²I mean this, that each of you says, "I follow Paul," or "I follow Apollos," or "I follow Cephas," or "I follow Christ." ¹³Is Christ divided? Was Paul crucified for you? Or, were you baptized in Paul's name? ¹⁴I thank God that I baptized no one except for Crispus and Gaius, ¹⁵so that no one may say that you were baptized in my name. ¹⁶I also baptized the household of Stephanus, but I do not know if I baptized anyone else. ¹⁷For Christ did not send me to baptize, but to proclaim the gospel, not with words of wisdom, so that the cross of Christ was not emptied of power.

CHRIST IS THE WISDOM OF GOD

¹⁸For the message of the cross is foolishness to those who are perishing, but to those who are being saved, it is the power of

---

1:1 Paul refers to himself as an *apostle*, which has both a technical meaning of one who was called of God to be an apostle of Jesus Christ and as a missionary who was sent out to proclaim the good news. Paul may be using the term in the latter sense. *Sosthenes* is probably the same person mentioned in Acts 18:17. **1:7** *Spiritual* was added to clarify the intent of the Greek word. *Gift from God* is also possible. **1:7–8** Paul appears to refer to the coming day of judgment, a day of wrath for those unprepared. **1:8** *Without blame* is a legal term that also appears in Doctrine and Covenants 4:2. **1:10–11, 26** Greek uses *brothers* generically to refer to *brothers and sisters*. **1:11** *Chloe's household* likely refers to the church that met in her home. This is the typical way that Paul speaks of the different house churches (see Romans 16:5, 11). There may have been several similar meeting places for early Christians in Corinth. **1:12** *Cephas* is Peter's Aramaic name. It is unusual that Paul would refer to him as such in a Greek-speaking Gentile city like Corinth. *Apollos* spent time at Corinth (Acts 18:24–19:1). The division in the church appears to be a breakdown of community and the rise of factions based on the prestige of the person who baptized them. However, this does not account for those who claim affinity with *Christ* unless they were claiming baptism by Jesus (John 3:22). Quoted in Doctrine and Covenants 76:99. **1:14** *Crispus's* conversion is told in Acts 18:8. *Gaius* is mentioned in Acts 19:29; 20:4 (but may not be the same person because he is from Derbe in Asia Minor). **1:17** *Of power* is added to help clarify the Greek, which literally says *so that the cross of Christ was not emptied*. **1:18** Paul divides all people into two classes: those who reject Christ and who are figuratively *perishing*, and those who accept Christ and are *being saved*. Paul conceives of the early Christian message as a *message of the cross*, thus highlighting the centrality of the crucifixion in his teaching.

God. [19]For it is written, "*I will destroy the wisdom of the wise, and I will nullify the understanding of the intelligent.*" [20]Where is the wise man? Where is the scribe? Where is the learned debater of this age? Has God not made the wisdom of the world foolish? [21]God was pleased to save those who believed in the foolishness of preaching, because in the wisdom of God the world did not know God through wisdom. [22]For Jews ask for signs, and Greeks seek wisdom. [23]But we declare to you a crucified Christ, to the Jews a scandal and foolishness to the Gentiles. [24]But to those who are called, Jews and Greeks alike, Christ is the power and wisdom of God. [25]For the foolishness of God is wiser than human wisdom, and the weakness of God is greater than human strength.

[26]Consider your calling, brothers and sisters, that there were not many who were wise according to human standards, not many were powerful, and not many were of noble birth. [27]But God chose the foolish of the world so that he might shame the wise, and God chose the weak of the world to shame the strong. [28]God chose what is low and despised in the world, those who are nothing, to bring to nothing what is regarded as something [29]so that no human being can boast in the presence of God. [30]And because of him you are in Christ Jesus, who became for us wisdom from God, righteousness, sanctification, and redemption, [31]just as it is written, "*Let the one who boasts do so in the Lord.*"

THE MESSAGE OF CHRIST CRUCIFIED

2 [1]When I came to you, brothers and sisters, I came not with excellent speech or wisdom as I proclaimed the mystery of God. [2]For I determined to know nothing among you except Jesus Christ and him crucified. [3]I was with you in weakness and fear, and in great trembling. [4]And my speech and my message were not with a persuasive word of wisdom but in a demonstration of the Spirit and power [5]so that your faith would not be in people but in the power of God.

THE WISDOM OF GOD

[6]But we speak wisdom among the mature, not the wisdom of this age or of the rulers of this age who will perish. [7]But we speak the wisdom of God hidden in a mystery, which God declared before the ages for our glory. [8]None of the rulers of this age

---

1:19 Quotation from Isaiah 29:14 (see also Isaiah 19:12; 22:18). Compare 2 Nephi 27:26. **1:23** Or *a crucified Messiah.* **1:24** *Called* is used synonymously with *believed.* **1:27** Doctrine and Covenants 35:13 draws upon the language of this verse. **1:29** *Human being* is *flesh* in Greek. Paul might be alluding to the idea that no mortal can withstand the presence of God, a topic that he will discuss later in 1 Corinthians 15:35–41. **1:30** *Sanctification* is to be made *holy* or *saintly* through accepting the preaching of Paul and others. **1:31** Quotation from Jeremiah 9:24.

2:1 Some early and good manuscripts read *the testimony of God* in place of *the mystery of God.* **2:6** The word translated as *mature* is difficult to render into a single English word. It ranges in meaning from *perfect* or *mature* to even one who is initiated into a Greco-Roman mystery religion. If Paul intended the latter meaning, then he was referring to those who had accepted Christ and were baptized. Roman society had a variety of mystery religions, where believers were initiated into the religion through rituals. Christianity may have appeared to be similar in some respects to one of the mystery religions. It is the same word used in Matthew 5:48 (translated as *perfect*). **2:6, 14** Paul appears to understand that the division in the church in Corinth has arisen, in part, through a misunderstanding between the *mature* believers and the *natural* believers. This is one of the first inner-church conflicts where believers were divided among themselves. **2:7** Paul declares that the gospel message had been decreed before the world began: *before the ages.*

understood this, for if they understood, they would not have crucified the Lord of glory. ⁹But, just as it is written, *"Things that no has eye seen, nor ear heard, nor has the heart of man imagined, God has prepared for those who love him."* ¹⁰God has revealed these things to us through the Spirit. For the Spirit searches all things, even the deep things of God. ¹¹For who knows a person's thoughts except the spirit of that person that is in him? So, too, no one knows the things of God except the Spirit of God. ¹²We have not received the spirit of the world but the Spirit of God so that we might understand the things freely given to us by God. ¹³And we speak about these things, not in words taught by human wisdom but in those taught by the Spirit, speaking spiritual things to those who are spiritual.

¹⁴The natural person does not accept the things of the Spirit of God, for they are foolish to him, and he is not able to understand them because they are discerned spiritually. ¹⁵But the spiritual person discerns all things, and he is scrutinized by no one. ¹⁶*"For who has known the mind of the Lord so as to instruct him?"* But we have the mind of Christ.

DIVISIONS IN CORINTH

3 ¹Brothers and sisters, I am not able to speak to you as spiritual people but as people of the flesh, as infants in Christ. ²I have fed you milk, not solid food, for you were not ready yet. And even now you are not ready, ³for you are still of the flesh. For where there is jealousy and division among you, are you not of the flesh and conduct yourselves in a human way? ⁴For when someone says, "I follow Paul," and another says, "I follow Apollos," are you not merely being human?

⁵What is Apollos really? What is Paul? Servants through whom you believed, and each as the Lord appointed. ⁶I planted, Apollos watered, but God caused it to grow. ⁷So, neither the one who plants nor the one who waters counts as anything, but only God who causes it to grow. ⁸The one who plants and the one who waters are one, and each will receive his own wages according to his labor. ⁹For we are God's fellow workers; you are God's field and God's building.

¹⁰According to the grace of God given to me, like a wise architect I established a foundation, and another is building the structure. Each one must be careful how he builds. ¹¹For no one can establish another foundation other than that which

---

2:9 Quotation from Isaiah 64:4. Valuable commentary on this Isaiah passage is found in 3 Nephi 17:16–17 (see also Doctrine and Covenants 76:10). **2:10–4:21** This section represents the first major issue addressed in Chloe's letter to Paul (see 1 Corinthians 1:11), and Paul deals with the general topic of divisions, suggesting he was establishing a foundation for his later response to Chloe's letter. **2:12** The *things freely given* uses a word that is elsewhere used to describe the giving of spiritual gifts (compare Romans 1:11). **2:14** This verse conceives of the natural man as resistant to the Spirit, and Mosiah 3:19 sees the natural man as an enemy to God. **2:16** Quotation from Isaiah 40:13. It is unclear what Paul might have meant by *we have the mind of Christ.* In his day, there were no written Christians texts (at least none have survived), and the Gospels had not been written. He may mean that we have access to the mind of Christ through the Holy Spirit.

3:1 Greek uses *brothers* generically to refer to *brothers and sisters.* A similar division between flesh and spirit is used by Nephi in 1 Nephi 22:1. **3:2** Alluded to in Doctrine and Covenants 19:22. **3:5** *Therefore, what is Apollos* is also possible. *Servants* is *deacons* in Greek. Paul's and Apollos's service in Corinth is one model that would later define the service of deacons in the church. **3:6** Because Paul *planted,* many scholars have understood Paul to be the founder of the church in Corinth. It appears likely that he was the first Christian missionary to visit the city. **3:8** This *grace* refers, in part, to Paul's call (Romans 1:5).

has been laid, which is Jesus Christ. ¹²If anyone builds upon the foundation using gold, silver, precious stones, wood, hay, or straw, ¹³each person's work will become manifest, and the day will make it manifest because it will be revealed by fire, and the fire will test each type of work and what each has done. ¹⁴If someone has built a work that remains, he will receive a reward. ¹⁵If someone's work is consumed in fire, he will suffer loss. He will be saved but only through fire.

¹⁶Do you not understand that you are God's temple and the Spirit of God dwells in you? ¹⁷If anyone destroys the temple of God, God will destroy him. For the temple of God is holy, as you are.

¹⁸Let no one deceive himself. If someone thinks he is wise in this age, let him be a fool so that he may become wise. ¹⁹For the wisdom of this world is foolishness with God. For it is written, "*He catches the wise in their cunning.*" ²⁰And again, "*The Lord knows that the thoughts of the wise are futile.*" ²¹So let no one boast about men.

For all things are yours, ²²whether Paul, or Apollos, or Cephas or the world or life or death or the present or what is to come. Everything is yours, ²³and you are Christ's, and Christ belongs to God.

APOSTLES AS EXAMPLES

4 ¹This is how one should regard us—as servants of Christ and stewards of the mysteries of God. ²It is required of stewards that they be found faithful. ³But with me, it is a small thing that I should be condemned by you or a human court. In fact, I do not condemn myself. ⁴I do not know of anything against myself, but I am not acquitted because of this. The one who judges me is the Lord. ⁵So do not judge anything before the time when the Lord comes, who will bring the things hidden in darkness to light, and he will reveal the desires of the heart. Then each will receive praise from God.

⁶I have applied these things to myself and to Apollos, brothers and sisters, for your benefit, so that you may learn

---

3:13 Many modern translations capitalize *Day* as a reference to the Day of Judgment, which will make the different works manifest. Perhaps an allusion to Malachi 3:2; Zechariah 13:9. **3:14** *Reward* can also be translated as *wages*, but the context here seems to favor *reward*. **3:15** *But only through fire* refers to torment that is like fire. **3:16** This verse is written in the second-person plural *you* and describes the members collectively as the *temple of God*. **3:17** The phrase *If anyone destroys the temple of God* envisions someone bringing down the church of God and deconstructing what God has built. Some older translations used the verb *defiled*, but the verb has nothing to do with defiling the edifice. Instead, it refers to tearing it down. God's action against that person is described using the exact same verb. Alluded to in Doctrine and Covenants 93:35. **3:19** Quotation from Job 5:13. **3:20** Quotation from Psalm 94:11. **3:21** Compare the similar criticism in 1 Corinthians 5:6. Alluded to in Doctrine and Covenants 76:59. **3:22** This verse is mentioned in Doctrine and Covenants 76:99.

4:1 The *mysteries* in this sense refer to the things that are not obvious or the things that have been revealed to the initiated, which in this case would refer to those who have accepted Christ and the associated ordinances. *Stewards* also means *servants* or *managers*. The word refers primarily to a household servant who oversees some aspect of production or management of the household. The Book of Mormon frequently draws upon the language of the *mysteries of God* (see 1 Nephi 1:1; 2:16; Mosiah 2:9). **4:3** This verse presents evidence that Paul was personally hurt by the accusations made against him. The word translated as *condemned* can equally be *judged* as well. The sharpness of the wording suggests that Paul felt condemned by some of the saints in Corinth for actions that were either incorrectly ascribed to him or for personal sin that was unfounded. **4:5** *Heart* is plural in Greek, perhaps indicating the desires of many different people. Greek also speaks collectively of the desires of the human *heart*. An allusion to this verse is found in Doctrine and Covenants 123:13. **4:6** Greek uses *brothers* generically to refer to

through us "*not to go beyond what is written*" so that none of you will be puffed up against one another. [7]What makes you distinct from anyone? What do you have that you have not received? If you received it, why do you boast as though it were not given to you? [8]You are already provided for; you are already rich! Without us you ruled like kings, and indeed I wish that you did reign so that we might reign with you. [9]For I think that God has exhibited us apostles last, as men condemned to death, because we have become a spectacle to the world, both to angels and to men. [10]We are fools for Christ, but you are wise in Christ; we are weak, but you are strong; you are praised, but we are in disrepute. [11]Up until the present hour, we have been hungry and thirsty, poorly clothed, mistreated, and homeless, [12]but we do hard work, laboring with our own hands. When we are verbally abused, we respond with a blessing; when persecuted, we endure; [13]when slandered, we comfort. We have become, and are now, the refuse and scum of the world.

PAUL'S INTENDED VISIT TO CORINTH

[14]I do not write these things to shame you but to exhort you as my beloved children. [15]For although you have countless guides in Christ, yet you do not have many fathers. For I became your father in Christ Jesus through the gospel. [16]Therefore, I encourage you to be imitators of me. [17]Because of this, I sent Timothy to you, who is my beloved and faithful son in the Lord, who will remind you of my ways in Christ Jesus, just as I teach them everywhere in every church. [18]Some are arrogant, as though I were not coming to you. [19]But I will come to you shortly, if the Lord is willing, and I will know not only the message of these arrogant people but also their power. [20]For the kingdom of God is not built on talk but on power. [21]What do you want? Shall I come to you with a rod to discipline or with love and the spirit of kindness?

SEXUAL IMPROPRIETY IN THE CHURCH

5 [1]It is actually reported that there is sexual impropriety among you, a kind of impropriety that does not exist among the Gentiles, for someone has married his father's wife. [2]But you are arrogant. Should you not have removed him who did this from among you and mourned instead? [3]For even though I am absent in body, I am present in spirit, and I have already judged the man who did this as though I were present. [4]When you gather in the

---

brothers and sisters. The phrase *not beyond what is written* is a quotation or slogan that Paul has cited in order to refute it. **4:9** Paul draws upon the language of the Roman arena and the condemned who are presented in the arena to fight to the death. The insinuation is that God is behind the act of making the apostles a spectacle to the world. Compare Doctrine and Covenants 42:48 for additional application of the meaning of this verse. **4:13** The language of *refuse and scum* are quite pointed in Greek and are not typical words used to describe friends and fellow believers. This strong language may demonstrate the depth of hurt that Paul feels. **4:16** Paul's encouragement that the Corinthian saints should emulate him is echoed in Galatians 4:12; Philippians 3:17; 4:9. **4:17** For Timothy's role in establishing the church in Corinth, see 2 Corinthians 1:19 (also Acts 16:1). **4:21** *To discipline* has been added to clarify that the rod spoken of here was to administer physical discipline.

5:1 This issue was brought to Paul's attention through Chloe's letter, or a verbal report from Chloe, and the problem was that a man had married his stepmother. It is not clear whether his father was still alive or if they had divorced, but Paul's shock at the situation suggests that he viewed this as a scandalous matter. Paul probably based his considerations on the precedent of Leviticus 18:8 (see also Leviticus 20:11; Deuteronomy 22:30; 27:20). **5:4–5** Paul appears to encourage the community to meet together to

name of our Lord Jesus and my spirit is there together with the power of our Lord Jesus, ⁵deliver this man to Satan for the destruction of the flesh, that his spirit may be saved in the day of the Lord.

⁶Your boasting is not good. Do you not understand that a little yeast leavens the entire lump of dough? ⁷Clean out the old yeast so that you have a new lump of dough, seeing that you are without yeast. For Christ, our Passover lamb, has been sacrificed. ⁸So let us celebrate the Passover not with old yeast, which is bad and wicked, but with the unleavened bread of sincerity and truth.

⁹I have written to you in a letter to not associate with immoral people, ¹⁰not in reference to the immoral of this world or the greedy, thieves, and idolaters, because then you would need to go out of the world. ¹¹But now I am writing to you to not associate with anyone who bears the name of brother or sister who is immoral, greedy, an idolater, verbally abusive, a drunk, or a thief. Do not even eat with such a person. ¹²For what do I have to do with judging those outside? Are you not the judge of those inside? ¹³God will judge those outside; *"remove the evil person from you."*

CHRISTIANS WHO SUE OTHER CHRISTIANS

6 ¹When any of you has a legal dispute with another, do you dare to go to court before the unrighteous and not before the saints? ²Do you not understand that the saints will judge the world? And if the world is to be judged by you, are you incapable of judging lesser things? ³Do you not understand that we will judge angels, to say nothing of ordinary matters? ⁴Then if you have ordinary matters, do you appoint judges from those who have no standing in the church? ⁵I tell you this for your shame. Is there not one among you who is wise enough to judge matters between one believer and another? ⁶Does a Christian sue another Christian and do this before unbelievers?

⁷Therefore, to have lawsuits against one another is already a show of defeat for you. Instead, why not suffer wrong? Why not rather be defrauded? ⁸But you wrong and defraud your brothers and sisters.

---

deal with the issue as a united body. **5:5** The meaning of this verse remains unclear. It appears to refer to excommunication from the community of the saints, and this is the meaning that the idea takes in the Book of Mormon (Alma 37:15) and the Doctrine and Covenants (78:12; 104:10). The language of the Book of Mormon and Doctrine and Covenants also has parallels to 1 Timothy 1:20. **5:7** Paul draws attention to Christ as the *Passover lamb*. For the symbolism of the *Passover* offering, see Exodus 12:1–27. Being without *yeast* refers to having no impurity (see verse 8). **5:8** *Unleavened bread* was understood to be without impurity. **5:9** This is a lost letter that Paul wrote to the saints previously. Many scholars have suggested that a portion of this letter is preserved in 2 Corinthians 6:14–7:1. The topics discussed in the passage from 2 Corinthians are similar to Paul's description here. **5:11** Greek uses *brother* generically for *brother or sister*. The allusion may be to partaking of the sacrament with that person rather than the avoidance of sharing any meals with him or her. **5:13** Quotation from Deuteronomy 17:7 (see also Deuteronomy 19:19; 22:21; 24; 24:7).

6:1 This is the second specific problem mentioned in Chloe's letter (see note on 5:1), and the problem seems to be that there were legal disputes among the believers and they had proposed taking their case to a Gentile or Roman court. No mention is made of what the legal dispute was about. Paul may have been drawing on the precedent of Matthew 18:15–17. **6:2** Compare Matthew 19:28. **6:6** The Greek says literally *does a brother sue a brother*, but the context is certainly an inner church dispute and Paul questions why Christians would sue one another in Gentile courts. **6:8** Greek uses *brothers* generically for *brothers and sisters*.

THE BODY AND SPIRIT

⁹Do you not understand that the unrighteous will not inherit the kingdom of God? Do not be deceived; neither the immoral nor idolaters nor adulterers nor male prostitutes nor sodomites ¹⁰nor robbers nor the greedy nor drunks nor verbal abusers nor thieves will inherit the kingdom of God. ¹¹Some of you were these things. But you were washed, you were made holy, and you were made righteous in the name of the Lord Jesus Christ and in the Spirit of our God.

¹²*"All things are lawful for me,"* but not all things are beneficial. *"All things are lawful for me,"* but I will not be controlled by anything. ¹³*"Food is intended for the stomach, and the stomach for food,"* but God will do away with both of these things. The body is not intended for immorality but for the Lord, and the Lord for the body. ¹⁴And God raised the Lord, and he will raise us through his power. ¹⁵Do you not understand that your bodies are members of Christ? Should I take the members of Christ and make them members of a prostitute? Certainly not. ¹⁶Or do you not understand that one who is joined with a prostitute is one with her? For it is said, *"The two will become one flesh."* ¹⁷But the one joined with the Lord is one in spirit with him. ¹⁸Flee immorality! *"Every sin a person commits is outside his own body."* But the immoral person sins against his own body. ¹⁹Do you not understand that your body is a temple of the Holy Spirit that is in you, whom you have from God? You are not your own, ²⁰for you were purchased with a price. Therefore, glorify God in your body.

QUESTIONS ABOUT MARRIAGE

7 ¹Concerning the things you wrote to me about, *"It is good for a man not to touch a woman."* ²But because of the potential for immorality, let each have his

---

6:10 *Verbal abusers* is sometimes translated as *revilers,* and the Greek word refers to someone who speaks against others in a hostile or abusive way. This teaching is echoed in 3 Nephi 11:33. **6:11** *Washed* likely refers to baptism. **6:12–13** Many scholars think this section of chapter 6 contains direct or nearly direct quotations from the letter delivered to Paul by Chloe (see note on 1:11; 5:1). These quotations do not represent assertions by Paul but rather the opinions of those in Corinth. The general consensus is that the quotation of the letter ends with *both of these things.* Paul's counsel thus begins with *the body is not intended,* where Paul counters the notion that *all things are lawful.* **6:15** *Members* refers to the parts of the body. **6:16** Quotation from Genesis 2:24. **6:18** Paul says literally *flee immoral behavior.* He uses a term (*porneia*) that refers to all types of sexual misbehavior, including adultery, lewdness, inappropriate sexual activity, and other actions that were considered ethically and sexually immoral. His views were likely informed by Leviticus 20:10–21 and Deuteronomy 22:13–30. Paul's counsel is intentionally directed at not only sexual misconduct but several behaviors that are also equally immoral (see verses 9–10). An additional issue in this verse is that it appears to contradict itself. Many scholars assert that the first phrase is a quotation from Chloe's letter (see 1:11), *Every sin a person commits is outside his own body.* The second phrase, translated as a second sentence, is Paul's argument against their position: *But the immoral person sins against his own body.* Paul appears to be trying to establish the notion that sin does affect the body in literal ways, and the Corinthians appear to have asserted that sin was an action done outside the body and therefore had no lasting effect on the person. **6:19** Doctrine and Covenants 18:32 echoes this verse. **6:20** This verse reflects an early view of the atonement as an act of purchasing wherein Christ, through the atonement, paid a price for sin. Some late and inferior manuscripts add to the end of this verse *and in your spirit, which are God's.*

7:1 The quotation from Chloe's letter is placed in italics to designate it as a direct quotation and not a summary or paraphrase (see 5:1; 6:12–13). *To touch a woman* is a phrase referring specifically to sexual relations. The question focuses on the idea of whether celibacy in marriage is appropriate.

own wife, and each woman have her own husband. ³A man should give his wife what is due sexually, and likewise a wife to her husband. ⁴The woman does not have authority over her own body, but her husband does. Likewise, the husband does not have authority over his own body, but his wife does. ⁵Do not deprive one another, except perhaps for a time by mutual agreement so that you may devote yourselves to prayer. Then come together again so that Satan may not tempt you because of your lack of self-control. ⁶I say this as a concession and not as a command. ⁷I wish that everyone were like me, but each has his own gift from God: one has this kind, another that kind.

⁸I say to the unmarried and the widows, it is good if they remain like me. ⁹If they cannot conduct themselves with self-control, let them marry. It is better to marry than to burn with passion.

¹⁰To the married I give this counsel, not I but the Lord: a wife should not divorce her husband ¹¹(but if she does so, she should remain unmarried or be reconciled with her husband), and a husband should not divorce his wife.

¹²To the rest I say, not I but the Lord, if any brother has a spouse who is a non-believer, and she agrees to live with him, he should not divorce her. ¹³And if any woman has a spouse who is a nonbeliever, and he agrees to live with her, she should not divorce him. ¹⁴For the nonbelieving husband is made holy because of his wife, and the nonbelieving wife is made holy because of her husband. Otherwise your children would be unclean, but now they are holy. ¹⁵But if the nonbeliever wants to divorce, let it happen. In such circumstances the brother or sister is not obligated. God has called you to peace. ¹⁶For how do you know, wife, that you will not save your husband? Or, how do you know, husband, that you will not save your wife?

LIVE IN YOUR CALLING

¹⁷Nevertheless, let each person walk as the Lord has assigned and as the Lord has called him. I instruct all the churches in this way. ¹⁸Was anyone called after being circumcised? Let him not try to reverse his circumcision. Was anyone called who was uncircumcised? Let him not be circumcised. ¹⁹Circumcision is nothing, and uncircumcision is nothing, but obeying the commandments of God is what matters. ²⁰Let each remain in the circumstance in which you were called. ²¹Were you a slave

---

7:3 Paul speaks specifically of what is owed to a spouse in marriage, referring to marital intimacy. **7:5** Paul warns those who have decided to forgo marital intimacy to beware that they will be tempted because during such times they lack *self-control*. Many later Greek manuscripts read *to prayer and fasting*. The addition likely reflects a later interest in asceticism or the interest to implement a more rigorous set of physical commandments. **7:6** Paul offers those who wish to forgo intimacy a concession in their request, but verse 7 makes it clear that he prefers they act otherwise. **7:8** From this verse, it is clear that Paul emphasized that he was not married at the time that he wrote the letter. It is unclear whether he was a widower or never married. **7:10** Paul's instruction is based on something the *Lord* commanded. Matthew 5:31–32; 19:3–9; Mark 10:7–12 likely reflect some of the teachings he was drawing upon in giving this counsel. **7:12** In this verse, *brother* refers to a member of the church and hence a Christian. *Live with him* is a euphemism for marriage. **7:14** Extensive commentary is given about this verse in Doctrine and Covenants 74:1–7. **7:15** The implication of Paul's counsel *God has called you to peace* is that rather than attempt to find a remedy for a marriage that has failed, the Christian should seek peace. **7:17** The instructions that Paul has given to *all the churches* is that all should be content with the calling they have received and with their station in life. This might reflect Paul's view of one of the causes leading to the divisions within the church at Corinth. **7:18** Some Jews, in attempting to assimilate into Roman culture, tried to physically reverse their circumcision.

when you were called? Do not worry about it. But if you are able to become free, make use of the opportunity. ²²For the one called in the Lord while yet a slave is a freedman of the Lord. Likewise, the one who was a freedman when called is a slave of Christ. ²³You were purchased with a price. Do not become the slaves of men. ²⁴In whatever situation you were called, brothers and sisters, let that person remain with God.

THE UNMARRIED AND WIDOWED

²⁵With regard to those who have not married, I have no command from the Lord. But I give my judgment as one who by the Lord's mercy is trustworthy. ²⁶I think it is good for you to remain as you are because of the impending distress. ²⁷If you are married, do not seek to divorce. The one who is divorced from a wife should not seek a spouse. ²⁸And if you marry, you have not sinned. And if someone who has never married marries, she has not sinned. Those who marry will have trials in the flesh, and I am trying to spare you. ²⁹I say this, brothers and sisters, the time remaining is short. From now on, let those who have wives live as though they had none, ³⁰and those who weep as though they were not weeping, and those who rejoice as though they were not rejoicing, and those who buy as those without possessions, ³¹and those who do business in the world as though they had no business. For the current form of the world is passing away.

³²I do not want you to be concerned. The unmarried person is concerned about the things of the Lord, how to please the Lord. ³³The married person is concerned with the things of the world, how to please his spouse, ³⁴and he is divided. An unmarried woman or a woman who has never married is concerned about the things of the Lord, to be holy in body and spirit. But the married woman is concerned with the things of the world, how to please her husband. ³⁵I say this to you for your own benefit and not to place any restraint on you so that you may serve the Lord without distraction with honor and constancy.

³⁶If anyone thinks he is acting inappropriately toward his fiancée, if his passions are too strong, and it seems to be necessary, let him marry as he wishes; this is not a sin. Let them marry. ³⁷If he stands firm in his heart and is not under necessity but has his passions under control and has determined in his own heart to keep her as his fiancée, he does well. ³⁸So the one who marries his fiancée does well, and the one who does not does better.

³⁹A woman is bound to her husband for the time that he is alive. But if her husband passes away, she is free to marry whom she wishes, only in the Lord. ⁴⁰According to my judgment, and I think that I have the Spirit of God, she is happier if she remains as she is.

FOOD SACRIFICED TO IDOLS

8 ¹Concerning what is sacrificed to idols, we know that we have knowledge. Knowledge makes us proud, but love builds up. ²If anyone thinks that he knows something, he does not yet know what he

---

7:24 Greek uses *brother* generically to refer to *brothers and sisters*. Compare 1 Corinthians 6:19. **7:28** The warning that they will have *trials in the flesh* is not a negative assessment of marriage but a concern about the coming distress (verse 26). **7:29** See note on 7:24. **7:29–33, 38** The Joseph Smith Translation interprets these verses as applicable to missionaries who travel. **7:36** The Greek literally says *virgin*, but the context indicates that Paul is speaking of those who are engaged or promised in marriage, and so *fiancée* better reflects the meaning. **7:39** *Only in the Lord* could refer to the marriage of another Christian or to making a covenant in the name of the Lord.

8:1 Many scholars suggest that the phrase *we know that we have knowledge* is a quotation from Chloe's letter (1:11). Chapter 8 addresses this concern with respect to eating meat that was previously offered in

needs to know. ³If anyone loves God, he is known by God.

⁴Therefore, concerning food sacrificed to idols, we know that an idol in the world is nothing and that there is no God but one. ⁵Even if there may be so-called gods in heaven or on earth (just as there are many gods and lords), ⁶however, there is one God for us, the Father, from whom are all things and for whom we exist, and one Lord, Jesus Christ, through whom all things are and through whom we exist.

⁷But knowledge is not shared by all. Some, who were formerly accustomed to idols, eat as though it were really a sacrifice to an idol, and their conscience, which is weak, is defiled. ⁸Food does not bring us near to God, nor if we do not eat are we inferior, nor if we eat are we better. ⁹Be attentive that this right of yours does not become a stumbling block to the weak. ¹⁰If anyone who has knowledge sees you dining in an idol's temple, will not his conscience, because he is weak, be emboldened to eat what is sacrificed to idols? ¹¹So by your knowledge this weak person is destroyed, namely the brother or sister for whom Christ died. ¹²Therefore, you sin against Christ when you sin against your brothers and sisters and wound their conscience when it is weak. ¹³Therefore, if food causes my brother or sister to stumble, I will never eat meat so that my brother or sister might not stumble.

PAUL'S DEFENSE AS AN APOSTLE

9 ¹Am I not free? Am I not an apostle? Have I not seen Jesus our Lord? Are you not my work in the Lord? ²If I am not an apostle to others, at least I am to you, for you are the seal of my apostleship in the Lord.

³This is my defense to those who judge me. ⁴Do we not have the right to eat and drink? ⁵Do we not have the right to have a spouse accompany us as the other apos-

---

sacrifice to a pagan god. This issue was addressed by a church council (see Acts 15:29). Some individuals in Corinth may have felt that they were exempt from the decisions of the church council because of their knowledge. **8:4** These two phrases are also likely quotations from Chloe's letter (1:11): *an idol in the world is nothing*, and *there is no God but one*. This latter phrase may contain an echo of Deuteronomy 6:4. **8:5** The wording of Paul's statement may suggest that he believed in the existence of other gods and lords, but such an interpretation of his words misses the criticism Paul is offering of those who believe in other gods. **8:6** The difference in the description between the *Father* and *Jesus Christ* is that all things came *from the Father*, but all things came *through Jesus Christ*. Mosiah 15:4 presents a similar idea regarding there being *one God*. **8:9** The *right* spoken of here is the right to eat any type of food, knowing that food does not bring us nearer to God (verse 7). **8:10** Paul's concern is that weaker Christians will see others eating in an *idol temple* and will thus be encouraged to also partake because they had seen other Christians doing so. One of the communal aspects of pagan temples was the opportunity to dine with fellow believers and to celebrate the influence of the deity in a person's life. This differs from the Jewish notion of temple. **8:11–13** Greek uses *brother* generically to refer to *brother or sister*.

9:1 The issue dealt with in this chapter also reflects a concern expressed in Chloe's letter (1:11; 5:1), although there are no obvious direct quotations. The question focuses on whether traveling missionaries should receive financial support or whether they should work for their own support. For Paul's other reference in this letter to seeing the Lord, see 1 Corinthians 15:8. **9:4** Paul's rebuttal to those who have taught things against his teachings and practices focuses initially on food concerns, suggesting that this was perhaps a debate about kosher foods. This was a matter of significant debate in the early church (see Acts 15:29; Galatians 2:11–12). **9:5** Earlier in the letter, Paul made it clear that he was unmarried (7:8), and therefore it is probable that one of his traveling companions traveled with a spouse. The *apostles and brothers of the Lord* are two distinct groups. The latter were Jesus's siblings (Matthew 13:55; Mark 6:3). Peter was married (Matthew 8:14; Mark 1:30), but the other apostles' spouses are never mentioned in

tles and brothers of the Lord and Cephas do? ⁶Or, is it only Barnabas and I who do not have the right to forgo working for a living? ⁷Who pays his own expenses as a soldier? Who plants a vineyard and does not eat its fruit? Or who shepherds a herd and does not get the milk?

⁸Am I saying this according to human authority? Or does the Law not say the same thing? ⁹For it is written in the law of Moses, "*You shall not muzzle an ox while it is treading the grain.*" Is God concerned with oxen? ¹⁰Or is he not speaking on our behalf? It was written for us, because the one who plows and threshes should work in hope of enjoying the harvest. ¹¹If we have sowed spiritual things among you, is it too great of a demand if we reap material benefits? ¹²If others enjoy this right among you, do we not even more?

But we have not made use of this right. Instead, we endure everything so that we may not be an obstacle to the gospel of Christ. ¹³Do you not understand that the priests who work in the temple eat the food from the temple and that those who serve at the altar receive a portion of the offerings? ¹⁴Thus, the Lord commanded that those who proclaim the gospel should get their living by the gospel. ¹⁵But I have not used any of these rights, nor am I writing these things so that this will happen for me in my case. For I would rather die than have anyone deprive me of my reason for boasting! ¹⁶For if I proclaim the gospel, I have no reason for boasting, for an obligation is laid on me. Woe to me if I do not proclaim the gospel! ¹⁷For if I do this of my own will, I have a reward, but if not of my own will, I am still entrusted with a responsibility. ¹⁸Therefore, what is my reward? That when I proclaim the gospel, I offer the gospel without charge and thereby do not make full use of my rights in the gospel.

¹⁹Because I am free from all, I have made myself a servant to all in order to gain more converts. ²⁰To the Jews I became

---

the New Testament. **9:6** The issue here is that some have complained that Paul ceased working and asked for assistance from the local churches to support him. He was criticized by some for doing so. For other references to Barnabas, see Acts 4:36–37; Galatians 2:1–10. **9:9** Quotation from Deuteronomy 25:4. **9:11–14** This is Paul's most spirited defense of the practice of local churches financially supporting traveling missionaries. **9:13** Guidelines for what the priests are permitted to consume are set forth in Deuteronomy 18:1–5. **9:14** This command may be based on Jesus's teachings to the disciples as they departed on their mission (Matthew 10:8–11; Luke 10:7). **9:15** This sentence is incomplete, although it has been translated as a complete sentence. Paul does not distinctly declare the object following *than* so that the sentence literally reads *For I would rather die than no one will deprive me of my reason for boasting!* **9:17** *Still* has been added to emphasize the structure of the Greek sentence, which includes the last phrase as a point of counteremphasis that if he did not work by his own will, he was still under obligation to proclaim the gospel. Earlier translations used the phrase *dispensation of the gospel* to render *a responsibility.* The word *gospel* does not appear in the Greek text, but the sense is that Paul was given a *responsibility* to proclaim the gospel or to serve or to administer, and hence older translations attempted to capture that meaning through *dispensation of the gospel.* That phrase appears also in Doctrine and Covenants 27:13; 110:12, 16, where it has a similar meaning to a *calling* or *responsibility* to proclaim the gospel. **9:19** Paul's truncated style of writing has left the final phrase of this sentence somewhat ambiguous. The Greek literally says *that I may win the more,* and it appears he is referring to winning more believers in Christ. **9:20** Paul distinguishes *Jews* and those *under the Law.* This may reflect those who accepted Christ but still insisted on observing portions of the law of Moses. Paul's statement that he became a *Jew* and acted as such among his countrymen helps explain his reasoning for requiring Timothy to be circumcised (Acts 16:3). Some late and inferior manuscripts omit *(although I myself am not under the Law).*

as a Jew so that I might gain Jews; to those under the Law I became as one under the Law (although I myself am not under the Law), that I might gain those under the Law. ²¹To those outside the Law I became as one outside the Law (although I am not free from God's law, but I am under Christ's law), that I might gain those outside the Law. ²²To the weak I became weak, that I might gain the weak. I have become all things to all people, that by all means I might save some. ²³I do all things for the gospel so that I might participate with them in it.

²⁴Do you not understand that the runners in a stadium all compete but one receives the prize? Run so that you may win. ²⁵Every athlete works at self-control in all things. They struggle in order to receive a perishable crown, but we struggle in order to receive an imperishable one. ²⁶So I do not run without direction, and I do not box as though I were punching air, ²⁷but I punish my body and make it a slave so that after proclaiming the gospel to others I will not be disqualified.

FLEE FROM IDOLATRY

10 ¹For I do not want you to be unaware, brothers and sisters, that all of our ancestors were under the cloud and traveled through the sea. ²And all were baptized into Moses in the cloud and in the sea, ³and everyone ate the same spiritual food, ⁴and all drank the same spiritual drink. For they drank from the spiritual rock that followed them, and the rock was Christ. ⁵But God was not pleased with most of them, and they were struck down in the desert.

⁶These things happened as an example for us so that we will not desire evil things as they did. ⁷Do not become idolaters as some of them did, as it is written, "*The people sat down to eat and drink and rose up to play.*" ⁸Let us not be immoral as some of them were, and twenty-three thousand fell in a single day. ⁹Let us not test Christ as some of them did and were destroyed by snakes. ¹⁰And do not complain as some of them did and were destroyed by the destroying angel. ¹¹These things happened to them to serve as an example, and they were written for our instruction, to whom the end of the ages has come. ¹²So, if one thinks he is standing, beware that he may fall. ¹³No temptation that is not common to humanity has seized you. God is faithful, and he will not permit you to be tempted beyond your ability, but with trial

9:24 Mosiah 4:27 is quite similar in conceiving life as a race where a prize is in sight. **9:25** The language of this verse also appears in Alma 38:10. *Temperate in all things* (following the King James translation) is discussed in both. **9:26** Paul's metaphor for the development of self-control is drawn from athletic competition in the boxing ring.

10:1 Greek uses *brothers* generically to refer to *brothers and sisters*. See Exodus 13:21–22; 14:22 regarding the stories referred to in this verse. This section of Paul's letter is not easily traceable to Chloe's letter, and instead 10:1–11:1 treat themes where Paul provided general counsel that he felt was timely, although idolatry punctuates the discussion. Verses 23 and 28 contain what are likely direct quotations of the letter. **10:2** *Into Moses* refers to being baptized into the law of Moses, his teachings, and precepts. Paul is drawing upon a figurative interpretation of the children of Israel passing through the Red Sea, which he saw as a symbol of the baptism that would be offered in Christ's name. **10:4** The *same spiritual drink* refers to Numbers 20:7–11. **10:5** Compare Doctrine and Covenants 68:31. **10:7** Quotation from Exodus 32:6. **10:8** Reference to Numbers 25:1–9. The story as recorded in Numbers refers to the death of 24,000, whereas Paul mentions 23,000. The difference may be a simple mistake, it may refer to a different event for which there is no record, or it may be that he counted the number of those who fell in a single day differently. **10:9** Reference to Numbers 21:5–9. **10:10** Reference to Numbers 16:41–50. **10:13** This teaching is alluded to in Alma 13:28; Doctrine and Covenants 64:20.

he will also provide a way out so that you can endure it.

¹⁴Therefore, my friends, flee from idolatry. ¹⁵I am speaking to wise people; judge what I am saying for yourselves. ¹⁶The cup of blessing which we bless, is it not sharing in the blood of Christ? The bread that we break, is it not sharing in the body of Christ? ¹⁷Because there is one bread, we who are many are one body, because we all partake of one bread. ¹⁸Consider the people of Israel. Are not those who eat the sacrifices partners of the altar? ¹⁹Then what am I saying? That food given to an idol is something? Or that an idol is something? ²⁰No, but pagans offer the things they sacrifice to demons and not to God. I do not want you to be partners with demons. ²¹You cannot drink the cup of the Lord and the cup of demons. You cannot share the table of the Lord and the table of demons. ²²Are we trying to provoke the Lord to jealousy? Are we stronger than him?

²³"*All things are lawful*," but not all things are necessary. "*All things are lawful*," but not all things are uplifting. ²⁴Let no one seek for his own good but for the good of another. ²⁵Eat everything that is sold in a market, not asking questions of conscience, ²⁶for "*the earth is the Lord's, and its fullness*." ²⁷If a nonbeliever asks you to go to dinner and you want to go, eat whatever is placed in front of you, not asking any question of conscience. ²⁸But if someone says to you, "This is from a sacrifice," do not eat it because of the one who told you and because of conscience. ²⁹I do not mean your conscience but the other person's. For why is my freedom being judged by another person's conscience? ³⁰If I partake with thankfulness, why am I slandered because of the food for which I give thanks?

³¹Whether you eat or drink, or whatever you do, do everything for the glory of God. ³²Do not become an offense to Jews, Greeks, and the church of God, ³³just as I seek to please everyone in all things. I am not seeking my own benefit but that of the many, that they may be saved.

11 ¹Be imitators of me as I am of Christ.

CULTURAL RELIGIOUS PRACTICES

²I commend you because you remember me in all things and maintain the

---

10:16–17 These verses represent one of the oldest surviving discussions of the sacrament and its meaning. Paul interprets the sacrament as participation in the body of Christ. **10:18** Paul refers to *Israel according to the flesh*, which is another way of saying *the people of Israel*. **10:20** The Greek text reads *they* in place of *pagans*. An allusion to Deuteronomy 32:17. **10:23** *All things are lawful* is a quotation from Chloe's letter, and Paul is offering criticism of the position of his opponents. Paul quotes their idea and then offers a counterargument detailing his own view, that all things that we do should be beneficial and uplifting. The segment of the letter that has been quoted from Chloe's letter is placed in italics to designate it as a direct quotation. **10:25** The *market* was a place where meat could be purchased, and some of the meat that was sold in the market would have been used in sacrifices to pagan deities, where the fat and bones were burned on the altar and the meat was sold to the public. **10:26** Quotation from Psalm 24:1. **10:28** Some late and less reliable manuscripts add the quotation from Psalm 24:1 to the end of this verse again (see 10:26). **10:30** *Food* is not specifically noted in the Greek text, but Paul is asking about being judged for eating food for which he has given thanks to God.

11:1 Verse 1 concludes Paul's thoughts from chapter 10, although the modern chapter divisions seemingly indicate otherwise. **11:2** *Maintain the traditions* refers to the ordinances and practices of the church. Although Paul does not specify what they are, they would include baptism, sacrament, practices and guidelines for meetings, and instructions for blessings. The theme of chapter 11 treats the subject of appropriate conduct at worship services and likely traces back to an issue raised in Chloe's letter (1:11; 5:1).

traditions just as I passed them on to you. ³But I want you to understand that Christ is the head of every man, and the man is the head of the woman, and God is the head of Christ. ⁴Any man who prays or prophesies with his head covered disgraces his head. ⁵Any woman who prays or prophesies with her head uncovered disgraces her head, for it is the same thing as having her head shaved. ⁶For if a woman will not cover her head, then she should cut her hair off. But if it is disgraceful for a woman to cut her hair or shave her head, let her cover her head. ⁷For a man should not cover his head, because he is in the image and glory of God, and a woman is the glory of a man. ⁸For man was not made from a woman but a woman from a man. ⁹Neither was a man created for the sake of a woman, but a woman for a man. ¹⁰Because of this, a woman should have the authority of a covering on her head because of the angels. ¹¹Nevertheless, a woman is not without a man, nor is a man without a woman in the Lord. ¹²For just as a woman was made from a man, a man is now born from a woman. And all things are from God. ¹³Judge for yourselves—is it appropriate for a woman to pray to God with her head uncovered? ¹⁴Does nature not teach you that it is dishonorable if a man wears long hair, ¹⁵but if a woman has long hair it is a glory to her? ¹⁶But if anyone is disposed to be contentious, we have no such custom, nor do the churches of God.

THE SACRAMENT

¹⁷But for the following instruction, I do not commend you because when you come together it is not for the better but for the worse. ¹⁸First, when you come together in the church, I hear that there are divisions among you, and I believe it in part. ¹⁹There must be divisions among you

---

11:3 The semantic range of meaning for *man* and *woman* in this verse can include *husband* and *wife*. The verse may include an allusion to Genesis 3:16. The statement comes in the context of questions about women in the church and their ability to prophesy (verse 5). The verse is unlikely to provide any direct evidence of Paul's view of men being superior or of his views on marriage. It appears that what is at stake here is whether the prophecy of a woman made in faith should be binding upon the church and how they should receive such prophetic counsel. **11:5** Paul speaks specifically of women *praying and prophesying* in the church. These may have been formal roles or spontaneous ones. Little is known about how these early meetings were conducted. Paul's concern is with head coverings, and differing traditions were at play where Jewish Christians would be inclined to see women cover their heads in worship and Greek or Roman Christians would not have expected them to cover their heads. This appears to be a conflict of cultural practices. Compare Joel 2:28 for women prophets. **11:6** Although the reasons for doing so remain unclear, the practice of shaving one's head in order to prophesy is what is at stake in the discussion. Women are encouraged to wear a head covering to imitate a man who has shaved his head. **11:7** Reference to Genesis 2:21–23. **11:7–10** These verses may offend modern sensibilities. They were delivered as Paul's reasoned explanation for why women should wear a head covering when prophesying in church services and not in the context of providing an explanation for the proper relationship between a man and a woman. Paul sought a scriptural explanation for a cultural practice. **11:10** The type of covering is unspecified. Scholars have suggested a veil, but Paul's intent remains unclear. **11:12** Paul's explanation now shifts to a biological approach where he finds parity for men and women. **11:13** Cultural practice would lead to differing answers to this question among the Pauline churches and between modern and ancient readers. **11:16** The matter of women prophets in the church had become a point of discussion, and Paul's reasoned explanation (verse 2–15) provides his effort to present a scriptural basis for head coverings for women. Paul seems to anticipate that the discussion would not be so easily resolved. **11:18** *I believe it in part* represents Paul's doubts that there are genuine divisions. He is not certain, but he partially believes there are divisions during meetings.

so that those among you who are genuine may be obvious. [20]When you gather together, it is not really to eat the Lord's supper. [21]For each of you eats his own supper when it is time to eat, and one is hungry and another is drunk. [22]Do you not have houses to eat and drink in? Or do you show contempt for the church of God by humiliating those who have nothing? What do I say to you? Should I praise you? In this matter, I will not praise you.

[23]For I received from the Lord what I have given to you, that the Lord Jesus on the night he was betrayed took bread, [24]and after he blessed it and broke it, he said, "*This is my body, which is for you. Do this in remembrance of me.*" [25]Likewise, for the cup after supper, saying, "*This cup is the new covenant in my blood. Do this each time you drink it, in remembrance of me.*" [26]Each time that you eat this bread and drink the cup, you proclaim the death of the Lord until he comes.

[27]Therefore, whoever eats the bread or drinks the cup of the Lord unworthily is guilty with respect to the body and blood of the Lord. [28]Let a person examine himself, and then let him eat the bread and drink the cup. [29]For the one eating and drinking without having considered the body, eats and drinks condemnation to himself. [30]This is why many among you are weak and ill, and some have died. [31]If we judged ourselves, we would not be judged. [32]When we are judged by the Lord, we are disciplined so that we are not judged together with the world. [33]So, my brothers and sisters, when you come together to eat, wait for one another. [34]If someone is hungry, let that person eat at home so that when you gather it does not result in your condemnation. I will give instructions about the other things when I come.

SPIRITUAL GIFTS

12 [1]Concerning spiritual gifts, I would not have you be unaware, brothers and sisters. [2]You understand that when you were pagans you were led astray by unspeaking idols, however you were led. [3]Therefore, I want you to know that no one who speaks with the Spirit of God says, "Jesus is cursed," and no one is able to say, "Jesus is Lord" except by the Holy Spirit.

[4]There are different spiritual gifts, but the same spirit, [5]and there are differences in service, but the same Lord, [6]and there are different types of activities, but it is the same God who does them all in everyone.

11:20 *Lord's supper* refers to the sacrament. **11:21–22** Paul was concerned about the practice of banqueting or feasting when the saints gathered to celebrate the sacrament. Culturally, Greeks and Romans would have been accustomed to participating in feasts at pagan temples, and this practice appears to have carried over into Christian worship services. Paul saw two issues of concern: (1) the disparity among what people in the church had to eat and (2) a lack of respect for the sacrament, where sobriety was required for respectful worship. He encourages those participating to wait until everyone has joined them and that they share their food (11:33–34). **11:24–25** These quotations are attributed to Jesus, but they differ slightly from the Gospel accounts of the Last Supper and the prayer for the bread and wine (compare Matthew 26:26–29; Mark 14:22–25; Luke 22:15–20). Third Nephi 18:7–14 contains similar teachings regarding remembering the Lord through the sacrament and obeying his commands. **11:25** The *new covenant* may allude to Jeremiah 31:31; 32:40. **11:26** The practice of celebrating the sacrament is to look forward to the return of the Lord. **11:27** Since Paul understood the celebration of the sacrament to be a partnership (1 Corinthians 10:16–18), partaking of the sacrament unworthily would in essence damage that partnership. **11:29** *The body* is ambiguous in this passage, and some later Greek texts attempted to clarify Paul's original writing by adding *of the Lord*. Compare 3 Nephi 18:29. **11:33** Greek uses *brothers* generically to refer to *brothers and sisters*. **11:34** *Your* has been added for clarity.

12:1 Greek uses *brothers* generically to refer to *brothers and sisters*.

[7]Each is given the manifestation of the Spirit for the common good. [8]To one, the word of wisdom is given through the Spirit, and to another the word of knowledge by the same Spirit, [9]to another faith by the same Spirit, to another gifts of healing by the one Spirit, [10]to another performing miracles, to another prophecy, to another discerning of spirits, to another different languages, to another the interpretation of languages. [11]All of these work together through one and the same Spirit, who gives to each person individually as he desires.

DIFFERENT GIFTS

[12]For just as the body is one and has many members, all the members of the body, although they are many, are one body; so it is with Christ. [13]For we are all baptized into one body in one Spirit, whether Jews or Greeks, slaves, or freedmen, we were all made to drink in the same Spirit.

[14]For the body is not one member but many. [15]Even if the foot says, "I am not a hand, I do not belong to the body," it does not cease to belong to the body just because of this statement. [16]And if the ear says, "I am not the eye, I do not belong to the body," it does not cease to belong to the body just because of this statement. [17]If the whole body were an eye, how would the body hear? If the whole body were an ear, how would the body have a sense of smell? [18]Now, God placed the members of the body, each according as he chose. [19]If all were one member, where would the body be? [20]Now there are many members but one body. [21]The eye cannot say to the hand, "I have no need you," nor can the head say to the feet, "I have no need of you." [22]Instead, the members of the body, even though they seem to be weaker, are essential, [23]and those members of the body that seem less honorable, we place greater honor on them, and our unpresentable body parts are clothed with greater respect, [24]which our more presentable parts do not need. But God has brought the body together, while giving greater honor to the lesser members [25]so that there may be no division in the body, but the members may care for one another in the same ways. [26]And if one member suffers, then every member suffers together, and if one member is glorified, then every member rejoices together.

[27]You are the body of Christ, and each member has a part. [28]And God has placed in the church, first apostles, second prophets, third teachers, then miracles, gifts of healing, helping, leadership, foreign languages. [29]Are all apostles? Are all prophets? Are all teachers? Do all work miracles? [30]Do all have gifts of healing? Do all speak languages? Do all interpret? [31]Seek for the greater gifts. And yet I will show you a more excellent way.

CHARITY

13 [1]If I speak the languages of men and angels but I do not have charity, I am like a brass horn or clanging cymbal. [2]If I have prophetic insight and I under-

---

12:7 This teaching is alluded to in Moroni 7:16. **12:7–11** A modern parallel to this section is found in Doctrine and Covenants 46:8–26. Compare the similar discussion in Moroni 10:8–17 that parallels 1 Corinthians 12:5–11. **12:8** *Word* in this verse can also mean *message* or *utterance*. Paul was likely referring to a person who could declare *words of wisdom* and *words of knowledge*. **12:9** *Gifts of healing by the one Spirit* may refer to healing multiple different types of illnesses but through the same Spirit. **12:10** The Greek text mentions the ability to speak foreign *tongues*, but this clearly refers to *foreign languages*. Compare Doctrine and Covenants 35:23 for the gift of *prophecy*. **12:21** The language of this verse shaped Doctrine and Covenants 84:109. **12:27** Compare Ephesians 4:12. **12:31** Compare Ether 12:11 for a similar usage of the idea of a *more excellent way*. Alluded to in Doctrine and Covenants 46:8.

13:1 Echoed in 2 Nephi 31:13. **13:2** *Charity* can also be translated as *love*, and the primary meaning is

stand all mysteries and knowledge and I have all faith so as to move mountains but I do not have charity, I am nothing. ³If I give away all that I have and hand over my body to be burned but I do not have charity, I gain nothing.

⁴Charity is patient; charity is kind; it is not jealous nor does it boast; it is not arrogant ⁵or rude. It is not self-serving; it is not resentful or spiteful. ⁶It does not rejoice in unrighteousness, but it rejoices in truth. ⁷Charity bears all things, believes all things, hopes all things, and endures all things.

⁸Charity never ends. But if there are prophecies, they will pass away; as for tongues, they will cease; as for knowledge, it will pass away. ⁹For we know in part, and we prophesy in part. ¹⁰When the fulfillment comes, the partial will pass away. ¹¹When I was a child, I spoke like a child, I thought like a child, I reasoned like a child. When I became an adult, I put away childish things. ¹²For we see dimly in a mirror, but then face to face. I know in part; then I will know fully even as I have been fully known. ¹³Now, faith, hope, and charity, these three abide, but the greatest of these is charity.

THE GIFT OF PROPHECY

14 ¹Pursue charity and seek for spiritual gifts, especially so that you may prophesy. ²For one who speaks in tongues does not speak to people but to God, for no one understands him, but he speaks the mysteries by the Spirit. ³But the one who prophesies speaks to people for their edification, encouragement, and comfort. ⁴The one who speaks in tongues edifies himself, but the one who prophesies edifies the church. ⁵I want you all to speak in tongues, but even more I want you to prophesy. The one who prophesies is greater than the one who speaks in tongues, unless someone interprets so that the church may be built up.

⁶Now, brothers and sisters, if I come to you speaking in tongues, how will I help you if I do not speak to you in a revelation or knowledge or prophecy or teaching? ⁷It is similar for lifeless instruments that make sound, like a flute or harp. If they do not make a distinct note, how can what is played on the flute or harp be understood? ⁸If the trumpet does not make a distinct sound, who will prepare for war? ⁹So it is with you, if with your tongue you do not speak in a way that is easily understood, how will anyone know what is being said? For you are speaking into the air. ¹⁰There are likely many different languages in the world, and none is without meaning. ¹¹Therefore, if I do not know the meaning of a language, I will be a foreigner to the speaker, and the speaker will be a foreigner to me. ¹²So it is with you, because you are

---

abstract love, similar to the love a person feels for an ideal, principle, or concept. It can also express love between individuals when there is no sexual component to that love. Perhaps an allusion to Matthew 21:21. This teaching is alluded to in 2 Nephi 26:30. Alma offers a different context for the phrase *I am nothing* (Alma 26:12). **13:2–7** Compare Moroni 7:44–46 **13:3** A number of early and reliable Greek manuscripts read *hand over my body to boast*. Although the reading does not appear to make sense, it has a strong likelihood of being original. **13:8** *Tongues* refers to the ability to speak foreign languages or possibly to the very existence of foreign languages. **13:12** Compare 2 Corinthians 3:18. The idea of seeing *dimly* is that an ancient mirror could only provide a poorly reflected image and not a clear image like a modern mirror can provide. **13:13** This teaching is echoed in Alma 7:24; Moroni 7:1; Doctrine and Covenants 4:5; 12:8 (compare also Galatians 5:5–6; 1 Thessalonians 1:3; 5:8).

14:1 *Charity* is the goal or purpose for which the spiritual gifts are given. Each of the gifts is considered in light of its ability to edify the members of the church. **14:2, 4, 13, 14, 19** The Joseph Smith Translation renders these verses to read *another tongue*. **14:6** Greek uses *brothers* generically to refer to *brothers and sisters*.

eager for the things of the Spirit, seek to abound in building up the church.

¹³Therefore, the one who speaks in a tongue should pray that he may interpret it. ¹⁴If I pray in a tongue, my spirit prays, but my mind is without benefit. ¹⁵Then what do I do? I will pray with my spirit, and I will pray with my mind; I will sing praises with my spirit, and I will sing praises with my mind. ¹⁶Otherwise, if you are giving thanks with your spirit, how can someone on the outside say "Amen" to your thanksgiving since he does not know what you are saying? ¹⁷You may be giving thanks in a good way, but the other person is not being edified. ¹⁸I thank God that I speak in tongues more than all of you. ¹⁹But in the church, I would rather speak five words using my mind in order to teach others than speak a myriad of words in tongues.

²⁰Brothers and sisters, do not be children in your thinking, but be infants in wickedness and mature in your thinking. ²¹In the Law it is written, *"By people of other tongues and by the lips of foreigners I will speak to this people, but they will not listen to me,"* says the Lord. ²²Thus, tongues are not a sign to those who believe but to the nonbelievers, whereas prophecy is not a sign to the nonbelievers but to the believers. ²³Therefore, if the whole church gathers and they all speak in tongues, and if nonbelievers and the uninformed enter, will they not say that you are mad? ²⁴But if all are prophesying and nonbelievers and the uninformed enter, they will be admonished and examined by all. ²⁵The secrets of his heart are made obvious, and thus by falling on his face he will worship God and proclaim that *"God is really among you."*

THE GIFTS IN THE CHURCHES

²⁶Then what do I do, brothers and sisters? When you assemble, each has a song of praise, each has a lesson, a revelation, a tongue, an interpretation. Let everything be for edification. ²⁷When someone speaks in a tongue, let there be two or at most three and each in turn, and have someone interpret. ²⁸If no one interprets, let him who speaks in a tongue remain silent in the church, but let him speak to himself and to God. ²⁹Let two or three prophets speak, and let the others judge what they say. ³⁰If someone sitting there receives a revelation, the one who was speaking should be silent. ³¹For you are each able to prophesy so that all may learn and all may be encouraged. ³²And the spirits of the prophets are subject to prophets. ³³For God is not a contributor to confusion but the author of peace.

As in all the churches of the saints, ³⁴let the women remain silent in the churches. For they are not permitted to speak but should be in submission just as the Law

---

14:13–17 The issue in these verses is offering silent prayers that others cannot hear. Paul is encouraging his readers to pray vocally so others are edified. **14:14** *Without benefit* is literally *without fruit*. **14:20** See note on 14:6. **14:21** Quotation from Isaiah 28:11–12. **14:24** The meaning of this verse as it relates to the gift of prophesy remains somewhat obscure. The two verbs at the end of the sentence indicate that prophecy will result in chastisement, convicting, examining, and admonishing others. The sentiments expressed seem to imply that prophecy as understood in this context could be better described as exhortation. **14:25** Quotation from Isaiah 45:14. **14:26** See note on 14:6. Paul speaks of *hymn* singing, which can also be translated as *psalm* singing. **14:29** Paul again uses prophecy in a way that would indicate his meaning was closer to exhortation or teaching, where individuals were encouraged to offer subsequent opinion regarding a prophecy (see verse 24). **14:30** The Greek says literally *the one speaking first*. In this instance, it appears that *revelation* takes precedence over teaching. **14:32** The intent is to declare that the spiritual promptings of the living prophets are subject to the writings of the former prophets. **14:34** Caution should be taken in directing this verse as a general directive prohibiting women from speaking in church since Paul elsewhere encouraged women to speak in the church (1 Corinthians 11:2–16).

says. ³⁵If they desire to learn anything, they should enquire of their husbands at home. For it is shameful for a woman to speak in church. ³⁶Did the word of God originate with you? Or did it come to you alone?

³⁷If anyone considers himself to be a prophet or a spiritual person, he should recognize that the things I write to you are a commandment of the Lord. ³⁸If anyone does not recognize this, he is not recognized. ³⁹Therefore, brothers and sisters, seek to prophesy and do not prohibit anyone from speaking in tongues. ⁴⁰Let everything be done in a decent and orderly manner.

THE RESURRECTION APPEARANCES

15 ¹Now I would remind you, brothers and sisters, of the gospel which we proclaimed to you, which you received, and in which you stand, ²by means of which you are being saved, if you hold firmly to the message I proclaimed to you, unless you believed in vain. ³For at first I gave to you what I received, that Christ died for our sins according to the scriptures ⁴and was buried and that he rose again on the third day according to the scriptures ⁵and that he appeared to Cephas, then to the twelve. ⁶Then he appeared to more than five hundred brothers and sisters at one time, the majority of whom are still alive, but some have passed away. ⁷Then he appeared to Jacob and then all of the apostles. ⁸Last of all, as an untimely birth, he appeared to me also. ⁹For I am the least of the apostles, unworthy to be called an apostle, because I persecuted the church of God. ¹⁰But by the grace of God I am what I am, and his grace to me has not been in vain. Indeed, I worked harder than any of them, but it was not me but the grace of God in me. ¹¹Whether it was I or they, we preached in this way, and so you believed.

QUESTION ABOUT THE RESURRECTION

¹²If Christ is proclaimed as having been raised from the dead, how can some say to you that there is no resurrection of the dead? ¹³If there is no resurrection from death, then not even Christ was raised. ¹⁴If Christ was not raised, then our message is in vain, and your faith is empty. ¹⁵We are found to be false witnesses of God because we have testified that God raised Christ, whom he did not truly raise if the dead are not raised. ¹⁶For if the dead are not raised, not even Christ has been raised. ¹⁷If Christ has not been raised, your faith is useless, and you are still in your sins. ¹⁸Those who have died in Christ have also perished. ¹⁹If we have hope in Christ for this life only, we are the most pitied of all people.

14:38 It appears that Paul intends to indicate that a person will no longer be *recognized* as a member of the community of believers. The sentence is built upon a play on words and is not easily translated into English. A possible translation of it could be *If anyone does not understand this, he is not recognized as one of us.*

15:1 Greek uses *brothers* generically to refer to *brothers and sisters*. This chapter appears to return to the issues raised in Chloe's letter (1:11; 5:11), and it treats the topic of the resurrection from the dead. **15:3** The *scriptures* referred to here would be passages such as Psalms 22; 69:9; 118:22; Isaiah 11:1–10; 53:1–12. **15:4** See Jonah 1:17. **15:5** Paul referred to Peter using his Aramaic name *Cephas* (Luke 24:34). **15:6** Greek uses *brothers* generically to refer to *brothers and sisters*. **15:7** This is *Jacob*, the brother of Jesus (Mark 6:3). The reference to the *twelve* in verse 5 is the designation used to refer to the disciples from Jesus's ministry. This verse refers to *all the apostles* indicating that the number had expanded beyond the twelve original disciples. The idea of additional *apostles* is the result of the early church calling missionaries, who were designated using the Greek noun *apostle* or *missionary*. There remained, however, a distinction between the original twelve and the others that were called later. **15:8** *Untimely birth* refers to a miscarriage. **15:9** See Acts 8:3. **15:14** This teaching is alluded to in Mosiah 16:7.

²⁰Now, Christ was in fact raised from the dead, the firstfruits of those who have died. ²¹For since death came through one person, the resurrection from the dead came through one person, ²²for just as in Adam all die, even so in Christ all will be made alive. ²³Each person in his own order—Christ as the firstfruit, then those who belong to Christ at his coming. ²⁴Then the end comes, when Christ hands over the kingdom to God the Father after ending all rule, and all authority and power. ²⁵For he must reign until he places all enemies under his feet. ²⁶Death is the last enemy to be destroyed, ²⁷for *"he has placed everything in subjection under his feet."* But when it says, *"everything has been placed in subjection,"* it is evident that the one who subjected all things is excluded. ²⁸When all things are subjected to him, then the Son himself will also be subjected to him who put all things in subjection under him, so that God is all in all. ²⁹Otherwise, why are they baptized on behalf of the dead? If the dead are not raised at all, why are they baptized on their behalf? ³⁰Why are we in danger every hour? ³¹I am dying every day. This is true, brothers and sisters, like my boasting of you which I have in Christ Jesus our Lord. ³²If I fought wild animals in Ephesus only as a man, what would I gain? If the dead are not raised, let us eat and drink, for tomorrow we die. ³³Do not be deceived: *"Bad company corrupts good morals."* ³⁴Sober up as is right, and cease sinning, for some have no understanding of God. I tell you this for your shame.

THE RESURRECTED BODY

³⁵But some will say, "How are the dead raised? In what body will they come?" ³⁶Fool, what you sow must die in order to come to life. ³⁷What you sow is not the body that is to be but a bare seed only, perhaps wheat or some other grain. ³⁸But God gives it a body as he desires, to each kind of seed its own body. ³⁹Not all flesh is the same flesh, but there is one kind for humans, and another flesh for animals, another for birds, and another for fish. ⁴⁰There are heavenly bodies and earthly bodies; however, the glory of the heav-

---

15:22 Paul is the only one in the New Testament to tie together the fall of Adam and the resurrection of Christ, though the concept is prevalent in the Book of Mormon (for example, 2 Nephi 2:25; Mosiah 3:16). **15:23** The technical term used to describe the *coming* of Christ is the *Parousia*. The word refers to the presence of a person, their arrival, or a visit. Sometimes the word is used to describe the *Second Coming of Christ*, but the New Testament does not use the word *Second* to describe that coming. Compare Doctrine and Covenants 88:60. **15:24** *All rule, and its associated authority and power* is also possible. **15:25** A phrase from this verse is quoted in Doctrine and Covenants 49:6 with expanded meaning. Compare Psalm 110:1; Doctrine and Covenants 58:22; 76:106. **15:27** Quotation from Psalm 8:6. **15:28** *All in all* refers to the idea that God the Father must remain above all, even with respect to the Son, and therefore the Son will eventually be subjected to the Father. Doctrine and Covenants 76:106 comments upon the meaning of this verse. **15:29** Paul does not specify who *they* are in this verse. The reference appears to be obvious to the Corinthian saints, and therefore it was likely that members of the church in Corinth who practiced baptism on behalf of the dead understood the reference. This is the only mention of the practice in the New Testament, and no guidelines or details associated with the practice have survived. Doctrine and Covenants 128:16 quotes this verse (compare Doctrine and Covenants 127:6). **15:31** Greek uses *brothers* generically to refer to *brothers and sisters*. **15:32** An allusion to Isaiah 22:13; 56:12. **15:33** A quotation from the Greek poet Menander from *Thais* (fragment 218). **15:37** *Only* is not noted in Greek. Paul is emphasizing that the mortal body is not like the eternal body we will possess but is rather only a seed of that body. The Greek says literally *a naked seed*. **15:40** The Joseph Smith Translation adds a third type of body to this list (telestial). Compare Doctrine and Covenants 76:78. **15:40–41** Doctrine and Covenants 76:96–8 expand the meaning of these verses.

enly body is of one type and the glory of the earthly another. [41]There is a glory of the sun, another glory of the moon, and another glory of the stars, for star differs from star in glory.

[42]So it is with the resurrection of the dead. What is sown is perishable. What is raised is imperishable. [43]What is sown in dishonor is raised in glory; what is sown in weakness is raised in power. [44]It is sown as a physical body; it is raised as a spiritual one. If there is a physical body, there is also a spiritual body. [45]As it is written, "*The first man Adam became a living soul.*" The last Adam became a life-giving spirit. [46]But it is not spiritual at first but physical, and then it is spiritual. [47]The first man is from the earth, from the dust, the second man is from heaven. [48]Like the one from the dust, so also are those who are from the dust, and like the man of heaven, even so are those who are from heaven. [49]For just as we wear the image of the dust, let us bear the image of heaven.

[50]This is what I am saying, brothers and sisters, that flesh and blood are not capable of inheriting the kingdom of God, nor does the perishable inherit the imperishable. [51]Behold, I tell you a mystery, not everyone will die, but all will be changed— [52]in a moment, in the blinking of an eye, at the last trumpet. For the trumpet will sound, and the dead will be raised imperishable, and we will be changed. [53]For this perishable body must put on an imperishable one, and this mortal body must put on an immortal one. [54]When this perishable body puts on an imperishable one, and the mortal body puts on an immortal one, then what is written will come to pass: "*Death is swallowed up in victory.* [55]*Where is your victory, death? Where is your sting, death?*" [56]The sting of death is sin, and the power of sin is the law. [57]Thanks be to God, who gives us the victory through our Lord Jesus Christ [58]so that, my dear brothers and sisters, you will become firm, immovable, abounding in the work of the Lord at all times, knowing that your labor is not in vain in the Lord.

THE COLLECTION FOR THE POOR SAINTS

16 [1]Concerning the collection for the saints, just as I directed the churches in Galatia, even so you should do also. [2]On the first day of every week, set aside, each one of you, a portion of your income to the extent you have been blessed so that there will be no collecting when I come. [3]When I arrive, I will send those whom you have approved with letters to carry your

---

15:42 Wording from this verse is echoed in Mosiah 16:10; Alma 5:15; Mormon 6:21. **15:44** This verse is commented upon and expanded in Doctrine and Covenants 29:43; 88:27–28. **15:46–48** Doctrine and Covenants 128:14 quotes these verses. **15:45** Quotation from Genesis 2:7. **15:50** See note on 15:31. **15:51** Paul offered a similar thought earlier in his ministry (1 Thessalonians 4:17). **15:51–52** Alluded to in Doctrine and Covenants 63:51; 101:31. **15:52** Compare 3 Nephi 28:8; Mormon 6:21; Doctrine and Covenants 29:26; 43:32; 63:51; 101:31. **15:53** Compare 2 Nephi 9:7; Alma 5:15; 40:2; Mormon 6:21. **15:54** Quotation from Isaiah 25:8 (also cited in Alma 27:28; compare Enos 1:27; Mosiah 16:10; Alma 41:4). **15:55** Quotation from Hosea 13:14 (also cited in Mosiah 16:7–8; Alma 22:14; Mormon 7:5). **15:56** Paul does not clarify whether he meant the law of Moses or more generally the idea of law. **15:58** See note on 15:31. A portion of this verse is also echoed in 1 Nephi 2:10; Mosiah 5:15; Alma 1:25.

16:1 *The collection for the saints* was intended to help the saints who had been severely affected by a famine in Judea. Paul had asked the saints in the various churches to donate generously and help alleviate their suffering (Romans 15:26–27; Galatians 2:10). **16:2** Paul had asked for the saints to save some money or to donate something one day each week. It is not clear that fasting accompanied their offering, and Paul specifically asked for them to set aside any additional income they could on that day. **16:3** *Letters* probably

gift to Jerusalem. ⁴If it seems wise for me to go also, they will travel with me.

Plan to Visit Corinth

⁵I will come to you when I travel through Macedonia, for I am going to Macedonia. ⁶Perhaps I will stay with you or pass the winter there so that you can send me on my travels wherever I might go. ⁷For I do not want to see you while in passing, but I hope to spend some time with you if the Lord allows. ⁸But I will stay in Ephesus until Pentecost, ⁹for a door of significant opportunity has been opened to me, but there are many enemies.

¹⁰When Timothy comes, see that he has nothing to fear among you, for he is doing the work of the Lord as I am. ¹¹Therefore, let no one treat him with contempt. Send him on his way in peace so that he may come to me, for I am anticipating him with the brothers.

¹²Concerning Apollos our brother, I strongly encouraged him to come to you with the brothers, but it was not his desire to come now. He will come when he has an opportunity.

Final Encouragement

¹³Be watchful; stand firm in the faith; be courageous; be strong. ¹⁴Let everything you do be done in love.

¹⁵You know the household of Stephanus, that they were the first believers in Achaia and they devoted themselves to the service of the saints. I encourage you, brothers and sisters, ¹⁶to submit to people like them and to every fellow laborer and everyone who works hard. ¹⁷I rejoiced at the arrival of Stephanus, Fortunatus, and Achaicus because they have made up for your absence. ¹⁸For they refreshed my spirit and yours. Therefore, recognize people like them.

¹⁹The churches in Asia greet you. Aquila and Prisca greet you warmly in the Lord, with the church that meets in their home. ²⁰All the brothers and sisters greet you. Greet one another with a holy kiss. ²¹I, Paul, write this greeting with my own hand. ²²If anyone does not love the Lord, let that person be accursed. Our Lord, come! ²³May the grace of the Lord Jesus be with you. ²⁴My love be with you all in Christ Jesus.

---

refers to letters of recommendation or explanation so that the saints in Jerusalem would know the source of the donation. **16:4** Paul had planned to send the collection with some of the saints from Corinth, but Acts hints that Paul went himself (Acts 21:17–20), a situation confirmed in Romans 15:25–29. **16:8** *Pentecost* took place fifty days after Passover, and thus Paul intended to stay in Ephesus until sometime in late May or early June. **16:9** Echoed in Doctrine and Covenants 112:19. **16:10** According to Acts 19:22, Paul sent Timothy from Ephesus to Macedonia, and in 1 Corinthians 4:17 it is clear that he has been sent to Corinth. Paul seems unclear when Timothy will arrive. **16:11** Paul does not specify who the *brothers* were that he was expecting in this verse. They appear to be known to the church in Corinth and were perhaps fellow missionaries. For this reason, *brothers* has been retained instead of translating it as brothers and sisters. **16:13** Similar language of standing in the faith is found in Mosiah 4:11; Alma 1:25. **16:14** *Love* can also be translated as *charity* (compare 2 Nephi 26:30). **16:15** Greek uses *brothers* generically to refer to *brothers and sisters*. The *service* of the household of Stephanus is described as the service of a deacon (see also Romans 16:5; 1 Corinthians 1:16). **16:19** Paul refers to her as *Prisca*, but Acts prefers Priscilla (see Acts 18:2; Romans 16:3–4; 2 Timothy 4:19). The *churches in Asia* would refer to those areas of the church in Asia Minor such as Ephesus and Miletus. **16:20** See note on 16:14. The *holy kiss* was a friendly greeting that included an embrace and kiss on the cheek or something similar. Paul sees it as a type of Christian fellowship (see Romans 16:16). **16:21** The concluding verses (21–24) were personally written by Paul. The remainder of the letter was dictated to a scribe. **16:22** Paul includes a transliteration into Greek of the Aramaic words (*Marana tha*). The words can mean *Our Lord, come!* or *Our Lord has come!*

2 CORINTHIANS

AUTHOR

This Pauline letter was sent to the church at Corinth together with Timothy (1:1), and it may have been the fourth letter that he wrote to the saints at Corinth (1 Corinthians, 2 Corinthians, 1 Corinthians 5:9; 2 Corinthians 2:3–4). The order of composition of the various letters to Corinth and the timing of their sending are matters of serious discussion today. What follows is a brief attempt to provide one solution that accounts for the existing facts, but it must be recognized that the matter is far from resolved.

At the conclusion of his second mission and while staying in Ephesus for nearly three years (Acts 20:31), Paul probably wrote the lost letter to the Corinthians (1 Corinthians 5:9), in which his tone was severe and stern. That letter was the first mentioned in his surviving letters, and it dealt with the topic of an immoral person in the community. Subsequently, Paul learned in a letter from Chloe that there were more significant problems in Corinth (1 Corinthians 1:11). The letter may have been delivered by Stephanus, Fortunatus, and Achaicus (1 Corinthians 16:17). In response to the dire report that he received from Chloe, Paul wrote 1 Corinthians. Paul then visited Corinth in person during what is known as his third missionary journey. That visit constituted his second visit to Corinth and may have been what Paul referred to as his painful visit (2 Corinthians 2:1). Following that visit, Paul wrote a letter of rebuke (2:3–4; 7:9) that Titus carried (7:5–8). After writing that letter of rebuke, which has not survived, Paul left Ephesus for Macedonia (Acts 20:1) and planned to meet Titus (2 Corinthians 2:12–13). Paul eventually met up with Titus, and after hearing his report of the situation in Corinth (7:6–16), Paul wrote 2 Corinthians. That final letter probably contains some responses to events that transpired during Paul's painful visit.

PURPOSE OF WRITING

Second Corinthians is a complex letter with multiple sections and themes, some of which are related and others which appear to be unrelated. Two chapters are devoted to the topic of the collection for the poor saints living in Judea (Galatians 2:10), and Paul is thankful that they were willing to donate their financial resources to another branch of the church, the members of which they had not met, thus challenging the fledgling

church with developing a sense of a global community. Also, Paul compares the generosity of two regions of the church, Macedonia and Corinth (2 Corinthians 8:1–3), to remind the Corinthians that they could be more generous in giving.

The tone of the letter takes a negative turn toward the end, when Paul challenges what he refers to as false apostles (11:1–15). Such a reference need not be taken to mean that some were masquerading as apostles of the Lord in a priesthood capacity but that there were some false missionaries (the meaning of the term *apostle*) traveling in the region with the intent to make money from unsuspecting believers. Paul felt that they had mocked his weak bodily presence, and they also challenged him because he would not accept financial support from the Corinthians, and therefore he was not to be considered a genuine apostle (11:7–11).

In the midst of his dispute with his opponents, Paul recounted a remarkable vision that he had experienced, one that introduced the topic of a *third heaven* (12:2), which Paul used as a means of saying that he had seen greater things and therefore wanted to turn the hearts of the saints toward those greater things and away from the claims of the false missionaries.

CONNECTION TO LATTER-DAY SAINT BELIEFS

Two teachings from 2 Corinthians have noteworthy connections to Restoration teachings and events. First, the Prophet Joseph Smith compared his own trials to those of Paul (6:4 and note). Both leaders had experienced severe trials, and if Joseph's comparison implied a more general pattern of similarity in their lives, then the end result of those trials would also be noteworthy as enemies eventually succeeded in taking their lives. A second point of connection is Paul's use of the term *third heaven* (12:2). The content of what Paul saw is passed over without comment in the letter, and unfortunately the reader is left to wonder what he saw and heard in the third heaven. Such a concept of three heavens must have been part of the groundwork that encouraged the revelation recorded as Doctrine and Covenants 76. The Bible is mostly silent on the topic of multiple heavens, but Paul unequivocally declares that he had seen into the third, a place that Joseph Smith would later refer to as the celestial kingdom. ❧

OPENING ADDRESS

1 ¹Paul, an apostle of Christ Jesus through the will of God, and Timothy our brother, to the church of God which is in Corinth, with all the saints in all Achaia: ²grace and peace to you, from God our Father and the Lord Jesus Christ.

THANKSGIVING

³Blessed be the God and Father of our Lord Jesus Christ, the Father of compassion and God of all comfort, ⁴who comforts us in all our trials so that we may be able to comfort those who are in any trial with the comfort with which we ourselves have been comforted by God. ⁵Just as Christ's sufferings abound toward us, even so our comfort through Christ abounds. ⁶If we experience trial, it is for your comfort and salvation; if we are comforted, it is for your comfort, which you will experience when you patiently endure the same sufferings that we suffer. ⁷And our hope for you is firm, knowing that you share in our sufferings; you will also share in our comfort.

⁸For we do not want you to be unaware, brothers and sisters, of our trial which came upon us in Asia, that we were weighed down tremendously so that we despaired even for life itself. ⁹But we felt we had a sentence of death passed upon us so that we would not trust in ourselves but in God who raises the dead, ¹⁰who delivered us from such a significant threat of death, and he will deliver us. We have placed our hope in him that he will yet deliver us. ¹¹You must help us by joining in prayer so that many may give thanks on our behalf for the great gift bestowed by us through the help of many.

¹²For our boasting is this, the testimony of our conscience that we acted in the world in holiness and sincerity from God, not in human wisdom but in the grace of God, especially toward you. ¹³For we do not write anything except what you can read and understand, and I hope that you fully understand, ¹⁴just as you understand us in part, that we are your boast even as you are our boast in the day of our Lord Jesus.

PAUL'S INTENDED VISIT

¹⁵With this confidence, I wanted to come to you first so that I would have a second opportunity to see you ¹⁶and through your assistance to travel to Macedonia and then back to you again from Macedonia and be helped by you on our way to Judea. ¹⁷Therefore, did I vacillate in my decision when planning this? Do I make my plan

---

1:1 Timothy was involved in the first visit to Corinth (Acts 18:5; 19:22). **1:4** *Trials* is singular in Greek, but English usage prefers the plural. **1:5** Paul speaks of *Christ's sufferings* in the plural, reflecting the idea that all his sufferings were for us. **1:6** This verse provides a brief glimpse into finding meaning through trial. The emphasis is not on understanding the purpose for which trial is given but *patiently* enduring. **1:8** Greek uses *brothers* generically to refer to *brothers and sisters*. **1:8–9** Paul does not specify what the event was, but it was life threatening. Scholars often suggest that this was an imprisonment in Ephesus, which is not attested elsewhere, and Paul may allude to this event in Philippians 1:12–26 (compare Acts 19:23; 1 Corinthians 15:32). **1:12** A number of early and important manuscripts read *pure motives* in place of *holiness*. **1:14** The pronoun *our,* in conjunction with *Lord Jesus*, is omitted in some early and important manuscripts. The textual tradition is mixed, and it is difficult to determine which reading is original. **1:15** The final phrase is somewhat unclear in Greek, and Paul says to *have a second grace*, which is used to describe looking forward to visiting the city again. **1:16** *Macedonia* includes Thessalonica and Philippi. **1:17** *In my decision* has been added to clarify Paul's intent to draw attention to his mental deliberations in planning to return to Corinth. The latter portion of the verse contains an allusion to Matthew 5:37 (also James 5:12). From the language of this verse, it appears that Paul sensed he was being criticized for not returning sooner to Corinth.

according to human considerations, ready to say, "yes, yes," and "no, no," at the same time? ¹⁸But God is faithful, and our message to you is not "yes" and "no." ¹⁹For the Son of God, Jesus Christ, whom we proclaimed among you, by Silvanus, Timothy, and I, was not "yes" and "no," but it has always been "yes" in him. ²⁰For in him, every one of God's promises is "yes." That is the reason why it is through him that we say "amen" to God for his glory. ²¹And God establishes us with you in Christ and has anointed us, ²²who sealed us and gave us his Spirit in our hearts as a promise.

²³I call on God as a witness against my soul: I did not come again to Corinth in order to spare you. ²⁴Not that we lord over your faith, but we are fellow workers in your joy because you stand firm in the faith.

2 ¹For I determined not to come to you again in sorrow. ²For if I make you sad, who would be left to cheer me up except the one whom I caused to be sad? ³I wrote this very thing to you so that when I came I would not feel pain for those who made me rejoice. For I am confident in all of you, that my joy would be the joy of you all. ⁴For I wrote in great trial and anguish of heart and with many tears, not to make you feel pain but to let you know the abundant love I have for you.

ACCEPTING THE REPENTANT

⁵If anyone made you feel pain, he has not caused me pain, but in some measure (not to exaggerate) he has caused all of you pain. ⁶This punishment inflicted by the majority is sufficient for him ⁷so that you ought to forgive and comfort him so that he may not be overwhelmed by excessive pain. ⁸So I urge you to reaffirm your love for him. ⁹For this reason I wrote to you, that I might test you to know if you are obedient in everything. ¹⁰Whomever you forgive I will also forgive, and whatever I have forgiven (if I have forgiven anything) has been for your sake in the presence of Christ ¹¹so that we would not be exploited by Satan, for we are not ignorant of his purposes.

TITUS

¹²When I came to Troas to proclaim the gospel of Christ, a door was opened to me in the Lord, ¹³but my spirit did not rest because I did not find my brother Titus

---

1:19 *Silvanus* is also referred to as *Silas* (1 Thessalonians 1:1; 2 Thessalonians 1:1 and possibly 1 Peter 5:12). He was a cofounder with Timothy and Paul of the church in Corinth (Acts 18:5). **1:21–22** The language of *anointing* and *sealing* probably corresponds to the covenant of baptism, where Christians accepted Christ and were sealed through the reception of the Holy Spirit. Some traces of an ordinance of *anointing* and *sealing* have survived in extracanonical sources, and their purpose seems to have been a formalizing of accepting Christ and being sealed through an anointing of oil. Little is known about how the practice was carried out. The anointing was probably similar to that of the priests who were anointed (Exodus 29:7; Leviticus 8:12). Paul elsewhere speaks of sealing metaphorically (Romans 4:11; 15:28; 1 Corinthians 9:2) **1:22** *Promise* can also be translated as *first installment* or *pledge*. Compare Ephesians 1:14.

2:1 Paul's visit *in sorrow* was his second visit to the city, and he is deliberating a third visit (2 Corinthians 12:14, 21; 13:1). Not much is known of Paul's second and most difficult visit to Corinth, but he wrote them a letter during this period, which is discussed in 2 Corinthians 1:23–2:4; 7:8, 12. **2:5** Paul appears to have a single individual in mind who has caused him pain, but the exact nature of the friction between them is not specified. **2:6–7** Whoever the person was, the members of the church appear to have excommunicated him through a majority decision. The saints are now encouraged to forgive that person, possibly indicating that he could rejoin them. **2:7** The verb of *forgiveness* in this verse can also mean *to pardon* or *to show kindness*. **2:10** *In the presence of Christ* is an allusion to judgment. **2:13** Paul's concern for Titus represents his genuine worry that something had happened to him because he did not meet with Paul at

there. So I departed from them and went to Macedonia.

PLEASING TO GOD

[14]But thanks be to God, who always leads us in triumphal procession and through us makes known the sweet smell that comes from knowing him, [15]because we are the aroma of Christ to God among those who are being saved and among those who are perishing, [16]to the one a smell of death to death, and to the other the fragrance of life to life. Who is equal to these things? [17]For we are not like so many others, merchants of the word of God for financial gain, but we speak as persons of sincerity in Christ, as persons sent from God and standing in his presence.

THE NEW COVENANT

3 [1]Are we beginning to commend ourselves again? Or do we need, as some do, letters of commendation to you or from you? [2]You are our letter of commendation, written upon our hearts, to be understood and read by all. [3]And you reveal that you are a letter from Christ, delivered by us, written not in black ink but in the Spirit of the living God, not on tablets of stone but on tablets of human hearts.

[4]We have this confidence in God through Christ. [5]Not that we are ourselves sufficient to claim anything as though it came from ourselves, but our adequacy is from God, [6]who made us competent to be ministers of a new covenant, not based on what was written but on the Spirit. For the letter kills, but the Spirit gives life.

[7]If the ministry that results in death, the one carved in letters on stone tablets, came in glory so that the Israelites were not able to gaze upon the face of Moses because of its glory, a glory that was concealed, [8]how much more glorious will the ministry of the Spirit be? [9]If the ministry of judgment had glory, the ministry of righteousness must abound in glory even more. [10]For

---

the planned rendezvous spot in Troas. Their reunion is described in some detail in 2 Corinthians 7:5–15. **2:14** The *triumphal procession* refers to the public displays of military victory that were celebrated across the Roman empire. **2:14–16** The concept of *smell*, *aroma*, and *fragrance* may allude to the use of incense in sacrifice or the sacrifice itself (Leviticus 1:9, 13; Philippians 4:18). **2:15** A similar division of people into those who are being *saved* and those who are *perishing* is found in 1 Corinthians 1:18. **2:16** *Who is equal to these things* refers to the requirements of service as a missionary and specifically to what Paul had sacrificed to serve the Corinthians (see 2 Corinthians 3:5).

3:1 The purpose of this chapter is to compare the inadequacy of the Sinai covenant to the covenant of the gospel or the new covenant. **3:3** An allusion to Exodus 24:12; Deuteronomy 9:10–11. Perhaps an allusion also to Ezekiel 11:19. **3:5** *Sufficient* and *adequacy* translate into the same Greek word. The fundamental idea is whether the believer is *adequate* to claim inspiration, revelation, prophecy, or other gifts or whether these come from God through the believer. An allusion to Jeremiah 31:33. **3:6** *New covenant* is an allusion to Jeremiah 31:31–34. *Servants* is a translation of the Greek word *deacons* (see also verses 7–9). Paul often seems to prefer the implications of referring to himself as a *deacon*, a person who serves the local branches rather than as an emissary, or messenger (i.e., an apostle). A *deacon* was connected to the everyday lives of the saints, whereas an apostle was sent to deliver a message and then depart. **3:7** The Greek text says *carved in stone*, but the reference is clearly to the *stone tablets* mentioned in verse 3. *A glory that was concealed* is an allusion to Exodus 34:35, when Moses covered his face with a veil so that he could continue speaking with the Israelites. Other translations render the phrase *fading away*. The primary meaning of the Greek verb is *to render ineffective*, and therefore the meaning is that Moses rendered the radiant glory of his face *ineffective* through the use of a veil (see also Exodus 34:29–30). A similar conceptualization of the law that leads to *death* is expressed later by Paul in Romans 7:10. **3:10** *Now* has been added to help clarify the temporal relationships in this verse. The verse declares the old covenant

what had been glorious has lost its glory because of the glory that now surpasses it. [11]For if that which became insufficient had glory, how much more glorious is that which remains constant.

[12]Therefore, because we have this hope we speak with great boldness [13]and not like Moses, who placed a veil over his face so that the Israelites might not gaze upon what was coming to an end. [14]But their minds were hardened. For until this day, the same veil remains when they hear the reading of the old covenant, because it is removed only in Christ. [15]But until this day, a veil lies over their hearts whenever Moses is read. [16]Whenever a person turns to the Lord, the veil is taken away. [17]The Lord is the Spirit, and where the Spirit of the Lord is there is freedom. [18]And all of us with unveiled faces and who behold the glory of the Lord are being transformed into the same image from one state of glory to another glory, for this comes from the Lord, the Spirit.

LET THE LIGHT SHINE OUT OF DARKNESS

4 [1]Because we have this ministry, just as we have received mercy, we do not lose heart. [2]But we have renounced shameful hidden things, and we do not practice cunning or falsify God's word, but by open proclamation of the truth we commend ourselves before God to everyone's conscience. [3]And if our gospel is veiled, it is veiled to those who are perishing, [4]in which case, the god of this world has blinded the minds of the unbelievers in order to stop them from seeing the light of the gospel of the glory of Christ, who is in the image of God. [5]For we do not proclaim ourselves, but we proclaim Jesus Christ the Lord and ourselves as servants for Jesus. [6]For it is God who said, "Let the light shine out of darkness," who has lighted our heart to shed light upon the knowledge of the glory of God in the face of Jesus Christ.

A TREASURE IN CLAY JARS

[7]We have this treasure in clay jars to demonstrate that this exceptional power belongs to God and is not from us. [8]We are tried in every way, but we are not crushed; we are perplexed but not driven to despair, [9]persecuted but not forsaken, struck down but not destroyed, [10]always bearing in our body the death of Jesus so that the life of Jesus might be manifest in our bodies. [11]For we who are living are always being handed over to death for Jesus's sake so that the life of Jesus may be manifest in

to have lost its glory because the new covenant far exceeds the glory of the old. **3:11** The comparison is between the ephemeral covenant delivered by Moses and the abiding covenant delivered through Jesus. **3:13** An allusion to Exodus 34:35. Paul's reasoning emphasizes the reality that the glory of Moses's face eventually faded, which he interprets as a sign of a fading Law and its effectiveness. **3:14** Paul laments that the reading of the old covenant, here interpreted as the law of Moses, does not lead directly to a belief in Jesus as the Messiah (Christ). **3:15** An allusion to Exodus 34:34. **3:18** *Behold* refers to seeing the glory of God in a mirror, so *reflect* is also possible. This verse conveys the underlying belief that a person is changed as a result of seeing the glory of the Lord, and therefore a person often sees the Lord through his reflection. *From one state of glory to another glory* is in Greek *from glory to glory*.

4:3 It remains unclear why Paul would describe the gospel as *veiled*. The reference appears to be a criticism of a position held by his opponents who thought he taught in convoluted ways. *Those who are perishing* are described as such because their rejection of Christ will result in their eventual demise. **4:4** *The god of this world* refers to the devil. **4:6** Allusion to Genesis 1:3. **4:7** The image of *clay jars* holding a treasure captures the difference in value between the body and the spirit: one is viewed as perishable, and one is viewed as eternal. **4:8–9** These sentiments appear to reflect Paul's encounters with persecution and trial, which have clearly affected him but have left him firm in the faith.

our mortal flesh. ¹²So that death works in us, but life is in you.

¹³Just as we have the same spirit of faith according to what was written, "*I believed, and I spoke accordingly,*" and so we believe and speak accordingly. ¹⁴We know that he who raised the Lord Jesus will raise us with Jesus and bring us with you into his presence. ¹⁵For everything is for you, so that as grace abounds to more people, it may increase thanksgiving, which is to the glory of God.

THE INNER SELF

¹⁶Therefore, we do not lose heart, but even if our physical self is wasting away, our inner self is being renewed day by day. ¹⁷For this minor, momentary trial is preparing us for an eternal weight of glory that is beyond all comparison, ¹⁸because we are not looking at what can be seen but at the things that are unseen—for what is seen is temporary, but the unseen things are eternal.

5 ¹For we know that if our earthly home, our tent, is destroyed, we have a building from God, a home not made with hands, eternal and in the heavens. ²For in this earthly home we groan because we desire to put on our heavenly dwelling, ³if indeed after putting it on we are not found to be naked. ⁴For while we are living in this tent, we groan, being burdened, not from a desire to be unclothed but to be clothed so that what is mortal may be swallowed up by life. ⁵God prepared us for this very thing and gave us the Spirit as a guarantee.

⁶Therefore, we are always confident, even knowing that while we are at home in the body we are away from the Lord ⁷because we walk by faith and not by sight. ⁸Indeed, we are confident, and we would rather be away from the body and at home with the Lord. ⁹Therefore, we strive to please him, whether at home or away from the body. ¹⁰For we must all appear before the judgment seat of Christ so that we may each receive what is due according to the things that have been done in the body, whether good or evil.

THE LOVE OF GOD ENCOURAGES US

¹¹Therefore, because we know the fear of the Lord, we persuade others, but we are well known to God, and I hope that we are also well known to your conscience. ¹²We are not commending ourselves to you again but are giving you reason to boast about us so that you have an answer to those who boast about outside appearance and not about what is in the heart. ¹³If we are out of our minds, it is for God, and if we are of sound mind, it is for you. ¹⁴For the love of Christ encourages us because we are convinced of this, that one died for

---

4:13 Quotation from Psalm 116:10. **4:14** This verse presents the believer as a coheir with Jesus Christ. Compare Romans 8:17. **4:17** The language of this verse is reflected in Doctrine and Covenants 63:66; 121:7.

5:1 The *building from God* describes our new bodies in the resurrection. The taking down of a tent can be an image referring to mortal death (LXX Isaiah 38:12). **5:2** The metaphor of groaning in our mortal bodies may reflect Paul's ailing physical body (2 Corinthians 12:7). **5:3** The concept of being *naked* after having clothed oneself may be an allusion to judgment and being unclothed or exposed in the presence of God. **5:4** *Tent* is a metaphor for the mortal body, which Paul longs to exchange for a more glorious immortal body. **5:10** *The judgment seat* was a common feature of a Greek city where some legal disputes were settled. Second Nephi 9:15 uses a similar concept of the *judgment seat*. Alluded to in 3 Nephi 28:31. **5:13** Paul may be referring to ecstatic spiritual experiences such as those mentioned in 1 Corinthians 14:26–33, but also he may have been referring to his earlier letter in which he wrote to them sorrowing that he may have been *out of his mind* with grief. **5:14** *For the love of Christ* could also be translated as *the love for Christ*.

all; therefore all have died. [15]And he died for all, so that those who are alive might no longer live for themselves but for him who died and was raised for them.

[16]From now on, we regard no one according to the flesh, even if we knew Christ according to the flesh at one time, we no longer know him in that way. [17]Therefore, if anyone is in Christ, that person is a new creation; the old has passed away, and, behold, the new has come. [18]All these things are from God, who changed us through Christ and gave us the ministry of reconciliation [19]so that in Christ, God was reconciling the world to himself, not accounting to them their sins, but entrusting the message of reconciliation to us. [20]Therefore, we are ambassadors for Christ, with God making his appeal through us. We strongly encourage you to be reconciled to God on behalf of Christ. [21]On our behalf, God made him who did not know sin to become sin so that we might become the righteousness of God.

6 [1]As fellow workers, we urge you not to embrace the grace of God in vain, [2]for he says, *"In a favorable time I listened to you, and I have helped you in the day of salvation."* Behold, now is the favorable time; now is the day of salvation! [3]We do not give a reason to stumble to anyone, so that no blame might be placed on the ministry, [4]but in every aspect we commend ourselves as servants of God, with great endurance, in trials, difficulties, calamities, [5]beatings, imprisonments, riots, hard work, sleepless nights, hunger, [6]by purity, knowledge, patience, kindness, the Holy Spirit, genuine charity, [7]speaking truth, and the power of God. With the weapons of righteousness in our right and left hands, [8]through glory and dishonor, through slander and praise, we are treated as imposters, but we are true, [9]as unknown, but we are well known, as dying, but behold we live, as scourged and not yet dead, [10]as sorrowful but always rejoicing, as poor but making many rich, as having nothing but having everything.

[11]We have spoken openly to you, Corinthians, our heart is open to you. [12]There is no limit in our compassion for you, but there is in yours for us. [13]In return (I am speaking as to a child), open your hearts also.

THE TEMPLE OF THE LIVING GOD

[14]Do not be equally yoked to nonbelievers, for what partnership does righteousness

---

5:16 From the wording of Paul's declaration in this verse, it is possible to understand that he or those with him *knew Christ according to the flesh.* This would contradict the description of Paul in Acts, but it may imply that some of his traveling companions had known Jesus in mortality. **5:17** Some manuscripts add *all* to the phrase *the new has come* so that it reads *all things have become new,* but the manuscripts that support this reading are later and less reliable. Doctrine and Covenants 29:24 expands the application of this verse. Compare Doctrine and Covenants 63:49. **5:18** *Changed* and *reconciliation* are based on the same root word, which means to *change, receive into favor,* and *reconcile.* The act of God reconciling us describes him changing us to conform to his person and attributes. **5:19** The implication of this verse is that God was not occupying himself with reckoning sin but rather in working toward the salvation of humanity. *The message of reconciliation* can also be translated as *the message of atonement.* **5:21** The phrase *who did not know sin to become sin* expresses the idea that Christ remained sinless but that he became an offering for sin for others (also expressed in Romans 8:3). In other words, he took sin upon him and thereby was sin (Leviticus 4:1–12).

6:2 Quotation from Isaiah 49:8. **6:4** Compare Doctrine and Covenants 127:2–3 for Joseph Smith's trials, which he compares to Paul's. **6:6** This verse is given a new context in Doctrine and Covenants 121:41–42, where both the King James Version and the Doctrine and Covenants use the phrase *love unfeigned.* **6:7** This teaching is echoed in 2 Nephi 1:23. **6:8–10** A possible allusion to Psalm 118:17–18. **6:14–7:1** Many scholars have questioned the originality of these verses because they appear to disrupt the logical flow of

have with lawlessness? Or what fellowship does light have with darkness? [15]What relationship does Christ have with Beliar? Or what part does a believer have with a nonbeliever? [16]What agreement does the temple of God have with idols? For we are the temple of the living God, just as God said, *"I will make my dwelling among them and will walk among them, and I am their God and they are my people."* [17]Therefore, *"Come out from among them and be separate, says the Lord, and touch nothing that is unclean, and I will welcome you."* [18]And, *"I will be a father to you, and you will be my sons and daughters, says the Lord Almighty."*

7 [1]Therefore, because we have these promises, beloved friends, let us cleanse ourselves from every defilement of body and spirit, and thereby accomplish holiness out of our fear of God.

[2]Make a space for us; we have not wronged anyone, we have not corrupted anyone, nor have we exploited anyone. [3]I do not speak to your condemnation, for I have said earlier that you are in our hearts, to die and live together. [4]I am

speaking with great boldness to you, and I have great pride in you. I am filled with comfort, overflowing with joy in all our trial.

EXPERIENCES IN MACEDONIA

[5]For when we came into Macedonia, our bodies had no rest, but we were in all kinds of danger, fighting without and fear from within. [6]But God, the one who comforts the grieving, comforted us at the arrival of Titus [7]and not only by his arrival but also by the comfort that he received from you when he told us of your longing, your mourning, and your zeal for me, so that I rejoiced even more. [8]Because if I made you sad with my letter, I do not regret it (although I did regret it when I saw that the letter made you sad, but only for a short time). [9]Now, I rejoice, not that you are sad but that you were sad, which led to repentance. For you felt godly sadness so that you experienced no harm from us. [10]For godly sorrow results in repentance, which leads to salvation and produces no regret, but worldly sorrow produces

---

the letter and they contain several terms not used elsewhere in Paul's letters. Verse 14 shifts away from Paul's personal defense of his ministry in Corinth and returns to a description of his earlier ministry there. **6:15** *Beliar* is also spelled *Belial* in some manuscripts. The word is a transliteration of the Hebrew word *worthlessness* or *good for nothing* and is used here as a reference to Satan. The word also appears in Judges 20:13 and is used only in this verse in the New Testament. **6:16** Quotation from Leviticus 26:12 (also Ezekiel 37:27). Some important Greek manuscripts read *you are* in place of *we are*. It is difficult to determine which was original because the manuscript evidence is equally divided. **6:17** Quotation from Isaiah 52:11 and Ezekiel 20:41. The wording of the quotation is slightly different from that of Ezekiel and probably represents a paraphrase of the text, possibly from memory. Alma 5:57 appears to also quote this same Old Testament passage, but its language is closer to 2 Corinthians (compare Leviticus 5:2). A similar thought is expressed in Moroni 10:30. **6:18** Quotation from 2 Samuel 7:14 and Isaiah 43:6. Paul has adapted this quotation of the Old Testament according to the situation in Corinth.

7:1 *Our* has been added to the text for clarification. This verse concludes the thoughts expressed in chapter 6. **7:2** Paul's intent may have been to say *receive us when we come*. **7:3** *I have said earlier* probably refers to 2 Corinthians 1:4–7. **7:4** This verse could be understood as a celebration at seeing the affliction of others, but Paul's intent seems to be to convey a sense of appreciation and joy at their joint suffering for Christ. **7:5** These appear to be the same trials as those discussed in 2 Corinthians 4:8. **7:6** Paul's feelings regarding *Titus* are expressed more fully in 2 Corinthians 8:23 (compare Galatians 2:3, where Paul reports that *Titus* was Greek). **7:8** This letter is also mentioned in 2 Corinthians 2:3. **7:11** *The matter* refers to a specific issue that Paul had held against the Corinthians saints, but now he has softened in his view.

death. [11]Look what diligence this godly sorrow has produced in you, what a reasoned defense, what indignation, what fear, what passion, what zeal, what punishment! In everything you have proved yourself to be without guilt in the matter. [12]So, although I have written to you, it was not on account of the one who did the wrong nor on account of the one who was wronged but that your diligence for us might be made manifest before God. [13]Because of this we are comforted. Apart from our own comfort, we rejoiced more at the joy of Titus, because you have all refreshed his spirit. [14]For if I have boasted anything to him about you, I have not been embarrassed. But just as everything we said to you was true, even so our boasting to Titus has proved to be true as well. [15]And his affection for you is greater, and he remembers the obedience of you all, how you received him with fear and trembling. [16]I rejoice because I have complete confidence in you.

GENEROSITY

8 [1]We want to make you aware, brothers and sisters, of the grace of God given to the churches in Macedonia [2]because during a severe trial their abundance of joy and their extreme poverty have overflowed in a wealth of generosity on their part. [3]As I can testify, they gave voluntarily according to their means and even beyond their means of giving, [4]begging us with great earnestness for the privilege of sharing this act of service to the saints. [5]And they did this not as we expected, but they gave themselves first to the Lord and then to us by the will of God. [6]So we encouraged Titus, just as he had begun, to complete this act of kindness for you. [7]But as you abound in everything, in faith, speech, knowledge, all diligence, and in our love for you, so we want you to abound in this act of kindness.

[8]I tell you this not as a command, but I am proving the genuineness of your love against the diligence of others. [9]For you know the grace of our Lord Jesus Christ, that although he was rich, he became poor for your sakes so that through his poverty you might become rich. [10]And in this matter, I give my opinion. This is a benefit to you, who began last year not only to produce an offering but also began in your desire to produce one. [11]Now, finish doing it as well so that your diligence in desiring it

---

7:12 The person who wronged Paul was discussed in 2 Corinthians 2:5–11. It remains unclear who this person was or what he had done to injure Paul.

8:1 Greek uses *brothers* generically to refer to *brothers and sisters*. **8:2** The references to *wealth* and *generosity* signal that Paul has turned to a discussion of the collection for the poor saints in Jerusalem, and he relates that the churches in Macedonia (verse 1) are ready to send their offering. Chapters 8–9 discuss issues associated with the collection, and the plan was to send it to Jerusalem to help the poor, perhaps those who were suffering from the effects of a famine there (Romans 15:25–32; 1 Corinthians 16:1–4). **8:3** The language suggests that the offering was spontaneous and not guided by principles of tithing. **8:4** The collection for the poor was understood also to be an act of solidarity that linked the Greek saints with the Jerusalem saints. This verse represents, in part, the development of the idea of a Christian community that had shared values and goals (see 1 Corinthians 10:16). **8:6** *Titus* was given the responsibility to oversee the collection for the poor and possibly to be in charge of delivering it to Jerusalem (compare 1 Corinthians 16:1, 5–10; Galatians 2:10). **8:7** Several early and important manuscripts read *your love for us* in place of *our love for you*. It is difficult to determine which reading is original. **8:8** The intent of this verse is to indicate that Paul is comparing the generosity of others (those of Macedonia, verse 3) with that of the Corinthians, who seemingly have not been as generous in their offerings. **8:9** *Rich* is used abstractly to refer to the wealth of the glory of Christ. This idea is expressed more clearly in Philippians 2:7. **8:12** Paul's guideline for giving is that the saints should not allow the offering of others to guide what

may be equal to completing it according to your means. [12]For if the diligence is there, it is acceptable according to what a person has and not according to what a person does not have. [13]I do not mean that there should be relief for others and trial for you, but it is a question of equality. [14]At present your abundance will supply their lack so that in the future their abundance will supply your lack and thereby there may be equality. [15]Just as it is written, "*The one who gathered much did not have too much, and the one who gathered little did not lack.*"

TITUS

[16]But thanks be to God, who put into the heart of Titus the same diligence that I have for you, [17]because he not only accepted the request, but now that he is even more eager, he is coming to you of his own volition. [18]We are sending with him the brother who is famous in spreading the gospel among all the churches. [19]And not only that, but he has been appointed by the churches as a fellow traveler while we administer this act of kindness to show our goodwill and for the glory of the Lord himself. [20]Our intent is that no one should blame us in regard to this act of kindness

we are administering. [21]For we intend to do what is right not only before the Lord but before all people. [22]And we are sending with them our brother whom we have often proved and found to be diligent in many matters and who is now more diligent than ever because of his confidence in you. [23]As for Titus, he is my partner and fellow worker to you; as for our brothers, they are apostles of the churches, to the glory of Christ. [24]Therefore, demonstrate before the churches your love and the reason for our boasting about you.

THE COLLECTION FOR THE POOR

9 [1]For it is not necessary for me to write to you concerning the service to the saints. [2]For I know your desire, about which I boast to the people of Macedonia, saying that the people of Achaia have been ready since last year. And your zeal has stimulated the majority of them. [3]But I am sending the brothers so that our boasting about you might not be in vain in this instance, so that you may be ready just as I told them. [4]If some of the Macedonians come with me and find that you are not prepared, we would be embarrassed (not to mention you also) because of the confi-

---

they offer, but rather they should make their offering according to their own financial means. This verse is alluded to in Doctrine and Covenants 64:34 (compare 1 Chronicles 28:9). **8:13–14** In the period after the demise of the church's effort to live a law of consecration (Acts 5:1–11), Paul advocates for a principle of financial equality. **8:15** Quotation from Exodus 16:18. **8:18** The identity of this brother is unknown. **8:19** *Appointed* refers to the act of voting by a raise of hands. **8:21** An allusion to Proverbs 3:4. **8:23** It is also possible that Paul intended the word *apostles* to be used generically in this verse to refer to *messengers*. Both translations are equally possible.

9:1 *The service to the saints* refers again to the collection for the poor (see 2 Corinthians 8:2–4 and notes), but in this instance Paul has changed the word used to describe the collection to be an act of *service*, or the act of a *deacon*. Because this chapter again treats the topic of the collection for the poor, some scholars have suggested that this chapter was a separate letter to the Corinthians encouraging them to donate to the collection. **9:2** *Achaia* refers to Greece and specifically in this instance Corinth. **9:3, 5** These *brothers* refer to missionaries whom Paul plans to send. They were likely male missionaries, and therefore *brothers* has been retained. **9:4** *The confidence we had in this* is in Greek *this confidence*, and the additional words have been supplied to clarify the meaning. **9:5** The *generous offering* is in Greek a *blessing*. The word *obligation* does not quite capture the sense of the Greek word, which implies that the saints in Corinth might feel that they were being extorted by the greed of Paul and others. English does not have a single word to describe this, and it can be rendered only through a longer phrase *as a gift given*

dence we had in this. ⁵Therefore, I thought it necessary to urge the brothers to come to you in advance and arrange ahead of time a generous offering that you had promised so that it may be ready as a gift and not an obligation.

⁶This is my point: the one who sows sparingly will reap sparingly, and the one who sows bountifully will reap bountifully. ⁷Each should give according to the heart and not out of sorrow or obligation, for "*God loves a cheerful giver.*" ⁸God is able to make grace abound for you so that you will have a sufficient amount of everything at all times and you will abound in every good work, ⁹just as it is written, "*He has scattered liberally; he gives to the poor; his righteousness remains forever.*"

¹⁰He who supplies the "*sower with seed and bread for food*" will supply and increase your seed for sowing and amplify the harvest of your righteousness. ¹¹You will be enriched in every way for your generosity, which through us will produce thanksgiving for God, ¹²because the service of this ministry is not only supplying the needs of the saints but also abounds with many thanks to God. ¹³Through the proof of this service, they will glorify God because of your obedience to your confession of the gospel of Christ and the generosity of your offering to them and to all others, ¹⁴and they long for you and pray for you because of the overwhelming grace of God that he has given you. ¹⁵Thanks be to God for his indescribable gift!

PAUL'S DEFENSE

10 ¹I, Paul, who am humble when in front of you but am bold when I am away, personally encourage you by the meekness and gentleness of Christ, ²and I ask you that while I am present that I might not need to be bold with such confidence as that I consider using against those who consider us as walking according to the flesh. ³For even though we walk in flesh, yet we do not fight like mortals do, ⁴for our weapons of war are not mortal weapons, but they have divine power to bring down strongholds. We bring down arguments ⁵and every prideful thing that is raised up against the knowledge of God, and we control every thought and make it obedient to Christ, ⁶and we are ready to punish every disobedience, when our obedience is complete.

⁷Look at what is in front of you. If someone is confident that he belongs to Christ, he should reconsider. Just as he belongs to Christ, so do we. ⁸For if I boast more abundantly than I should about our authority that the Lord gave us for building you up and not tearing you down, I will not be ashamed. ⁹I do not want to seem as though I am terrifying you with my letters. ¹⁰For they say, "His letters are weighty and strong, but his bodily presence is sickly, and his speech is of no account." ¹¹Let them consider this, that what we say by letters when absent, we likewise do when present.

¹²We would not dare to classify or compare ourselves with those who recommend

---

through covetousness where the giver gives with remorse. **9:8** Compare Alma 7:24; 1 Corinthians 13:13. **9:9** Quotation from Psalm 112:9. This quotation, although given in a context where God is the subject of the sentence (verse 8) refers to the cheerful giver (verse 7). **9:10** Quotation from Isaiah 55:10 (compare Hosea 10:12). **9:11** *To God* is also possible, but the case of the Greek noun is better rendered in the sense of thanksgiving for what God has bestowed.

10:6 *When our obedience is complete* is temporally connected to the first phrase of this verse. **10:9** Paul implies that by this stage of his missionary work he had written multiple letters. **10:10** *They* refers to Paul's opponents in Corinth, but he does not give any specific indications concerning their identity. *Sickly* can also be translated as *weak in bodily appearance* (compare Galatians 4:13). **10:12** Paul does not explain what type of letters his opponents were using to justify their actions, but he calls attention to the practice and denounces it.

themselves, but they measure themselves against one another and compare themselves with themselves, and they are not wise. [13]But we will not boast beyond limit, and we will observe the limits God has appointed to us which reaches as far as you. [14]For we were not overextending ourselves when we reached you, because we were the first to come to you with the gospel of Christ. [15]We did not boast beyond limit with regard to the labor of others, but we have hope that as your faith grows, our work among you may be greatly enlarged [16]so that we may proclaim the gospel in regions beyond, without boasting of work already done in another person's area. [17]*"Let the person who boasts, boast in the Lord."* [18]For it is not the person who recommends himself that is accepted, but the person the Lord recommends.

THE FALSE APOSTLES

11 [1]I wish that you would bear with me in a little folly, and indeed you are bearing with me. [2]For I have the zeal of God for you because I betrothed you as a chaste virgin to Christ, who is your only husband. [3]And I am afraid that as the serpent beguiled Eve through subtlety, your minds may be corrupted from the simplicity and purity that is in Christ. [4]For if someone comes and proclaims another Jesus whom we have not proclaimed or you receive another spirit that you have not received or you receive another gospel that you have not received, you endure it well enough. [5]For I do not consider myself to be inferior to the superlative apostles. [6]If I am unskilled in speaking, I am not unskilled in knowledge, but we have made this plain to you in all things.

[7]Have I committed a sin in humbling myself so you might be exalted because I proclaimed the gospel of God to you without cost? [8]But I have robbed the churches, receiving money from them so that I could serve you. [9]When I was with you and was in need, I did not burden anyone because my needs were met by the brothers who came from Macedonia. I refrained from burdening you, and I will refrain from burdening you in any way. [10]As the truth of Christ is in me, this personal boasting will not be silenced in the regions of Achaia. [11]Why? Because I do not love you? God knows I do.

[12]And what I am doing I will continue to do so that I may cut off the opportunity to those who want to be recognized as equals to us in what they boast about. [13]For

---

10:17 Quotation from Jeremiah 9:24. This scripture reference appears to convey Paul's concern about working in areas where others have already proclaimed the gospel, possibly a result of trials he had experienced when he taught where others had taught (2 Corinthians 1:1–17). **10:18** Compare Luke 18:14.

11:3 Some manuscripts omit *and purity*, but the words are present in the best manuscripts. Compare Mosiah 16:3 for the idea that Satan was the serpent in Eden. **11:4** *Another Jesus, another spirit*, and *another gospel* characterize the contrary teachings of Paul's opponents in Corinth. They most likely represent differing interpretations of Jesus and his gospel, but Paul does not clarify the precise content of their teachings. A similar expression occurs in Galatians 1:6 to describe alternate views about Jesus. **11:5** *Superlative apostles* is spoken in irony and used to describe Paul's opponents. It is not clear to whom he is referring, but he may not have intended the word *apostle* to be used in its technical sense. It probably refers to *missionaries*, and Paul is disparaging their reputation as *superlative missionaries* (see verse 13). **11:6** *Unskilled* refers to professional training, and in the context of speech this would refer to training in rhetoric. **11:7, 9** The implication is that some have complained that by not asking for financial assistance, Paul was not a legitimate missionary/apostle. Paul criticizes this view and offers his willingness to work as a sign of his genuineness. See 1 Corinthians 9:18, 1 Thessalonians 2:9. **11:9** See note on 2 Corinthians 9:3, 5. **11:13** *For such are false missionaries* is also possible. Paul's intent may have been to compare his opponents to the called and appointed missionaries of the church, and the

such are false apostles, deceitful workers, masquerading as apostles of Christ. [14]And no wonder, for Satan masquerades as an angel of light. [15]Therefore, it is not surprising if his servants also masquerade as servants of righteousness. Their end will be according to their deeds.

I AM A FOOL

[16]I tell you again, let no one think that I am foolish. But if they do, accept me even as a fool so that I may also boast a little. [17]I am speaking with this boastful confidence as the Lord would but as a fool. [18]Because many boast according to human standards, I too will boast. [19]Because you are wise, you will bear fools gladly. [20]For you endure it when someone makes slaves of you or devours you or takes advantage of you or someone behaves arrogantly or if someone strikes you in the face. [21]To my own shame, I must say that we were too weak for that.

But whatever else someone may dare boast of, I am speaking foolishly, I dare to boast also. [22]Are they Hebrews? So am I. Are they Israelites? So am I. Are they descendants of Abraham? So am I. [23]Are they servants of Christ? (I am speaking like I am out of my mind.) I am these things even more, with more abundant labors, in a greater number of imprisonments, in more severe beatings, facing death more of-

ten. [24]I received thirty-nine lashes from the Jews on five occasions. [25]Three times I was beaten with rods; once I was stoned. Three times I was shipwrecked, and a night and a day I spent in the sea. [26]I have frequently been on journeys, in dangers from rivers, from robbers, from my countrymen, from Gentiles, in the city, in the desert, at sea, and from false brothers. [27]I have worked hard and labored; I have passed sleepless nights; been hungry and thirsty, without food many times, and exposed without clothing. [28]Apart from other things, there is the daily burden of anxiety for all the churches. [29]Who is weak, and am I not weak? Who stumbles and I do not subsequently grow indignant?

[30]If boasting is necessary, I will boast about the things pertaining to my weakness. [31]The God and Father of the Lord Jesus, who is blessed for eternity, knows that I am not lying. [32]In Damascus, the governor under King Aretas was guarding the city of Damascus in an attempt to seize me, [33]but I was let down in a basket through an opening in the wall, and I fled out of his hands.

THE THIRD HEAVEN

12 [1]It is necessary to boast. Although it is not profitable, I will go on to visions and revelations of the Lord. [2]I know a man in Christ who fourteen

---

word *apostle* is ambiguous in this verse regarding whether it technically refers to an *apostle* who is called or to a *missionary*. **11:13–15** The meaning of the Greek verb translated as *masquerade* in these verses can also mean *disguised* and is used to describe Paul's opponents who *masquerade* as true apostles and Satan who also *masquerades* as an angel. **11:14** The term *angel of light* appears in 2 Nephi 9:9 (see also Alma 30:53). Alluded to in Doctrine and Covenants 128:20; 129:8. **11:15** *Servants* is the Greek word *deacons*. **11:24** For the practice, see Deuteronomy 25:3. **11:25** Perhaps a reference to the events described in Acts 14:19; 16:22. **11:26** Alluded to in Doctrine and Covenants 122:5. **11:27** This verse is technically a clause that is dependent upon the main verb of verse 26, which has been repeated at the beginning of this verse and which has also been translated as a new sentence. **11:32** This event is also described in Acts 9:23–25. *The governor* was technically an *ethnarch*, or local leader appointed by the king. In this instance, the name of the governor is unknown. *King Aretas* refers to *Aretas IV Philopatris*, who died in 40 CE and was a Nabatean king. There is some dispute whether he had jurisdiction in Damascus, and it may be that he had control only of the Nabatean population in the region.

12:2 The Prophet Joseph Smith used similar language to describe his revelation of the celestial kingdom

years ago was caught up into the third heaven (whether in the body or not, I do not know, but God knows). ³And I know that this man (whether in the body or apart from the body, I do not know, but God knows) ⁴was caught up to paradise, and he heard things that cannot be put into words, which are not lawful for a human to speak. ⁵I will boast on this person's behalf, but on my own account I will not boast except about my weaknesses. ⁶Although if I desire to boast, I will not be a fool, because I am speaking the truth. But I refrain from doing so in order that no one may think of me beyond what he sees in me or hears from me, ⁷even in light of the extraordinary revelations. Therefore, so that I would not be arrogant, there was given to me a thorn in the flesh, a messenger of Satan to harass me so that I would not be arrogant. ⁸I called on the Lord three times about this, that it might leave me. ⁹And he said to me, "My grace is sufficient for you, for my power is made perfect in weaknesses." Therefore, I will boast more gladly in my weaknesses so that the power of Christ resides in me. ¹⁰Therefore, I am satisfied with my weaknesses, insults, difficulties, persecutions, and calamities for the sake of Christ. For when I am weak, then I am strong.

¹¹I have become a fool. You pushed me to it, for I should have been commended by you. For I am not inferior to the superlative apostles, even though I am nothing. ¹²The signs of an apostle were performed among you with great patience, with signs, wonders, and powerful actions. ¹³For how were you treated inferior to the other churches, except that I was not a burden to you personally? Forgive me of this injustice!

PAUL'S VISIT TO CORINTH

¹⁴This is the third time that I have come to you, and I will not be a burden, for I do not seek your possessions, but I seek for your welfare. For children should not have to save for their parents but the parents for their children. ¹⁵I will gladly spend my life and be spent for your souls. If I love you more, am I to be loved less? ¹⁶And be that as it is, I have not burdened you. But being crafty, I took you in by deceit. ¹⁷Did I take advantage of you by any of those whom I sent you? ¹⁸I encouraged Titus to visit and sent the brother together with him. Did Titus take advantage of you? Did we not act in the same spirit? Did we not act in the same way?

¹⁹Have you been thinking for a long time that we have been defending ourselves to you? We are speaking before God

---

(Doctrine and Covenants 137:1). The *third heaven* likely refers to the highest heaven, although it could refer to the lowest, depending on the order the sequence is counted. **12:2–3** Echoed in 3 Nephi 28:13–15; Doctrine and Covenants 137:1. **12:2–4** Although he speaks of the person who saw the vision in the third person, his parenthetical remarks clarify that the vision was his own. **12:4** The word *paradise* seems to be a metaphor for the *third heaven* mentioned in verse 2. In Luke 23:43 it refers to the place where the righteous dead reside before the judgment. *Cannot be put into words* can also be translated as *unable to speak*. The wording suggests that the human tongue is not capable of reproducing the things that were heard. **12:7** Paul does not clarify the nature of his *thorn in the flesh*, but scholars have suggested an illness, eye disease, and opposition from Jewish Christians. **12:9–10** Similar language appears in Ether 12:26–27; Doctrine and Covenants 17:8; 18:31. **12:11** See note on 2 Corinthians 11:5. These *superlative apostles* could be missionaries who thought they were exceptional and that Paul was inferior to them. **12:13** *Forgive me of this injustice* is said in irony. **12:14** The emphasis is on the idea that little children cannot and should not care for the financial needs of their parents. **12:15** *My life* has been added for clarification. **12:18** For *Titus*, see 2 Corinthians 8:16–9:5. The *brother* mentioned in this verse is otherwise unknown.

in Christ, and everything that we do we have done to edify you, dear brothers and sisters. ²⁰For I am afraid that somehow when I come I will not find you as I wish, and you may find me not as you wish, that somehow there may be infighting, jealousy, anger, hostility, defaming, slander, pride, and instability. ²¹I am afraid that when I come again, my God may humble me before you and I may have to mourn for many of those who sinned previously and have not repented of impurity, sexual impropriety, and lust that they have practiced.

Examine Yourselves

13 ¹This is the third time that I am coming to you. "*By the mouth of two or three witnesses every matter will be established.*" ²I said before when I was with you during my second visit, and although I am absent, again I say to those who previously sinned and to the others: if I return I will not be lenient, ³because you seek for proof that Christ is speaking through me. He is not weak toward you, but he is powerful among you. ⁴For he was crucified in weakness, but he lives in the power of God. For we are weak in him, but we will live with him because of God's power toward you.

⁵Put yourselves to the test to determine if you are in the faith; examine yourselves! Or do you not know this about yourselves, that Jesus Christ is in you unless indeed you fail the test. ⁶I hope that you know that we have not failed the test. ⁷But we pray to God that you may not do wrong, not so that we may appear to have passed the test but only for the sake of the truth, even if we appear to have failed the test. ⁸For we cannot do anything against the truth but only for the truth. ⁹For we rejoice when we are weak but you are strong. We pray for this, that you may be fully strengthened. ¹⁰Therefore, I write these things while I am away, that when I come I may not need to treat you harshly by using my authority. The Lord gave it to me to edify and not to tear down!

Final Encouragement

¹¹Finally, brothers and sisters, rejoice. Put things in order, be comforted, be of the same mind, be at peace, and the God of love and peace will be with you. ¹²Greet one another with a holy kiss. All the saints greet you. ¹³May the grace of the Lord Jesus Christ, and the love of God, and the fellowship of the Holy Spirit be with you all.

13:1 Quotation from Deuteronomy 19:15. The same Old Testament passage is also quoted in Doctrine and Covenants 6:28, but the language is clearly that of 2 Corinthians (compare also Matthew 18:16); Doctrine and Covenants 128:3 similarly treats this subject, but it quotes from Matthew 18:16. **13:2** Paul's patience appears to have grown thin, and he plans to deal harshly with those who have sinned if they have not repented when he visits Corinth for the third time. **13:4** *Crucified in weakness* may refer to the idea that Christ was crucified in the weakness of being in a body of flesh. **13:5** The Greek verb *test* can also mean *trial* or *temptation*. The meaning of Paul's injunction is that the saints should carefully examine their own souls to determine whether they stand in the faith. **13:9** *Fully strengthened* can also mean *perfected* or *fully instructed*. **13:11** Greek uses *brothers* generically to refer to *brothers and sisters*. **13:12** For the *kiss*, see Romans 16:16. It was a form of friendly greeting in ancient Mediterranean cultures. **13:12–13** Some translations divide these two concluding verses into three verses, although the content is the same.

GALATIANS

AUTHOR

Paul is listed as the sole author and sender of this letter (1:1), and it is written to a region and a group of churches rather than to a single location. The recipients are clearly Gentiles to whom the recounting of Peter's actions in Antioch would make sense, and most likely they are the saints living in Iconium, Lystra, and Derbe, where Paul and Barnabas traveled on their first missionary journey (Acts 14:1–23). Paul's perspective in this letter is that he has recently returned from the Jerusalem conference (Acts 15:1–29), and therefore in his mind the decision of whether Gentile members needed to be circumcised had been resolved. However, despite the clear decision made by Peter and Jacob in Acts 15, Paul writes with a tone of frustration that subsequent events threatened to undo the momentum of good will toward Gentiles following the decision of the conference.

Titus traveled with Paul, as did Barnabas (Galatians 2:1), and in Jerusalem they met with Peter, Jacob the brother of the Lord, and John. Paul also took time in this letter to provide an account of his conversion and of the events that immediately followed the revelation on the road to Damascus. Paul saw himself as successful in his ancestral religion (1:14), and he used the language of a prophetic call rather than the language of conversion (1:15) to describe what he had experienced. Subsequent to the revelation on the road to Damascus, Paul then traveled in Arabia (1:17) and then to Jerusalem to find answers from the apostles (1:18–19). In sum, Paul is reflective in this letter, offering personal commentary on his previous life and existence.

PURPOSE OF WRITING

The most obvious reason for writing is to express a sense of outrage and frustration that Peter had eaten with Gentiles but then after the arrival of individuals from Jerusalem, Peter would no longer eat with Gentiles (2:1–14). Paul seemed to believe that his work in Galatia had been threatened by Peter's actions, which must have had some public component to them for them to be so offensive. From the existing letter, there is no evidence that Paul attempted to understand why Peter acted in the way he did, nor does he report anything in Peter's defense. Paul's tone is accusatory and frustrated.

That tone of frustration quickly gives way to a reflection on what it means to be a believing Gentile and to be accepted into the covenant of Christ (5:2–15). Paul develops the idea of there being two covenants that are interrelated and connected in fundamental ways. He finds in the story of Abraham a type of the two covenants. Famously, Paul concludes that Jews and Gentiles are saved by faith: "I have been crucified with Christ, but it is no longer I who live, but Christ lives in me. Now, the life I live in the flesh I live by faith in the Son of God, who loved me and gave himself for me" (2:19–20). Galatians demonstrates that religious innovation was borne out of trial and affliction.

CONNECTION TO LATTER-DAY SAINT BELIEFS

Following the King James translation, one of the most influential verses from Galatians states, "Wherefore the law was our schoolmaster to bring us unto Christ, that we might be justified by faith" (3:24). In the current translation, these words appear thus: "So that the Law was our guardian until Christ came so that we might be made righteous by faith." The thought expressed in this verse is that the Law served only for a time and that it was subsequently done away with, a concept that is now referred to as supersessionism. The idea is that the law of Moses has been superseded or replaced in its entirety by the gospel or new covenant. Critics of that concept note that it has permitted the persecution and marginalization of Jews because they had effectively been replaced in God's covenant. Many modern religions debate to what degree their views are supersessionist, and Latter-day Saints have tended to be stronger in their supersessionist views. A healthy discussion regarding the negative consequences of historical attitudes toward Jews has begun, and hopefully older attitudes can be replaced by more healthy attitudes. ॐ

OPENING ADDRESS

1 ¹Paul, an apostle, not from men or through a man but through Jesus Christ and God the Father, who raised him from the dead, ²and through all the brothers and sisters who are with me, to the churches of Galatia: ³grace and peace to you from God our Father and the Lord Jesus Christ, ⁴who gave himself for our sins, to rescue us from the present age of evil according to the will of our God and Father, ⁵to whom be glory forever and ever, amen.

SOME ARE TROUBLING YOU

⁶I am amazed at how quickly you are deserting the one who called you in the grace of Christ and are following another gospel, ⁷not that there is another gospel, but there are some who are troubling you and want to turn you away from the gospel of Christ. ⁸But even if we or an angel from heaven proclaims to you a different gospel than the one we preached to you, let that person be accursed. ⁹As we have said previously and I say to you again, if someone proclaims a different gospel to you than the one you received, let that person be accursed.

PAUL'S TIME AS A PERSECUTOR

¹⁰Am I trying to persuade people or God? Or am I seeking to please people? If I am still pleasing people, I would not be a servant of Christ. ¹¹For I would have you understand, brothers and sisters, that the gospel proclaimed by me is not according to human sensibilities. ¹²For I did not receive it from a human source, nor was it taught to me, but I received it through a revelation of Jesus Christ. ¹³For you have heard of my former conduct in Judaism, how I violently persecuted the church of God and tried to destroy it. ¹⁴And I was advancing in Judaism beyond many of my peers among my nation, being extremely zealous for the traditions of my ancestors. ¹⁵But when God, who set me apart from the womb and called me by his grace, was pleased ¹⁶to reveal his Son in me so that I might proclaim him among the Gentiles, I did not confer with flesh and blood, ¹⁷nor

---

1:1 *Not from men or through a man* seems to call attention to the fact that Paul was made an *apostle* through other means—namely, through his personal experiences with the risen Lord. Paul draws upon the concept that an *apostle* was a special witness of Christ. **1:2** The Greek text mentions only *brothers*, and Paul may have intentionally meant only the *brothers* who were traveling with him. However, the word frequently refers to *brothers and sisters*, and the form of the address indicates that those who were with Paul when he wrote the letter are sending their greetings along with Paul, and hence these are the members of the church. *Galatia* refers to the Roman province of *Galatia*, and the region included several cities visited during Paul's first missionary journey with Barnabas (Psidian Antioch, Lystra, Derbe, Iconium; Acts 13:13–14:28). **1:4** The concept that Christ *gave himself for our sins* is not frequently mentioned in Paul's letters, and it conceptualizes the atonement of Christ as a personal offering for the sins of others. *The present age of evil* is ending, a fact that is connected to the atonement of Jesus Christ. **1:5** Typically, in Paul's letters the opening introduction is followed by several verses of praise. Instead, Paul rebukes the Galatians. This is the only letter to lack these verses of praise and thanksgiving. **1:6** The use of the word *gospel* implies that Paul was concerned about alternate teachings about the Lord rather than about the Galatian saints falling away from the faith (compare 2 Corinthians 11:4). **1:7** *To turn you away* translates a Greek verb that in this context can also mean *distort* or *corrupt*. **1:11** Greek uses *brothers* generically to refer to *brothers and sisters*. **1:12** *Of Jesus Christ* can mean *about Jesus Christ* or *from Jesus Christ*. This verse is echoed in Doctrine and Covenants 128:8 (compare 1 Peter 1:13; Revelation 1:1). **1:13** Paul's persecution of the church is also noted in Acts 9:21. **1:15** *God* is omitted in some early and important manuscripts, but other early ones include it. Scribes may have added the divine noun to clarify an ambiguous *he*. Paul's call may intentionally be modeled on Jeremiah 1:5. **1:17** *Arabia* is the

did I travel to Jerusalem to those who were apostles before me, but I traveled to Arabia and returned again to Damascus.

[18]Then after three years, I traveled to Jerusalem to become acquainted with Cephas, and I stayed with him for fifteen days. [19]But I did not see any of the other apostles except Jacob, the brother of the Lord. [20]I assure you before God that I am not lying in what I wrote to you. [21]Then I went to the regions of Syria and Cilicia. [22]But I was not known by sight to the churches of Christ that were in Judea. [23]They were only hearing "The one who once persecuted us is now proclaiming the faith he once tried to destroy." [24]And they glorified God because of me.

PAUL'S JOURNEY TO JERUSALEM AFTER HIS CONVERSION

2 [1]Then after fourteen years, I went up again to Jerusalem with Barnabas, taking Titus with me also. [2]I went up according to revelation, and I set out for them (though privately to those who were prominent among them) the gospel that I proclaim among the Gentiles so that I might not run, or had run, in vain. [3]But Titus who was with me, being a Greek, was not compelled to be circumcised. [4]And a discussion arose because of false brothers who secretly entered in order to spy on our freedom which we have in Christ Jesus, that they might enslave us, [5]to whom we did not subject ourselves for a moment, in order that the truth of the gospel might reside in you.

[6]But from those who were prominent—whatever they were makes no difference to me, God shows no partiality—they added nothing to me. [7]But when they saw that I was entrusted with the gospel to the uncircumcised just as Peter was with the circumcised [8](for he who worked through Peter in the ministry of an apostle to the circumcised also worked through me to the Gentiles), [9]and when Jacob, Cephas,

---

region to the east of Palestine and Jerusalem and extending south into the Arabian Peninsula. The region would have included the site of Jesus's baptism. There remains some ambiguity concerning the precise location Paul intended. **1:18** Paul uses Peter's Aramaic name *Cephas*, probably because his audience was more familiar with it than the name Peter, although he does use both. This visit may also be described in Acts 9:26. **1:19** For *Jacob, the brother of the Lord*, see Acts 15:13–21; Mark 6:3. **1:20** The concern about *lying* may have arisen because of the accusation that Paul was made an apostle not through his vision of Jesus Christ but through appointment by others. **1:21** *Syria and Cilicia* would include Antioch and Tarsus (Paul's hometown, Acts 21:39).

2:1 For *Barnabas*'s role in Paul's missions, see Acts 11:22, 25; 12:25; 15:36–39. For *Titus*, see 2 Corinthians 2:13; 7:6–14. **2:2** The *prominent* are almost certainly the leaders of the church in Jerusalem. Paul's description makes it appear that there were significant factions within the church and that he had to report his experiences in nuanced ways to different groups. **2:3** The issue of whether Greek-born converts were required to be circumcised was settled at a church conference (Acts 15:5, 11). The policy was for Jewish converts to undergo circumcision, but for Greeks it was not required. **2:4** *A discussion arose* has been added to clarify missing words. Paul simply says *because of false brothers*, but in the context of having reported his missionary activity privately, the subject is clearly Paul's reference to being required to make different reports to different groups. Paul seems to be drawing attention to the fact that the Jerusalem church had previously endorsed his mission to the Gentiles. The *false brothers* are separate from the leaders of the Jerusalem church. The Joseph Smith Translation reads at the beginning of this verse *Notwithstanding there were some brought in by false brethren unawares.* **2:6** An allusion to Deuteronomy 10:17. **2:7** Paul speaks of his calling to the Gentiles in 1 Corinthians 9:17. **2:9** *Pillars* is a respectful description of the leaders of the church (see verse 2) and may refer to the pillars of the Jerusalem temple. *Jacob* is Jesus's sibling (Mark 6:3). Paul's use of *seemed* may indicate turmoil among the leaders in Jerusalem and the presence of significant factions there. The word *seemed* may also be translated as *acknowledged*.

and John perceived the grace that had been given to me—they seemed to be the pillars—they gave to Barnabas and me the right hand of fellowship so that we would go to the Gentiles and they would go to the circumcised. [10]They requested only that we would remember the poor, the very thing that I was eager to do.

PAUL CONFRONTS PETER

[11]But when Cephas came to Antioch, I opposed him to his face because he was at fault. [12]For before some people from Jacob came, he ate with the Gentiles, but when they came, he drew back and recused himself, fearing those of the circumcision. [13]And the remaining Jews were also caught up in this hypocrisy so that even Barnabas was carried away by their hypocrisy. [14]But when I saw that they did not act uprightly toward the truth of the gospel, I said to Cephas in front of them all, "If you are a Jew and live like a Gentile and not like a Jew, how can you compel the Gentiles to live like Jews?"

MADE RIGHTEOUS THROUGH FAITH

[15]We are ethnically Jews and not sinful Gentiles, [16]yet we know that a person is not made righteous by works of the Law but through the faith of Jesus Christ, and we have believed in Christ Jesus so that we might be made righteous by faith in Christ and not by works of the Law, because by works of the Law no person is made righteous. [17]But if in our seeking to be made righteous in Christ, we ourselves are found to be sinners, is Christ then a servant of sin? Certainly not. [18]For if I build up the things I once tore down, then I prove myself to be a transgressor. [19]For through the Law I died to the Law so that I might live in God. [20]I have been crucified with Christ, but it is no longer I who live but Christ lives in me. Now, the life I live in the flesh I live by faith in the Son of God, who loved me and gave himself for me. [21]I do not set aside the grace of God, for if righteousness came through the Law, then Christ died undeservedly.

2:11 *Cephas* refers to the apostle Peter. See note on 1:18. **2:12** Jews were not specifically forbidden from eating with Gentiles. The likely issue was with what was being eaten, and Peter withdrew from a dinner where unclean foods were being consumed. **2:13** *Even Barnabas* indicates the expectation that Barnabas would have been sensitive to the needs of the Gentile mission, and Paul expresses concern that a fellow missionary to the Gentiles would act against the needs and perceptions of the Gentile members. **2:14–16** Paul's report of his own words to Peter may extend through verse 16. **2:15** *We are ethnically Jews* is in Greek *we who are Jews by nature.* **2:16** Paul appears to have the law of Moses in mind here, and hence *Law* instead of *law.* Some translators prefer *justified* in place of *made righteous. Through the faith of Jesus Christ* can also be translated as *through the faith in Jesus Christ.* The issue is whether Paul directed us to have faith *in Jesus Christ* or whether he intended us to draw upon the *faith of Jesus* as an example. Both translations are equally possible. The Book of Mormon uses the phrase *the faith of Christ* similarly (Alma 27:27). Compare Philippians 3:9. **2:19** A similar expression regarding the law of Moses is found in 2 Nephi 25:25. **2:20** The idea of being *crucified with Christ* is more fully discussed in Romans 6:5–6. Some important manuscripts read *God and Christ* in place of *the Son of God.* It is difficult to determine which is the original reading given the nearly equal textual evidence. **2:21** A similar sentiment is expressed in Mosiah 13:28.

ABRAHAM BELIEVED

3 ¹Oh foolish Galatians, who has bewitched you? Jesus Christ was carefully portrayed as crucified before your eyes. ²The only thing I want to learn from you is this: did you receive the Spirit from works of the Law or from hearing with faith? ³Are you so foolish, having begun in the Spirit are you now ending with the flesh? ⁴Did you experience so much for no gain? If indeed it was for no gain. ⁵Therefore, does God who supplies you with the Spirit and works miracles among you do so from works of the Law or from hearing with faith?

⁶Thus, Abraham *"believed God and it was reckoned to him as righteousness."* ⁷Therefore, you understand that those who believe are the children of Abraham. ⁸The scripture, foreseeing that God would make the Gentiles righteous by faith, proclaimed the gospel to Abraham beforehand, saying, *"All the Gentiles will be blessed in you,"* ⁹so that those who have faith are blessed with Abraham who had faith.

¹⁰For all of those who rely upon the works of the Law are under a curse, for it is written, *"Cursed are all who do not abide by all things that are written in the book of Law and do them."* ¹¹And it is evident that no one is made righteous in the Law before God, for *"the one who is righteous will live by faith."* ¹²But the Law is not built on faith, but *"the one who does them will live by them."* ¹³Christ redeemed us from the curse of Law by becoming a curse for us, as it is written, *"Cursed is everyone who hangs on a tree,"* ¹⁴so that the blessing of Abraham might come to the Gentiles in Christ Jesus so that we may receive the promise of the Spirit through faith.

WHY THE LAW?

¹⁵Brothers and sisters, I am speaking in human terms—after a person has ratified a contract, no one can void it or add to it. ¹⁶The promises were made to Abraham and his descendants. It does not say, "And to his descendants," referring to many, but to one, *"And to your descendant,"* who is Christ. ¹⁷I mean this, the Law that came four hundred and thirty years later, does not nullify a covenant previously ratified by God so as to void the promise. ¹⁸For if the inheritance is by the Law, it is no longer by promise, but God graciously gave it to Abraham through the promise.

3:1 Some late and inferior manuscripts add *to not obey the truth* following the phrase *who has bewitched you*. The addition appears to be later, possibly added as an explanation to the meaning of *bewitched*. The Greek verb implies *casting a spell* or *charming* someone. Many translations prefer *publicly portrayed/exhibited* in place of *carefully portrayed*. The Greek verb implies a written description that is done with care and refers to Paul's detailed proclamation of the crucified Christ drawing upon scripture. **3:6** Quotation from Genesis 15:6. **3:8** Quotation from Genesis 12:3; 18:18 (see also Genesis 22:18). **3:10** Quotation from Deuteronomy 27:26; 28:58. **3:10–13** Paul set forth the argument that unless a person lives according to every precept of the Law, that person is under a curse (verse 10). The argument then proceeds to work under the notion that all are therefore cursed, not being able to live up to every precept of the Law. To redeem us, Christ became that curse for us by becoming cursed according to the definition set forth in Deuteronomy 21:23. As such, Christ was effectively able to end the curse by dying on our behalf, or as embodying the curse, Christ died, thus ending the curse. **3:11** Quotation from Habakkuk 2:4. **3:12** Quotation from Leviticus 18:5. **3:13** Quotation from Deuteronomy 21:23 (compare Deuteronomy 27:26). **3:15** Greek uses *brothers* generically to refer to *brothers and sisters*. The *contract* in question may be a personal will. **3:16** Quotation from Genesis 12:7; 13:15; 24:7. The language of this verse is echoed in Doctrine and Covenants 107:40, where the meaning is applied in a new context. **3:17** Some later manuscripts read *by God in Christ*, but the addition appears to be a later attempt at clarification of Christ's participation in the process of ratification. A reference to Exodus 12:40.

[19]Why then the Law? It was added because of transgressions, until the descendant arrived to whom the promise had been made, and it was ordained by angels through an intermediary. [20]Now, an intermediary implies more than one, but God is one. [21]Therefore, is the Law contrary to the promises of God? Certainly not. If a law that could grant life had been given, then righteousness would have been built upon the Law. [22]But the scripture has encircled everyone by sin so that the promise would be given by faith in Jesus Christ to those who believe.

[23]Before faith came, we were held in custody by the Law, being held as prisoners until faith would be revealed, [24]so that the Law was our guardian until Christ came so that we might be made righteous by faith. [25]Now that faith has come, we are no longer under a guardian. [26]For you are all the children of God through faith in Christ Jesus. [27]For as many of you as were baptized in Christ have clothed yourself in Christ. [28]There is no longer Jew or Greek, nor is there slave or free, nor male or female, for all of you are one in Christ Jesus. [29]And if you belong to Christ, you are descendants of Abraham, heirs according to the promise.

HEIRS OF GOD

4 [1]And I say that for the time that the heir is a minor, he is no different from a servant even though he is the lord of everything, [2]but he is under overseers and stewards until the date set by the father. [3]So it is for us when we were minors, we were under the natural forces of the world. [4]When the appropriate time came, God sent his Son, born from a woman and under the Law [5]in order to redeem those under the Law so that we might receive adoption as children. [6]And because you are children, God sent the Spirit of his Son into our hearts, crying, "Abba, Father!" [7]So that you are no longer servants but children, and if children, then heirs through God.

HOW CAN YOU TURN BACK?

[8]When you did not know God, you were enslaved to those who are not gods by their nature. [9]Now that you have come to know God, or rather you are known by God, how can you turn back to the weak and impoverished elements, which you desire to serve again? [10]You observe days, months, seasons, and years. [11]I fear that my labor on your behalf has been in vain.

3:20 The Joseph Smith Translation of this verse reads *Now this mediator was not a mediator of the new covenant, but there is one mediator of the new covenant, who is Christ, as it is written in the law concerning the promises made to Abraham and his seed. Now Christ is the mediator of life, for this is the promise which God made unto Abraham.* **3:22** This verse is interpreted in Doctrine and Covenants 49:8 (compare Romans 3:9). **3:24** For the purpose of the law of Moses, see 2 Nephi 11:4. **3:27** To be *clothed in Christ* is to *put him on* or to be *endowed in Christ.* The Greek verb *endow,* used here, refers to the act of putting on clothing (see Luke 24:49). **3:28** The promise of the covenant being extended to all is expressed in similar language in 2 Nephi 10:16; 26:33; Alma 1:30.

4:3, 9 *Natural forces* and *elements* translate to the same Greek word, which refers to the natural world, its elements, and elemental powers. **4:4** Some earlier translations preferred *fullness of time* in place of *appropriate time.* The Greek phrase is an idiom referring to the completion of time. Compare 2 Nephi 2:3, 26; 11:7. It is used temporally to refer to our day and age in the Doctrine and Covenants (see 112, 30–31; 128:18, 20–21). *Born from a woman* has a distinctly negative connotation in Job 14:1; 15:14; 25:4, which is the only place this precise phrase occurs in the Bible. **4:5** *Adoption* in this verse is a legal term referring to receiving the full rights of children. **4:6** *Abba* is the Greek transliteration of the Aramaic invocation *father.* Compare Mark 14:36. **4:10** The criticism that they observe *days, months, seasons, and years* refers to the observance of religious days, either Jewish or pagan. The issue is the astronomical

PAUL'S PERSONAL APPEAL

¹²I beg you: become as I am, for I have become even as you are, brothers and sisters. You have done me no wrong! ¹³You know that through a physical illness I proclaimed the gospel to you at first. ¹⁴And although my physical ailment was a test to you, you did not despise or reject me, but you received me as an angel of God, as Christ Jesus. ¹⁵Therefore, where is your feeling of blessedness? For I testify that if it were possible, you would have torn out your eyes and given them to me. ¹⁶Have I become your enemy by speaking the truth? ¹⁷They seek after you but not for good; they desire to exclude you so that you would seek for them. ¹⁸It is good to be sought after at all times with respect to what is good and not only when I am present before you. ¹⁹My children, I am again feeling the pains of birth for until Christ is formed in you. ²⁰I want to be with you and change my tone, for I am in doubt about you.

HAGAR AND SARAH

²¹Tell me, you who desire to be under the Law, have you not listened to the Law? ²²For it is written that Abraham had two sons, one from the slave woman and one from the free woman. ²³But the one from the slave woman was born according to the flesh, and the one from the free woman

was born through promise. ²⁴These things are an allegory. These women are two covenants. One is from Mount Sinai bearing children into slavery; she is Hagar. ²⁵Hagar is Mount Sinai in Arabia, and she corresponds to present-day Jerusalem, for she is enslaved with her children. ²⁶But the other woman corresponds to Jerusalem above that is free, and she is our mother. ²⁷For it is written, "*Rejoice, O barren one who does not bear, break forth and shout, you who are not in labor, because the children of the desolate one are more than the children of her who is married.*" ²⁸But we, brothers and sisters, are children of the promise like Isaac. ²⁹But just as at that time he who was born according to the flesh persecuted him who was born according to the Spirit, so it is now also. ³⁰But what does the scripture say? "*Cast out the slave woman and her son, for the child of the slave shall not inherit with the son of the free woman.*" ³¹So, brothers and sisters, we are not children of the slave woman, but of the free woman.

5 ¹For freedom Christ has made us free; therefore, stand and do not submit to the yoke of slavery.

CIRCUMCISION

²Behold, I, Paul, tell you that if you accept being circumcised, Christ will be of no benefit to you. ³I again testify to every man who is circumcised that he is obligated to

---

calculation of religious holy days. Paul returned to this topic in his later epistle to the Romans (14:5–6). **4:12** Greek uses *brothers* generically for *brothers and sisters*. The Joseph Smith Translation reads *Brethren, I beseech you to be perfect as I am perfect; for I am persuaded as ye have a knowledge of me, ye have not injured me at all by your sayings.* **4:13** Paul discussed his physical ailment elsewhere (1 Corinthians 2:3; 2 Corinthians 10:10). **4:14** *Physical ailment* is in Greek simply *flesh.* The context makes it obvious that Paul was referring to something wrong with his physical body, which was visually obvious to the Galatians. **4:15** This verse has led many commentators to suggest that Paul suffered from an eye ailment, one that was visible (verse 14), and one that perhaps resulted in diminished eyesight. **4:17–18** The precise meaning of these two verses remains obscure. Compare Doctrine and Covenants 58:27 for verse 18. **4:22** The slave woman refers to Hagar (Genesis 16:1–3) and the free woman to Sarah (Genesis 17:15–21). **4:27** Quotation from Isaiah 54:1. **4:28** See note on 4:12. Some early and reliable manuscripts read *you* in place of *we*. **4:30** Quotation from Genesis 21:10. **4:31** See note on 4:12.

5:1 A similar injunction to being *made free* is used in Doctrine and Covenants 88:86; Mosiah 23:13. Alma 58:40 alludes to this verse following the King James translation. **5:2–3** Paul narrows his argument

obey the entire Law. [4]You who would be made righteous by the Law are cut off from Christ; you have fallen from grace. [5]For by faith we wait in the Spirit for a hope of righteousness. [6]For in Christ Jesus neither circumcision nor uncircumcision benefits us, but only faith enacted through love.

[7]You were running well. Who hindered you from obeying the truth? [8]This kind of hindering does not come from the one who calls you. [9]A little yeast causes the entire dough to rise. [10]I am confident in the Lord that you will not think otherwise, and the one who troubles you will bear the penalty, whoever he is. [11]But if I, brothers and sisters, still preach circumcision, why am I still persecuted? In that case, the offense of the cross has been removed. [12]I wish that those who trouble you would castrate themselves.

SERVE ONE ANOTHER THROUGH LOVE

[13]For you were called to freedom, brothers and sisters; only do not use your freedom to satisfy your flesh, but to serve one another through love. [14]For the entire Law is fulfilled in one word: "*You shall love your neighbor as yourself.*" [15]If you bite and devour one another, beware that you are not consumed by one another.

[16]But I say, walk by the Spirit and do not give in to the desires of the flesh. [17]For the desires of the flesh are contrary to the Spirit, and the desires of the Spirit are contrary to the flesh, for these are opposed to one another so that you may not do what you desire. [18]But if you are led by the Spirit, you are not under the Law. [19]The works of the flesh are clear: sexual impropriety, uncleanness, lust, [20]idolatry, sorcery, enmities, contention, jealousy, anger, dissension, factions, [21]envy, murder, drunkenness, reveling, and similar things, which I am warning you about, just as I previously warned you. Those who practice such things will not inherit the kingdom of God.

[22]For the fruit of the Spirit is charity, joy, peace, patience, kindness, generosity, faithfulness, [23]gentleness, and self-control. There is no law against such things. [24]Those who belong to Christ have crucified the flesh with its passions and desires. [25]If we live by the Spirit, let us also follow the Spirit. [26]Let us not become conceited, competing against one another, envying one another.

BEAR ONE ANOTHER'S BURDENS

6 [1]Brothers and sisters, if anyone is caught in sin, you who are spiritual should

---

to circumcision, likely indicating that his opponents in Galatia were Jewish Christians who desired to have all converts circumcised contrary to the decision made in Acts 15:19–21. **5:4** Compare Doctrine and Covenants 20:32–34. **5:8** *The one who calls you* refers to Jesus Christ, and the call that the saints received is contrasted with human efforts to hinder the saints in their faith. **5:10** A single individual appears to have been the source of the problems in Galatia. **5:11** Greek uses *brothers* generically to refer to *brothers and sisters*. *The offense of the cross* summarizes a fundamental component of Paul's teachings, which is lost or *removed* if *circumcision* is still required. **5:12** This verse preserves Paul's rudest comment in all his letters and demonstrates the passion he felt about the topic of living a new life in Christ and leaving behind a life in the law of Moses. Some older translations attempted to soften the language by insinuating that Paul was encouraging that the agitators in Galatia be cut off from fellowship in the church, but the verb clearly implies self-castration. See Galatians 1:8–9 for Paul's concern that someone in Galatia was preaching another gospel. **5:13** See note on 5:11. **5:14** Quotation from Leviticus 19:18. This teaching of Jesus was captured in Matthew 22:39. **5:18** This practice is observed in Doctrine and Covenants 20:45; 28:4. Nephi uses the language of being *led by the Spirit* (1 Nephi 4:6; compare Luke 4:1). **5:21** Some early and excellent manuscripts omit the word *murder*, but it appears that it was omitted through scribal error.

6:1 The language of this verse is quoted in Doctrine and Covenants 20:80, following the language of the

restore such a one in a spirit of gentleness, guarding yourselves so that you are not also tempted. ²Bear one another's burdens, and in doing so you will fulfill the law of Christ. ³For if anyone thinks he is something even though he is nothing, he deceives himself. ⁴Let each person examine his own work, and then he will have a reason to boast to himself only, and not in regard to the work of others. ⁵For each person will have to bear his own load.

⁶Let the one who is instructed in the word share in all good things with the person who is teaching. ⁷Do not be deceived. God is not mocked, for what a person sows, that he will also reap. ⁸For the one who sows according to his own flesh reaps corruption from the flesh, but if a person sows by the Spirit, he will reap eternal life from the Spirit. ⁹So let us not grow tired of doing good, for if we do not give up we will reap during the harvest. ¹⁰Therefore, when we have an opportunity, let us work for the good of all, and especially for those who belong to the family of faith.

FINAL ENCOURAGEMENT

¹¹Look at what large letters I write to you with my own hand. ¹²Those who desire to make a good show in the flesh desire to compel you to be circumcised, but they do so in order to avoid being persecuted for the cross of Christ. ¹³For those who are circumcised do not obey the Law themselves, but they desire you to be circumcised so that they can boast about your flesh. ¹⁴I will certainly not boast except in the cross of our Lord Jesus Christ, through which the world has been crucified to me and I to the world. ¹⁵For neither circumcision nor uncircumcision benefits us. What matters is a new creation. ¹⁶And those who follow this rule, may peace and mercy be upon them and upon the Israel of God.

¹⁷From now on, let no one trouble you, for I bear the marks of Jesus in my body.

¹⁸May the grace of our Lord Jesus Christ be with your spirit, brothers and sisters. Amen.

King James translation. **6:2** Compare Mosiah 18:8. **6:6** This verse may be an encouragement to help assist the apostles and missionaries financially. Compare Doctrine and Covenants 50:22. **6:7** Echoed in Doctrine and Covenants 6:33. **6:9** This verse is partially quoted in Doctrine and Covenants 64:33. **6:11–18** These verses were almost certainly written by Paul personally, whereas the remainder of the letter was dictated to a scribe. Paul signals that his own writing is in *large letters*, which may indicate that he had difficulty seeing. **6:12** Paul ascribes the motive for teaching circumcision to a desire to avoid being persecuted for teaching the more problematic doctrine of the cross of Christ. Therefore, they were attempting to placate those who accepted Judaism but who were concerned about Christianity. **6:15** Paul later returned to the topic of *a new creation* (2 Corinthians 5:17). **6:18** Greek uses *brothers* generically to refer to *brothers and sisters*.

EPHESIANS

AUTHOR

Paul worked in Ephesus for over two years (Acts 19:10), and at some point following his third missionary journey he wrote this general letter to the saints living in Ephesus. Some of the letter is impersonal (3:2; 4:21), but it is generally upbeat and encouraging (1:3–23). Given that the letter describes circumstances that are similar to Colossians, such as Paul being in prison (3;1; 4:1; 6:20) and his experiencing affliction (3:13), many have supposed that he wrote this letter around the same time that he wrote Colossians.

Paul is the sole author of the letter (1:1), and the style of the letter favors long, complex sentences with richly textured expression. The letter is directed toward a Gentile audience (2:11), and Paul has sent Tychicus, a man with a common slave name, to report on his well-being and health (6:21–22). Paul's outlook is positive, and he implies that the Gentile community has struggled as a result of opposition from local Jews (2:11–13), and he encourages them to think of themselves in the following way: "you are no longer foreigners and noncitizens, but you are fellow citizens with the saints and household of God" (2:19). Because many of the expressions used in this letter are similar to Colossians, and because the style of writing is markedly different from the majority of Paul's letters, scholars have questioned whether Paul wrote this letter. The difference in style and vocabulary is a recognized fact, and if Paul wrote it, then he did so in different circumstances from those of his earlier letters.

PURPOSE OF WRITING

In the letter Paul consistently returns to the theme of the riches of Christ, encouraging the saints in Ephesus to "put on the new person, which was created in the image of God in righteousness and holiness of truth" (4:24). The letter contains few quotations or allusions to the Old Testament, confirming that the recipients were Gentiles who sought a new existence in Christ apart from the law of Moses. Paul frequently draws upon the language of redemption and inheritance, suggesting that the letter was seen as a means of encouraging a community to stand firm in faith. There are some concerns expressed in the letter (5:3–21), but the tone of the letter is not one of concern for a major schism in the branch but rather a general tone of counsel to live a new life in Christ.

It is unclear how Paul's statements regarding his troubles in Asia are reflected in this letter, but at one point he wrote to the saints in Corinth concerning a trial that was so severe that he thought he would perhaps die as a result: "For we do not want you to be unaware, brothers and sisters, of our trial which came upon us in Asia, that we were weighed down tremendously, so that we despaired even for life itself. But we felt we had a sentence of death passed upon us" (2 Corinthians 1:8–9). That trial most likely took place in Ephesus given the amount of time that Paul spent in the city. The letter to the saints is, however, mostly positive, suggesting that this trial did not damage his relationship with the saints or darken his feelings toward the community there.

CONNECTION TO LATTER-DAY SAINT BELIEFS

The letter to the Ephesians has been extremely important for shaping Latter-day Saint identity regarding the organizational structure of the church (2:20; 4:11). In trying to settle a series of disputes that had arisen in the branch, Paul encouraged them to rely on sound doctrine as taught by apostles and prophets. Early recipients of these letters would have understood those terms to refer to the missionaries who had been sent to them—the primary meaning of the term *apostle*—and Christian prophets who helped guide early worship services. Paul was intentionally emphasizing a hierarchy that developed out of the Holy Spirit (1:13), and Paul desired the community to rely on the Spirit instead of human wisdom. A second important connection is the now famous counsel to "clothe yourselves in the armor of God so that you are able to stand against the schemes of the devil" (6:11). Those verses vividly describe a defensive posture that the believer should adopt in confronting the forces of evil in the world. ⁊

OPENING ADDRESS

1 ¹Paul, an apostle of Jesus Christ through the will of God, to the saints, the faithful in Christ Jesus, who are in Ephesus: ²grace and peace to you from God our Father and the Lord Jesus Christ.

³Blessed is God the Father and our Lord Jesus Christ, who has blessed us with every spiritual blessing in Christ, who is in heavenly places, ⁴just as he chose us to be holy and blameless before him in Christ before the foundation of the world. In love ⁵he foreordained us for adoption through Jesus Christ, according to the good pleasure of his will, ⁶to the praise of his glorious grace, which he graciously gave to us in his beloved Son, ⁷in whom we have redemption through his blood and forgiveness of sins, according to the wealth of his grace, ⁸which he bestowed upon us abundantly in all wisdom and insight. ⁹He made the mystery of his will known to us, according to his good pleasure that he set forth in Christ, ¹⁰as a means to administer the fullness of time, to gather all things in Christ, things in the heavens and things upon the earth. ¹¹In Christ we have obtained an inheritance, having been foreordained according to the plan of him who accomplishes all things according to the counsel of his will, ¹²so that we who were the first to hope in Christ might contribute to the praise of his glory. ¹³When you heard the word of truth, the gospel of your salvation, and after you believed in him you were sealed by the promised Holy Spirit, ¹⁴who is the first installment of our inheritance for our redemption as God's possession to the praise of his glory.

PAUL'S PRAYER FOR THE SAINTS IN EPHESUS

¹⁵I have heard of your faith in the Lord Jesus and your love for all the saints; because

---

1:1 A number of early and reliable manuscripts lack the words *in Ephesus*, but other early and reliable manuscripts preserve it. It appears that the evidence slightly favors omission, and one early Christian author (Marcion) labeled it the *letter to the Laodiceans* (see Colossians 4:16). The omission of the name of a city or region leaves a void in the logic of the opening address. **1:3** The precise meaning of *heavenly places* remains obscure, and it is not used in Paul's other letters. The context suggests either that the saints are *blessed in heavenly places* or that we are blessed *in Christ*, who resides in *heavenly places*. **1:3–14** These verses form a single sentence in Greek, and the translation has attempted to create shorter sentences to help clarify the meaning. **1:4** Joseph Smith also traced his calling to *before the foundation of the world* (Doctrine and Covenants 127:2). **1:5** Greek makes no distinction between *foreordain* and *predestine*. The two words have taken on nuanced meanings in theological discussions which are foreign to Paul's writings, and Paul uses the word in a sense of preplanning or preparing. **1:5–6** These verses promote the ideal that God foreordained the saints to follow him in order that they would praise *his grace*. Although this statement simplifies the complexity of righteousness and a life in Christ, it highlights the importance of *grace* in God's plan. **1:6** The Greek mentions only *beloved*, so *beloved Son* and *Beloved* are both possible translations. **1:9** *The mystery of his will* is the revelation of the gospel through Jesus Christ. **1:10** The concept of the administration of *the fullness of time* refers to the idea that God had a *plan* for a certain time or age to administer it according to his will. Some older translations preferred the idea of a dispensation of the fullness of times, which conveyed the concept of a period of time with a unique administrative approach. The language of dispensations is used in Doctrine and Covenants 121:31; 124:41 (compare 2 Nephi 2:3). Portions of this verse are quoted and interpreted in Doctrine and Covenants 27:13. **1:13** Some translations attempt to convey the Greek word order through the title the Holy Spirit of Promise. The phrase refers specifically to the promise of the Holy Spirit, something that believers look forward to receiving after they have believed in Christ. Echoed in Doctrine and Covenants 88:3; 124:124. **1:14** This verse envisions a path to salvation where the first step is the reception of the *Holy Spirit*. **1:15** Paul does not appear to know the recipients of the letter personally, which may indicate that the letter was

of this ¹⁶I do not cease to give thanks for you when mentioning you in my prayers. ¹⁷I pray that the God of our Lord Jesus Christ, the Father of glory, might give you a spirit of wisdom and revelation in knowing him, ¹⁸thereby having the eyes of your heart enlightened that you may know the hope of his calling, the glory of his inheritance in the saints, ¹⁹and what is the incomparable greatness of his power for us who believe, according to the working of his mighty power, ²⁰which he exercised in Christ when he raised him from the dead and seated him at his right hand in the heavenly realms ²¹above all rule, authority, power, and dominion, and every name that is named, not only in this age but in the one to come. ²²And he put all things under his feet and made him the head of all things for the church, ²³which is his body, the fullness of him who fills all in all.

THE INCOMPARABLE WEALTH OF HIS GRACE

2 ¹And you were dead while in your transgressions and sins ²in which you previously walked after the pattern of the age of this world, according to the ruler of the kingdom of the air, the spirit that is now working in the children of disobedience, ³among whom we all at one time lived our lives in the desires of the flesh, pursuing the will of the flesh and the mind, and we were by nature children of wrath as the others were. ⁴But God being rich in mercy, because of his great love by which he loved us, ⁵even when we were dead in our transgressions, made us alive together in Christ (you have been saved by grace), ⁶and he raised and seated us with him in the heavenly realms in Christ Jesus ⁷so that in the ages to come he will show the incomparable wealth of his grace in kindness toward us in Christ Jesus. ⁸For you have been saved by grace through faith, and this is not on your own; it is the gift of God, ⁹not a result of works, so that no one may boast. ¹⁰For we are his workmanship, being created in Christ Jesus for good works that God prepared beforehand so that we might walk in them.

APOSTLES AND PROPHETS

¹¹Therefore, remember that you were Gentiles in the flesh once, called "uncircumcision" by those called "circumcision" that is performed by human hands. ¹²Remember that you were apart from Christ at that

written to a number of churches and not simply to the Ephesians. **1:20** A similar thought is expressed in Philippians 2:9. **1:21** Similar language to that found in this verse is used when Nephi spoke of the return of the Lord in the latter days (1 Nephi 22:24). **1:22** An allusion to Psalm 8:6.

2:1–3 These verses compose a single Greek sentence that lacks a finite verb. The author does not conclude the thought that was begun in verse 1 but instead characterizes our former behavior as wicked. **2:2** *The ruler of the kingdom of the air* is Satan, although this way of describing him is unique to Ephesians. *The children of disobedience* (literally *sons of disobedience*) is an idiom referring to all those who act unrighteously. The theme of *the children of disobedience* is discussed in Doctrine and Covenants 121:17. **2:3** *We were by nature* supposes that conversion to or acceptance of Christ results in a changed nature. The author includes himself among those who lived after *the desires of the flesh*. **2:5** Believers were at one time *dead in our transgressions*, and Christ *made us alive* with the result that the believers are *saved by grace*. The parenthetical note defines the phrases immediately preceding it, thus making it clear what the salvation *by grace* looks like to the believer. **2:6** The meaning of this verse remains obscure, and the author does not clarify what is intended by the seating *in heavenly realms*. Matthew 16:19 may provide the context for interpreting this verse. **2:10** *Walk in them* refers to *good works* earlier in the verse. **2:12** The language of not belonging to Israel and the covenants is heavily influenced by ethnic boundaries, and the words *alienated*, *apart*, and *foreigners* all describe people who were ethnically different. Such divisive language was a common feature of Jewish descriptions of foreigners in the first century.

time, alienated from the society of Israel and foreigners to the covenants of promise, without hope and without God in the world. ¹³But now in Christ Jesus you who were at one time far away are now brought near by the blood of Christ. ¹⁴For he is our peace, the one who made both into one and broke down in his flesh the dividing wall of hostility, ¹⁵doing away with the law of commandments and ordinances, that he might establish in himself one new person out of the two, thus producing peace, ¹⁶and he reconciled us both to God in one body through the cross, thereby ending hostility. ¹⁷And he came and proclaimed peace to you who are far and near. ¹⁸Therefore, through him we both have access to the Father in one Spirit. ¹⁹Therefore, you are no longer foreigners and noncitizens, but you are fellow citizens with the saints and household of God, ²⁰being built upon the foundation of apostles and prophets, with Christ Jesus himself being the corner-

stone, ²¹in whom the entire building being joined together grows into a holy temple in the Lord, ²²in whom you are also built together for a habitation for God in the Spirit.

PAUL, A PRISONER OF CHRIST JESUS

3 ¹For this reason, I, Paul, am a prisoner of Christ Jesus on behalf of you Gentiles— ²if indeed you have heard of the administration of the grace of God that was given to me for you— ³that by revelation he made known the mystery to me, as I wrote briefly before. ⁴When you read this, you will be able to understand my knowledge of the mystery of Christ, ⁵a mystery that was not made known to people in other generations as it is now revealed to his holy apostles and prophets by the Spirit. ⁶The mystery is that the Gentiles are fellow heirs, fellow members, and fellow participants of the promise in Christ Jesus

Such language may signal that while Gentiles had accepted Christ they were of one ethnic group since the author seems to assume that they are separate from Israelites but that they are ethnically homogenous among themselves. The dividing lines between these groups are removed in verses 18–19. *Without God in the world* also appears in Mosiah 27:31. Compare Alma 41:11. **2:13** *Are near* contrasts the idea in the previous verse that we were at one time *apart* from Christ. **2:14** *Both into one* envisions bringing those who were apart from Christ (verse 12) and those who were near Christ (verse 13) into one body of believers. **2:15** *New person* is literally *new man* in Greek. The concept of a *new person in Christ* is discussed again in Ephesians 4:24. The concept of doing away with the *law of commandments and ordinances* emphasizes that the new covenant is simpler with fewer *ordinances* such as baptism and the sacrament. **2:16** The hostility mentioned in verse 14 is resolved in this verse. The theme of hostility is fundamental to this chapter, where the tension between the former self and the believing self introduce the chapter. The second part of the discussion moves to hostility that exists between nonbelievers and believers. **2:19–22** Some scholars⁵ have suggested that these verses represent a fragment of an early Christian hymn. The verses do contain a number of terms that are atypical of Paul's other letters, and the thoughts are different from those in his other letters. **2:20** Perhaps an allusion to Isaiah 28:16. If the author had intended to refer to the *prophets* of the Old Testament and the *apostles* of the New Testament, then the word order would be reversed. The suggestion is that these are Christian prophets. Two named prophets in the New Testament are Agabus (Acts 11:23) and Anna (Luke 2:36). **2:21** The text omits *the* in connection with the *holy temple*, suggesting the author had in mind a new building.

3:1 No details are known about this imprisonment, and it could refer to several different imprisonments (for example, 2 Corinthians 6:5; Philippians 1:13–14; Philemon 1:9; Acts 21:21–36). **3:3** *Wrote before* can also be translated as *wrote above* or *earlier*, and in this case it likely refers to the contents of Ephesians 1:9 instead of a lost writing on the topic of the mystery of God. **3:4** Paul spoke similarly of the *mystery* of God in Romans 16:25.

through the gospel, [7]of which I became a servant according to the gift of the grace of God that was given to me, which was given to me by the working of his power.

[8]Although I am the very least of all the saints, this grace was given to me to proclaim the unsearchable riches of Christ to the Gentiles [9]and to enlighten everyone about the plan for the mystery that for ages was hidden away in God, who created all things [10]so that now the variety of the wisdom of God might be made known to the rulers and authorities in heavenly places through the church. [11]This was according to the plan for the ages which he accomplished in Christ Jesus our Lord, [12]in whom we have boldness and access to God with confidence because of Christ's faithfulness. [13]Because of this I ask you not to lose heart over what I am suffering on your behalf, which is for your glory.

PAUL'S PRAYER

[14]For this reason I bow my knees before the Father, [15]by whom every family in the heavens and upon the earth are named,

[16]so that he may give to you according to the riches of his glory to be strengthened with power through his Spirit in your inner being, [17]that through faith Christ may dwell in your hearts, that you may be rooted and founded in love, [18]that you may have strength to comprehend with all the saints what is the breadth, length, height, and depth, [19]to know both the love of Christ that surpasses knowledge so that you may be filled with all the fullness of God.

[20]To him who is powerful to do more abundantly than all that we ask or think, according to the power working in us, [21]to him be glory in the church and in Christ Jesus through all generations, forever and ever. Amen.

APOSTLES, PROPHETS, EVANGELISTS, SHEPHERDS, AND TEACHERS

4 [1]Therefore, as a prisoner for the Lord, I encourage you to walk worthily of the calling to which you have been called, [2]with all humility and gentleness, with

---

3:7 *Servant* is the Greek word *deacon* (compare 1 Corinthians 3:5). **3:9** The *mystery* is the *plan*, or at least information about the plan. The author suggests that the concept of *mystery* describes God's current plan of administering salvation through the gospel of Jesus Christ, whereas he had previously administered it through the law of Moses. The gospel *plan* is the *mystery* that has been reserved for later ages. **3:10** The use of the word *variety*, also translated as *multifaceted* or *manifold*, signals that the author recognizes that God has worked differently across the ages. Although this has been a subtly suggested message, it is here directly engaged. The phrase *made known to the rulers and authorities in heavenly places* points to the declaration of God's plan to *rulers and authorities* in heaven. **3:12** The translation of the end of the verse could also be *because of faith in him*. The Greek is ambiguous, and in this instance it appears that the believer has access to God because Christ led the way, and therefore *Christ's faithfulness* better represents the context. A similar issue appears in Romans 3:22, 26; Galatians 2:16, 20, 3:22; Philippians 3:9. **3:13** *What I am suffering* can also be translated as *what trials I am experiencing*. In this context, *suffering* better captures the point of emphasis. **3:14** Following *Father*, some late manuscripts add the phrase *of our Lord Jesus Christ*. The addition was likely made by scribes who wished to include Christ in personal prayer. **3:14–21** Although not technically the end of the letter, these verses conclude a major section of the letter (Paul's defense and description of his ministry). **3:15** *Heavens* is a plural noun, but Greek often uses it to indicate the singular concept of *heaven*. **3:16** *Inner being* could refer to the conscience or to self-will and self-control. **3:21** Similar terminology is used in Doctrine and Covenants 76:112.

4:1 *Worthily* has been substituted for the expected *righteously*. The two terms have different connotations, and righteousness in Paul's letters often describes a relationship to the Law, whereas *worthiness* is often a moral term describing upright conduct in relation to God, self, and others (Colossians 3:12–13).

patience, bearing with one another in love, [3]being diligent to maintain the unity of the Spirit in the bond of peace. [4]There is one body and one Spirit, just as you were called to the one hope that is associated with your call: [5]one Lord, one faith, one baptism, [6]one God and Father of all, who is over all and through all and in all. [7]And grace was given to each one of us according to the measure of Christ's gift. [8]Therefore, it says, "*When he ascended on high he captured those who were captive; he gave gifts to men and women.*" [9]What does "*he ascended*" mean except that he also descended into the lower regions of the earth? [10]He who descended is the same as the one who ascended above all the heavens so that he may fill all things. [11]And he gave some apostles, prophets, evangelists, shepherds, and teachers, [12]to equip the saints for the work of ministry, for building up the body of Christ, [13]until we all arrive at the unity of faith and the knowledge of the Son of God, at being a mature person at the measure of the stature of the fullness of Christ [14]so that we are no longer infants, tossed back and forth by the waves and carried about by every wind of teaching, by the cunning of people who with craftiness carry out deceitful schemes. [15]While speaking the truth in love, we will grow up to Christ in all things, who is the head, [16]from whom the whole body, being joined together and united through every associated joint, when each works according to its own association it makes the body grow so that it establishes itself in love.

A NEW CHRISTIAN LIFE

[17]Therefore, I speak and testify in the Lord, that you must no longer walk as the Gentiles walk in the vanity of their thinking. [18]They are darkened in their understanding, alienated from the life of God because

---

4:5 *One faith* and *one baptism* appear in Mosiah 18:21. **4:5–6** These verses preserve what may have been one of the earliest declarations of faith for Christians entering baptism. The two verses lack a verb and declare the fundamentals of Christian identity. The context suggests that *your call* of verse 4 is being defined using this statement of faith. **4:8** Quotation from Psalm 68:18 (with variation from the Hebrew and Greek texts of the Old Testament). The Old Testament text that has been passed down reads *he received gifts* instead of *he gave gifts*, as quoted here. The Greek text of the quotation mentions *men* specifically, but this noun often refers to both *men and women*. Doctrine and Covenants 88:6 offers important commentary on the themes of this verse. **4:9** The interpretation of Psalm 68:18 includes the idea that Christ ascended and that he also descended. The descent of Christ into the lower regions of hell is recorded more fully in 1 Peter 3:19–20; 4:6. These verses (7–10) are an attempt to draw upon the known belief of Christ's descent into hell and to teach its corollary—namely, Christ's ascent into heaven above all things. Some later and less reliable manuscripts read *first descended*. The likely original reading is provided in the translation. **4:11** *Shepherds* is often translated as *bishops*, which the term seems to represent. The original word has been translated as it appears in Greek to represent the early church's view of bishops who were described figuratively as *shepherds*. An evangelist should probably be translated as *missionary*, or someone who proclaims the gospel in a local area, which is the primary meaning of the Greek term. An *apostle* is also a missionary but on a larger scale. The *apostles* appear to have had a worldwide calling to declare the gospel. **4:12** *Ministry* represents the work of *service*, much like the word *ministry* is founded upon the notion of ministering to others. One of the apostles' duties was to train others for the ministry. This verse is applied to priesthood offices in Doctrine and Covenants 124:143. **4:14** *Teaching* can also be translated as *doctrine*. The primary meaning of the noun is a *thing that is taught*. Doctrine has taken on the meaning of a more formal teaching or belief. Doctrine and Covenants 123:12 echoes this verse. **4:18** *Because of their ignorance* is literally *because of the ignorance in them*. This verse is quoted in Doctrine and Covenants 10:2.

of their ignorance, a result of the hardness of their heart. ¹⁹They are callous, giving themselves over to lust, for the working of all kinds of uncleanness motivated by greed. ²⁰But you did not learn about Christ in this way ²¹if indeed you heard about him and were taught in him, just as the truth is in Jesus, ²²to lay aside your former self, which belongs to your earlier way of life and is corrupted according to deceitful desires, ²³and to be renewed in the spirit of your minds. ²⁴Put on the new person, which was created in the image of God in righteousness and holiness of truth.

²⁵Therefore, having set aside falsehood, *"you will speak the truth, each with his neighbor,"* for we are members belonging to one another. ²⁶*"Be angry and do not sin,"* and do not let the sun set on your anger. ²⁷Do not give the devil an opportunity. ²⁸The one who steals must no longer steal; rather he should labor, working with his own hands for good so that he might have something to share with someone in need. ²⁹Do not let a corrupt word exit your mouth, but only what is good for the building up of someone in need so that it may give grace to those who hear you. ³⁰Do not offend the Holy Spirit of God, by whom you were sealed for the day of deliverance. ³¹Let all bitterness, anger, wrath, dissension, and slander be set aside. ³²But be kind to one another, compassionate, and forgiving one another just as God in Christ forgave you.

5 ¹Therefore, become imitators of God, as beloved children, ²and walk in love, just as Christ loved us and gave himself for us, an offering of sacrifice and a sweet-smelling offering to God.

DO NOT BE PARTAKERS WITH THEM

³Let there not be sexual impropriety, uncleanness of any kind, or greed among you, as is fitting for the saints. ⁴Neither should there be vulgar speaking, foolish talk, or rude humor, which are out of place, but rather there should be thanksgiving. ⁵For you know this, that no person who is immoral, unclean, or greedy (that person is an idolater) has an inheritance in the kingdom of Christ and God. ⁶Let no one deceive you with empty words, for because of

---

4:19 *Motivated by greed* represents the Greek *with greediness*. The relationship of greed to *all kinds of uncleanness* is not clear, and the translation has attempted to capture the nuance of the author's intent of saying *uncleanness with greed as motive*. Compare 1 Nephi 17:45 (*they are callous*, which is rendered in the King James translation as *past feeling*). **4:22** This idea is expressed more clearly in Romans 6:6. **4:25** Quotation from Zechariah 8:16. **4:26** Quotation from Psalm 4:4. The word *angry* includes the emotions of wrath, anger, or visceral hatred and reflects the language of the Psalm. **4:27** Paul rarely refers to the adversary as the *devil* (1 Corinthians 10:20–21), preferring the term *Satan* (Romans 16:20). In the New Testament period, the two terms were used interchangeably, but the word *devil* originally meant the *slanderer*. **4:29** *You* has been added to the end of the verse to clarify the meaning. **4:30** Perhaps an allusion to Isaiah 63:10. Alluded to in Doctrine and Covenants 30:30.

5:2 Christ's love for us is defined as him giving his life for us. This definition of love may be implied in Ephesians 5:25, 28, and 33. **5:4** The author offers advice on proper and acceptable speech. The guiding principle in this exhortation is the concept of what is *fitting for the saints* (verse 3). **5:5** The word *immoral* represents a Greek term that is difficult to convey in English. Immorality is a much larger concept in English, including concerns such as justice, mercy, doing good to others, caring for others, etc. The Greek word is largely limited to sexual behaviors that are inappropriate. Alma's words, *no unclean thing can inherit the kingdom of heaven*, draw on the language of this verse (Alma 11:37) and report the wording as a quotation. The phrase *kingdom of Christ* is unique to Ephesians (compare 2 Peter 1:11). **5:6** *Children of disobedience* is literally the *sons of disobedience*, but in English this is a gendered concept, whereas the Greek is an idiom describing all who are disobedient regardless of gender.

these things the wrath of God comes upon the children of disobedience. [7]Therefore, do not be partakers with them. [8]For you were at one time in darkness, but now you are a light in the Lord; walk as children of the light. [9]For the fruit of the light is in all that is good, right, and true, [10]and try to learn what is pleasing to the Lord. [11]And do not partner with those who work the barren works of darkness, but rather expose them. [12]For the things they do secretly are shameful even to mention, [13]and all things exposed by the light are made obvious. [14]For everything that is made obvious is light. Therefore, it says, "Awake, O sleeper, and rise from the dead, and Christ will shine on you." [15]Therefore, be careful how you live your life, not as the unwise but as the wise, [16]using the time wisely because the days are evil. [17]For this reason, do not be foolish, but understand what the will of the Lord is. [18]And do not get drunk with wine, in which there is debauchery, but be filled with the Spirit, [19]speaking to one another in psalms, hymns, and spiritual odes, singing and making psalms to the Lord with your heart, [20]giving thanks to God the Father in the name of our Lord Jesus Christ, always and for all things, [21]submitting to one another out of reverence for Christ.

HOUSEHOLD GUIDELINES

[22]Wives, submit to your husbands as to the Lord, [23]because the husband is the head of the woman as Christ is the head of the church, of which body he is the savior. [24]But as the church submits to Christ, even so women should submit to their husbands in all things. [25]Husbands, love your wives just as Christ loved the church and gave himself for her [26]in order to sanctify her by cleansing her, washing her with water in the word, [27]so that he might present the church to himself in glory, without spot or wrinkle or anything similar, but holy and without blemish. [28]Thus, men ought to love their wives as they love their own bodies. The one who loves his wife loves himself. [29]For no one ever hated his own flesh, but he nourishes and cares for it, just as Christ did for the church, [30]because we are members of his body. [31]*For this reason a man shall leave his father and mother and be joined to his wife, and the two will become one flesh.* [32]This mystery is great; I am speaking about Christ and about the church. [33]However, each one of you must also love his own wife as he loves himself, so that his wife may respect her husband.

5:14 The quotation is given as though it has been quoted from a known source, although no surviving source for it exists. The language of the verse has conceptual parallels to Isaiah 60:1. **5:15** The Greek specifically says *beware how carefully you walk*, but the verb of walking also refers to a person's way of living. **5:21** This verse may represent a general principle that guides the following discussion (5:22–33). **5:22–24** The call for wives to be subject to their husbands is unique to Ephesians (among Paul's letters), and therefore it is difficult to understand the purpose for which these verses were written and included in the letter. They may represent a response to a specific question or issue that arose in Ephesus or the surrounding region (see note on 1:1) and may not have been intended as general counsel. The larger discussion is developed through an analogy of Christ's relationship to the church (verses 22–33). **5:26** Baptismal imagery is expanded to included *washing* and *cleansing*. **5:30** Some manuscripts add the phrase to the end of this verse *of his flesh and of his bones*, but the manuscript evidence is mixed, and it is difficult to determine which reading is original. **5:31** Quotation from Genesis 2:24.

COUNSEL TO CHILDREN AND PARENTS

6 [1]Children, obey your parents in the Lord, for this is right. [2]*"Honor your father and mother"* (this is the first commandment given with a promise), [3]*so that it may go well for you and you may live long upon the land."* [4]And, fathers, do not provoke your children to anger, but raise them up in the education and instruction of the Lord.

COUNSEL REGARDING SLAVES

[5]Servants, obey your earthly masters with fear and trembling, with the sincerity of your heart as though for Christ, [6]not to be seen to be as people pleasers, but as servants of Christ doing the will of God from the soul. [7]Do your work with enthusiasm, as though you were serving the Lord and not people, [8]knowing that whatever good each person does, he will receive the same from the Lord, whether servant or free. [9]And masters, do the same for them, not threatening them, because you know that there is the same Lord in heaven for both of you, and there is no partiality with him.

THE ARMOR OF GOD

[10]Finally, be strengthened in the Lord and in the strength of his power. [11]Clothe yourselves in the armor of God so that you are able to stand against the schemes of the devil [12]because we do not wrestle against flesh and blood but against rulers, authorities, the cosmic powers of this time of darkness, and the spiritual forces of evil in the heavenly places. [13]For this reason take up the armor of God so that you will be able to stand in the day of wickedness, having done all to stand firm. [14]Therefore, stand, having fastened the belt of truth around your waist, having put on the breastplate of righteousness, [15]by putting shoes on your feet in preparation for the gospel of peace, [16]and in all things, taking up the shield of faith, by which you are able to extinguish all the fiery arrows of the evil one. [17]And take the helmet of salvation and the sword of the Spirit, which is the word of God.

[18]In every prayer and entreaty at all times, pray in the Spirit, and to this end, be alert with all determination and supplication for all the saints. [19]And pray on my behalf, so that I may be given the message when I open my mouth boldly to proclaim the mystery of the gospel, [20]for which I am an ambassador in chains so that I may declare it boldly as I ought to speak.

6:1 *In the Lord* is omitted in some early and reliable manuscripts, but it also has excellent manuscript support. The evidence favors its inclusion in the text. **6:2** Quotation from Exodus 20:12; Deuteronomy 5:16. **6:3** Quotation from Deuteronomy 5:16. **6:4** Many modern translators favor *discipline* in place of *education*. First-century educational practices favored discipline as a method of learning, but the goal of that discipline was improved learning and education. Compare Enos 1:1. **6:5–9** These verses represent the author's attempt to deal with the nearly ubiquitous practice of slavery in the first century. The author promotes the development of a work ethic in Christ and a reduction in violence toward slaves (compare Colossians 3:22–4:1). These verses remain problematic in the modern era. **6:9** An allusion to Deuteronomy 10:17. **6:11** *Clothe yourselves* is also *endow yourselves* (the Greek verb *endow* means *to put on clothing* or *to assume the position of another person*). An earlier version of this teaching is found in 1 Thessalonians 5:8. Compare Luke 24:49. **6:12** Heavenly and earthly forces are joined together, suggesting collusion and shared efforts to thwart God's plan. **6:13–17** Doctrine and Covenants 27:15–18 offers valuable commentary on these verses. **6:14** Alluded to in Doctrine and Covenants 38:9. **6:16** This verse is echoed in Doctrine and Covenants 3:8; 27:17 (compare 1 Nephi 15:24). **6:17** *The helmet of salvation* is an allusion to Isaiah 59:17.

CONCLUDING REMARKS

²¹So that you may know how I am and what I am doing, Tychicus, the beloved brother and faithful servant in the Lord, will tell you everything. ²²I have sent him to you for this reason so that you may know about us and that he may encourage your hearts.

²³Peace to the brothers and sisters, and love with faith from God the Father and the Lord Jesus Christ. ²⁴Grace be with you all who love our Lord Jesus Christ with incorruptible love.

6:21 For *Tychicus*, see Acts 20:4; Colossians 4:7–9. **6:23** Greek uses *brothers* generically to refer to *brothers and sisters*. *Love* is a noun connected with *faith* so that God sends the *brothers and sisters* his *love with faith*. The earliest and best manuscripts do not conclude the letter with *Amen*, but some later and less reliable ones do so.

PHILIPPIANS

AUTHOR

Paul and Timothy are listed as co-senders of the letter, which was written to a newly formed community of believers that had been created during Paul's second missionary journey. The city of Philippi was located along the Ignatian Way and was populated by Latin-speaking former Roman soldiers who had been granted special privileges such as not having to pay poll or land taxes and receiving the favored status of citizen. According to Acts, Silas accompanied Paul during his work in Philippi, where both were eventually imprisoned (Acts 16:16–26). Timothy was also with Paul during his initial visit to the city (Acts 16:1–2), and Luke also traveled with Paul at that time (Acts 16:10–17). Although Luke plays no obvious role in the letter to the Philippians, the famous "we" passages (see introduction to Acts) begin around the time that Paul traveled into Macedonia and Philippi. Despite being imprisoned when he wrote, Paul enjoyed considerable freedom to write and communicate freely (1:7, 13–14, 17). Because of the descriptions of the "imperial guard" and "Caesar's household" (4:22), many have thought that Paul was in prison in Rome, which would indicate that the letter was written in the early 60s CE and after the account of Acts 28.

Paul is mostly positive and thankful in this letter, and despite what appears to be a death sentence he is optimistic in his ability to obtain his freedom (1:19–24), but he narrates it as though the outcome is up to him to decide. Describing a historical situation where Paul would have had the option of choosing life or death is difficult to do, and perhaps he was considering whether to offer a defense or to allow the charges against him to stand. In either case, he appears to have decided to continue living with the intent that he would be able to continue teaching the gospel.

PURPOSE OF WRITING

The most obvious purpose in writing was to offer thanks to the saints for the money they had sent to Paul (1:5, 7; 4:15). During Paul's time in Corinth, he was pressured to earn a living, and rather than ask the saints in Corinth to help him financially, Paul received funds from Philippi. This letter is Paul's formal expression of thanks for that offering. Paul also wanted to offer thanks for the work of Epaphroditus (4:10–20) and to note that

Epaphroditus had become ill (2:26–27), but now that he is well again he is returning with the letter to the Philippians (2:25).

Paul also expresses some concern about a faction within the community, and he uses strong language to describe them. He refers to them as "dogs" (3:2–4) and hints that the problem lies with those who wished to influence Christian belief according to Jewish sensitivities, sometimes referred to as a Judaizing influence (3:2, 18–19). The language of criticism is quite pointed, suggesting that Paul had someone specific in mind, perhaps even an individual. His willingness to criticize his opponents in Philippi led Paul to boast about his own heritage (3:4–8), which also led Paul to reveal his former status as a Pharisee. In assessing his former life, Paul used an economic metaphor to describe his current thinking: "But these things that were gains to me became liabilities because of Christ" (3:7). The language of debt thereby emerges as a component of Paul's religious vocabulary.

Connection to Latter-day Saint Beliefs

The obvious connection between this letter and Latter-day Saint belief is found in 4:8, which provides the basis for the thirteenth article of faith. The article of faith quotes the language of Philippians using the King James translation and adds to it the note that these ideas belong to Paul. A second important connection is the embedded hymn found in 2:6–11 (compare Colossians 1:13–20), which documents the early Christian belief in the divinity of Jesus Christ. In succinct form, it presents the doctrine of Christ, his descent to the earth, and his exaltation, which provide a pattern for Latter-day Saint teachings on the topic. ⁂

OPENING ADDRESS

1 [1]Paul and Timothy, servants of Christ Jesus, to all the saints in Christ Jesus who are in Philippi, with the bishops and deacons: [2]grace and peace to you from God our Father and the Lord Jesus Christ.

[3]I thank my God for all my memories of you, [4]always praying with joy in every prayer of mine for all of you [5]because of your participation in the gospel from the first day until now. [6]I am certain of this, that he who began a good work among you will perfect it until the day of Christ Jesus, [7]just as it is right for me to feel this about all of you because I have you in my heart, in my imprisonment, in my defense, and in my confirmation of the gospel; all of you became partners in grace. [8]For God is my witness, how I yearn for you with the compassion of Christ Jesus. [9]And I pray for this, that your love will increase more and more in knowledge and in being full of discernment [10]for you to differentiate what is good and bad so that you may be pure and blameless in the day of Christ, [11]filled with the fruit of righteousness that comes through Jesus Christ to the glory and praise of God.

CIRCUMSTANCES OF PAUL'S IMPRISONMENT

[12]I want you to know, brothers and sisters, that the things that have happened to me have resulted in the spread of the gospel [13]so that my imprisonment in Christ has become known by the entire imperial guard and to everyone else. [14]And the majority of the brothers and sisters have become confident in the Lord because of my imprisonment, and now they are more daring in speaking the word without fear.

[15]Some proclaim Christ from envy and rivalry, some from goodwill. [16]They do so out of love, knowing that I have been placed in this situation for the defense of the gospel. [17]Others proclaim Christ out of envy, not sincerely, because they think they can increase my suffering in my imprisonment. [18]What is the result? Only that in every way, whether out of false motives or true, Christ is proclaimed, and I rejoice in that.

I will continue rejoicing, [19]for I know that through your prayers and the assistance of the Spirit of Jesus Christ, this will result in my deliverance, [20]as it is my eager expectation and hope that I will not be ashamed at all, but in all boldness now and always, Christ will be magnified in my body, whether through life or through death. [21]To me, to live is Christ, and to die is an advantage. [22]If I am going to live in

---

1:1 *Timothy* joined with Paul in sending this letter as he did in 2 Corinthians (1:1). *Philippi* was a Roman colony in Macedonia and was inhabited by Roman soldiers with a large Greek population as well. The letter is also sent by the *bishops and deacons*, suggesting that these are now formal offices in the church. The Greek word translated as *bishops* refers primarily to *overseers*. **1:3** Greek uses a singular (*memory*), while English usage prefers a plural. **1:6** Paul was the first missionary to bring the gospel message to Philippi (Acts 16:12). *Until the day of Christ* refers to the return of Christ (compare 1 Corinthians 1:8). **1:7** Paul was imprisoned in Philippi (Acts 16:23–40), Caesarea Maritima (Acts 23:23–26:32), and Rome (Acts 28:16–31). **1:12** Greek uses *brothers* generically to refer to *brothers and sisters*. **1:13** The *imperial guard* can refer to the troops given the assignment to protect the emperor or to the Roman provincial governor's personal residence. The phrase can be used as an indication that Paul was imprisoned in Rome, but this is not the only possible interpretation (see note on verse 7). **1:14** See note on 1:12. **1:19** Perhaps an allusion to Job 13:16. **1:20–22** The language of choosing life or death suggests that Paul is making a personal decision about the matter, perhaps wondering whether he should offer a defense of his actions or allow the charges against him to go unanswered.

the flesh, that means productive labor for me, but I do not know what I prefer. ²³I am pressed to decide between the two, having a desire to return and be with Christ, which is greater by far, ²⁴but to remain in the flesh is more beneficial for you, ²⁵because I am convinced of this: I know that I will remain and continue with all of you for your progress and joy in the faith ²⁶so that your boasting of me may abound in Christ Jesus when I come to you again.

²⁷Only let the way you live your life be worthy of the gospel of Christ so that whether I come and see you or whether I am away I might hear about you, that you stand united in one Spirit, with one mind, contending together for the faith of the gospel ²⁸and not being frightened by your adversaries. This is proof to them of their destruction, but to you it is proof of your salvation, and this is from God. ²⁹For it has been granted to you for the sake of Christ, not only that you should believe in him but also that you should suffer for him, ³⁰having the same conflict that you saw in me and now you hear that I still have.

A HYMN TO CHRIST

2 ¹Therefore, if there is any comfort in Christ, if there is any consolation in love, if there is any sharing in the Spirit, if there is any kindness and compassion, ²make my joy complete by being of the same mind, and having the same love, being of one accord and one mind. ³Do nothing out of selfish ambition or conceit, but in humility treat one another as more important than yourselves. ⁴Each of you should consider the interests of others and not your own interests. ⁵Have this in mind among you as it was in Christ Jesus,

⁶who was in the form of God,
did not suppose that equality with God
was a prize to be seized,
⁷but he poured himself out
and took the form of a slave,
and he was born like human beings.
And he was found in human form;
⁸he humbled himself
and was obedient to the point of death:
death on the cross.
⁹Therefore, God exalted him on high
and freely bestowed on him the name
that is above every name
¹⁰so that in the name of Jesus
every knee should bend in worship
in the heavens, on earth,
and among those who dwell beneath
the earth
¹¹and every tongue will confess
the Lord Jesus Christ,
to the glory of God the Father.

1:27 *Only let the way you live your life* is in Greek *to live like free citizens*. It is both a call to live uprightly and to live freely.

2:6 *Was in the form of God* suggests condescension on Christ's part (compare 1 Nephi 11:16–21). **2:6–7** A similar teaching is found in Mosiah 13:34. **2:6–11** These verses preserve what scholars have suggested was an early Christian hymn sung to Christ or about Christ. Some early Christian hymns are embedded in the New Testament text (for example, see John 1:1–18). The hymn, because it is pre-Pauline, represents one of the earliest Christian writings to have survived. **2:7** The belief that Jesus *poured himself out* implies that Jesus took up his abode among humans by means of his divine nature entering or being poured into a human body. **2:9** *The name above every name* is probably a play on the title *Lord*, which refers to someone who is in charge of others. The precise name is likely to be Jesus (compare Hebrews 1:4). **2:10–11** Similar phrases appear in Mosiah 27:31; echoed in Doctrine and Covenants 88:89, 104.

WORK OUT YOUR OWN SALVATION

[12]Therefore, my beloved, just as you have always obeyed, not only when I was with you, but now even more in my absence, work out your own salvation with fear and trembling. [13]For God is at work in you, bringing out both the desire and effort to do his will.

[14]Do all things without murmuring or hesitation [15]so that you may become blameless and innocent, children of God without blemish in the midst of a crooked and perverse generation, in which you shine as lights in the world, [16]by holding fast to the word of life so that in the day of Christ I can boast that I did not run or labor in vain. [17]But if I am poured out as an offering upon the sacrifice and offering of your faith, I am glad and rejoice together with you all. [18]And in the same way you should also be glad and rejoice with me.

TIMOTHY AND EPAPHRODITUS

[19]I hope in the Lord Jesus to quickly send Timothy to you so that I may be encouraged by hearing news of you. [20]For I have no one like him who will be anxious for your welfare. [21]For they all look after their own concerns and not the things of Jesus Christ. [22]But you know his worth, that as a father and son he has served with me for the gospel. [23]Therefore, I hope to send him as soon as I see how things will go with me, [24]although I am persuaded in the Lord that I will also come soon.

[25]I have determined that it is necessary to send Epaphroditus to you, for he is my brother, coworker, and fellow soldier, your messenger and minister to my need. [26]For he has been longing for all of you, and he was concerned because you heard that he was ill. [27]Indeed, he nearly died, but God had mercy on him, not on him only but on me also, so that I should not have one sorrow after another. [28]Therefore, I am more eager to send him so that upon seeing him you may rejoice again and I can be free from sorrow. [29]Therefore, receive him in the Lord with all joy, and honor such people [30]because he almost died for the work of Christ, risking his life so that he

---

2:12 Compare Alma 34:37; Mormon 9:27. **2:13** *His will* can also be translated as *good pleasure*. The noun means fundamentally the things that are pleasing to God. **2:15** An allusion to Deuteronomy 32:5, which is also quoted in Doctrine and Covenants 34:6. **2:17** The imagery of this verse is that of a liquid offering, usually wine or oil, made in connection with ancient sacrifices. It is not specific to either Judaism or pagan religious practices. **2:19** The verb *hearing* has been added to clarify the meaning. Paul has obviously been away from Philippi for some time, and he is anxious to send Timothy (Acts 16:3, 12; 19:22) to determine how the Philippian saints were doing. This mention of sending Timothy does little to clarify where Paul was at the time of writing, and Timothy was certainly with Paul when he wrote (Philippians 1:1). **2:21** This is one of the first hints that Paul's fellow traveling companions or close associates have begun to lose interest in the missionary work (see 2 Timothy 4:10). **2:23** *How things will go with me* probably refers to *how things will go concerning my trial and court case*. Paul remains positive in the outcome of his trial or his difficult circumstances, but there is still some possibility that his life will remain in jeopardy. **2:25** *Epaphroditus* may be the same person as *Epaphras*, although that suggestion is now considered by scholars to be unlikely (Colossians 1:7). He is mentioned in only this letter (2:25; 4:18), and he bears a Greek name and was likely a Gentile convert. He is called an *apostle*, translated as *minister* in this verse, but the context suggests that Paul used the term generically as *messenger* or *missionary*. **2:30** The reference to the Philippian saints' inability to provide for Paul remains unclear. It is possible that he was referring to financial support that they had promised him or that he took care of the collection for the poor that they were not able to complete or send. Philippians 4:10 mentions the reception of support, probably financial, thus suggesting that the collection for the poor is the likely

might complete the service you were unable to provide for me.

WARNINGS

3 ¹Finally, my brothers and sisters, rejoice in the Lord. To write the same things to you is not a burden to me, and it is a safe measure for you.

²Beware of dogs, beware of evil workers, and beware of those who mutilate the flesh! ³For we are the circumcision, the ones who worship God in the Spirit, boast in Christ Jesus, and do not have confidence in the flesh, ⁴even though I have confidence in the flesh. If anyone thinks he has confidence in the flesh, I have more; ⁵I was circumcised on the eighth day, from the people of Israel and the tribe of Benjamin, a Hebrew born of Hebrews; according to the Law, I was a Pharisee. ⁶In my zeal, I persecuted the church; according to the righteousness which is in the Law,

I was blameless. ⁷But these things that were gains to me became liabilities because of Christ. ⁸But more than that, I now count everything as loss because of the superior value of knowing Christ Jesus my Lord, for whom I have suffered the loss of all things. I regard them as dung so that I may gain Christ ⁹and be found in him, while not having my own righteousness from the Law but that which comes through the faith of Christ, the righteousness from God that relies on faith. ¹⁰I want to know Christ and the power of his resurrection and the sharing in his sufferings and to be like him in his death ¹¹if somehow I might achieve the resurrection from the dead.

I SEEK FOR THE GOAL

¹²Not that I have already received it or that I have already been perfected, but I seek to obtain that which Christ Jesus obtained for me. ¹³Brothers and sisters, I do

reference here (see Philippians 2:25; 2 Corinthians 8–9).

3:1 Greek uses *brothers* generically to refer to *brothers and sisters*. **3:2** This series of warnings probably has a single person or belief in mind, and they are considered to be *dogs, evil workers,* and *those who mutilate the flesh*. The word *mutilate* is in Greek *to emasculate* or *destroy by circumcision*. Paul is being rude in his speech, and he is passionate in his warning to avoid those who wish to continue the practice of circumcision. The term *dogs* is derogatory (Mark 7:27–28) and could have ethnic connotations. **3:5** The Pharisees play only a peripheral role in Acts and in Paul's letters, but they were a significant factor in the Gospels. Little is known about Paul's time as a Pharisee or whether he came from a family of Pharisees. The reference is placed between his description of his own zeal and his being born of Hebrew parents, suggesting that he was raised a Pharisee. The Pharisees believed in a resurrection and had several other beliefs that were similar to early Christian beliefs. For the requirement of circumcision, see Genesis 17:12; Leviticus 12:3. On the special place of Benjamin, see 1 Kings 12:21. **3:5–6** This pedigree of former righteousness demonstrates an early segment of Paul's spiritual development and, while provided as irony, demonstrates Paul's former assessment of his spirituality. **3:8** The word translated as *dung* is the vulgar word for fecal matter, and it was probably used here for emphasis to accurately describe the contrast between the value Paul placed on his knowledge of Christ and the low value he placed on his former sense of achievement. Mosiah 2:34 encourages us to understand ourselves as debtors. **3:9** *Faith of Christ* can also be translated as *Christ's faithfulness*. The difference in meaning is important here because *faith of Christ* would imply the inherent faith we have in Christ and his gospel or even the faith we have in him; the second changes the meaning to Christ becoming an example of faith, and the believer is literally supposed to look to Christ's example of faithfulness. **3:10** Similar ideas are expressed in 2 Nephi 10:25. **3:11** The verb *achieve* also means *attain* or *accomplish*. It is unclear what Paul meant by this phrase, but the wording suggests he wanted to attain a level of righteousness that permitted him to be resurrected. This interpretation becomes clear in verse 12–13. **3:13** Greek uses *brothers* generically to refer to *brothers and sisters*.

not consider myself to have obtained this. But I do one thing, forgetting what is in the past and striving for what lies ahead, ¹⁴I seek for the goal, for the prize of the calling of God from above in Christ Jesus. ¹⁵Therefore, those who are mature should think this way. And if you think otherwise, God will reveal this to you also. ¹⁶Likewise, let us hold fast to what we have attained.

¹⁷Be imitators of me, brothers and sisters, and observe those who live in this manner just as you have us as an example. ¹⁸For many live as enemies of the cross of Christ, as I often told you about them and now I tell you with tears. ¹⁹Their end is destruction; their god is their belly and their glory is their shame, with their thoughts on earthly concerns. ²⁰For our citizenship is in heaven, and we are waiting for a Savior from there, the Lord Jesus Christ, ²¹who will change our lowly body to be like his body of glory according to his power by which he subjects all things to himself.

4 ¹Therefore, my beloved brothers and sisters whom I long for, my joy and crown, stand firm in the Lord, my beloved.

REJOICE IN THE LORD

²I encourage Euodia and Syntyche to be of the same mind in the Lord. ³Yes, I ask you also, faithful companion, help them, for they have struggled alongside me and Clement and my other fellow workers in the ministry of the gospel, whose names are written in the book of life.

⁴Rejoice in the Lord always, and I say again, rejoice. ⁵Let your kindness be known to everyone. The Lord is near. ⁶Do not worry about anything, but in all things let your requests be known to God by means of prayer and supplication with thanksgiving. ⁷And the peace of God that surpasses all understanding will guard your hearts and thoughts in Christ Jesus.

⁸Finally, beloved, whatever is true, honorable, just, pure, lovely, commendable, if something is excellent or praiseworthy, think about these things. ⁹And what you learned, received, heard, and saw in me, do these things, and the God of peace will be with you.

THANKS

¹⁰I rejoice in the Lord greatly because now at last you have renewed your concern for

---

3:14 Many translations render *calling from above* as *upward call*, but the context suggests a heavenly call, and therefore *calling from above* appears to capture the sense. It may also be an allusion to Paul's own call (Acts 9:1–9). **3:15** The reference to *this* in the phrase *God will reveal this to you also* is the teaching found in verses 13–15. The emphasis of those verses is the encouragement to seek the goal and prize of a calling from God (verse 14). The word translated as *mature* can also mean *perfect* or *complete* but not *flawless* or *blameless*. The context suggests that Paul was speaking of the saints who were *mature* in their faith. **3:17** Greek uses *brothers* generically to refer to *brothers and sisters*. Paul often drew upon himself as an example (1 Corinthians 4:16; 11:1). **3:19** Paul also considers the consequence of sin in 2 Corinthians 11:15. **3:20** *Our citizenship* recalls the encouragement to live like citizens (see Philippians 1:27 and note). **3:21** The power of the resurrection is associated with the power of subjecting all things to Christ. Doctrine and Covenants 19:2 uses a similar concept of subjecting or subduing all things.

4:1 Greek uses *brothers* generically to refer to *brothers and sisters*. **4:2** Nothing else is known of these two women, but Paul knows them personally. **4:3** The name of the *faithful companion* is unknown, although Timothy is a possible reference. The Greek adjective is masculine, but little else is known about his identity. The *book of life* imagery is found in Exodus 32:32–33, but the title is frequently used in Revelation (3:5; 13:8; 17:8, etc.). **4:5** *The Lord is near* can refer to his imminent return in the sense that the Lord is at hand. **4:8** Article of Faith 13 is based on this verse. **4:9** Paul earlier encouraged the saints of Thessalonica in similar ways (1 Thessalonians 4:1). **4:10** *To express it* has been added to clarify the Greek, which states

me, but you have lacked an opportunity to express it. [11]I am not saying that I am in need, because I have learned to be content with whatever I have. [12]I have known what it is to have little, and I have known times of abundance, and in any and every circumstance I have learned the secret of having plenty and facing hunger, of having an abundance and being in need. [13]I can do all things through him who strengthens me.

[14]Nevertheless, you did well to share in my trials. [15]But you Philippians, know that at the beginning of my ministry in the gospel I came from Macedonia. No church shared with me in a partnership of giving and receiving, except you alone. [16]Even in Thessalonica you sent me assistance for my needs more than once. [17]Not that I seek for a gift, but I seek the interest that would add to your account. [18]I have received everything, and I have an abundance. I am content because I received from Epaphroditus what you sent, a sweet-smelling offering, an acceptable sacrifice that is pleasing to God. [19]And my God will provide for all your needs according to the glory of his riches in Christ Jesus. [20]May glory be given to God our Father forever and ever. Amen.

FINAL GREETINGS

[21]Greet all the saints in Christ Jesus. Those brothers and sisters who are with me greet you. [22]All the saints greet you, especially those of Caesar's household.

[23]May the grace of the Lord Jesus Christ be with your spirit.

only *you lacked an opportunity*. **4:15** For Paul's call to preach the gospel in Macedonia, see Acts 16:9–12. **4:16** For Paul's early ministry in Thessalonica, see Acts 17:1–9. **4:17** The language of this verse is informed by the harvest of fruit. Paul conceptualizes the conversion of Gentiles as bearing fruit (Romans 15:28). **4:18** A similar thought regarding sacrifice is expressed in Ephesians 5:2. **4:21** See note on 4:1. **4:22** *Caesar's household* refers to a number of different institutions and groups living both in Rome and the provinces, and it does not necessarily refer to the emperor's household in Rome. The phrase does, however, indicate a close connection between some of the Philippians saints to the emperor, his slaves, or servants (see Philippians 1:13). The mention of a palace in the first chapter and *Caesar's household* would fit Caesarea Maritima (Acts 23:23–26:32) and Rome (Acts 28:16–31).

COLOSSIANS

AUTHOR

This short letter to the community of saints living in Colossae, a city in the Lycus Valley with Hierapolis and Laodicea, was written by Paul and Timothy, who are listed as co-senders (1:1). Acts does not record any information about the spread of the gospel in the city, but Colossians reports that Epaphras brought the gospel there (1:7). Epaphras was also influential in building the community (4:13), and he may have met Paul in Ephesus and then brought the gospel message back to his hometown. When Paul wrote, he was in prison (4:3, 18).

The writing style of Colossians is similar to Ephesians, with which it shares a significant amount of terminology (Ephesians 6:21–22; Colossians 4:7–9). The author also favors long and complex sentences and the development of ideas. The differences in vocabulary and the style of writing have led scholars to suggest that the same person wrote both Ephesians and Colossians but that a different person wrote the other Pauline letters (Romans through 2 Thessalonians and Philemon). The style is markedly different, enough to suggest that Paul did not write this letter in the same way he wrote many of his other letters. If Paul wrote the letter, he probably did so from Rome during his imprisonment there as described in Acts 28:16–28 or perhaps from a later Roman imprisonment.

PURPOSE OF WRITING

The reason for writing this letter is related to a growing schism or heresy that had taken root among the community. The number of saints involved in the faction remains an unanswerable question, but it is clear that some had become concerned with esoteric teachings (2:8–18), angel worship (2:18), and asceticism (2:20–23). Those who promoted such ideals are sometimes referred to as "Gnostics," a later movement that did emphasize the worship of angelic intermediaries, private or mystical knowledge, and the concept of physically rigorous spirituality. Today, scholars tend not to describe the movement in Colossae as a form of early Gnosticism and the heresy as different from the problems faced in the other Pauline branches of the church. The problem might be described as an emphasis on wisdom and personal spirituality, and Paul does associate the movement with Jewish ideas (2:13, 16).

Paul countered the ideas of those who were troubling the branch with a declaration of what he defined as true spirituality (3:5–10) and what amounts to a declaration of the nature or essence of Christ (1:16–18). This declaration is founded upon an early Christian hymn, the author of which remains unknown, but whom Paul quoted in the service of teaching about Christ and his eternal nature. The letter concludes with a long list of Pauline associates and friends (4:7–18), including well-known individuals such as Mark, Onesimus, and Luke. Furthermore, Paul encouraged the communities at Laodicea and Colossae to exchange letters (4:16). The letter to the Laodiceans is now lost unless it is the same as the letter to the Ephesians (see note on Ephesians 1:1).

CONNECTION TO LATTER-DAY SAINT BELIEFS

This letter has had no direct influence on Latter-day Saint practice and belief. Its doctrines and teachings are widely read and studied, and the letter demonstrates the difficulties that new communities of believers faced in a challenging social world like the Roman Empire. ⸾

OPENING ADDRESS

1 ¹Paul, an apostle of Christ Jesus through the will of God, and Timothy our brother, ²to the saints in Colossae and the faithful brothers and sisters in Christ: grace and peace to you from God our Father.

THANKSGIVING

³We always thank God the Father of our Lord Jesus Christ when we pray for you ⁴since we heard of your faith in Christ Jesus and the love which you have for all of the saints, ⁵because of the hope that is laid up for you in heaven, which you have heard about in the word of truth, which is the gospel. ⁶The gospel has come to you, and just as it is bearing fruit and growing in all the world, it has done so for you from the day when you heard and truly understood the grace of God. ⁷You learned the gospel from Epaphras, our beloved fellow servant, who is a faithful servant of Christ on our behalf, ⁸who made your love in the Spirit known to us.

⁹Because of this, we also, from the day when we heard about you, have not ceased praying for you and asking God that you may be filled with knowledge of his will in all spiritual wisdom and understanding ¹⁰so that you may live worthily of the Lord, being pleasing in all things, bearing fruit in every good work and increasing in the knowledge of God, ¹¹being strengthened in all power according to the power of his glory for all endurance and patience, ¹²giving thanks with joy to the Father who prepared us to share in the inheritance of the saints in the light. ¹³He saved us from the power of darkness and transferred us to the kingdom of his beloved Son, ¹⁴in whom we have redemption, meaning forgiveness of sins.

A HYMN ABOUT CHRIST

¹⁵He is the image of the unseen God,
the firstborn of all creation, ¹⁶because all things in heaven were created by him—in heaven and upon the earth, what is seen and unseen, whether thrones or dominions, whether rulers or authorities, all things were created through him and for him.
¹⁷He is before all things, and all things are held together by him,

---

1:1 *Colossae* was a Greek city in Asia Minor and near the city of Laodicea. Paul had not visited the city (verse 4), but in the letter to Philemon, Paul expressed an interest to visit there (1:22). It is not clear at what point Paul wrote to the saints in Colossae if this letter was written by him (see introduction). **1:2** Some early and reliable manuscripts add *and the Lord Jesus Christ* to the end of the verse. **1:3–8** These verses are a single sentence in Greek, and they have been divided into smaller units to represent better English style. **1:7** *Epaphras* is otherwise unknown, but he played an important role in the evangelization of the saints in Colossae (see Colossians 4:12; Philemon 1:23). *Our behalf* is *your behalf* in some later and less reliable manuscripts. **1:9** Doctrine and Covenants 84:98 (compare Habakkuk 2:14 also) echoes the language of this verse but in a different context. *Spiritual wisdom* is a new concept for Paul. First Corinthians 2:13 presents the contrast of wisdom that is taught by the Spirit and human wisdom. The wording allows for two types of wisdom: spiritual and human. **1:14** Some very late and less reliable manuscripts add *through his blood* following *redemption*. This addition was likely added for doctrinal reasons. The language of *redemption* is built upon the concept of a manumission of a slave or the paying off of a debt (compare Romans 5:11; Galatians 3:22). **1:15** Jesus is called the *firstborn*, which may signal that he was being praised as the firstborn king (Psalm 89:27). For the idea that God is *unseen*, see Hebrews 11:27. Compare Mosiah 7:27, where Christ takes on the image of a man. **1:15–20** These verses preserve a fragment of an early Christian hymn or psalm. These hymns are difficult to recover because they may have been paraphrased or the author may have added or removed words from the original. These hymns reflect some of the earliest teachings about Jesus (John 1:1–18; Philippians 2:6–11).

[18]and he is the head of the body—the church—he is the beginning, the firstborn from the dead, so that he may become first in all things.

[19]For God was pleased to have his fullness reside in him

[20]and through him to reconcile all things to himself, making peace through the blood of his cross, whether things on earth or things in heaven.

PAUL'S CONCERN FOR THE SAINTS OF COLOSSAE

[21]And you were once strangers and enemies in your thoughts, as demonstrated through evil deeds, [22]but now he has reconciled you by his body of flesh through death in order to present you holy, pure, and blameless before him, [23]if indeed you remain in the faith, being established and steady, not shifting from the hope of the gospel that you heard, which has been proclaimed among all creations under heaven, and I Paul have become its servant.

[24]Now I rejoice in my sufferings on your behalf, and I am filling up in my physical body what was lacking in the sufferings of Christ, to assist his body, which is the church, [25]for which I became a servant according to the stewardship from God that was given to me to fulfill the word of God, [26]which is the mystery that has been hidden away for ages and generations, but now it has been revealed to his saints. [27]God wanted to make known to them the riches of the glory of this mystery among the Gentiles, which is Christ in you, the hope of glory. [28]We declare him by teaching all people with all wisdom so that we present every person who is mature in Christ. [29]For this purpose I also labor, struggling according to his power that so powerfully works in me.

2 [1]For I want you to know what great agony I have for you and for those in Laodicea and also for those who have not seen me face to face [2]so that their hearts may be comforted, joining together in love to obtain all the wealth of full understanding and the knowledge of God's mystery, which is Christ, [3]in whom are hidden all the treasures of wisdom and knowledge. [4]I say this so that no one will deceive you

---

1:18 *The church*, a phrase that interrupts the flow of the hymn, may have been added by the author. **1:19** *To have his fullness reside in him* refers to God's fullness residing in Christ. **1:20** The Greek manuscripts are very nearly equally divided between those which read *whether things on earth or things in heaven* and those that read *through him, whether things on earth or things in heaven*. The second reading makes little sense, which is often a hallmark that it was original (scribes often removed words and phrases that were confusing), but in this instance *through him* does not appear to add to the meaning of the verse in any obvious way. **1:21** *As demonstrated through* has been added to clarify the Greek. The text says literally *and enemies of thought in works of evil*. **1:22** *Pure* can also be translated as *without spot or blemish*. In the context of *holy* and *blameless*, both words that denote purity, the word *pure* better approximates the sense of the noun. **1:23** *Creations* is singular in Greek, but English usage prefers the plural. *Which has been proclaimed among all creations under heaven* seems to refer to a later stage of Paul's missionary work when the gospel had spread beyond the few cities in the Eastern Mediterranean basin. *Servant* is the Greek word *deacon*, but the author appears to be using it in a generic sense. **1:27** *Which is Christ in you* interrupts the flow and logic of the verse, and the author interprets the revelation of the mystery of God as *Christ for you* or *Christ in you*. **1:28** *That we present* refers to the act of presenting someone before a ruler or standing beside someone in support. *Mature* can also be translated *perfect*, but the emphasis is on stability and maturity.

2:1 Acts does not mention that Paul traveled to *Laodicea*, and his letters do not mention any trips there. Laodicea was located a little over ten miles (seventeen kilometers) to the west of Colossae (compare Revelation 1:11). **2:3** An allusion to Isaiah 11:2.

with persuasive speech. ⁵Although I am absent in body, I am with you in spirit, rejoicing in seeing your character and the firmness of your faith in Christ.

WARNING

⁶Therefore, just as you received Christ Jesus the Lord, live in him, ⁷being rooted, built up in him, and established in the faith just as you have been taught while abounding in gratitude. ⁸Beware not to let anyone lead you captive through an empty and deceitful philosophy, according to human tradition, according to the elemental forces of the world and not according to Christ, ⁹because in him dwells all the fullness of deity in bodily form, ¹⁰and you have been filled in him, who is the head of all rule and authority. ¹¹You have been circumcised in him, but not by a circumcision done by human hands but by setting aside the mortal body in the circumcision of Christ, ¹²having been buried with him in baptism, in which you were also raised through your faith in the power of God's work, who raised him from the dead. ¹³And you who were dead to sins and to the uncircumcision of your flesh, God made you alive together with him, forgiving you of all your sins, ¹⁴having wiped out the handwritten accusation of debt made against us. He removed it by nailing it to the cross. ¹⁵He disarmed the rulers and authorities and put them to public shame, triumphing over them in the cross.

¹⁶Therefore, do not let anyone judge you with regard to food or drink or with respect to a feast, new moon, or Sabbath, ¹⁷which are a shadow of things to come, but the reality belongs to Christ. ¹⁸Do not allow anyone to deceive you, insisting on humility and the worship of angels,

---

2:5 The word translated as *character* sometimes refers to a soldier's willingness to hold a position in line or to the general concepts of order or discipline. **2:8** The translation of this verse significantly departs from other translations in the phrase *captive through an empty and deceitful philosophy*. Other translations prefer *captive through philosophy and empty deceit*. The two nouns share a single definite article, thus indicating that they modify one another (*the philosophy that is deceitful*). The phrase *elemental forces* is difficult to translate in this sentence because its precise meaning is unclear. Some translators suggest that the author was speaking of *elemental spirits* or *spiritual forces*. The word often refers to the elemental building blocks of matter in philosophical discussions, and here it seems to represent the author's criticism of philosophical concern with matter in place of God. *Philosophy* is used as an equivalent of teaching. **2:9** The author uses a Greek word, *pleroma* (translated as *fullness*), that became part of Gnostic thinking and speculation. The word refers to the fullness of all life, matter, existence, and being, and it clearly engages questions about the fundamental nature of God. This is one of the few verses in the New Testament that discusses the nature of God (John 1:1; Hebrews 1:3–4). **2:10** *Rule and authority* may refer to earthly dominions but also heavenly ones (see verse 15). **2:11** This verse presents several new concepts, particularly the *setting aside the mortal body* and the *circumcision of Christ*. *Setting aside the mortal body* probably refers to setting aside the interests and desires of the body and not promoting a desire to die and be with God. The *circumcision of Christ* can refer to the actual circumcision of Jesus (Luke 2:21–22) or to the symbolic circumcision that he performed on human hearts. **2:12** This verse presents the idea that baptism is a symbol of dying to the old self and becoming a new person in Christ. The Book of Mormon fundamentally understands baptism as a covenant (Mosiah 18:10, 13–14, compare Romans 6:4). **2:15** The Greek construction allows for *in the cross* to also be translated as *in him (Christ)*. **2:16** Ezekiel rejected similar concerns (45:17). These concerns appear to be Jewish in origin with an emphasis on the timing or date of holy days, Sabbath days, and festivals, which were calculated using lunar cycles. **2:17** Mosiah 16:14 echoes the language of this verse (compare Mosiah 13:10). **2:18** *Humility*, which is connected to the practice of worshipping angels, in this verse is a negative concept, and perhaps *false humility* better captures the nuance.

promoting visions, puffed up without reason by human thinking, [19]and not holding tightly to the head, from whom the entire body, connected and joined together through its ligaments and sinews, grows with an increase that is from God.

[20]If with Christ you have died to the natural forces of the world, why do you live in the world and remain subject to them? [21]"Do not handle; do not taste; do not touch!" [22]These are all things that will pass away with use, according to human commands and teachings. [23]These have an appearance of wisdom in promoting a self-interested worship and humility, and bodily asceticism, but they are not of any value in guarding against self-indulgence.

SEEK WHAT IS FROM ABOVE

3 [1]Therefore, if you were raised with Christ, seek what is from above, where Christ is, seated at the right hand of God. [2]Think about what is from above and not about what is on the earth. [3]For you have died, and your life is hidden with Christ in God. [4]When Christ appears—your life—then you will also appear in glory with him.

[5]Therefore, put to death your attributes that belong to the earth: sexual impropriety, uncleanness, lust, evil desire, and greed, which is idolatry. [6]Because of these things, the wrath of God is coming upon the children of disobedience. [7]You walked in these ways at one time when you lived among them. [8]But now you must put them all aside—wrath, anger, evil, slander, rude speech from your mouth. [9]Do not lie to one another after having put off the old self with its practices [10]and having put on the new self, which is being renewed in knowledge according to the image of the one who created it. [11]There is neither Greek nor Jew, circumcised nor uncircumcised, foreigner, Scythian, slave, free, but Christ is all and in all.

[12]Therefore, clothe yourselves as the elect of God, holy and beloved saints, with compassionate hearts, kindness, humility, meekness, and patience, [13]bearing with one another and forgiving one another if anyone has a complaint against another person. Just as the Lord has forgiven you, likewise forgive one another. [14]Above all these things, clothe yourselves in love, which is a bond of perfection. [15]And let the peace of Christ guide your hearts, for which peace

---

2:20 The Joseph Smith Translation adds to the very end of the verse *ordinances, which are after the doctrines and commandments of men.* **2:21** These words are quotations from those who have advocated for positions different than those that aligned with Paul's teachings. **2:22** A similar concern is expressed in Matthew 15:9. An allusion to Isaiah 29:13. **2:23** The author endorses the concept that curbing physical desires will promote greater spiritual awareness and focus, but in this verse *asceticism* is negative because it is not done with an eye to God.

3:4 English usage would prefer *when Christ appears, who is your life*, but the author has constructed the sentence so that *your life* becomes the point of emphasis. **3:5** *Your attributes* are literally *your members*, referring to *members of the body*. **3:6** The phrase *upon the children of disobedience* is lacking in a couple of early and reliable manuscripts, but the overwhelming majority of manuscripts contain it. The omission makes the verse general in application. **3:7** The translation *among them* assumes that *children of disobedience* was the original reading (see note on 3:6). If not, then the translation would be amended to *lived in those ways*. **3:9** Compare Mosiah 3:19, which engages similar themes in greater depth. **3:11** In Greek literature, the *Scythians* were those who lived north of the Black Sea. They may have been included in the list as the least likely and last to accept the gospel. **3:12** The directive to *clothe yourselves* is also to *endow yourselves*. The primary meaning of the verb is to put something on, particularly clothing. **3:14** Doctrine and Covenants 88:125 quotes a portion of this verse and expands its original context.

you were called to be one body, and be thankful. [16]Let the word of Christ richly dwell in you, and in all wisdom teach and encourage each other with psalms, hymns, spiritual songs, with thanks in your hearts to God. [17]And whatever you do, in speech or work, do all things in the name of the Lord Jesus, giving thanks to God the Father through him.

HOUSEHOLD GUIDELINES

[18]Wives, submit to your husbands, as is fitting in the Lord. [19]Husbands, love your wives and do not treat them with anger. [20]Children, obey your parents in all things, for this is pleasing in the Lord. [21]Fathers, do not provoke your children so that they may not become discouraged. [22]Servants, obey your earthly masters in all things, not to be seen as people pleasers but with a sincere heart, fearing the Lord. [23]Whatever you do, work with your whole soul, working for the Lord and not for people, [24]knowing that you will receive an inheritance from the Lord as a reward. You are serving the Lord Christ. [25]For the person who does wrong will be paid back for the wrong he has done, for there is no partiality.

4 [1]Masters, treat your servants with justice and fairness, knowing that you too have a Master in heaven.

CONCLUDING REMARKS

[2]Continue in prayer, being watchful in it, praying with thanksgiving. [3]At the same time, pray for us too so that God may open a door to us for the word, to speak the mystery of Christ, on account of which I am in prison. [4]Pray that I may make it manifest as I ought to do. [5]Live in wisdom toward those who are outsiders, making the most of your time. [6]Let your speech always be gracious, seasoned with salt, so that you may know how you ought to respond to one another.

[7]Tychicus, a beloved brother, faithful minister and fellow servant in the Lord, will tell you all things about me. [8]I sent him to you for this reason so that you would know about us and that he might encourage your hearts [9]with Onesimus, the faithful and beloved brother who is from among you. They will tell you everything that is happening here.

[10]Aristarchus, my fellow prisoner, greets you, as does Mark, the cousin of Barnabas (about whom you received directions); if he comes to you, welcome him. [11]And

---

3:16 *The word of Christ* appears only here and in Romans 10:17. Compare Ephesians 5:19 for a similar directive to sing *psalms* and *hymns*. **3:18–22** There is a similar section encouraging wives to submit and children to obey in Ephesians 5:22–6:9. The parallel section in Colossians is much shorter. These words of counsel are based on the concept of harmony between a father, mother, children, and household servants. The structure of a Roman household functioned on the father maintaining a position of authority over all members in the household. The author is encouraging his readers to find value in working together for the same purpose (verses 22–23) and not relying on authority, anger, and harshness to direct the affairs of the household. These words of advice have little to do with the dynamics of modern families, although the encouragement to act in *love* does cross cultural boundaries. **3:23** *Your whole* has been added to capture the nuance of the Greek, which says literally *work with soul*. **3:25** An allusion to Deuteronomy 10:17 (compare Romans 2:11; Doctrine and Covenants 1:35).

4:1 This verse may be a restatement of Leviticus 25:43. **4:6** Probably an allusion to Leviticus 2:13 (compare Exodus 30:35). **4:7** For *Tychicus*, see Ephesians 6:21–22. The word translated as *minister* is the Greek word *deacon*. The word in this context appears to have a generic meaning and not to the office of a deacon. **4:9** *Onesimus*, whom Paul met in prison, was a servant of Philemon. Paul wrote to Philemon on his behalf (Philemon 1:8–18). **4:10** For *Aristarchus*, see Acts 27:2. For *Mark*, see Acts 15:37–39; 2 Timothy 4:11. He may be the same person who wrote the Gospel of Mark. **4:11** *They are the only*

Jesus who is called Justus greets you. They were of the circumcision, and they are the only fellow workers in the kingdom of God, and they were a comfort to me. [12]Epaphras, who is one of you, a servant of Christ Jesus, greets you. He is always struggling for you in his prayers so that you may stand mature and fully convinced in all the will of God. [13]For I can testify that he has worked hard for you and for those in Laodicea and Hierapolis. [14]Luke, the beloved physician, greets you, as does Demas. [15]Greet the brothers and sisters at Laodicea, and Nympha and the church that meets at her house. [16]And when the letter has been read to you, have it also read in the church of the Laodiceans. And see that you read the letter from Laodicea also. [17]And tell Archippus, "See that you complete the ministry that you have received in the Lord." [18]I, Paul, write this greeting with my own hand. Remember my imprisonment. May grace be with you.

---

fellow workers in the kingdom of God probably intends to convey the idea that these individuals are the only Jewish converts in the region who were also fellow workers. **4:12** For *Epaphras*, see Philemon 1:23. Some early and reliable manuscripts omit *Jesus* in this verse, but equally early and reliable manuscripts preserve it. **4:14** For *Luke*, see 2 Timothy 4:11. This Luke may have been the author of the Gospel of *Luke*. For *Demas*, see 2 Timothy 4:10; Philemon 1:24. **4:15** Greek uses *brothers* generically to refer to *brothers and sisters*. Some manuscripts indicate that *Nympha* was a male, but the better reading appears to be that the name represented a female believer. The *church that meets at her house* refers to a local gathering of Christians. The groups were usually identified by the name of the owner of the house. **4:16** The letter to the *Laodiceans* has been lost unless it is the same as Ephesians (see note on Ephesians 1:1). **4:17** For *Archippus*, see Philemon 1:2.

1 THESSALONIANS

AUTHOR

Paul, together with Silvanus (Silas) and Timothy, wrote this letter to the community of saints living in Thessalonica shortly after his departure from the city during his second missionary journey. The letter was perhaps written around 49–51 CE while Paul was in Corinth and when he learned how the saints were doing from an oral report he received from Timothy and Silvanus. Paul's tone is warm and friendly, especially in its opening verses (1:2–10), and those verses demonstrate a sense of deep affection for the faith of the new community of believers who had only recently accepted Jesus Christ as Lord. The community was located in Macedonia and was composed of Greek-speaking Gentiles who would have had consistent contact with the Latin-speaking west. The saints were Greek, and there are few references to the law of Moses or Judaism, suggesting that few of them had contact with Judaism or diaspora Jews. Today, most scholars accept this book as the oldest writing preserved in the New Testament, making it the first Christian writing to be preserved.

PURPOSE OF WRITING

According to Luke's account in Acts 17:1–10, the saints in Thessalonica were persecuted, but Luke reports that the persecution arose from the Jews living in the city. Their complaint is that Paul's teachings were subversive and undermined Roman authority. As a result of the persecution that Paul and his companions faced in Thessalonica, he traveled to Beroea and then sent Timothy back to check on the saints (Acts 17:10–15). Timothy then caught up with Paul again in Athens, and then Paul sent him back immediately to check on their welfare (3:1–2). Paul then traveled to Corinth, where Timothy and Silvanus met him (Acts 18:1–5). Based on the letter, it appears that Timothy gave a positive report about the community (3:6–7). Timothy's report seems to have triggered the writing of 1 Thessalonians, which is mostly positive, but there are some items of concern.

One of the major areas of concern resulted from a question posed to Paul concerning the fate of the living and the dead at the Second Coming (4:13–5:11). The precise question is difficult to unravel given that the letter only preserves Paul's response, but the intent of the question seems to be whether the living saints or the deceased would

have any prioritized position in God's kingdom when the Son returned in glory. Paul assured them that both would be equally represented and cared for, and in responding he seems to imply that he would live to see the day of the return (4:15, 17 and notes). A second concern was that some of the saints were not willing to work for their own living (4:9–12). It remains unclear what led to this phenomenon, and Paul's counsel on the matter seeks to restore harmony in the community.

CONNECTION TO LATTER-DAY SAINT BELIEFS

Given that this is probably the earliest Christian writing in the New Testament and the fact that it predates the writing of the Gospels, the letter should be an important source of information for Latter-day Saints on the consequences of faith. The letter preserves the words of a deeply concerned missionary, Paul, who wrote to a small community of saints. Paul attempted to balance providing corrective counsel with encouragement to stand firm in the faith. The fact that the theme of persecution and affliction so fully permeate the message of both 1 and 2 Thessalonians provides valuable insight into the challenges faced by those who have recently accepted the Lord Jesus Christ. ❧

OPENING ADDRESS

1 ¹Paul, Silvanus, and Timothy, to the church of the Thessalonians in God the Father and the Lord Jesus Christ. Grace and peace to you.

THE CHURCH IN THESSALONICA

²We always thank God for all of you, constantly mentioning you in our prayers, ³remembering before God our Father your work of faith and labor of love and steadfastness of hope in our Lord Jesus Christ. ⁴We know, brothers and sisters, loved by God, that he has chosen you, ⁵inasmuch as our gospel did not come to you in word only but in power and the Holy Spirit and with full conviction, just as you know how we acted among you and on your behalf. ⁶And you became imitators of us and of the Lord after you received the message in great trial and with joy from the Holy Spirit ⁷so that you became an example to all those who believe in Macedonia and Greece. ⁸For the word of the Lord has sounded out from you not only in Macedonia and Achaia, but word of your faith in God has traveled to every place, and we do not need to say anything. ⁹For they report about us the kind of reception we have among you and how you turned to God from idols to serve the true and living God ¹⁰and to wait for his Son from heaven, whom he raised from the dead, Jesus, the one who delivers us from the coming wrath.

PAUL'S MINISTRY TO THESSALONICA

2 ¹For you know, brothers and sisters, that our coming to you was not in vain. ²Although we suffered and were treated shamefully in Philippi, as you know, we were bold in our God to declare the gospel of God with much opposition. ³For our appeal is not based on error, impurity, or deceit, ⁴but just as we have been approved by God to be entrusted with the gospel, even so we speak, not to please people but to please God, who examines our hearts. ⁵For we never came with words of flattery, as you know, nor with a pretext for greed—God is witness to this. ⁶Nor did we seek glory from people, whether from you or others, ⁷although we could have been a burden to you as apostles of Christ. Instead, we became like little children among you, like a nursing mother caring for her children. ⁸Thus, having affection for you, we were pleased to impart

---

1:1 Thessalonica was a city in Macedonia (northern Greece). Paul visited the city on his second missionary journey. Scholars widely agree that this is the earliest Christian writing to survive. Paul refers to the *church of the Thessalonians*, indicating that he wrote some time later when a church group had been organized. Acts does not report that Paul had significant success there (Acts 17:1–9). This verse may have included *from God our Father and the Lord Jesus Christ* at the end of the verse. Some early and reliable manuscripts omit this phrase, but it appears that the addition was intended to bring it into harmony with Paul's other letters (compare 1 Corinthians 1:3). The name *Silvanus* is sometimes shortened to *Silas* (Acts 15:22; 16:19; 17:4, 10). *Timothy* was also with Paul on his second missionary journey (Acts 16:1–2). **1:4** Greek uses *brothers* generically to refer to *brothers and sisters*. **1:7** The believers in *Macedonia and Greece* would include those in Philippi, Athens, Corinth, and Beroea. **1:8** *The word of the Lord* may recall Genesis 15:1. **1:9** This verse is alluded to in Doctrine and Covenants 20:19 (compare Jeremiah 10:10). **1:10** The idea of *the coming wrath* of God is a significant theme in Paul's letters (Romans 1:18; 2:16; Colossians 3:6).

2:1 Greek uses *brothers* generically to refer to *brothers and sisters*. **2:2** This story is told in Acts 16:19–24. **2:7** The title *apostles* is used to refer to the three senders of the letter (Timothy, Silvanus, and Paul) and is probably used in the sense of missionary or emissary, the primary meaning of the Greek noun *apostle*. **2:8** In one of Paul's latest letters, he returned to the idea that his life would be taken as a result of his service (Philippians 2:17).

not only the gospel of God to you but also our own souls because you had become so beloved to us.

[9]For you remember, brothers and sisters, our work among you and our distress, working night and day that we might not be a burden to any of you while we proclaimed the gospel of God. [10]You are witnesses, and God also, to how holy, righteous, and blameless our conduct was toward you who believe. [11]You know that we were like a father with his children with each one of you. [12]We entreated and encouraged you, urging you to live worthily of God, who calls you into his own kingdom and glory.

[13]Because of this we thank God constantly that when you received the word of God that you heard from us, you accepted it not as a human message but as what it really is, the word of God, which is working in you who believe. [14]For you became imitators, brothers and sisters, of the churches of God that are in Judea in Christ Jesus, because you also suffered the same things from your own countrymen, as they did from the Jews, [15]who killed the Lord Jesus and the prophets and drove us out. They displease God, and they opposed all people [16]by hindering us from speaking to the Gentiles so that the Gentiles might be saved. Therefore, they always fill up the measure of their sins. But wrath has come upon them at last.

CONCERNS AFTER PAUL'S DEPARTURE

[17]But when we were away from you, brothers and sisters, for a short time, in person but not in heart, we were more eager and greatly desirous to see you in person [18]because we wanted to come to you. I, Paul, wanted to come again and again, but Satan hindered us. [19]For who is our hope, our joy, our crown to boast of before our Lord Jesus at his coming? Is it not you? [20]For you are our glory and joy.

3 [1]Therefore, when we could no longer bear it, we decided to stay in Athens alone, [2]and we sent Timothy, our brother and fellow servant for God in the gospel of Christ, to establish you and comfort you concerning your faith [3]so that no one would be moved by these persecutions. For you know that this is our determined outcome. [4]For when we were with you, we told you before it happened that we would suffer persecution, and it happened as you know. [5]Because of this, when I could no longer bear it, I sent to know about your faith. My concern was that somehow the tempter had tempted you and our labor among you had been in vain.

[6]But Timothy has come to us from being with you, and he has told us the good news about your faith and your love. He also told us that you always remember us with affection and long to see us, just as we long to see you. [7]Therefore, brothers and sisters, we have been comforted by

---

2:9, 14, 17 See note on 2:1. **2:14–15** The Greek represents a restrictive relative clause as Paul draws attention to the *Jews, the ones who killed the Lord Jesus and the prophets*. The phrase should not be taken as a condemnation of all Jews. **2:15** Some scribes attempted to clarify that the Jews had killed their own prophets. The earlier and better manuscripts omit the addition of *their own*. **2:18** For a similar view of Satan's ability to hinder Paul's missionary work, see 2 Corinthians 2:11. **2:19** The word translated as *coming* is the technical term used for the return of Christ at his Second Coming (see 1 Thessalonians 3:13; 4:15; 5:23).

3:1 This probably describes Paul's second missionary journey, when he remained in Athens and then sent Timothy back to Thessalonica to determine how things had transpired during his absence. Paul describes the event in slightly different terms than Acts does (17:14–15). **3:6** Timothy's return is reported in Acts 18:5. This would indicate that Paul probably wrote 1 Thessalonians while in Corinth. **3:7** Greek uses *brothers* generically to refer to *brothers and sisters*.

you in all our distress and persecution because of your faith, ⁸because now we live if you stand firm in the Lord. ⁹For how can we sufficiently thank God for you, for all the joy we feel before our God because of you? ¹⁰We pray earnestly night and day to see you in person and to mend whatever is lacking in your faith.

¹¹May God our Father himself and our Lord Jesus direct our way to you. ¹²May the Lord cause you to increase and to abound in love for one another and for all, just as we do for you, ¹³so that your hearts are strengthened in holiness and that you may be blameless before God our Father at the coming of our Lord Jesus with all his saints. Amen.

AN UPRIGHT LIFE

4 ¹Finally, brothers and sisters, we ask and encourage you in the Lord Jesus, that just as you learned from us how you ought to live and please God, just as you are doing, you should do so more and more. ²For you know what instructions we gave you through the Lord Jesus.

³For this is the will of God, your being made holy, that you stay away from sexual misbehavior, ⁴that each of you understands how to possess his own body in holiness and honor, ⁵not in lust and desire like the Gentiles who do not know God, ⁶that no one exploit or take advantage of a brother or sister, because the Lord is an avenger of all these things, just as I told you earlier and solemnly warned you. ⁷For God did not call us to uncleanness but to holiness. ⁸Therefore, the one who rejects this is not rejecting human authority but God, who gives his Holy Spirit to you.

⁹Now, concerning the topic of brotherly love, you do not have a need to have anyone write to you, for you yourselves are taught by God to love one another. ¹⁰For indeed you are doing this for all the brothers and sisters in all of Macedonia. And we encourage you, brothers and sisters, to do this more and more, ¹¹to aspire to live quietly, to attend to your own business, and to work with your own hands, just as we commanded you, ¹²so that you will live an upright life with respect to outsiders and not be dependent on anyone.

THE RETURN OF THE LORD

¹³We do not want you to be uninformed, brothers and sisters, concerning those who have died so that you will not grieve

---

3:10 Paul's hope to *mend whatever is lacking in your faith* is probably an indication of the newness of their faith and the need for further instruction in the gospel. **3:13** Some early and reliable manuscripts omit *Amen*, but given its placement in the middle of the letter, it appears to not have been added as a customary designation to signal the end of the letter. A similar encouragement is found in 1 Corinthians 1:7–8.

4:1 Greek uses *brothers* generically to refer to *brothers and sisters*. *Learned* in this verse is frequently translated as *received*, but the context indicates that this is learning through the passing on of traditions and teachings, and therefore *received* works also. **4:3** Many commentators see in this verse a general disdain for Roman cultural attitudes toward sex. The verse may therefore have the ideal in mind of distancing themselves from worldly ways. **4:4** The translation *each of you understands how to possess his own body* can also be rendered as *each of you marries his own wife*. The verb of *possessing* is the same verb that describes *marrying* or *taking a wife*. The translation provided is preferable because the word for *body* or *vessel* is not a euphemism for a spouse. **4:5** *Gentiles who do not know God* is probably intended to distinguish the Thessalonian saints who were Gentiles who did accept the gospel message. **4:6, 10, 13** See note on 4:1. **4:9** *Brotherly love* could also be rendered as *care for a brother or sister* or even *almsgiving*. **4:11–12** These verses promote Greco-Roman ideals of a good life, one that is lived in mutual respect for believers and nonbelievers. The phrase *and not be dependent on anyone* is an encouragement to not be brought into bondage to anyone or to any vice. **4:13** The phrase *those who have died* is in Greek *those who have fallen asleep*.

as the others who have no hope. [14]For we believe that Jesus died and rose again and that through Jesus, God will bring with him those who have died. [15]For we tell you this by the word of the Lord, that we who are alive and who remain until the coming of the Lord will not precede those who have died. [16]For the Lord himself will descend from heaven with a shout of command, with the voice of an archangel, and with the sound of God's trumpet, and the dead in Christ will rise first. [17]Then we who are alive and who are left, we will be caught up together with them in the clouds to meet the Lord in the air, and thus we will always be with the Lord. [18]Therefore, encourage one another with these words.

THE DAY OF THE LORD

5 [1]Concerning the times and seasons, brothers and sisters, you do not need anything to be written to you. [2]For you know well that the day of the Lord will come as a thief comes in the night. [3]When they say, "There is peace and security," then sudden destruction comes upon them just like a labor pain for a pregnant woman, and they will not escape. [4]But you, brothers and sisters, are not in darkness so that the day does not seize you like a thief. [5]For you are all children of the light and children of the day. We are not of the night or darkness. [6]Therefore, let us not sleep as

others do, but let us be alert and sober. [7]For those who are sleeping do so at night, and those who get drunk do so at night. [8]But we are of the day, and let us be sober by putting on the breastplate of faith and love and the helmet of hope for salvation. [9]For God has not destined us for wrath but to gain salvation through our Lord Jesus Christ, [10]who died for us so that whether we are alert or asleep, we may live together with him. [11]Therefore, encourage one another and build up each other just as you are doing.

FINAL ENCOURAGEMENT

[12]We ask you, brothers and sisters, to respect those who work among you and who preside over you in the Lord and admonish you [13]and to esteem them very highly in love because of their work. Be at peace among yourselves. [14]We encourage you, brothers and sisters, to admonish the disorderly, comfort the discouraged, help the weak, and be patient with them all. [15]See that no one returns evil for evil to anyone, but always seek to do good to one another and everyone. [16]Rejoice always; [17]pray without ceasing; [18]in all circumstances give thanks. For this is the will of God in Christ Jesus for you. [19]Do not suppress the Spirit. [20]Do not despise prophecies, [21]but test everything and hold tightly to what is good. [22]Abstain from every form of evil.

4:15 The phrase *for we tell you this by the word of the Lord* is meant to distinguish what follows from Paul's own thoughts. It effectively draws attention to the following words as inspired counsel. The technical usage of *the word of the Lord* is found in Genesis 15:1. **4:15, 17** The Joseph Smith Translation changes these two passages so that rather than referring to Paul and his fellow saints in the first-person plural (*we*), the passages are rendered as predictions of the future and *those who remain*. **4:16–17** Alluded to in Doctrine and Covenants 45:45. **4:17** Compare Doctrine and Covenants 109:75.

5:1, 4, 12, 14, 25–27 Greek uses *brothers* generically to refer to *brothers and sisters*. **5:2** The allusion to the Lord coming *as a thief in the night* is repeated in Doctrine and Covenants 45:19; 106:4. **5:3** *Peace and security* were part of Roman imperial propaganda to promote the rule of law. **5:4** The final sentence states in Greek *you are not in darkness for the day to seize you like a thief*, but the English translation has been rendered as a negative statement to clarify the meaning. Alluded to in Doctrine and Covenants 106:5. **5:5** Compare John 12:35–36, which provides counsel on becoming *children of the light*. **5:8** An allusion to Isaiah 59:17. Compare Ephesians 6:11–18. **5:9** Compare 1 Thessalonians 1:10.

²³May the God of peace make you completely holy, and may your spirit, soul, and body be kept blameless for the coming of our Lord Jesus Christ. ²⁴The one who calls you is faithful, and he will accomplish this. ²⁵Brothers and sisters, pray for us as well.

²⁶Greet all the brothers and sisters with a holy kiss. ²⁷I solemnly charge you by the Lord that this letter be read to all the brothers and sisters. ²⁸May the grace of our Lord Jesus Christ be with you. Amen.

5:23 Paul recognizes the tripartite identity of humanity: *body*, *soul*, and *spirit*. Doctrine and Covenants 88:15 adds that the spirit and body are the soul of a person. These two different views are not opposed to one another. Paul's statement appears to be a statement of the constitution of human existence, whereas the Doctrine and Covenants appears to be a purpose statement, the body and soul work together to become the soul of a person. **5:26** A *kiss* was a common form of greeting and salutation in the Greco-Roman world (Romans 16:16; 1 Corinthians 16:20) and may have been part of the way that Christians identified one another. **5:27** A number of early and reliable manuscripts read *holy brothers and sisters*. A decision as to which reading is original is difficult in this situation, although the evidence tends to favor its omission.

2 THESSALONIANS

AUTHOR

Paul and two of his traveling companions, Silvanus and Timothy, are listed as authors of this short epistle to the saints living in the Greek-speaking community located in Thessalonica (1:1). To what extent Paul is the sole author is unknown, and the letter reportedly provides counsel from all three leaders equally. The letter was penned shortly after the first letter was written, but news of a new and emerging problem had reached Paul (3:11).

The letter bears a striking resemblance to 1 Thessalonians, and the two letters are clearly written in close chronological proximity to one another, a fact demonstrated by the shared structure and similarity of expression. The sequence of events appears to be that Paul had departed from Thessalonica during his second missionary journey and that shortly after his departure he wrote 1 Thessalonians. Later, upon learning of problems among the members regarding idleness and other issues, Paul wrote a short letter hoping to settle the problem. Part of the issue appears to be that some had expected the return of the Lord would take place shortly (2:1–12), and Paul attempted to assure them that there were some events that would still take place prior to the Second Coming.

PURPOSE OF WRITING

This letter is not a treatise on a doctrinal theme or concept, but it is a short directive that intentionally encourages the saints to live in harmony. The saints had continued to face persecution, but Paul does not indicate the source of the persecution. The language of wrath and punishment in the context of trial and affliction (1:3–12) suggests that the problem was acute. The letter concludes with a lengthy section on idleness (3:6–15), and many commentators have suggested that some members of the community had ceased working in anticipation of the Second Coming of the Lord. This may represent the historical situation in Thessalonica, but it may also represent the fact that some members of the community wished to receive financial support from other members of the community. Early Christian communities were eager to offer financial support to widows and others, and some may have taken advantage of that support.

CONNECTION TO LATTER-DAY SAINT BELIEFS

Perhaps the most important link to this letter for Latter-day Saints is the conceptualization of the apostasy or rebellion that would occur before the return of the Lord. Paul specifically mentions that in the coming days there will be a rebellion or mutiny among the members, the two most common translations of the word *apostasy*. The recipients of the letter would have received such counsel as a warning against internal dissension and discord because the word used by Paul insinuates internal strife. Latter-day revelation has drawn attention to this concept as a building block for the necessity of the Restoration of the gospel and to explain how precious truths have been lost. ❧

Opening Address

1 [1]Paul, Silvanus, and Timothy to the church of the Thessalonians in God our Father and Lord Jesus Christ. [2]Grace and peace to you from God our Father and the Lord Jesus Christ. [3]We must thank God for you always, brothers and sisters, which is right to do because your faith is growing and each person's love for one another is growing. [4]Therefore, we boast about you in the churches of God for your endurance and faith in all kinds of trials and afflictions that you are enduring.

The Coming Judgment

[5]This is evidence of a righteous judgment of God and for the purpose of making you worthy of the kingdom of God, for which you suffer. [6]For it is just of God to repay those who trouble you with affliction [7]and to provide relief to the afflicted and to us when the Lord Jesus is revealed from heaven with his mighty angels, [8]in flaming fire, inflicting vengeance on those who do not know God and who do not obey the gospel of our Lord Jesus. [9]These ones will pay the price of eternal destruction, being separated from the presence of the Lord and from the glory of his might [10]when he comes to be glorified by his saints and marveled at by all those who believe because you believed our witness on that day. [11]For this we pray for you always so that our God will make you worthy of his call-ing and fulfill every good desire and work of faith by his power [12]so that the name of our Lord Jesus Christ may be glorified among you, and you in him, according to the grace of our God and the Lord Jesus Christ.

The Day of the Lord: Apostasy

2 [1]We ask you, brothers and sisters, re-garding the coming of our Lord Jesus Christ and our being gathered together to him, [2]not to be quickly disturbed in mind or alarmed by a spirit, word, or letter as though from us to the effect that the day of the Lord is already here. [3]Let no one de-ceive you by any means, because that day will not come until the apostasy comes first and the man of lawlessness, who is the son of perdition, is revealed. [4]He sets himself in opposition and raises himself up above every so-called god or object of worship so that he sits in the temple of God declaring himself to be God. [5]Do you not remember that when I was with you I told you about these things? [6]And now you know what holds him back so that he will be revealed in his own time. [7]For the mystery of lawlessness is already at work, but the one who restrains him will do so until he is taken out of the way, [8]and then the lawless one will be revealed, whom the Lord Jesus will destroy by the word of his mouth, abolishing him by the presence of his coming. [9]The coming of the lawless one is made clear in the works of Satan in all

---

1:3 Greek uses *brothers* generically to refer to *brothers and sisters*. **1:4** These events are described in part in Acts 17:1–13. **1:8** An allusion to the fulfillment of Jeremiah 10:25. **1:9** An allusion to Isaiah 2:10, 19, 21. **1:10** A possible allusion to Isaiah 66:5. The passive construction, *our witness was believed by you on that day*, has been changed into an indicative construction to make the meaning clearer.

2:1, 13, 15 Greek uses *brothers* generically to refer to *brothers and sisters*. **2:3** The word *apostasy* in Greek refers to a *rebellion* or *mutiny*. Paul appears to be hinting at a rebellion in the church when there would be a division, fight, or apostasy of its members. *The man of lawlessness* is in some early manuscripts *the man of sin*. The better manuscripts read *lawlessness*, which is likely the original reading. *The son of perdition* is *the son of destruction* (the same title is used of Judas Iscariot in John 17:12). Latter-day Saint vocabulary has favored the word *perdition*, and the word fundamentally means *lost to destruction*. **2:4** An allusion to Isaiah 14:13–14; Daniel 11:36. **2:9** The Joseph Smith Translation reads *Yea, the Lord, even Jesus, whose coming is not until after there cometh a falling away, by the working of Satan with all power and signs and lying wonders.*

power, signs, and false miracles [10]and with every kind of wicked deception aimed at those who are perishing because they rejected the love of the truth that would save them. [11]Because of this, God sends a powerful delusion to them so that they believe what is false [12]and so that all of them who have not believed the truth and have enjoyed wickedness will be judged.

AN ETERNAL COMFORT

[13]We must always give thanks to God for you, brothers and sisters, beloved by the Lord, because from the beginning God chose you for salvation through being made holy by the Spirit and faith in the truth. [14]He called you through our gospel for this purpose so that you may possess the glory of our Lord Jesus Christ. [15]Therefore, brothers and sisters, stand firm and hold tightly to the things that you have been taught by us, whether by speech or by letter. [16]And may our Lord Jesus Christ himself and God our Father, who loved us and gave us an eternal comfort and good hope through grace, [17]comfort your hearts and strengthen you in every good work and word.

PRAY FOR US

3 [1]Finally, brothers and sisters, pray for us so that the word of the Lord may spread quickly and be glorified just as it was among you [2]so that we may be delivered from wicked and evil people, for not everyone has faith. [3]The Lord is faithful; he strengthens us and guards us from evil. [4]We are confident in the Lord concerning you, that you are doing and will continue to do the things we command. [5]May the Lord direct your hearts to the love of God and to the patience of Christ.

WARNING ABOUT IDLENESS

[6]Now, we command you, brothers and sisters, in the name of our Lord Jesus Christ, to stay away from a brother or sister who lives in idleness and not according to the tradition received from us. [7]For you know how you ought to imitate us, because we have not been idle when we were among you, [8]and we did not eat anyone's bread without paying for it, but in toil and labor, night and day, we worked so that we would not be a burden for any of you, [9]not because we did not have the right but so that we might be an example for you to imitate. [10]For even when we were with you, we gave you this instruction, that if anyone did not want to work he should not eat. [11]For we hear that some live among you without working, not actually working but nearly working. [12]In the Lord Jesus Christ we command and exhort such people to work in silence and eat their own bread. [13]But you, brothers and sisters, do not be weary in doing good. [14]But if any-

---

2:13 Some manuscripts read *firstfruits* in place of *from the beginning*. It is unlikely that Paul would refer to the saints in Thessalonica as the *firstfruits* in the gospel. Instead, given the context, it seems more likely that he was speaking specifically to those who accepted the gospel on his first missionary visit to the city. The manuscript evidence supports the reading provided in the translation. 2:16 *Comfort* can also be translated as *calling*, but its usage in the next verse suggests that the intended meaning is *comfort*.

3:1, 6, 13 Greek uses *brothers* generically to refer to *brothers and sisters*. 3:5 The verse may also be translated as *may the Lord direct your hearts to God's love and to Christ's endurance*. The meaning of the verse would, as a result, be significantly different. If this translation is adopted, then the meaning would be for the believer to look to God's love as an example and to Christ's act of endurance, perhaps in reference to his sacrifice in Gethsemane. 3:6 Some later manuscripts add *you received (from us)*. Alma 1:24 reads *withdraw themselves from among them*, perhaps echoing this concept. 3:11 *Without working* can also be translated as *in idleness*. There is a play on words in Greek at the end of the verse, which is difficult to render into English. The meaning is close to *not working but near-working*. 3:13 Compare Galatians 6:9 for a similar injunction.

2 THESSALONIANS 3 | 377

one does not obey our instruction through this letter, take note of that person, and do not associate with him so that he may be ashamed. [15]Do not consider him an enemy, but exhort him as a brother.

CONCLUDING REMARKS

[16]May the Lord of peace himself give you peace at all times and in every way. May the Lord be with you all. [17]I, Paul, wrote this greeting with my own hand, which is a sign in every letter that I write. [18]The grace of our Lord Jesus Christ be with you all.

3:16 Perhaps an allusion to Isaiah 9:6. **3:17** A number of other letters contain similar personal indicators of authorship (1 Corinthians 16:21; Galatians 6:11; Colossians 4:18).

1 TIMOTHY

AUTHOR

Paul writes to Timothy as "an apostle of Jesus Christ" (1:1), and in the letter he adopts the tone of both a friend and an ecclesiastical leader. Paul penned three such personal letters—a fourth personal letter (Philemon) is not grouped with these three because it does not deal with matters of church practice and governance. These three have generally been grouped together and referred to as the "Pastoral Epistles." Each of these epistles, 1–2 Timothy and Titus, discusses matters of church practice such as the calling of bishops and elders, and each also conveys personal counsel to the recipients.

In the modern era, scholars began questioning the authorship of the Pastoral Epistles because they use a significant number of words that are not found in Paul's other letters, they all seem to describe events that took place after Acts 28, and the style of writing is markedly different from Paul's other writings. However, each of the three letters also specifically refers to Paul as author. Bound up with this question of authorship is the question of authority and importance if someone wrote the letters in Paul's name. In other words, in the modern world, writing in someone else's name is considered forgery. Despite the objections, which are genuine, the letters do not advance a markedly different doctrinal position from Paul's other letters, although they do share different perspectives. The reason for this may be that someone gathered Paul's known writings and composed these on behalf of Paul, or even under his direction. One reasonable solution is to accept them as representations of what Paul counseled Timothy and Titus to do, while noting that he did not likely write them in the same way he wrote his other letters.

PURPOSE OF WRITING

The most explicit purpose of all three pastoral letters is to aid Timothy and Titus in their efforts to fend off false teachings and to call ecclesiastical leaders. According to the few historical reminiscences that remain, the letters assert that Paul had left Timothy in Ephesus while he traveled to Macedonia (1:3), and Paul feared that he would not return to Ephesus in the near future (3:14–15). Titus was left alone in Crete, but he was encouraged to visit Paul in Nicopolis for the winter (Titus 1:5). Both of these situations appear to describe events after Acts had concluded its retelling of Paul's life.

According to Acts, Timothy was born to a Greek father and Jewish Christian mother (Acts 16:1), and the pastoral letters indicate that he had been taught from the Old Testament (2 Timothy 1:5; 3:15). During Paul's second missionary journey, Timothy taught in Macedonia and Greece (Acts 17:14–15; 18:5; 19:22), and he traveled from Ephesus to Macedonia to Corinth (Acts 20:1–6). Furthermore, Philippians 1:1 and Philemon 1:1 may indicate that Timothy was with Paul during his Roman imprisonment. In his letter to the Romans, Paul indicated that if the opportunity arose he intended to travel to Spain after visiting Rome (Romans 15:23–29). Ultimately, the historical situation described in the letters matches some events described in Paul's letters, but they seem to come from a later time, and perhaps Paul was released from his Roman imprisonment and then returned to Greece and Crete to further his missionary efforts in those regions.

Much of 1 Timothy deals with the problem of false teaching (1:3–7; 4:1–8; 6:3–5), but the challenge of calling church leaders is also mentioned (3:1–13; 5:17–25). These topics would suggest that Timothy was young in his faith or in need of counsel on these topics. First Timothy 1:12–20 also contains a powerful reflection on Paul's time as a persecutor of the Christian faith. In sharing that story with Timothy, he may have been suggesting that his opponents could likewise turn around from their opposition to the faith.

CONNECTION TO LATTER-DAY SAINT BELIEFS

The Pastoral Epistles have not been overtly influential in the Restoration, but Latter-day Saints will find in them support for the sixth article of faith: "We believe in the same organization that existed in the Primitive Church, namely, apostles, prophets, pastors, teachers, evangelists, and so forth." These letters provide information about the organization of the early church. They indicate that bishops worked in conjunction with elders and deacons, and they provide information about how bishops were encouraged to conduct themselves among the saints. ⁊

OPENING ADDRESS

1 [1]Paul, an apostle of Christ Jesus according to the command of God our Savior and Christ Jesus our hope, [2]to Timothy, my genuine child in the faith: grace, mercy, and peace from God the Father and Christ Jesus our Lord.

WARNING

[3]Just as I entreated you to remain in Ephesus while I traveled to Macedonia, I urge you to instruct certain people not to spread false teachings [4]or to pay attention to myths and endless genealogies that raise questions rather than the redemptive plan of God that is in faith. [5]But the purpose of our message is love from a pure heart and a good conscience and sincere faith. [6]Some have strayed from these things and have turned toward vain discussion, [7]wanting to be teachers of the Law, not understanding what they are saying or the things they confidently assert.

[8]We know that the Law is good if someone lives it properly [9]because we know this, that the Law is not set up for a just person but for the lawless and the disobedient, for the ungodly and sinners, for the unholy and profane, for those who kill fathers or mothers, for murderers, [10]for the sexually immoral, sodomites, kidnappers, liars, perjurers, and whatever else is opposed to sound teaching, [11]in accordance with the glorious gospel of the blessed God, with which I was entrusted.

A FORMER PERSECUTOR

[12]I am thankful to the one who strengthened me in this, our Lord Christ Jesus, because he considered me to be faithful by appointing me to the ministry, [13]although I was formerly a blasphemer, persecutor, and a prideful man. But I received mercy because I acted without faith, [14]and the grace of our Lord was abundant for me, with faith and love that was in Christ Jesus. [15]This saying is trustworthy and worthy of full acceptance, "Christ Jesus came into the world to save sinners, of which I am the foremost!" [16]Because of this I received mercy so that Christ Jesus would show in me, the foremost sinner, his perfect patience as an example for those who would believe in him for eternal life. [17]To the eternal king, the immortal, unseen and

---

1:1 God is rarely called our *Savior*, but 1–2 Timothy and Titus do so six times (Luke 1:47; 1 Timothy 2:3; 4:10; Titus 1:3; 2:10; 3:4; Jude 1:25). **1:2** For *Timothy*, see Acts 16:1–4; 1 Corinthians 4:17. **1:3** The command given to Timothy in this verse does not fit easily into Paul's life as described in the book of Acts. Many have supposed, therefore, that this event describes Paul's actions after he traveled to Rome and possibly after his first Roman imprisonment. **1:4** The reference to *endless genealogies* has caused some scholars to suggest that the letter is confronting the heresy of Gnosticism. In verse 7, however, the same individuals hope to be teachers of the Law, and therefore the problem appears to be more nuanced. These individuals, whoever they may have been, were interested in promoting the law of Moses, speculating about *genealogies* (probably from the Old Testament, or perhaps Jesus's own genealogy), and they taught things referred to as *myths*. For information on Gnosticism, see 1 Timothy 6:20 and note. **1:6** *Vain discussion* is also *empty discussion*. **1:7** The *Law* probably refers to the law of Moses (see verse 8). **1:10** *Sodomites* refers specifically to the dominant male in same-sex sexual activity. It seems to derive from the practice of male prostitution. **1:11** This verse follows the thought expressed in verse 8. **1:12** *The ministry* can also be translated as *the service*. The Greek noun is in other contexts translated as *deacon* and describes the primary service of a deacon, or one who serves the church. **1:13** For Paul to refer to himself as a *blasphemer* makes little sense. He may have blasphemed Jesus's name prior to his conversion (Acts 26:9), but the general categorization of his actions as blasphemy is not found in his other descriptions of his earlier beliefs and practices. **1:17** *And only* is *and wise* in some early manuscripts. The earliest and best manuscripts read *only*, and the change to *wise* may have arisen from the parallel in Romans 16:27.

only God, honor and glory forever and ever. Amen.

[18]This charge I give to you, my son, Timothy, according to the prophecies given about you, that being encouraged by them you may fight the good fight, [19]having faith and a good conscience. Some have rejected their conscience and thereby suffered a shipwreck with their faith, [20]some of whom are Hymenaeus and Alexander, whom I have delivered to Satan so that they may learn not to blaspheme.

COUNSEL ON PRAYER

2 [1]First of all, I urge that entreaties, prayers, petitions, and thanks be made on behalf of all people, [2]on behalf of kings and all those who are in positions of authority, so that we may live a peaceful and quiet life, godly and respectable in every way. [3]This is good and acceptable in the presence of God our Savior, [4]who desires that all people are saved and that they may come to a knowledge of the truth. [5]For there is one God and one intermediary between God and humanity, the human Christ Jesus, [6]who gave himself as a ransom for all, as a testimony at the proper time. [7]For this purpose I was appointed as a preacher and apostle (I am telling the truth; I am not lying), a teacher of the Gentiles in faith and truth.

[8]Therefore, I want the men in every place to pray, lifting up holy hands without anger or dispute. [9]Likewise, the women are to dress in appropriate dress with modesty and moderation, not with braided hair, gold, pearls, and expensive clothing. [10]But they should dress with what is proper for women who profess piety—with good works. [11]A woman must learn in quietness and all obedience. [12]I do not allow a woman to teach nor to govern a man; she is to be silent. [13]For Adam was created first

---

1:18 The *prophecies* spoken to Timothy are also mentioned in 1 Timothy 4:14. Alma 1:1 reads *wars a good warfare.* **1:19** *Their* has been added before *conscience* to help clarify the meaning. It appears that they have rejected the promptings of their own conscience. **1:20** Being *delivered to Satan* is a metaphor to describe the distancing or temporary excommunication of an individual from the body of the saints in order to provide the individual a time to repent (see 1 Corinthians 5:5). Little is known about how this practice was administered or how it was decided upon. The terminology was also used in the early days of the Restoration (Doctrine and Covenants 78:12; 104:9–10). Little is known about *Hymenaeus and Alexander* (see 2 Timothy 2:17).

2:1–2 These verses are a request for Rome in particular to maintain the public peace so that the saints may continue to thrive and grow. **2:3** For *God our Savior,* see 1 Timothy 1:2. **2:5** The emphasis in the Greek sentence is to draw attention to the mortality of Jesus Christ and not his gender. Many translations choose to render the final phrase *the man Christ Jesus,* but the word choice reflects a contrast with divinity, and therefore *human* is a better choice. **2:6** The word *ransom* reflects the idea that Jesus paid a price for sin by offering himself in place of what the law of Moses would require as a suitable offering for sin. **2:7** *Preacher and apostle* could also be translated as *herald and missionary.* **2:8** Some manuscripts read *to pray in Christ,* but the majority of early and reliable manuscripts omit this addition. Alluded to in Doctrine and Covenants 60:7. **2:8–10** These verses contain teachings that are problematic for the modern reader because they reflect older cultural attitudes about hairstyles (*braided hair*) and certain types of jewelry. The emphasis of verse 10 presents a contrast to the counsel on proper attire, when Paul notes that a woman should wear the attire of *good works.* **2:11–15** These teachings are tied to a historical situation that is no longer known or understood. It remains unclear why Paul would instruct women to remain silent and to learn in *all obedience.* From the tone of the verses, it appears that Paul was attempting to settle a dispute in the community, although these verses may represent common cultural attitudes. The fact that Paul uses the sequence of Eve's creation as an argument that she is inferior to Adam does not represent the Genesis account or other scriptural teachings (compare 1 Corinthians 14:34–35).

and then Eve. [14]Adam was not deceived, but the woman was deceived and became a transgressor. [15]She will be saved in bearing children if she remains in faith, love, and holiness with self-control.

THE CALLING OF BISHOPS

3 [1]The saying is true, "If someone desires the office of bishop, that person desires a good work." [2]Therefore, a bishop must be above reproach, the husband of one woman, clear thinking, self-controlled, respectable, hospitable, a capable teacher, [3]not inclined to being drunk, not violent but gentle, not argumentative, not a person who loves money. [4]He must establish his own household well, keeping his children submissive while maintaining complete dignity [5](if a person does not know how to establish his own household, how will that person care for the church of God?). [6]He should not be a recent convert, so that he does not become arrogant and fall into the condemnation of the devil. [7]Those outside the church must hold him in good standing so that he may not fall into disgrace and into the trap of the devil.

QUALIFICATIONS FOR DEACONS

[8]Deacons must also be dignified, not deceitful, not inclined to too much wine, not greedy for profits, [9]holding to the mystery of the faith with a clear conscience. [10]And they ought to be tested first, and then let them serve as deacons after they are proven blameless. [11]Their wives must also be dignified, not slanderers, self-controlled, faithful in all things. [12]Deacons must be the husbands of one wife, managing well their children and their own households. [13]For those who have served well as deacons place themselves in good standing and great boldness in the faith that is in Christ Jesus.

THE MYSTERY OF GODLINESS

[14]I write these things to you while hoping to come to you soon, [15]and if I am delayed, you may know how one ought to act in the household of God, which is the church of the living God, a pillar and foundation of the truth. [16]We agree that the mystery of godliness is great:

He was revealed in the flesh,
vindicated by the Spirit

2:14 The word translated as *transgressor* is different from the usual word for *sinner*. This word signifies someone who disregards the law of the Lord and who transgresses the commandments while conscious of it being a sinful action.

3:1 It remains unclear if Paul is citing a commonly held belief or if he is the author of the saying. The structure of the Greek suggests that it is a quotation, although it could equally refer to the statement in 1 Timothy 2:15. A *bishop* is literally an *overseer*. **3:2** *Hospitality* was an important attribute according to ancient societies (see also Romans 12:13). **3:5** This verse appears to be the basis for the instruction given in Doctrine and Covenants 93:43. **3:7** The concern regarding what *outsiders* will think about Christian bishops may indicate growth in the church and greater visibility. **3:8** Most often the word *deacon* seems to refer simply to a servant. In a few instances, it appears to refer to an office (Romans 16:1; Philippians 1:1; 1 Timothy 3:8). **3:11** The deacons mentioned are married men, but the Greek may also refer to female deacons. The structure of the Greek makes it possible that female deacons must have the qualities outlined in verses 11–13. Modern readers will undoubtedly think of *deacon* as a priesthood office and therefore as a male-only calling. The primary meaning of the word *deacon* is servant or one who serves others, and therefore female deacons were likely as common as male deacons. The callings held by female deacons in the local branches could have been described under the general term *deaconess*. **3:16** Or *vindicated in spirit*. This verse is often considered to be a hymn fragment (for example, see Philippians 2:6–11 and note) that Paul quoted. Nothing is known of its origin or authorship. Doctrine and Covenants 19:10 offers commentary upon the meaning of *the mystery of godliness*. Similar teachings are found

seen by angels,
proclaimed among the nations,
believed on in the world,
taken up in glory.

ASCETIC TENDENCIES AMONG BELIEVERS

4 ¹And the Spirit explicitly says that in the latter days some will depart from the faith and will devote themselves to deceiving spirits and the teachings of demons, ²following the hypocrisy of liars whose consciences are seared. ³They forbid marriage and abstain from some foods that God has created to be received with thanksgiving by those who believe and know the truth. ⁴For every creation of God is good, and nothing is to be rejected if it is received with thanksgiving. ⁵For it is made holy through God's word and prayer.

BE AN EXAMPLE

⁶By presenting these things to the brothers and sisters, you will be a good minister of Christ Jesus, being nourished by the words of faith and the good teachings that you have followed. ⁷But reject those myths of the ungodly and gullible. Train yourself for piety. ⁸For "bodily exercise is of little value, but godliness is valuable in every way because it has the promise of life now and in the future." ⁹This saying is trustworthy and worthy of all acceptance. ¹⁰For this is why we toil and struggle, because we have hope in the living God, who is the Savior of all humanity, especially for those who believe.

¹¹Command and teach these things. ¹²Do not permit anyone to look down on you because you are young, but be an example to the believers in speech, in conduct, in love, in faith, and in purity. ¹³Until I come, pay attention to reading scripture publicly, to exhortation, and to teaching. ¹⁴Do not neglect your spiritual gift which was given to you through prophecy by means of the laying on of hands by the elders. ¹⁵Pay attention to these things; commit yourself to them so that your progress may be visible to everyone. ¹⁶Pay attention to yourself and to the content of what you teach. Continue doing this, and you and those who listen to you will be saved.

---

in 1 Nephi 10:11, and a summary of Jesus Christ's mortal ministry is found in that verse (also 2 Nephi 6:9). The hymn contains a synopsis of what the early saints believed.

4:1 Compare Doctrine and Covenants 46:7. **4:3** Doctrine and Covenants 49:15, 18–19 offers commentary on those who forbid to marry and who forbid to eat certain foods. These concerns represent a shift toward idealizing asceticism, or rigorous physical practices that define Christian identity and belief. **4:6** Greek uses *brothers* generically to refer to *brothers* and *sisters*. The word translated as *minister* is the Greek word *deacon*, but it appears to be used here in a general sense. **4:7** *Gullible* is literally *relating to elderly women*, which the author uses as a negative stereotype to describe those who would believe unsubstantiated stories. The word *train yourself* is built from the Greek verb referring to athletic training and physical fitness. **4:8** This saying (referred to as a saying in verse 9) is from an unknown source, perhaps coming directly from Paul but also possibly from a source. **4:12** Timothy's youth solicits a comment from the author because it is implied that Timothy has been treated differently as a result. The Greek term cannot be used to identify a specific age but only that he is considerably younger than Paul. This would also indicate a time earlier in Paul's ministry (see note on 1 Timothy 1:3). **4:13** The text does not mention *reading scripture publicly* but only *reading scripture*. The verse describes an early Christian meeting practice where a scriptural text was read and then commented upon. Private reading was not a common feature of early Christian life and practice, and at least one early commentator noted that those who read privately were suspicious. **4:14** The text mentions laying on of hands by the *elder*, referring to the council of elders or quorum of elders. Doctrine and Covenants 49:14 and 76:52 as well as article of faith 3 refer to the practice of laying on of hands.

GENERAL COUNSEL

5 ¹Do not rebuke an older man, but encourage him like a father. Treat young men as brothers, ²older women as mothers, young women as sisters, and treat everyone with purity.

³Honor widows who are truly widows. ⁴But if a widow has children or grandchildren, they should first learn to live their religion in their household and thereby make some repayment to their parents. For this is pleasing before God. ⁵And the woman who is truly a widow and completely alone has hoped in God and continues in appeals and prayers night and day. ⁶But the widow who lives for pleasure is dead even while alive. ⁷Declare these teachings so that they will be blameless. ⁸But if someone does not provide for his own, especially those of his own household, he has denied the faith and is worse than an unbeliever.

⁹A widow should not be enrolled if she is under sixty years of age. She must have been the wife of one husband ¹⁰and have a reputation of good works: if she raised children, if she showed hospitality, if she washed the feet of the saints, assisted those in distress, and pursued every kind of good work. ¹¹But do not permit younger widows to enroll because their sexual desires lead them away from Christ and they want to marry ¹²and so incur judgment for casting aside their first faith. ¹³And at the same time they wander from house to house learning to be idle, and not only that but they learn to be gossipers and busybodies, saying things that are not theirs to discuss. ¹⁴Therefore, I want the younger women to marry, raise children, and manage a household in order not to give the adversary an opportunity to revile us. ¹⁵For some have wandered away after Satan. ¹⁶If a believing woman has widows in her household, let her assist them so that the church is not burdened so that it may help those who are really in need.

¹⁷The elders who lead well are worthy of a double honor, especially those who labor in speaking and teaching. ¹⁸For the scripture says, *"Do not muzzle an ox while it is treading out the grain,"* and *"The laborer is worthy of his pay."* ¹⁹Never accept any charge against an elder except on the evidence of two or three witnesses. ²⁰Those who continue to sin must be rebuked before all, so that the others may stand in fear. ²¹In the presence of God and Christ Jesus and the elect angels, I charge you to obey these instructions without partiality or favoritism. ²²Do not ordain anyone hastily or share in another person's sins. Keep yourself pure.

²³Do not drink water only, but use a little wine for the sake of your stomach and because of your frequent illnesses. ²⁴The sins of some people are conspicuous, going before them to judgment, but for some their sins follow them to judgment. ²⁵Likewise, good works are conspicuous, and even when they are not they cannot be hidden.

5:3 The word *honor* implies both honor and respect as well as offering financial assistance. The instructions to care for widows may have been based on the teachings of Deuteronomy 24:17–22. The practice was begun in Acts 6:1–6. **5:4** *Live their religion* is to fulfill their religious duty. **5:8** A person's *household* includes everyone in the house, including extended family, married children, and servants. **5:9** The early church cared for the widows financially, and women were enrolled into this program. Paul provides an outline of requirements for those who can be enrolled. **5:11–12** The widows were required to remain celibate and unmarried in order to remain under the church's care. **5:18** Quotation from Deuteronomy 25:4 and Luke 10:7. **5:19** An allusion to Deuteronomy 17:6; 19:15. **5:22** *Do not ordain* is literally *do not lay hands on.* The issue seems to be hasty ordinations, but it could refer to hasty blessings as well.

6 ¹All those who are under the yoke as slaves should regard their own masters as worthy of all honor so that the name of God and our teaching are not slandered. ²But those who have believing masters should not be disrespectful to them because they are brothers, but rather they should serve them all the more because those who benefit from their service are believers and beloved.

CONTEND FOR THE FAITH

Teach these things and exhort them. ³If someone teaches otherwise and does not agree with the sound words of our Lord Jesus Christ and with the teaching that is according to godliness, ⁴he is conceited and understands nothing but has a fascination with controversy and verbal disputes, from which come envy, contention, slander, evil suspicions, ⁵and arguments among those who are corrupt in their mind, devoid of the truth, thinking that godliness is a means of turning a profit. ⁶There is great profit in godliness combined with being content. ⁷For we brought nothing into the world, so we cannot take anything out of it. ⁸But we have food and shelter, with which we will be satisfied. ⁹Those who desire to be rich fall into temptation and are ensnared by many senseless and damaging desires that plunge them into ruin and destruction. ¹⁰For the love of money is the root of all evil, and in their yearning to be rich some have wandered from the faith and they have pierced themselves with many sorrows.

¹¹But as a person of God, flee from these things, and pursue instead righteousness, godliness, faith, love, patience, and kindness. ¹²Contend for the good fight of the faith; take hold of eternal life, to which you were called and about which you made your good confession before many witnesses. ¹³I encourage you before God, who gives life to all, and before Christ Jesus, who made his good confession before Pontius Pilate, ¹⁴to obey the commandments without spot or blame until the appearing of our Lord Jesus Christ, ¹⁵which he will show forth at the right time—the blessed and only Sovereign, the King of kings and Lord of lords, ¹⁶who alone has immortality, who lives in unapproachable light, whom no human has seen or is able to see. To him be honor and eternal power. Amen.

¹⁷Concerning the rich in this present age, charge them to not be proud or to set their hopes upon uncertain riches but on God, who richly provides for us in all things for our enjoyment. ¹⁸Charge them to do good, to be rich in good works, to be generous and sharing with others, ¹⁹thereby setting aside treasure for themselves as a good foundation for the future so that they will lay hold of what is truly life.

6:1–2 The counsel given to slaves is directed at individuals in a household who were servants to an estate. The practice was common in the Roman empire, and Paul's instruction was based on maintaining what he felt was a harmonious social order, especially in situations where the slave and master were both believers and therefore participation in church services could alter the dynamics of the household hierarchy. Such servitude should, however, be unequivocally condemned in the modern era. **6:2** The implication is that they are *brothers* in the faith of Christ. **6:5** Following the word *godliness*, some manuscripts add a parenthetical remark *stay away from such things*. This remark appears to have originated as a marginal note that eventually crept into the text in later copies, but it should be understood as a later addition. **6:10** Echoed in Doctrine and Covenants 1:3. **6:13** Doctrine and Covenants 88:17 may allude to this verse using the language of the King James Version. Pontius Pilate (26–36 CE) was the prefect of Judea when Jesus was crucified. **6:16** The Joseph Smith Translation alters this verse to allow for those who have *the light, and the hope of immortality* to see God. **6:19** Doctrine and Covenants 4:4 echoes this verse.

386 | 1 Timothy 6

CONCLUSION

[20]Timothy, guard what has been entrusted to you. Avoid the useless babbling and contradictions of what is falsely called knowledge, [21]which some have professed and have deviated from the faith as a result. Grace be with you all.

6:20 The word translated as *knowledge* (Greek *gnosis*) has often been linked with a second-century movement referred to in modern times as Gnosticism. The term, however, can refer to religious *knowledge* generally, to specific *knowledge* relating to Judaism, for example, or to an emphasis on *knowledge* needed for salvation. It remains unclear whether Paul was referring to a movement that can be defined as Gnosticism. It appears more likely that he was criticizing the rise in emphasis on *knowledge* as a means of salvation.

2 TIMOTHY

AUTHOR

The opening verse mentions that Paul was writing directly to his "beloved child" (1:2), sending Timothy a personal letter of instruction and encouragement to visit Paul for the upcoming winter season. Overall, Paul was lonely when he wrote, and he saw in Timothy an ally who would help him through his difficult circumstances. The historical events depicted in this letter do not fit easily within the framework of Acts or Paul's other letters, which has caused some scholars to question whether Paul wrote this letter. Scholars have also pointed out that the style of writing is different, and the author used phrases and terms that are different from Paul's other letters. The question of Paul's authorship cannot be settled simply. The ideas are closely connected with Paul's other writings, and the letter is a type of last will and testament written by Paul shortly before he passed away (4:13). Paul had faced an initial hearing of his case (4:16–18), and because of its results (4:6) he was not overly optimistic about the outcome.

Paul did not indicate his specific location, although Rome makes sense in the context of the variety of clues regarding a trial that could result in his death. The letter preserves a touching display of an aging missionary who sincerely desired that his final days be spent in companionship with a close and trusted friend.

PURPOSE OF WRITING

According to the few clues remaining in the letter, Paul had previously visited Troas (4:13), and he desired that Timothy would bring some items that he had left there. The request suggests that Paul had at some point spent a significant amount of time in Troas, perhaps describing events that occurred after Acts 28. After Paul's departure from Troas, some fellow missionaries had abandoned Paul (1:15; 4:9–12), and Paul mentions them by name. The peculiar wording of 4:10 hints that Demas had forsaken Paul but that others had departed from Paul for unspecified reasons, perhaps also deserting Paul. The extent of Paul's personal longing is felt in the phrase *only Luke is with me* (4:11). Paul was expecting to die (4:6–8) as a result of the charges made against him, and he saw Timothy and Luke as stalwart companions in faith.

There are numerous references to Timothy in Paul's letters, and reconstructing his travel is complicated. Timothy was with Paul in Philippians 2:19–24 when Paul was facing his first major Roman imprisonment. In that letter, Paul had wanted to go to Macedonia (Philippians 2:24), but there were already problems in Ephesus, which necessitated Paul's staying in Ephesus for some time. According to this letter, which seems to describe a different trip through the region, Paul had spent some time in Corinth and Miletus (4:20), both of which were cities visited at the end of the third mission. Given that this letter is a last will and testament, it is unimaginable that Paul viewed his future so uncertainly at the conclusion of that mission. This letter must describe a later visit to those cities and then a subsequent arrest and trial.

CONNECTION TO LATTER-DAY SAINT BELIEFS

The final chapter shows Paul's optimism about his eternal future, declaring, "I have competed well; I have finished the race; I have kept the faith. Finally, a crown of righteousness is reserved for me" (4:7–8). The language is influenced by athletic competition and hints at the concept of endurance and trial. Paul now looks forward to a glorious eternal life, which he has been awarded as a prize for a life of competition. The metaphor is important given Paul's earlier emphasis on grace, and here he connects works to grace unequivocally. A similar concept is found in the Book of Mormon: "For we know that it is by grace that we are saved, after all we can do" (2 Nephi 25:23). The language of 2 Timothy does not shape this Book of Mormon declaration, but the concepts are remarkably similar. ⸙

OPENING ADDRESS

1 ¹Paul, an apostle of Christ Jesus through the will of God according to the promise of life in Christ Jesus, ²to Timothy, my beloved child: grace, mercy, peace from God the Father and Christ Jesus our Lord.

THANKSGIVING

³I am thankful to God, whom I serve with a clear conscience as my ancestors did, when I remember you unceasingly in my prayers night and day. ⁴While remembering your tears, I desire to see you so that I may be filled with joy. ⁵I am reminded of your sincere faith, a faith that first resided in your grandmother Lois and your mother, Eunice. I am confident it now resides in you. ⁶Therefore, I remind you to rekindle the gift of God which is in you through the laying on of my hands, ⁷for God did not give us the spirit of cowardice but a spirit of power, love, and self-control.

⁸So do not be ashamed of testifying about our Lord, or about me his prisoner, but participate in the suffering of the gospel in the power of God, ⁹who saved us and called us by a holy calling, not according to our works but according to his own purpose and grace, which Christ Jesus gave to us before the ages began ¹⁰and now has appeared through the manifestation of our Savior Christ Jesus, who abolished death and brought life and immortality to light through the gospel, ¹¹for which I was appointed a preacher, apostle, and teacher. ¹²Because of this, in fact, I suffer these things, but I am not ashamed, for I know in whom I have believed, and I am convinced that he is able to protect what has been entrusted to me until that day. ¹³Hold to the example of sound words that you heard from me in faith and love which are in Christ Jesus. ¹⁴Guard the good that you have been entrusted with through the Holy Spirit who resides in us.

¹⁵You know that all who are in Asia have turned away from me, among whom are Phygelus and Hermogenes. ¹⁶May the Lord provide mercy to the house of Onesiphorus, because he often lifted me up and was not ashamed of my imprisonment, ¹⁷but when he arrived in Rome he sought me out eagerly and found me. ¹⁸May the Lord grant that he will find mercy from the Lord in that day! You know well how much service he rendered in Ephesus.

COUNSEL TO TIMOTHY

2 ¹Therefore, my child, be strong in the grace that is in Christ Jesus, ²and what you heard from me, accompanied by many

---

1:4 Acts 20:36–38 describes a tearful departure from Ephesus that may be in mind in this verse. **1:5** *Eunice* is mentioned in Acts 16:1 but not by name. **1:6** The wording of this sentence indicates that Paul bestowed a spiritual gift upon Timothy through the laying on of hands. **1:8** Paul was imprisoned when he wrote 2 Timothy but not when he wrote 1 Timothy. His personal situation has changed dramatically, but little is known of the historical details. The imprisonment is probably Roman (1 Timothy 4:17), and Paul seems to expect his own death (4:6–8). **1:9–10** These verses may preserve part of a sermon or early Christian liturgy. They differ in language and style from the surrounding verses and probably represent a core teaching that both Paul and Timothy knew well. **1:9** For Paul's emphasis on *works*, see Romans 3:28; Galatians 2:16. Echoed in 3 Nephi 26:5. **1:11** The word *apostle* in this verse is probably used in a generic sense to refer to Paul's work as a missionary, which is the primary meaning of the noun *apostle*. Some manuscripts add *of the Gentiles* following the word *teacher*. This seems to be a harmonization to 1 Timothy 2:7. **1:12** Perhaps an echo of Romans 1:16. **1:15** *Asia* would include Ephesus and the cities of the Roman province of Asia Minor visited on Paul's missionary travels (Miletus, Troas, etc.). **1:15–16** *Phygelus and Hermogenes* are otherwise unknown, but the house of *Onesiphorus* is mentioned also in 1 Timothy 4:16. These two groups appear to be opposing factions in a schism that took place, perhaps in Ephesus (see verse 18).

witnesses, entrust to faithful people who will be able to teach others as well. [3]Participate in suffering as a good soldier of Christ Jesus. [4]No one serving as a soldier gets entangled in the mundane concerns of life, but the soldier's concern is to please the one who recruited him. [5]And if someone is an athlete, he will not be crowned a victor if he does not compete by the rules. [6]A farmer who labors should receive the first portion of the crops. [7]Consider what I am saying, for the Lord will give you understanding in all things.

[8]Remember Jesus Christ, raised from the dead, a descendant of David—that is my gospel [9]for which I suffer, even to the point of imprisonment as a criminal. But the word of God is not bound. [10]Therefore, I endure all things for those who are chosen so that they may also obtain salvation with eternal glory in Christ Jesus. [11]The saying is trustworthy,

For if we died in him, we will also live with him,
[12]if we endure, we will also reign with him, if we deny him, he will also deny us,
[13]if we are without faith, he remains faithful, for he cannot deny himself.

[14]Remind them of these things and warn them before God not to argue over words, which does no good, but only destroys those who listen to it. [15]Be diligent to present yourself before God as a proven work beyond reproach, correctly explaining the word of truth. [16]Avoid useless babbling, for it will lead people to greater and greater impiety, [17]and their message will spread like gangrene, among whom are Hymenaeus and Philetus. [18]They have deviated from the truth, saying that the resurrection has already occurred, and they are overturning some people's faith. [19]However, God's firm foundation stands, having this seal: "*The Lord knows those who are his*," and "*Let everyone who names the name of the Lord depart from wickedness*."

[20]In a large house there are not only utensils of gold and silver but also of wood and clay, and some are used for distinguished purposes and some are used for mundane purposes. [21]Therefore, if someone cleanses himself from these things, he will be a vessel for distinguished purposes, dedicated for the use of the master of the house, prepared for every good work. [22]Flee from youthful desires and pursue righteousness, faith, love, and peace, with those who call on the Lord from a pure heart. [23]Have nothing to do with stupid and ignorant controversies, because you know they generate infighting. [24]And the Lord's servant must not be confrontational, but kind to everyone, an able teacher, patient, [25]correcting opponents with gentleness. Perhaps God will grant them the chance to repent and come to know the truth [26]and that they may escape the snare of the devil, where they have been held captive to do his will.

2:9 *As a criminal* signals Paul's disparagement of the charges made against him, but the word is generic and does little to clarify the charges that were made against Paul. **2:11–13** These verses preserve a hymn fragment from an otherwise unknown author (see Philippians 2:6–11). The composition is in the first-person plural, suggesting audience participation in the declarations made in the hymn. **2:14** The argument *over words* implies problems similar to those mentioned in 1 Timothy (1:3–7). Some later manuscripts read *before the Lord*, but *before God* is more widely attested. **2:17** For *Hymenaeus*, see 1 Timothy 1:20. **2:19** Quotation from Numbers 16:5. The second quotation combines elements from Isaiah 26:13 and Job 36:10. **2:22** For Timothy's age, see 1 Timothy 4:12. **2:25** Many translations favor *grant them repentance*, but this promotes the idea that God is responsible for their ability to repent. Such a translation, however, does accurately represent the noun form used in the Greek sentence.

DIFFICULT TIMES
IN THE LAST DAYS

3 ¹But know this, that difficult times will come in the last days. ²For people will be self-centered, lovers of money, boasters, arrogant, abusive, disobedient to parents, ungrateful, unholy, ³unloving, unbending, slanderers, without self-control, vicious, opposed to what is good, ⁴treacherous, reckless, conceited, loving pleasure rather than loving God, ⁵having a form of godliness but denying its power. Avoid such people. ⁶For among them are those who creep into houses and captivate weak women who are burdened with sins and led around by various passions, ⁷who are ever learning but are never able to arrive at a knowledge of the truth. ⁸Just as Jannes and Jambres opposed Moses, these men oppose the truth, men of corrupt minds and counterfeit faith. ⁹But they will not progress further, for their lack of understanding will be obvious to everyone, as it came to be for these two men.

¹⁰You have followed my teachings, my way of life, my conduct, my faith, my patience, my love, my endurance, ¹¹my persecutions, and my suffering that happened to me in Antioch, Iconium, and Lystra. What persecutions I endured! Yet the Lord delivered me from all of them. ¹²And all who desire to live a godly life in Christ Jesus will be persecuted. ¹³But wicked people and imposters will go from bad to worse, deceiving and being deceived. ¹⁴But for you, continue in what you have learned and believed, knowing from whom you learned ¹⁵and that from infancy you have known the sacred writings, which provide wisdom for salvation through faith in Christ Jesus. ¹⁶Every scripture is inspired by God and is useful for teaching, reproof, correction, and for instruction in righteousness, ¹⁷that the person of God may be complete, equipped for every good work.

TIMOTHY'S CHARGE

4 ¹I charge you before God and Christ Jesus, who will judge the living and the dead, and by his appearing and his kingdom—²proclaim the word, be ready in season or out of season, reprove, admonish, and exhort with complete patience and teaching. ³For the time is coming when people will not tolerate sound teaching but will follow their own desires, accumulating teachers for themselves because they have itching ears, ⁴and they turn away from listening to the truth and turn aside to myths. ⁵But as for you, always be circumspect, endure suffering, do the work of an evangelist, fulfill your service.

⁶For I am already being poured out as an offering, and the time for my departure is

---

3:5 A portion of this verse is quoted in Joseph Smith—History 1:19 following the wording of the King James translation. **3:8** *Jannes and Jambres* are the traditional names of the priests of Pharaoh who opposed Moses (see Exodus 7:11–12). Their names are not given in the Old Testament, but they are named in later pseudepigraphical texts such as *The Apocryphon of Jannes and Jambres the Magicians*. **3:9** Doctrine and Covenants 35:7; 63:15; 136:19 may echo this verse. **3:11** The persecutions that took place in these cities (*Psidian Antioch, Iconium, and Lystra*) are reported briefly in Acts 13:50–51; 14:5–6, 19–21. **3:15** *The sacred writings* refer to the scriptures, which in this verse would imply all the writings of the Old Testament and possibly some others that were also considered sacred (see note on verse 8). Paul indicates that when those texts are read *through faith in Christ Jesus*, they become valuable for salvation. **3:16** The idea that the scriptures are *inspired* arises from the idea that God breathed into them, as Paul describes them in this verse.

4:5 *Your service* can be translated as *your service as a deacon*. The meaning of the Greek word *evangelist* indicates that Paul was encouraging Timothy to preach the word as a missionary, proclaiming the gospel (see verse 2). An *evangelist* may have been a local missionary or one who was commissioned and sent out by a local community. **4:6** A similar sentiment is expressed in Philippians 2:17.

at hand. [7]I have competed well; I have finished the race; I have kept the faith. [8]Finally, a crown of righteousness is reserved for me, which the Lord, the righteous judge, will give me in that day, and not only to me but to all who love his appearing.

SOME HAVE FORSAKEN PAUL

[9]Make every effort to come to me quickly. [10]For Demas has deserted me because he loves the present age, and he traveled to Thessalonica, Crescens went to Galatia, and Titus to Dalmatia. [11]Only Luke is with me. Get Mark and bring him with you, for he is useful to me for the ministry. [12]I have sent Tychicus to Ephesus. [13]When you come, bring with you the cloak that I left in Troas with Carpus and also the scrolls and, above all, the parchments. [14]Alexander the coppersmith did me great harm; the Lord will repay him for his actions. [15]Be on guard regarding him, for he strongly opposed our message. [16]In my first defense, no one was with me, but everyone deserted me. May they not be held accountable. [17]But the Lord stood by me and strengthened me so that through me the message would be fully proclaimed for all the Gentiles to hear. I was delivered from the lion's mouth! [18]The Lord will deliver me from every evil action and bring me safely into his heavenly kingdom. To him be glory forever and ever. Amen.

CONCLUSION

[19]Greet Prisca and Aquila, and the household of Onesiphorus. [20]Erastus stayed in Corinth, and I left Trophimus ill in Miletus. [21]Make every effort to come before winter. Eubulus, Prudens, Linus, Claudius, and all the brothers and sisters greet you. [22]The Lord be with your spirit. Grace be with you.

4:8 Compare Doctrine and Covenants 25:15; 29:13. **4:10** The Greek construction can be translated to mean that *Demas, Crescens,* and *Titus* have all deserted Paul. The translation has opted for the meaning that Demas has deserted Paul and that the other two are simply away and not able to comfort Paul. Demas is mentioned in Colossians 4:14; Philemon 1:24. **4:11** *Mark* is mentioned in Colossians 4:10. **4:12** *Tychicus* is mentioned frequently in other letters (Acts 20:4; Ephesians 6:21; Colossians 4:7). **4:13** The *scrolls* and *parchments* probably are intended to refer to two different types of writing: one on papyrus and the other on animal skin. Parchment, made from animal skin, was generally more expensive to produce. Both could refer to sacred writings from early Christians or Old Testament writings. **4:14** An allusion to Psalm 28:4. Alexander's actions are described in Acts 19:33 (see 1 Timothy 1:20). **4:16** Paul's *first defense* may refer to his time in Caesarea Maritima (see Acts 25) or possibly Rome. **4:19** Prisca and Aquila are mentioned in Acts 18:18, 26; Romans 16:3; 1 Corinthians 16:19. **4:20** *Erastus* was apparently from Corinth (see Romans 16:23). For *Trophimus,* see Acts 20:4; 21:29. **4:21** Greek uses *brothers* generically to refer to *brothers and sisters.*

TITUS

AUTHOR

Paul refers to himself as "an apostle of Jesus Christ" in this letter (1:1), providing strong evidence that the letter is directly connected to Paul. The historical information provided in the letter regarding where Paul was at (Crete and Nicopolis), in addition to the author's use of terms and phraseology that are significantly different from Paul's other letters, have led scholars to suggest that this letter was not written personally by Paul but perhaps by a scribe. Others have rejected the notion that the letter is not from Paul, and they contend that the events described in the letter took place years after Luke wrote the end of Acts. If this is so, Paul was released from his Roman imprisonment and then he traveled back to Greece and Crete to do further missionary work there. Such a scenario is not unimaginable, but it remains difficult to conclude that the style of Greek in Titus was produced by the same person who wrote Romans, for example. Given that the letters do treat topics that are familiar from Paul's letters, it seems reasonable to conclude that however they were composed, whether through a scribe or someone else who gathered together Paul's personal letters to Titus to create this letter, that the thoughts and ideas are most likely Paul's from a period late in his life.

PURPOSE OF WRITING

When Paul left Antioch to travel to Jerusalem to seek input regarding the continued practice of circumcision (Acts 15:1), he took Titus with him (Galatians 2:1–3). Paul noted that he had not required Titus to be circumcised because he was a Gentile (Galatians 2:3–5), which was an important point of discussion at the conference. At least on some level, Paul was comfortable with Titus and appreciated him as a fellow missionary and traveling companion. Later, Titus was with Paul during the third missionary journey (2 Corinthians 2:12–13; 7:5–7; 8:6), and in this letter Paul wanted Titus to visit him in Nicopolis (3:12). Paul had left Titus in Crete (1:5), and therefore Paul had been there previously but had departed to do work in other places. Given this set of historical clues, it appears that Paul wanted Titus with him as Paul continued to preach the gospel in other cities and towns.

The reason for writing can be described both in positive and negative terms. There was a growing problem with false teachers and dissenters, some of whom taught circumcision (1:5, 10–11, 2:1–8, 15; 3:1–15). Specifically, Paul refers to those of the "circumcision faction" (1:10). Whether these were individuals within the church who insisted that all male members be circumcised or whether they were Jews who pressured Christians to be circumcised is unclear. Regardless, Paul saw them as a source of problems within the church. Paul is also reflective, stating, "For we were once foolish also, disobedient, led astray, enslaved to various passions and pleasures" (3:3). Paul occasionally reflected on his own life prior to Damascus, but this letter is unique in calling that old life "foolish, disobedient," and "led astray." Finally, the letter provides counsel on calling elders and bishops in the church (1:5–9). The counsel is brief, but it carries with it a powerful purpose statement that guides those who serve as bishops, "that he may be able to exhort with sound teaching and to correct those who contradict it" (1:9).

CONNECTION TO LATTER-DAY SAINT BELIEFS

This letter is important to Latter-day Saint belief and practice in two distinct ways. First, it helps provide a blueprint for the organization of the early church and for the calling of elders and bishops. Although the letter provides few details, it does seem to indicate that an elder should preside in every city and guide the affairs of the church there. Bishops are envisioned as teachers who would promote belief in Christ in sound ways. The second important connection is the testimony that Jesus Christ is Deity, "while we wait for the blessed hope and appearing of the glory of our great God and Savior, Jesus Christ" (2:13). This is one of the clearest statements in the New Testament that Jesus Christ is Deity. ⁊

OPENING ADDRESS

1 ¹Paul, a servant of God and an apostle of Jesus Christ for the faith of God's elect and knowledge of the truth, which is according to godliness, ²in hope of eternal life, which God, who does not lie, promised before time began. ³But he has now manifest his word in his own time through the preaching with which I have been entrusted according to the command of God our Savior. ⁴To Titus, my genuine child in common faith: grace and peace from God the Father and Christ Jesus our Savior.

TITUS'S MINISTRY IN CRETE

⁵This is why I left you in Crete, so that you might put the remaining matters in order and appoint elders in every town as I instructed you to do. ⁶An elder must be blameless, the husband of one woman, with faithful children who cannot be charged with unruly living and insubordination. ⁷For the bishop should be blameless as a steward of God, not arrogant, not prone to anger, not a drunk, not violent or greedy for gain, ⁸but hospitable, a lover of goodness, wise, righteous, holy, and self-controlled. ⁹He must hold firmly to the faithful word of God that has been taught so that he may be able to exhort with sound teaching and to correct those who contradict it.

¹⁰For there are many disobedient people, empty talkers and deceivers, especially those from the circumcision faction, ¹¹who must be reduced to silence because they turn entire households upside down, teaching what they should not be teaching for dishonest gain. ¹²One from among them, one of their own prophets, said "Cretans always lie, evil beasts, lazy gluttons." ¹³This testimony is true. For this reason, rebuke them sharply so that they may be healthy in the faith ¹⁴and not pay attention to Jewish myths and the commandments of people who turn away from the truth. ¹⁵All things are pure to the pure, but

---

1:1 *Elect* can also be translated as *chosen*. **1:4** *Titus* was a frequent traveling companion of Paul's, but his movements and travels are not well known. In this letter, Titus is in Crete (verse 5). He traveled with Paul to Jerusalem at the end of the first mission (Galatians 2:1), and Paul was deeply worried when Titus did not arrive in time on a planned trip to Corinth (2 Corinthians 7:6, 13–14). Titus also traveled to Dalmatia (2 Timothy 4:10), but the peculiar wording of that passage suggests that Titus may have become disaffected. **1:5** The wording suggests that Paul intended that an *elder* would remain in each city to direct the affairs of the church there. There is little evidence to suggest whether this was a result of small branches of the church or whether this was standard practice in all the areas where Paul visited. Titus is given instruction on calling bishops (verse 7). The hierarchical structure appears to be that of a bishop acting as an overseer-shepherd with the elders seeing to the affairs of the church in a local branch and deacons serving the most basic needs of the church. Paul mentions the act of *appointing* elders to serve. Older translations refer to this using the verb *ordain*. The meaning of the word is to *establish, set up*, or even to *place in order*. **1:6** The Greek construction of this verse is somewhat ambiguous, and the verse begins *if anyone is blameless*, but it is clearly a continuation of verse 4, and therefore it describes anyone who is an elder. **1:7–9** A similar list of requirements for service as a *bishop* is found in 1 Timothy 3:1–7. **1:9** *Of God* has been added for clarity. The Greek says simply *the faithful word* or *the faithful message* without clearly referring to it as God's word. **1:10** The Greek notes only *from the circumcision*, the precise meaning of which remains obscure. It may be that Paul was referring to Christians who insisted on circumcision for their male children and obedience to the law of Moses, or these may have been Jews who wanted Christians to abide the Jewish Law. **1:12** The quotation is attributed to the Greek poet Epimenides of Crete (sixth century BCE), although Epimenides was not from the circumcision faction (see note on verse 10), but he was from Crete. This may indicate that the circumcision faction was composed of people from Crete. **1:15** Why Paul would declare that *all things are pure to the pure* remains unclear.

to the corrupt and unfaithful nothing is pure, but their minds and consciences are corrupted. [16]They profess to know God, but they deny him by their works. They are despicable and disobedient and unfit for any good work.

ENCOURAGE AND REPROVE

2 [1]But, as for you, teach what is consistent with sound teaching. [2]Older men are to be temperate, serious, sensible, sound in faith, in love, and in endurance. [3]Likewise, the older women are to be reverent in behavior, not slanderers or slaves to drink but teaching what is good [4]so that they train the young women to love their husbands and children, [5]to be sensible, holy, good managers of a household, kind, and submissive to their own husbands so that the message of God may not be slandered.

[6]Likewise, encourage the younger men to act sensibly, [7]showing yourself to be an example of good works in every way, and in your teaching show integrity, reverence, [8]and sound speech that cannot be criticized so that anyone opposed will be put to shame, having nothing evil to say about us.

[9]Servants are to be subject to their own masters in everything, and do what is expected and not talk back, [10]not stealing but showing forth complete and perfect fidelity

so that in everything they may be an ornament to the teaching of God our Savior.

[11]For the grace of God has appeared, bringing salvation to all. [12]It teaches us to reject impiety and worldly desires and to live self-controlled, righteous, and godly lives in the present age [13]while we wait for the blessed hope and appearing of the glory of our great God and Savior, Jesus Christ. [14]He gave himself for us so that he might redeem us from all lawlessness and to purify for himself a people of his own who seek to do good. [15]Speak these things; encourage and reprove with all authority. Let no one look down on you.

REMIND THEM TO BE OBEDIENT

3 [1]Remind them to be subject to rulers and authorities, to be obedient, and to be prepared for every good work, [2]to not slander, to avoid fighting, to be gentle, and to show kindness to everyone. [3]For we were once foolish also, disobedient, led astray, enslaved to various passions and pleasures, leading our lives in malice and envy, being hated and hating one another. [4]But when the goodness and loving kindness of our God and Savior appeared, [5]he saved us, not as a result of works we did in righteousness but according to his mercy, by means of the washing of rebirth and renewal of the Holy Spirit. [6]He poured the Spirit out upon us richly through Jesus Christ our Savior [7]so that we might be

---

The word can also mean *clean*, and possibly relates to foods and concerns with clean and unclean foods. The meaning would then be that Paul was declaring all foods to be clean for the pure (see Mark 7:18–19).

2:5 The word *submissive* represents the idea that a woman is *subject to* or acts with the husband as a manager of the household. This recommendation has strong cultural underpinnings and conveys a common cultural attitude toward women and men. **2:9–10** These verses preserve a first-century endorsement of slavery that is inappropriate in the modern age. Paul was endorsing cultural practices of his day, and the dynamics and nuances of that conversation should not be used to promote servitude in the modern age. **2:13** Jesus is unequivocally called *God*, an important statement on the acceptance of Jesus Christ as both God's Son and as God himself. The coming of Christ described in this verse has parallels to the First Vision appearance to the Prophet Joseph Smith.

3:1 This verse has parallels to article of faith 12. **3:5** *The washing of rebirth* may be a baptismal image or an interpretive metaphor meant to explain one of the outcomes of baptism. **3:7** Doctrine and Covenants

made righteous in his grace and become heirs according to a hope of eternal life. [8]The saying is trustworthy.

I want you to insist on these things so that those who have come to believe in God may be thoughtful in engaging in good works. These things are good and helpful for all people. [9]But avoid foolish controversies, genealogies, infighting, and fights about the Law because they are useless and empty. [10]Avoid a divisive individual after warning him one or two times [11]because you know that such a person is twisted and sinful, being self-condemned.

CONCLUDING REMARKS

[12]When I send Artemas to you, or Tychicus, do your best to come to me in Nicopolis, for I decided to spend the winter there. [13]Make every effort to send Zenas the lawyer and Apollos, and see that they lack nothing. [14]And let our people learn to dedicate themselves to good works, in order to meet urgent needs and that they may not be unproductive.

[15]All who are with me greet you. Greet those in the faith who love us. Grace be with all of you.

70:8 speaks of *heirs according to the laws of the kingdom*. **3:8** The saying referred to is contained in verse 4–7. The saying differs in style and content from the body of the letter and is probably a quotation from an unknown source. The contents of these verses suggest it is a quotation from a declaration (or creed) of faith. **3:9** *Infighting* may also be translated simply as *fighting* or *quarreling*. **3:10–11** The example given presupposes an individual has been reproved by the church but is still unwilling to change behavior. **3:12** For Tychicus, see Acts 20:4; Ephesians 6:21; Colossians 4:7–9. *Nicopolis* is not mentioned in any of Paul's letters or in Acts, and it is unclear when Paul may have visited this Greek city. The note that Paul wants to *spend the winter* in Nicopolis appears to convey a personal decision to do so and not that he was forced to do so. This information does not fit easily into the information described in Acts and may postdate Paul's travels as described in Acts.

PHILEMON

AUTHOR

Paul wrote this short letter to a private individual, Philemon, regarding a runaway slave named Onesimus whom Paul had converted while in prison (1:10). Paul intended to return Onesimus to Philemon, and in doing so he also made a plea for Onesimus's well-being and care. Hints in the language of the epistle suggest that Onesimus may have worked in the textile trade as Paul did (Acts 18:3) and that Paul may have worked with Onesimus as an apprentice: "I wanted to keep him with me so that he might serve me on your behalf in my imprisonment for the gospel" (1:13). The language of this verse is also used in apprenticeship arrangements, and by this stage in Paul's life he may have been working as an entrepreneur and employing others for commissioned textile work. Paul's reference to Onesimus as a "companion" (1:7) and the frequent business language further suggest that Philemon also worked in the textile industry and that perhaps this was how Paul came to know him.

PURPOSE OF WRITING

The letter is a strong statement of Paul's personal concern for Onesimus and of his personal contact with Philemon, whom Paul proposes to visit soon (1:22). The recipient of the letter was well-known to other Pauline missionaries such as Mark and Epaphras. The most significant question of interpretation comes down to what Paul wanted Philemon to do once Onesimus returned to him. The language of 1:18 suggests that apart from Onesimus running away, he may also have stolen something or wronged Philemon in some way. Paul was willing to repay that debt from his personal funds (1:19). Paul encouraged Philemon to receive him back, "not as a slave but more than a slave, as a beloved brother, especially to me and even more so to you both in the flesh and in the Lord" (1:16). This phrase demonstrates one of the interesting social dynamics of conversion to early Christianity where a master-slave relationship could be transformed into a new relationship between Christian brothers or sisters. In this situation, it remains unclear whether Onesimus would continue to serve as a slave to Philemon or whether Philemon would accept Onesimus as a free person and fellow believer in Christ.

CONNECTION TO LATTER-DAY SAINT BELIEFS

There is nothing uniquely connected to Latter-day Saint practice or belief in this letter. However, in it Paul writes as an aging leader (1:9) who shows parental care and a willingness to reach out and help an individual whom he had come into contact with. The letter is a powerful statement on the intersection of pastoral and personal interest and, as such, can guide others in developing such instincts. ॐ

OPENING ADDRESS

1 [1]Paul, a prisoner of Christ Jesus, and Timothy, a brother, to Philemon, a friend and fellow worker, [2]to Apphia our sister, and Archippus our fellow soldier, and the church that meets in your house: [3]grace to you and peace from God our Father and the Lord Jesus Christ.

THANKSGIVING

[4]I thank my God when I remember you in my prayers [5]because I hear of your love and faith that you have for the Lord Jesus and for all the saints. [6]And I pray that the faith you share will be helpful in your knowledge of everything good and which is in you in Christ. [7]For I have much joy and comfort because of your love, for the hearts of the saints have been refreshed because of you, brother.

PAUL'S REQUEST TO PHILEMON FOR ONESIMUS

[8]Although I have great boldness in Christ to command you to do what is required, [9]I would rather encourage you through love, as I, Paul, an old man and now also a prisoner of Christ Jesus, [10]am encouraging you on account of my child Onesimus, whose father I became while imprisoned [11](he was previously useless to you, but he is now useful to you and me). [12]I am sending him back to you, and he is my very heart.

[13]I wanted to keep him with me so that he might serve me on your behalf in my imprisonment for the gospel, [14]but I determined to do nothing without your knowledge so that your good act is not done out of necessity but instead voluntarily.

[15]Perhaps for this reason he was separated from you for a little while so that you might have him back forever, [16]not as a slave but more than a slave, as a beloved brother, especially to me and even more so to you, both in the flesh and in the Lord. [17]Therefore, if you regard him as a companion, receive him as you would receive me. [18]If he has wronged you in anything or owes you, put it on my account. [19]I, Paul, am writing this with my own hand, I will repay it. I could also add that you owe me your very self. [20]Yes, brother, I receive a benefit from you in the Lord. Refresh my heart in Christ. [21]Having confidence in your obedience, I write to you, knowing that you will do more than I have asked. [22]At the same time, prepare a place for me to stay, for I hope that through your prayers I will be given back to you.

CONCLUDING REMARKS

[23]Epaphras, my fellow prisoner in Christ Jesus, greets you. [24]Mark, Aristarchus, Demas, and Luke, my companions greet you also. [25]The grace of Lord Jesus Christ be with your spirit.

1:1 *A prisoner of Christ Jesus* implies that Paul was imprisoned for his belief in, or efforts to preach, Jesus Christ as Lord. The location and date of this imprisonment are unknown. **1:2** In the earliest period when the gospel began to spread, Christian meetings were held in houses. The house church mentioned is the one that meets in Philemon's home, but the city is unknown. The named individuals were acquaintances of Paul, but they are not mentioned in his other letters. *Apphia* may be the spouse of Philemon. *Archippus* is mentioned in Colossians 4:17. **1:9** For *a prisoner of Christ Jesus*, see note on verse 1. **1:10** *Onesimus* is mentioned in Colossians 4:9. *Onesimus* accepted the gospel while both he and Paul were in prison. **1:11** The statement that Onesimus was previously useless is a play on the idea that now that Onesimus is a fellow laborer in the gospel, he is much more useful to their shared purpose of spreading the faith. **1:15** The wording may suggest that *Onesimus* would be Philemon's slave *forever*. This is unlikely to be the meaning. **1:19** What precisely Philemon owes Paul is uncertain, but the wording hints that Paul helped facilitate Philemon's conversion to the gospel. **1:23** *Epaphras* is possibly the same person as *Epaphroditus* (see Philippians 2:25; Colossians 1:7; 4:12). **1:24** *Aristarchus* is mentioned in Acts 27:2; Colossians 4:10. *Demas* is mentioned in Colossians 4:14; 2 Timothy 4:10.

HEBREWS

AUTHOR

In one of the earliest Greek manuscripts (Chester Beatty papyrus 46), this epistle is included immediately following Romans, indicating that whoever made that copy of the New Testament felt that Paul was the author of the work because the scribe placed the book alongside the other Pauline letters. This would indicate that the sentiments expressed at the end of the epistle (13:22–25) are those of Paul and that they represent a time in Paul's life that is similar to his concerns and state of mind during the late second mission and third missionary journey. However, there are also significant concerns regarding Paul's authorship of the letter, and the style of Hebrews and the quality of the Greek writing is so markedly different from Paul's other letters as to suggest that Paul certainly did not write the letter in the same way and under the same circumstances that he wrote his other letters.

Modern concerns with authorship have connected the importance of the epistle's message with the question of authorship. In other words, if Paul did not write Hebrews, then somehow the message of the epistle is diminished or even of no value. Tradition suggests that Paul wrote Hebrews, which is a reasonable assumption; the evidence is fairly conclusive that an early Christian author who was connected to Timothy wrote this epistle with the intent of addressing the topic of Christ for a Jewish Christian audience.

The epistle is only marginally a letter in its style and structure. The book begins with a strong statement that God now speaks through the Son, that the Son is a faithful high priest (2:17), and that Moses had prefigured the ministry of Christ. The book maintains a focus on Christ throughout, drawing upon concepts such as Melchizedek as a type of Christ (7:1–28), the new covenant (9:15–22), and encouragement to endure trial (10:26–12:13). The language is elegant and well considered, suggesting that the author had in mind a powerful defense of his belief in Christ in light of differing opinions.

PURPOSE OF WRITING

There is significant deliberation regarding whether the letter was written to a Gentile Christian community or a Jewish Christian community. The author specifically encourages readers, "Let us hold tightly to our confession" (4:14) and "Let us approach with confidence the throne of grace" (4:16). Both of these injunctions argue for stability and continuity in living a Christian life. Remaining faithful is also a significant concern (3:1–4:3). These directives and points of focus indicate that the author was attempting to turn Christians in a direction that would help them not "drift away" (2:1).

The author richly weaves Jewish scripture into his counsel (see notes) and is particularly influenced by the books of Genesis and Psalms. In at least one sense, the author was establishing a clear precedent that Christ could be found in the messages of the Old Testament. Such an understanding would have made this work valuable for teaching and missionary work among Jews. The author enjoys expanding older concepts into newer ones, where Christ is described as "the apostle and high priest whom we confess" (3:1), and he is a priest like Melchizedek (5:10). Such considerations are unique in the New Testament and show how thoroughly the author understood the Old Testament and also his willingness to put that understanding to service in explaining the doctrine of Christ.

CONNECTION TO LATTER-DAY SAINT BELIEFS

Latter-day Saints will find immediate connections to the Christology of Hebrews—the study of the nature, person, and divinity of Jesus Christ—which is quite similar to modern ways of speaking of Christ. For example, God speaks through his Son, who is literally "the character of his essence" (1:3). Christ is greater than the angels, and he is an example to all believers while also being a Savior to all. Additionally, the author chooses to draw upon the story of Melchizedek as it is told in Genesis, where very little is known of his origins, upbringing, or priesthood. The author uses this to draw attention to the fact that just as Melchizedek had no father or mother in the stories that are told about him, Jesus Christ also received his priesthood not from his parents or lineage, but rather directly from God. Also like Melchizedek, to whom Abraham paid tithes, Jesus Christ was a priest greater than the Levitical priests. The author understood that Melchizedek was greater than Abraham and therefore he uses that comparison to draw attention to the fact that Jesus was greater than the priests living in his day.

Latter-day Saints will also be drawn to the forward-looking nature of the book, where the author encourages readers to see their faith and its future in the story of Mount Zion: "But you have come to Mount Zion, the city of the living God, the heavenly Jerusalem, and to a myriad of angels in a celebratory gathering, and to the assembly of the firstborn who are enrolled in heaven, and to God, the judge of all, and the spirits of righteous people made perfect, and to Jesus, the mediator of the new covenant, and to the spilled blood that speaks something better than Abel's offering does" (11:4). Thus, in some respects, the message of the book is hopeful, focusing faith on a future existence with Christ. ⁂

GOD NOW SPEAKS BY HIS SON

1 ¹A long time ago God spoke to our fathers by the prophets in many and various ways. ²In these last days he has spoken to us by his Son, whom he established as heir of all things, through whom he created the world. ³The Son is the radiance of his glory and the character of his essence, and he supports all things through the word of his power. After he made purification for sins, he sat down on the right hand of the Majesty on high. ⁴By this he became far greater than the angels, just as he inherited a name that is greater than theirs.

THE SUPERIORITY OF THE SON

⁵To which of the angels has God ever said, *"You are my Son; today I have begotten you"*? Or again, *"I will be a father to him, and he will be a son to me"*? ⁶When he brings his firstborn into the world again, he says, *"Let all the angels of God worship him!"* ⁷And he says to the angels, *"He makes his angels spirits and his ministers a flame of fire."* ⁸But regarding the Son he says, *"Your throne, God, is forever and ever, and the scepter of righteousness is the scepter of your kingdom. ⁹You loved righteousness and hated lawlessness. Because of this, God, your God, has anointed you with the oil of rejoicing beyond your companions."*

¹⁰And, *"You founded the earth, Lord, from the beginning, and the works of your hands are the heavens. ¹¹They will perish, but you will remain, and all will grow old like a garment of clothing; ¹²like a robe you will fold them up, and like a garment they will be changed, but you are the same, and your years will not end."* ¹³But to which of the angels has he ever said, *"Sit at my right hand until I make your enemies a footstool for your feet"*? ¹⁴Are the angels not all ministering spirits sent out to serve those who are to inherit salvation?

CONFIRMED WITH SIGNS, WONDERS, AND MIRACLES

2 ¹Because of this we must pay closer attention to what we have heard so that we do not drift away from it. ²Since the message spoken through angels proved to

---

1:1 The *many and various ways* in which God speaks is meant to include God's word to all nations and peoples. Such an inclusive message may signal that the author was reaching out to Gentiles. **1:2** The author refers to his day as *these last days*, emphasizing the idea that they were living in the time before Christ came again. *The world* is literally *the ages* in Greek, but in this context it appears to refer to the creation of the material realm, its times and ages. **1:3** *Character of his essence* refers to the very nature of God himself, and Jesus Christ as Son is the embodiment or precise representation of God's essence. Similar language is found in Moroni 7:27 (compare Hebrews 10:12) and Doctrine and Covenants 20:24. *Purification for sins* refers to the act of washing away the effects of sin or the consequences of sin. An allusion to Psalm 110:1. **1:4** The *name* referred to here may also be that mentioned in Philippians 2:9–10. That name in Philippians is *Jesus*, which is given special power and authority by God. **1:5** Quotation from Psalm 2:7 (also quoted in Acts 13:33; Romans 1:4); 2 Samuel 7:14. **1:6** The word *again* signals that this verse refers to the return of the Son or to his Second Coming. Quotation from Deuteronomy 32:43 (LXX); Psalm 97:7. **1:7** Quotation from Psalm 104:4. **1:8–9** Quotation from Psalm 45:6–7. The Psalm is quoted to indicate that the Son is God. **1:10** This verse is echoed in Doctrine and Covenants 67:2. **1:10–12** Quotation from Psalm 102:25–27. **1:12** The words *like a garment* are omitted in some manuscripts, possibly because scribes realized that these words are not part of Psalm 102:26, the source of the quotation in this verse. It is more likely, however, that they are original, and therefore they have been included in the translation. **1:13** Quotation from Psalm 110:1. **1:14** This verse is quoted in a new context in Doctrine and Covenants 7:6, see Hebrews 1:7. The *ministering spirits* serve those who will receive salvation. Compare Doctrine and Covenants 76:88.

2:2 *The message spoken through angels* refers to the law of Moses (Deuteronomy 33:2; Acts 7:38, 53).

be so well established that every transgression and disobedience received a just punishment, ³how will we escape if we neglect such great salvation? It was first declared by the Lord and then proclaimed to us by those who heard him, ⁴while God confirmed their witness together with them with signs, wonders, various miracles, and by the gifts of the Holy Spirit that he distributed according to his will.

A MERCIFUL AND
FAITHFUL HIGH PRIEST

⁵For he did not place the world to come, about which we are speaking, under the direction of the angels. ⁶But it has been testified about somewhere, *"What is man, that you remember him or the son of man that you care for him? ⁷You made him lower than the angels for a little while; you crowned him with glory and honor; ⁸You put all things under his feet."* For when he placed all things under his direction, he left nothing outside of his direction.

Now, we do not see that all things are under his direction, ⁹but we see him who was made lower than the angels for a little while, namely Jesus, who was crowned with glory and honor because of the suffering of death so that by the grace of God he may taste death for everyone. ¹⁰For it was fitting that he, for whom and through whom all things exist, in bringing many sons and daughters to glory, should make the prince of their salvation perfect through sufferings. ¹¹For the one who makes holy and those who have been made holy all have one origin, and so he is not ashamed to call them brothers and sisters, ¹²saying, *"I will declare your name to my brothers, and in the midst of your gathering I will sing your praise."* ¹³And again, *"I will put my trust in him,"* and again, *"Behold, I am with the children God has given me."* ¹⁴Therefore, since the children share blood and flesh, he also shared in the same experience so that through death he would destroy the one who has the power of death, which is the devil, ¹⁵and deliver those who were held in slavery to a

---

The idea is that the validity of the law of Moses was such that disobedience to its principles and statutes received *a just punishment.* **2:3** The author is establishing the idea that God spoke to his children through prophets in past dispensations, setting up the idea that more recently he has spoken through his Son and that the message of the Son has now been declared by those who heard him. **2:5** The English phrase *the world to come* may appear to refer to the world after this one, but the idea is of the world that came into existence, and hence the inhabited world. **2:6** The author uses an unexpected introduction for rhetorical effect: *it has been testified about somewhere.* Both *man* and *the son of man* refer to humanity generally. **2:6–8** Quotation from Psalm 8:4–6. **2:7** This verse represents a quotation from the LXX translation of Psalm 8:5, which reads *you made him lower than the gods [Elohim].* An impressive group of manuscripts add *you have given him dominion over the works of your hands* at the end of verse 7, but it appears that this was added by scribes to correct the quotation to the text of Psalm 8:6. A number of early and important manuscripts omit the phrase, likely signaling their attempt to convey the original wording of the author. **2:8–9** These two verses contain commentary on Psalm 8:4–6 and adopt many terms from the Psalm. **2:8–10** These verses present the idea of the descent of the Son of God, and how that descent enabled him to atone for sins. **2:10** The Greek text mentions only *sons,* but it is used generically in this verse to refer to all of God's children. The phrase *perfect through sufferings* can also be translated as *complete through sufferings.* **2:11** Origin has been added to clarify the Greek, which says only *all have one.* Greek uses *brothers* generically to refer to *brothers and sisters.* **2:12** Quotation from Psalm 22:22. The word *brothers* has been retained instead of rendering it more inclusively because this is an Old Testament quotation, and thus the original meaning of the Hebrew text has been retained. **2:13** Quotation from Isaiah 8:17–18.

fear of death all their lives. ¹⁶For certainly it is not angels that he helps but the descendants of Abraham. ¹⁷Therefore, he was obligated to be made like his brothers and sisters in every way so that he would become a merciful and faithful high priest in the things of God, to make an offering for the sins of the people. ¹⁸For he personally suffered when tempted; he is able to help those who are tempted.

LIKE MOSES

3 ¹Therefore, holy brothers and sisters, partners in the heavenly calling, consider the apostle and high priest whom we confess, Jesus, ²who is faithful to him who appointed him just as *Moses was faithful in all of God's house*. ³For Jesus was counted worthy of more glory than Moses, like a builder who has much more honor than the house itself. ⁴For every house is built by someone, but God is the builder of all things. ⁵*Moses was faithful in all of God's house* as a servant, to testify of things that would be said later, ⁶but Christ is in charge as a son over God's house, and we are his house if we hold tightly to our confidence and pride that belong to hope.

WARNING

⁷Therefore, just as the Holy Spirit says, "*Today, if you hear his voice, ⁸do not harden your hearts as in the rebellion on the day of testing in the desert ⁹where your ancestors tested me and saw my works for forty years. ¹⁰Therefore, I was provoked with that generation, and said, 'They always wander in their heart, they have not known my ways.' ¹¹As I swore in my wrath, 'They will not enter into my rest.'*"

¹²Be watchful, brothers and sisters, so that there is not anyone among you who has an evil, unfaithful heart that stands apart from the living God. ¹³But exhort one another every day, as long as it is called "*today*," so that no one from among you is hardened by the deception of sin. ¹⁴For we have become partners with Christ if we hold tightly to our original confidence in him to the end. ¹⁵As it says, "*Today, if you hear his voice, do not harden your hearts as in the rebellion.*" ¹⁶For which ones heard and still rebelled? Was it not all who came out of Egypt under Moses's direction? ¹⁷And with whom was he angry for forty years?

2:18 Doctrine and Covenants 62:1 quotes from this verse using the King James Version language. That Jesus *suffered when tempted* signals that he had the ability to succumb to the temptation (he *suffered*) and to fall as a result of succumbing. The wording does not suggest a passive or abstract experience but a genuine bout with temptation and its effects.

3:1 Greek uses *brothers* generically to refer to *brothers and sisters*. This is the only instance of Jesus being referred to as an *apostle*. The title is used as a technical term in this instance and not in its more general sense of one who is sent out to proclaim the gospel. It may refer to Jesus's position as an emissary of God or the one who was sent out from God's presence. **3:2, 5** Quotation from Numbers 12:7. **3:6** *But Christ is in charge as a son* refers to being in charge as an heir of the house. Some early and important manuscripts read *if we hold tightly until the end*. The evidence for this phrase is mixed and has been omitted from the translation with some hesitation. **3:7–11** Quotation from Psalm 95:7–11. **3:8** Exodus 17:7 is echoed in this verse (Meribah means *rebellion*, and Massah means *testing*). Compare Psalm 95:7–8, 11; Jacob 1:7; 6:6. **3:9** The Greek text includes *for forty years* as the beginning of verse 10. **3:11** Compare Alma 12:35; see also Psalm 95:11. Commentary on this event is found in Doctrine and Covenants 84:24. **3:12** Perhaps an allusion to Numbers 14:9. **3:13** The language of this verse is echoed in Doctrine and Covenants 45:6. **3:15** Quotation from Psalm 95:7–8. **3:17** This story is told in Numbers 14:29, 37.

Was it not with those who had sinned, whose bodies fell in the desert? [18]And to whom did he swear that they would not enter his rest except those who were disobedient? [19]And we see that they were not able to enter because of unbelief.

GOD'S REST

4 [1]Therefore, let us be attentive, while the promise of entering into his rest is open to us, lest any of you should seem to have fallen short of it. [2]For we received the good news just as they did, but the message that they heard did not help them because they were not united with those who heard it in faith. [3]For we who believe enter that rest, just as he said, "*As I swore in my wrath, 'They will not enter into my rest,*" even though his works were accomplished from the foundation of the world. [4]For he has spoken somewhere about the seventh day in this way: "*God rested on the seventh day from all his works.*" [5]Again in this passage he said, "*They will not enter into my rest.*" [6]Therefore, since it remains for some to enter it still and those who previously had it proclaimed to them did not enter because of disobedience, [7]God again appointed a certain day—"*Today*," speaking through David after such a long time, just as it has been said before, "*To-day, if you hear his voice, do not harden your hearts.*" [8]For if Joshua had provided them rest, God would not have spoken of another day later on. [9]So then there remains a Sabbath rest for the people of God, [10]for the one who enters into God's rest has himself rested from his works just as God rested from his own works.

[11]Therefore, let us work to enter into that rest so that no one may fall by the same type of disobedience. [12]For the word of God is living and active, sharper than a two-edged sword, piercing to the point of dividing soul and spirit, joints and marrow, and judging the desires and thoughts of the heart. [13]No creature is hidden from his presence, but all are naked and exposed to the eyes of him to whom we will give an account.

JESUS THE GREAT HIGH PRIEST

[14]Therefore, having a great high priest who has passed through the heavens, Jesus, the Son of God, let us hold tightly to our confession. [15]For we do not have a high priest that cannot be influenced by our weaknesses but one who was tempted in all things just as we are but without sin. [16]Therefore, let us approach the throne of grace with confidence so that we may receive mercy and grace to help us in a time of need.

3:18 This story is told in Numbers 14:29, 32. The *rest of the Lord* is explained in Doctrine and Covenants 84:24.

4:1 The author appears to place a time constraint on the duration of the promise of God. This appears to be a rhetorical device to encourage repentance. **4:2** The author possibly has in mind events such as those described in Deuteronomy 1:20–21. The *good news* is synonymous with the term *gospel*. **4:3** Quotation from Psalm 95:11 (quoted also in Hebrews 3:11). Compare Doctrine and Covenants 84:24. **4:4** Quotation from Genesis 2:2. **4:5** Quotation from Psalm 95:11. **4:7** The quotation to which the author refers, *just as it has been said before*, is found in Hebrews 3:7 and in Psalm 95:7–8. **4:12** The language of this verse is used frequently in the Doctrine and Covenants (6:2; 11:2; 12:2; 14:2; 33:1, also Helaman 3:29). A portion of this verse is also echoed in Doctrine and Covenants 6:16. Compare Psalm 149:6; Proverbs 5:4. **4:14** Compare Hebrews 3:1 for the idea of our *confession*. Jesus acts as our *high priest* to help us enter the presence of God. **4:15** The author draws out an emotional connection between the believer and Jesus, who is able to feel or to be *influenced by our weaknesses*. The word translated as *tempted* can also be translated as *tried*. The believer has a personal and direct connection with a tempted high priest who leads by example. **4:16** The *throne of grace* appears to be God's throne, and the believer is encouraged to approach God through the guidance and direction of Jesus.

5 ¹For every high priest who is taken from among the people is appointed to represent them to God so that he offers gifts and sacrifices for sins. ²He can act with compassion for the ignorant and wayward because he is subject to weakness. ³And because of this he is obligated to offer sacrifice for his own sins as well as for the people. ⁴And no one receives this honor except those who are called by God just as Aaron was. ⁵And thus Christ did not glorify himself in becoming a high priest but was glorified by the one who said to him, "*You are my Son; today I have begotten you.*" ⁶Also in another place he says, "*You are a priest forever after the order of Melchizedek.*" ⁷While in the days of his mortality, Jesus offered both prayers and supplications, with loud cries and tears, to the one who was able to save him from death. He was heard because of his reverence and faith. ⁸Although he was a son, he learned obedience from the things he suffered. ⁹And being made perfect, he became the source of eternal salvation for all who obey him,

¹⁰being designated by God as a high priest after the order of Melchizedek.

YOU NEED MILK

¹¹We have much to say about this, and it is difficult to explain because you have become dull of hearing. ¹²And for this reason you ought to be teachers at this time, but you need someone to again teach you the fundamental principles of the things God has spoken. You now need milk, not solid food. ¹³For everyone who lives on milk is unskilled in the word of righteousness, for that person is a child. ¹⁴But solid food is for the mature, the ones who have their abilities of perception trained to discern both good and evil.

MATURITY IN FAITH

6 ¹Therefore, we must move beyond the basic teaching about Christ. Let us move on to maturity, not establishing the foundation again: repentance from dead works and faith in God, ²teaching about baptisms, laying on of hands, resurrection

---

5:1 The word *appointed* was often translated as *ordained* in older translations. The Greek verb means to *establish, place in a position,* or *appoint.* See Mark 3:14. **5:3** The practice described in this verse is mentioned in Leviticus 4:2–3; 9:7. **5:4** Aaron's call is used as a pattern for others who are called (Leviticus 8:1–9). **5:5** Quotation from Psalm 2:7. **5:6** Quotation from Psalm 110:4. Little is known about the historical person Melchizedek (see Genesis 14). Compare Doctrine and Covenants 107:9, 29. **5:7** *Reverence and faith* represent a single Greek word, which means *devotion, reverence, piety,* and *caution.* This verse appears to allude to the accounts describing Christ's prayers in Gethsemane, particularly Matthew 26:39–45 (compare Mark 14:32–41; Luke 22:40–46). **5:7–8** The Joseph Smith Translation indicates that these two verses are a parenthesis referring to Melchizedek. **5:8** The emphasis is placed on Jesus being a mortal *son* and not the *Son* of God, and therefore the noun has not been capitalized. **5:9** *Being made perfect* can also be translated as *being made complete.* **5:10** Being *a high priest after the order of Melchizedek* is an important point in the author's discussion because Jesus was not of priestly lineage (meaning he did not belong to a priestly tribe or family), and therefore his priesthood was not a result of him serving as a priest in the Jerusalem temple. **5:12** The theme of *milk* versus *solid food* is used in 1 Corinthians 3:2–3; 1 Peter 2:2; Doctrine and Covenants 19:21–22.

6:1 The phrase *doctrine of Christ* (2 Nephi 31:2, but compare 2 John 1:9) is used in the King James translation for this verse. The text omits the word *doctrine* or *teaching* (as rendered in this translation) and says simply the *basic thing about Christ.* **6:1–2** The author has set out the idea that the doctrines listed in these verses are the *basic teaching about Christ* and that the discussion will now turn to teachings that are beyond the basics of the gospel. **6:2** *Baptisms* is plural, suggesting multiple baptisms, perhaps those for the living and those for the dead (1 Corinthians 15:29). The New Testament provides a few examples of

of the dead, and eternal judgment. ³And we will do this if God permits. ⁴For it is impossible for those who have once been enlightened, tasted of the heavenly gift, become partners of the Holy Spirit ⁵and tasted of the good word of God and the miracles of the age to come ⁶and then to have fallen, to restore them again to repentance because they are recrucifying the Son of God for themselves and holding him up to public shame. ⁷For a land that has soaked up the rain that often falls on it and produces a crop useful for the sake of the one who cultivated it receives a blessing from God. ⁸But if it bears thorns and thistles, it is useless and near to being cursed, and its end is to be burned.

⁹ But we are persuaded about you, dear friends, that things are better in relation to your salvation even though we speak this way. ¹⁰For God is not so unjust as to overlook your work and your love which you have shown for his name because you have served the saints and you continue to serve the saints. ¹¹We desire each of you to demonstrate the same eagerness for the fulfillment of hope until the end, ¹²so that you will not become sluggish but imitators of those who inherit the promises through faith and patience.

THE PROMISE TO ABRAHAM

¹³When God made a promise to Abraham, he swore by himself because he could swear by no one greater, ¹⁴saying, "*Surely, I will bless you and multiply you.*" ¹⁵And thus he waited patiently and obtained the promise. ¹⁶For people swear by something that is greater than them, and the confirmation of the oath is an end of all dispute. ¹⁷So when God wanted to show the unchangeable nature of his will more clearly to the heirs of the promise, he administered it with an oath ¹⁸so that we who have fled for refuge in him may find strong encouragement to hold tightly to the hope set before us, which is established by two unchangeable things, in which it is not possible for God to lie. ¹⁹We have this hope as a fixed and sure anchor for the soul that reaches inside the veil, ²⁰where Jesus our forerunner entered for us, and he became a priest after the order of Melchizedek forever.

THE MELCHIZEDEK PRIESTHOOD

7 ¹For this "*Melchizedek, king of Salem, priest of the Most High God, met Abraham as he was returning from defeating the kings and blessed him.*" ²And to him, Abraham apportioned a tenth of everything. First, his name means king of righteous-

---

laying on of hands (Acts 8:17; 19:6). The practice is more established in Restoration scripture (Doctrine and Covenants 107:67). **6:4–6** Alma 24:30 provides teachings that are similar to these verses. **6:6** This verse is clearly echoed in Doctrine and Covenants 76:35. It is difficult to determine how much a person has *fallen*. This verse seems to present the idea that a person has little hope of returning to the faith after falling from a position of faith, suggesting that this is not merely a period of weakened faith or questioning. **6:8** Doctrine and Covenants 104:3 echoes this verse (following the King James translation). A possible allusion to Genesis 3:18. **6:11** The author encourages the reader to rely on *hope* to carry a person through to the end. This emphasis on *hope* is an important part of this chapter. It becomes an *anchor for the soul* of the believer (verse 19). **6:13** This story is told in Genesis 22:16–18. **6:14** Quotation from Genesis 22:17. **6:19** This *veil* is the one that separates the Holy of Holies in the temple from the other chambers of the temple. It created a partition so that a priest or anyone else could not see into the Holy of Holies (Exodus 26:31–33). Echoed in Ether 12:4. **6:20** Allusion to Psalm 110:4. Compare Alma 13:9.

7:1 Paraphrase of Genesis 14:17–20. **7:1–5, 17** Compare Alma 13:9, 15–18, which discusses similar concepts. **7:2** *His name* refers to the name Melchizedek. The author is providing two different interpretations of the name.

ness, then king of Salem, which is king of peace; ³without father or mother, without a genealogy, he has no beginning of days or end of life, but similar to the Son of God, he remains a priest forever.

⁴See how great this man was to whom Abraham the patriarch gave him a tenth of his plunder. ⁵And those who are the descendants of Levi who receive the priesthood have a commandment according to the Law to receive a tithe from the people—that is, from their brothers and sisters—even though they are also descended from Abraham. ⁶But Melchizedek, who does not descend from the same people, received tithes from Abraham and blessed him who had the promises. ⁷Without any controversy, the lesser was blessed by the greater, ⁸and in the one case tithes are received by mortal men, while in the other case they are received by him who is confirmed to be alive. ⁹One might even say that Levi, who received tithes, paid tithes through Abraham. ¹⁰For he was still unborn, in Abraham's loins when Melchizedek met him.

¹¹On the one hand, if perfection through the Levitical Priesthood were possible (for the people received the Law under it), why would there still have been a need for another priest after the order of Melchizedek

and not named after the order of Aaron? ¹²For when the priesthood changes, there must also be a change in the Law. ¹³But the one about whom these things are spoken, he belonged to another tribe, a tribe from which no one has ever served at the altar. ¹⁴For it is certain that our Lord descended from Judah, and Moses said nothing about priests in that tribe. ¹⁵And this is even clearer if another priest like Melchizedek arises, ¹⁶one who has not become a priest by legal requirement concerning physical descent but by the miracle of an indestructible life. ¹⁷For it is witnessed about him that *you are a priest forever according to the order of Melchizedek.* ¹⁸For on the one hand, an earlier commandment was set aside because of its weakness and uselessness ¹⁹(for the Law made nothing perfect), but on the other hand a better hope was introduced, through which we draw near to God. ²⁰And it was not without an oath, for the former priests became such without an oath, ²¹but Jesus was made a priest by an oath by the one who said to him, *"The Lord has sworn, and he will not change his mind, 'You are a priest forever.'"* ²²Accordingly, this makes Jesus the guarantor of a better covenant. ²³And there were many who were priests formerly, but they were prevented by death from continuing

---

7:3 The discussion of Melchizedek lacking a *father, mother, a genealogy,* etc., reflects Melchizedek's story as told in the Old Testament, where nothing is known of his ancestry, descendants, or death. The Joseph Smith Translation interprets this verse as referring to the priesthood, which has no *father, mother, genealogy,* etc. It reads *For this Melchizedek was ordained a priest after the order of the Son of God, which order was without father, without mother, without descent, having neither beginning of days, nor end of life; and all those who are ordained unto this priesthood are made like unto the Son of God, abiding a priest continually.* On the practice of choosing a high priest, see Leviticus 21:10. Echoed in Doctrine and Covenants 78:16; 84:17. Alma 13:9 refers to Christ as being *without beginning of days of end of years.* **7:4** Allusion to Genesis 14:20. **7:5** *Their brothers and sisters* can in this instance also be translated as *fellow countrymen.* The tithe collected by the priests is set forth in Numbers 18:21–32. **7:6** Even though the author had stated that Melchizedek's ancestry was unknown, he notes here that he was not an Israelite. **7:14** The reference to Judah may arise from Isaiah 11:1 and Micah 5:2. Jesus was from the tribe of Judah (Romans 1:3; Matthew 1:1). **7:16** Many translations favor *power of an indestructible life,* but the Greek word can also mean the *power to perform a miracle.* The idea is that Melchizedek is a priest forever (see verse 17), an unlikely achievement for a mortal, and hence the word *miracle* seems to better capture the force of the Greek phrase. **7:17** Quotation from Psalm 110:4. **7:21** Quotation from Psalm 110:4.

in office, ²⁴but Jesus holds his priesthood permanently because he remains forever. ²⁵So he is able to save completely those who come near to God through him because he always lives to intercede for them. ²⁶For it is indeed fitting for us to have such a high priest, holy, innocent, unstained, separate from sinners, exalted above the heavens. ²⁷He has no need, like the former high priests, to offer sacrifices each day first for their own sins and then the sins of the people because he did this once and for all in offering himself. ²⁸For the Law appoints men who are prone to weakness as high priests, but the word of the oath which came after the Law appoints a Son who has forever been made perfect.

A BETTER COVENANT ESTABLISHED UPON BETTER PROMISES

8 ¹The point of what we are saying is this, we have a high priest who sat down on the right hand of the throne of the Majesty in heaven, ²a minister in the holy places, in the true tabernacle which the Lord, and not a mortal, set up. ³For every high priest is appointed to offer gifts and offerings; therefore, it is necessary for him to have something to offer. ⁴Therefore, if he were on earth, he would not be a priest because there are priests who offer gifts according to the Law. ⁵They serve as a type and shadow of heavenly things just as Moses was warned by God when he was about to erect the tabernacle. For he says, "*See that you make everything according to the pattern that was shown to you in the mountain.*" ⁶But now Jesus has obtained a greater ministry because the covenant he mediates is better and it is established upon better promises.

⁷For if the first covenant had been without fault, no one would have sought for a second one. ⁸For he finds fault when he says, "*Behold, the days are coming, says the Lord, when I will establish a new covenant with the house of Israel and with the house of Judah, ⁹not like the covenant I made with their ancestors on the day I took them by the hand to bring them out of the land of Egypt. Because they did not remain in my covenant, and so I had no regard for them, says the Lord. ¹⁰Because this is the covenant that I will make with the house of Israel after those days, says the Lord. I will put my laws into their minds, and I will write them upon their hearts, and I will be their God and they will be my people. ¹¹And they will certainly not teach each person his neighbor, and each person will not teach his brother, saying, 'Know the Lord,' because they will all know me, from the least until the greatest among them. ¹²For I will be merciful toward their evil deeds, and their sins I will no longer remember.*"

¹³In speaking of a new covenant, he makes the first covenant obsolete. And

---

7:24 Perhaps an allusion to Psalm 89:36. 7:25 To *intercede for them* refers to the act of Jesus pleading and praying to the Father on behalf of those who have come to him. 7:27 *Former* has been added to clarify that the author is referring to the Levitical high priests.

8:1 Allusion to Psalm 110:1. 8:3 The phrase *for him* is *this one* in Greek, and refers to the high priest who offers gifts and sacrifices. 8:4 The logic of this statement is that if Christ were a *priest on earth*, he would effectively be redundant because there were already priests who were appointed to fill that position. The Joseph Smith Translation reads *Therefore, while he was on the earth, he offered for a sacrifice his own life for the sins of the people. Now every priest under the law must needs offer gifts, or sacrifices, according to the law.* 8:5 Quotation from Exodus 25:40. 8:8–12 Quotation from Jeremiah 31:31–34. This is the longest Old Testament quotation in the New Testament. 8:12 Doctrine and Covenants 38:14 speaks of being *merciful unto your weaknesses.* Compare Doctrine and Covenants 58:42. 8:13 The *new covenant* spoken of by Jeremiah (see note on 8:8–12) is often associated with the promise of Christianity and the new covenant to come with Christ. This is one of the strongest statements in the New Testament regarding the dissolution or abandonment of the old covenant.

what is becoming obsolete and growing old is ready to disappear.

THE TWO SANCTUARIES

9 ¹Now, the first covenant had regulations for worship and its earthly sanctuary. ²For a tent was prepared with the outer partition, in which were the lampstand, the table, and the presentation of the loaves. It was called the holy place. ³After the second curtain was a tent called the Holy of Holies. ⁴It had the gold altar of incense and the ark of the covenant covered all over in gold. In the ark was a gold bowl containing the manna and Aaron's staff that budded and the tablets of the covenant. ⁵Above the ark were the cherubim of glory overshadowing the mercy seat. Now is not the time to speak of these in detail.

⁶With these things being prepared in this way, the priests would enter the outer partition regularly to perform their duties, ⁷but only the high priest entered into the second partition, once a year, and not without blood, which he would offer for himself and for the unintentional sins of the people. ⁸The Holy Spirit demonstrated that the way into the holy place had not yet been made apparent as long as the first tabernacle was standing, ⁹which is symbolic for the present age. In this way, gifts and sacrifices were offered that could not perfect the conscience of the worshipper. ¹⁰Their purpose was for food and drink and various washings, which are human regulations that were set in place until the time of reformation.

¹¹But Christ has come as high priest of the good things to come, passing through the greater and more perfect tent not made with hands, which is not of this creation. ¹²And he entered the holy place once and for all, not by means of the blood of goats and calves but by his own blood, thus securing an eternal redemption. ¹³For if the blood of goats and bulls and the ashes of a young heifer sprinkled on the defiled sanctifies them so that they are purified, ¹⁴how much more will the blood of Christ, who through the eternal Spirit offered himself without blemish to God, purify our conscience from dead works to worship the living God.

¹⁵Because of this, he is the mediator of the new covenant; those who are called may receive an eternal inheritance because a death has occurred that sets them free from the transgressions of the first covenant. ¹⁶For if there is a will, the death of the person who made it must be proven. ¹⁷For a will goes into effect at death, since it has no power while the one who made it is still living. ¹⁸Not even the first covenant was initiated without blood. ¹⁹For when

---

9:1 For information regarding the tabernacle, its rights and practices, and a description, see Exodus 25–27. **9:2** The translation of *tent* instead of *tabernacle* is intended to convey the author's interest in discussing the tabernacle in the wilderness. The *outer partition* is called in Greek the *first partition*. The *lampstand* was the menorah. **9:3** The author understood the *Holy of Holies* to be a separate *tent*. **9:4** For Aaron's budding *staff*, see Numbers 17:1–11. **9:5** For the *cherubim*, see Exodus 25:18–20. **9:8** The translation has adopted the position that the author is referring to the entire *tabernacle* in the phrase *first tabernacle*. It is possible that the author intended only the first part of the tabernacle, the outer partition mentioned in verses 2 and 6. In that case, the translation should be *outer tent*. **9:10** *Various washings* is literally *various baptisms* in Greek. The ritual washings that the priests performed were referred to using the Greek term *baptism*, which denotes submersion and complete washing. The *time of reformation* refers to the time in the future when things would be *set in order*. **9:12** See Leviticus 16:5–15. **9:13** See Leviticus 4:5–6; Numbers 19. **9:16–17** Abinadi's death is framed on the principles set forth in these verses. **9:19** Described in Exodus 24:8; Leviticus 14:2–7; Numbers 19:9, 18, 20. *Hyssop* is an herb used in cooking and for treating some ailments.

every commandment of the Law had been spoken by Moses to all the people, he took the blood of calves and goats and he sprinkled the book and all the people with water and red wool and hyssop, ²⁰saying, "*This is the blood of the covenant that God has commanded you to obey.*" ²¹And likewise he sprinkled both the tabernacle and all the utensils of worship with blood. ²²And with blood almost all things are purified according to the Law, and without the shedding of blood forgiveness does not come.

CHRIST PUT AWAY SIN

²³Therefore, it is necessary for the types and shadows of the things in heaven to be purified through these practices, but the heavenly things needed better sacrifices than these. ²⁴For Christ has not entered holy places made with hands, which are types and shadows of true things, but into heaven itself. Now he appears in the presence of God on our behalf. ²⁵He did not enter so that he would offer himself repeatedly, just as the high priest enters the holy place every year with blood that is not his own, ²⁶since he would have to suffer repeatedly from the foundation of the world. Now he has appeared once and for all at the end of the ages to put away sin by sacrificing himself. ²⁷And as it is appointed for a person to die once and then be judged, ²⁸even so Christ was offered once to bear the sins of many, and he will appear a second time, not to deal with sin but to bring salvation to those who eagerly await him.

SACRIFICES AND OFFERINGS

10¹For the Law is a type of good things to come, but it is not the reality itself. The Law is not capable of perfecting those who come to worship by the same sacrifices offered continually every year. ²Otherwise, they would not have ceased to be offered because the worshippers would have been cleansed once and for all and would no longer have a consciousness of sins. ³But in the sacrifices there is a reminder of sins year after year. ⁴For the blood of bulls and goats cannot take away sins.

⁵Therefore, when Christ came into the world, he said, "*You have not desired sacrifice and offering, but a body you have prepared for me; ⁶in burnt offerings and in sin offerings you have not taken pleasure. ⁷Then he said, 'Behold, I have come, as it is written of me in the scroll of the book, to do your will, God.'*"

⁸When it says above, "*Sacrifices and offerings and burnt offerings and sin offerings, you did not desire nor take delight in them*" (which are offered according to the Law), ⁹then he says, "*Behold, I have come to do your will,*" he abolishes the first in order to establish the second. ¹⁰In his will we are made holy because of the offering of the body of Jesus Christ once and for all.

¹¹And every priest stands daily at his service, offering repeatedly the same sacrifices, which can never take away sins. ¹²But when Christ had offered one sacrifice for sins for all time, he sat down at the right hand of God, ¹³waiting until his enemies are made a footstool under his feet. ¹⁴For in one offering he has per-

---

9:20 Quotation from Exodus 24:8. **9:23** *The types of the things in heaven* refers to the utensils used in temple service which are patterned on heavenly examples. **9:27** A more detailed discussion of this teaching is found in Alma 12:27. **9:28** An allusion to Isaiah 53:12.

10:5 The Greek text simply says *he* in place of *Christ*. **10:5–7** Quotation from Psalm 40:6–8. **10:7** Doctrine and Covenants 99:5 quotes this verse in a new context. **10:8–9** The author quotes portions of Psalm 40:6–8 and adds commentary. **10:12** The Greek text says *this one* in place of *Christ*. An allusion to Psalm 110:1. **10:13** An allusion to Psalm 110:1.

fected those who are made holy for all time. [15]And the Holy Spirit testifies to us, for after he says, [16]"*This is the covenant which I will make with them, after those days, says the Lord. I will put my laws in their hearts, and I will write them on their minds.*" [17]Then he says, "*I will not remember their sins and their lawlessness any longer.*" [18]Where there is forgiveness of these things, there is no longer an offering for sin.

A LIFE IN CHRIST

[19]Therefore, brothers and sisters, because we have confidence to enter the holy place by the blood of Jesus, [20]by the new and living way he initiated for us through the veil (that is, through his flesh), [21]and since we have a great high priest over the house of God, [22]let us approach with a true heart and the full assurance of faith, with our hearts sprinkled from a wicked conscience and our bodies washed in pure water. [23]Let us hold tightly without wavering to the confession of hope, for the one who gave the promise is faithful. [24]And let us consider how to encourage one another to love and to do good works, [25]not abandoning our meetings, as is the habit for some, but encouraging one another, and even more so because you see the day drawing near.

[26]For if we continue sinning willfully after receiving the knowledge of the truth, there is no longer a sacrifice for sins [27]but a certain fearful expectation of judgment and the fury of fire that will consume God's enemies. [28]A person who rejected the law of Moses was put to death without mercy on the evidence of two or three witnesses. [29]How much worse of a punishment do you think that person deserves who has rejected the Son of God and profanes the blood of the covenant that made that person holy and also insults the Spirit of grace? [30]For we know the one who said, "*Vengeance is mine, and I will repay,*" and again, "*The Lord will judge his people.*" [31]It is a fearful thing to fall into the hands of the living God.

[32]Remember the former days: when you were enlightened, you endured a great conflict of suffering. [33]Sometimes you were publicly exposed to abuse and trials, and at other times you were partners with those who were treated that way. [34]For you showed compassion to the imprisoned, and you accepted the seizure of your property with joy, knowing that you yourselves had a great possession and one that abides. [35]Therefore, do not throw away your confidence, which has a great reward. [36]For you need endurance so that when you do the will of God you will receive what is promised. [37]For "*yet a little while, the coming one will come without delay,* [38]*but my righteous one will live by faith, and if he shrinks back, my soul has no pleasure in him.*" [39]We are not those who shrink back and are destroyed, but we are among those who have faith and preserve their souls.

10:16 Quotation from Jeremiah 31:33. Doctrine and Covenants 49:9 speaks of the *everlasting covenant* in terms that are broadly similar to those in Hebrews. **10:17** Quotation from Jeremiah 31:34 with differences from the Hebrew text. **10:19** Greek uses *brothers* generically to refer to *brothers and sisters*. **10:20** An allusion to the tearing of the temple veil (Matthew 27:51; Mark 15:38; Luke 23:45). **10:22** The phrase *with our hearts sprinkled* refers to the cleansing of the heart through sprinkling with water. The practice of priests washing before entering the inner sanctuary is described in Leviticus 16:4; Numbers 8:7. **10:27** An allusion to Zephaniah 1:18; Isaiah 26:11. Compare Alma 40:14. **10:28** Allusion to Deuteronomy 17:6. **10:30** Quotation from Deuteronomy 32:35–36; Psalm 135:14. **10:37** The prophecy of the *coming one* is also mentioned in Matthew 3:11; 11:3; 21:9. **10:37–38** Quotation from Isaiah 26:20; Habakkuk 2:3–4.

EXAMPLES OF FAITH

11 [1]Faith is being confident in what we hope for, being convinced of things we do not see. [2]For by this the people of old received a commendation by God. [3]By faith we understand that the ages of the world were established by God's word so that what is seen was not made from visible things. [4]By faith Abel offered a better sacrifice than Cain, for which he was commended as being righteous. God commended him for his gifts. And through this sacrifice he still speaks, even though he is dead. [5]By faith Enoch was lifted up so that he did not see death, and he was not found because God lifted him up. For before he was lifted up, he was commended because he pleased God. [6]Without faith it is impossible to please him, for the one who approaches God must believe that God exists and that he rewards those who seek after him. [7]By faith Noah, being warned about events that were not yet seen, in reverent regard built an ark for the salvation of his family. Through faith he judged the world, and he became an heir of righteousness through faith.

[8]By faith Abraham obeyed when called to go to a place that he would receive as an inheritance, and he went not knowing where he was going. [9]By faith he departed to live in the land of promise as a foreigner in a foreign country, living in tents with Isaac and Jacob, who were heirs with him of the same promise. [10]For he was looking for the city that has foundations, whose architect and builder is God. [11]By faith he received power to conceive, even though he was too old and Sarah was barren, because he considered the one who made the promise to be faithful. [12]Therefore, from one man, and this one as good as dead, were born descendants just like the stars of heaven in number and just like the innumerable grains of sand by the seashore.

[13]These men all died having faith, not receiving the things that were promised, but they saw them at a distance and welcomed them, confessing that they were strangers and foreigners on the earth. [14]For those who say these things make it obvious that they are seeking a homeland. [15]And if they had been thinking about the land that they had left, they would have had a chance to return. [16]Now they desire a better homeland; that is, a heavenly one. Therefore, God is not ashamed to be called their God, for he has made a city ready for them.

[17]By faith Abraham, when he was tested, offered up Isaac because he received the promises, but he was ready to sacrifice his only son. [18]For God said to him, *"In Isaac your descendants will be named."* [19]And Abraham reasoned that God was able to raise him from the dead, and, figuratively speaking, he received him back. [20]By faith Isaac blessed Jacob and Esau about their future. [21]By faith Jacob, while dying, blessed each of the sons of Joseph and worshipped as he leaned on the top of his staff. [22]By faith Joseph, near the end of his life, referred to the exodus of the Israelites and gave instructions concerning his bones.

11:1 Compare Alma 32:21; Ether 12:6. **11:2** *By God* has been added to clarify that the *people of old* were not simply given public commendation for their faith. **11:4** For Abel, see Genesis 4:4. **11:5** For Enoch, see Genesis 5:22–24. **11:6** Echoed in Doctrine and Covenants 63:11. **11:7** For Noah, see Genesis 6:13–9:17. **11:8** For Abraham, see Genesis 12:1–5. **11:9** For the modern *land of promise*, see Doctrine and Covenants 38:18. See Genesis 25:27 for the period when they lived in tents. **11:11** For Sarah, see Genesis 17:19; 21:2. **11:12** An allusion to Genesis 22:17. **11:13** Doctrine and Covenants 45:13 quotes this verse. **11:15** Perhaps an allusion to Genesis 24:5–8. **11:17** This event is described in Genesis 22:1–9. **11:18** Quotation from Genesis 21:12. **11:19** *Abraham* has been added to clarify the Greek pronoun *he*. **11:20** The story is told in Genesis 27:27–40. **11:21** An allusion to Genesis 47:31. The story is told in Genesis 48:8–22. **11:22** See Genesis 50:25.

²³By faith Moses, when he was born, was hidden for three months by his parents because they saw that the child was beautiful and were not afraid of the king's edict. ²⁴By faith Moses, when he was grown, refused to be called the son of Pharaoh's daughter ²⁵and chose rather to be mistreated with the people of God than to enjoy sin's fleeting pleasure. ²⁶He considered the reproach experienced for Christ to be greater than the treasures of Egypt, for he was looking for the reward. ²⁷By faith he departed from Egypt, not fearing the wrath of the king, for he persevered as though he could see the invisible one. ²⁸By faith he kept the Passover and sprinkled the blood so that the destroyer of the firstborn would not touch them.

²⁹By faith they crossed the Red Sea as though it were dry land, but when the Egyptians tried they were drowned. ³⁰By faith the walls of Jericho fell when they marched around them for seven days. ³¹By faith Rahab the prostitute did not die with those who were disobedient, because she received the spies in peace.

³²And what more will I say? For time will fail me in recounting Gideon, Barak, Samson, Jephthah, David and Samuel, and the prophets, ³³who through faith conquered kingdoms, administered justice, obtained promises, shut the mouths of lions, ³⁴quenched the power of fire, escaped the edge of the sword, became strong from their weaknesses, grew strong in war, and put foreign armies to flight. ³⁵Women received their dead who were raised to life, but some were tortured, not accepting release so that they might rise again in a better life. ³⁶Others suffered mocking and scourging and even chains of imprisonment. ³⁷They were stoned, sawn in two, killed by the sword. They went around in sheepskins and goatskins being destitute, afflicted and ill treated ³⁸(the world was not worthy of them), wandering around in deserts and mountains and in caves and caverns in the earth. ³⁹And these were all commended because of their faith, but they did not receive what was promised. ⁴⁰For God has provided something better for us so that they would not be made perfect without us.

JESUS, THE ARCHITECT OF OUR FAITH

12 ¹Therefore, since we are surrounded by such a great cloud of witnesses, we must put off every weight and sin that clings closely to us and run with endurance the race that is set out before us, ²looking to Jesus, the architect and perfecter of our faith, who for the joy set out before him suffered a cross despite its shame, and he has sat down on the right hand of the throne of God. ³Consider the one who endured such contempt against himself from

---

11:23 See Exodus 2:2. **11:24** See Exodus 2:10. **11:29** See Exodus 14. **11:31** See Joshua 2:1–11. **11:32** For Gideon (Judges 6–8), Barak (Judges 4), Samson (Judges 13–16), Jephthah (Judges 11–12), David and Samuel (1–2 Samuel). **11:33** Perhaps an allusion to Daniel 6:19–23. **11:34** Perhaps an allusion to Daniel 3:27. **11:35** Jacob 4:11 speaks of rising in the resurrection in a way that is similar to this verse. Jacob speaks of *obtaining a resurrection*, which the King James translation uses in this verse. The concept is that of rising to a better life and striving to obtain it. **11:37** Perhaps an allusion to 2 Chronicles 24:21 (stoned), 2 Kings 2:8–13; Zechariah 13:4 (sheepskins). Some important manuscripts read (*they were*) *tempted* in place of (*they were*) *sawn in two*, but the better reading is the one given in the translation. Tradition holds that Isaiah was sawn in two. **11:40** The Joseph Smith Translation reads *God having provided some better things for them through their sufferings, for without sufferings they could not be made perfect.*

12:1 Nephi uses a similar phrase (2 Nephi 4:18) to describe his struggle with sin. Compare Alma 7:15. **12:2** An allusion to Psalm 110:1. Moroni 6:4 refers to *the author and finisher of their faith*. The clause *endured the crosses of the world* appears in 2 Nephi 9:18.

sinners so that you may not grow tired in your souls and give up.

⁴You have not resisted to the point of bloodshed in your struggle against sin. ⁵And have you forgotten the exhortation that called you as children? *"My child, do not disregard the Lord's discipline or be weary when reproved by him. ⁶For the Lord disciplines the one he loves and chastises every child whom he receives."*

⁷Endure trials for the purpose of discipline; God is treating you as children. For what child is there that a father does not discipline? ⁸If you are without discipline, which is something all children have shared, then you are illegitimate and not true children. ⁹Indeed, we have had mortal fathers who disciplined us, and we respected them. Shall we not be much more subject to the Father of spirits and live? ¹⁰For they disciplined us for a little while according to what seemed appropriate to them, but he disciplines us for our good so that we may share in his holiness. ¹¹All discipline seems to be painful at the time and not joyful, but later it produces the peaceful fruit of righteousness for those who have learned by it.

¹²Therefore, *"lift up your hands that hang down and strengthen your weak knees,"* ¹³and make straight the paths of your feet so that what is weak may not be thrown out of joint but be healed.

WARNINGS

¹⁴Seek for peace with everyone and for the holiness without which no one will see the Lord. ¹⁵See to it that no one falls short of the grace of God, that no one is like a bitter root sprouting up and causing trouble, and through him many become defiled. ¹⁶And make sure that no one is immoral or unholy like Esau, who sold his birthright for a single meal. ¹⁷For you know that later, when he wished to inherit the blessing, he was rejected, for he found no opportunity to repent even though he sought for it with tears.

¹⁸For you have not come to something that can be touched, to a burning fire, darkness, gloom, and a tempest, ¹⁹and the sound of a trumpet and a voice speaking, which caused the hearers to beg that a word might not be spoken to them. ²⁰For they could not bear what was commanded, *"If even an animal touches the mountain, it must be stoned."* ²¹And the sight was so terrifying that Moses said, *"I am trembling with fear."* ²²But you have come to Mount Zion, the city of the living God, the heavenly Jerusalem, and to a myriad of angels in a celebratory gathering ²³and to the assembly of the firstborn who are enrolled in heaven and to God, the judge of all, and the spirits of righteous people made perfect ²⁴and to Jesus, the mediator of the new covenant, and to the spilled blood that speaks something better than Abel's offering does.

12:5 The Greek noun *children* is *male children*, but in this instance it refers to both sons and daughters. **12:5–6** Quotation from Proverbs 3:11–12. **12:12** Quotation from Isaiah 35:3 (compare Doctrine and Covenants 81:5). **12:13** An allusion to Proverbs 4:26. **12:15** An allusion to Deuteronomy 29:17. **12:16** An allusion to Genesis 27:34–41. The *immorality or unholy* actions of Esau are not sexual in nature. The author uses a broader definition of *immorality*. **12:17** See Genesis 27:34–38. **12:18** *Something that can be touched* is Mount Sinai (Exodus 19; Deuteronomy 4:11–12). **12:19** See Exodus 20:19. **12:20** Quotation from Exodus 19:12–13. The quotation provides the author's understanding of why the Israelites were afraid to hear the voice of the Lord. **12:21** Quotation from Deuteronomy 9:19. **12:22–24** Commentary on these verses is given in Doctrine and Covenants 76:66–69. Compare Doctrine and Covenants 93:22; 107:19; 138:12. Perhaps an allusion to the *myriad angels* in Daniel 7:10. **12:23** Doctrine and Covenants 76:66–69 and 107:19 allude to this verse.

²⁵See that you do not reject the one who is speaking. For if they did not escape when they rejected the one who warned them on earth, how much less will we, if we reject the one who warns from heaven? ²⁶Then his voice shook the earth, and now he has promised, saying, "*I will once more shake not only the earth but heaven also.*" ²⁷This phrase *once more* indicates the removal of what is shaken (that is, the things that have been made) in order that what cannot be shaken may remain. ²⁸Therefore, since we are receiving an unshakable kingdom, let us give thanks, through which we may serve God pleasingly with devotion and awe. ²⁹For our "*God is a consuming fire.*"

CHRISTIAN LIFE

13 ¹Brotherly love must continue; ²do not neglect to show hospitality, for by doing so some have welcomed angels as guests without knowing it. ³Remember those who are in prison as though you were in prison with them and those who were mistreated because you also have a body. ⁴Marriage must be honored by all and the marriage bed be undefiled, for God will judge the immoral and adulterous. ⁵Your behavior must be free from the love of money, and you must be content with what you have now. For he has said, "*I will never leave you or forsake you.*" ⁶Because of this we can say with confidence, "*The Lord is my helper, and I will not fear. What can a man do to me?*"

⁷Remember your leaders, the ones who spoke the word of God to you, and consider their behavior and imitate their faith. ⁸Jesus Christ is the same yesterday, today, and forever. ⁹Do not be led away by diverse and strange teachings, for it is good for the heart to be established in grace, not in foods, which have not benefited those who participated in them. ¹⁰We have an altar that those who serve in the tabernacle have no authority to eat from. ¹¹For the bodies of those animals whose blood is brought into the holy place by the high priest as an offering for sin, they are burned outside of the camp. ¹²Jesus also suffered outside the gate so that he might make the people holy through his own blood. ¹³Therefore, let us go to him outside the camp and bear the abuse he suffered. ¹⁴For we have no lasting city here, but we will seek the one to come. ¹⁵Therefore, through him let us continually offer a sacrifice of praise to God, which is the fruit of the lips that give thanks to his name. ¹⁶Do not neglect to do good and share in the common good, for God is pleased with such sacrifices.

¹⁷Obey your leaders and submit to them, for they are watching over your souls, as ones who provide an account of things. Let them do this with joy and without making a complaint, for this would be of no advantage to you.

¹⁸Pray for us, for we are certain that we have a clear conscience, desiring to act uprightly in every way. ¹⁹I encourage you to do this all the more so that I may more quickly be restored to you.

12:26 Quotation from Haggai 2:6. Alluded to in Doctrine and Covenants 84:118. **12:29** Quotation from Deuteronomy 4:24; 9:3.

13:2 The author may have in mind the story of Abraham and Sarah (Genesis 18:2–15) or Lot (Genesis 19:1–14), who received angels as guests. **13:5** Quotation from Deuteronomy 31:6, 8. **13:6** Quotation from Psalm 118:6. **13:8** The phrase *the same yesterday, today, and forever* is used only once in the Bible but frequently in the Book of Mormon (1 Nephi 10:18; 2 Nephi 2:4; 27:23; 29:9; Alma 31:17; Mormon 9:9; Moroni 10:19). See also Doctrine and Covenants 20:12; 35:1. **13:9** A similar teaching is found in Ephesians 4:14; Colossians 2:8. **13:12** The practice is described in Leviticus 4:12. John 19:17–20 emphasizes Jesus's death outside the city walls of Jerusalem. **13:15** An allusion to Hosea 14:2.

CONCLUDING REMARKS

[20]May the God of peace, who brought our Lord Jesus again from the dead, Jesus the great shepherd of the sheep, by the blood of the eternal covenant, [21]equip you with every good thing in order to do his will, working in us that which is pleasing in his presence, through Jesus Christ, to whom be glory forever and ever. Amen.

[22]I call on you, brothers and sisters, to bear my message of exhortation, for I have written to you briefly. [23]Understand that our brother Timothy has been released, and if he comes soon I will see you together with him. [24]Greet all your leaders and all the saints. The saints from Italy greet you. [25]May grace be with all of you.

13:20 For shepherding imagery, see Isaiah 40:11; Ezekiel 34:23; John 10:11. **13:20–25** Hebrews has very few features suggesting that it was originally a letter, but the final verses are standard for a letter. **13:22** Greek uses *brothers* generically to refer to *brothers and sisters*. **13:23** Hebrews is formally anonymous and the only direct connection to Paul is the reference to Timothy, a traveling companion of Paul's. Timothy may also have been connected to other church leaders, and the text may have been written by someone who was similarly close to Timothy (compare Acts 16:1–3).

THE EPISTLE OF JAMES

John 7:5
1 Corinthians 15:7
Galatians 1:19

AUTHOR

Jacob—or James, as the name is most often translated—was the brother of the Lord (Matthew 13:55; Mark 6:3) and, according to later Christian sources, a leader in the Jerusalem community of believers (see also Galatians 2:9). There is a strong series of parallels in language between Acts 15:13–21, a speech in Jerusalem by Jacob, and the letter bearing his name, suggesting to many that this letter represents an early, but not dependent, account of Jacob's view of early church practice and belief. Moreover, the author knew teachings from the Sermon on the Mount (see notes) but not in the form those teachings are recorded in the Gospels of Matthew and Luke. This is a further suggestion that the letter may be potentially quite early, perhaps from the 60s or 70s CE.

Despite being written by a widely recognizable figure from the New Testament, the Epistle of James struggled to be accepted into the canon. Several fourth-century lists of the canon (Muratorian, Cheltenham, and Mommensianus) lack the book. It is difficult to know why a book by one of Jesus's siblings would have been slow to be widely accepted. One feature of the letter is that it emphasizes the balance between works and grace differently than the Pauline letters (2:14–26) and thus probably appealed directly to Christian Jews, who had a heritage in the law of Moses. Gentile Christians may have found such teachings more difficult to accept, or they may have preferred Paul's greater emphasis on grace.

PURPOSE OF WRITING

The letter is intentionally written to Christian Jews, "to the twelve tribes of the diaspora," (1:1) and, as such, is probably to be understood as the New Testament's most clear assertion of a Jewish Christian position of faith in Jesus Christ. In 2:19, Jacob asks, "Do you believe there is a God?," which can also be translated as "Do you believe that God is one?" This is a quotation of the Shema (Deuteronomy 6:4) and would have been recognizable to all Jews. Within this context, the encouragement to "ask God" (1:5) is a directive to help the believer understand the importance of Judaism in a Christian's life.

Much of the letter is devoted to ethical advice, encouragement to seek for self-control, and care for others. Such advice envisions a community of committed believers striving

to make themselves better and to formalize their outward commitment to the Lord through righteous actions. Saints are advised to act like saints, and, as such, their faith will grow. Those who wander are mentioned, and believers are called on to lead those persons back to faith (5:19). With such a strong emphasis on a Jewish Christian perspective, and given the community-centered language, it seems possible that the letter was specifically written with Jerusalem in mind where nearly all Christians would have been Christian Jews. This would particularly fit the counsel on riches, given the difficult circumstances the saints in Jerusalem faced under the emperor Claudius (Acts 11:27–30).

CONNECTION TO LATTER-DAY SAINT BELIEFS

The most obvious connection to Latter-day Saint beliefs, and indeed the most important connection, is the famous directive "If anyone lacks wisdom, let that person ask God, who gives to everyone generously and without reproach, and it will be given to him" (1:5). In the context of the letter, the counsel is understood as a way for the believer to sift through differing interpretations of what it means to be Christian and also within the context of overcoming trial. Those words led a young Joseph Smith Jr. to ask God and seek for the very type of clarification that Jacob was speaking about. The verses following it further make that point, "for the one who doubts is like a wave of the sea that is driven and tossed by wind" (1:6), which the author hopes the believer can avoid if she or he will only ask God for guidance. ॐ

OPENING ADDRESS

1 ¹Jacob, a servant of God and the Lord Jesus Christ, to the twelve tribes in the diaspora, greetings.

²Consider it complete joy, brothers and sisters, when you fall into various kinds of trials, ³knowing that the test of your faith produces endurance. ⁴Let endurance have its full effect, so that you might be perfect and complete, lacking in nothing. ⁵If anyone lacks wisdom, let that person ask God, who gives to everyone generously and without reproach, and it will be given to him. ⁶Let a person ask in faith, without doubting, for the one who doubts is like a wave of the sea that is driven and tossed by wind. ⁷For that person must not suppose that he will receive something from the Lord, ⁸for that man is double-minded, unstable in all his ways.

Ὑποκριτε

ENDURING TRIAL

⁹Let the humble brother boast in his high position ¹⁰and the rich in his hum-ble position because like a flower of grass he will pass away. ¹¹For the sun rises with burning heat and dries up the grass; its flower falls, and its beauty perishes. It is likewise for the rich: while living a busy life, they will pass away.

¹²Blessed is the person who endures trial because after that person is proven to be acceptable, he will receive the crown of life, which God promises to those who love him. ¹³Let no one say when he is tempted, "I am being tempted by God." For God cannot be tempted with evil, and he tempts no one. ¹⁴But each person is tempted when he is lured and trapped by his own desires. ¹⁵When desire seizes a person it gives birth to sin, and when it is fully grown it gives birth to death.

¹⁶Do not be led astray, my beloved brothers and sisters. ¹⁷Every good gift and every perfect gift is from above, descending from the Father of lights, for whom there is no variation or shadow of change. ¹⁸By his will he brought us forth by the

---

1:1 *James* is the name *Jacob* in Hebrew, but modern convention renders it as *James*. The *diaspora* refers to Jews living outside of Judea and Galilee. **1:2** Greek uses *brothers* generically to refer to *brothers and sisters*. **1:4** The Epistle of James has numerous parallels to the Sermon on the Mount (Matthew 5–7; 3 Nephi 12–14), suggesting that the author was broadly familiar with its teachings. The parallels are not worded precisely as Matthew wrote them, but the concepts are similar (see Matthew 5:48). **1:5** See Matthew 7:7. This verse led Joseph Smith to enter the Sacred Grove and ask God for himself (Joseph Smith—History 1:11). Similar wording is used by the Lord in Doctrine and Covenants 42:68. A similar injunction is found in 2 Nephi 4:35. **1:8** The *double-minded* individual has two distinct identities, and the word is similar to the modern meaning of a hypocrite. **1:9** *Humble* is intended to refer to *poverty*, as the comparison to the rich in verse 10 makes clear. **1:10** Perhaps an allusion to Isaiah 40:6–8. *Flower of grass* may have referred to a specific type of flower common to meadows, but the exact reference is no longer clear. **1:12** Many early and important manuscripts lack the noun *God* and simply state *he*. This is probably the original reading, but the noun has been supplied for clarity. **1:12–13** The words *trial* and *temptation* are the same in Greek and can be used interchangeably in the translation. Modern translations favor the word *temptation* in verse 13, but *trial* in verse 12. The reason for doing so is the phrase *for God cannot be tempted with evil*, which appears to be a clarification that God can try a person but not be tempted by evil. Greek does not distinguish between the efforts of the devil to tempt and the efforts of God to try humankind. **1:12–14** These verses are delivered in the third-person singular and may refer to a male or female believer. Changing the verbs to plurals to capture both male and female believers loses the emphasis on the personal challenge of facing trial. **1:16** See note on 1:2. **1:17** The title *Father of lights* is used in Doctrine and Covenants 67:9. The idea that God is unchangeable is also found in Mormon 9:9, which uses the phrase *no variableness neither shadow of changing*.

word of truth in order for us to be a kind of firstfruits of his creations.

QUICK TO LISTEN

[19]Know this, my beloved brothers and sisters, let every person be quick to listen, slow to speak, slow to wrath. [20]For human wrath does not accomplish God's righteousness. [21]Therefore, put away all filth and evil excess, and welcome with meekness the word implanted in you, which can save your souls. [22]Become doers of the word and not merely hearers who deceive themselves [23]because if anyone is a hearer and not a doer, he is like a person who looks at his own image in a mirror. [24]For he carefully considers himself and then departs and immediately forgets what type of person he is. [25]But the one who carefully looks at the perfect law, the law of liberty, and abides in it, not being a forgetful hearer but a doer who acts, he will be blessed in his doing. [26]If anyone thinks he is religious and does not bridle his tongue but deceives his heart, his religion is worthless. [27]Pure and undefiled religion before God the Father is this: to visit the orphans and widows in their trials and to keep oneself unspotted from the world.

DO NOT SHOW PARTIALITY

2 [1]My brothers and sisters, do not possess partiality in your faith in our Lord Jesus Christ, the Lord of glory. [2]For if someone enters your gathering wearing a gold finger ring with fine clothing and a poor man in filthy clothing also enters, [3]if you pay attention to the one wearing fine clothing and say, "You sit here in a good place," but to the poor man you say, "You stand over there," or "Sit down near my feet," [4]have you not made distinctions in yourselves and become judges with evil reasoning? [5]Listen, my beloved brothers and sisters, has God not chosen the worldly poor to be rich in faith and heirs of the kingdom, which he has promised to those who love him? [6]But you have dishonored the poor. Are the rich not oppressing you and dragging you to the courts? [7]Are they not slandering the good name by which you were called?

[8]If you fulfill the royal law according to the scripture, "*You shall love your neighbor as yourself,*" you are doing well. [9]But if you show partiality, you are committing sin and are convicted by the law as transgressors. [10]For the one who obeys the whole Law but stumbles in one thing is guilty of the entire Law. [11]For he who said, "*Do not commit adultery,*" also said, "*Do not murder.*" If you do not commit adultery but you do commit murder, you have become a transgressor of the Law.

[12]So speak and act like those who will be judged by the law of liberty. [13]For judgment is merciless to the one who has not shown mercy. Mercy triumphs over judgment.

1:19 See note on 1:2. **1:22** See Paul's parallel teaching in Roman 2:13. **1:27** This verse is quoted in Doctrine and Covenants 59:9, where it is applied to the context of the Sabbath. A similar injunction is given in Doctrine and Covenants 44:6.

2:1 *Partiality* conveys the idea of preference for the wealthy believer over the poor believer in Christ. **2:1, 5, 14** Greek uses *brothers* generically to refer to *brothers and sisters*. **2:5** The *worldly poor* can also be translated as *the poor in the world*. There is perhaps an allusion to Matthew 11:5 and potentially a self-reference to the early believers being financially poor. **2:8** Quotation from Leviticus 19:18. The idea of a *royal law* is to connect the law to the king or perhaps even the law of the land. In this context it refers to the command to love one another, which is interpreted as God's law of the land. **2:9** An allusion to Deuteronomy 1:17. **2:10** See Matthew 5:19. **2:11** Quotations from Exodus 20:13–14; Deuteronomy 5:17–18.

FAITH WITHOUT WORKS IS DEAD

[14]What good is it, my brothers and sisters, if someone says he has faith but he does not have works? Is faith able to save him? [15]If a brother or a sister is poorly clothed and lacking daily food, [16]and someone from among you says, "Depart in peace; be warm and eat well," but you do not give them the things needed for the body, what good comes from it? [17]Thus faith by itself, if it does not have works, is dead.

[18]But someone will say, "You have faith, and I have works." Show me your faith without works, and I will show you my faith by my works. [19]You believe that there is a God, you do well. Even the demons believe and are struck with fear.

[20]Do you want to know, you empty person, that faith without works is useless? [21]Was our father Abraham not made righteous by works when he offered his son Isaac upon the altar? [22]You see that faith was working in tandem with his works, and his faith was made perfect by works. [23]And the scripture was fulfilled that says, *"Abraham believed God, and it was counted to him for righteousness,"* and he was called a friend of God. [24]You see that a person is made righteous by works and not by faith only. [25]Likewise, was not Rahab the prostitute also made righteous by works when she received the messengers and sent them out by another way? [26]For just as the body without the spirit is dead, even so faith without works is dead.

THE TONGUE IS A FIRE

3 [1]Not many of you should become teachers, my brothers and sisters, knowing that we who teach will receive the harsher judgment. [2]For we all stumble in many ways, and if anyone does not stumble in what he says, he is a perfect man and is also able to bridle his whole body also. [3]If we put bits into the mouths of horses so that they obey us, then we guide their whole bodies. [4]Look at the ships. Although they are quite large and driven by strong winds, they are steered by a small rudder wherever the desire of the pilot steers them. [5]Thus the tongue is a small member and boasts of great things. Look how such a small flame burns a large forest. [6]And the tongue is a fire. The tongue makes itself an unrighteous world among our members: it defiles the entire body and

---

2:16 See Doctrine and Covenants 104:18, where the Lord commands us to care for the poor. Compare Doctrine and Covenants 38:35; 42:30. **2:17** The idea that faith without works *is dead* implies that faith alone does not have sufficient power to save a person. **2:18** It is not certain where the quotation ends, but the translation follows current scholarly thinking on the issue. **2:20** Some early and important manuscripts read *faith without works is dead*, while some read *faith without works is useless*. Although not based on the strongest textual support, the translation opts for what appears to be the original reading. The word *dead* probably arises from the parallel in verse 17 and 26. The other reading (*useless*) has weaker textual support. **2:21** This story is told in Genesis 22:9–14. **2:21–22** *Faith* and *works*, according to Jacob, work in tandem for the salvation of the believer. This perspective relies heavily on the concept of obedience to law and the commandments. **2:23** Quotation from Genesis 15:6. The last part of the verse is an allusion to Isaiah 41:8. **2:25** Rahab's story is told in Joshua 2.

3:1 *Teachers* are discussed in a general sense and not as a priesthood office. Doctrine and Covenants 82:3 also speaks of *harsher judgment* or *greater condemnation*. It is unclear why teachers will receive a greater condemnation unless Jacob is insinuating that teachers have a greater potential to lead believers astray. **3:6** *Hell* in this verse is *Gehenna*, a reference to the *Hinnom Valley* on the south side of the city of Jerusalem. The valley became a metaphor for *hell* because there were possibly human offerings made in the valley (Jeremiah 7:31), and later trash was dumped in the valley. The strong criticism of the *tongue*, or the things a person says, suggests that Jacob has a specific event in mind. This criticism is particularly pointed.

sets on fire the cycle of human existence, and it is set on fire by hell.

[7]For every type of animal and bird, reptile and sea creature, is subdued and has been subdued by humankind. [8]But no one is able to tame the tongue; it is a tireless evil, full of deadly poison. [9]With it we bless the Lord and Father, and with it we curse people who are made in God's image. [10]From the same mouth come blessing and cursing. These things should not be so, my brothers and sisters. [11]Can a spring bring forth sweet and bitter water out of the same opening? [12]Can a fig tree, my brothers and sisters, make olives? Or can a grape vine make figs? Neither can a saltwater spring make fresh water.

WHO IS WISE?

[13]Who is wise and understanding among you? Let his good conduct demonstrate his works done in the kindness of wisdom. [14]But if you have bitter jealousy and selfishness in your hearts, do not boast and lie against the truth. [15]This wisdom does not descend from above but is earthly, human, and demonic. [16]For where there is zeal and selfishness, there is discord and every wicked practice. [17]But the wisdom from above is first of all pure, then peaceable, gentle, open to persuasion, full of mercy and good fruits, impartial, and sincere.

[18]And the fruit of righteousness is sown in peace by those who make peace.

BE HUMBLE

4 [1]What is the source of conflicts and fights among you? Is it not from your passions at war within you? [2]You want something but you do not have it, so you murder. And you covet something but you cannot obtain it so you fight and quarrel. You do not have it because you do not ask. [3]You ask and do not receive because you ask wrongly so that you can waste it on your passions. [4]Adulterers, do you not understand that friendship with the world is enmity toward God? Therefore, whoever desires to be a friend with the world, makes himself an enemy of God. [5]Or do you think that the scripture says without meaning it that "the spirit that lives in us has an envious desire"? [6]But he gives greater grace; therefore, it says, "*God opposes the proud, but he gives grace to the humble.*" [7]Therefore, submit to God, but resist the devil, and he will flee from you. [8]Draw near to God, and he will draw near to you. Cleanse your hands, sinners, and purify your hearts, you double-minded. [9]Grieve, mourn, and weep, and let your laughter turn to mourning and your joy into heaviness. [10]Be humble before the Lord, and he will exalt you.

3:10 Greek uses *brothers* generically to refer to *brothers and sisters*. **3:11** Compare Moroni 7:11. **3:12** See Matthew 7:16. **3:16** *Zeal* can also be translated as *jealousy*.

4:1 Or *at war in your members*. The question posed by Jacob implies that there has been infighting among the Christian communities to whom he was writing. The problem appears to have originated from false teachers (see chapter 3). **4:3** This verse is quoted in Doctrine and Covenants 46:9 following the language of the King James translation. Compare 2 Nephi 4:35; Mormon 9:28. **4:4** The wording suggests that the community of the faithful had come to see the world as its enemy, perhaps as a result of persecution or rejection for believing in Jesus. **4:5** The source of this quotation is unknown, but it is clearly a quotation from a source (see Proverbs 21:10). It may represent a lost scripture, but it may also be a summary of various scriptural ideas. The passage also has several textual variants that make it clear that scribes had trouble with the passage. The older and most reliable manuscripts read *the spirit that God caused to live in us has an envious desire*. The translation favors the reading of later manuscripts in order to make sense of the unclear passage, and the sentence lacks a clear subject, so *God* must be supplied to complete the meaning. **4:6** Quotation from Proverbs 3:34. **4:8** For the term *double-minded*, see note on James 1:8.

DO NOT SPEAK AGAINST A BROTHER OR SISTER

[11]Do not speak against one another, brothers and sisters. The one who speaks against a brother or sister judges his brother or sister and speaks against the Law and judges the Law. But if you judge the Law, you are not a doer of the Law but a judge. [12]There is one lawgiver and judge, the one who is able to save and destroy. But who are you to judge your neighbor?

BOASTING

[13]Come now, you who say, "Today or tomorrow we will enter into such and such a town and will stay there a year and trade and turn a profit." [14]But you do not know about tomorrow. What is your life? For you are a swirl of smoke that appears for a short time, and then it vanishes. [15]Instead, you should say, "If the Lord desires it, then we will live and do this or that." [16]But now you boast in your arrogance. All such boasting is evil. [17]Therefore, whoever knows how to do what is good and does not do it, for that person it is sin.

PROBLEMS WITH RICHES

5 [1]Come now and weep and wail over the miseries that are coming upon you who are rich. [2]Your riches have rotted, and your clothing is moth-eaten. [3]Your gold and silver have rusted, and their rust will be a sign against you, and it will eat your flesh like fire. You have stored up your treasure in the last days. [4]Behold, the wages you withheld fraudulently from the laborers who reaped your fields, they cry out against you, and their shouts have reached the ears of the Lord of hosts. [5]You have lived in luxury and self-indulgence on the earth. You have fattened your hearts in a day of slaughter. [6]You have condemned and murdered the righteous person, but he does not resist you.

BE PATIENT

[7]Therefore, be patient, brothers and sisters, until the coming of the Lord. Behold how the farmer waits for the precious fruit of the earth, remaining patient until he receives the early and late rains. [8]Be patient also and strengthen your hearts because the coming of the Lord draws near. [9]Do not grumble against one another, brothers and sisters, so that you are not judged. Behold, the one who judges is standing at the doors. [10]Brothers and sisters, take the prophets who spoke in the name of the Lord as an example of suffering and patience. [11]Behold, we regard those who endured as blessed. You have heard of Job's endurance and have seen the Lord's purpose, that the Lord is full of compassion and mercy. [12]Above all, my brothers and sisters, do not swear by heaven or by the earth or with any other oath, but let your "yes" be yes and your "no" be no, so that you do not fall under condemnation.

CONFESS YOUR SINS

[13]Is anyone among you suffering? Let him pray. Is anyone in good spirits? Let

---

4:11 Greek uses *brothers* generically to refer to *brothers and sisters*. The word *law* in this verse is used in the sense of the *commandments* so that a person speaks against the validity of the commandments, or the law of God. Jacob may also have intended the reader to think of the law of Moses. Many of the statutes of the law of Moses were still in effect for early Christian believers. **4:12** See Matthew 7:1.

5:4 An allusion to Isaiah 5:9 and the law found in Leviticus 19:13. Many translations have used the phrase *Lord Sabaoth*, which means the *Lord of armies*, or *Lord of the heavenly host*. This verse is echoed in Doctrine and Covenants 87:7; 95:7; 98:2 (compare Romans 9:29). **5:5** An allusion to Jeremiah 12:3. **5:7, 9–10, 12, 19** Greek uses *brothers* generically to refer to *brothers and sisters*. **5:8** Quoted in Doctrine and Covenants 106:4. **5:10** Compare Abinadi's sufferings as described in Mosiah 17:13–15. **5:11** An allusion to Exodus 34:6. **5:12** See Matthew 5:34–37.

him sing. ¹⁴Is anyone ill among you? He should call on the elders of the church and let them pray over him, anointing him with oil in the name of the Lord. ¹⁵And the prayer of faith will save the one who is sick and the Lord will raise him, and if he has committed sins, he will be forgiven. ¹⁶Therefore, confess your sins to one another and pray for one another in order that you might be healed. The effective prayer of a righteous person has great power. ¹⁷Elijah was a man with passions like ours, and he prayed earnestly that it would not rain, and there was no rain on the land for three years and six months. ¹⁸And he prayed again, and the heaven gave rain and the earth brought forth its fruit.

¹⁹My brothers and sisters, if anyone among you wanders from the truth and someone brings him back, ²⁰let him know that the person who brings him back from his wandering path will save that person's soul from death and will cover a multitude of sins.

5:14 Compare Doctrine and Covenants 42:44. **5:15** Doctrine and Covenants 104:80 echoes this verse. **5:17–18** The story is told in 1 Kings 17:1; 18:42–45.

1 PETER

AUTHOR

In the first sentence of the letter, the author identifies himself as "Peter, an apostle of Jesus Christ," who was writing to a number of communities in Asia (modern Turkey). The language of the letter is Greek, and it is some of the best Greek in the New Testament, a significant departure from the quality of Greek in 2 Peter. A variety of historical considerations have led scholars to question the authorship of 1 Peter. The major concerns are that the Greek seems too sophisticated for a Galilean fisherman who was "uneducated," according to Acts 4:13. The writer also omitted any significant discussion of the life of Jesus and accompanying miracles or events, and the author quoted from the Greek translation of the Old Testament rather than the Hebrew. Against this view, scholars have noted that early Christians consistently attributed this book to Peter, that other methods of writing and transmission could account for the elevated Greek such as the use of a scribe, and that even if the letter were written by another Christian on Peter's behalf, the ideas and concepts are still traceable to Peter.

A decision on this matter is hardly possible given the lack of information in our historical record. An important consideration in this discussion is the concept of intent in writing a letter in another person's name. The practice of writing a letter on someone else's behalf would be described by modern literary theory as manipulation and deception. However, the historical situation is much more complex than that, and the document may have indeed been written by someone else on Peter's behalf after that individual had compiled the available source documents, read the existing writings attributed to Peter, and then put together what he or she felt was the most accurate representation of those ideas.

PURPOSE OF WRITING

In this epistle, Peter writes from a position of awareness that the saints are experiencing persecution and suffering. The letter addresses the problem of persecution generally and specifically, suggesting that there were both specific events in mind and a general sense of how that persecution had affected the saints. Specifically, the saints faced challenges to their belief (3:15), and they suffered abuse as a result (3:14–16; 4:4, 14–16). Other

advice in the letter should be interpreted in light of the overarching context of persecution. The question "Who will harm you if you seek what is good?" (3:13) draws attention to the fact that the persecution they suffered was most likely a result of the accusation of being malefactors or evildoers. The general accusation of wickedness is probably not tied to an official, empire-wide persecution but rather a localized experience where a community suffered at the hands of their neighbors.

In a related way, Peter also seems to hint that the saints might be close to failure. The closing lines offer encouragement through a promise of reward: "And the God of all grace, who has called you to his eternal glory in Christ, after you have suffered a little while, will restore, confirm, strengthen, and establish you" (5:10). The context seems to be that if the saints can hold out for a short time, then they will be delivered or saved, but the encouragement also suggests a hint of fear that perhaps the saints will not endure long enough.

CONNECTION TO LATTER-DAY SAINT BELIEFS

One of the more powerful connections to the Restoration is found in the second chapter, where Peter compares the community of saints to the old system of priests and encouraged them to become a "holy priesthood" (2:5) that is capable of offering "spiritual sacrifices that are acceptable to God through Jesus Christ" (2:5). The language of this passage is not gender specific and should not be taken as a directive only to male saints but to all saints, who are to become like the priests of the Levitical order. The saints are to offer a new type of offering to God, "a chosen race, a royal priesthood, a holy nation, a people acquired" (2:9). That new offering is idealized in the advice to the saints, telling them "that you may spend the remainder of your time in the flesh no longer according to human desires but according to the will of God" (4:2). Such a vision for the community of believers encourages everyone to seek for the holiness that the priests had obtained, and now the new community emerges as a people of priesthood devoted to offering themselves to God through Jesus Christ. First Peter also played a foundational role in the revelation of Doctrine and Covenants 138, when President Joseph F. Smith pondered the meaning of 1 Peter 3:18–20 and 1 Peter 4:6. ❧

Opening Address

1 ¹Peter, an apostle of Jesus Christ, to the elect who are exiles in the diaspora, in Pontus, Galatia, Cappadocia, Asia, and Bythinia, ²who are chosen according to the foreknowledge of God the Father and consecrated by the Spirit for obedience and sprinkling with the blood of Jesus Christ: may grace and peace be multiplied to you.

The Test of Faith

³Blessed be the God and Father of our Lord Jesus Christ. According to his great mercy he gave us new birth into a living hope through the resurrection of Jesus Christ from the dead ⁴into an inheritance that is imperishable, undefiled, and unfading, reserved in heaven for you, ⁵who by God's power are guarded through faith for a salvation that is prepared and to be revealed in the last time. ⁶In this you rejoice, although you have been grieved, if necessary, for a little while by various trials ⁷so that the test of your genuine faith is much more precious than gold—gold that is tested by fire even though it perishes—and may result in praise, glory, and honor when Jesus Christ is revealed. ⁸You have not seen him, but you love him. Although you do not see him now, you believe and rejoice with a joy that is indescribable and glorious, ⁹a result of obtaining the outcome of your faith, the salvation of your souls.

¹⁰Concerning this salvation, the prophets who foretold the grace that would come to you searched and inquired diligently, ¹¹inquiring what person or time the Spirit of Christ was indicating when he testified beforehand concerning the sufferings of Christ and their attendant glories. ¹²It was revealed to them that they were not serving themselves but you with respect to the things now declared to you through those who proclaimed the gospel to you by the Holy Spirit sent from heaven, things about which the angels desire to glimpse.

1:1 This letter was addressed to saints living outside of Judea using language that is usually reserved for describing Jews who live outside of Judea in what was called the diaspora. The opening verse suggests that the Christian homeland was also Judea. *Apostle* is used in a technical sense in this verse, referring to a wider authority to preach the gospel. **1:2** *Chosen* in this context can mean selected or even *choice* or *preeminent.* **1:3** This *new birth* is likely a reference to baptism that signals a new beginning in the quest for salvation. **1:4–5** These verses describe in general terms the heavenly gift of salvation that awaits the righteous. **1:7** Ether 12:6 also speaks of a trial or *test of faith* as a singular moment. **1:8** Alluded to in Helaman 5:44. **1:9** The word *outcome* can also be translated as the *end, result,* or *purpose.* **1:10** The word translated as *salvation* also means *safety* or *deliverance.* A person's *salvation* is something that is granted to them by God as a means of protecting and delivering them.

Diaspora Communities
Map by Brandon Whitney, ThinkSpatial, BYU Geography

You Shall Be Holy

[13]Therefore, prepare your minds for action and, being sober in mind, place your hope completely upon the grace that will be brought to you with the revelation of Jesus Christ. [14]As obedient children, do not be conformed with the evil desires of your earlier ignorance, [15]but just as the one who called you is holy, be holy also in all your conduct [16]because it is written, "*You shall be holy, for I am holy.*" [17]And if you address him as a Father who judges impartially according to each person's actions, live the time of your earthly residence in fear. [18]You know that you were ransomed from your empty life inherited from your ancestors, not by perishable things like silver or gold [19]but with the precious blood of Christ like that of an unblemished and spotless lamb. [20]He was foreknown before the foundation of the world, but he was made manifest in the last times for you, [21]who through him are believers in God, who raised him from the dead and gave him glory so that your faith and hope are in God.

[22]You have purified your souls in obedience to the truth in order to show mutual love, so love one another earnestly from a pure heart. [23]You have been born again, not from perishable seed but from imperishable seed through the living and abiding word of God. [24]For "*all flesh is like grass, and all its glory is like the flower of grass. The grass withers and the flower falls,* [25]*but the word of the Lord abides forever.*" And this is the word that was proclaimed to you.

A Royal Priesthood

2 [1]Therefore, put aside all evil, deceit, hypocrisy, envy, and all slander. [2]Like newborn infants, yearn for the pure, spiritual milk so that in it you may grow into salvation, [3]if indeed *you have tasted the Lord's goodness.*

[4]As you approach him, a living stone on the one hand rejected by men, but chosen and honored by God on the other, [5]as living stones you yourselves are established as a residence of the Spirit to be a holy priesthood to offer spiritual sacrifices that are acceptable to God through Jesus Christ. [6]For as it stands in scripture, "*Behold, I am laying a stone in Zion, a cornerstone chosen and honored, and whoever believes in him will not be put to shame.*" [7]Therefore, he is precious to those who believe, but for those who do not believe, "*the stone that the builders rejected has become the cornerstone,*" [8]and "*a stone of stumbling, and a rock of offense.*" They stumble because they refuse to believe the word, as they were destined to do. [9]But you are a chosen race, a royal priesthood, a holy nation, a people acquired so that you declare the virtues of the one who called you from darkness to his amazing light. [10]Once you were not a

---

1:14 This verse seems to indicate that the recipients of this letter were not formerly obedient to God's counsels and that therefore they were likely Gentiles before accepting the faith of Christ. **1:16** Quotation from Leviticus 11:44; 19:2; 20:7. **1:19** See Deuteronomy 15:21 for the command to use an *unblemished lamb.* **1:24–25** Quotation from Isaiah 40:6, 8.

2:3 Quotation from Psalm 34:8. **2:4–5** An allusion to Psalm 118:22, but Peter changes the allusion to refer to *living stones.* Christians are to model their actions on the *living stone,* who is Jesus (verse 4). **2:5** *Holy priesthood* refers to the actions and duties of the priests. The allusion to the priests of Levi calls to mind a course of service that is holy and led by the Spirit. The human *spirit* is also possible. **2:6** Quotation from Isaiah 28:16. **2:7** Quotation from Psalm 118:22. **2:8** Quotation from Isaiah 8:14. The word *destined* also means *set in place, established,* or *ordained.* **2:9** *Race* can refer to a people or ethnic group. Peter is suggesting that the believers in Christ have become a new people or race. Allusions to Exodus 19:6; Deuteronomy 7:6; Isaiah 43:20–21. **2:10** An allusion to Hosea 1:9; 2:23. The reference to *mercy* implies caring for the poor or showing *mercy* to those in need. The physical act of showing *mercy* is often translated as *giving alms* or *showing compassion.*

people, but now you are God's people, and once you were shown no mercy, but now you have received mercy.

ACCEPT AUTHORITY

[11]Beloved, I encourage you as foreigners and exiles to stay away from fleshly desires that are at war with the soul [12]and maintain your good conduct among the Gentiles so that when they speak against you as evildoers they will look upon your good works and give glory to God in the day of visitation.

[13]Be subject to every human institution for the Lord's sake, whether to the king as supreme [14]or to governors as those who are sent to punish evildoers and to praise those who do good, [15]because this is the will of God, that by doing good you may put the misunderstanding of foolish people to silence. [16]Be like those who are free, not using your freedom for evil, but be like God's servants. [17]Honor all people; love the family of God; fear God; honor the king.

COUNSEL ABOUT SERVANTS

[18]Household servants, be subject to your masters with complete respect, not only to the good and gentle but also to the unfair.

[19]For this pleases God if a person endures grief while suffering unjustly as a consequence of conscience toward God. [20]For what credit is it if, when you sin and are beaten as a result, you endure? But if when you do good and suffer for it you endure, this is pleasing before God. [21]For this you have been called because Christ also suffered for you, leaving an example for you so that you might follow in his steps. [22]*"He committed no sin, nor was deceit found in his mouth."* [23]He was abused but did not respond with reviling. When he suffered, he did not threaten, but he gave himself to the one who judges righteously. [24]He himself bore our sins in his body on the tree so that we may cease to sin and live to righteousness. By his wounds you have been healed. [25]For you were wandering like sheep, but now you have turned back to the shepherd and guardian of your souls.

COUNSEL FOR WIVES AND HUSBANDS

3 [1]Likewise, women, be subject to your own husbands so that even if some do not obey the word, they will be won over without a word by the conduct of their spouses [2]when they see your respectful and holy conduct. [3]Do not let your adornment be external—braiding of hair,

---

2:11 *Soul* refers to the spiritual component of the person. Restoration scripture often speaks of the spirit in this way. **2:12** An allusion to Isaiah 10:3. **2:13** The word *institution* refers to things that were created for the benefit and governance of humankind. It includes *civic*, *public*, and even *private* institutions that are established for the betterment of humankind. The *king* is probably *Caesar* or *the emperor* (see also verse 17). **2:17** *The family of God* in Greek is *the brotherhood*. The word refers to *the brotherhood and sisterhood*, and therefore the phrase *family of God* best captures the inclusive sense of the term. The *king* may refer to the *emperor*. **2:18** The injunction to *household servants* was likely given in an interest to protect the social balance between Christians and the communities where they resided. The interest appears to be an effort to not draw attention to the house churches and new communities of believers. These interests, however, should not excuse the practice of slavery nor should it soften modern attitudes to this abhorrent practice. Peter draws upon the example of Christ as one who suffered without reacting against his abusers. **2:22** Quotation from Isaiah 53:9. **2:23** An allusion to Isaiah 53:7. **2:24** An allusion to Isaiah 53:4–5, 12. **2:25** An allusion to Isaiah 53:6. The word *guardian* is the Greek word *overseer* or *bishop*.

3:1–7 Peter uses the context of mutual influence to propose his guidelines on women in marriage. His counsel is similar to Paul's (1 Corinthians 7:1–16), and it is also typical of the first century. Common cultural perceptions such as referring to a woman as *the weaker vessel* inform this advice. Peter's approach

wearing gold jewelry, and wearing fine clothing—[4]but let it be the adornment of the inner person of the heart, the incorruptible beauty of the meek and quiet spirit, which is precious in God's sight. [5]For thus the holy women who long ago hoped in God used to adorn themselves by being subject to their own husbands, [6]as Sarah obeyed Abraham by calling him Lord. And you are her children when you do what is good and do not fear anything threatening.

[7]Likewise, men, live together in understanding with the weaker vessel, showing honor to your spouse as fellow heirs of the grace of life so that your prayers will not be hindered.

SUFFERING AS A RESULT OF BEING RIGHTEOUS

[8]Finally, all of you have unity in thought, sympathy, brotherly love, kind hearts, and humility. [9]Do not return evil for evil or reviling for reviling, but rather bless because you were called to inherit a blessing. [10]For *"whoever desires to love life, and see good days, let him keep his tongue from evil, and his lips from speaking deceit. [11]Let him turn away from evil and do good; let him seek peace and pursue it, [12]because the eyes of the Lord are upon the righteous, and his ears are open to their prayer, but the face of the Lord is against those who do evil."* [13]And who will harm you if you seek what is good? [14]But if you were to suffer for the sake of righteousness, you are blessed. *"Do not be afraid of them or be shaken."* [15]But hold Christ as holy in your hearts, always being prepared to offer a defense to anyone who asks you for a reason for the hope that is in you, [16]but do so with meekness and fear, maintaining a good conscience so that those who speak against your behavior in Christ may be put to shame when they slander you. [17]For it is better to suffer for doing good, if it is God's will, than for doing evil. [18]Because Christ also suffered for sins once for all, the just for the unjust, in order to bring you to God by being put to death in the flesh and by being made alive in the spirit, [19]in which he entered and preached to the spirits in prison [20]when they were formerly disobedient, when God waited patiently in the days of Noah as the ark was being prepared, in which a few, specifically eight persons, were carried safely through water. [21]This is a type of baptism that now saves you, not washing away physical dirt but as an appeal to God for a clear conscience through the resurrection of Jesus Christ, [22]who entered into heaven and is on the right hand of God with angels, authorities, and powers subject to him.

---

seems to be an effort to maintain current social boundaries and relationships with a concern for internal harmony. **3:10–12** Quotation from Psalm 34:12–16. The context of Peter's advice is expanded to include the scriptural injunction that the Lord looks favorably upon those who do not act with deceit and practice evil. **3:14** Quotation from Isaiah 8:12. **3:15** An allusion to Isaiah 8:13. **3:15–16** The believer is encouraged to offer a rational defense of the faith that will withstand the scrutiny of critics. **3:18** An allusion to Isaiah 53:11–12. Peter may have intended *Spirit*, but the parallel to *flesh* in the same verse suggests that he intended the life-giving spirit that permeates the created world and not the *Holy Spirit*. **3:18–19** Many scholars regard these verses as an early Christian hymn or a poetic section (see note on Philippians 2:6–11). Echoed in Doctrine and Covenants 67:11. The intent may be to imply a work through the *Holy Spirit* rather than through the *spirit* as translated here. **3:18–20** Quoted in Doctrine and Covenants 138:7–9. **3:19** Alluded to in Doctrine and Covenants 76:73 (compare Doctrine and Covenants 138:28). **3:20** See Genesis 8:1. **3:22** The reference to *angels, authorities, and powers* is ambiguous. Christ's position above the *angels* is clearly in view, while the other two terms appear to refer to different aspects of God's work on the earth.

Stewards of God's Grace

4 ¹Therefore, because Christ suffered in the flesh, arm yourselves also with the same mind, for the one who suffered in the flesh has ceased from sin ²in order that you may spend the remainder of your time in the flesh no longer according to human desires but according to the will of God. ³For the time that has passed was enough to accomplish the desire of the Gentiles, living in unbridled lust, passions, drunkenness, revelry, carousing, and lawless idolatries. ⁴They are surprised that you do not join together with them in the same outpouring of wickedness, and they slander you. ⁵They will give an account to the one prepared to judge the living and the dead. ⁶For this is the reason the gospel was preached also to those who are dead, so that they may be judged in the flesh by human standards, and they may live according to God's standards.

⁷For the end of all things is near; therefore, be self-controlled and circumspect in your prayers. ⁸Above all things, continue loving one another, because *love hides a multitude of sins.* ⁹Show hospitality to one another without complaining. ¹⁰Just as each person has received a gift, serve one another as good stewards of God's varied grace. ¹¹Whoever speaks, let it be the words of God; whoever serves, let it be done with the strength that God provides so that in everything God will be glorified through Jesus Christ, who is the glory and the power forever and ever. Amen.

Suffering

¹²Dear friends, do not be surprised as though some strange thing were happening to you when the fiery trial that comes upon you to test you. ¹³But rejoice inasmuch as you share in the sufferings of Christ so that in the revelation of his glory you may rejoice and be glad. ¹⁴If you are reproached for the name of Christ, you are blessed because the Spirit of glory, who is *the Spirit of God, rests* upon you. ¹⁵But let no one among you suffer as a murderer, thief, evildoer, or troublemaker. ¹⁶If anyone suffers as a Christian, let that person not be ashamed, but let that person glorify God in that name. ¹⁷Because it is the time for the judgment to begin with the household of God, and if it begins with us, what will be the end for those who do not obey the gospel of God? ¹⁸And "*if the righteous are barely saved, what will become of the ungodly and sinners?*" ¹⁹So, let those who suffer according to the will of God entrust their souls to a faithful creator while at the same time doing good.

A Crown of Glory

5 ¹I encourage the elders among you, as a fellow elder and a witness of the suffering of Christ and as one who shares in the

---

4:1 The language of combat is implied, and the believer is to take up the shield of faith in Christ, who set an example. **4:3** Peter reminds his readers the time of sin has passed, and a new age of righteousness has begun in preparation for the return of the Lord. **4:6** Quoted in Doctrine and Covenants 138:10 (compare Doctrine and Covenants 76:73; 88:99). **4:7** A possible allusion to Genesis 6:13. **4:8** Quotation of Proverbs 10:12. **4:10** *Varied grace* can also be translated as *multicolored* or *variegated grace.* It seems to imply that grace is granted differently to each believer. **4:12** The singularity of *the fiery trial* hints that Peter had a specific event in mind. **4:14** Quotation from Isaiah 11:2. **4:15** The meaning of the noun *troublemaker* in Greek is uncertain and may refer to someone who spies on other people. The intent of this verse is to encourage Christians to cast out the wicked from their community. The language does not refer to excommunication but rather social distancing of the wicked. **4:16** The title *Christian* occurs only two other times in the New Testament (Acts 11:26; 26:28). **4:18** Quotation from Proverbs 11:31.

5:1 The term *elder*, like apostle, deacon, and teacher, can have both a priesthood and mundane meaning. In this verse, it may refer to those who are elderly and who have been followers of Christ for some time.

glory that will be revealed. ²Shepherd the flock of God that is among you, watching over not by compulsion but willingly, as God would have it, not for shameful profit but eagerly. ³Do not lord over those in your charge, but be examples to the flock. ⁴And when the chief Shepherd appears, you will receive the unfading crown of glory. ⁵Likewise, you who are younger, be subject to the elders. Clothe yourselves, all of you, with humility toward one another, for "*God opposes the proud but gives grace to the humble.*"

⁶Therefore, humble yourselves beneath the powerful hand of God so that he may exalt you in the proper time ⁷by throwing on him all your burdens because he cares about you. ⁸Be sober-minded; be watchful. Your enemy the devil prowls like a roaring lion, seeking for someone to consume.

⁹Stand against him, strong in the faith, knowing that your brothers and sisters throughout the world are experiencing similar suffering. ¹⁰And the God of all grace, who has called you to his eternal glory in Christ, after you have suffered a little while, will restore, confirm, strengthen, and establish you. ¹¹To him is the power forever. Amen.

FINAL GREETINGS

¹²I have written briefly to you through Silvanus, whom I consider a faithful brother, encouraging and testifying that this is the true grace of God; stand firm in it. ¹³The church in Babylon, who is also chosen, greets you, as does Mark, my son. ¹⁴Greet one another with a kiss of love. Peace to all of you who are in Christ.

The comparison to Peter suggests that it is being used as an age distinction (verse 5 appears to confirm that he is speaking to the elderly). The office of *elder* in the early church was modeled on the role of the *elderly*, particularly those who had been early followers of Christ. This verse is alluded to in Doctrine and Covenants 66:2. **5:2** *Shepherd the flock* implies acting as an overseer or bishop over the faithful. **5:4** Christian shepherds are to take their example from the *chief Shepherd*, who is Christ. **5:5** Quotation from Proverbs 3:34. **5:7** An allusion to Psalm 55:22. **5:8** An allusion to Psalm 22:13. *Lions* were a serious threat to people living in parts of Judea and near the Jordan River Valley, and therefore the image is one that first-century readers would have been familiar with. **5:9** Instead of saying *brothers and sisters*, Peter speaks of *brotherhood and sisterhood* throughout the world. **5:12** This is likely to be the same *Silvanus* mentioned in Paul's letters (Acts 15:40; 2 Corinthians 1:19; 1 Thessalonians 1:1), and he is the letter carrier for 1 Peter. **5:13** The word *church* is not present in Greek, which states literally *the one in Babylon*. The Greek feminine article could refer to the church or to a woman in Babylon. Most scholars assert that *Babylon* refers to the city of Rome. For Mark, see Acts 12:12–17; 15:37.

2 PETER

AUTHOR

Second Peter is a short letter written by Simon Peter, Jesus's disciple, to an unidentified group of recipients who are likewise believers in Jesus Christ. The letter takes the form of a final testament of Peter's steadfast faith in light of his impending death (1:13–14). The letter is frequently written in the first-person singular ("I") but occasionally uses the first-person plural ("we," 1:16–19; 3:13). Much of the letter centers on the return of the Lord and the attitudes and behaviors that will be prevalent at that time. The author feels a personal concern to warn the faithful and to bear testimony of his beliefs.

Many scholars today think that 2 Peter was not personally written by Peter but by a later disciple who collected and transmitted Peter's teachings after his death. Peter's teachings are at the heart of the letter, but the style of writing departs so dramatically from 1 Peter as to suggest two different authors. Regardless of who penned the letter, the thoughts recorded in 2 Peter are presented as the apostle's counsel on the Second Coming.

If Peter personally wrote the letter, then the date of the writing of 2 Peter would be no later than 64/65 CE, when tradition holds that Peter died in Rome during the reign of the emperor Nero (died 9 June 68 CE). If the letter was written after Peter's death with the intent to gather the apostle's thoughts and was subsequently sent out as a reminder to be faithful and patient in waiting for the return of the Lord, then perhaps the latter two decades of the first century are likely.

The author speaks of a first letter (3:1), and it appears that some have begun to lose hope that the Lord would return. According to 3:4, some Christians have died ("since our ancestors died"), suggesting that some time has passed between the death of Jesus and his expected return. This could describe events in the mid-60s, but it more accurately describes the events of the 90s when the emperor Domitian (died 18 September 96 CE) openly persecuted Christians, and some subsequently began to lose hope.

A date in the mid-90s is the most likely, given the intense focus on the Second Coming, and the purpose for which the letter was written was to call attention to the words of Peter in an age when many or nearly all from the eyewitness generation had passed away. Peter's teachings are accepted as authoritative, and his words are carefully presented.

PURPOSE OF WRITING

Although written as a letter, 2 Peter is more formally a last will and testament expressing Peter's final words to the saints before his expected death. Prophetic teachings are defended (1:20–21), scoffers are condemned (3:3–10), and the faithful are encouraged to be prepared because the Lord will come as "a thief" (3:10). The author concludes with a warm sendoff describing shared faith while also reintroducing the familiar theme of warning (3:17).

The main organizing feature of the letter is the epistle of Jude, which is quoted extensively in 2 Peter 2:3–18; 3:1–3. Scholars largely agree that 2 Peter quotes Jude and not vice versa, but admittedly there is no clear evidence as to which letter was the first to be written and which one quoted the other. If 2 Peter quotes Jude, then it is likely that the teachings of Jude were also associated with Peter because the quotations from Jude appear in 2 Peter as direct counsel from Peter.

CONNECTION TO LATTER-DAY SAINT BELIEFS

Perhaps the most profound connection between this short letter and the Restoration is the usage of the phrase *calling and election* (1:10). In the context of this letter, the phrase refers to seeking to confirm one's place in the kingdom and to avoid falling into sin. *Calling and election* is not a technical term in the letter, but it refers to the process of being called of God where God personally *calls* or *invites* a believer to become part of the *chosen* or *elected*. The topic of receiving one's calling and election is discussed in Doctrine and Covenants 131:5, which comments specifically upon the wording of 2 Peter 1:19. The concept presupposes that the recipients of the letter were seeking to assure or confirm their election. These individuals wished to assure their standing in the kingdom, to find a sure foothold of faith in their lives, and the attributes listed in 2 Peter 1:5–8 promise just such a foothold. ࿇

GREETINGS

1 ¹Simon Peter, a servant and apostle of Jesus Christ, to those who obtained faith equal to ours through righteousness in our God and Savior Jesus Christ: ²may grace and peace be increased in you through the knowledge of God and of Jesus our Lord.

THE VIRTUES OF A CHRISTIAN LIFE

³His divine power has given us all things necessary for life and godliness through the knowledge of him who called us by his own glory and goodness, ⁴by which he has given us his great and precious promises so that through them you may become participants in the divine nature after having escaped from the corruption in the world generated by lust. ⁵For this reason, make every effort to supplement your faith with goodness, and goodness with knowledge, ⁶and knowledge with self-control, and self-control with perseverance, and perseverance with godliness, ⁷and godliness with brotherly kindness, and brotherly kindness with love. ⁸For if these attributes are yours and are increasing in you, they will keep you from being ineffective and unfruitful in the knowledge of our Lord Jesus Christ. ⁹Whoever lacks these things is nearsighted, or even blind, having forgotten about the cleansing of past sins. ¹⁰Therefore, brothers and sisters, be more diligent to confirm your calling and election, for if you do this you will never stumble. ¹¹For in this way, an entryway into the eternal kingdom of our Lord and Savior Jesus Christ will be richly provided for you.

PETER'S EYEWITNESS TESTIMONY

¹²Therefore, I intend to remind you always of these attributes, even though you know them and are established in the truth that you have now. ¹³I think it right, while I am

---

1:1 *Apostle* is used here in a technical sense to refer to Peter as one who is both a servant and messenger of the teachings of Jesus Christ. His pairing of the two terms *servant* and *apostle* may join the Old Testament concept of *the servant of the Lord* (2 Kings 10:10; James 1:1) and an *apostle*, the term used foremost in Acts to refer to Jesus's disciples (compare Luke 6:13; Acts 1:2). *God and Savior Jesus Christ* refers only to Jesus Christ in this passage, and this verse unequivocally testifies of the belief that Jesus is Deity. **1:2** *Of God and of Jesus Christ our Lord* in this verse refer to God the Father and Jesus Christ (see note on verse 1). **1:3** *Called us by his own glory* could also be rendered as *called us through his glory*. Some important early manuscripts change the reading so that *through* is the only possible translation. The meaning is that the faithful have been called by seeing the glory of Jesus Christ. **1:4** *Participants* also means *users* and *sharers*; thus the meaning is that the believer can share and draw upon the blessings of the divine nature. The phrase *divine nature* refers to the material and spiritual existence of God, and Peter invites the recipients of the letter to have a part in the nature of God's existence. **1:5–8** These verses are reflected in Doctrine and Covenants 4:5–6; 107:30–31. **1:7** *Brotherly* includes *men* and *women*. The word translated as *love* can also mean *charity*, and it is the most important virtue in the list of attributes. **1:8** The knowledge mentioned in this verse and 1:2 implies more than simple abstract knowledge of facts but a knowledge of Jesus Christ personally, of who he is, and what is required to believe in him. **1:9** The verse specifically mentions *cleansing* from sins and not forgiveness of sins, perhaps to emphasize the state of being completely free and clean from sin as a result of the waters of baptism. **1:10** The Greek here uses *brothers* collectively to refer to *brothers and sisters. Calling and election* are used generally to reflect those who have accepted the call to faith and have lived a Christian life defined by the attributes of verses 5–8 and who are cleansed from sin (verse 9). Romans 11:11 discusses the possibility of losing one's election. *Stumble* can also mean *to stumble in sin* or *fall*. **1:13** Peter uses *tent* in place of the words translated as *mortal body*, and a similar allusion can be found in 1 Corinthians 3:16. Compare 1 Nephi 2:24.

in this mortal body, to awaken the memory in you [14]because I know that the laying down of my body will come soon, as our Lord Jesus Christ has made it clear to me. [15]And I will make every effort so that after my death you may be able to remember these things.

[16]For we did not follow wisely developed myths when we made known to you the power and coming of our Lord Jesus Christ, but we were eyewitnesses of his majesty. [17]For he received honor and glory from God the Father when the voice came to him in sublime glory, "This is my beloved Son, in whom I am well pleased." [18]We ourselves heard this voice from heaven when we were with him on the holy mountain. [19]And we have the prophetic word more fully confirmed. You would do well to heed this as you would a lamp shining in a dark place until the day dawns and the morning star rises in your hearts, [20]knowing this first of all, that no prophecy of scripture comes from one's own interpretation [21]because no prophecy ever came by the will of a man but rather by

men and women moved by the Holy Spirit speaking from God.

FALSE PROPHETS AND TEACHERS

2 [1]But false prophets were also among the people, just as there will be false teachers among you who will secretly bring destructive heresies, even denying the Lord who purchased them, thus bringing swift destruction upon themselves. [2]Many will follow them in their debauched lifestyles, and because of them the way of truth will be slandered. [3]And in their greed they will take advantage of you with deceptive words. Their condemnation that was pronounced long ago is not waiting idly, and their destruction is not asleep.

[4]If God did not spare the angels when they sinned, but he cast them into hell and put them in chains of total darkness to be kept until the judgment, [5]and he did not spare the ancient world, but he saved Noah, a preacher of righteousness, together with seven others, when he brought a flood upon an ungodly world, [6]and if he turned the cities of Sodom and Gomorrah

---

1:17 Peter alludes to events that took place on the Mount of Transfiguration (Matthew 17:1–8). Many translations refer to *the Majestic Glory* in place of what is translated here as *sublime glory*. The issue is whether the author intended the word *glory* to be a title referring to God. Compare 3 Nephi 11:7. **1:19** An allusion to Numbers 24:17 and the star that would arise out of Jacob. The mention of the *prophetic word* being confirmed is made in the context of wisely developed myths. Peter equates seeing or being an eyewitness (verse 16) with having a better knowledge of the prophetic word. This verse forms the basis for the question and answer found in Doctrine and Covenants 131:5. The Joseph Smith Translation reads *We have therefore a more sure knowledge of the word of prophecy, to which word of prophecy ye do well that ye take heed.* **1:20–21** The concern of these verses is to distinguish private and personal interpretation of scripture from prophetic and inspired revelation. Peter defines scripture as the revealed word of God. **1:21** The Greek has only *men*, but it is used inclusively to refer to *men and women*. The future when *men and women* are moved upon by the Holy Spirit may allude to Joel 2:28, where a similar prophecy is reported. For female prophets, see Luke 2:36; Acts 21:9; 1 Corinthians 11:5.

2:1 The fundamental idea behind the *destructive heresies* is that of *false choices* or *false options* that supposedly lead to belief in God. **2:4** *Cast them into hell* is in Greek *cast them into Tartarus*. This is the only place in the New Testament where hell is described using the mythical *Tartarus*, or the deep abyss of punishment from Greek mythology. Echoed in Doctrine and Covenants 38:5. **2:4–10** This is a single conditional sentence in Greek listing abhorrent actions that will result in judgment. These events are similarly noted in Jude 1:6–7. The cursing of the fallen angels is in reference to Genesis 6:1–4. **2:5** For Noah's *righteousness*, see Genesis 6:18; 7:1. **2:6** Some manuscripts read *condemn them to destruction*, but several important early witnesses omit *to destruction*. The addition appears to be a redundancy added by scribes

to ashes when he condemned them, and he made them an example of what is coming to the ungodly, [7]and if he rescued Lot, a righteous man who was distressed over the lifestyle of the lawless in their depravity [8](that righteous man, living among them day after day, was distressed by the lawless actions he saw and heard), [9]then the Lord knows how to rescue the godly from temptation and to reserve the unrighteous for condemnation until the day of judgment, [10]particularly those who gratify their physical lust and who think little of authority.

Bold and headstrong, they are not afraid to slander celestial beings, [11]but even the angels, despite their greater strength and power, do not bring a slanderous judgment against them before the Lord. [12]These people are like irrational animals, creatures of instinct that are born to be hunted and killed. They slander the things they do not understand, and they will be completely destroyed like the beasts, [13]suffering for the pain they have inflicted. They count it a pleasure to revel in the daylight. They are stains and blemishes, reveling in their deceits when feasting with you. [14]They have eyes full of adultery, unstoppable in sin, alluring unstable people. They have habituated their hearts in greed, these cursed children. [15]They have abandoned the straight way and gone astray through the way of Balaam, son of Bosor, who loved the wages of unrighteousness, [16]and was chastised for his own sin when a speechless donkey spoke with a human voice and curtailed the prophet's madness.

[17]These false teachers are springs without water, mists driven by a storm, for whom the most profound darkness has been reserved. [18]By making eloquent and empty claims, through desires of the flesh, they entice people who have just escaped from those who live in error. [19]They promise them freedom, but they are enslaved to corruption. (Whatever overpowers a person, to that a person is enslaved). [20]For if after they have fled the defilement of the world through the knowledge of our Lord and Savior Jesus Christ, they are again entangled and are overcome, then their last stage is worse for them than the first.

---

to make the condemnation more explicit. **2:7** For *Lot's* righteousness, see Genesis 18:23–25. **2:8** This verse is a parenthetical explanation regarding Lot. **2:9** *Temptation* can also be translated as *trial*. This verse is echoed in Doctrine and Covenants 38:5. **2:10** The meaning of the Greek *celestial beings* is unclear. The Greek simply notes *glorious ones*, thus implying angels or heavenly beings. **2:11** A parallel situation is found in Zechariah 3:1 (compare Jude 1:9). **2:12** *Irrational* in this context means *unable to speak* or *use reason*. The last phrase of this verse is ambiguous in Greek and appears to indicate that the false teachers (2:1) will suffer the same fate as the irrational creatures who will be destroyed. **2:13** The Greek can also mean *suffering harm* instead of the more abstract *suffering* as translated here. There is a pun here with the words *deceits* and *feasts* (rendered as *feasting with you*) in Greek. The word *feasts* in certain contexts refers to Christian gatherings where the sacrament (or Eucharist) was celebrated (compare Jude 1:12). **2:14** *Their* is lacking in Greek. **2:15–16** For the story of Balaam and his talking donkey, see Numbers 22:21–35 (compare Jude 1:11). **2:16** *Prophet* is not used positively of Balaam, nor is it a tacit acceptance of his attempted cursing of Israel. He serves in these verses as an example of the misguided individual who presumes to speak for the Lord. **2:17** The Greek notes simply *these*, but the reference appears to be the false teachers of 2:1. The King James Bible uses the phrase *mist of darkness* in this verse. That phrase is foundational for Nephi's account of the tree of life (1 Nephi 8:23–24). For the idea of knowledge, see note on 2 Peter 1:8. **2:18** *Who have just escaped from those who live in error* describes the attempt to deceive those who have recently *just escaped* the world and have come to follow God. **2:20** *Defilement* is plural in Greek, but it appears to denote a general state of pollution or corruption in this context. **2:20–21** These verses are commented on and expanded in Doctrine and Covenants 76:34–35, which also blends the language of Hebrews 6:6.

²¹For it would have been better for them to have never known the way of righteousness than, after knowing it, to turn away from the sacred commandment given to them. ²²It happened to them according to the true proverb, "*A dog returns to its own vomit*," and "A washed sow will wallow in the mud."

THE COMING OF THE LORD

3 ¹Beloved, this is now the second letter that I am writing to you. In both, I am stirring up your pure mind as a reminder ²that you should recall the predictive teachings of the holy prophets and the commandment of the Lord and Savior through your apostles, ³knowing this first of all, that scoffers will come in the last days ridiculing, pursuing their own wicked interests, ⁴and saying, "Where is the promise of his coming? Since our ancestors died, all things continue as they were from the beginning of creation." ⁵For they willingly overlook this fact, that the heavens existed a long time ago, and the earth was formed by the word of God out of water and by means of water. ⁶The world existing at that time was destroyed because of these things when it was flooded with water. ⁷But now the heavens and the earth by the same word have been reserved for fire, being preserved for the day of judgment and for the destruction of the ungodly.

⁸Now, beloved, do not let this escape your notice, that one day is like a thousand years with the Lord, and a thousand years are like a single day. ⁹The Lord does not delay his promise as some count slowness, but he is patient with you because he does not want any to perish, but rather that all should come to repentance. ¹⁰But the day of the Lord will come as a thief, and when it comes the heavens will pass away with a rushing sound, and the elements will melt with burning heat, and the earth and every action done on it will be made manifest.

¹¹Since all these things are to dissolve in this way, what type of people must we be, living our lives in holiness and godliness, ¹²waiting for and yearning for the coming of the day of God? Because of this the heavens will be burned up and dissolved, and the elements will melt as they are burned up. ¹³We are waiting, according to

---

2:22 The first quotation comes from Proverbs 26:11, but the second is from an unknown source. Echoed in 2 Nephi 31:14. Third Nephi 7:8 also quotes the proverb of a dog turning to its vomit.

3:1 First Nephi 2:24 uses the phrase *stir them up in the ways of remembrance*. **3:2** This is one of the earliest places where the testimony of the apostles is declared to be authoritative (see also 2 Peter 1:16–18). **3:4** This quotation exemplifies the idea that some believe the Lord has delayed his return and that therefore they have assumed that he will not return. This chapter attempts to put forward another way to understand what has been perceived as a delay in the return of the Lord. **3:5** Perhaps an allusion to Genesis 1:6–7. **3:6** An allusion to Genesis 7:11. The Greek is ambiguous regarding what *these things* refers to, but they most likely refer to their actions described in verse 3. **3:7** The Greek says *ungodly men*, but the phrase is generic and refers to the destruction of all the ungodly. **3:8** This idea of a thousand years being like a single day with the Lord is found also in Abraham 3:4 (compare Psalm 90:4). **3:9** *Does not want any to perish* is a declaration of God's will. His will is to offer salvation to all. *Repentance* is the Greek word *to change one's mind*. **3:10** The word translated as *elements* may refer to *heavenly bodies* such as the stars and planets. If *heavenly bodies* are intended, then there is a clear allusion to Isaiah 34:4. Some late and inferior manuscripts read *as a thief in the night* (compare Doctrine and Covenants 101:25; 106:4–5; 1 Thessalonians 5:2). This verse is echoed in 3 Nephi 26:3; Mormon 9:2, which also blends the language of Isaiah 34:4. **3:11** Some manuscripts construct this verse in the second-person plural *you* so that Peter says *what type of people must you be*. The earliest and best manuscripts lack any pronoun, although one needs to be supplied. Because the author includes himself among the righteous, *we* seems to be the best translation. **3:12** Echoed in Doctrine and Covenants 101:25. **3:13** The promise is first found in

2 PETER 3 | 441

his promise, for new heavens and a new earth on which righteousness resides.

CONCLUDING EXHORTATION

[14]Therefore, beloved, because you are waiting for these things, be diligent to be found spotless and without blemish and at peace in his presence. [15]And consider the patience of our Lord as an opportunity for salvation, just as our beloved brother Paul wrote to you according to the wisdom given to him, [16]as he wrote in all his let- ters when he speaks of these things. There are some difficult things to understand in them, which the ignorant and unstable distort to their own destruction, and they also set aside the other scriptures. [17]There- fore, beloved, knowing beforehand, be watchful that you are not led astray by these lawless people and lose your own firm foundation. [18]But grow in grace and knowledge of our Lord and Savior Jesus Christ. To him is the glory now and to the day of eternity. Amen.

Isaiah 65:17; 66:22. Greek often uses the plural *heavens* in places where modern English would prefer a singular. **3:14** *In his presence* is conveyed by a single word in Greek and can also mean *by him*. Echoed in Doctrine and Covenants 38:31. **3:15** The Greek says simply *consider the patience of our Lord as salvation*, but the meaning seems to be that the delay of the Lord's coming provides an opportunity for salvation. **3:15–16** The reference to Paul speaking of similar things most likely refers to 2 Thessalonians 2:1–7. **3:16** Echoed in Alma 13:20; Doctrine and Covenants 10:63. **3:17** *Firm foundation* can also be translat- ed as *firmness* or *steadfastness*. **3:18** Doctrine and Covenants 50:40 alludes to this verse.

1–3 John

Author

Given the language, style of writing, and ideas of 1–3 John, it is assumed that the same author wrote all three books. Two of the works (2–3 John) are letters in a proper sense, with 2 John being written to an otherwise unknown "elect lady" and 3 John being written to an individual named Gaius. The author refers to himself as "the elder" (2 John 1:1; 3 John 1:1) but does not specifically identify himself by name in 1 John. Tradition has associated the author of the three letters with the author of the Gospel of John and the book of Revelation. It is possible that the author who wrote the letters was the same as the one who wrote the Gospel, but the ideas in the letters are expressed in ways that are less refined than in the Gospel. In some instances, it appears that the author was attempting to follow the style and prose of the Gospel of John. If the same author wrote all these books, the Gospel and 1–3 John, then there may have been a significant passage of time between the writing, as well as changes in historical circumstances.

Purpose of Writing

The epistles of 2–3 John deal specifically with the issue of dissension among the community of believers. Some problematic individuals are listed by name such as Diotrephes (3 John 1:9), and 1 John 2:19 indicates that "they departed from us," suggesting that there was a genuine rift in the community where some members no longer wished to associate with the community of believers. First John, however, does not directly address the topic of their departure, and instead it is a sermon on love. This may indicate what the author saw as the principal reason for the problems that arose among them, and the author also encouraged the saints to test the spirits so that they could identify the spirit of the antichrist (1 John 4:3). The picture is one of distress and intrigue created by a community that had lost some of its founding members and therefore was facing serious questions about its ability to thrive in the faith. The author seems duly concerned and hopes to visit the saints in person (2 John 1:12; 3 John 1:14). The author also raises the question of belief—namely, that some no longer believed that Jesus came in the flesh (1 John 4:1–3).

CONNECTION TO LATTER-DAY SAINT BELIEFS

These letters are important to Latter-day Saints because they continue the thread of discussion from the Gospel of John concerning the new commandment to love one another (1 John 2:7–17). The declaration of a new commandment was made on the eve of Jesus's death (John 13:34). These injunctions are, in part, a reminder to live the commandment first issued in Leviticus 19:18, and thus these letters form part of the development of an early Christian ethic of love that connects both the Old and New Testaments. The letters are also important for understanding the influence of the beloved disciple, John the son of Zebedee, in early Christian thought. ❧

THE WORD OF LIFE

1 ¹That which was from the beginning, which we have heard, which we have seen with our eyes, and which we have looked upon and touched with our hands concerning the word of life—²and the life was made manifest, and we have seen, testify, and proclaim to you the eternal life that was with the Father and was made manifest to us—³that which we have seen and heard we proclaim to you also so that you may have fellowship with us. Indeed, our fellowship is with the Father and with his Son Jesus Christ. ⁴And we are writing these things so that our joy might be complete.

⁵And this is the message that we have heard from him and that we proclaim to you, that God is light and there is no darkness in him at all. ⁶If we say that we have fellowship with him while we walk in darkness, we lie and do not live according to truth. ⁷If we walk in the light, as he himself is in the light, we have fellowship with one another, and the blood of Jesus his Son cleanses us from all sin. ⁸If we say that we have no sin, we deceive ourselves and the truth is not in us. ⁹If we confess our sins, he is faithful and just and will forgive us of our sins, cleansing us from all unrighteousness. ¹⁰If we say that we have not sinned, we make him a liar and his word is not in us.

AN ATONING SACRIFICE

2 ¹My little children, I am writing these things to you so that you may not sin, but if someone sins, we have an advocate with the Father, Jesus Christ the just, ²and he himself is the atoning sacrifice for our sins, and not for us only but for the sins of the entire world.

³And by this we know that we have come to know him, if we obey his commandments. ⁴The one who says, "I have come to know him," but does not obey his commandments is a liar, and the truth is not in him. ⁵To the one who obeys his word, the love of God is truly perfected in him. By this we know that we are in him. ⁶The one who says he abides in him ought to walk in the same way that he walked.

I AM WRITING A NEW COMMANDMENT

⁷Beloved, I am not writing to you concerning a new commandment but regarding an

---

1:1 This letter is written by at least one eyewitness, but the perspective is that of the eyewitness generation *we have heard . . . we have seen*. The author does not list his name, but tradition has ascribed this letter and two others (2–3 John) to John the Beloved, one of Jesus's twelve disciples (see Matthew 17:1). **1:1–5** These verses are a single sentence in Greek, and they constitute one of the most difficult sentences in the entire New Testament. **1:4** Some manuscripts read *your joy*, but the better reading is *our joy*, based on the manuscript evidence. **1:5** Perhaps an allusion to John 8:12. The word *message* is a cognate with the noun *gospel* and may be intended as such in this verse. *Him* may refer to either the Father or the Son, but *we have heard* likely clarifies that John intended it to refer to the Son. Doctrine and Covenants 88:12 clarifies what it means for God to be light. **1:8** This verse seems to intentionally counter the claims of some who had departed from the faith and who appear to have claimed that they were free from sin (1 John 2:19). **1:9** *Confess* can also be translated as *declare*. *Cleanse from all unrighteousness* is alluded to in Alma 7:14; Doctrine and Covenants 76:41.

2:1 The word *advocate* is the same as the one used to describe the Holy Spirit in John 14:16, 26; 15:26; 16:7 (compare Hebrews 7:25). Doctrine and Covenants 29:5 and 110:4 contain additional teachings about having an *advocate with the Father*. **2:2** The idea of an *atoning sacrifice* is found in Numbers 5:8; Psalm 49:7–8; Ezekiel 44:27. *Sins of the world* appears in 1 Nephi 11:33. **2:3** The antecedent of *him* is ambiguous and could refer to God or Jesus Christ. Given the reference to *his commandments* it appears the author intended the reference to be to God. **2:6** The *same way he walked* is *the same way Jesus walked*. **2:7** Compare the teaching on the new commandment in John 13:34.

that you have had from ... old commandment is ... you have heard. [8]Likewise, ... new commandment to you ... him and in you, because the ... ding and the true light is al- ... ng. [9]The one who says he is in ... and hates his brother or sister is ... arkness. [10]The one who loves his ... abides in the light, and there is ... son for stumbling in him. [11]But the ... ho hates his brother or sister is in the ... ness, and he walks in the darkness, and ... oes not know where he is going be- ... e the darkness has blinded his eyes. [12]I am writing to you, little children, because your sins are forgiven through his name. [13]I am writing to you, fathers, because you know him who is from the beginning. I am writing to you, young people, because you have overcome evil. [14]I have written to you, children, because you know the Father. I have written to you, fathers, because you know him who is from the beginning. I have written to you, young people, because you are strong, and the word of God abides in you, and you have overcome evil.

[15]Do not love the world or the things in the world. If someone loves the world, the love of the Father is not in him, [16]because all that is in the world, the desire of the flesh and the desire of the eyes and the pride associated with life, is not from the Father but it is from the world. [17]And the world and its passions fade, but the person who does the will of God abides forever.

THE ANTICHRIST IS COMING

[18]Children, it is the last hour, and just as you have heard that the antichrist is coming, even so many antichrists have already come; therefore, we know that it is the last hour. [19]They departed from us, but they were not of us. For if they were of us, they would have remained with us, but they departed from us in order to show that all of them are not of us. [20]And you have been anointed by the Holy One, and you all know. [21]I have not written to you because you do not know the truth but because you know it and because no falsehood is of the truth.

[22]Who is the liar except the person who denies that Jesus is the Christ? This is the antichrist—the one who denies the Father and the Son. [23]Everyone who denies the Son does not have the Father either. The one who confesses the Son has the Father also.

[24]You have heard from the beginning what must abide in you. If what you heard from the beginning abides in you, you will abide in the Son and in the Father. [25]This is what he himself promised us—eternal life.

2:8 Compare Doctrine and Covenants 50:24. The Joseph Smith Translation reads *Again, a new commandment I write unto you, which thing was of old ordained of God.* **2:9** Greek uses *brother* generically to refer to *brothers and sisters.* **2:10–11** Doctrine and Covenants 95:12 uses similar language to teach the principle of the Father's love (see verse 15 also). **2:13–14** The noun *evil* refers to the *evil one* or Satan. **2:14** Some translations alter the verse division of verses 13–14. The translation follows the standard Greek text used today. **2:15** *The love of the Father* can refer to the Father's love abiding in a person that the Father bestows on that person or the love a person feels for the Father. **2:18** *The last hour* refers to the end times or the end of the world. *Anti-* refers to being opposed to something, and hence an *antichrist* is someone who is opposed to the genuine Christ. See 1 John 2:22 for John's definition of the term *antichrist.* The term is also used to describe those who fought against John's teachings (1 John 4:2–3; 2 John 1:7). Compare Jacob 7:1–23; Alma 1:2–16; 30:6–60. **2:19** This is the reason that John has written, to deal with the division that has occurred and to explain why some of the members had departed. **2:20** The *anointing* spoken of in this verse (and 2:27) may refer to baptism and the reception of the Holy Spirit. Some manuscripts read *you know all things,* but that reading appears to be a later attempt to clarify the meaning. The oil used for anointing is described in Exodus 30:25–31 (compare Exodus 29:7). **2:25** Doctrine and Covenants 88:4 offers commentary on this verse.

[26]I have written these things to you concerning those who are trying to deceive you, [27]but the anointing you have received from him abides in you, and you have no need that anyone should teach you. But as his anointing teaches you about all things, it is true and it is not a lie, just as it has been taught to you, abide in him.

THE CHILDREN OF GOD

[28]And now, little children, abide in him so that when he appears we may have confidence and not shrink in shame from him at his coming. [29]If you know that he is just, you also know that everyone who lives in righteousness is born of him.

3 [1]We love what the Father has given to us so that we may be called the children of God, and so we are. This is the reason the world does not understand us, because it did not understand him. [2]Beloved, now we are God's children, and what we will be has not yet been revealed. We know that when he appears we will be like him, because we will see him as he is. [3]And everyone who has hope in him purifies himself just as he is pure.

[4]Everyone who practices sin also practices lawlessness; sin is lawlessness. [5]You know that he appeared so that he might take away sins, and there is no sin in him. [6]No one who abides in him sins; everyone who sins has neither seen him nor known him.

[7]Children, let no one deceive you. The person who practices righteousness is righteous, just as he is righteous. [8]The person who practices sin is of the devil, because the devil continues in sin from the beginning. The Son of God was revealed for this reason, in order to destroy the works of the devil. [9]Everyone who has been born of God does not continue in sin, because God's seed abides in him, and he is not able to sin because he has been born of God. [10]By this it is evident who the children of God and who the children of the devil are. The one who does not practice righteousness is not of God and also the one who does not love his brother and sister.

BELIEVE IN THE NAME OF HIS SON

[11]For this is the message that you have heard from the beginning so that we might love one another. [12]We should not be like Cain, who was from the evil one and murdered his brother. And why did he murder him? Because his actions were evil and his brother's actions were righteous.

[13]Do not be surprised, brothers and sisters, if the world hates you. [14]We know that we have passed from death into life because we love our brothers and sisters. The one who does not love abides in death. [15]The one who hates his brother is a murderer, and you know that no murderer has eternal life abiding in him. [16]By this we know love because he laid down his life for us, and we ought to lay down our lives for our brothers and sisters. [17]If a person has the possessions of the world and sees a brother or sister in need and closes his heart against him, how does God's love abide in him? [18]Little children, let us not love in word or speech but in action and truth.

[19]By this we know that we are of the truth and will confirm our hearts in his presence, [20]that whenever our hearts condemn us, God is greater than our hearts and he knows everything. [21]Beloved, if our hearts do not condemn us, we have confidence before God. [22]And we receive whatever we ask from him because we obey his

---

3:2–3 A portion of these verses appear with a similar meaning in Moroni 7:48; Doctrine and Covenants 130:1. **3:7** *Just as he is righteous* means *just as Jesus is righteous.* **3:9** *Born of God* is echoed in Alma 5:14. **3:10** The Greek text mentions only *brother.* **3:13–14, 16–17** Greek uses *brothers* generically to refer to *brothers and sisters.* Compare John 15:18. **3:14, 16** The word *our* has been added to clarify that the *brothers and sisters* spoken of are fellow believers. Compare John 5:24.

commandments and do the things that are pleasing to him.

²³And this is his commandment, that we believe in the name of his Son Jesus Christ and love one another, just as he commanded us. ²⁴The one who obeys his commandment abides in God, and God in him. And by this we know that he abides in us, by the Spirit he has given to us.

TEST THE SPIRITS

4 ¹Beloved, do not believe every spirit, but test whether the spirits are from God because many false prophets have gone into the world. ²By this you know the Spirit of God. Every spirit that confesses that Jesus Christ has come in the flesh is from God, ³and every spirit that does not confess Jesus is not from God. And this is the spirit of the antichrist, which you have heard is coming and is now already in the world.

⁴You are from God, little children, and you have conquered them because the one who is in you is greater than the one who is in the world. ⁵They are from the world; because of this they speak of the world and the world listens to them. ⁶We are from God. The one who knows God listens to us. Whoever is not from God does not listen to us. By this we know the spirit of truth and the spirit of deceit.

LOVE ONE ANOTHER

⁷Beloved, let us love one another, because love is from God, and everyone who loves has been born of God and knows [...] ⁸The one who does not love does not k[...] God, because God is love. ⁹By this the [...] of God was manifest among us, beca[...] God sent his only begotten Son into [...] world so that we might live through hi[...] ¹⁰In this is love, not because we have love[...] God, but because he loved us and sent hi[...] Son to be an atoning sacrifice for our sins[...] ¹¹Beloved, if God so loved us, we ought to love one another. ¹²No one has seen God at any time. If we love one another, God abides in us, and his love is perfected in us. ¹³By this we know that we abide in him and he in us, because he has given us his Spirit. ¹⁴And we have seen and testify that the Father sent his Son to be the Savior of the world. ¹⁵Whoever confesses that Jesus is the Son of God, God abides in him and he in God. ¹⁶And we have come to know and to believe the love that God has for us. God is love, and the one who abides in love, God abides in him. ¹⁷By this, love is perfected among us so that we have confidence in the day of judgment; because just as he is, we are also in this world. ¹⁸There is no fear in love, but perfect love casts out fear, because fear has to do with punishment. The one who fears punishment has not been perfected in love. ¹⁹We love because he first loved us. ²⁰If anyone says, "I love God," and hates his brother or sister, he is a liar. For the one who does not love his brother or sister whom he has seen cannot love God whom he has not seen. ²¹And this is the commandment we have from

---

3:24 *God* has been added to clarify what would otherwise be ambiguous pronouns in English.

4:1 The testing of the *spirits* of the *false prophets* probably draws on the precedent set forth in Deuteronomy 13:1–5. Extensive commentary on the principle presented in this verse is found in Doctrine and Covenants 50:1–3, 31–35. **4:2–3** One of the reasons that John has written is that some have denied the physical existence of *Jesus Christ*, although the wording of these verses insinuates that they did not deny the existence of *Jesus Christ* in heaven. **4:9** This verse is echoed in Doctrine and Covenants 49:5. **4:10** See note on 1 John 2:2. **4:12** An allusion to John 1:18. The idea that no one has seen God appears to directly contradict Exodus 33:11 and Isaiah 6:1 and suggests that John was speaking of something other than prophets seeing the Lord. The Joseph Smith Translation reads *No man hath seen God at any time, except them who believe.* **4:18** *Fear has to do with punishment* may mean *fear is a consequence of punishment.* Compare Moroni 8:16. **4:20–21** Greek uses *brothers* generically to refer to *brothers and sisters.*

him, that the one who loves God should love his brother and sister also.

BORN OF GOD

5 ¹Everyone who believes that Jesus is the Christ is born of God, and everyone who loves the Father loves the child born from him. ²By this we know that we love the children of God, when we love God and keep his commandments. ³For this is the love of God, that we obey his commandments. And his commandments are not burdensome ⁴because everyone that has been born of God conquers the world. And our faith is the victory that overcomes the world. ⁵Who is it who conquers the world except the one who believes that Jesus is the Son of God?

⁶This is he who came by water and blood, Jesus Christ, not by water only but by water and blood. And the Spirit is the one who testifies, because the Spirit is truth. ⁷Because there are three that testify—⁸the Spirit, the water, and the blood—and these three agree. ⁹If we accept the testimony of people, the testimony of God is greater, because this is the testimony of God that he gave concerning his Son. ¹⁰The one who believes in the Son of God has the testimony in himself. The one who does not believe in God has made him a liar because he has not believed the testimony that God has given concerning his Son. ¹¹And this is the testimony, that God gave us eternal life

and this life is in his Son. ¹²The one who has the Son has life; the one who does not have the Son of God does not have life.

CONCLUDING REMARKS

¹³I have written these things to you who believe in the name of the Son of God so that you may know that you have eternal life. ¹⁴And this is the confidence that we have in him, because if we ask anything according to his will, he listens to us. ¹⁵And if we know that he listens to us with respect to what we ask, then we know that we have obtained the requests we have made of him. ¹⁶If someone sees his brother or sister sinning, but it is not a deadly sin, he will ask and God will give him life for those who do not commit a sin leading unto death. There is a sin that leads to death, and I do not say that he should ask about that. ¹⁷All unrighteousness is sin, but there is sin that is not a deadly sin.

¹⁸We know that everyone who is born of God does not sin, but God protects the one he has fathered so that the evil one cannot touch him. ¹⁹We know that we are of God, and the whole world lies in the power of evil. ²⁰We know that the Son of God has come and given us understanding so that we know him who is true, and we are in him who is true, and in his Son Jesus Christ. This one is the true God and eternal life. ²¹Little children, guard yourselves from idols.

5:6 *Water and blood* refer to the mortal life of Jesus, who experienced birth like other mortals (see note on 1 John 4:2–3). Compare Moses 6:59. **5:7–8** Immediately before the phrase *the Spirit, the water, and the blood*, some medieval manuscripts add an extra verse that reads *in heaven, the Father, the Word, and the Holy Spirit, and these three are one. And there are three that testify on earth.* The text then continues with *and these three agree*, as is rendered in the translation. This insertion is noteworthy because of the popularity of the King James translation, which used a Greek text that contained this spurious reading. However, the earliest manuscript to contain the Greek text of this additional verse is from the fourteenth century, and it is clearly a verse that was added many years after the letter was originally composed. The wording of verse 7 is similar to 2 Nephi 31:21; 3 Nephi 11:27; Mormon 7:7 (compare also Matthew 28:19). **5:9** The Greek text reads *the testimony of men*, but it is used to refer generally to humans and not men specifically. **5:16** Greek uses *brother* generically to refer to *brothers* and *sisters*. **5:17** Doctrine and Covenants 64:7 also speaks of a sin unto death or a *mortal sin*. **5:19** Compare Doctrine and Covenants 84:49. **5:20** John encourages us to believe in the *Father* (*him who is true*) through the Son.

2 JOHN

OPENING ADDRESS

1 ¹The elder to an elect lady and her children, whom I love in truth, and not I alone but all who know the truth, ²because the truth abides in us and is with us forever: ³grace, mercy, and peace be with us from God the Father and from Jesus Christ the Son of the Father, in truth and love.

WARNING ABOUT
THE DECEIVERS

⁴I rejoiced greatly to find some of your children walking in truth, just as we have received the commandment from the Father. ⁵And now I ask you, dear lady, not that I am writing a new commandment to you but one we have had from the beginning, so that we love one another. ⁶And this is love, that we walk according to his commandments. This is the commandment; just as you have heard from the beginning, even so that you should walk in it.

⁷For many deceivers have entered the world who do not confess Jesus Christ has come in flesh; such a person is a deceiver and antichrist. ⁸Look out so that you do not lose what we have worked for but may receive a full reward. ⁹Everyone who goes out and does not abide in the teaching of Christ does not have God. The one who abides in the teaching has both the Father and the Son. ¹⁰If someone comes to you and does not bring this teaching, do not receive him into your house and do not greet him. ¹¹For the one who greets him shares in his wicked work.

CONCLUSION

¹²Though I have much to write to you, I do not want to do so with papyrus and ink, but I hope to come to you and speak face to face so that your joy is full.

¹³The children of your elect sister greet you.

1:1 For a note on the authorship of 1–3 John, see note on 1 John 1:1. The author refers to himself simply as *the elder*. Some scholars suggest that this letter is addressed to a woman named Kyria, or perhaps even to a church using the female addressee as a metaphor for the church. The word *Kyria* means *lady*. Echoed in Doctrine and Covenants 25:3. **1:3** Some early manuscripts read *Lord Jesus Christ*, but the evidence is in favor of the shorter title. **1:5** The *new commandment* is also mentioned in John 13:34–35; 1 John 2:7. **1:6** *Walk in it* refers to walking in love. **1:12** The author refers to the implements of writing, specifically referring to what was commonly used to compose personal letters. The location of the sender and recipient are unknown.

3 JOHN

OPENING ADDRESS

1 ¹The elder to the beloved Gaius, whom I love in truth.

²Beloved, I pray that all may go well for you and that you may enjoy good health, just as it is well with your soul. ³For I rejoiced greatly when the brothers and sisters came and testified of your commitment to the truth, just as you walk in truth. ⁴I have no greater joy than this, that I hear my children walk in truth.

CONGRATULATIONS

⁵Beloved, you act faithfully by what you do for the brothers and sisters, even though they are foreigners. ⁶They have testified about your love before the church. You will do well to send them on their way in a manner that is worthy of God. ⁷For they have departed for the sake of his name, receiving nothing from the Gentiles.

⁸Therefore, we should support such individuals, so that we might be fellow workers in the truth.

DIOTREPHES

⁹I have written something to the church, but Diotrephes, who loves to be first, does not acknowledge us. ¹⁰Therefore, if I come, I will remember what he is doing, making empty charges against us. And not satisfied with that, he not only refuses to accept the brothers and sisters himself, but he hinders those who want to receive them, and he casts them out of the church. ¹¹Beloved, do not imitate the evil but the good. The one who does good is from God, and the one who does evil has not seen God. ¹²Demetrius has received the testimony of everyone, even the truth itself. We also testify, and you know that our testimony is true.

1:1 For a note on the authorship of 1–3 John, see note on 1 John 1:1. Gaius is otherwise unknown and is probably not the same individual mentioned in Paul's letters (1 Corinthians 1:14). **1:2–4** The reason for writing this letter is to congratulate Gaius on his success for an event about which John held some concerns. **1:3, 5, 10** Greek uses *brothers* generically to refer to *brothers and sisters*. **1:5** The phrase *even though they are foreigners* can be translated as *especially to foreigners*. The one-sided nature of this letter makes it difficult to reconstruct the historical circumstances behind it, but this verse implies that the saints had warmly welcomed foreign saints into their community. **1:9–12** Diotrephes has refused to show hospitality to some, and John condemns him for doing so.

CONCLUSION

[13]I have many things to write to you, but I do not want to do so with pen and ink. [14]I hope to see you soon, that we may speak face to face. [15]Peace to you. The friends greet you. Greet the friends by name.

JUDE

AUTHOR

The author of the book identifies himself as Jude, the common English rendering of the name *Judah* or *Judas* (1:1). He is also the brother of Jacob, thus potentially making him the brother of Jesus (Matthew 13:55; Mark 6:3). If he is the brother of the Lord, then Paul may have been referring to him and the other brothers of the Lord in 1 Corinthians 9:5. According to Paul, the brothers of Jesus traveled around proclaiming the gospel message and sharing their faith with Greek-speaking communities in the Mediterranean basin. The author's Greek is sophisticated, and this may indicate that the author had assistance in crafting his message. The form of the document is a personal letter to a community, but the author moves quickly past the customary greetings to warn his audience of unchecked sin.

PURPOSE OF WRITING

The purpose of writing is one of concern that some individuals have entered the community of believers and have promoted ideals and practices that may lead to "unbridled lust" (1:4). The letter quickly turns to the idea of divine restraint, and Jude encourages his readers to recognize that God's previous restraint in dealing with sin cannot be assumed in the future. Jude retells the stories of Israelites and non-Israelites who were punished for sins, specifically the people of Sodom and Gomorrah, suggesting again that he was concerned with matters of sexual misbehavior. Much of the letter is repeated in 2 Peter 2–3, indicating that the problem may have been more widespread than one short letter might indicate.

CONNECTION TO LATTER-DAY SAINT BELIEFS

Perhaps the most important connections to Latter-day Saint belief are the role that Michael the archangel plays in the dispute about the body of Moses and the several allusions to the writings of Enoch. Michael plays a prominent role in the revelations of the Doctrine and Covenants (27:11; 88:112–13; 107:54), and his role in this letter parallels his position in modern revelation. Also, the letter briefly quotes from the noncanonical 1 Enoch (2:6, 14–15) as well as the Assumption of Moses. These quotations demonstrate that the author accepted a broader canon than what was eventually passed down to us as the twenty-seven books of the New Testament. ❧

OPENING ADDRESS

1 ¹Jude, a servant of Jesus Christ and brother of Jacob, to those who are called, beloved by God the Father and kept for Jesus Christ: ²mercy and peace to you, and love be multiplied.

UNGODLY HAVE ENTERED AMONG YOU

³Beloved, although I have been anxious to write to you about our shared salvation, I feel it is necessary to write encouraging you to contend for the faith that was once entrusted to the saints. ⁴For certain men have secretly slipped in among you, men who were designated for this condemnation a long time ago, ungodly men who have changed the grace of our God into unbridled lust, and they deny our only Master and Lord, Jesus Christ.

⁵I want to remind you, although you knew it fully at one time, that Jesus saved the people from the land of Egypt and later destroyed those who did not believe. ⁶You know that the angels who did not keep their own dominion but rather left behind their own habitation, he has kept in everlasting chains until the judgment in the great day, ⁷just as Sodom and Gomor-rah and the neighboring cities, which likewise engaged in sexual improprieties and went after other flesh. They are an example by suffering a punishment of eternal fire.

⁸Likewise, those who also rely on their dreams defile the flesh, reject authority, and slander the glorious ones. ⁹But Michael the archangel, when contending with the devil and arguing about the body of Moses, did not bring a slanderous judgment but said, *"May the Lord rebuke you."* ¹⁰But these individuals slander everything they do not understand, and, like irrational animals, they are destroyed by all the things they should naturally understand. ¹¹Woe to them because they walked in the way of Cain, and they abandoned themselves in Balaam's error because of greed, and they perished in the rebellion of Korah. ¹²These individuals are hidden shoals at your love feasts, feasting without fear, shepherds to themselves, clouds without water, driven by winds, autumn trees without fruit, twice dead, uprooted, ¹³raging waves of the sea, foaming out their own shame, wandering stars for whom the depth of eternal darkness has been kept.

¹⁴Enoch, the seventh from Adam, prophesied about these things, saying, "Behold, the Lord is coming with a myriad

---

1:1 *Jude*, traditionally thought to be one of Jesus's siblings (Matthew 13:55: Mark 6:3), introduces himself simply as *Judas*, which has been anglicized to *Jude*, the brother of *Jacob*, also thought to be Jesus's sibling. **1:4** Compare 2 Peter 2:1–2. **1:5** Compare 2 Peter 2:4. This verse specifically declares that *Jesus* was responsible for bringing the children of Israel out of Egypt, an act that was done by *YHWH*, or *Jehovah* in the Old Testament (Deuteronomy 1:31–32). Some later manuscripts use *the Lord* in place of *Jesus*. **1:6** The King James translation uses the phrase *first estate* (*own dominion*), which is echoed in Abraham 3:26, where the *first estate* is also spoken of. The *dominion* or *estate* is a sphere of authority and power. **1:7** Doctrine and Covenants 76:105 alludes to this verse. **1:8** Compare 2 Peter 2:10–11, which implies that the *glorious ones* are the angels of glory. **1:9** Quotation from Zechariah 3:2. This verse is echoed in Doctrine and Covenants 50:33 (compare 2 Peter 2:11). There may also be a paraphrase of the apocryphal work entitled the Assumption of Moses. **1:10** *Naturally* refers to something that is understood *by nature* or *instinctively*. **1:11** For *Cain*, see Genesis 4:1–16; for Balaam, see Numbers 22–24; for *Korah*, see Numbers 16. **1:12** *Love feasts* refers to early Christian worship gatherings where the sacrament was celebrated. Compare 2 Peter 2:13, 17. **1:13** Perhaps an allusion to Isaiah 57:20. **1:14** *Enoch* is the *seventh* (Adam, Seth, Enos, Cainan, Mahalalel, Jared, Enoch). The quotation appears to come from the pseudepigraphical work 1 Enoch 1:9. The quotation does not align perfectly with the Greek text of 1 Enoch that has survived, and the passage may therefore have been quoted from memory.

of his holy ones, [15]to execute judgment against all, and to convict every person of all the ungodly actions that they have done in an ungodly manner, and for all the offensive things that ungodly sinners have spoken against him." [16]They are complainers, discontents, who go around pursuing their own desires, who speak extravagant words, putting people in awe for their own advantage.

A CHRISTIAN RESPONSE TO DISSENSION

[17]But you, beloved, remember the words spoken previously by the apostles of our Lord Jesus Christ. [18]For they said to you, "In the last time there will be scoffers pursuing their own ungodly desires." [19]For they are divisive people, worldly, devoid of the Spirit. [20]But you, beloved, build yourselves up in your most holy faith by praying in the Holy Spirit. [21]Keep yourselves in God's love, waiting for the mercy of our Lord Jesus Christ that leads to eternal life. [22]And have mercy on those who separate themselves, [23]and save others by snatching them from the fire. Have mercy coupled with respect, hating even the clothing defiled by the flesh.

[24]To the one who is able to guard you from falling and to cause you to stand without blemish before his glorious presence while rejoicing, [25]to the only God, our Savior through Jesus Christ our Lord, be glory, majesty, power, and authority, before all time and in the present, and for all eternity. Amen.

Myriad can refer to 10,000 but also to thousands upon thousands. **1:15** Echoed in Doctrine and Covenants 99:5. **1:16** Compare 2 Peter 2:18. **1:17** Compare 2 Peter 3:2. **1:18** The source of this quotation is unknown, but it is attributed to the *apostles*. **1:22** Jude encourages his readers to be merciful to those who have left the faith and have departed from the community. **1:23** This verse is echoed in Doctrine and Covenants 36:6. The meaning of *hating even the clothing defiled by the flesh* could also be *hating even the clothing touched by bodies*.

REVELATION

AUTHOR

The author of the book of Revelation formally introduces himself as *John* (Revelation 1:1). Based on the contents of the book, the author was also a Christian prophet who intentionally shared the contents of a spectacular vision relating to seven churches in western Asia Minor (modern Turkey). Tradition asserts broadly that John is to be identified with John the son of Zebedee (Matthew 10:2) and that the same author also wrote the Gospel of John and 1–3 John. Based on the style and substance of the writing, it is clear that the author was a native Hebrew/Aramaic speaker who probably moved to western Asia Minor and wrote his book in Greek to the churches in that region. The language is simple, revealing the words of an individual who had not been trained in Greek. From a scholarly perspective, it seems almost impossible to suggest that the same person wrote the Gospel of John, 1–3 John, and Revelation in the same way. More than likely, all of these compositions have historical connections to the apostle John, the son of Zebedee, though he did not write them personally. They all share ideas and concepts, but they were likely written at different times by different people.

PURPOSE OF WRITING

The book of Revelation shares many parallels with Daniel and Ezekiel and is formally a "revelation," a term taken from the first word of the book, which calls the work an "apocalypse." The book is divided into several smaller sections, with a brief introduction to the book (1:1–11), the message to the seven churches (1:12–3:22), the main body of the work or central section (4:1–22:5), and a conclusion (22:6–11). The contents of the revelation are intended both to rebuke and comfort, and each of the seven churches in Asia receives counsel on what they are doing well (except Laodicea) and what needs to be improved. That counsel is framed in the context of the return of the Lord, and therefore there is a sense of immediacy and distress throughout the work.

Much of the language of the book is couched in metaphor and symbol within the context that what is retold will be fulfilled in the "near" future (Revelation 1:3). The language is that of resistance to encroachment of wicked ways and political forces that seek to extinguish Christian faith. The author even worried that individuals would

attempt to tamper with the book (Revelation 22:18–19). The book helped shape the identity of a community that felt persecuted, and the life of the faithful as described in the book is one of persecution with a hope in eventual redemption. Evidence within the book suggests that it was written during the time of the emperor Nero (ca. 68 CE) or the emperor Domitian (ca. 96 CE), but the evidence is ambiguous, suggesting that perhaps it contains details from both periods.

CONNECTIONS TO LATTER-DAY SAINT BELIEFS

Latter-day Saints have several strong connections to the book, and a section of the Doctrine and Covenants (77:1–15) is devoted to answering questions about the book; 1 Nephi 14:20–27 connects the author of the book with the apostle John, the son of Zebedee; and the Doctrine and Covenants quotes from the book frequently. Perhaps the most influential component of the book is the concept of dispensations or periods of the earth's existence, and the idea that one of the final dispensations will be a millennial period when Christ will again visit the earth. Latter-day Saints look forward to that millennial reign and also expect cataclysmic events to precipitate the return of the Lord in glory (Doctrine and Covenants 45).

Believers may also find hope in the idea of an eventual triumph. In the closing chapters (19–21), Satan is bound and Christ reigns in glory and power as the bridegroom. While there is no promise of immediate safety in the final scenes of the earth's existence, there is a promise of eventual victory. ⚘

OPENING ADDRESS

1 ¹The revelation of Jesus Christ, which God gave to him to show his servants what was about to happen. He made it known by sending his angel to his servant John, ²who testified of the word of God and of the testimony of Jesus Christ in all that he saw. ³Blessed is the one who reads aloud, and blessed are those who listen to the words of this prophecy and who obey what is written in it, for the time is near.

⁴John to the seven churches that are in Asia: grace and peace to you from him who is, who was, and is to come and from the seven spirits who are before his throne, ⁵and from Jesus Christ, the witness, the faithful one, the firstborn from the dead, the ruler of the kings of the earth. To him who loved us and freed us from our sins by his blood, ⁶and who made us a kingdom, priests to his God and Father, to him be glory and might forever and ever. Amen. ⁷*Behold, he is coming with the clouds, and every eye will see him, even those who pierced him, and all the tribes on earth will mourn because of him.* So it will happen. Amen.

⁸"I am Alpha and Omega," says the Lord God, who is and was and is to come, the Almighty.

In a number of very late manuscripts, the book of Revelation is entitled *The Revelation of John the Theologian and Evangelist* or *The Revelation of Saint John the Apostle and Evangelist and Theologian.* Earlier manuscripts entitled it simply *The Revelation of John.* The identity of John is ambiguous, and later scribes sought to clarify that John the evangelist, author of the Gospel of John, was the author (see Revelation 1:10). **1:1** The word translated as *angel* can also be translated as *messenger.* Compare verse 20, where the word is used again and where it seems to refer to *angels* who have the responsibility of being *messengers.* The angel of this verse reappears in Revelation 22:6–9. The *revelation of Jesus Christ* can refer to the revelation about Jesus or the revelation of him personally. Nephi appears to have the revelation of John in mind as connected to his own vision (1 Nephi 14:18–27). The language of this verse is alluded to in Doctrine and Covenants 88:79. *Servants* can also be translated as *slaves.* **1:3** The mention of reading the book to others points to this book being part of worship services. Early Christian meetings were defined by reading from the scriptures, a practice that was adopted from the synagogue. **1:4** *Asia* refers to the Roman province of Asia (see map). The cities listed in verse 11 were all in *Asia.* **1:5** Some later manuscripts change *freed us* to *washed us.* The later reading is clearly secondary and probably has baptism in mind. **1:6** This verse is alluded to and expanded in its meaning in Doctrine and Covenants 76:56 (see also Revelation 5:10). Compare Exodus 19:6 for a similar promise. The new kingdom with priests is modeled on the kingdom of Israel with the priests of Levi. **1:7** The quotation is assembled from Daniel 7:13 and Zechariah 12:10. **1:8** The quotation is given as a direct quotation of words that were spoken to the author. The *Almighty* is the title *pantokrator,* which can be translated also as the *All-Powerful. Omnipotent* is a synonym (Mosiah 3:5). Compare Revelation 21:6; Doctrine and Covenants 19:1; 35:1; 38:1. *Alpha and Omega* are the first and last letters of the Greek alphabet.

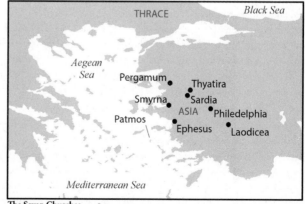

The Seven Churches
Map by Brandon Whitney, ThinkSpatial, BYU Geography

A PERSONAL VISION OF THE RESURRECTED CHRIST

⁹I, John, your brother and partner in trials, in the kingdom, and in endurance in Jesus, was on the island called Patmos because of the word of God and for the testimony of Jesus. ¹⁰I was in the Spirit on the Lord's day and heard a loud voice like a trumpet behind me, ¹¹saying, "Write what you see on a scroll and send it to the seven churches: to Ephesus, Smyrna, Pergamum, Thyatira, Sardis, Philadelphia, and Laodicea."

¹²I turned to see the voice that was speaking to me, and after turning I saw seven gold lampstands, ¹³and in the middle of the lamps, one like a son of man, and he was wearing a robe that extended to his feet, and he wore a gold sash around his chest. ¹⁴And his head and hair were white like wool, as white as snow, and his eyes were like a fiery flame. ¹⁵And his feet were like polished metal refined in a furnace, and his voice was like the sound of many waters. ¹⁶He held seven stars in his right hand, and from his mouth came a sharp two-edged sword, and his face was like the sun shining in its strength.

¹⁷And when I saw him, I fell at his feet as though dead, and he placed his right hand on me, saying, "Do not fear. I am the first and the last. ¹⁸I am the living one. I was dead, but, behold, I am alive forever and ever, and I have the keys of death and Hades. ¹⁹Therefore, write what you saw, things which are and which are about to take place after this. ²⁰The mystery of the seven stars that you saw in my right hand and the seven gold lampstands, the seven stars are the messengers of the seven churches, and the seven lampstands are the seven churches."

EPHESUS

2 ¹"To the angel of the church in Ephesus write, 'These are the words of him who holds the seven stars in his right hand, who walks in the midst of the seven gold lampstands. ²I know your works and labor and your patient endurance and that you cannot support evil. You have tested those who call themselves apostles but are not, and you have found that they are false. ³I know that you have endured patiently and have tolerated much because of my name,

---

1:9 Little is known about Patmos at the time of the revelation, and John may have been banished there. **1:10** *The Lord's day* is Sunday and not the Jewish Sabbath (Saturday). Christians began celebrating the day of the resurrection (Sunday) instead of the Jewish Sabbath. **1:11** *Laodicea* was mentioned in Colossians 2:1; 4:15–16. **1:12** These were likely to be menorahs (Leviticus 24:2–4). **1:13** The one like a human or *a son of man* is an allusion to Daniel 7:9, 13; 10:5–6. **1:14** A similar visionary description is given in Doctrine and Covenants 110:3 (compare Revelation 19:12). **1:15** The word translated as *polished metal* is not used in any other Greek text, so its meaning is unclear. It is clearly some type of metal, perhaps bronze and polished like a mirror. Compare Doctrine and Covenants 110:2–3; 133:22. **1:16** Joseph Smith gave a similar description (Joseph Smith—History 1:16–17). **1:17–18** These verses are quoted in Doctrine and Covenants 110:4. **1:18** *Hades* was the place in Greek mythology where the dead resided. In the New Testament it can refer to the abode of the wicked after death (Matthew 11:23; Luke 10:15; Acts 2:27, 31). **1:19** Nephi records a similar injunction using the language of this verse (1 Nephi 14:21–22). **1:20** *Angels* can also be translated as *messengers* (see verse 1). The Joseph Smith Translation changes them to *servants*.

2:1 The Joseph Smith Translation changes the word *angel* in chapters 2 and 3 to *servant*. *These are the words* intentionally follows the pattern in the Old Testament: *The Lord says* (Exodus 4:22). *In the midst of the seven gold lampstands* probably refers to being among the gold menorahs, and hence in the temple. In Revelation 1:20 the *lampstands* symbolize the churches, so the image refers symbolically to being among the churches. **2:1–3:22** The seven messages to the individual churches are not technically letters, but they are closer to public announcements or edicts. Each follows a similar pattern. **2:2** *False apostles* are also mentioned in 2 Corinthians 11:13 and probably refer to false missionaries.

and you have not grown weary. ⁴But I have something against you, that you have departed from your first love. ⁵Therefore, remember from what position you have fallen and repent and do the works that you did formerly. If not, I will come to you and remove your lampstand from its place, if you do not repent. ⁶But you have this, you hate the works of the Nicolaitans, which I also hate. ⁷The one who has an ear, let that person hear what the Spirit says to the churches. I will grant the one who conquers to eat from the tree of life, which is in the paradise of God.'"

SMYRNA

⁸"And to the angel of the church in Smyrna write, 'These are the words of the first and the last, who was dead but now lives. ⁹I know your suffering and poverty (but you are rich), and the slander from those who say they are Jews but are not. They are the synagogue of Satan. ¹⁰Do not fear what you are about to suffer. Behold, the devil is about to cast some of you into prison so that you might be tested, and you will experience a trial for ten days. Be faithful to the point of death, and I will give you the crown of life. ¹¹The one who has an ear, let that person hear what the Spirit says to the churches. The one who conquers will not be hurt by the second death.'"

PERGAMUM

¹²"And to the angel of the church in Pergamum write, 'These are the words of the one who has the sharp two-edged sword. ¹³I know where you live; it is where the throne of Satan is. You held tightly to my name, and you did not deny my faith in the days of Antipas, my faithful witness, who was killed among you, where Satan lives. ¹⁴But I have a few things against you, you have some there who hold tightly to the teaching of Balaam, who taught Balak to throw a stumbling block in front of the children of Israel, to eat what was sacrificed to idols and to commit sexual sins. ¹⁵Thus you have some who hold tightly to the teaching of the Nicolaitans. ¹⁶Therefore, repent. If not, I will come to you quickly and make war against them with the sword of my mouth. ¹⁷The one who has an ear, let that person hear what the Spirit says to the churches. I will give him some of the hidden manna to the one who conquers, and I will give him a white stone, and upon that stone a new name will be written which no one knows except the person who receives it.'"

THYATIRA

¹⁸"And to the angel of the church in Thyatira write, 'These are the words of the Son of God, who has eyes like a fiery flame and his feet are like polished metal. ¹⁹I know your works, love, faith, service, and patient

---

2:6 *The Nicolaitans* were a group that taught that sins were not held against a person and that sin had no consequence. Some scholars have connected them with Nicolas of Acts 6:5. **2:7** *The tree of life* is mentioned in Genesis 2:9; 3:22–24. *Paradise* is a Greek word referring to a place of peaceful existence or where the righteous dead reside. Here it is connected to Eden through the reference to *the tree of life* (compare 2 Nephi 2:19, 22). **2:9** The *synagogue* was a gathering place for Jews to worship (Mark 1:21). The specificity of the language of this verse suggests that the author had a specific community in mind. **2:10** The enemy is called *the devil*, a Greek word meaning *the slanderer*. A similar promise to that found in this verse is made in Doctrine and Covenants 20:14. **2:11** The theme of a *second death* is common in the Book of Mormon (Jacob 3:11; Alma 12:16). **2:13** The word translated as *witness* can also equally be translated as *martyr*, but nothing is known of Antipas or how he died. **2:14** The story of *Balaam* and *Balak* is told in Numbers 22–24. **2:17** The *white stone* is explained in Doctrine and Covenants 130:10–11. *Manna* is mentioned in Exodus 16:4.

endurance, and your recent works are greater than the first. ²⁰But I have something against you, that you support that woman Jezebel, who calls herself a prophetess, and she teaches and deceives my servants to commit sexual sins and to eat things sacrificed to idols. ²¹I have given her time so that she may repent, and she did not want to repent from her sexual sins. ²²Behold, I will throw her onto a sickbed, and I will throw those who commit adultery with her into great affliction if they do not repent from her works. ²³And I will put her children to death. And all the churches will know that I am the one who searches minds and hearts, and I will give you each according to your works. ²⁴But to the rest of you in Thyatira, to those who do not accept this teaching, and to the ones who have not learned what they call the deep things of Satan, I say that I do not place any burden on you. ²⁵Only hold tightly to what you have until I come. ²⁶And to the one who conquers and who continues to the end in my works I give him authority over the nations. ²⁷And *"he will rule over them with an iron rod, and he will break them into pieces like clay jars."* ²⁸Just as I have received authority from my Father, I will give to that person the morning star. ²⁹The one who has an ear, let that person hear what the Spirit says to the churches.'"

SARDIS

3 ¹"And to the angel of the church in Sardis write, 'These are the words of the one who has the seven spirits of God and the seven stars. I know your works, and you have a name of being alive, but you are dead. ²Wake up and strengthen what remains and is about to die, for I have not found your works complete before my God. ³Therefore, remember what you received and heard, and obey it and repent. Therefore, if you will not wake up, I will come as a thief, and you will not know what hour I will come against you. ⁴But you have a few names in Sardis of people who have not stained their clothes, and they will walk with me dressed in white because they are worthy. ⁵The one who conquers will be clothed in white clothing like them, and I will never blot his name from the book of life, and I will confess his name before my Father and before his angels. ⁶The one who has an ear, let that person hear what the Spirit says to the churches.'"

PHILADELPHIA

⁷"And to the angel of the church in Philadelphia write, 'These are the words of the holy one, the true one, who has the key of David, and who opens and no one will shut, and who shuts and no one will open. ⁸I know your works. Behold, I have placed in front of you an open door that no one can shut, because you have a little strength and you have obeyed my word and have not denied my name. ⁹Behold, I will make those of the synagogue of Satan, who say they are Jews but they are lying; behold, I will make them come and bow down before your feet, and they will know that I

2:20 Jezebel was famous for her sins (1 Kings 18–19). The condemnation is not for her actions as a prophetess but probably for sexual sins. *Servants* can also mean *slaves*. **2:26** The word *nations* can also be translated as *Gentiles*. It is unclear which meaning was intended. **2:27** Quotation from Psalm 2:9. The Joseph Smith Translation changes this to read *he will rule them with the word of God; and they shall be in his hands as the vessels of clay in the hands of a potter; and he shall govern them by faith, with equity and justice, even as I received of my Father.* **2:28** Similar imagery is used in 2 Peter 1:19.

3:1 The precise meaning of the phrase *you have a name of being alive* is unclear. **3:3** The theme of Christ's return as a thief is found in the Gospels and letters of Paul also (Matthew 24:42–44; Luke 12:39–40; 1 Thessalonians 5:2; 2 Peter 3:10). **3:5** For *the book of life,* see Exodus 32:32; Daniel 12:1. **3:7** *The key of David* is mentioned also in Isaiah 22:22.

loved you, [10]because you have obeyed my word about patient endurance. I will keep you from the hour of temptation that is about to come upon the whole world, to try those who live upon the earth. [11]I am coming quickly. Hold tightly to what you have so that no one takes your crown. [12]The one who conquers, I will make that person a pillar in the temple of my God, and he will not exit it. I will write upon that person the name of my God and the name of the city of my God, the new Jerusalem, which descends from heaven from my God, and my own new name. [13]The one who has an ear, let that person hear what the Spirit says to the churches.'"

LAODICEA

[14]"And to the angel of the church in Laodicea write, 'These are the words of the Amen, the faithful and true witness, the beginning of God's creation. [15]I know your works, that you are neither cold nor hot. I wish that you were cold or hot. [16]So, because you are lukewarm, neither hot nor cold, I am about to spit you out of my mouth. [17]Because you say, 'I am rich and have prospered, and I do not have any need,' you do not realize that you are miserable, pitiful, poor, blind, and naked. [18]I counsel you to buy from me gold that was refined by fire so that you may be rich, and buy from me white clothing so that you may be clothed and the shame of your nakedness will not be made obvious, and

buy from me salve to anoint your eyes so that you may see. [19]Everyone that I love, I chastise and discipline. Therefore, be eager and repent. [20]Behold, I am standing at the door and I am knocking. If anyone hears my voice and opens the door, I will come in and dine with him, and he with me. [21]The one who conquers, I will grant him to sit with me on my throne just as I conquered and sat with my Father on his throne. [22]The one who has an ear, let that person hear what the Spirit says to the churches.'"

ONE SEATED UPON THE THRONE

4 [1]After these things, I looked and behold a door was opened in heaven, and the first voice, which I heard speaking like a trumpet, said, "Come up here, and I will show you what must happen after these things." [2]Immediately I was in the Spirit and a throne stood in heaven, and someone was seated upon it! [3]And the one seated upon it was like jasper and carnelian in appearance, and around the throne was a rainbow that had the appearance of emerald. [4]And the throne was encircled by twenty-four thrones, and upon the thrones were twenty-four elders seated and clothed in white robes, and upon their heads were gold crowns. [5]And from the throne came flashes of lightning, rumblings and thunder, and seven flaming lamps were in front of the throne that were the seven spirits of

---

3:11 The theme of the quick return of the Lord is expanded in its application in Doctrine and Covenants 87:8. **3:12** This may be a foreshadowing of Revelation 14:1. A dedication to God was written on the high priest's hat (Exodus 28:36–38). For *new Jerusalem*, see Galatians 4:26; Philippians 3:20. Isaiah also spoke of a *new name* (Isaiah 62:2). **3:14** The *words of the Amen* refer to the words of the one who is true. **3:18** The verse hints at a powerful force of refinement prior to being clothed in white. The anointing of the eyes appears to be for the purpose of alleviating pain and making it easier to see. **3:21** This verse may look toward the fulfillment of Psalm 110:1.

4:2 The one seated on the throne is God. **4:3** *Jasper* was a semiprecious gemstone, probably green; *Carnelian* was also semiprecious and is usually red. A possible allusion to Ezekiel 1:28. **4:4** This verse is explained in Doctrine and Covenants 77:5. The number *twenty-four* may correspond to the twelve apostles and the representatives from the twelve tribes (Joshua 3:12). **4:5** The various emanations coming from the throne appear to describe different voices.

God, ⁶and it was like a sea of glass in front of the throne, like crystal.

And in the midst of the throne and in a circle around it were four living creatures full of eyes in front and back. ⁷The first living creature was like a lion, and the second living creature was like an ox, and the third living creature had the face of a man, and the fourth living creature was like an eagle in flight. ⁸And the four living creatures each had six wings and were full of eyes all around and within, and they did not pause day or night from saying,

"*Holy, holy, holy*
is the Lord God Almighty,
who was and is and is to come."

⁹And when the living creatures gave glory and honor and thanks to the one seated on the throne, who is alive forever and ever, ¹⁰the twenty-four elders fell in front of the one seated upon the throne, and they worshipped him who is alive forever and ever. They threw their crowns before the throne, saying,

¹¹"You are worthy, our Lord and God,
    to receive glory, honor, and power
because you created all things,
        and because of your will they existed and were created."

A SCROLL WITH WRITING ON IT

5 ¹And I saw a scroll written on the inside and outside and sealed with seven seals in the right hand of the one seated upon the throne. ²And I saw a mighty angel declaring in a loud voice, "Who is worthy to unroll the scroll and break its seals?" ³And no one in heaven, on the earth, or under the earth was able to unroll the scroll or to see inside it. ⁴So I began to weep profoundly because no one was found who was worthy to unroll the scroll or see inside it. ⁵One of the elders said to me, "Do not weep. Behold, the lion of the tribe of Judah, the root of David, has conquered, and therefore he has succeeded in unrolling the scroll and breaking its seven seals."

⁶And I saw in the midst of the throne and of the four living creatures and in the midst of the elders a Lamb standing, as though he had been slain, having seven horns and seven eyes, which are the seven spirits of God sent to all the earth. ⁷He came and took the scroll from the right hand of the one seated upon the throne. ⁸And after he had taken the scroll, the four living creatures and the twenty-four elders knelt before the Lamb. They each had a harp and gold bowls full of incense, which are the prayers of the saints. ⁹And they sang a new song, saying,

"You are worthy to receive the scroll
and open its seals because you were killed,
and by your blood you ransomed people for God from every tribe and language and people and nation,

---

4:6 *Like crystal* can also be translated as *like ice*. Compare Ezekiel 1:5–14. This verse is explained in Doctrine and Covenants 77:1–4. **4:8** Quotation from Isaiah 6:3. *Holy, holy, holy is the Lord* is often called the *Trisagion*. The portion of the quotation not in italics includes a quotation from Revelation 1:8. First Nephi 1:14 and 2 Nephi 9:46 also reflect on the title *the Lord God Almighty*.

5:1 An allusion to Ezekiel 2:9–10. This verse is explained in Doctrine and Covenants 77:6–7. **5:3** The *seven seals* appear to represent seven different places in the scroll that were sealed rather than a scroll that was sealed in one place seven times. **5:5** An allusion to Isaiah 11:1, 10 (compare Genesis 49:9). **5:6** The *Lamb* is the most important title for Jesus in the book of Revelation. **5:8** The *harp* is technically a *kithara*, a stringed instrument that could produce a melody. **5:9** A *new song* is mentioned in Isaiah 42:10; Psalm 96:1; 144:9. *Because you were killed* is literally *because you were slaughtered*. The imagery is intentionally violent.

¹⁰and you made them a kingdom and priests to our God,
and they will rule upon the earth."

¹¹And I looked, and I heard the voice of many angels encircling the throne and the living creatures and elders. Their number was myriad upon myriad and thousands upon thousands, ¹²and they were saying in a loud voice,

"Worthy is the Lamb, who was killed,
to receive the power, wealth,
wisdom, strength, honor, glory, and praise!"

¹³And I heard every creature which is in heaven and upon the earth and under the earth and in the sea and everything in them, saying,

"To the one seated upon the throne and to the Lamb be praise, honor, glory, power, forever and ever."

¹⁴And the four living creatures said, "Amen," and the elders knelt and worshipped.

THE SEVEN SEALS

6 ¹I saw that the Lamb opened one of the seven seals, and I heard one of the four living creatures saying in a voice like thunder, "Come." ²And I looked and saw a white horse, and the one sitting upon it had a bow, and a crown was given to him, and he went out conquering and to conquer.

³And when he opened the second seal, I heard the second living creature saying, "Come." ⁴And out came another horse, a burning red one, and the one sitting upon it was given permission to take peace from the earth so that they would murder one another, and he was given a large sword.

⁵And when he opened the third seal, I heard the third living creature, saying, "Come." And I looked and saw a black horse, and the one seated upon it had a balance scale in his hand. ⁶And I heard something like a voice in the midst of the four living creatures, saying, "A measure of wheat will cost a silver coin, and three measures of barley will cost a silver coin, and do not harm the olive oil and wine."

⁷And when he opened the fourth seal, I heard the voice of the fourth living creature, saying, "Come." ⁸And I looked and saw a pale horse, and the one seated upon it had the name of death, and Hades followed after him, and authority was given to them over the fourth part of the earth to kill with a sword, famine, disease, and by the wild animals of the earth.

⁹And when he opened the fifth seal, I saw under the altar the souls of those who were murdered because of the word

---

5:10 Some later manuscripts read *made us* instead of *made them*. **5:11** Some translations prefer ten thousand times ten thousand in place of *myriad upon myriad*. The Greek term loosely refers to ten thousands in monetary contexts but is often a general term for many thousands. **5:13** This verse is quoted and adapted to a new context in Doctrine and Covenants 124:101 (compare Doctrine and Covenants 76:119).

6:1 An explanation of the *seals* is given in Doctrine and Covenants 77:7. Modern scripture looks at the seals as representing seven periods of the earth's existence. The book of Revelation focuses on events in the sixth and seventh seals. **6:2** The things that are given to the rider signify the possession of a kingdom. **6:4** Doctrine and Covenants 1:35 considers the time when *peace* will be taken from the earth. Compare Zechariah 1:8. *Fiery red* is possible in place of *burning red*. **6:6** A *measure* was equal to about a quart or about .95 liters. The prices are considerably higher than usual and suggest inflated prices or prices that are the result of a famine or dearth. The *silver coins* mentioned are denarii. **6:8** *Disease* is the Greek word *death*, and it is used in this sentence in the sense of dying by disease or pestilence. *Death* and *Hades* are personifications of wickedness. **6:9** Using the imagery of this verse, Doctrine and Covenants 135:7 describes Joseph and Hyrum Smith as under the *altar*.

of God and because of the testimony they had given. ¹⁰And they cried out in a loud voice, saying, "How long, Lord, holy and true, will you not judge and avenge our blood upon those who live on the earth?" ¹¹And to each of them was given a white robe, and they were told to rest for a little longer until their fellow servants and their brothers and sisters reached the full number of those who were going to be killed as they had been.

¹²And I saw when he opened the sixth seal that there was a great earthquake, and the sun became like a sackcloth of hair, and the entire moon became like blood, ¹³and the stars of heaven fell to the earth, like a fig tree lets its late summer figs fall when shaken by a great wind. ¹⁴And heaven was separated like a scroll being rolled up, and every mountain and island was moved from its place. ¹⁵And the kings of the earth and the great ones and the military leaders and the rich and powerful, and everyone, slave and free, hid themselves in the caves and among the rocks of the mountains, ¹⁶and they said to the mountains and rocks, "Fall upon us and hide us from the face of him who is seated upon the throne and from the wrath of the Lamb ¹⁷because

the great day of his wrath has come, and who is able to stand?"

THE SEALING OF THE 144,000

7 ¹After this I saw four angels standing at the four corners of the earth, holding the four winds of the earth so that the wind did not blow upon the earth nor upon the sea nor upon any tree. ²And I saw another angel descending from the east, who had the seal of the living God, and he cried out in a loud voice to the four angels who were permitted to harm the earth and the sea, ³saying, "Do not harm the earth nor the sea nor the trees until we seal the servants of our God upon their foreheads." ⁴And I heard the number of those who were sealed, one hundred and forty-four thousand, sealed from all the tribes of Israel,

⁵From the tribe of Judah, twelve thousand were sealed,
from the tribe of Reuben, twelve thousand,
from the tribe of Gad, twelve thousand,
⁶from the tribe of Asher, twelve thousand,
from the tribe of Naphtali, twelve thousand,

6:10 The title *Lord* is different from that used in the majority of instances in the New Testament. This word often means *master* or even *leader*. 6:11 Greek uses *brothers* generically to refer to *brothers and sisters*. The destruction will take place until a *complete* or *full* number had been killed, indicating that the number of slain had been known beforehand. 6:12 Commentary on this verse is given in Doctrine and Covenants 77:10. Compare Doctrine and Covenants 29:14; 45:42 for a similar prophecy. 6:13 Doctrine and Covenants 88:87 provides commentary on this verse. 6:14 This verse is quoted in Doctrine and Covenants 88:95. The act of rolling up a scroll would signal the end of a story or account. 6:16 Alma 12:14 uses language that is similar to this verse in describing the dread of being condemned. This verse, which preserves a quotation of the personified wicked, also contains an allusion to Hosea 10:8. A possible allusion to Psalm 76:7. Their fear is the result of not being covered by the white robe (see 3:18).

7:1 This verse is explained in Doctrine and Covenants 77:8. The timing of this chapter is discussed in Doctrine and Covenants 77:10. The *wind* alluded to in this verse is the drying and destructive wind that destroyed crops and killed vegetation. 7:2 *The seal of the living God* may refer to baptism (2 Corinthians 1:21–22) as well as other ordinances whereby a person receives God's seal, technically a stamp from his personal seal. This verse is explained in Doctrine and Covenants 77:9. 7:3 An allusion to Ezekiel 9:4. Those who have the seal of God are protected from plague and calamity. 7:4 The 144,000 are explained in Doctrine and Covenants 77:11. 7:5–8 The tribe of Dan is missing from the list.

from the tribe of Manasseh, twelve thousand, [7]from the tribe of Simeon, twelve thousand, from the tribe of Levi, twelve thousand, from the tribe of Issachar, twelve thousand, [8]from the tribe of Zebulun, twelve thousand, from the tribe of Joseph, twelve thousand, and from the tribe of Benjamin, twelve thousand were sealed.

THE ONES WHO CAME FROM THE GREAT TRIBULATION

[9]After this I saw a large crowd that no one could number, from every nation, tribe, people, and language, and they stood in front of the throne and in front of the Lamb, and they wore white robes, and they had palm branches in their hands. [10]And they cried out in a loud voice, saying,

"Salvation belongs to our God, who is seated on the throne, and to the Lamb."

[11]And all of the angels were standing in a circle around the throne, the elders, and the four living creatures, and they fell down on their faces in front of the throne and worshipped God, [12]saying,

"Amen! Praise, glory, wisdom, thanks, honor, power, and strength belong to our God forever and ever. Amen."

[13]And one of the elders replied to me, saying, "Who are these who are dressed in white robes, and where did they come from?" [14]And I said to him, "My lord, you know." And he said to me, "These are the ones who came from the great tribulation, and they washed their robes and whitened them in the blood of the Lamb. [15]Because of this they are in front of the throne of God, and they minister to him day and night in his temple, and the one seated upon the throne will shelter them. [16]They will not be hungry or thirsty again, nor will the sun beat down upon them, nor any burning heat [17]because the Lamb in the midst of the throne will shepherd them, and he will lead them to a fountain of life-giving waters, and God will wipe away every tear from their eyes."

THE OPENING OF THE SEVENTH SEAL

8 [1]When he opened the seventh seal, there was silence in heaven for about a half hour. [2]And I saw the seven angels who stand before God, and seven trumpets were given to them. [3]And another came

---

7:9 For the purpose of the *white robe*, see 3:18. **7:14** John speaks to a servant of the Lord here, and therefore *lord* is used instead of Lord. A similar description of the saints is given in 1 Nephi 12:10–11; Alma 13:11; 3 Nephi 27:19. Washing in blood contrasts the typical process of whitening clothing. **7:15** *Shelter them* refers to the act of covering them with a tent. Similar throne imagery is used in Doctrine and Covenants 88:13. *Because of this* signals that they were given that position because they had been martyrs for the testimony of the Lord. **7:16** An allusion to Isaiah 49:10. **7:17** An allusion to Isaiah 25:8. The image of a shepherd points to Jesus Christ, who was frequently described using shepherding terms (John 10:2). *Life-giving waters* can refer to waters that have the power to give eternal life or to waters that sustain life. A similar promise is given in John 4:14, and perhaps an allusion to Jeremiah 2:13; 17:13.

8:1 The timing of the fulfillment of the events in this chapter are discussed in Doctrine and Covenants 77:12. This chapter introduces plagues and calamities that intervene in the description of the opening of the seals. The imagery has parallels to the plagues of Egypt (Exodus 7–12). A similar division of time is used in Doctrine and Covenants 88:95. **8:2** The meaning of the trumpets is provided in Doctrine and Covenants 77:12. **8:3** *A gold censer* was a bowl used for burning incense. The idea that the angel needed

and stood at the altar having a gold censer, and much incense was given to him so that he might offer it with the prayers of all the saints upon the gold altar before the throne, [4]and the smoke of incense offered with the prayers of the saints ascended to God from the hand of the angel. [5]Then the angel took the censer and filled it with fire from the altar and threw it upon the earth, and there were flashes of thunder, voices, lightning, and an earthquake.

SEVEN TRUMPETS

[6]And the seven angels, the ones having the seven trumpets, prepared to blow them. [7]And the first blew his trumpet, and there was hail and fire mixed with blood, and it was thrown upon the earth, and a third of the earth was burned up, and a third of the trees were burned up, and all the green grass was burned up.

[8]And the second angel blew his trumpet, and something like a great mountain burning with fire was cast into the sea, and one-third of the sea became blood. [9]A third of all the living creatures in the sea were destroyed, and a third of the ships were destroyed.

[10]And the third angel blew his trumpet, and a huge star burning like a torch fell from heaven, and it fell upon a third of the rivers and the springs of water. [11]And the name of the star was called Wormwood, and a third of the waters became wormwood, and many people died from the water that was poisoned.

[12]And the fourth angel blew his trumpet, and a third of the sun was struck, and a third of the moon and stars as well so that a third of them were darkened. A third of the daylight was lost, and likewise a third of the night. [13]And I saw and heard an eagle flying directly overhead, crying in a loud voice, "Woe, woe, woe to those living on the earth because of the remaining voices of the trumpets of the three angels who are about to blow them."

9 [1]And the fifth angel sounded his trumpet, and I saw a star had fallen from heaven to the earth, and he was given the key to the shaft of the abyss. [2]And he opened the shaft of the abyss, and smoke went out of the shaft like the smoke of a large oven, and the sun and the sky were darkened from the smoke from the shaft. [3]Locusts came out of the smoke onto the earth, and they were given power like the power of earthly scorpions. [4]They were told not to harm the grass of the earth or any green plant or any tree, but only those

---

much incense implies a corresponding increase in the number of saints offering prayers. **8:4** The imagery of the prayers of the saints being mixed with the smoke of incense is found in Psalm 141:2. The altar of incense, described in this verse, was located in the Jerusalem temple, and incense was offered on it twice daily. **8:5** Doctrine and Covenants 88:90 draws upon the language of this verse. **8:7** This plague is similar to one of the Egyptian plagues (Exodus 9:18–25). The destruction of a third part of humanity is a theme found also in Ezekiel 5:2–12. **8:8** An allusion to one of the Egyptian plagues (Exodus 7:20–21), similar imagery is used in Psalm 46:2. **8:11** *Wormwood* is the Greek word *Absinthe*. The plant was used to make a highly potent alcoholic beverage that is still produced today. The extract of the plant was extremely bitter, and some have attributed medicinal qualities to the plant. The image depicted in this verse suggests that its intoxicating powers were at play in altering the fresh water. *Poisoned* is literally *bitter* in Greek, but it is an idiom referring to something that is poisonous to consume. **8:12** This plague has some similarities to an Egyptian plague (Exodus 10:21). **8:13** Doctrine and Covenants 88:92; 133:36 alludes to this verse.

9:1 *The abyss* is used by Paul to refer to the place where the wicked reside (Romans 10:7). Compare Exodus 10:4–20 for similarities to one of the Egyptian plagues. **9:2** *The shaft of the abyss* likely portrays the entranceway into the realm of the dead, or spirit prison. The smoke that billows out of the abyss implies that the dead are being tortured in flames. **9:3** *Locusts* were particularly destructive of crops. These

people who did not have the seal of God upon their foreheads. ⁵They were not permitted to kill them, but to harass them for five months, and their torment was like a scorpion when it stings a person. ⁶And in those days people will seek death and not find it, and they will want to die but death will flee from them.

⁷The locusts looked like horses made ready for battle, and upon their heads they had something like crowns of gold, and their faces looked like the faces of people. ⁸They had hair like women's hair, and their teeth were like lions' teeth. ⁹They had breastplates like iron breastplates, and the sound of their wings was like the sound of many horse-drawn chariots going to war. ¹⁰They had tails and stingers like scorpions, and their power to harm people for five months was in their tails. ¹¹They had a king over them, the angel of the abyss, whose name in Hebrew is Abaddon, and in Greek his name is Apollyon.

¹²The first woe has passed. Behold, two woes are coming after these things.

¹³And the sixth angel blew his trumpet, and I heard a voice from the four horns of the gold altar before God, ¹⁴saying to the sixth angel who had the trumpet, "Release the four angels who are bound at the great river Euphrates." ¹⁵So the four angels, who were prepared for that hour and day and month and year, were released to kill one third of humanity. ¹⁶And the number of the soldiers on horseback was two hundred million; I heard their number. ¹⁷And this is what the horses looked like in my vision and those who rode upon them. They had breastplates that looked like fire, dark blue, and sulfur in color, and the heads of the horses were like lions' heads, and fire, smoke, and sulfur came out of their mouths. ¹⁸One-third of humanity was killed by these three plagues, by the fire, smoke, and sulfur issuing from their mouths. ¹⁹For the power of the horses is in their mouths and in their tails, for their tails are like snakes with heads that inflict harm.

²⁰The remaining people who were not killed in these plagues did not repent from the works of their hands, and they did not cease worshipping demons and idols made of gold, silver, bronze, stone, and wood, idols that cannot see or hear or walk. ²¹Neither did they repent of their murders or their sorceries or their sexual sins or their thefts.

THE LITTLE SCROLL

10 ¹And I saw another mighty angel descending from heaven wrapped in a cloud, and a rainbow over his head, and his face was like the sun, and his legs were like pillars of fire. ²And he had in his hand a little scroll that was open, and he placed his right foot upon the sea and his left foot on the land. ³And he cried out in a loud voice just like a lion, and when he cried out the seven thunders replied in their voices. ⁴And when the seven thunders

---

insects are prone to large swarms. **9:7** The Greek reads *the faces of men*, but it appears to be used generically to refer to humans or to *the faces of people*. The imagery may come from Joel 2:4. **9:7–10** The author appears to be describing a barbarian or foreign army. **9:9** The imagery may come from Joel 2:5–7. **9:11** The Hebrew term *Abaddon* means *ruin* or *destruction*, and the Greek term *Apollyon* means *destroyer* (compare Job 26:6). **9:13** The *horns of the altar* were attached to the four corners of the altar. **9:14** The *Euphrates* stood as the natural boundary between Rome and its eastern rival Parthia. **9:16** This army is much larger than the entire population of the Roman Empire and far beyond the size of any earthly army of the day. **9:20** This is similar to the response to the Egyptian plagues (Exodus 7:13, 22; 8:15). **9:21** *Sorceries* refers to drug-induced spells.

10:1 There are many similarities to events described in this chapter and Daniel 12:1–13. **10:2** Compare Ezekiel 2:9–10 for the use of a visionary scroll containing information about the history of the earth. *Open* in this case would refer to being unrolled. **10:4–7** Compare Daniel 12:4–9 for a similar vision.

spoke, I was about to write, but I heard a voice speaking from heaven, "Seal up what the seven thunders have said, and do not write it." ⁵And the angel, which I saw standing upon the sea and the land, raised his right hand to heaven, ⁶and he swore by the one who lives forever and ever, who created the heaven and what is in it and the earth and what is on it and the sea and what is in it, that there will be no more delay. ⁷But in the days when the seventh angel is about to sound his trumpet, the mystery of God will be completed just as he declared it to his servants the prophets.

⁸And the voice that I heard from heaven spoke to me again, saying, "Go, and take the scroll that is opened in the hand of the angel who is standing upon the sea and the land." ⁹And I went to the angel and told him to give me the little scroll, and he said to me, "Take it and eat it. It will be bitter to your stomach, but it will be sweet like honey in your mouth."

¹⁰And I took the little scroll from the hand of the angel and ate it, and it was sweet like honey in my mouth, but when I ate it, it was bitter in my stomach. ¹¹And they said to me, "You must prophesy again about many people, nations, languages, and kings."

THE TWO MARTYRS

11 ¹Then a measuring rod like a staff was given to me, saying, "Rise and measure the temple of God and the altar, and number those who worship in it. ²But do not measure the outer courtyard outside the temple; leave it out because it is given to the Gentiles, and they will trample the holy city for forty-two months. ³And I will give authority to my two witnesses that they will prophesy for 1,260 days while clothed in sackcloth."

⁴These are the two olive trees and the two lamps standing before the Lord of the earth. ⁵And if anyone desires to harm them, fire comes from their mouth and consumes their enemies. And if anyone desires to harm them, this is how that person must die. ⁶They have authority to shut the sky so that no rain falls in the days of their prophesying, and they have authority over the waters to change them into blood and to strike the earth with whatever kind of plague as they desire. ⁷And when they have completed their testimony, the beast that rises from the abyss will make war with them and conquer and kill them, ⁸and their corpses will lie in the street of the great city which spiritually is called Sodom and Egypt, where the Lord was crucified. ⁹Some of the people, tribes,

---

10:5 The meaning of this verse is greatly expanded in Doctrine and Covenants 88:110. The angel raises his hand to signal the swearing of an oath. **10:6** *That there will be no more delay* may be a continuation of what was spoken by the heavenly voice in verse 5 so that it would be translated *There will be no more delay.* **10:8** Interpreted in Doctrine and Covenants 77:14. **10:9** The word translated as *bitter* can also mean *poisonous.* The act of eating *the little scroll* is to accept a prophetic call (Ezekiel 2:8). **10:10** This verse is explained in Doctrine and Covenants 77:14. **10:11** It is unclear who *they* refers to because the preceding verses have only mentioned a single angelic intermediary.

11:1 Some unreliable Greek manuscripts add *and the angel stood.* The area around the *altar* is sometimes referred to as the court of the priests. **11:2** These two witnesses are mentioned in Isaiah 51:19; Zechariah 4:3, 11, 14; 2 Nephi 8:18–20 (which quotes Isaiah 51). **11:3** The time frame given here is the same as Daniel 7:25; 12:7 and refers to a period of approximately three and a half years. The *sackcloth* was sometimes made of hair (Isaiah 50:3). An explanation is given in Doctrine and Covenants 77:15. **11:6** An allusion to Exodus 7:17–25. The Greek wording suggests that they have been given *power* or *authority* to shut the heavens in the way that a person might close a door. **11:7** The reference to the *beast* may be an allusion to Daniel 7:3–7. **11:8** Some modern translations prefer *symbolically* in place of *spiritually.* The Greek word is *spiritually,* but the meaning in this context may include the notion that Jerusalem is

languages, and nations will stare at their corpses for three and a half days, and they will not permit them to be placed in a tomb. [10]Those who live on the earth will rejoice over them and will celebrate and give gifts to one another, because these two prophets had tormented those who live on the earth. [11]But after three and a half days, a breath of life from God entered into them, and they stood upon their feet, and great fear seized those who were watching them. [12]Then they heard a loud voice from heaven saying to them, "Come up here!" And they ascended to heaven in a cloud, and their enemies stared at them. [13]Then there was a great earthquake in that hour, and a tenth of the city fell and was killed in the earthquake. Seven thousand people died, and the remainder were afraid and gave glory to the God of heaven.

[14]The second woe has passed; behold, the third woe comes quickly.

THE SEVENTH TRUMPET

[15]And the seventh angel blew his trumpet, and there were loud voices in heaven, saying,

"The kingdom of the world
has become the kingdom of our Lord
and his Christ,
and he will rule forever and ever."

[16]And the twenty-four elders who were seated before God on their thrones fell down upon their faces, and they worshipped God, [17]saying,

"We thank you, Lord God Almighty,
the one who is and was,
because you have taken your great
power and started to rule.
[18]And the nations raged,
but your wrath has come,
and the time for the dead to be judged
has come and for rewarding your servants, the prophets and saints,
and those who fear your name,
the small and the great,
and the time has come for destroying
those who destroyed the earth."

[19]Then God's temple in heaven was opened, and the ark of his covenant was seen in his temple, and there were flashes of lightning, voices, thunders, an earthquake, and a great hailstorm.

SIGNS IN HEAVEN

12 [1]And a great sign appeared in heaven, a woman wearing the sun with the moon beneath her feet, and upon her head a crown of twelve stars. [2]She was pregnant, and she cried out in pain and in labor to give birth. [3]And another sign appeared in heaven: behold, a huge red dragon with seven heads and ten horns, and upon his heads were seven diadems. [4]And the dragon's tail swept away a third of the stars of heaven and threw them to the earth. Then the dragon stood before the woman, who was about to give birth

---

being referred to in a symbolic way as *Sodom* and *Egypt* (compare Isaiah 1:10; 19:1). Compare Doctrine and Covenants 77:15. **11:11** This verse borrows heavily from Ezekiel 37:5, 10. **11:13** For a similar prophesy of a great earthquake, see Doctrine and Covenants 88:87–90. **11:19** An allusion to Ezekiel 13:13 (compare Doctrine and Covenants 29:16). For *the ark of his covenant*, see Exodus 25:10–22.

12:1 Perhaps an allusion to Genesis 37:9. The Joseph Smith Translation indicates that the figures and images depicted in this chapter are signs of things that were to take place upon the earth. **12:2** An allusion to Isaiah 66:7–9. **12:3** *Diadems* refers to the crowns of monarchs. The word *dragon* arises from the Greek translation of the Old Testament where the term for Leviathan is translated as *dragon* (Job 41:1; Isaiah 27:1). The *ten horns* derive from Daniel 7:7, 20, 24. **12:4** Doctrine and Covenants 29:36–38 expands the context and meaning of this verse, but it may also be dependent upon Moses 4:1–4 (see also Isaiah 14:12–13).

so that he might eat her child when it was born. ⁵And she gave birth to a male child, who was about to shepherd all the nations with a rod of iron. Then her child was caught up to God, before his throne, ⁶and the woman fled into the desert, where there was a place prepared for her by God so that she might be cared for there for 1,260 days.

MICHAEL FIGHTS THE DRAGON

⁷Then there was a war in heaven. Michael and his angels fought against the dragon, and the dragon and his angels returned the fight. ⁸But the dragon was defeated, and there was no longer any place for them in heaven. ⁹Then the huge dragon was thrown out, that ancient snake who is called the devil and Satan, who deceives the entire world, was thrown down to the earth and his angels with him. ¹⁰And I heard a loud voice in heaven, saying,

"The salvation and the power,
and the kingdom of our God,
and the authority of his Christ have come,
because the accuser of our brothers and sisters,
the one who accuses them before our God

night and day has been thrown down.
¹¹But they conquered him because of the blood of the Lamb,
and because of the word of the message of their testimony,
and they did not love their lives enough to avoid death.
¹²Rejoice, heavens, because of this,
and all those who live in them.
But woe to the earth and the sea
because the devil has descended upon you; he is terribly angry because he knows that he only has a little time left."

THE DRAGON FIGHTS AGAINST THE WOMAN

¹³And when the dragon saw that he was thrown down to the earth, he pursued the woman who had given birth to the male child. ¹⁴But the woman was given two giant eagle's wings so that she could fly to the desert to the place prepared for her, where she would be cared for away from the snake, for a time, times, and half a time. ¹⁵Then the snake spit water like a river from his mouth to sweep away the woman with a flood. ¹⁶But the earth helped the woman, and the earth opened its mouth and swallowed the river that the dragon spit from his mouth. ¹⁷And the dragon was angry with the woman, and

---

12:5 An allusion to Psalm 2:9 (compare Isaiah 66:7). This psalm is also alluded to or quoted in Revelation 2:27 and 19:15. Compare 1 Nephi 11:25 for the image of *the rod of iron*. **12:6** Doctrine and Covenants 33:5 reports the fulfillment of this image (compare also Doctrine and Covenants 86:3). **12:7** *Michael* is an important figure in Daniel (10:13, 21; 12:1) and the Restoration (Doctrine and Covenants 88:112–13; 107:54; 128:20–21). **12:8** The Joseph Smith Translation reads *And the dragon prevailed not against Michael; neither the child, nor the woman, which was the church of God, who had been delivered of her pains, and brought forth the kingdom of our God and his Christ.* **12:9** In 2 Nephi 9:8–9, the *devil* falls rather than being *thrown out*. Similar imagery regarding the *devil* is found in 2 Nephi 2:18. The fall of the *devil* may be built upon Isaiah 14:12–15. Compare Doctrine and Covenants 29:37; 76:28; 88:110. **12:10** Greek uses *brothers* generically to refer to *brothers and sisters*. Satan *accuses* as a means of challenging the children of God. **12:11** The faithful conquer Satan through the *blood of the Lamb*. **12:14** *A time, times, and half a time* is another way of referring to 1,260 days (see Revelation 12:6). The phrase derives from the idea of a year of 360 days plus two years of 360 days each plus half of year (180 days). See also Revelation 11:3. The image of a rescuing eagle is an allusion to Exodus 19:4. **12:16** A possible allusion to Exodus 15:12. **12:17** An allusion to Daniel 7:21. The idea of those who *obey the commandments and the testimony of*

he went to make war with her other descendants, those who obey the commandments of God and have the testimony of Jesus. [18]And the dragon stood upon the sand of the seashore.

THE FIRST BEAST

13 [1]And I saw the beast arising from the sea, having seven heads and ten horns, and upon his horns he had ten diadems, and upon his heads was a blasphemous name. [2]And the beast that I saw was like a leopard, and his feet were like a bear's feet, and its mouth was like a lion's mouth. And the dragon gave him his power, his throne, and great authority. [3]And one of his heads was wounded and near death, and his wound of death was healed. Then the whole earth followed the beast in amazement. [4]And they worshipped the dragon because he gave authority to the beast, and they worshipped the beast, saying, "Who is like the beast, and who is able to make war against him?"

[5]He was given a mouth to speak important things and blasphemies, and he was given authority for forty-two months. [6]And he opened his mouth to speak blasphemies against God, to blaspheme his name and his place of dwelling; that is, those who dwell in heaven. [7]And he was permitted to make war against the saints and to conquer them. And authority was given to him over every tribe, people, language, and nation, [8]and everyone living on the earth will worship him, everyone whose name was not written before the foundation of the world in the book of life of the Lamb who was killed. [9]If anyone has an ear, let that person hear.

> [10]If anyone is to be taken captive,
> let that person be taken into captivity;
> if anyone is to be killed by the sword,
> let that person be killed by the sword.

These circumstances require the endurance and faith of the saints.

THE SECOND BEAST

[11]Then I saw another beast ascending from the earth, and he had two horns like a lamb, but he spoke like a dragon. [12]And he had all the authority on behalf of the first beast, and he made the earth and those who live on it worship the first beast, whose deadly wound had been healed. [13]He performed great miracles so that he made fire come down from heaven to the earth in front of people, [14]and he deceived those who live on the earth because of the miracles he was permitted to perform on behalf of the beast. He told those who live

---

Jesus refers to those who remained obedient to the Law while also accepting Jesus as Lord. Many Christians obeyed portions of the law of Moses while also accepting Christ. **12:18** Some modern translations include this verse as the first verse of chapter 13.

13:1 A reference to Revelation 12:3. Some manuscripts read *blasphemous names*. It is unclear what this name might be. Compare Daniel 7:3–8 for a similar vision. **13:4** This could be a criticism of the Roman practice of worshipping the emperor and giving him divine honors. **13:5** Compare Revelation 11:2. **13:7** *And he was permitted to make war against the saints and to conquer them* is lacking in some early manuscripts, but due to what appears to be a copying error, most scholars assume that the phrase is original. Some early manuscripts do preserve the phrase. **13:8** Some translations have rendered the phrase *before the foundation of the world* as modifying the *Lamb who was killed*. However, the phrase fits better with *whose name was not written*. This idea is also expressed in Revelation 17:8. **13:10** This saying may be a reflection on Matthew 26:52 (compare Jeremiah 15:2). First Nephi 14:4 conceives of captivity in a similar way. The final sentence of this verse appears to be a direct warning to the reader. **13:12** *Authority* can also be translated as *power*. **13:14** The idea that deception will be used against the saints is a common theme in Restoration scripture (2 Nephi 28:21; Doctrine and Covenants 52:14).

on the earth to make a statue to the beast who had been wounded by the sword but lived. ¹⁵He was given power to give life to the statue of the first beast so that it could speak and could cause those who would not worship the statue of the beast to be killed. ¹⁶And he made everyone, small and great, rich and poor, free and slave, to receive a mark upon their right hand or upon their forehead ¹⁷so that no one was permitted to buy or sell unless he had the mark of the beast, his name or his number. ¹⁸Here is wisdom: Let the one who has understanding calculate the number of the beast, for it is the number of a man, and his number is 666.

THE 144,000

14 ¹And I looked, and, behold, the Lamb was standing upon Mount Zion, and with him were one hundred forty-four thousand who had the name of his Father written on their foreheads. ²Then I heard a voice from heaven like the sound of many waters and the sound of loud thunder. And the sound that I heard was like harpists playing their harps, ³and they were singing a new song before the throne, and before the four living creatures, and the elders. And no one was able to learn the song except the one hundred forty-four thousand who had been redeemed from the earth. ⁴These are the ones who have not defiled themselves with women, for they are virgins. They follow the Lamb wherever he leads them; they were redeemed from humanity as the first fruits to God and the Lamb. ⁵No lie was found in their mouth, for they are blameless.

THE THREE ANGELS

⁶And I saw another angel flying directly overhead, having the eternal gospel to proclaim to those living on the earth, and to every nation, tribe, language, and people, ⁷saying in a loud voice, "Fear God and give him glory because the hour of his judgment has come, and worship the one who made heaven and earth and the sea and the springs of water."

13:15 *Give life* is in Greek *give breath*. **13:18** Some important and early manuscripts and patristic writers indicate that the number is 616 instead of 666. The variant number may have come about as scribes attempted to calculate the number of the beast by converting different names to numbers, a result of adding up the numeric value of their names (in Greek, A=1, B=2, G=3, etc.). The practice is called isopsephy and was regularly used to create riddles and obscure hidden messages. Nero Caesar's name adds up to 616 (if using the Latin spelling of his name) and 666 (if using the Greek spelling of his name). It remains unclear whether the author intended to refer to Nero using the number 666 or whether it refers to the *number of humanity*, a possible translation of the Greek *number of a man*.

14:1 The location of *Mount Zion* as used in this verse is probably the temple mount (see Isaiah 60:14; Hebrews 12:22–23), but it may refer to the hill located in the city of David on the southwestern perimeter of the old city wall. Further context for this verse is provided in Doctrine and Covenants 133:18. **14:2** Compare Doctrine and Covenants 133:22 for a discussion of this verse. **14:3** Some manuscripts read *something like a new song*, but the better and earlier manuscripts preserve the reading provided in the translation. **14:4** *Defiled* can also be translated as *stained* or *polluted themselves with*. The opening lines of the song promote asceticism and celibacy. The defilement mentioned in these verses is not improper sex but sex of any kind. This type of encouragement to remain *virgins* is a feature of apocalyptic visions and later Christian writings. It may have something to do with the context of the last days. **14:5** An allusion to Zephaniah 3:13; Isaiah 53:9. For the 144,000, see Doctrine and Covenants 77:11. **14:6** Partial fulfillment of this verse is found in Doctrine and Covenants 133:36–39. First Nephi 5:18 divides the world similarly into *nations, tribes, languages, and people*. **14:7** An allusion to Nehemiah 9:6. This verse is echoed in Doctrine and Covenants 88:104 and quoted in Doctrine and Covenants 133:38.

⁸And a second angel followed, saying, "Fallen, Babylon the great is fallen! She has made all the nations drink of the wine of her immoral passion."

⁹And a third angel followed them, saying in a loud voice, "If anyone worships the beast and his statue and receives a mark in his forehead or upon his hand, ¹⁰that person will drink from the wine of the wrath of God, poured out undiluted into the cup of his anger, and he will be harassed by fire and sulfur in the presence of holy angels and in the presence of the Lamb. ¹¹And the smoke of their torment ascends forever and ever, and they have no rest day and night, they who worship the beast and his statue, and whoever receives the mark of his name." ¹²This requires the endurance of the saints, those who obey the commandments of God and have faith in Jesus.

¹³And I heard a voice from heaven saying, "Write this: 'Blessed are the dead who die in the Lord from this time forward.'" "Yes," says the Spirit, "so that they may rest from their labors, for their actions follow them."

¹⁴Then I saw a white cloud, and seated upon the cloud was one like a son of man, and he had a gold crown upon his head and a sharp sickle in his hand. ¹⁵And another came from the temple, crying out in a loud voice to him who sat on the cloud, "Put in your sickle and reap because the hour has come, for the harvest of the earth is ready." ¹⁶Then the one seated upon the cloud swung in his sickle across the earth, and the earth was reaped.

¹⁷Then another angel came from the temple in heaven, and he also had a sharp sickle. ¹⁸And another angel came from the altar, and he was in charge of the fire, and he called out in a loud voice to the one who had the sharp sickle, "Put in your sickle and gather the clusters of grapes from the vineyard of the earth, because the grapes in it are ripe." ¹⁹Then the angel swung in his sickle across the earth, and he gathered the grapes from the vineyard of the earth, and he threw them into the large winepress of the wrath of God. ²⁰And the winepress was trampled outside the city, and blood came out of the winepress to the height of horses' bridles for a distance of about two hundred miles.

THE FINAL PLAGUES

15 ¹Then I saw another great and amazing sign in heaven, seven angels who have seven final plagues, and in them the wrath of God is ended.

²Then I saw something like a sea of glass mixed with fire as well as those who conquered the beast and its statue and the

---

14:8 Some manuscripts read *another* in place of *a second*, but the evidence for *a second* is better. A partial fulfillment of this verse is found in Doctrine and Covenants 88:94, 105 (compare Doctrine and Covenants 35:11). **14:10** This verse is quoted in Doctrine and Covenants 115:6 (compare 29:17). Doctrine and Covenants 43:26; Mosiah 3:26 may contain allusions to these concepts. **14:10–11** Mosiah 3:27 and Alma 12:17 allude to these concepts. **14:11** The term *ascendeth up unto God forever and ever* appears in 1 Nephi 15:30. **14:13** Doctrine and Covenants 59:2; 63:49; 124:86 may allude to this verse. **14:14** An allusion to Daniel 7:13. The image in Daniel refers to a human, and hence the comparison is to a human and not the *Son of Man*. **14:15** The language of gathering with a *sickle* was used in the early days of the Restoration to describe missionary work (Doctrine and Covenants 12:4; 31:5). **14:18** *He was in charge of the fire* refers to the angel responsible for fires. **14:19** A partial explanation of this verse is given in Doctrine and Covenants 88:106. The image of a *winepress* in judgment is found in Isaiah 63:1–3 and Doctrine and Covenants 76:107. **14:20** The Greek measurement is 1,600 stadia, which is about 184 miles/296 kilometers (a stadion was about 600 feet or 185 meters). The *height of horses' bridles* is the distance from the ground to the mouth of a horse, or approximately four to five feet or a meter and a half.

15:2 The *sea of glass* is also mentioned in Revelation 4:6 (compare Doctrine and Covenants 130:7).

number of its name, standing next to the sea of glass and having harps provided by God in their hands. ³And they sing the song of Moses, the servant of God, and the song of the Lamb, saying,

> "Great and amazing are your works,
> O Lord God Almighty!
> Just and true are your ways,
> O King of the nations!
> ⁴Who does not fear you, O Lord,
> and give glory to your name?
> For you alone are holy?
> All nations will come
> and worship in your presence,
> because your righteous actions have been revealed."

⁵Then after these things I looked, and the temple, which is the tent of testimony, was opened in heaven, ⁶and the seven angels who had the seven plagues came out of the temple, and they were dressed in clean, bright linen with gold sashes around their chests. ⁷And one of the four living creatures gave to the seven angels seven gold bowls filled with the wrath of God, who lives forever and ever. ⁸Then the temple was filled with smoke from the glory of God and from his power, and no one was able to enter the temple until the seven plagues of the seven angels were completed.

THE SEVEN BOWLS

16 ¹Then I heard a loud voice from the temple saying to the seven angels, "Go and pour out the seven bowls containing the wrath of God upon the earth."

²And the first went and poured out his bowl upon the earth, and there were harmful and painful sores on the people who had the mark of the beast and those who worshipped his statue.

³And the second angel poured his bowl upon the sea, and it turned to blood and looked like a corpse, and every living creature that was in the sea died.

⁴And the third angel poured his bowl upon the rivers and the springs of water, and they turned to blood. ⁵Then I heard the angel of the waters saying,

> "You are just, who is and who was, the Holy One, because you delivered these judgments.
> ⁶They have poured out the blood of the saints and prophets, and you have given them blood to drink. They received what they deserved."

⁷And I heard the altar saying,

> "Yes, Lord God Almighty,
> your judgments are true and just."

⁸And the fourth angel poured out his bowl upon the sun, and it was permitted to scorch people with fire. ⁹And people were scorched with intense heat, and they blasphemed the name of God, who has the authority over these plagues, and they would not repent and give him glory.

¹⁰And the fifth angel poured out his bowl upon the throne of the beast, and his kingdom was darkened, and they began to bite their tongues from the pain. ¹¹Then they blasphemed the God of heaven because of their pain and their sores, but they did not repent from their works.

15:3 *Nations* can also be translated as *Gentiles*. *The song of Moses* is found in Deuteronomy 32:1–43 (compare Exodus 15:1–18). 15:5 *The tent of testimony* is a frequent description used in Exodus (see 27:21). 15:7 These bowls are similar to those that were used to catch the blood of animals that were sacrificed in the Jerusalem temple. 15:8 An allusion to Exodus 40:34–35.

16:2 Compare Exodus 9:8–9 for a similar Egyptian plague. 16:3–4 Compare Exodus 7:14–25 for a similar Egyptian plague. 16:5–7 These interjections into the narrative probe the question of the justice of the slaughter of so many people, animals, and plants.

[12]And the sixth angel poured out his bowl upon the great river Euphrates, and its water was dried up in order to prepare a way for the kings from the east. [13]And I saw three unclean spirits that looked like frogs coming out from the mouth of the dragon and from the mouth of the beast and from the mouth of the false prophet. [14]For they are demonic spirits, who go out to the kings of the whole world, performing miracles to gather them for war on the great day of the Almighty God. [15]("Behold, I will come like a thief. Blessed is the one who is awake, keeping his clothing on, so that he does not go about naked and they see his shameful condition.") [16]And they gathered them to a place called Armageddon in Hebrew.

[17]Then the seventh angel poured out his bowl into the air, and a loud voice came from the throne in the temple, saying, "It is completed." [18]And there were flashes of lightning, and voices, thunder, and a great earthquake such as there had not been since people were on the earth, so great was the earthquake. [19]And the great city was divided into three parts, and the cities of the nations fell, and Babylon the great was remembered in God's presence and was given the cup filled with the wine of God's wrath. [20]And every island fled, and no mountains were to be found. [21]And large hailstones, weighing about one hundred pounds each, fell from heaven on the people, but they blasphemed God because of the plague of hailstones that was so terrible.

THE PUNISHMENT OF THE PROSTITUTE

17 [1]Then one of the seven angels who had the seven bowls came to me and said, "Come, I will show you the punishment of the great prostitute who sits upon many waters, [2]with whom the kings of the earth acted immorally, and those who live on the earth have become drunk with the wine of her sexual impropriety." [3]And he carried me in the Spirit to a desert, and I saw a woman sitting upon a red beast that was full of blasphemous names and had seven heads and ten horns. [4]And the woman was dressed in purple and red and was also wearing gold, jewels, and pearls, and she held in her hand a gold cup full of abominations and uncleanness associated with her sexual impropriety. [5]And upon her forehead was written a name that was

---

16:12 The *Euphrates* served as a boundary to the eastern part of the Roman empire, and in this part of the vision a way is opened up for the eastern empire to be attacked. **16:13** *The false prophet* is mentioned in Revelation 13:11–18. **16:14** Similar battle scenes are depicted in Ezekiel 38–39; Zechariah 12:1–9. **16:15** The theme of the Lord coming as *a thief* is also found in Luke 21:35–36 and Revelation 3:3. This verse interrupts the telling of the pouring out of the bowls and is given in first-person singular, thus indicating that the Lord is speaking. **16:16** The transliteration *Armageddon* refers to the Mount of *Megiddo*, or the *Har-Megiddo*. This area was located in central Palestine, south of the Sea of Galilee. The area witnessed several devastating battles (2 Kings 23:29–30; Judges 4:16). **16:19** *The great city* is Jerusalem. **16:21** The *hailstones* weigh *about a talent*, which is approximately 40 kilograms, or about 100 pounds. See Doctrine and Covenants 29:16 for another prophesy of a hailstorm.

17:1 Perhaps an allusion to Jeremiah 51:13. The theme of comparing Israel to a *prostitute* is common (Isaiah 1:21; Jeremiah 3:1–2; Hosea 1:2). Compare 1 Nephi 14:11–12; Doctrine and Covenants 29:21. **17:2** First Nephi 14:9–13 uses similar terminology in describing the final battle scenes of this earth's existence. The word *immorally* derives from a Greek verb meaning *filthiness, prostitution,* or *sexual deviance.* **17:3** Nephi was also carried away *in the Spirit* (1 Nephi 14:30). This same beast is also found in Revelation 13:1. **17:4** Wearing *purple* would make her appear to be dressed like royalty. **17:5** Compare Doctrine and Covenants 88:94 for engagement with these prophecies. First Nephi 14 consistently speaks of the *mother of harlots*.

a mystery, "Babylon the great, the mother of prostitutes and the abominations of the earth." ⁶And I saw the woman, drunken from the blood of the saints and the blood of the martyrs to Jesus. After I saw her, I marveled greatly.

⁷Then the angel said to me, "Why are you amazed? I will tell you the mystery of the woman and of the beast with the seven heads and ten horns that carries her. ⁸The beast that you saw was, and is not, but is about to ascend out of the abyss and then go to destruction. Those who live on the earth and whose names are not written in the book of life from the foundation of the world will marvel after seeing the beast because it was and is not and is to come. ⁹(This needs a wise mind.) The seven heads are seven hills that the woman sits upon. They are also seven kings, ¹⁰five of whom have fallen. One is living; the other has not come yet, and when he comes he must remain for a short time only. ¹¹And the beast which was and is not, it is an eighth king, but it is also one of the seven, and it is going to destruction. ¹²And the ten horns that you saw are ten kings who have not received a kingdom, but they will receive authority as kings for a single hour together with the beast. ¹³These kings have a single purpose: they give their power and authority to the beast. ¹⁴They make war with the Lamb, and the Lamb will conquer them because he is his Lord of lords and King of kings, and those who are with him are called, chosen, and faithful."

¹⁵And the angel said to me, "The waters that you saw and where the prostitute sits are peoples, crowds, nations, and languages. ¹⁶And the ten horns and the beast that you saw, they will hate the prostitute and make her desolate and naked, and they will consume her flesh and burn her with fire. ¹⁷For God put it into their hearts to accomplish his purpose by being of one mind and giving their kingdom to the beast until the words of God are fulfilled. ¹⁸And the woman which you saw in the great city, she has power to rule over the kings of the earth."

THE FALL OF BABYLON

18 ¹After these things, I saw another angel descending from heaven having great authority, and the earth was lightened by his glory. ²And he cried out in a powerful voice,

"Fallen! Babylon the great is fallen.
She has become the dwelling place for demons,
a prison for every unclean spirit,
a prison for every unclean bird,

17:6 The Greek reads *the martyrs of Jesus*. These individuals have given their lives for being *saints* while others have lost their lives for having borne witness to Jesus. Similar imagery regarding *the blood of the saints* is found in 2 Nephi 26:3. **17:8** For a note on the *abyss*, see Revelation 9:1. The beast has no past because it *was and is not*. **17:9** Most scholars agree that the seven kings are the Roman emperors, possibly seven specific emperors or an idealized representation of them. *This needs a wise mind* is direct counsel given to the reader. **17:9–10** Given that *five* of the kings have fallen, it appears that the author is signaling the time when the book was received. Depending on whether the author referred to Julius Caesar as the first on the list, or Augustus, it appears that the revelation was received sometime shortly after Nero's reign (the five dead emperors would be: Julius Caesar, Augustus, Tiberius, Gaius, and Claudius). This would place the reception of the revelation in the late 60s CE, but this remains only a conjecture. **17:11–12** These verses seek to expand the interpretation of Daniel 7:24. **17:12** These client kings would be placed in authority by Caesar (see note on 17:9). **17:16** Jezebel suffered a similar fate (1 Kings 21:23–24). This verse depicts a civil war when the people of the empire turn on Rome.

18:2 An allusion to Isaiah 21:9 (compare Isaiah 13:21; 34:11). Some manuscripts omit *a prison for every unclean and hated beast*.

a prison for every unclean and hated beast,

³because all the nations have fallen
as a result of the wine of her immoral passion,
and the kings of the earth have been immoral with her,
and the merchants of the earth have grown rich from the power of her luxurious living."

⁴And I heard another voice from heaven, saying,

"Come out of her, my people,
so that you do not participate in her sins,
and you do not share in her plagues.
⁵Because her sins are piled high to heaven,
and God has remembered her unrighteous actions.
⁶Repay her as she repaid others,
even double for her actions;
mix a double portion for her in the cup she mixed.
⁷As she gave glory to herself and lived in luxury,
likewise give her torment and grief,
because she says in her heart,
'I sit like a queen,
I am not a widow,
and I will never see mourning.'
⁸Because of this her plagues have arrived in a single day,
death, mourning, and famine,
and she will be consumed with fire,
because the Lord God, who has judged her, is powerful."

⁹Then the kings of the earth who were immoral with her and lived in luxury with her will weep and wail for her when they see the smoke from the fire that consumes her. ¹⁰They will stand at a distance because they fear her torment, and they will say,

"Woe, woe to the great city,
Babylon, the strong city,
because your judgment has come in a single hour."

¹¹And the merchants of the earth will weep and mourn for her because no one buys their goods any longer: ¹²goods of gold, silver, precious stones, pearls, costly linen, purple, silk, scarlet, all kinds of items made from citron wood, and all kinds of objects made from ivory, and all kinds of items made from fine wood, bronze, iron, and marble, ¹³cinnamon, spice, incense, myrrh, frankincense, wine, olive oil, fine flour, wheat, cattle and sheep, horses and chariots, slaves and human lives.

¹⁴"The fruit which your soul desired has left you,
and all your fine things and delights have gone from you,
and they will no longer be found."

¹⁵The merchants who sold these things, those who became rich from her, will stand at a distance because they fear her torment. They will weep and mourn, ¹⁶saying,

"Woe, woe, to the great city,
dressed in fine linen, purple, and red,
wearing gold, precious stones, and pearls,

18:3 *The nations* can also be translated *Gentiles*. Compare Doctrine and Covenants 35:11. Much of the condemnation and judgment found in this chapter is associated with *merchants*, the class of individuals who provided goods for Rome's insatiable appetite for foreign and domestic products and luxuries. **18:4** Perhaps an allusion to Isaiah 48:20 (compare Jeremiah 1:8). **18:8** The idea of a future burning is further developed in Doctrine and Covenants 64:24. **18:12** *Citron wood* is a wood from the citrus family, and therefore it yields a dense hardwood that was used for specialty applications. A similar list of goods is given in 1 Nephi 13:7. **18:12–13** This list of goods may be derived from Ezekiel 16:9–13; 27:5–24. **18:13** *Myrrh* was often used for the preparation of the body of deceased person.

[17]because in a single hour this wealth has been destroyed!"

And every ship's captain and seafaring men, sailors and all those who work on the sea, will stand at a distance [18]and cry out when they see the smoke of her burning,

"What was the great city like?"

[19]And they will throw dust on their heads and cry out, weeping and mourning,

"Woe, woe to the great city,
in which all those who had ships on the sea got rich from her wealth,
because in a single hour she has been destroyed!"

[20](Rejoice over her, heaven, saints, apostles, and prophets, because God has judged her on your behalf.) [21]Then one strong angel lifted a stone like a millstone and threw it into the sea, saying,

"Thus will Babylon the great city be thrown down with violence,
and she will no longer be found.
[22]The sound of harpists and musicians,
of flute players and trumpeters
will never be heard among you again.
No tradesperson who has any skill
will ever be found among you again;
the sound of a mill will never be heard among you again.
[23]Even light from a lamp
will not appear among you again,
and the sound of a bridegroom and bride will not be heard among you again,
because your merchants were the important people of the earth,
and all nations were deceived by your sorcery.
[24]And in her the blood of prophets and saints was found,
as well as all who have been killed on the earth."

CELEBRATION IN HEAVEN

19 [1]After this I heard something like a loud voice of a large audience in heaven, saying,

"Hallelujah! Salvation, glory, and power belong to our God,
[2]because his judgments are true and just,
because he judged the great prostitute, who corrupted the earth with her sexual impropriety,
and he avenged the blood of his servants upon her."

[3]And a second time they shouted,

"Hallelujah! The smoke from her ascends forever and ever!"

[4]And the twenty-four elders and the four living creatures fell down and worshipped God who was seated upon the throne, saying, "Amen! Hallelujah!" [5]And a voice came from the throne, saying,

"Praise our God,
all his servants;
and fear him,
small and great."

[6]And I heard something like a voice of a great audience, and it was like the sound of

---

18:20 This verse interrupts the flow of the narrative with a call to rejoice. Some translations place this verse in quotation marks, indicating that it is a continuation of the thought expressed in verse 19.

19:1 *Hallelujah* is a Hebrew word meaning *Praise Yahweh* or *Praise God*. **19:2** The Greek of the final clause, *avenged the blood of his servants upon her*, reads literally *avenged the blood of his servants by her own hand*. Compare Doctrine and Covenants 29:21 for commentary on this verse (compare 1 Nephi 14:10–12). **19:3** The *smoke* that *ascends forever* is from the burning corpse of the great prostitute (Revelation 18:9). **19:6** The phrase *the Lord God Almighty* (the *Lord God Omnipotent* in the King James Version) is also used in Mosiah 3:5, 17–18, 21; 5:2, 15.

many waters and like the sound of mighty thunder, speaking,

"Hallelujah!
Because the Lord our God the Almighty rules.
[7]Let us rejoice and exult and give him glory,
because the wedding of the Lamb has arrived,
and his bride has made herself ready.
[8]She was permitted to clothe herself in fine linen, bright and pure."
(The fine linen is the righteous actions of the saints.)

[9]And the angel said to me, "Write, Blessed are those who are invited to the marriage feast of the Lamb." And he said to me, "These are the true words of God." [10]Then I fell at his feet to worship him, but he said to me, "Do not do this. I am a fellow servant with you and your brothers and sisters who have the testimony of Jesus. Worship God, for the testimony about Jesus is the spirit of prophecy."

THE WHITE HORSEMAN RETURNS

[11]Then I saw heaven opened, and, behold, a white horse, and the one seated upon it is called Faithful and True, and in righteousness he judges and makes war. [12]His eyes were like a flame of fire, and on his head were many diadems, and he has a name written that no one knows except him. [13]And he wears a robe that has been dipped in blood, and he is called the Word of God.

[14]The armies which are in heaven were dressed in white and clean fine linen, and they followed him upon white horses. [15]From his mouth comes a sharp sword with which he can strike down the nations. He will shepherd them with a rod of iron, and he tramples the winepress of the fury of the wrath of the Almighty God. [16]He has written on his robe and his thigh a name: King of kings and Lord of lords.

THE DEFEAT OF THE BEAST

[17]And I saw an angel standing in the sun and crying out in a loud voice, saying to all the birds that fly directly overhead, "Come, gather for the great feast of God [18]to eat the flesh of kings and military officers, the flesh of the strong horses, and those who ride them, and the flesh of all people, slave and free, small and great." [19]And I saw the beast and the kings of the earth and their armies assembled to make war against him who is seated upon the horse and against his army. [20]The beast was captured and with him the false prophet who performed the miracles on his behalf, miracles by which he deceived those who received the mark of the beast and who worshipped his statue. These two were thrown into the lake of fire burning with sulfur. [21]And the remainder were killed by the sword that came from the mouth of the one who rode upon the horse, and all the birds consumed their flesh.

19:9 *The marriage feast of the Lamb* is also discussed in Doctrine and Covenants 58:11. **19:10** Greek uses *brothers* generically to refer to *brothers and sisters*. **19:12** For a note on *diadems*, see Revelation 12:3. Compare Revelation 3:12 for God's *name that no one knows*. Doctrine and Covenants 110:3 quotes a portion of this verse. **19:13** Some manuscripts change *dipped* to *sprinkled*, probably in an attempt to allude to Isaiah 63:2–3. *The Word of God* is an allusion to John 1:1. See Doctrine and Covenants 88:106; 133:48–51 for additional information about these events. **19:15** *The rod of iron* is an allusion to Psalm 2:9. Quoted in Doctrine and Covenants 76:107 (compare Doctrine and Covenants 88:106). **19:18** The *military officers* in this verse are commanders of one thousand soldiers. **19:19** Echoed in 1 Nephi 11:34. **19:20** Echoed in Doctrine and Covenants 76:36. **19:21** Compare Doctrine and Covenants 29:20.

THE MILLENNIUM

20 ¹Then I saw an angel descending from heaven, having the key of the abyss in his hand and a large chain. ²And he seized the dragon, that old snake who is the devil and Satan, and tied him up for a thousand years. ³And he threw the dragon into the abyss and locked and sealed it on him so that he would no longer deceive the nations until the thousand years were completed. After this he must be let go for a short time.

⁴And I saw thrones, and seated on them were those who had been given the authority to judge, and I saw the souls of those who had been beheaded for the testimony of Jesus and for the word of God, and who also had not worshipped the beast nor his statue and had not received the mark on their forehead nor on their hands. They lived and ruled with Christ for a thousand years. ⁵And the remaining dead did not live until the thousand years were completed. This is the first resurrection. ⁶Blessed and holy are those who have a part in the first resurrection. The second death has no power over them, but they will be priests of God and Christ, and they will rule with him for a thousand years.

THE FALL OF SATAN

⁷When the thousand years are completed, Satan will be let go from his prison, ⁸and he will go out to deceive the nations at the four corners of the earth. Gog and Magog will gather them for war, and their number is as the sand of the sea. ⁹They will march on a broad plain of the earth and encircle the camp of the saints and the beloved city, and fire will come down from heaven and consume them. ¹⁰And the devil, the one who deceived them, will be thrown into a lake of fire and sulfur, where the beast and the false prophet will be, and they will be tormented day and night forever and ever.

JUDGMENT

¹¹Then I saw a large white throne and the one seated upon it, and earth and heaven fled from his presence, and no place was found for them. ¹²And I saw the dead, both the great and the small, standing

---

20:1 Doctrine and Covenants 76:48 contains information about the depth and misery associated with hell. **20:2** Doctrine and Covenants 84:100 describes the end of Satan. Compare Doctrine and Covenants 45:55; 76:27–29; 88:110. **20:3** Doctrine and Covenants 43:31 quotes portions of this verse and discusses its fulfillment. Echoed in Doctrine and Covenants 29:22; 88:111. **20:4** This likely refers to the disciples (Matthew 19:28). The time span of a thousand years is not found elsewhere in the Bible with reference to the millennium (see Doctrine and Covenants 88:101). Those who are *beheaded* may allude to the deaths of Roman citizens. Such a punishment was not typical of the more tortuous forms of execution, like crucifixion, reserved for noncitizens. **20:5** Doctrine and Covenants 43:18 and 88:101 seem to have this verse in mind when they speak of the sinners who sleep until the return of the Lord. **20:5–6** Similar language associated with *the first resurrection* is found in Mosiah 18:9. **20:6** The word *power* can also be translated as *authority*. Echoed in Doctrine and Covenants 63:18; 76:64. **20:7** Alluded to in Doctrine and Covenants 29:22. **20:8** This battle is depicted in Ezekiel 38. The final battle between the forces of good and evil is sometimes referred to as the battle of *Gog of Magog*. The *four corners of the earth* are also mentioned in 2 Nephi 21:12. **20:9** Allusion to 2 Kings 1:10, 12; Daniel 12:2. The *beloved city* is Jerusalem. **20:10** The end of Satan is described in Doctrine and Covenants 19:3. For the punishment of the wicked, see 2 Nephi 9:16; Doctrine and Covenants 76:36, which draw upon the imagery of this verse. **20:12** An allusion to Daniel 7:10. Doctrine and Covenants 137:9 adds *the desire of their hearts* as a basis for the final judgment. Doctrine and Covenants 128:6–7 offers commentary on this verse. Doctrine and Covenants 138:11 uses similar terms as this verse to describe the dead. The fact that multiple *books were opened* may signal that there were books containing the records of the righteous and wicked.

before the throne. And the books were opened, and another book was opened, which is the book of life. Then the dead were judged from what was written in the books according to their actions. ¹³And the sea gave up the dead that were in it, and death and Hades gave up the dead in them, and they were each judged according to their actions. ¹⁴And death and Hades were thrown into the lake of fire. This is the second death, the lake of fire. ¹⁵And if anyone's name was not found written in the book of life, that person was thrown into the lake of fire.

A NEW HEAVEN AND EARTH

21 ¹And I saw a new heaven and new earth, for the first heaven and first earth had departed, and the sea was no longer present. ²And I saw the holy city, the new Jerusalem, descending out of heaven from God, prepared like a bride adorned for her husband. ³And I heard a loud voice from the throne, saying, "Behold, the dwelling place of God is with humanity, and he will live among them. They will be his people, and God himself will be with them. ⁴And he will wipe away every tear from their eyes, and death will no longer exist, nor mourning, crying, or pain, for the former things have ceased."

⁵And the one seated upon the throne said, "Behold, I am making all things new." Then he said, "Write this, because these words are faithful and true." ⁶And he said to me, "It is done. I am Alpha and Omega, the beginning and the end. I will give water from the spring of life as a gift to those who are thirsty. ⁷The one who conquers will inherit these things, and I will be his God, and he will be my child. ⁸But as to the cowardly, the faithless, the polluted, murderers, the sexually immoral, the sorcerers, idolaters, and all liars, their part will be in the lake that burns with fire and sulfur. This is the second death."

NEW JERUSALEM

⁹Then one of the seven angels who had the seven bowls full of the seven final plagues, spoke with me, saying, "Come, I will show you the bride, the wife of the Lamb!" ¹⁰Then he led me in the Spirit to a great and high mountain, and he showed to me the holy city, Jerusalem descending out of heaven from God, ¹¹having the glory of God, its radiance like a precious stone, like a jasper and crystal clear. ¹²It had a great and high wall, and it had twelve gates, and at the gates it had twelve angels, and the names of the twelve tribes of the people of Israel were written on the gates. ¹³On the east side there were three gates, and on

---

20:13 *Death and Hades* are personified in this verse and the next (compare 1 Corinthians 15:54). Second Nephi 28:23 appears to paraphrase these concepts, particularly the personification of *death*. **20:13–14** A similar depiction of judgment is found in 2 Nephi 9:12. **20:14** Jacob 3:11 and Doctrine and Covenants 63:17 allude to this verse. **20:15** Doctrine and Covenants 85:9, 11 speaks of being cut off because a person's name is not written in the *book of the law*, whereas reference here in verse 15 is to the *book of life*.

21:1 The *new heaven and new earth* are a result of the previous ones fleeing the presence of God (compare Isaiah 65:17; 2 Peter 3:13). See Ether 13:9 (compare 2 Corinthians 5:17); Doctrine and Covenants 29:23–24. **21:2** The *new Jerusalem* is also mentioned in Galatians 4:24–27; Philippians 3:20; Hebrews 11:10, 14–16; Ether 13:10. **21:3** This *dwelling place* is literally God's *tent* or *tabernacle* (compare Ezekiel 37:26). In this verse it appears to refer to the literal place where he lives. Some later manuscripts add to the end of this verse *as their God*. **21:4** An allusion to Isaiah 25:8. Echoed in Doctrine and Covenants 88:116. **21:7** An allusion to 2 Samuel 7:14. **21:8** The phrase *lake of fire and brimstone* appears in Jacob 3:11; 6:10; Doctrine and Covenants 63:17. **21:10** First Nephi 11:1 describes Nephi's vision in similar terms (compare 1 Nephi 1:4, which echoes this verse). **21:11** *Jasper* is not typically clear or crystal-like. **21:12** A similar description is given in Ezekiel 48:30–35.

the north side there were three gates, and on the south side there were three gates, and on the west side there were three gates. ¹⁴The wall of the city had twelve foundations, and the twelve names of the twelve apostles of the Lamb were written on them.

¹⁵And the one speaking with me had a measuring stick of gold so that he could measure the gates and walls of the city. ¹⁶The city was laid out in a square with equal length and width. He measured the city with the measuring stick at fourteen hundred miles—its length, width, and height were equal. ¹⁷He measured its wall at one hundred forty-four cubits according to human measurement, which is also the angel's measurement. ¹⁸The wall was built of jasper, and the city was made of pure gold like clear glass. ¹⁹The foundations of the city wall were adorned with all kinds of precious stones. The first was jasper, the second sapphire, the third agate, the fourth emerald, ²⁰the fifth onyx, the sixth carnelian, the seventh chrysolite, the eighth beryl, the ninth topaz, the tenth chrysoprase, the eleventh jacinth, and the twelfth amethyst. ²¹And the twelve gates were twelve pearls, and each one of the gates was made from a single pearl. The main street of the city was pure gold like clear glass.

²²I did not see a temple in the city, for the Lord God Almighty and the Lamb are its temple. ²³The city does not need the sun or moon to light it, for the glory of God lights it, and its lamp is the Lamb. ²⁴And the nations will walk according to its light, and the kings of the earth will bring their glory to it, ²⁵and its gates will not be closed by day, and there will be no night there. ²⁶They will bring the glory and honor of the nations to it. ²⁷And nothing unclean will ever enter it, nor anyone who is a pollution or false, but only those who are written in the book of life of the Lamb.

THE RIVER OF LIFE

22 ¹Then he showed me a river of life, which had crystal clear water, flowing from the throne of God and the Lamb, ²running down the middle of the main street. On either side of the river there is a tree of life producing twelve crops of fruit according to each month and its season. The leaves of the tree of life are for healing the nations. ³And there will no longer be any curse, and the throne of God and the Lamb will be in the city, and his servants will worship him, ⁴and they will see his face, and his name will be upon their foreheads. ⁵And there will no longer be night, and they will not need the light of a lamp or the light of the sun because the Lord

---

21:14 The phrase *the twelve apostles of the Lamb* is also used in 1 Nephi 11:34–36. **21:16** The measure of the city was 12,000 *stadia*, where a *stadion* is equal to 607 feet or 185 meters. The new city is enormous, spanning thousands of square miles. **21:17** The measure of *144 cubits* (approximately 216 feet tall or 65 meters tall), is referred to as a *human measurement*, indicating that perhaps this is a symbolic number. The angel is the same height as the city wall. **21:19–20** The stones mentioned in these verses are all semiprecious stones used for making jewelry, personal care products, and windows (compare Isaiah 54:11–12). They range in colors, and many are quite common. The less well known ones are *carnelian* (a red-colored stone), *chrysolite* (a type of quartz or possibly topaz), *beryl* (a green-colored stone), *chrysoprase* (a green quartz), and *jacinth* (a blue stone). **21:21** A similar description of the heavenly city is given in Doctrine and Covenants 137:2–4. **21:24** Compare Isaiah 49:22. **21:25** An allusion to Isaiah 60:11. **21:26** *Nations* can also be translated as *Gentiles*.

22:1–2 An allusion to Ezekiel 47:7–10. **22:2** The *tree of life* is mentioned in Genesis 2:9 with an allusion to the tree in Ezekiel 47:12. Lehi's vision is also focused on the *tree of life* (1 Nephi 8:1–11). **22:4** This privilege is a reversal from Exodus 33:20; Deuteronomy 4:12. This promise is extended to the believing in Doctrine and Covenants 38:8.

God will give light to them, and they will rule forever and ever.

⁶Then he said to me, "These words are faithful and true, and the Lord, the God of the spirits of the prophets, sent his angel to show his servants what must soon take place."

⁷"Behold, I am coming quickly. Blessed are those who obey the words of the prophecy of this book."

CONCLUDING REMARKS

⁸I, John, am the one who heard and saw these things, and when I heard and saw, I fell down to worship at the feet of the angel who was showing these things to me. ⁹But he said to me, "Do not do this. I am your fellow servant with your brothers the prophets and with those who obey the words of this book. Worship God."

¹⁰And he said to me, "Do not seal the words of the prophecy of this book, for the time is near. ¹¹Let the wicked still act wickedly, and the filthy continue to be filthy. Let the one who is righteous still do right, and let the holy continue to be holy."

¹²"Behold, I am coming quickly, and my reward comes with me so that I can pay each person according to this his actions. ¹³I am Alpha and Omega, the first and the last, the beginning and the end."

¹⁴Blessed are those who wash their robes so that they are permitted to go to the tree of life and enter the gates of the city. ¹⁵Outside are dogs, sorcerers, the sexually immoral, murderers, idolaters, and all who love practicing falsehood.

¹⁶"I, Jesus, sent my angel to testify to you about these things for the churches. I am the root and the descendant of David, the bright morning star." ¹⁷And the Spirit and the bride say, "Come." And let the one who hears say, "Come." And let the one who is thirsty come, and let the one who wants the water of life to receive it as a gift.

¹⁸I testify to everyone who hears the words of the prophecy of this book. If anyone adds to them, God will place the plagues that are written in this book upon that person. ¹⁹And if anyone removes anything from the words of the book of this prophecy, God will remove his part from the tree of life and his part in the holy city, which are described in this book.

²⁰The one who testifies about these things says, "Yes, I am coming soon. Amen. Come, Lord Jesus!"

²¹May the grace of Lord Jesus be with everyone.

22:6 An injunction to search what is written using the language of this verse is found in Doctrine and Covenants 1:37. The concept of *soon* or *shortly* is also used in Restoration scripture (Doctrine and Covenants 88:79). **22:7** This verse is an interjection where the Lord speaks personally in the first person. Many translations separate the two quotations in verses 6 and 7, as has been done here, to show the two different speakers. The language of this verse appears to have influenced the revelation in Doctrine and Covenants 51:20. **22:11** The concept of the *filthy* is discussed in 1 Nephi 15:33; 2 Nephi 9:16; Alma 7:21; Mormon 9:14. **22:12** Doctrine and Covenants 54:10 quotes this verse (compare Doctrine and Covenants 85:9). **22:13** Compare Doctrine and Covenants 45:7 for the usage of the title *Alpha and Omega* in a revelation about the end of time. A similar injunction is given in Doctrine and Covenants 68:34–35. **22:14** Some very late manuscripts read *obey his commandments* in place of *wash their robes*. **22:15** Alluded to in Doctrine and Covenants 76:103. **22:16** An allusion to Isaiah 11:1–2; 53:2. **22:17** Partaking of *the waters of life* appears in Alma 42:27; Doctrine and Covenants 10:66. **22:18** The warning of this verse is discussed in Doctrine and Covenants 20:35–36. **22:19** The King James translation contains an error in this verse when it translated *tree of life* as *book of life*. The error has no ancient support and has been removed for modern translations.

SYNOPSIS
OF MATTHEW, MARK, AND LUKE
WITH ADDITIONS FROM JOHN

Passages in parentheses indicate sections not designated with a heading but incorporated into another section.

The passages from the Gospel of John are included only when there is a parallel in Matthew, Mark, or John.

	Matthew	Mark	Luke	John
The Prologue Hymn				1:1–18
Introduction	(1:1)	(1:1)	1:1–4	
The Promise of John's Birth			1:5–25	
The Annunciation of Jesus's Birth			1:26–38	
Mary's Visit to Elizabeth			1:39–56	
The Birth of John the Baptist			1:57–80	
The Genealogy of Jesus	1:1–17		3:23–38	
The Birth of Jesus	1:18–25		2:1–7	
The Shepherds			2:8–20	
The Magi Bring Gifts	2:1–12			
Jesus's Presentation at the Temple			2:21–38	
The Escape to Egypt	2:13–18			
The Move to Nazareth	2:19–23		2:39–40	
Jesus in the Temple			2:41–52	
John the Baptist	3:1–12	1:1–8	3:1–18	1:19–28
The Baptism of Jesus	3:13–17	1:9–11	3:21–22	(1:29–34)

	Matthew	Mark	Luke	John
The Temptation of Jesus	4:1–11	1:12–13	4:1–13	
The Early Galilean Ministry	4:12–17	1:14–15	4:14–15	(4:1–3, 43–46)
Jesus Calls His First Disciples	4:18–22	1:16–20	5:1–11	1:35–51
Healing of a Man with an Unclean Spirit		1:21–28	4:31–37	
Healing of Peter's Mother-in-Law	8:14–17	1:29–34	4:38–41	
Jesus Departs from Capernaum		1:35–39	4:42–44	
Healing of a Man with Leprosy	8:1–4	1:40–45	5:12–16	
The Centurion's Son Is Healed	8:5–13		7:1–10	(4:46–54)
Foxes Have Holes	8:18–22		9:57–62	
The Mission of the Seventy			10:1–12	
Healing of a Paralyzed Man	9:1–8	2:1–12	5:17–26	(5:8–9)
The Call of Matthew/Levi	9:9–13	2:13–17	5:27–32	
A Question about Fasting	9:14–17	2:18–22	5:33–39	
Come unto Me	11:28–30			
The Son of Man Is Lord of the Sabbath	12:1–8	2:23–28	6:1–5	
Healing of a Man with a Withered Hand	12:9–14	3:1–6	6:6–11	
My Servant	12:15–21			
Early Miracles	4:23–25	3:7–12	6:17–19	
The Beatitudes	5:1–12		(6:20–23)	
Salt and Light of the World	5:13–16			
The Law and the Prophets	5:17–20			
Perspectives on the Law	5:21–48		(6:27–35)	
Offerings and Prayer	6:1–15		11:1–13	
On Fasting	6:16–18			
On Discipleship	6:19–34		12:22–34	
On Judging	7:1–12	(4:24–25)	(6:37–42)	
Warnings	7:13–29		(6:43–49)	
The Sermon on the Plain			6:20–49	
Healing of the Widow's Son at Nain			7:11–17	
Jesus Calls the Twelve	10:1–4	3:13–19	6:12–16	
Beelzebul	12:22–32	3:19b–30	11:14–28	
A Tree and Its Fruit	12:33–37		(6:43–45)	
The Family of Jesus	12:46–50	3:31–35	8:19–21	(15:14)
Female Followers			8:1–3	

	Matthew	Mark	Luke	John
The Parable of the Sower	13:1–9	4:1–9	8:4–8	
The Reason for Teaching in Parables	13:10–17	4:10–12	8:9–10	
The Parable of the Sower Explained	13:18–23	4:13–20	8:11–15	
The Parable of the Weeds among the Wheat	13:24–30			
A Lamp under a Basket		4:21–25	8:16–18	
The Parable of the Growing Seed		4:26–29		
The Parable of the Mustard Seed	13:31–32	4:30–32	13:18–19	
The Parable of the Leaven	13:33		13:20–21	
Teaching in Parables	13:34–35	4:33–34		
Explanation of the Weeds among the Wheat	13:36–43			
Parables of the Field, the Pearl, and the Net	13:44–50			
New and Old Treasures	13:51–52			
The Stilling of the Storm	8:23–27	4:35–41	8:22–25	
Healing of a Man at Gadara/Gerasa	8:28–34	5:1–20	8:26–39	
Jairus's Daughter and a Woman Healed	9:18–26	5:21–43	8:40–56	
Healing of Two Blind Men	9:27–31			
Healing of a Mute Individual	9:32–34			
The Harvest Is Great	9:35–38			(4:35)
Rejection of Jesus at Nazareth	13:53–58	6:1–6	4:16–30	
Sending Out the Twelve	10:5–15	6:7–13	9:1–6	
Herod's Confusion	(14:1–2)	(6:14–16)	9:7–9	
Do Not Fear	10:26–33		12:2–12	
The Parable of the Rich Fool			12:13–21	
The Cost of Discipleship	10:34–39		12:49–59	
			14:25–35	
The Parable of the Barren Fig Tree			13:1–9	
Jesus Heals a Woman on the Sabbath			13:10–17	
The Narrow Door			13:22–30	
A Warning to Herod			13:31–33	
Welcoming a Prophet	10:40–42			(13:20)
John's Disciples Visit Jesus	11:1–6		7:18–23	
Jesus Declares John to Be Elijah	11:7–19		7:24–35	
Woes on Galilean Cities	11:20–24		10:13–16	

	Matthew	Mark	Luke	John
The Return of the Seventy			10:17–24	
The Parable of the Good Samaritan			10:25–37	
Mary and Martha			10:38–42	
Jesus Heals a Man on the Sabbath			14:1–6	
On Humility			14:7–14	
The Parable of the Lost Coin			15:8–10	
The Parable of the Prodigal Sons			15:11–32	
The Parable of the Unjust Steward			16:1–13	
Teachings about the Pharisees			16:14–18	
The Rich Man and Lazarus			16:19–31	
Unprofitable Servants			17:1–10	
Jesus Heals Ten with Leprosy			17:11–19	
The Coming of the Kingdom of God			17:20–37	
The Parable of the Widow			18:1–8	
The Pharisee and the Tax Collector			18:9–14	
John the Baptist Arrested	(14:3–4)	(6:17–18)	3:19–20	
The Death of John the Baptist	14:1–12	6:14–29	(9:9)	
Feeding the Five Thousand	14:13–21	6:30–44	9:10–17	6:1–15
Jesus Walks on Water	14:22–33	6:45–52		6:16–21
Healing in Gennesaret	14:34–36	6:53–56		(6:22–25)
Eating with Unwashed Hands	15:1–20	7:1–23	(11:37–41) (6:39)	
The Syrophoenecian Woman's Daughter	15:21–28	7:24–30		
Healing of a Deaf Person	15:29–31	7:31–37		
Feeding of the Four Thousand	15:32–39	8:1–10		
The Pharisees Seek a Sign	12:38–45	(8:11–13)	(11:29–32)	
The Signs of the Times	16:1–4	8:11–13	(12:54–56)	
The Yeast of the Pharisees	16:5–12	8:14–21	12:1	
A Blind Man Healed at Bethsaida		8:22–26		
Peter's Declaration at Caesarea Philippi	16:13–20	8:27–30	9:18–22	(6:67–71)
Jesus Foretells His Death and Resurrection	16:21–23	8:31–33	(9:22)	
Taking Up a Cross	16:24–28	8:34–9:1	9:23–27	
The Mount of Transfiguration	17:1–8	9:2–8	9:28–36	
The Coming of Elijah	17:9–13	9:9–13		
A Boy Is Healed	17:14–21	9:14–29	9:37–43a	

	Matthew	Mark	Luke	John
Jesus Foretells His Passion Again	17:22–23	9:30–32	9:43b–45	
The Temple Tax	17:24–27			
On Greatness	18:1–5	9:33–37	9:46–48	
The Other Healer		9:38–41	9:49–50	
A Samaritan Village Rejects Jesus			9:51–56	
Causing Others to Stumble	18:6–9	9:42–50		
The Parable of the Lost Sheep	18:10–14		15:1–7	
Judging a Brother or Sister	18:15–20			
Forgiveness	18:21–22			
The Parable of the Unforgiving Servant	18:23–35			
Instructions about Divorce	19:1–12	10:1–12		
Jesus Blesses Little Children	19:13–15	10:13–16	18:15–17	
The Rich Young Man	19:16–30	10:17–31	18:18–30	
The Parable of the Laborers in the Vineyard	20:1–16			
Jesus Foretells His Death a Third Time	20:17–19	10:32–34	18:31–34	
The Request of Jacob and John	20:20–28	10:35–45	22:24–27	
The Healing of Bartimaeus/The Healing of Two Blind Individuals	20:29–34	10:46–52	18:35–43	
Zacchaeus			19:1–10	
The Triumphal Entry	21:1–11	11:1–11	19:28–40	12:12–19
Jesus Weeps for Jerusalem			19:41–44	
Cursing a Fig Tree	21:18–22	11:12–14		
Cleansing the Temple	21:12–17	11:15–19	19:45–48	2:13–22
Meaning of the Fig Tree	(21:20–22)	11:20–26		
The Question about Authority	21:23–27	11:27–33	20:1–8	
The Parable of the Two Sons	21:28–32			
The Parable of the Wicked Tenants	21:33–46	12:1–12	20:9–19	
The Parable of the Wedding Feast	22:1–14		14:15–24	
A Question about Taxes	22:15–22	12:13–17	20:20–26	
A Question about the Resurrection	22:23–33	12:18–27	20:27–40	
The Greatest Commandment	22:34–40	12:28–34	(10:25–28)	
The Question about David's Son	22:41–46	12:35–37	20:41–44	
Denunciation of the Scribes and Pharisees	23:1–36	12:38–40	11:29–54	
Denunciation of the Scribes			20:45–47	
Jesus's Lament over Jerusalem	23:37–39		13:34–35	

	Matthew	Mark	Luke	John
The Widow's Offering		12:41–44	21:1–4	
The Destruction of the Temple Foretold	24:1–8	13:1–8	21:5–11	
Persecution Foretold	10:16–25 24:9–14	13:9–13	21:12–19	(13:16)
The Desolating Sacrilege	24:15–28	13:14–23	21:20–24	
The Coming of the Son of Man	24:29–31	13:24–27	21:25–28	
The Meaning of the Fig Tree	24:32–35	13:28–31	21:29–33	
The Need to Be Watchful	24:36–44	13:32–37	12:35–48 21:34–38	(13:4–5)
The Faithful Servant	24:45–51		(12:41–48)	
The Parable of the Ten Maidens	25:1–13			
The Parable of the Talents/Pounds	25:14–30		19:11–27	
The Parable of the Sheep and Goats	25:31–46			
The Plot to Kill Jesus	26:1–5	14:1–2	22:1–6	
Jesus Is Anointed at Bethany	26:6–13	14:3–9	7:36–50	12:1–8
Judas Betrays Jesus	26:14–16	14:10–11	(22:3–6)	
Preparation for the Passover	26:17–19	14:12–16	22:7–13	
Passover and Betrayal Foretold	26:20–25	14:17–21		(13:21–30)
The Sacrament	26:26–30	14:22–26	22:14–23	
Peter's Denial Foretold	26:31–35	14:27–31	22:31–38	13:36–38
Jesus Prays in Gethsemane	26:36–46	14:32–42	22:39–46	17:1–26(?)
The Arrest	26:47–56	14:43–52	22:47–53	18:1–11
Jesus Interrogated	26:57–68	14:53–65	22:54–71	18:12–24
Peter Denies Jesus	26:69–75	14:66–72	(22:56–62)	18:25–27
Jesus before Pilate	27:1–2, 11–14	15:1–5	23:1–5	18:28–38
Jesus before Herod Antipas			23:6–12	
Pilate Declares Jesus to Be Innocent			23:13–16	
Pilate Delivers Jesus to Be Crucified	27:15–26	15:6–15	23:17–25	(18:39–40; 19:16)
The Death of Judas Iscariot	27:3–10			
Soldiers Mock Jesus	27:27–31	15:16–20		(19:2–3)
Simon of Cyrene	(27:32)	(15:21)	23:26–31	
The Crucifixion	27:32–44	15:21–32	23:32–43	19:17–27
The Death of Jesus	27:45–56	15:33–41	23:44–49	19:28–30
The Burial	27:57–61	15:42–47	23:50–56	19:38–42

	Matthew	Mark	Luke	John
The Guard at the Tomb	27:62–66			
The Resurrection	28:1–10	16:1–8	24:1–12	20:1–10
Report on the Empty Tomb	28:11–15			
The Longer Ending of Mark	28:9–20	16:9–20	24:13–52	
Jesus Appears to Mary Magdalene	(28:9–10)	16:9–11		20:11–18
Jesus Appears to Two Disciples		16:12–13	24:13–35	
Jesus Appears to His Disciples in Jerusalem			24:36–49	20:19–29
The Great Commission	28:16–20	16:14–18		
The Ascension		16:19–20	24:50–52	

ABOUT THE TRANSLATOR

Thomas A. Wayment is a professor of classical studies at Brigham Young University, where he previously worked as a professor of ancient scripture and as publications director of the Religious Studies Center. He received his BA in Classics from the University of California at Riverside and his MA and PhD in New Testament studies from the Claremont Graduate School. Dr. Wayment's research interests include the historical life of Jesus, New Testament manuscript traditions, papyrology, the life of Paul, and the Joseph Smith Translation of the Bible. He has published an important study that was published in *Novum Testamentum* that examines evidence culled from a third-century papyrus fragment, P. Oxy. 2383 (P69), which raises some important questions about the text of Luke 22. This study has made a significant contribution to the wider academic conversation regarding the events germane to the suffering of the Savior in Gethsemane. The tripartite series *The Life and Teachings of Jesus Christ: From Bethlehem through the Triumphal Entry*, which Dr. Wayment edited with BYU colleague Richard Neitzel Holzapfel, includes essays examining historical and doctrinal aspects surrounding the Savior's mortal ministry. His collaboration with BYU faculty has also produced *Jesus Christ and the World of the New Testament*, in which he, along with Dr. Holzapfel and Dr. Eric Huntsman, addresses the historical context in which the events related in the New Testament took place. He has also published *From Persecutor to Apostle: A Biography of Paul*. His work with textual analysis and the Joseph Smith Translation of the Bible led him to edit *The Complete Joseph Smith Translation of the New Testament* and *The Complete Joseph Smith Translation of the Old Testament*.